African American Religious Studies

African American Religious Studies

An Interdisciplinary Anthology

Edited by Gayraud Wilmore

Duke University Press   Durham and London 1989

© 1989 Duke University Press
All rights reserved
Printed in the United States of America
on acid-free paper ∞
Library of Congress Cataloging-in-Publication Data
appear on the last printed page of this book.
Permissions to reprint selections appear at the end
of this book.

Contents

Part Three   Theological and Ethical Studies

Part Four   Historical Studies

Part Five   Mission and Ministry Studies

Preface

The idea for this book grew out of a course that I taught at New York Theological Seminary entitled "Critical Issues in African American Religious Studies." Students were introduced to the field by reading selected articles and were encouraged to think about what would be the appropriate form and content of a course in Black religion, given the problems of ministry in the Black Church and the current state of African American religious scholarship, in the context of the struggle against racism and oppression. The purpose of the course was two-fold: to help students preparing for ministry in the Black community to develop a coherent, interdisciplinary theory of the African American religious experience, and to utilize the knowledge and insights gained to design a demonstration project or course of study for action/reflection experimentation with lay people in a local congregation.

The latter purpose may seem somewhat askew from the tradition of religious studies research in most American and Canadian seminaries, but many African American scholars in the United States agree that there is little justification for theory without practice in the Black Church. The stakes are simply too high. The purpose of graduate theological education in this context is to prepare men and women to convey the results of their academic research and reflection to people who have no degrees, and in many cases not even a decent secondary education. I wanted my students to be able to translate the language, concepts, and issues of the theological academy into the language, concepts, and issues of the folk, for the purpose of both edification and liberation. I wanted them to be able to investigate, order, and explicate a certain body of data and skills related to both the interdisciplinary study of the religions of people of African descent and the practice of professional ministry in Black congregations that ought to be committed to the radical transformation of persons and institutions in American society.

There is at present no single text on African American Religious Studies encompassing all of these problematic purposes and goals. This anthology was compiled to fill what is a conspicuous gap in the literature on the Black religious experience in the United States. Since the publication of *The Black Experience in Religion* (Garden City, N.Y.: Anchor Press, 1974), edited by C. Eric Lincoln, we have urgently needed another volume on problems and issues incident to the investigation of the phenomena of African American religions and the development of an interdisciplinary theory and praxis for persons going into the ministry at various levels in the life and mission of the Black Church.

It should be obvious also that such a book has long been needed by our white colleagues, particularly those teaching in predominantly white seminaries where there continues to be woeful ignorance about how to structure the curriculum to meet the special needs of minority students. Moreover, we have known for some time that no well-informed American, much less a theological student, can afford to be ignorant about the faith and practice of more than eighteen million African American church members, organized in approximately thirty-five denominations and 65,000 individual congregations, exercising a considerable moral influence on this nation. African American religion, in all of its colorful and multiform variety, is too massive a reality in American social, political, economic, and cultural affairs not to be understood and valued, if only for the power it wields, by those who may be expected to be the leaders of American religious institutions in the twenty-first century.

There are two major sources of the problems, issues, and opinions expressed in these pages. All of them have, at one time or another, been discussed and debated in meetings of the Society for the Study of Black Religion, which was founded in 1970 to bring together college and seminary teachers particularly interested in working on questions related to the academic study of Black religion. Second are the two periodicals, the *Journal of Religious Thought* of Howard University School of Religion, and the *Journal of the Interdenominational Theological Center*, which have done so much to promote the study of African American religion in the United States. I am deeply indebted to the editors of both of these distinguished journals for permission to reprint many of the articles in this book.

In addition to reprints of important articles from these and other journals, I have selected a few chapters from books and several hitherto unpublished manuscripts. As always with anthologies, the problem has been to decide what otherwise useful contributions would have to be sacrificed in the interest of space. Unfortunately it has not been possible to acknowledge the broader scope of African American Religious Studies by including articles investigating issues especially pertinent to the study of Islam, Black Judaism, Afro-Caribbean, and Black Latin American folk belief systems, as well as revitalized African Traditional Religions that have been transplanted in more recent years in the Black ghettoes of the United States. Such a project would require several volumes and must await the prodigious effort of future scholars of the whole panorama of diasporic studies in religion.

The present work should, nevertheless, introduce the reader to several important areas of Black faith in the Western hemisphere. From it we may glean something of the restive scholarship of the African American theological community in the United States, its dissatisfaction with the present state of ethnic studies in the majority of theological seminaries, its provisional revision of some of the standard disciplines of the academy, and its feeling of urgency about sending into professional ministry men and women who thoroughly understand and appreciate the problems and opportunities of African American Christians and their religious institutions.

Knowledge of God and of one's own history are not only the beginning of wisdom. They are also the beginning of self-understanding and the *sine qua non* of true liberation. One day an intelligent slave named Frederick Douglass concluded that what made whites the masters and Blacks the slaves was ignorance—the lack of self-respecting, self-determining knowledge. He wrote in his autobiography:

> I was told, too, that God was good, and that He knew what was best for me, and best for everybody. . . . Once, however, engaged in the inquiry, I was not very long in finding out the true solution of the matter. It was not color, but crime, not God, but man, that afforded the true explanation of the existence of slavery; nor was I long in finding out another important truth, viz: what man can make, man can unmake.

The purpose of this book is the studious unmaking of intellectual bondage to schools of scholarship that have too long ignored, discredited, and subordinated the religious experience of Black believers. To put the matter more positively, it is about the making of an intelligent and robust faith for a previously submerged people: faith that will be rooted in the heritage of ancestors, but informed by an up-to-date interdisciplinary theory about how it should be understood, appropriated, and made efficacious in a struggle for identity, integration, and liberation that has all appearances of continuing into an indefinite future.

Many colleagues and friends have had something to do with the development of this work. I am particularly grateful to those who prepared original manuscripts in response to my nagging requests and to those who gave me permission to reprint their articles and book chapters. I acknowledge with thanks the help of those who read all or parts of the finished manuscript, and of the students at New York Theological Seminary and the Interdenominational Theological Center in Atlanta who struggled in my classes with the xeroxed prototype of this book and made many helpful criticisms and suggestions. Particularly helpful in the final stages were James T. Roberson in New York and Jimmie Hawkins in Atlanta. Special thanks are due to Lee Wilmore, C. Eric Lincoln, and T. Richard Snyder for constant encouragement; to Gemma Barrow, who did much of the correspondence and retyping of manuscripts; and to Joanne Ferguson, of Duke University Press, for guiding me through the whole process with sage advice. Notwithstanding all assistance, I accept full responsibility for whatever is not as it should be.

*

Gayraud Wilmore

What Is African American Religious Studies?

African American Religious Studies refers to a field of teaching and research that suddenly burst upon graduate theological education in the late 1960s.[1] Serious inquiry and debate about the religious sentiments of Black slaves and free persons in the Americas date from a much earlier period. However, it was not until the Black Studies movement, the artistic and intellectual efflorescence of the civil rights period, erupted on seminary campuses where there were critical masses of Black students that we began to hear of Black Church Studies, or African American Religious Studies programs.[2] Because various terms have been used to denote academic interest in the religions of African Americans and the requirements for an effective ministry in most Black congregations, differences of opinion remain about the precise nature of the field. We begin, therefore, with a working definition of what is meant in this book by African American Religious Studies. A few preliminary remarks are necessary before presenting a definition that encompasses the variety of documents in this anthology.

First of all, while it was inevitable that the earliest investigations of Black religions would probably occur in the context of scientific research under the direction of scholars such as W. E. B. DuBois, Carter G. Woodson, Ruby F. Johnston, E. Franklin Frazier, and Benjamin E. Mays, it would have been strange indeed if they had remained at that level of disinterestedness. The practical needs of the Black Church and community were too pressing. The extraordinary influence of the church could not but help make the training of pastors a dominating consideration shaping courses of religious studies in the Black academy. African Americans have rarely been able to afford the luxury of "scientific studies" of religion unconcerned with social action and the training of a professional leadership class. After all, excluding the family, the church has always been the most important institution in the personal and collective lives of Black people in this country.

Second, with the possible exception of the famous Myrdal studies,[3] the most serious investigations of African American religions in this century were done over many years by students and professors at Gammon Theological Seminary in Atlanta and the Howard University School of Religion in Washington, D.C., the first fully accredited, predominantly Black graduate schools of religion. Most of those studies have either disappeared with the passing years or are now buried in neglected archives, having served the eminently practical purpose of "equipping the saints for ministry" in days long past.

Third, the comprehensive cultural and holistic character of African American religion itself militates against the epistemological split that often characterizes much of what is called Religious Studies in the prestigious white theological schools and university departments of religion. The best religious scholarship in the Black academy is, perforce, "believing scholarship," accepting all the risks that such a position entails. It could not be otherwise. The centuries-old struggle for Black humanity in a racist environment has not encouraged the development of a dispassionate, armchair science of religion for preparing the leadership of the Black Church in North America. Whatever the titles of programs designed for the study of the religions of the African diaspora in the New World, most of them have in common the ultimate purpose of faithful and practical service to the people.

The definition that follows will reflect this commonsense attitude toward research that comes out of the ethos of the historic Black community and the struggle for freedom. Briefly stated, African American Religious Studies investigates the religions of people of African descent and their practice of ministry. As we shall soon see, however, in this book the field takes on richer, interdisciplinary implications and practical uses that involve all levels of education among Black believers, regulate a certain cultural and religious interaction between Blacks and others, and facilitate the deployment of the Black Church as an agency of social, political, and economic change. Hence, most of the contributors to this volume would agree that a more comprehensive definition is desirable. It may be stated as follows:

African American Religious Studies refers to the investigation, analysis, and ordering of a wide variety of data related to the religions of persons of African descent for the purpose of authenticating and enriching personal faith and preparing both clergy and laity for a ministry in the Black Church and community, understood in terms of competent and faithful leadership in worship, nurture, education, and corporate action in behalf of God's mission of liberation for all people.

The definition is, of course, heuristic—open for experimentation and revision as we gain greater experience in teaching and research. It also presupposes provisional answers to several questions which the documents in this book will be able only barely to touch upon. For example, what is an acceptable definition for Black or African American *religions*? Acceptable, by the way, by whose standards? What is the place of ethnicity and commitment to special-group interests in theological education? What are the appropriate pedagogical requirements of graduate theological education? What is the relationship between African American Religious Studies in the seminary and Religious Studies in the university, or in the university-related divinity school? What is the scope of African American Religious Studies? Should it include, for example, courses in Black Judaism, Islam, neo-African religions, and new urban sects and cults in the Black community? Finally, how does African American Religious Studies relate to Black Studies, African Studies, and to the research on Hispanic, Asian, native American, and other Third World religions?

This introductory essay must remand most of those questions to a future book. My intention now is to concentrate on the single task of unpacking the above definition in order to lay the groundwork for (1) an interdisciplinary theory which explains the nature and significance of the Black religious experience in North America; (2) exploring some aspects of an experimental model for teaching and researching Black religion from the perspective of both the theological and secular disciplines in order to help revitalize religion in the Black Church and community; and (3) presenting a critique of American cultural, political, and economic conditions implicit in an approach which posits Black Churches as agents of social change toward a more just society.

What our own definition intends to suggest, therefore, is a theoretical prolegomenon and context for understanding the unifying substance and underlying purpose of the articles contained herein, and to test their capacity to do what African American Religious Studies has always been about —helping Black people to think more systematically about God; who they are as a people; what their condition is in a world dominated by white people; and how they can, with the help of their historic religious institutions, participate more meaningfully and effectively in God's mission of liberation from the power of racism and oppression.

Let us begin, therefore, by turning to the definition itself to ascertain whether or not it lends itself to the pursuit of these objectives and what problems will be encountered along the way.

I

African American Religious Studies refers to the investigation, analysis, and ordering of a wide variety of data related to the religions of persons of African descent.

The emphasis here is upon the systematic examination and presentation of what we already know and still need to learn about the nature of religion and its relationship to other cultural phenomena in the African American subcommunity. Obviously one of the first tasks is to design a heuristic definition of Black religion itself. We use the singular here to indicate that our search is for a definition broad enough to include a variety of experiences that reflect the collective consciousness of a more or less common "ultimate concern," while at the same time being narrow enough and sufficiently committed to the Christian worldview to be able to utilize the traditional disciplines of the American "theological encyclopedia."[4]

In the search for such a definition I have used the approach of symbolic anthropologists like Clifford Geertz, John Morgan, and Ann Marie Powers. In an attempt to break away from a narrow functionalist explanation of religion, these writers have sought to penetrate its meaning as a system or mosaic of symbols by which people "communicate, perpetuate, and develop their knowledge about and attitudes toward life," continuously shaping reality as well as being shaped by it.[5] Geertz's paradigm for the study of religion as a cultural system describes how sacred symbols serve to synthesize a people's ethos with their operative worldview in such a way that makes for a subtle circularity—a reciprocal confirmation or coherence between how they live (i.e., their patterned behavior) and what they actually believe about the world in which they exist (i.e., their specific belief system or, one might say, their operative metaphysics). Religion, therefore, in Geertz's understanding is "a system of symbols which acts to establish powerful, pervasive, and long-lasting moods and motivations in men by formulating conceptions of a general order of existence and clothing these conceptions with such an aura of factuality that the moods and motivations seem uniquely realistic."[6]

Such a definition has the advantage of giving us a useful model for developing a more specific understanding of Black religion as a *particular* symbol system, marginal to the mainstream of American culture, but characteristically exhibiting an extraordinary relationship to the African American subculture as a whole. For it seems quite clear that religion has played a role in Black America that is considerably more holistic and effectual than its more segmented role in most white communities. The focus of the symbolic anthropologists upon the relationship between religion and culture has helped us understand how Black faith extracts meaning out of the depths and crises of oppression under the dominating culture and pours it into the cultural molds of the Black ghetto. At the same time African American religion itself is being molded, for both good and ill, for accommodation and protest, compromise and resistance, by the social, economic, and political realities of Black existence.[7]

Obviously, such an understanding of Black religion and culture cannot be validated without reference to a variety of academic disciplines from both the theological seminary and the university. The basic orientation is anthropological, but history, sociology, psychology, political science, literature, and ethnomusicology are all relevant to this task. When we add biblical studies, church history, theology, ethics, and "practicum" in preaching, counseling, and church administration to the "secular" disciplines, it becomes clear what broad perspectives are needed to traverse the full range of belief, experience, and practice within the boundaries of the critical ethnic designation— "persons of African descent." What it actually means to be a person of African descent is not altogether clear, but most of us generally recognize some notable differences as well as similarities between such persons and persons of British, German, or Italian descent. The argument about the retention of attenuated African elements in Black culture and religion is not yet conclusive. Thus, the question of the relationship of Africa to African American Religious Studies remains problematic, but it cannot be avoided. To give only one illustration: debatable on several counts is the extent to which a three-year seminary curriculum should be able to trace the movement of Egyptian, Ethiopian, and Nubian Christianity from east to west, its decay, diffusion, and Islamization among the African Traditional Religions in the cultural areas from whence the majority of slaves were brought to the Americas, and then follow the course of its Americanization in the United States under the pressure of slavery, ghettoization, and secularization. But the problems in such a course of study do not disqualify it. They merely illustrate the magnitude and complexity of any search for a comprehensive, interdisciplinary theory of the origin, evolution, and structure of the belief systems and ritual patterns of the adherents of the historic African American religions.

Difficulties notwithstanding, the task of collecting, sorting out, and analyzing all kinds of data related to religion that are embedded in the social-structural and personality systems of Black Americans will require an unparalleled collaboration between subject matters as diverse as the archaeology of West Africa and the hermeneutics of three centuries of Black American music, dance, and literature. Out of the welter of evidence, both ancient and modern, we may be able to verify the multiform character of African American religion and—what is more important for activist scholarship—catch a glimpse of the common thread of ethnic suffering and struggle in migration, slavery, decolonization, and detribalization that binds together Black believers still in Africa and the American diaspora in a seamless garment of pragmatic spirituality. It should be mentioned here that such work is not the exclusive domain and task of Black scholars. Others who are committed to correcting years of neglect and distortion in the study of Black culture will join in this enterprise. Indeed, some are already at work.

To conclude this discussion of the first clause in our definition of African American Religious Studies, let us propose the forthright proposition that the field involves, at least, the *academic* analysis of data—from an interdisciplinary perspective—dealing with the system of sacred symbols that people of African descent pass down from generation to generation and have given meaning and direction to their lives in this hemisphere for more than four hundred years.

II

. . . for the purpose of authenticating and enriching personal faith and preparing both clergy and laity for a ministry in the Black Church and community . . .

Here we come to a highly debatable question that must separate African American Religious Studies, as understood by most of the contributors to this anthology, from Religious Studies in most predominantly white seminaries and universities. Our focus unabashedly seeks to authenticate and enrich personal faith. This point is critical. We mean to help students move from an *academic conceptualization* to an *experiential appropriation*. This requires taking the student's personal faith and life experiences, and the life and faith of the local congregation he or she serves during the seminary years, with utmost seriousness. The object is the enhancement of personal faith, not only by the acquisition of abstract knowledge, but by the appropriation of *meaning* for life and vocation. It means not only the "re-conversion" of the student, but concern about the process by which the student's faith is tested, corrected, and ultimately verified by the gospel, and is instructive to the Black Church and community. We want to subject the academic conceptualization of the student to both the authority of the Christian message and the priority of the valid religious and cultural experiences of the people. In this view theological education will have failed, despite having expertly decoded the Black experience by means of an interdisciplinary theory, if there is no faith-decision, no new and enriching sentiment embraced by the student. The seminary always fails to fulfill its mission whenever what it teaches is left untouched by the experiences of those it serves, both students and congregations, as they struggle for faith, hope, self-determination, and love in a world of white oppression and hostility.

It should be clear that the discussion thus far has suggested two dimensions, or levels, of African American Religious Studies. On the first level the question is what do these subjects and academic disciplines teach about the origin, nature, development, and influence of religion in the culture of persons of African descent, particularly in the United States? On the second level, what precisely does this knowledge have to do with my conviction (or lack of conviction) that Jesus is Lord and Savior, and that his messiahship is imperfectly but consistently expressed in the historic affirmations, yearnings, and strivings of the Black Church and community where I serve?

The latter question relates to the reason why some Black Christian scholars insist upon the existential appropriation, authentication, and enrichment of Black faith as one of the objectives of African American Religious Studies. We are obliged to be what we are—*Black* Christians. We begin with the assumption that the gospel itself stands in judgment upon all human knowledge and endeavor and that we must permit it to authenticate our academic enterprise. Second, we assume that there is an important work of translation and interpretation to be done in two directions: from the graduate theological seminary to the Black community and from the Black community to the seminary. Inherent in the latter assumption is the recognition of the equal relevance of the Black religious experience for the education of white men and women preparing for ministry. It is, in other words, important for everyone involved in theological education that the religious experience of Black people—to whatever extent possible—be translated into the language and thought-forms of the academy. But of even greater import is that scholarly judgments and valuations be first communicated to Black congregations in such a way that the folk recognize the essential integrity between what they believe and practice—by the authority of Scripture, the Holy Spirit, and the African American tradition—and what their half-educated, sophisticated, but inexperienced student pastors espouse. This does not mean that what the folk already believe should always be the final authority. Rather it means that, as far as we are concerned, the burden is on graduate theological education and educators to make themselves understood and validated by Black people who are familiar with both the sanctuary and the streets.

> "Aunt Jane" is still in the pew on Sunday morning. Today she may have a high school or even a college diploma, a late model car in the church parking lot, and other appurtenances of the Black middle class, but she still has a no-nonsense attitude about her religion. She wants it straight, no chaser. She remembers what racism and oppression are like and sees their more subtle and disguised manifestations crippling her children and grandchildren. She knows that Jesus, the Holy Ghost, and the struggle for survival are real, and she expects her seminary-trained preacher to "tell the story" in symbols and images that rise to the heights of passion and creative imagination without losing a grip on the practical requirements of daily life—on whatever Black people have to do to remain sane in this world and secure for the world yet to come.[8]

Certainly African American Religious Studies must be critical of both the Black Church *and* "Aunt Jane," but it must also have its academic feet on the ground upon which they stand. Propositions and presuppositions need to be tested by the people's faith that has "brought them a mighty long way," enabling them somehow to survive the dehumanization of racism. What we are describing in this book as African American Religious Studies cannot exist without a dynamic relationship between the student, the classroom, the congregation, and the community—with God at the center. The student, as scholar and professional in training, should be taught to understand the nature of all religions in general and of Black religion in particular. But what is ultimately desirable is what might be called a "second conversion experience"—away from a naive faith, unduly influenced by white evangelicalism appropriated during slavery—to a new persona grounded in a mature and learned reappropriation of faith in the "God of our weary years . . . of our silent tears . . . who has brought us thus far along the way." The liberating God of Africa and of Afro-America: this God alone is the source of the power that holds the entire system of faith and praxis together, with creative energies flowing back and forth between the student, the classroom and the congregation; all within the context of a specific sociopolitical situation and analysis.

III

. . . [ministry] understood in terms of competent and faithful leadership in worship, nurture, education, and corporate action in behalf of God's mission of liberation for all people.

Here "leadership" refers to both the professional clergy and the laity, each of whom need African American Religious Studies in their respective contexts. In other words, the climax of this definition stresses the instruction and guidance of the Black Church and community in liberating experiences of worship, study, and social action. Everything points to the goal of equipping "the saints" for ministry (Eph. 4:12). More specifically—everything points to preparation for a ministry of social transformation and liberation from the dehumanizing forces of institutional racism, economic injustice, and political oppression.

This brings us to a necessary historical excursus. African American Religious Studies, as we understand it today, evolved from the Black Studies movement of the 1960s. In his contribution to this anthology James H. Evans compares the critique by the death-of-God theologians of the absence of a theoretical basis for American religious practices with the less-celebrated critique by Black college students during the same period of abstract academic theory in white universities. Black students, led by Bob Moses, Stokely

Carmichael, H. Rap Brown, and James Forman, pronounced their anathemas on any educational program that had no practical consequences for the freedom and welfare of the community. One of the primary emphases of the Black Studies movement was education for liberation, i.e., for service (in our terms, ministry) in the Black community. Manning Marable, in a perceptive essay on the African American intellectual tradition, concludes that "Black Studies reveals the historical evolution and social reality of American capitalist society from the perspective of 'the bottom up.' It embraces the totality of the social sciences and the humanities, and seeks to restructure the method and content of American education from the vantage point of the oppressed."[9]

African American Religious Studies programs in American theological seminaries were similarly motivated. In the late 1960s and early 1970s Black seminarians startled white faculties and boards of trustees with the declaration that theological education which presumed to prepare men and women for ministry among Blacks had a moral obligation to give Black students the requisite knowledge and skills for the radicalization of the Black Church as an institution for social transformation. They followed the leadership of the militant undergraduates who were forcing the concept of Black Studies upon secular institutions.

The definition with which we are working ends on this familiar note that other Black intellectuals had sounded over more than two hundred years before the idea of Black Studies had been conceived. But the need for the study of Black religion to motivate and instruct the laity for struggle has never been more urgent than it is today. With the waning influence of the traditional civil rights organizations, the closing of historic Black colleges, and the alarming decrease of Black public school teachers, the Black Church may be the last bastion of Black culture and consciousness for the masses of African Americans. The Black preacher, therefore, has no option but to become once again the teacher, role model, and mentor of those who are looking for a more radical analysis of the Black condition. Such an analysis, and its implications for collective action, seem unlikely at the grass-roots level unless the future leadership of Black congregations, denominations, and various religious organizations will have been exposed to an African American Religious Studies program or emphasis that is based upon some version of the interdisciplinary, faith-oriented, political-activist theory of education being explored in this introduction.

The need is for practical application of the study of religion to the mission and ministry of the Black Church that will engage a cadre of committed adults who have been taught by professionals who have themselves been grounded in this field. Thus, the teaching responsibility of Black preachers becomes one of the highest priorities for theological education. Such teaching should not be limited to what is conventionally called Christian education. Only to the extent that the entire worship life of the congregation, its participatory activities, and its community outreach are permeated with questions and answers about the meaning of the Black past and how to think theologically about the present and future will the Black Church be enabled to experience the impact it once had upon the lives of African Americans and the nation as a whole.

The object is to invest the worship, intellectual, and participatory life of the congregation with consciousness of a spiritual and political vocation that is capable of critiquing the connection between Euro-American capitalism, bourgeois democracy, poverty, sexism, and racism in the United States and throughout the world. Only such people are able to mount an inspired and sustained attack on global exploitation and oppression. African American Religious Studies is the first stage of such an attack, but it cannot be restricted to the seminaries. It must also have access to colleges and universities, local churches, block clubs and neighborhood associations, the Black family, and other cultural, political, and economic structures of the community. The important point is not to try to force everyone into some dogmatic mold, but to help future generations of African Americans synthesize conceptualizations of Black reality, personal faith, and day-to-day experiences in a way that brings theory and praxis together, that makes academic study and religious education an experience of both personal transformation and participation in the mission of human liberation. Thus, African American Religious Studies becomes something more than another sequence of ego-massaging exercises leading to a professional degree. It becomes, at one and the same time, intellectually responsible preparation for ministry and the existential experience of ministry itself—employing all the disciplines of the academy and the wisdom of the streets for the work of humanization and liberation. Such a program of reflection and action will attempt to maintain, between the Black Church and the academy, a shared responsibility in which Black congregations are continuously drawn into the process of theological education and the seminary into the ambit of personal rehabilitation and societal transformation.

Notes

1. Despite the warning of St. Clair Drake that the North American diaspora never developed an *African American* culture (*The Redemption of Africa and Black Religion* [Chicago: Third World Press, 1970]: 19), we are using the term in most contexts as interchangeable with *Afro-American* because it is gaining vogue in many Black communities today and bespeaks a certain ideological orientation toward African identity that has almost always been a desideratum of the Black Church.

2. The two terms are not, of course, strictly synonomous. Black Church Studies has an institutional focus upon Christianity. African American Religious Studies is concerned about the full spectrum and phenomenology of Black religions in the New World. However the terms are often used interchangeably and we do so here.

3. Gunnar Myrdal, *An American Dilemma* (New York: Harper & Bros., 1944). See vol. 2, chap. 40, "The Negro Church."

4. This should not be taken as a uncritical endorsement of the present fourfold division of the curriculum of most seminaries. It is rather a recognition of the status quo and a conscious decision not to make a frontal attack upon the traditional disciplines the major confrontation with a theological education elite which already suspects African American Religious Studies of being dangerously nontraditional.

5. Clifford Geertz, *The Interpretation of Cultures* (New York: Basic Books, 1973): 89. See also John H. Morgan, ed., *Understanding Religion and Culture: Anthropological and Theological Perspectives*, (Washington, D.C.: University Press of America, 1979).

6. Geertz, p. 90.

7. Following Geertz's paradigm I have used the following operational definition of Black religion: "By Black religion reference is made to a system of symbols deeply embedded in the culture of people of African descent. This symbol system, formed in slavery from remnants of African religions and preserved in the historic Black Christian churches, acts to establish powerful psychosomatic moods and motivations in believers by evoking conceptions of a generally hostile world, which Blacks frequently attribute to white oppression and in which both provisional accommodation and protest are found to be so effective for survival and liberation, with the help of mystical or divine Powers, that the psychosomatic moods and motivations seem uniquely appropriate for overcoming present realities and guaranteeing a joyous and eternal existence in a world yet to come."

8. Gayraud Wilmore, "Tension Points in Black Church Studies," *The Christian Century*, April 11, 1979.

9. Manning Marable, "Black Studies: Marxism and the Black Intellectual Tradition," in Bertell Ollman and E. Vernoff, eds., *The Left Academy*, vol. 3 (New York: Praeger, 1986): 57.

Part One

Origins, Context and

Conceptualization

The academic study of the religion of African Americans, not related to efforts of Christian evangelization, did not begin until the first half of the twentieth century when a few folklorists, anthropologists, sociologists and psychologists began to debate such issues as the provenience and meaning of the African American religious experience.[1] The most recent and productive development in this field, however, began between 1950 and 1970 with the emphasis on Black Studies in the United States. During this period Black seminarians and their professors expressed a new pride in the African and African American religious past; they began to demand that it be subjected to thorough investigation and that the seminaries give special attention to the needs of Black religious institutions as agencies of social change.[2]

In March 1959 a consultation on "The Negro in the Christian Ministry," called by the National Council of Churches at Seabury House in Connecticut, raised questions about the putative theological education of Black ministers, particularly the desirability of bringing together academic reflection and social action for dealing with the problems of the African American Church and community.[3] Out of this meeting came the first impulse for radical revision of African American graduate theological education. Three important events followed: the inauguration of the Benjamin E. Mays Fellowship of the Fund for Theological Education at Princeton in 1960, the first national conference of Black seminarians in Boston in 1968, and the establishment of a special committee on "The Black Religious Experience and Theological Education" under the chairmanship of C. Shelby Rooks by the American Association of Theological Schools (AATS) in 1970.[4] It was under these auspices that intellectual activity began to build around questions that concern us in part one of this book: what are the origins of the Black religious experience? in what context did scholarly interest in it unfold? and how shall its various issues and problems be conceptualized and systematized for academic study?[5]

It seems advisable to begin with a historical essay. Chapter one, by C. Eric Lincoln, deals with the earliest development of Judeo-Christian religion related to Black people and gives us important insights into Christianization efforts in the New World. Lincoln is the author of many books and articles on African American religion and teaches in the field of the Sociology of Religion at Duke University in Durham, North Carolina. His contribution to this volume introduces the question of neglected origins and points toward the necessity of a certain interdisciplinary context for properly addressing substantive issues in African American Religious Studies.

Chapter two, which takes up this question, was written by James H. Evans, Jr., the Martin Luther King, Jr., Memorial Professor of Black Church Studies at Colgate Rochester/Bexley Hall/Crozer Theological Seminary in Rochester, New York. Evans teaches systematic theology at that seminary where the first Black Church Studies Program was organized in 1969. He has published two books on contemporary Black theology.

Chapter three continues to explore questions of origin and context for the study of African American religion. The author, Charles H. Long, is the Jeanette K. Watson Professor of the History of Religions at Syracuse University, Syracuse, New York. For several years he has been president of the Society for the Study of Black Religion and is a past-president of the American Academy of Religion.

With chapters four, five, and six we take a somewhat different tack to introduce some basic perspectives that have developed in recent years on three major groupings related to African American Christianity: Black folk religion, or the tradition of the mass Black churches of the nineteenth and twentieth centuries; the extraordinary quasi-religious movement founded by Marcus M. Garvey; and the little-known but continuous congeries of churches outside mainstream Christian orthodoxy that may be very roughly categorized for the purposes of this section as belonging to the Spiritual-Holiness-Pentecostal family.

Chapter four is an excerpt from a pivotal book in the literature, *Black Religion: The Negro and Christianity in the United States* (Boston: Beacon Press, 1964), by Joseph R. Washington, Jr., who directs the Afro-American Studies Program of the University of Pennsylvania in Philadelphia. In this essay he raises a highly controversial but persuasive argument about the nature of Black folk religion and its dysfunctionality.

The next contribution is also an excerpt from a larger work that has made its mark on the current generation of religious scholars. Chapter five is the second chapter of *Garveyism as a Religious Movement: The Institutionalization of a Black Civil Religion* (Metuchen, N.J.: Scarecrow Press, 1978), by Randall K. Burkett. In this study Burkett convincingly demonstrates his thesis that Garvey was a theologian and any investigation of twentieth-century religious movements must include the Universal Negro Improvement Association. Randall Burkett is director of the W. E. B. DuBois Institute at Harvard University and editor of the newsletter of the Afro-American Religious History Group of the American Academy of Religion.

Part one concludes with chapter six, a new essay by Hans A. Baer, professor in the Department of Anthropology at the University of Arkansas in Little Rock. Baer explores African American religion as a response to oppression by examining the history, organizational structure, and role of "spiritual" or "psychic" phenomena in the African American urban community. In 1984 the University of Tennessee published his *The Black Spiritual Movement: A Religious Response to Racism*.

Thus we begin our study with an emphasis on the contributions of several social sciences to the knowledge of African American religion in the United States. With some understanding of the origins of Black faith in the world of the Bible and in Africa, its second birth in Puritan America, and the problems and issues of how it is dealt with in the theological curriculum, along with a few basic conceptualizations of its problematic history, sociology of religion and anthropology, we are ready to begin our introduction to African American Religious Studies with some normative data in hand, and some clarification of the state of current scholarship.

Notes

1. See, for example, W. E. B. DuBois, *The Souls of Black Folk* (Greenwich, Conn.: Fawcett Publications, 1961), originally published in 1903; Newbell N. Puckett, *Folk Beliefs of the Southern Negro* (Chapel Hill: University of North Carolina Press, 1926); Melville Herskovits, *The Myth of the Negro Past* (Boston: Beacon Press, 1958) first published in 1941: Raymond J. Jones, *A Comparative Study of Religious Cult Behavior Among Negroes with Special Reference to Emotional Group Conditioning Factors* (Washington, D.C.: Howard University, 1939); E. Franklin Frazier, *The Negro Church in America* (Liverpool: University of Liverpool Press, 1963); C. Eric Lincoln, *The Black Church Since Frazier* (New York: Schocken Books, 1974); Ruby F. Johnston, *The Religion of Negro Protestants* (New York: Philosophical Library, 1956); Yosef ben-Jochannan, *African Origins of the Major "Western Religions"* (New York: Alkebu-lan Books, 1970); George

E. Simpson, *Black Religions in the New World* (New York: Columbia University Press, 1978); and Gayraud S. Wilmore, *Black Religion and Black Radicalism* (Maryknoll, N.Y.: Orbis Books, 1983), first published in 1973.

2. C. Shelby Rooks, "Vision, Reality and Challenge: Black Americans and North American Theological Education, 1959–1983," in *Theological Education*, vol. 20, no. 1 (Autumn 1983): 49.

3. Ibid., 48–49.

4. See the report in *Theological Education*, vol. 6, no. 3, supplement (Spring 1970).

5. Such questions began to receive more sustained attention after the founding of the Society for the Study of Black Religion by C. Shelby Rooks, Charles E. Long, C. Eric Lincoln, and others in 1970. This brought together most of the less than a hundred African American faculty members in American theological seminaries and university departments of religion. The Society continues to meet annually to discuss members' papers and consider issues related to the field.

1

The Development of Black Religion in America

C. Eric Lincoln

When Zedekiah, last king of Judah delivered Jeremiah up to the nervous rabble of his decaying establishment, those so-called "princes," too cowardly to murder the prophet out-right, dumped him into the muck of an abandoned well instead and waited for nature to take its course. Tradition has it that Ebedmelech, the African, rescued Jeremiah and was rewarded by God's promise that in the terrible prospects of the destruction of Jerusalem and the Babylonian captivity then in the offing, he, Ebedmelech, would not be delivered into the hands of strangers.[1] There is another tradition that six centuries later, another African whose name was Simon helped Jesus struggle up Mount Calvary under the burden of the cross[2] that was to become the symbol of a New Jerusalem. Somewhere between Jeremiah and Jesus, somewhere between God's promise to Ebedmelech and Simon's travail on the way to Golgotha, somewhere between the death of the Jewish nation and the birth of the Christian religion, tradition takes on a compelling significance, the ramifications of which are now, two thousand years later, set in insistent reverberation. At stake is the religious commitment and the religious identity of millions of Black Christians who want to shuck off their identification with white, American Christianity because the white expression of the faith is not always flattering to Black people and frequently demeaning to them. What Black Americans are now in search of is the reconstruction of an alternative circuitry that avoids the embarrassment of their association with American Christianity and re-establishes their connection with the faith through new understandings of God's will for man and man's willingness to assume responsibility for his dignity and his destiny on earth.

Hence Pentecost takes on new meaning, for among those "devout men from every nation under heaven"[3] who heard Peter proclaim the promise to them and to their children[4] were men from Africa.[5] But as if to underscore divine intention that *Black*[6] Africa, which first touched the destiny of Israel when Abraham came out of Ur and settled in Egypt and continued through all the centuries thereafter, should be a direct and unequivocal heir to that promise, the divine imperative came to the evangelist Philip directing him toward a rendezvous with the destiny of a people. "Take the desert road that leads towards Gaza," he was told. Waiting for him there with a copy of Isaiah in his hand was a high-born African, treasurer to Her Majesty Candace, Queen of Ethiopia. He invited Philip to join him in his chariot, received the good news from his lips, and accepted baptism at this hand,[7] an act that from the beginning symbolizes the African involvement in the new faith that was to spread throughout the world as "Christianity."

This must be reckoned a momentous event in the history of African Christianity. Whether it has a probable significance for the present mood of Black Americans must depend upon the examination of an extended spectrum of additional factors still to be introduced. At a minimum, however, there is the fact that Christianity found an early and fertile establishment in North Africa, in Egypt, and in Ethiopia, and that the church in Africa gave back to the universal church an extraordinary interest on its investment. We are reminded that during the three hundred years from the third through the fifth century when the church wrestled with its most critical theological formulations, of the eighteen or twenty most prominent leaders, no fewer than nine were African: Clement, Origen, Tertullian, Cyprian, Dionysius, Athanasius, Didymus, Augustine, and Cyril. Cyprian and Augustine were the great intellectuals who worked out the basic political and theological doctrines of the Western Church.[8] How ironic are the whimsicalities of history that so much light should come from so "dark" a continent, and that it should bring sufficient illumination to an incipient faith in an indeterminate culture as to eventuate in a civilization called "the Christian West"; and that in time the Christian West, goaded by an insatiable economic self-interest would turn again to Africa, not to bless her, but to suck her blood. But such are the inexplicables of human history. We soon learn that neither the light of reason nor the illumination of the Spirit is a sure hedge to the predaceousness that is ever the corollary of power; and this irrespective of any categories of race, or geography, or nationality. As fate would have it, the men who caught men (or bought them), and the men who were caught (or bought), were destined to play out their generations against the backdrop of the faith they came to share in a new world informed by latter-day apostles whose understanding of that faith was clouded by an incipient racism, a degraded economics, and an illusion of manifest destiny.

I have said that Africa knew the Hebrew nation in its infancy—from Abraham even—and the civilizations of Africa were ancient even then. It is sometimes necessary to remind Christians in the West that Egypt is in Africa, and that Egyptians are Africans, and that no one in ancient Egypt had the clairvoyance to exclude the Black Africans from history-in-the-making in order to accommodate the wish-theories of our latter-day historians. This could hardly have been accomplished anyway, since the Egyptians themselves are racial hybrids representing a fusion of Black peoples from the South with lighter-skinned races from the North.[9] But the racial composition of the Egyptian people is for our present purposes somewhat beside the point, except that the peculiar convergence of events that brought Africans and American Christianity into a strange concubinage for three and a half centuries tends to bypass and ignore the Black African's ancient role in the development of Egyptian civilization in an effort to deny the Black African a role in human progress and development. This is a perspective that is helped along by practically all Western scholarship through a concerted pedagogical effort to remove Egypt from the continent of Africa and suspend it somewhere between earth and sky until "all the facts are in," which in translation means until some miracle of historical research resolves once and for all the troublesome question of Black influence and participation in the great civilizations of the Nile.

As a matter of fact, the Blacks who came to this country as slaves did not come from Egypt. And few would press such a claim. They did not come from Ethiopia. They came from the coastal states of West Africa. But the Black presence in Egypt, long before the white man came to Africa, whether to conquer, as did the Greeks and the Romans, or to deal in human chattels, as did most of the rest of Western Europe, seems well established. And this despite the frustration it poses for "scholars" with preconceived conclusions about Black history and Black achievement. It is not my present task to seek to validate the relevance of the Black experience in Egypt, but to address another aspect of Black history which begins with the rape of Africa at the hands of successive waves of Christian slavers, and continues to this day in the bifurcation of religious understanding and expression wherever there are white and Black Christians. Our present attention, then, is directed to the Motherland of the Black diaspora, that tortured and plundered Western Shore from which the sea captains of Europe and America took, in the course of four centuries, unnumbered tons of gold, uncounted shiploads of ivory, and millions upon millions of men and women. Black men and women. To the plunderers, Africa was the "Gold Coast"; the "Ivory Coast"; the "Slave Coast." It was never a community of people.

From 638 the Christian influence in Africa was muted by the vast hegemony of Islam.[10] History had to wait for Prince Henry the Navigator, that half-English, half-Portuguese Grand Master of the Order of Christ,[11] to open up the "dark continent" for Christ and commerce, to see the slave trade established in medieval Europe fifty years before Columbus would discover a new Europe where slavery would become normative to the culture[12] for the better part of three hundred years. But Portuguese Christianity cannot support an unchallenged claim to bringing Black slavery to Europe, for, under Enrique III of Castile, gold and slaves from Africa were marketed in Seville in the last decade of the 15th century, and although good Queen Isabella, that canny and daring patron of Columbus, sought unsuccessfully to kill the practice before it was well rooted, she failed in the end. She failed because the prevailing sentiment of the Roman Catholic Church was that it was better for a "heathen" to have his body bound and his soul free than vice versa. So, by 1501 it was possible and profitable for the Spanish crown to issue an edict permitting not only "freshly caught" Africans, but those born in Christianity as well, to be sold in America. At first the notion seemed to be that Christianized Blacks could better convert the Indians, although it was never quite clear why "savages and heathens" should promise greater success in the conversion enterprise than Christians with the seasoning of centuries. Perhaps the fact that slaves from Guinea brought four times as much as Indian slaves in the American market was not altogether irrelevant.[13]

Impressed by the Spanish success, by the end of the fifteenth century Portugal had developed a voracious parasitism which she has continued to indulge since, with only such modifications as changing times and world sentiment have induced her to make. With Africa as an inexhaustible source of supply for free Black labor, Portugal contracted with Spain to provide the Spaniards with slaves for markets Spain had developed in the New World—an obvious Portuguese stratagem to maintain a monopoly on her own very profitable procurements in human flesh. But the neighboring states of Western Europe smelled a good thing, and the Portuguese monopoly was soon fractured by Spanish, English, French, Dutch, Danish, and American competition for live, black bodies from Africa. Labor was short and the market was aggressive. As a result there were 500,000 slaves in the American colonies by the time of the Revolution—an embarrassing statistic patently inconsonant with the brave rhetoric of the founding fathers, to say nothing of the moral principles of an avowedly Christian nation.[14]

Few if any of the slaves brought into the English colonies were Christian, but there were Black Christians with the Spanish adventurers in South and Central America, in Mexico, and in the Spanish settlements in Florida from the very beginning. Not all of them were slaves. Pedro Alonza was captain of Columbus' flagship, the *Nina*. Estevanica, who explored parts of Mexico and the Southwest with De Vaca, led an expedition into what is now New Mexico and Arizona, where he discovered the Zuni Indians and planted the first wheat crop in America in 1539. Whatever their motives, the Catholic countries —Portugal and Spain especially, were generally anxious to see their slaves baptized; the Anglo-Saxon peoples were not. The Catholics, it seemed, gave a first consideration, however perfunctory, to the demands of the Church. We are told that the Portuguese

> sold the performers of heathen rites and gave the proceeds to the poor. The numbers were so great that the slaver depended on the missionary to complete his cargo. Merolla sold a slave for a flask of wine for the sacraments. Even if Negroes had been baptized, the (Catholic) missionary saw no sin in enslaving them. In reality, however, baptism encouraged and sanctioned slavery for it made the Negro a Christian and a man *nolens volens*, while the Christian slave trade was a beneficent agency to bring black barbarians into Christian civilization. Only, let not the slave be sold to heretics, for then he would be doubly damned.[15]

This was representative Catholicism at work in the slave trade. A bow toward Rome and on with the business at hand, being careful only to have no dealing with the heathen Mohammedans, lest the poor Black souls, already damned for being Black, be damned again for falling into the hands of Muslims. The Protestants bowed only to an incipient racism which, ere long, would develop a ponderous psychology of justification which would burden church and society for generations. The Englishman considered *himself* first, above all. And when he contemplated his own perfection, he saw the heathenism of the Blacks as being but one aspect of a generalized disparity. Blacks were not simply non-Christian and thereby capable of being made whole through the saving ministry of Jesus Christ. They were beings apart which no amount of grace could raise to a level consistent with the Anglo-Saxons' concept of themselves. Says Winthrop Jordan, "Heathenism was from the Anglo-Saxon's point of view, not so much a specifically religious defeat but as one manifestation of a general refusal to measure up to proper standards, as a failure to be English. . . . Being Christian was not merely a matter of subscribing to certain doctrines; it was a quality inherent in oneself and one's society. It was interconnected with all the other attributes of normal and proper men."[16]

It was an aspect of the Black man's depraved condition. Since he was not and could not become an Englishman his importance and his place in the Englishman's scheme of things was already determined: for from so haughty and preclusive a perspective the Anglo-Saxon could scarcely be expected to develop a warm appreciation of the African's humanity, his native religion, or his capacity to benefit by Christian instruction.

If the Anglo-Saxon's racial and cultural arrogance had been less peremptory and less categorical, it is possible that he could have learned something from the African which might have given him cause for reflection. The Africans he dismissed arbitrarily as heathen did, as a matter of fact, believe in one supreme God. Above the intermediary gods and spirits which distressed the white man so was always the One God who was the giver and sustainer of life. What the white man dismissed as African ancestor worship was a highly sophisticated expression of love and respect for the family and the recognition of the continuity of its relationships — an observation strangely and unaccountably lost on a people so irrevocably committed to the importance of family continuity as are the Anglo-Saxons. What is more, the African moral codes were consistent with the notion of One God of all people.[17] The slave trader saw none of this. He understood less than he saw, and cared about less than he understood. After all, "the English errand in Africa was not (the search for) a new or perfect community, but a business trip."[18] The great civilizations the Africans had raised at Ghana, at Melle, at Jenne, Songhay and Timbuktu, their art, their religion meant nothing to the men who came bringing chains and Bibles.

In the final analysis, as slavery went, the English were probably no worse than the worst and certainly no better than the best, and the line that separated the one from the other is scarcely discernible from any perspective of human responsibility. Whether Saxon, Spaniard, or Dane, Portuguese,

Dutch, or American, these men wasted Africa, decimated her towns and villages, corrupted her politics, destroyed her economy, and hauled her people away wholesale to a distant land where those who survived were reduced to servility and "unconditional submission."[19] It is not a question of whether the Anglo-Saxon was better or worse. What is important is that America is the place where white Christians and Blacks still confront each other in the continuing conflicts of culture and the differences of religious interests that have their roots in the response of the Anglo-Saxon establishment to the humanity of Black people. That response was initiated when, by whatever agency of the moment, the African peoples were herded into the holds of the stinking ships that reeked of blood and excrement and consigned to America. They were destined to be the Black African diaspora: the Mandingos, the Ibos, the Fulani, the Hauseas, the Makalolus, the Kaffirs, the Senegalese, the Iboni, Ibani, the Ashanti, the Wysyahs, the Bossutas—chained neck to neck, wrist to wrist, and ankle to ankle, and shipped off into a new kind of Babylonian captivity in Christian America. They left their gods, but not their God: Muslim, Christian, and heathen alike. Chained body to body between decks four feet high, if they survived the darkness, the filth, the horror, and the death of the "middle passage," they would arrive by and by in the land of the American Christians: the Congregationalists, the Presbyterians, the Roman Catholics, the Quakers, the Lutherans, the Baptists, the Methodists, and, of course, the Anglicans once-removed.

The arrival of the Blacks in America was not an occasion for the American colonists to interrupt the routine of their perceived manifest destiny. In the words of one observer, "The colonists generally made little conscious effort to assess the nature of the people they enslaved and took to bed . . . both the Negro and slavery were self explanatory. Negroes were people from Africa brought for the purpose of performing labor. What fact could be more obvious and natural, less demanding of an explanation?"[20]

Ironically, the time would come when what seemed so natural in the beginning would be challenged in the end. In the most solemn assemblies the most learned divines would eventually address themselves to the question of whether these people from Africa had souls in those bodies the colonists took to bed, and whether in fact they were truly people in the sense that whites were people. The theologians never did resolve the question of souls to everyone's satisfaction, but the "people" issue was settled finally by a political agreement between the North and the South that a slave was equal to three-fifths of a man.

There was no great hurry to make Christians of the Africans once they were landed in America. The social ethics of Puritanism were directed toward the acquisition and proper stewardship of wealth as outward symbols of God's favor and the consequent salvation of the individual. Hence the colonization of America by Protestant separatists of the Calvinistic tradition did not particularly contemplate Christianization or salvation of native people (i.e., the Indians), or others. As a matter of fact, the Puritan church was a closed-membership organization, even excluding from membership certain classes of whites. In consequence, there was no tradition in Puritanism that would justify the expectation that Blacks, when introduced into the colonies as slaves, would be evangelized.

Not all of the early colonial settlers were of Puritan stock, of course. The middle-Atlantic colonies and the Carolinas were settled largely by Anglicans, Pennsylvania by Quakers, and Maryland by Catholics. Although each of these religious groups responded differently to the questions of the propriety (and the practicality) of bringing the gospel to the slaves, all three groups held slaves. The dearth of labor was a universal problem in colonial America and, indeed, with the traditional under-employment of Black Americans, the labor supply never caught up with demand until the turn of the twentieth century when the labor market reached a saturation point through the influx of Southern and Eastern Europeans. The industrialized economy of the North was said to be "not compatible to slavery," but for a time at least the "Puritan North" no less than the "Anglican South" experimented with both Indian and African slavery. The indenture system which permitted the bonding of Europeans up to a period of seven years was common to all the colonies.

The Christianization of slavery meant, first of all, the sanctification of the practice of slave-holding as having biblical precedent and spiritual merit. It implied the approval, even the favor of God for saving the African from a life of savagery. It meant the implementation of a curse on the "sons of Ham" who are destined forever to be "hewers of wood and drawers of water." Also a part of the rationale of slavery was the belief that the enslavement of the "lesser breeds" was an inevitable and necessary step toward the fulfillment of the white race's "manifest destiny," a destiny which somehow converted the Black man's labor into the white man's burden.

Christianization also meant the evangelization of individual slaves. In the Latin countries where the Catholic church sought to extend the universality of the church by bringing the slaves into the fold, it was soon discovered that slaves who were Christianized became more tractable and less troublesome. Nevertheless the Protestant Americans rejected the evangelization of their slaves for three principal reasons: (1) the hearing of the gospel required time that could be economically productive; (2) slaves gathered together in a religious assembly might become conscious of their own strength and plot insurrections under cover of religious instruction; (3) there was an English tradition of long-standing that once a slave became a Christian he could no longer be held a slave.

In the end these objections were overcome and the s.p.g. (Society for the Propagation of the Gospel, organized in England in 1701) sent out hundreds of missionaries to work among the Blacks (after work with the Indians proved less than satisfactory). The southern planters were particularly resistant to having their slaves exposed to the gospel because of the fear of being required to release them should they become Christians. The s.p.g. assured the planters through a series of tracts that such was not the case. "The Liberty of Christianity is entirely spiritual," declared William Fleetwood, the Bishop of Aspaugh, and masters "are neither prohibited by the Laws of God nor those of the land from keeping Christian slaves."[21] There the matter might well have rested, but most of the colonies made the bishop's spiritual assurances a matter of law. Only then did the prohibitions against evangelizing the slaves begin to relax. But there were other obstacles.

One real fear of the slave owner was that the Christian slave might forget his or her place in the scheme of things. Peter Kalm, a Swedish observer visiting America during the colonial period wrote that opposition was "partly by the conceit of its being shameful to have a spiritual brother or sister among so despicable a people; partly because they would not be able to keep their negroes so subjected afterwards, and partly through fear of the negroes growing too proud on seeing themselves upon a level with their masters in religious matters."[22]

One slave-owning mistress became quite agitated over the possibility of having to share the comforts of heaven with Black people. "Is it possible," she inquired, "that any of my slaves could go to Heaven and must I see them there?"[23] And Morgan Godwyn, a graduate of Oxford University serving churches in Virginia around 1665, wrote that masters were commonly affronted by the suggestion that their slaves be Christianized. They would commonly exclaim, he said, "What, such as they? What, those black dogs be made

Christians? What, shall they be like us?"[24] The essential factor at work here was an Anglo-Saxon tribalism militated against the creation of opportunities for sharing the in-group experience even temporarily, *even* for the propagation of faith. Social distance must not be impaired under the ordinary amenities of common worship. Three hundred years later the churches of America would still be in embarrassed debate over the same issues. There would be kneel-ins, and lock-outs, and Black caucuses and the demand for reparations, and a variety of other forms of behavior, which in the context of Christianity must appear to be strange. But in the context of history, they may well have been predictable.

For example, a convocation of Anglican ministers meeting at Oxford, Maryland, in 1731 revealed a sad record of disinterest among planters in having their slaves exhorted at all.

> Mr. Fletcher said his parishioners were generally so brutish that they would not suffer their Negroes to be instructed, catechized, or baptized. . . . Mr. Airey finds the people of his parish very inclined to have their Negroes instructed, but they will not be at any pains and trouble of it. . . . Mr. Mamadier has often pressed on his people their obligation to instruct their Negroes, but yet they are very remiss and neglectful . . . Mr. Nichols says . . . he has from the pulpit and in conversation been Instant with his Parishioners to instruct their Negroes, in order to their being made Christians but that the best answer he can get, even from the best people, is that they are very sorry, and Lament that they cannot comply with it . . . Mr. Cox has urged the necessity of instructing the negroes, but 'tho his Parishioners allow it to be a good thing, yet they generally excuse themselves as thinking it to be impracticable. . . .[25]

If the experiences of these ministers were typical of the colonial spirit, and the overwhelming evidence suggests such to be the case, then the notion that American slavery was preeminently or even initially an altruistic endeavor to save the heathen Africans from the consequences of Black sin is quite badly in need of demonstrative support. But then perhaps it is unChristian to lay the burden of such support upon the Anglican church, which was for the most part dominated by slaveholders. It has been argued that although the Anglicans were the "established" church in the five southern colonies, the institutional weakness of Anglicanism during the colonial period made it improbable that a church which had grown moribund in England would have sufficient fire to warm the hearts of the planter aristocracy in America. The Bishop of London could (and did) issue whatever pronouncements he might choose, but the real control of the parish churches was in the hands of the vestrymen—who in most cases turned out to be the principal slaveholders. It is charged that the "absence of educated, self-denying and upright men from the mass of the Anglican ministers and missionaries before 1783, and the failure of their worthy members to influence the Negro made Black Episcopalians as scarce as white blackbirds."[26] In Virginia, which had the largest slave population of any of the colonies, the Anglican churches were as independent as the Congregational churches in New England. By the eighteenth century the development of a peculiarly "American" Christianity was under way in the North and in the South and on the issue of race the philosophical differences between Puritan and Anglican were not extreme.

The tribalistic spirit in New England Puritanism was perhaps more disguised than that in Southern Anglicanism, but it was no less powerful in drawing the line between Anglo-Saxon and non-Anglo-Saxon. Contrary to popular belief, it was not the Puritan's Calvinism which excluded Blacks from the circle of the elect, but his unwillingness to accept the Black man's capacity for meaningful spiritual instruction and refined religious behavior. Cotton Mather complained that "'poor Negroes especially are kept Strangers to the way of life' because their master made 'pretense' that they were 'dull.' 'They are kept only as Horses or Oxen to do our Drudgeries,' Mather went on, 'but their Souls, which are white and good as those of other nations . . . but are Destroyed for lack of knowledge. This is a desperate Wickedness. But are they dull? Then instruct them rather; that is the way to sharpen them.'"[27]

Despite the urgings of Mather and others, Puritan New England refused to become exercised over the souls of Black folk. The Puritan's concept of God was ever a reflection of his own self-image, and the trend toward racial exclusiveness in colonial New England differed from the tribalism of the Southern planters in the nature of its expression, but hardly in the nature of its conviction. As late as 1680, the governor of Massachusetts could report of the Black population "none baptized that I ever heard of."[28]

The Quakers alone were ardent advocates of extending full religious communion to Blacks during the colonial period, possibly because of the memory of their recent persecution in the English Civil War, and possibly because they themselves had an established tradition regarding the principle of religious equality. George Fox, who had seen the horror of slavery in the West Indies as well as in the United States, admonished his followers that the gospel was for everyone. "'And so now, consider,' he wrote in 1676, 'do not slight them.'"[29] No Quaker held slaves after 1787, but the Quaker influence beyond their own small group was not considerable.

It is difficult to determine with exactness the point in the religious history of America at which the unconcern and the negativism of the American churches towards the Black presence among them began to change. It is apparent, however, that just as the Black man's condition as a slave was an overriding consideration that originally influenced his exclusion from the church, it was his condition as a slave and the desire to make that condition more secure that finally influenced his Christianization. A quote from Cotton Mather, the Puritan pastor who was New England's foremost advocate for raising the heathen blacks through the instrumentality of the Christian church, will be illustrative. Mather's essay on *The Negro Christianized* was published in 1743 and addressed to Boston slavemasters. It extols the following benefits:

> Oh that our neighbors would consider the incomparable Benefits that would follow upon your Endeavors to Christianize your Negroes. . . . Oh the consolations that will belong to you! . . . Your Negroes are immediately raised unto an astonishing felicity. They are become amiable spectacles such as the Angels of God would repair to the windows to look down upon. Tho' they remain your servants, yet are they become the children of God. Tho' they are to enjoy no Earthly Goods, but the small allowance that your Justice and Bounty shall see proper for them . . . Tho' they are your Vassals, and must with a profound subject wait upon you, yet the Angels of God now take them under their Guardianship. Oh what you have done for them. Happy Masters! . . . it will not be long before you and they come . . . together in the Heavenly City . . . and (you) hear them forever blessing the gracious God for the Day when He first made them your servants.[30]

Mather also promised that "even in this life" there would be a "Sensible Recompense" for those who "here instituted their servants in Christian Piety," for they would be "the more Serviceable, and Obedient, and obliging . . . filled with Goodness . . . and exceeding Dutiful unto their Masters, exceeding Patient, . . . exceeding Faithful . . . and afraid of speaking or doing anything that may justly displease you."[31]

Mather organized a Society of Negroes, membership in which was restricted to slaves who were personally acceptable to him, who had their master's permission to attend the services, and who promised to "avoid all wicked companies." The principal intent of the society was to "make the slaves exemplary servants." The meetings were held in Mather's home from seven to nine o'clock each Sunday evening to avoid conflict with work requirements, and each meeting was monitored by "some wise and good man of the English" to preclude the possibility that the gathering could become an occasion for plotting rebellion or escape.[32] In his catechism prepared for his Society of Negroes, Mather prepared a table of Ten Commandments which demanded of the slave obedience, respect and fidelity to his master, patience and contentment with his own condition as God-willed and God-ordained. His reward would be a mansion in heaven where he would be the companion of angels in a glorious paradise.

When the Society for the Propagation of the Gospel in Foreign Parts, an agency of the Anglican Church, sent missionaries to the colonies to work among the slaves and Indians, the New England colonies were as unreceptive to the s.p.g. as were the Southern planters. This was, of course, consistent with the Puritans' general distrust of the Anglicans, whom they feared intended to establish an English Episcopate in America. In consequence, contact between the society and the New England slaves was difficult, and the results were inconsiderable. The records of the s.p.g. reveal that in 1729 their agent in Boston, one Dr. Cutler, baptized only one slave. Thirty-one years later, in 1750, he could boast of having baptized five Black children, one of whom was a slave, during the seven months preceding his report. The Society's laborers in neighboring Connecticut fared little better. The Reverend Samuel Seabury of New London noting in his report of November 12, 1739, that in the latter half of that year he had added to Christ's meager company of Blacks in America one mulatto servant and one Negro child.[33]

In the South, after strong initial opposition from the Southern slave-masters who accused the English missionaries of being meddling outsiders, the Society for Propagation of the Gospel was permitted eventually to work among the slaves—but only after the legal issue of holding *Christian* slaves had been settled to the satisfaction of the slave owners and only upon the assurance that the Blacks would be taught nothing which might be inimical to their status as slaves. That courtesy extended to racial slavery on the part of Christian ministers, South or North, was seldom violated. Nothing in the

typical sermon addressed to Black ears could have provided any encouragement to any spark of intuition a Black man may have had that his enslavement
was somehow inconsistent with the notion of a just God who was the common father of all men. Here is a typical sermon preached to a Maryland slave
congregation in 1743:

> I now come to lay before you your duties to your masters and mistresses
> on earth. And for this you have one general rule you ought always to
> carry in your minds: — and that is, — *to do all service for them as if you did it
> for GOD, himself.* — Poor creatures! You little consider, when you are idle
> and neglectful of your master's business — when you *steal* and *waste,* and
> hurt any of their substance, — when you are *saucy* and *impudent,* — when
> you are telling them *lies,* and deceiving them, — or when you prove
> *stubborn* or *sullen* and will not do the work . . . (these) are faults against
> God himself who hath set your masters and mistresses over you, in his
> own stead. . . . 'Servants, be obedient to them that are your masters
> according to the flesh with fear and trembling, in singleness of your
> heart as unto Christ. . . .'[34]

Whatever the white American's motivation in his shift from a pronounced
reluctance to a manifest eagerness to see the Black man Christianized, the
Black man did not in fact find a significant involvement in American Christianity until the revival fever of the "Great Awakening" signaled the redefinition
of American Protestantism in the early 1740s. The established communions
remained aloof and quite firm in their commitment to the notion that religion
was a privilege, conversion was a process, and the church was a closed society.
But the people themselves defected from the damp formalism of New England
Congregationalism and from the musty stuffiness of Southern Anglicanism
alike to seek regeneration in the powerful preaching of Tennent and Whitefield
and Wesley. The Blacks, too, found themselves included in the spirit of the
"Awakening," which caused one minister to complain, "Nay the very Servants
and Slaves pretend to extraordinary inspiration, and under the veil thereof
cherish their idle dispositions and in lieu of dutifully minding their respective
businesses, run rambling about to utter enthusiastic nonsense."[35]

Another divine was even more outraged to discover that ". . . Negroes
have (even) taken upon themselves to do the business of preaching."[36] Large
numbers of Blacks, slave and free, were accepted into the Baptist and Methodist communions. Wesley himself baptized the first Black Methodist in 1758;

and in 1766 the first Methodist congregation to be established in America included on its rolls a Black woman.[37]

By 1816 there were 42,000 Blacks in the Methodist church alone, and 30,000 of these were Southern slaves. By the time the Methodist church split over the issue of slavery in 1844, its Black membership was up to 150,000. There were probably as many Blacks in the Baptist churches, but few could be counted among the Congregationalists, the Episcopalians, the Presbyterians, or Lutherans although the Presbyterians and particularly the Congregationalists were later to rival the Methodists in their concern for the *education* of Black people. Considering its power and its scope, the Roman Catholic Church in America does not appear to have been a factor of marked significance in either the Christianization nor the education of the Black American, its principal ministry being confined to ethnics of European descent.

Serious efforts to Christianize the Blacks did not begin to bear fruit until 1740. There were, of course, many individual efforts throughout the colonial period, North and South, and some minor successes of a local nature do occasionally spangle a spiritual firmament which might otherwise have been a total blackout. One of the first Black churches in America was established through the benign interest of a Georgia planter who permitted George Liele to be baptized and preach in a church Liele's master built for him near Savannah around 1788. A school to train Blacks in missionary work was established in Charleston in 1743. Lemuel Haynes pastored an all-white congregation in Hartford, Connecticut, and William Lemon was called to pastor a white church in Gloucester, Virginia, in 1801. As Bishop Asbury traveled the circuits of Methodism in the late eighteenth century attended by his servant Black Harry, the churches were crowded with people who came to shake hands with the bishop and to hear Black Harry preach.

The fact remains that when the colonial era ended a century and a half after they were first brought involuntarily to live among the English colonists, by far the greater portion of the Blacks were untaught and unchurched. Those who were members of the white man's churches, or who heard the white American's gospel preached to them, were given no occasion to know the full, rich range of possibilities for brotherly love, personal freedom, and human dignification inherent in the *whole* gospel. When they worshipped in the white man's church, they were assigned a *place*—a place of contempt and indignity intended to reinforce the place assigned them in the secular world. Even in the churches of Massachusetts they had no vote. Everywhere they

were made to worship in "nigger heaven" up among the rafters of the church
—albeit up there separated from the contemptuous Christians they
served they were perhaps closer to God than might otherwise have been the
case. They were segregated even in death except when, through some occasional romantic caprice, one might be buried near his Christian master—no
doubt as a convenience to his master's call for a continuing service in some
other world.

In the main the message the American Christians communicated to the
African diaspora was a gospel distorted by an insidious racism and compromised by self-conceit and economic self-interest. It made God a party to the
white man's cupidity and laid on Him a false ordinance of human separation
and a spurious consignment of a whole people to perpetual indignity rather
than lifting up His common fatherhood and publishing His commandment
to love. Such was the genesis of the Black religious experience in America, an
experience which did much to shape our common destinies and to set us
firmly on a treadmill that covers the same ground, year after year, century after
century, and from which Black Christians have so recently launched a final
effort to disengage.

Notes

Adapted from *The Black Church and Black Religion.* C. Eric Lincoln Series on Black Religion
(New York: Doubleday, 1973).

1. Jer. 38:1–13; 39:15–18.

2. Mark 15:21. There is an heretical tradition that Simon the African was crucified instead of
Jesus. See Frederick Perry Noble, *The Redemption of Africa*, vol. 1 (Chicago: Fleming H. Revell
Co., 1899):16.

3. Acts 2:5.

4. Acts 2:39.

5. Acts 2:10.

6. Cf. Noble, 7. Says Noble: "In the Egyptians we have a dark race originating from the
mingling of black and white races. If these blacks were Negroes or like Negroes—and the best
authorities regard this as the case. . . . the civilization of Egypt is only less Negro than
(Caucasian)." Obviously, the present writer accepts the dictum of the best authorities.

7. Acts 8:26–39.

8. Noble, 33–34.

9. See note 7.

10. Noble, 85.

11. Ibid., 128.

12. Saunders Redding, *They Came in Chains* (Philadelphia: Lippincott, 1950).

13. Noble, 139.

14. Winthrop D. Jordan. *White over Black* (Chapel Hill: University of North Carolina Press, 1968).

15. Noble, 134–35.

16. Jordan, 24.

17. Cf. Thomas Patrick Melady, *House Divided* (New York: Sheed and Ward, 1969):28.

18. Jordan, 27.

19. Kenneth M. Stampp, *The Peculiar Institution* (New York: Knopf):141.

20. Jordan, 179.

21. H. Shelton Smith, *In His Image, But* (Durham, N.C.: Duke University Press, 1972):9.

22. Jordan, 183.

23. Smith, 11.

24. Ibid.

25. Jordan, 186.

26. Noble, 2:481.

27. Jordan, 190.

28. Lorenzo J. Greene, *The Negro in Colonial New England* (New York: Columbia, 1968):237.

29. Jordan, 194.

30. Gilbert Osofsky, *The Burden of Race* (New York: Harper & Row, 1967):35–36.

31. Ibid., 36.

32. Greene, 266.

33. Ibid., pp. 271–72.

34. Osofsky, 39–40.

35. Greene, 276.

36. Jordan, 212.

37. Noble, 493.

2

Black Church Studies
and the Theological Curriculum

James H. Evans, Jr.

Introduction

The purpose of this essay is to address the role of the study of the African American religious tradition and experience in the curricular life of the graduate theological school. What are the problems and possibilities of Black church studies within this educational paradigm? To set this question in its broader context I will briefly describe what I see to be the general problematic in contemporary graduate theological education and define Black church studies as a response, at least in part, to that problematic, both in terms of the curriculum and the ethos of theological education. In concluding I will venture some observations on the challenges and future of Black church studies as an educational enterprise.

Graduate theological education is presently experiencing an anxiety just short of crisis. The number of students enrolling in theological institutions is declining and even the temporary, and not always welcomed, influx of women and older students with their precious tuition dollars will not provide a long-term solution. But the problem goes deeper than enrollments and tuition. The problem lies at the very heart of the educational enterprise itself.

There are two historical sources to this problematic. The first is seen in the origins of theological education in this country. Higher education in America as a whole had its beginnings in the desire of the early colonialists to ensure a learned ministry for future generations. Thus, for instance, etched on the gateway at Harvard University are these words:

After God had carried us safe to New England & wee had builded our houses provided necessaries for our livelihood reard convenient places for Gods worship and settled the civill government one of the next things we longed for and looked after was to advance learning and perpetuate it to posterity dreading to leave an illiterate ministry to the churches when our present ministers shall lie in the dust.

Harvard College was established as a result in 1631. Its purpose was to provide for the churches a ministry with a liberal education. Therefore all students, whether they were preparing for ministry or not, took the same courses. They included mathematics, logic, and rhetoric (the trivium), as well as Latin, Hebrew, Greek, and "the Divinity subjects." In the latter part of the eighteenth century the divinity requirements for all students were modified and finally abolished altogether.

Harvard College was also the center of the liberal wing of Puritan church theology and by 1808 the more conservative wing of the Congregational church, fearing that the distinctiveness of their religious perspective was being usurped by the gluttonous liberalism of Harvard, founded a separate seminary in Andover, Massachusetts. Not to be outdone, in 1819 Harvard formally established the divinity school as a distinct, but not independent, department of the university. This event is significant because the issues of institutional control and intellectual independence that afflict theological education today have their roots here. Although the early colonialists saw no inherent conflict between the maintenance of the churches and the benefits of a liberal education, they based their understanding on the European model where the churches along with the state controlled higher education. In America that would not be the case and the churches and state would become occasional antagonists rather than allies. Harvard, representing the canons of liberal learning as authoritative guides to truth, established a divinity school that would never forsake the quest in the academy for the truth. Andover, representing the canons of doctrinal teaching as authoritative guides to truth, established a seminary that would never forsake its fidelity to the churches. Of course here Harvard and Andover are functioning as grounded metaphors, or analogies, for a much broader reality. Nevertheless in them the paradigm was set: there were (and to a large extent still are) two types of theological institutions. The first is the "divinity school," which is associated with a university. Its curriculum and pedagogical direction is set by the standards of the academy. The second is the "theological seminary," which is associated with a denomination. Its curriculum and pedagogical direction is set by the standards of orthodoxy of the church.

Here is the origin of one of the tensions in graduate theological education: who decides when people are fit for ministry and on what basis does one make this decision? On one extreme the seminary could imagine a divinity school granting a degree to a person with no interpersonal skills, no sensitivity to the suffering of others, no understanding of what it means to have a disciplined spiritual life or be a part of the community of faith, but who did get straight A's in his or her courses. On the other extreme the divinity school could imagine a "seminary" granting a degree to a person who is completely incapable of abstract thought, logical reasoning, written communication, or scholarly research, but who wholeheartedly buys the demand for doctrinal fidelity to the church. These are the extremes and somewhere between them graduate theological education is struggling for equilibrium and trying to avoid the bequest of the Enlightenment: that there is a fundamental contradiction between faith and truth.

The second historical source of the contemporary problematic for graduate theological education can be found in the chronologically brief, but substantively crucial, period between 1961 and 1968. In this period the hegemony of both the church and the university as "establishment institutions" was called into question. In 1966 three prominent Christian theologians declared that God is dead. William Hamilton, Gabriel Vahanian, and T. Thomas Altizer, the death-of-God theologians, as they came to be called, stated that the reality to which the word God refers no longer attracts the requisite emotional and intellectual response from modern people. Like Nietzsche before them, they stated we must wean ourselves from this dependency on religion and the church. Instead we must maturely face a world without God. This theological movement was a response to secularism. The death-of-God theologians, rather than fight godlessness, decided to embrace it. As a result the church became irrelevant to modern people. Also in 1966 Stokely Carmichael, a former member of Martin Luther King, Jr.'s civil rights movement, declared that African Americans needed "Black Power." The Black Power, or Black consciousness, movement was the signal of the awakening of oppressed people to the true nature of politics, economics, and education in this country. Many of these Black radicals, along with the white radical left, directed their attention to universities noting that the educational paradigm operative on most predominantly white campuses had nothing to do with the reality of Black folks' lives. Thus they called for the establishment of Black Studies departments, in some instances separate from the main campus and relatively free of institutional control. This educational movement was a response to the resurgent quest for freedom in the Black community both here and abroad. The result was that the existing university system was seen as irrelevant to Black concerns.

There are several important features to the coincidence of these events. First, the death-of-God movement belonged to the white community and it met with derision in the Black community, especially among church folk. Thus while a segment of the white community was lamenting the death of its God, rising secularity among its youth, and loss of American world-prestige, the Black community, or a segment thereof, was celebrating the resurrection of a radical consciousness both inside and outside the churches. Second, both the church and the university were condemned as being irrelevant. That is, no longer were they considered to be central sources of authority and meaning. The problem with both centered around the relation between theory and praxis. The death-of-God theologians observed that modern Christians performed religious practice without seeing that the theoretical basis for that practice no longer existed. African American reformers observed that students attending white universities imbibed abstract theory with no relation to the actual practice of living in a racist society. In both cases the fundamental relation between theory and praxis had been obscured. For theological education the challenges raised by this period in our past wrought many changes, some of which were, as it turns out, ill-advised. In the quest for relevancy to the modern world, many institutions, especially "divinity schools" threw their curricula to the wind, allowing students to determine from among available courses which combination would best equip them for life in the modern world. A few of these same institutions established Black Church Studies programs as a response to the need for relevance to the struggle of oppressed Christians.[1] However, in dismantling a highly structured curriculum, theological educators chose to exchange identity for relevance, but ended up with neither. Both students and faculty began to wonder what distinguished theological education from graduate study of religions or professional social work education. Theology no longer seemed to speak to the totality of lived experience and was therefore reducible to abstract theory. Theology also no longer seemed to address that unspoken point of reference (God) and was therefore reducible to superficial practice. In short, the study of theology was threatened with anonymity and irrelevance.[2]

However, important theological work was going on among a people well accustomed to the challenges of anonymity and irrelevance. Black Church

Studies emerged as a special concern for the theological education of Black students. Let me now move on to a definition of Black Church Studies.[3]

What is Black Church Studies?

When one thinks of Black Church Studies, the two disciplines that most readily come to mind are Black Church history and Black theology. Though Black Church Studies has come to designate a broad range of disciplines and perspectives within theological education, the distortion and silence that were encountered relating to the religious history and experience of African Americans were the impetus for thinking about Black Church Studies as a special concern. Moreover, the need to understand the phenomenon of African American Christianity means that indigenous and distinctive ways of articulating and plumbing the depths of Black religious experience are required.

There are several ways to describe Black Church Studies. For some people it is any theological or religious research engaged in by African American scholars. Thus *the Black scholar* is the focal point of Black Church Studies. For other people it is any theological or religious research which takes as its subject *Black religious experience*. Thus the subject matter is the distinguishing characteristic of Black Church Studies. For a third group it is the *methodological* advocacy that sets Black Church Studies apart. That is, it is a way of doing theological research which is aimed ultimately at the liberation of African Americans from economic, social, and political oppression. It is the *telos*, or goal, of Black Church Studies that gives it its uniqueness.

Clearly all of the above tasks are the ideal desiderata of Black Church Studies. However the distinctiveness of Black Church Studies is its liberating analysis of the situation of oppression in which African Americans find themselves and its critical praxis in the midst of that oppression. A liberating analysis is one which is directed toward the deliverance of African American experience from the corruption of neglect and willful misinterpretation. This is the reason that Black religious history was one of the first disciplines to arise out of the turbulence and reawakening of the 1960s. A critical praxis is one directed toward the destruction of the situation of oppression. By engaging in the struggle for liberation from oppression one can then—in reality —understand it. This is the reason that Black Theology evolved the way it did in the 1960s. Black Theology was for racist America what Marxist philosophy was for capitalist Europe—not a way to merely understand the world, but the attempt to change it. A liberating analysis and a critical praxis are the methods, or tools, of Black Church Studies. Through this liberating analysis provided by the study of Black Church history the Black past can be redeemed and through this critical praxis provided by Black Theology the present can be renamed.

Reclaiming the Past

The reclamation of the past of African Americans is difficult, ambitious and necessary. It is difficult because the noble origins of African Americans have been encrusted under layers of neglect, misinterpretation, and outright lies. The myth of the happy slave evaporates when one discovers that there were so many slave insurrections in Virginia in the nineteenth century that they were not all recorded for fear that the magnitude of the Black quest for freedom might overwhelm the slaveowners. The reclamation of the past is ambitious because the amount of material and information to be examined is voluminous. The surface has barely been scratched in this area. The reclamation of the past is necessary because there is an ineluctable relation between a people's history and their hope. Without the salvage of Black history, Black hope withers.

There are three areas in which this reclamation project is taking place. The first is the revalorization of Africa. Africa must be reclaimed as a place where three of the great world religions met: Judaism, Islam, and Christianity. Moreover it must be seen as the appropriate place to begin study of African American religion. The second area is the recovery of the genius of slave religion. Slave religion must be seen as a cultural response to a situation of almost intolerable oppression. To take slave religion out of the economic, social, and political context to which it was a response is to distort it. Slave religion cannot be understood apart from the liberation struggle of the enslaved African. The third area is the reclamation of the influence of the Black Church on American Christianity. In spite of the segregation forced upon it, the Black Church was not completely outside of the American mainstream. Nor was the Black Church exclusively the passive recipient in any cultural exchange. The white church in America cannot be adequately assessed apart from the presence of millions of African American Christians. It follows that the recovery of African American religious history is a primary task for Black Church Studies.

The reclamation of the past, however, has a second dimension that is often overlooked. In the frenzied and justified effort to reassemble the jigsaw puzzle of the collective African American past, the personal and spiritual dimension of this project is often undervalued. The recovery of the past must not become private or individualistic, but it can be personal. In the collective historical task the liberating analysis is stressed. In this second personal task, the critical praxis is stressed. This second task involves the attempt to plumb the depths of African American experience in search of the hidden testimony of a people to the God of Abraham and Sarah, Isaac and Rachel, Jacob and Rebecca. The testimonies, narratives, autobiographies, prayers, and sermons of ancient African American Christian witnesses can lead the scholar into the presence of the joy and sorrow of the moment. These texts may recreate the *zeitgeist* of their inception. They can lead the scholar into historical solidarity with the sufferer. This is the effect of Frederick Douglass' *Narrative* of 1845, the *Autobiography* of Amanda Smith, and the account of *Elizabeth: A Colored Minister of the Gospel, Born in Slavery*. A critical praxis seeks understanding through solidarity. This is the ciphered meaning of the Negro spiritual "Were You There When They Crucified My Lord?" African slaves in eighteenth- and nineteenth-century America could understand the writings of a condemned Jew in first century Palestine because they had been to the cross.

Renaming the Present

The second task of Black Church Studies is to rename the present. It requires more than a passionate appeal to the moral sensibilities of others, however. What is needed is a concrete analysis of the oppressive structures of our society. This means that those who engage in Black Church Studies must assess all of the available methods for completing that analysis. The primary approach has been a cultural analysis of oppression. This is quite understandable because African American culture has been a source of identity for Black Americans. The distinctiveness of slave culture has survived to some degree in the uniqueness of contemporary African American culture. Within that cultural context Black religion developed so it is not surprising that the early emphasis in Black Church Studies has been placed on a cultural analysis of the predicament of African Americans. But still heard are questions about the sufficiency of a cultural analysis alone to name the demons afflicting African American life. Can we understand racism outside the complex infrastructure of corporate capitalism? Can we understand racism without a concrete analysis of the social arrangement? These are difficult, and often unpopular, questions. But difficulty and rebuke have historically been the lot of African American Christians concerned about the demons of physical oppression. The task of renaming the present brings Black Church Studies squarely into the political arena in which Black people live. Attempting a political analysis of American society means taking sides. Resistance to this task may come from people who see no connection between the religious and political dimensions of life; it may also come from people who see no connection between the academic and political dimensions of scholarship. Despite this resistance, scholars working in the area of Black Church Studies cannot be concerned about religious or academic propriety if it is not related to the historic African American struggle for liberation. One result of this analysis of oppression by Black Church Studies scholars will be a clearer perception of its link to analyses made by other scholars in Black Studies programs. The ferment of the 1960s, which gave rise to Black Studies programs in colleges and universities, also spawned Black Church Studies programs in predominantly white seminaries and divinity schools. Unfortunately no comprehensive dialogue has taken place between both types of programs. A few years ago I attended a conference on Black Studies at Cornell University at which representatives from programs across the nation were present. To my knowledge I was the only person in attendance from a Black Church Studies program. This incident suggests some dialogue between Black scholars in the university and those in the seminary is needed. A second result of a comprehensive analysis of oppression will be a global understanding of the Christian faith. The liberating faith of African Americans can be shared with sisters and brothers in Africa, the Carribean, Asia, and South America. The common denominator of that faith is a concern for the manifestation of justice in a society where the maldistribution of power and wealth often veils the reality that we are all created in God's image.

Conclusion

There are, as we have discovered, two crucial and interrelated problems in theological education today: the *identity* of theology and its *relevance* to contemporary human experience. Attempts at curricular reforms are often partial and inadequate responses to one or the other of these problems. When institutions are concerned with the *identity* of their educational enterprise, the solution most often suggested is a return to orthodoxy. In this instance the school names the *church* as its primary public. The goal of this educational process is most often to conform the student to the needs of the churches and emphasize the student's behavior within the vocation of ministry. Students are trained to function efficiently and effectively as ministers of the churches. In this schema education is viewed as the preservation and transmission of the tradition of the churches, following a distinctive, unchanging body of theological knowledge given to the churches by divine revelation and not available anywhere else. Thus the church employs its educational arm, the seminary, to guard and promote that special knowledge. The result being a theological curriculum almost completely prescribed. Required courses in polity, denominational history, and church doctrine, along with biblical languages and exegesis, often leave little chance for the student to take other subjects. In this way the institutional control of the seminary is squarely in the hands of the churches: the formation of the student is directed by the needs of the churches, the knowledge imparted is controlled by the churches, and the curriculum is shaped by the churches. The identity of theological education is reclaimed, but at the price of relevance to contemporary human experience.

When institutions are concerned with the *relevance* of their educational enterprise, the solution most often suggested is a return to liberalism. In this instance the school names the *university* as its primary public. This means that the school shapes its educational program around the needs and requirements for a well-rounded, learned leadership for churches and other institutions, i.e., business, medicine, law, and universities. The goal of this educational process is most often to inform the student of the broader dimensions of intellectual and moral life. The emphasis is on the capacity of the student to think critically about the more important ethical and religious issues of human existence. Students are encouraged to understand the nature of reality itself. In this schema, education is viewed as opening the religious traditions to critical inquiry and analytical thought. There is no special body of theological knowledge, but all pursuit of knowledge attempts to understand the same reality. Knowledge is *paideia*, belles lettres, or the human sciences. Thus, the university employs its theological arm, the divinity school, to relate the understanding of the Christian faith to understanding in general. The result is that the theological curriculum is almost completely open. There are very few required courses and students may complete their divinity studies with a substantial number of offerings within other divisions of the university. In this way the institutional control of the seminary is squarely in the hands of the university: the formation of the student is directed by the requirements of the university, the knowledge imparted is controlled by the university, and the curriculum is shaped by the university. The relevance of theological education to broader human concerns is reclaimed, but at the price of a distinctive identity.

The point of this essay is that Black Church Studies represents a way between the "rock" of identity without relevance and the "hard place" of relevance without identity. Black Church Studies challenges mindless allegiance to the standards of the academy or university. Michele Russell, a feminist scholar, puts it this way:

> How will you refuse to let the academy separate the dead from the living, and then yourself declare allegiance to life? As teachers, scholars, and students, how available will you make your knowledge to others as tools for their liberation? This is not a call for mindless activism, but rather engaged scholarship.[4]

In terms of its sources, methods, pedagogy, and curricular structure, Black Church Studies refuses to be guided exclusively by the concerns of the university. On the other hand, Black Church Studies challenges the narrowness and myopia of religious institutions in their claim to a special knowledge of important issues of human existence. Mercy Amba Oduyoye, an African woman and theologian, asks:

> Can we comprehend God outside events in human life? Can we find God apart from our human experience? . . . Some criticism suggests that we could do theology outside the events of our times, that there is a metaphysical revealed knowledge available to us in sacred scripture, quite apart from . . . what we have in the Bible and in the articles of faith formulated in the formative age of the church.[5]

In terms of its breadth, scope, pedagogy, and curricular structure, Black Church Studies affirms that God is the foundational factor in human life and experience. It is significant that both Michelle Russell and Mercy Amba Oduyoye are speaking from the perspective of groups which have not normally been considered as important either to the church or the academy. Women and their concerns have been considered marginal to the life of the church and academy. People of African descent have been considered "invisible" to the American churches and the academy. Therefore the point of reference, the oppressed, their experiences and traditions, is crucial in understanding the educational tasks of Black Church Studies. From this point of reference both identity and relevance can be reclaimed for theological education.

In conclusion, let me suggest how Black Church Studies exemplifies an approach to theological education that affirms *both* identity and relevance. The primary public for Black Church Studies is the Black community. The African American churches certainly embody, in a specific way, the concerns and aspirations of African Americans. Yet one cannot understand or assess the Black Church outside of the Black community. Nor can one fully understand the Black community without attention to the Black Church. Therefore students are equipped to fill the needs of Black churches for trained leadership and they are also encouraged to subject the total economic, social, cultural, and political experience of Black people to critical analysis. The goal of this educational process is the transformation of the structures of injustice afflicting Black people both in and out of the church. The emphasis is on praxis and critical reflection within the biosphere of African Americans. In *this* schema education is viewed as "advocacy scholarship." There is no neutral or disinterested learning: all learning and teaching either supports or opposes the status quo. Because Black Church Studies begins with the Black community as the locus of struggle and redemption, theological knowledge is always both critical and constructive. This knowledge destroys stereotypes and false images. It also brings to light the hidden resources and potential of the Black community. The kind of curriculum that results from this perspective is a *directed* curriculum. The curriculum is directed toward presenting and discovering usable knowledge for the Black community and, by extension, for humanity at large. This knowledge is identified with the traditions of an important segment of American society, and is relevant to all of American society. The Bible tells the story of God's redemption of all humanity through the life of one person. Perhaps all of American theological education may be enriched through the particular struggle of African Americans.

Notes

1. A few Black theologians raised the question of the relevance of graduate theological education in America to the emergence of Black radicalism in the 1960s. Unfortunately their analysis of the plight of seminary education was not taken seriously by the majority of theological

educators. See James H. Cone, "Black Power, Black Theology and the Study of Theology and Ethics," *Theological Education* 6 (Spring 1970): 202–15.

2. This problem of the orientation of the study of theology is addressed by Gerhard Ebeling in his book, *The Study of Theology* (Philadelphia: Fortress Press, 1978). However it never seems to occur to Ebeling that the source of the apparent irrelevance and anonymity of the study of theology may be its lack of prophetic witness in an unjust world. More recently Edward Farley addressed the problem of unity and identity in the study of theology in his book *Theologia: The Fragmentation and Unity of Theological Education* (Philadelphia: Fortress Press, 1983). He states that Black theology is "severely critical of traditional Western 'academic' theology [but] has yet mounted almost no serious criticism of or proposals about theological study" (p. 21). This statement in itself reveals an inexplicable ignorance on Farley's part of the existing literature on Black theological education or the existence of viable Black Church Studies programs in graduate theological schools. Thus most of the treatments of the problems within theological education fail to discuss the political dimensions of the issues.

3. For an analysis of Black Church Studies based on empirical research, see my article "'I Rose and Found My Voice': Black Church Studies and Theological Education." *Theological Education* 21 (Spring 1985): 49–72.

4. Michelle Russell, "An Open Letter to the Academy." Cited in Elisabeth Schussler-Fiorenza, *In Memory of Her*. (New York: Crossroad Publishing Co., 1984):xxii.

5. Mercy Amba Oduyoye, "Who Does Theology? Reflections on the Subject of Theology," in *Doing Theology in a Divided World*, ed. V. Fabella and S. Torres (Maryknoll, N.Y.: Orbis Books, 1985):145ff.

3

Assessment and New Departures for a Study of Black Religion in the United States of America

Charles H. Long

Assessment

Though the present interest in the study of Black religion in the United States within the theological community must be seen within the context of the programmatic theological statements of Professor James Cone, his work does not constitute the beginnings of the study of Black religion in the United States by Black scholars within the theological tradition.

Prior to the work of Cone several works dealing with some aspect of Black religion published by Black scholars appeared. I refer to W. E. B. DuBois's *The Negro Church* (1903), Carter G. Woodson's *The History of the Negro Church* (1921), Benjamin Mays and Joseph Nicholson's *The Negro's Church* (1933), Mays's *The Negro's God* (1938), and E. Franklin Frazier's *The Negro Church in America* (1955). In addition, two dissertations from the University of Chicago were Carleton L. Lee's *Patterns of Leadership Among Negroes* (1950), and Miles Mark Fisher's *Negro Slave Songs in the United States* (1953). Even closer in time are C. Eric Lincoln's *The Black Muslims in America* (1961) and Joseph Washington's *Black Religion* (1964). On the specifically theological level the works of Howard Thurman have for some time set forth a distinctively new interpretation of Black religious experience.

If Cone's work does not constitute an absolutely new beginning, it does represent a shift that might form a watershed in the study of Black religion. From the work of Cone one is able to set forth a basis from which we might assess the works prior to his time and to plot new and different trends in the study of Black religion.

Professor Cone's book, *Black Theology and Black Power* (1969), is unique in several ways. He is not, however, the first one to make the point that Jesus or God might be Black; a long line of Blacks have asserted this slogan, from

Bishop William McNeal Turner to Marcus Garvey. Cone is distinctive in that his understanding of the Blackness of the godhead is carried on within the context of a systematic apologetic theology that argues from within the theological tradition for its cogency. This work should be seen as part of the civil rights movement and of the change of context from civil rights integrationism to Black Power. I quote from the first section of this work, where Cone says, "If, as I believe, Black Power is the most important development in American life in this century, there is need to begin to analyze it from a theological perspective. In this work an effort is made to investigate the concept of Black Power, placing primary emphasis on its relationship to Christianity, the Church and contemporary American theology." (p. 1)

He continues, "It is my thesis, however, that Black Power, even in its most radical expression, is not an antithesis to Christianity, nor is it a heretical idea to be tolerated with painful forbearance. It is, rather, Christ's central message to twentieth-century America. And unless the empirical denominational church makes a determined effort to capture the man Jesus through a total identification with the suffering poor as expressed in Black Power, that church will become exactly what Christ is not." (p. 2)

Even this emphasis is not new. The same kind of overtone is present in the works of Eric Lincoln and Joseph Washington, and of course, these particular phrases remind us of the work of Howard Thurman, *Jesus and the Disinherited* first published in 1949. In this work Thurman stated, "The significance of the religion of Jesus to people who stand with their backs against the wall has always seemed to me to be crucial. It is one emphasis which has been lacking—except where it has been part of a very unfortunate corruption of the missionary impulse, which is, in a sense, the very heartbeat of the Christian religion. The basic fact is that Christianity as it was born in the mind of this Jewish thinker and teacher appears as a technique of survival for the oppressed." (p. 29)

So the theme of Blackness and the oppressed in Cone's work is not novel. As I said before, the distinctiveness of his work is in the sustained systematic exposition, but there is yet another distinction: Cone, though acknowledging the oppression, mounted a theological critique of the oppressors from the stance of Power! To be sure, the power, as far as the text is concerned, is present in its rhetorical style, its open accusation, its prophetic pronouncements. It issued a challenge—a challenge to Black and white churchmen, and a challenge to American theology, and, for that matter, all Christian theology.

It was a book published by the right person at the right time and in the right place. It caught up with some of the themes of previous Black scholars of religion from the sociological and Christian ethics perspectives as well as the theological trends that were emerging within social ethics. It formed a continuity and a discontinuity with that milieu; it made clear a place on which to stand and thus it became a pointer, and if not a culmination, a hiatus. Its culmination lies in the theological statements that summarize the protest for justice in the history of Black scholarship in religion, its hiatus in the self-conscious theological assertiveness. If *Black Theology and Black Power* makes a clarion call and if its appearance on the scene was one of audacity, Cone's work of 1970, *A Black Theology of Liberation*, is a different kind of theological work. Its style is different; it sets about to fill in the blank spaces created by his previous work. It moves more carefully through the theological method and defines itself as part and parcel of a theology of liberation. Its more sober tone reminds one that additional theological work remains to be done and Cone sets forth those elements that must be dealt with within the complete corpus of a Black Theology of liberation.

In the meanwhile, the Fund for Theological Education had shifted resources to the support of doctoral studies in religion for Black students; the Society for the Study of Black Religion was organized and out of this ferment critical analyses and discussion of Cone's work and the rediscovery of other works published previous to Cone's *Black Theology* were brought to bear on the discussion. So, coincidentally and causally related to these two works, we are able to see the formation of a new discourse that brings older works into a new milieu and points to trends in other directions—directions stemming from this new discourse.

Major critical and alternate statements on the definition of Black Theology were contributed by Major Jones and Deotis Roberts. The most trenchant critique of Black Theology is probably that of William Jones's *Is God a White Racist? A Preamble to Black Theology* (1973). This work by Jones raises the essential issue of theodicy. Put simply it is this question: Is suffering, Black suffering, crucial for the Black theologian? To regard liberation as the summum bonum and sine qua non necessitates the opposite, suffering as oppression, as an aspect of the *summum malum*. The precondition for Black liberation as the objective for Black Theology is the prior affirmation of Black suffering as oppressive.

This is a crucial argument for it raises questions concerning not simply the enterprise of Black Theology, but of the Christian structure of existence itself; it forces one to ask whether the structure of Christian existence is capable of defining or expressing freedom for those who suffer.

While theologians were discussing Blackness within the context of theologizing, Gayraud Wilmore put out a kind of theological history of the Black Church. In his *Black Religion and Black Radicalism* (1972), Wilmore traced the history of the Black Church and its leaders as they responded to the various historical manifestations of racism in America. Though churches and church leaders took different stances during different periods, one is able to see a thread of continuity in the manner in which, in every case, the two structures of survival and protest constituted a kind of baseline around which these stances were taken. Again I see a skeletal structure in this work that should lead and has led in some quarters to more detailed historical studies of the Black Church. In part the works of James Washington and Albert Raboteau are already filling in some of the flesh of this sturdy skeleton erected by Wilmore.

A special word must be said about C. Eric Lincoln. The publication of his *Black Muslims in America* was a signal that something new was going to happen in the religious life of Black Americans. Lincoln has always been ahead of everyone else. He has a peculiar intellectual intuition about matters of this kind. Not only has he written extensively on the sociology of Black religion and the Black Church, giving us a reassessment of E. Franklin Frazier, and an excellent book of readings on *The Black Experience in Religion* (1974), he has encouraged and presided over the publication of several volumes which might not have seen the light of day apart from his confidence and faith in the authors. Not only for his own works but equally for this task and his hand in the works of others do we owe him a special thanks. This kind of genius is as much needed as the great intellectual ideas and to find both of these in one person is much more than one would expect.

With the mention of Lincoln, let me move on to another phase by way of a comment based upon his edited work, *The Black Experience in Religion*. If we examine this text we see that it covers a very wide range of materials and interpretations: articles on the Black Church, preachers and preaching, Black Theology, Black sects and cults, and on Caribbean and African religions. From this work it is clear that Eric Lincoln has not confined the Black experience to the Christian churches in North America, nor is the attention to the Black churches in North America limited to a theological interpretation of their histories. "Black experiences" seems to constitute a world system, or a potentially world system, of communication and soteriological meaning. This was already a leitmotif in his work on the Black Muslims, for he saw the existence of Black Muslims at once as a protest against American racism and the expression of an alternate system of world communication. One may come at this point in another way if one looks at the activities and the work just put out by Gayraud Wilmore and James Cone. In their *Black Theology, A Documentary History, 1966–1979* (1979), the authors document the history of this movement and provide critical comments regarding Black Theology over this period of time, but they also include in this volume those meanings of Black Theology as a theology of liberation and thus the conversation and dialogue of Black Theology and theologians with Africans, Europeans, and Latin Americans extends the range of this soteriological communication.

A crucial issue will, in my opinion, emerge at this point. Is theology in any of its manifestations capable of sustaining this conversation or will it be sustained at another level that grows out of a more difficult conversation—a conversation that is an attempt to communicate the religious elements of one's cultural experience to another? To put it bluntly, how long will Jürgen Moltman and Paul Holmer be able to maintain themselves in this conversation, or, if they are able to do so, will they prevent other Africans or Latin Americans from speaking? How continuous is the discussion with variant structures of liberation theology and how much will the cultural-historical experience form a discontinuity?

One of the themes running through a great deal of the interpretations of Black Theology and Black religion is the assertion that the Black community did not and does not make distinctions between the secular and the sacred and that it follows from this assertion that the Black Church is and has been the locus of the Black community. If this is so, then it means that the church is the locus of the expression of Black cultural life. Politics, art, business, and all other dimensions of the Black community should thus find their expression as aspects of the religious experience of Black folks. To test out this assertion Black scholars in religion should be conversant with works that deal with the wider ranges of Black experience. To some extent the society has a few members who were not trained in theological schools, but only a few. Only one of two sociologists of religion, no anthropologist of religion, poet, novelist, political scientist, or economist is among us. We must do the best we can to become conversant with them through their writings.

Harold Cruse, in his wonderful tour de force book of 1967 *The Crisis of the Negro Intellectual*, had asserted that only Blacks in America could make a cultural revolution and he called upon the Black intellectuals to develop what he called a Black cultural methodology. By this he meant a critical and creative hermeneutic that was capable of taking a stance within the American and Western tradition affirmatively and critically. It would involve not simply criticism of racial oppression but an identification within that culture while at the same time undercutting the very stance of one's authenticity with that tradition in status quo.

In another vein Cruse was stating in our times the issue that DuBois raised in *Souls of Black Folk* (1903) as the double consciousness. But before I can give this discussion solidity, I must interject some other literature. First of all, there is a body of literature that deals with us explicitly and contingently, a body of scholarly works by Blacks and others that bear on our situation. These exist in contrast to a body of general American texts—texts that tell the American story, the American ideology, George Washington, the founding fathers, Thanksgiving, the Fourth of July, etc., etc., etc. In one way or other we were all educated in this mode so I don't need to go any further. We should, however, be aware of the internal critiques of myth-history. As far as history is concerned, let me mention only a few works: first, Francis Jennings's *The Invasion of America: Indians, Colonialism, and the Cant of Conquest* (1975), *Savagism and Civility* (1978) by Bernard Sheehan, and *Sons of the Fathers* (1976) by Catherine Albanese. Studies of this kind form a critique of the early American tradition and open the possibility for another mode of interpretation of American experience in terms of the new data and methods. These works should be read alongside the works of Vine Deloria. On Mexico I would recommend Jacques LaFaye's *Quetzcatacoatl and Guadulupe* (1978). I think that these should be decisive for any critical cultural methodology that undertakes the analysis of the nature and reality of the world of the colonized during the colonial period. Millions of people were in fact colonized during the period of late Western expansion, but the progeny of these colonizers, at least at this time, did not have an imperialism over the methods and theories regarding the realities of persons and cultures during this period. As far as a philosophical critique is concerned, I would recommend the work of David Brion Davis, especially his *The Problem of Slavery in an Age of Revolution* (1975).

Closer to home there are a host of works by Black novelists, historians, anthropologists, sociologists, political scientists, etc. John Hope Franklin's editions of Black biographies from University of California Press include James Weldon Johnson, William Wells Brown, Ida B. Wells, T. Thomas Fortune, and Henry Ossawa Tanner. And even closer there are the works of John Lovell, Jr., and Eileen Southern on Black music or A. Leon Higginbotham's study of Blacks and the legal process. Works of this kind will help us make sense of the claim of a pattern of experience and expression within the Black community.

But there is another body of literature that is in one sense as close and in another sense quite distant from our work. It is close because it purports to deal with many of the same issues that face us and distant because it does not arise out of the primordium of cultural passions that generates our work. Therefore, while these works are exceedingly competent in terms of the questions that they pose and resolve, the very questions are structures of the alienation. I am speaking here of works such as Eugene Genovese's *Roll, Jordan, Roll* (1974), and Lawrence Levine's *Black Culture and Black Consciousness* (1977).

Eugene Genovese's *Roll, Jordan, Roll* is part of an oeuvre that includes *The Political Economy of Slavery* (1967) and the subtitle of *Roll, Jordan, Roll* is "The World the Slaves Made." This is in a dialectical relationship with the former work. It is an extremely valuable text and continues a line of interpretation from Newbell Niles Puckett's *The Magic and Folk Beliefs of the Southern Negro* (1969) through Kenneth Stampp's *The Peculiar Institution* (1956) to *Time on the Cross* by Robert Fogel and Stanley Engerman (1974).

Genovese's method carries strong overtones of the dialectic of Hegel and Marx and in carrying through this method he makes a major revision of the religion of the slaves. The problem with this text is hermeneutical. What is his stance before our history? What is most lacking is any possibility for the discussion of the experience of slavery and of the slave in the terms of a transcendent meaning of freedom. The dialectic of master-slave allows only for the discussion of the meaning of freedom and obligation within the structure of paternalism. The meaning of the religion of the slaves is too closely tied to and reduced to the structures of the economy. Though admitting the formation of a new consciousness, it remains rooted in the structures of materiality and transcendent meanings are projections of this rootedness. The subtlety of DuBois's delineation of the double consciousness that tended to undercut its own formation is not an element of this analysis.

Levine's work, though bearing the title *Black Culture and Black Consciousness*, misses the point in the same manner—lack of participation as hermeneutical issue: the issue of living in and thinking about. Let me state what I have in mind at this point by reference to DuBois's notion of the double consciousness. In one sense it is the issue of objectivity and subjectivity. The true rendering of Black experience and expression is not a privileged position for Black scholars. At the same time there is room for and necessity for historical and humanistic studies that combine the "thinking about," with the lived in participation. This methodological issue will become increasingly important in the work of Black scholars.

Let me give an example of what I have in mind by using Hegel's master/ slave dialectic from this point of view:

Even when the slave, ex-slave, or colonized person becomes aware of the autonomy and independence of his consciousness, he finds that, because of the economic, political and linguistic hegemony of the master, there is not space for the legitimate expression for such a human form. The desire for an authentic place for the expression of this reality is the source of the revolutionary tendencies in these religions. But on the level of human consciousness religions of the oppressed create in another manner. The hegemony of the oppressors is understood as a myth—myth in two major senses, as true and as fictive. It is true as a structure with which one must deal in a day-by-day manner if one is to persevere, but it is fictive as far as any ontological significance is concerned.

But such a procedure does not define a simple dichotomy, for the day-to-day existence is in fact his labor—labor from which his autonomy arises; therefore his own autonomy takes on a fictive character. The truth of his existence must necessarily involve not only the change of this consciousness but the realization of the true and fictive consciousness of the oppressor. This drama is carried out again and again in the religions of the oppressed. But the basic structure of such meanings approximates the myth, for only the consciousness as myth can express the full range of this dialectical mode of being.

The oppressed must deal with both the fictive truth of his status as expressed by the oppressor, i.e., his second creation, and the discovery of his own autonomy and truth—his first creation. The locus for this structure is the mythic consciousness which dehistorizes the relationship for the sake of creating a new form of humanity—a form of humanity which is no longer based on the master-slave dialectic. The utopian and eschatological dimensions of the religions of the oppressed stem from this modality.

The oppressive element in the religions of the oppressed is the negation of the image of the oppressor and the discovery of the first creation. It is thus the negation that is found in community and seeks its expression in more authentic forms of community, those forms of community which are based upon the first creation, the original authenticity of all persons which precedes the master-slave dichotomy. There is thus a primordial structure to his consciousness, for in seeking a new beginning in the future it must perforce imagine an original beginning. (Long, 1976, pp. 411-2)

Leonard Barret's discussion of the Cumina-Pukkumina in C. Eric Lincoln's *The Black Experience in Religion* expresses the meaning of this dialectical mode of consciousness at the level of ritual action and his analysis might well carry over into some aspects of religious worship on the North American continent and allow us to rethink the impact of the Great Awakening on the slaves and other Black persons.

More congruent to, but offering a different methodological stance than either Genovese or Levine, is Roger Bastide's the *African Religions of Brazil* (1978). In this work Bastide employs an intensive participant-observant *verstehen* method in accumulating his data. He was actually initiated into *candomble* and this initiation was more than and deeper than that cute kind of story often related by anthropologists at cocktail parties. It was an expression of what he called a crisis of consciousness of a personal level and on the level of his scholarly discipline, comparative sociology; it raised the issue of the very raison d'être for study. It may be the case that such intimacy allowed for better understanding, but, what is more important, it prepared him to understand the dialectical modality of consciousness that while present in the *candomble* was at the same time an experience of modernity—that *candomble* and himself were struggling with similar problems. This is a masterful work by one who stands outside a tradition to study it in context.

What can one make of these various studies, presenting us with new data and new methods in light of the programmatic structures of Black Theology? First of all, though Black Theology is the most sustained protestant movement in Black religious thought, it has not picked up or fully exploited the social-ethical emphases of former Black religious thinkers and therefore has not made full use of a particular tradition in Black religious thought.

In connection with this point Black Theology, though making one of its resources the Black Christian institutional churches, had made hardly any inroads within these churches. The Black churches have not seen fit to affirm or to critically evaluate the project of Black Theology.

Neither Black Theology nor attendant works dealing with Black religion and Black culture have developed a general interpretative framework in which their interpretation makes for a distinctively new evaluation of religion and culture. (See Howard Dodson, "Needed: A New Perspective on Black History," 1981.) Is it possible for new works about Blacks to stay within the same framework that just a few years ago thrived on their exclusion? Responses to these questions lead to the next section of this paper.

Departures

We should wish to know, for example, how it would be possible to tolerate, and to justify, the sufferings and annihilation of so many peoples who suffer and are annihilated for the simple reason that their geographical situation sets them in the pathway of history; that they are neighbors of empires in a state of permanent expansion. How to justify for example, the fact that southwestern Europe had to suffer for centuries —and hence to renounce any impulse toward a higher historical existence, toward spiritual creation on a universal plane—invaders and later of the Ottoman empire? And in our day, when historical pressure no longer allows any escape, how can man tolerate the catastrophies and horrors of history—if beyond them he can glimpse no sign, no transhistorical meaning; if they are only blind play of economic, social, or political forces, or, even worse, only the result of "liberties" that a minority takes and exercises directly on the stage of universal history? (Eliade, p. 151)

The Negro is sort of a seventh son, born with a veil, and gifted with second-sight in this American world—a world which yields him no true self-consciousness, but only lets him see himself through the revelation of the other world. It is a peculiar sensation, this double consciousness, this sense of always looking at one's self through the eyes of the others, of measuring one's soul by the tape of a world that looks on in amused contempt and pity. One feels this two-ness—as American, as Negro; two souls, two thoughts, two unreconciled strivings; two warring ideals in one dark body, whose dogged strength alone keeps it from being torn asunder. The history of the American Negro is the history of this strife —this longing to attain self-conscious manhood, to merge this double self into a better truer self. In this merging he wishes neither of the older selves to be lost. He would not Africanize America, for America has too much to teach the world and Africa. He would not bleach his Negro soul in a flood of white Americanism, for he knows that Negro blood has a message for the world. . . . (DuBois, pp. 3–4)

These two epigraphs form the context for this section. They are from the pens of two very dissimilar, from a conventional point of view, scholars. Eliade is the Rumanian-American émigré historian of religions, and the quotation comes at the end of his work *Cosmos and History* (1959) in the section entitled, "The Terror of History." W. E. B. DuBois is the Black American scholar, leader, agitator, and historian; his quotation is taken from the very first section of the chapter entitled, "Of Our Spiritual Strivings," in his *Souls of Black Folk*.

There are, however, in the face of these dissimilarities several commonalities. Both of the statements are from a genre of literature that falls between scholarship and autobiography. They represent hermeneutical probings in which the stance and point of view exposed reveal a lived experience as the source of the probing. Both deal with human time as that temporal order that is the increment of imperialism and world systems that order through military, economic, and political power, such that they smother the time and histories of all who come into contact with them. Eliade raises the question of the philosophical justification of this kind of power in the terms of the apologia for it, and DuBois's statement represents an assessment of the possibility of freedom once this power has effected its purpose. Both are interpretations of religion.

The bifurcation of the world that is coincidental to enslavement and conquest produces not only differing rhythms of the temporal sequences but also different meanings of the manifestation of world, the epistemologies for knowing it, and the practical activities for deciphering the meanings of cultural destinies. Invariably a normative meaning of history is supported and justified by the ideologies of conquest. And these ideologies are not simply the crass and crude slogans of blood and soil or manifest destiny. In the period of late Western expansion these philosophical ideologies were, more often than not, part and parcel of the enunciation of a universal humanism, making claims as it did for the essential status of all human beings. This is as true for the French philosophes, Montesquieu, Montaigne, Rousseau, as it for the German philosophers from Kant to Hegel, and the English empiricists.

These philosophical ideologies must be seen as sometimes forming the foundation for, and at other times serving as the correlate of, the modern university disciplines that undertook the task of studying, classifying, and understanding the lives and cultures of those who had to undergo the histories of the conquerors, or in Eliade's term, the "terror" of their histories. What is remarkable on the epistemological level in these early new social sciences (and we might say almost to the present) is the fact that they hardly make mention of the contact situation itself, the fact of mutual discovery of the two cultures in the situation of colonialism—what Francis Jennings has called mutual discoveries. This is even more remarkable when we observe that one of the basic ingredients within the philosophical and cultural meaning of the conquerors is the evaluation of history. By history in this sense, I don't mean that valuation of temporality that is a pervasive characteristic of human existence. I mean a particular and peculiar interpretation and point of view regarding time, justified in many instances through recourse to progress, civilizing missions, and Christian theologies; it finds its supporters among the technological positivists of the left and the right.

Those who are forced to undergo this history are not subjected simply to economic and political exploitation; they are simultaneously forced to undergo an evacuation of their cultural meaning and the possibility for cultural creativity and stability. This evacuation of cultural meaning forced by the conqueror is matched by the presentation of the conquered people and culture as "problems of knowledge" in a special sense. They are "problems of knowledge" not so much in the conventional sense, but classified as special categories of this kind of problem. The taxonomies used to describe them allow them to become normal special problems, or normal exotic problems, and thus disciplinary structures need not fear their disappearance, for they were created by and for the disciplines and tend to exist as eternal intellectual problems. One of the most general and pervasive structures of this kind of problem revolves around the distinction primitive/civilized. (See my article

"Primitive/Civilized: The Locus of a Problem," *History of Religions* 19, no. 6 [November 1980].) I show how meanings regarding a European discourse on wild men, women, and the insane, became the normative language for the discussion of the new geographies and cultures discovered by the Europeans from the fifteenth century to the present. This language still pervades many of our common disciplinary fields and it is one of those forms of cultural language that has defined explicity and adumbrated a range of meanings and interpretative schema concerning Blacks in the United States. Critical and precise hermeneutical attention must be given to this level of our cultural and disciplinary languages as part of the creativity of Black scholarship if this scholarship is ever to form a new framework of interpretation. In this connection I have found that some of the philosophical positions set forth by Jacques Derrida are quite congruent with DuBois's notion of a double consciousness. Especially in his program of deconstruction do I see a meaning of radical critique and creativity. I am pleased to find that younger scholars such as Cornel West at Union Seminary are of the same opinion.

Another area pertinent to this topic has to do with the general interpretation of American culture itself. If this culture is continually understood simply as the culture of Europeans who came to a virgin land all subsequent interpretations will tend to be wrong-headed. I have experimented with the most general categorization of American culture as an aboriginal-Euro-African culture.

In making this assertion or operating with this presupposition, I am trying to mitigate the notion that Euro-Americans serve as the reality principle for American culture and that others are not real until contact has been made with the Euro-Americans. All are real, but in differing modes. To decipher this meaning methodologically, I have had recourse to models from structural linguistics, where I employ the meanings of synchrony, diachrony, and silence as basic elements for a total language.

At another level attention should be directed towards a comparative history of the religions of the oppressed. Vittorio Lanternari's work of this title (*Religions of the Oppressed*, 1963) is suggestive but its heavy-handed Marxism suffocates any genuine religious interpretation. Given the general context of oppression, what mode of consciousness emerges, what epistemological resources are created, and what meanings of world are actual and possible?

One of the problems of Black Theology is that none of its protagonists have attempted to delineate the meaning of power in our present situation.

Power is assumed to be an eternal neutral category that can be had or grasped by the group or person lucky or militant enough to handle it. Power is a pervasive dimension of human existence but its constellation, locus, and influence is contextually situated. Paul Tillich's essay on the "End of the Protestant Era," in his *The Protestant Era* (1948) should complement W. E. B. DuBois's statement of the twentieth century and the "rising tide of color." What is the meaning of power at the end of the protestant era? Do the oppressed slaver for the old capitalist protestant power or has a new locus and formation of power appeared to them? These are crucial issues and since religion is also a concern about power, its origins and its forms, such questions cannot be avoided.

My own work at this point has been at the level of what I call ideograms, (to borrow a term from Rudolf Otto). I have been concerned to pay close attention to the concrete expressions from this level to conceptualization in either the theological or philosophical mode, I have developed the liminal ideogram, a meaning that emerges from concreteness but is not yet a concept. The ideogram allows for religious experience to adumbrate other dimensions of human existence in a preconceptual form raising the wider issues of reality, world, epistemology, etc. Conceptual structures arising from these ideograms ought then to be constructive and critical. At the present time I am working with the passivity of power, the opaqueness of reality, the percussive nature of existence, and the rhythms of time.

The study of Black religion cannot be provincialized. Africans were brought to the New World as part and parcel of an international system of trade and communication; the meanings of the cultures of the former, colonized in the modern world, carry the same implications. Religious forms and expressions are the sources of new worlds of meaning; the study and understanding of Black religion has much to contribute to our future.

References

Albanese, Catherine. *Sons of the Fathers*. Philadelphia: Temple University Press, 1976.

Bastide, Roger. *African Religions of Brazil*. Baltimore: Johns Hopkins University Press, 1978.

Cone, James. *Black Theology and Black Power*. New York: Seabury Press, 1969.

————. *A Black Theology of Liberation*. Philadelphia and New York: Lippincott, 1970.

Cruse, Harold. *The Crisis of the Negro Intellectual*. New York: William Morrow, 1967.

Dodson, Howard. "Needed: A New Perspective on Black History," *National Endowment for the Humanities*, 2, no. 1 (February 1981): 1, 2.

DuBois, W. E. B., *The Negro Church*. Atlanta: Atlanta University Press, 1903.

————. *Souls of Black Folk*. Chicago: A.C. McClurg & Co., 1903. Reprint. New York: Fawcett Publications, 1961.

Eliade, Mircea. *Cosmos and History*. New York: Harper Torch Books, Harper & Row, 1959.

Fisher, Miles Mark. *Negro Slave Songs in the United States*. New York: Citadel Press, 1963.

Frazier, E. Franklin. *The Negro Church in America*. 1955. Reprint. Liverpool: University of Liverpool Press, 1963.

Fogel, Robert and Stanley Engerman. *Time on the Cross*. Boston: Little, Brown, 1974.

Genovese, Eugene D. *The Political Economy of Slavery*. New York: Random House, 1967.

————. *Roll, Jordan, Roll*. New York: Random House, 1974.

Higginbotham, A. Leon, Jr. *In the Matter of Color*. New York: Oxford University Press, 1978.

Jennings, Francis. *The Invasion of America: Indians, Colonialism, and the Cant of Conquest*. Chapel Hill: University of North Carolina Press, 1975.

Jones, William. *Is God a White Racist? A Preamble to Black Theology*. Garden City, New York: Doubleday/Anchor, 1974.

LaFaye, Jacques. *Quetzcatacoatl and Guadulupe*. Chicago: University of Chicago Press, 1978.

Lanternari, Vittoria. *Religions of the Oppressed*. New York: Alfred A. Knopf, 1963.

Lee, Carleton L. *Patterns of Leadership Among Negroes*. Ph.D. diss., University of Chicago Press, 1950.

Levine, Lawrence. *Black Culture and Black Consciousness*. New York: Oxford University Press, 1977.

Lincoln, C. Eric. *The Black Muslims in America*. Boston: Beacon Press, 1961.

————. *The World the Slaveholders Made*. New York: Random House, 1969.

————, ed., *The Black Experience in Religion*. Garden City, N.Y.: Doubleday/Anchor, 1974.

Long, Charles H., "Oppression in Religion, and the Religions of the Oppressed," *Harvard Theological Review*. 69, no. 3–4 (1976): 397–412.

————. "Primitive/Civilized: The Locus of a Problem," *History of Religions*, 19, no. 6 (November 1980).

Lovell, John, Jr., *Black Song, the Forge and the Flame*. New York: Collier-Macmillan, 1972.

Mays, Benjamin E. and Joseph W. Nicholson. *The Negro's Church*. New York: Institute of Social and Religious Research, 1933.

————. *The Negro's God*. Boston: Chapman & Grimes, Inc., 1938.

Philips, Ulrich B. *American Negro Slavery*. Baton Rouge: Louisiana State University Press, 1966.

————. *The Slave Economy of the Old South*. Baton Rouge: Louisiana State University Press, 1968.

Puckett, Newbell Niles. *The Magic and Folk Beliefs of the Southern Negro*. New York: Dover Publications Inc., 1969.

Stampp, Kenneth. *The Peculiar Institution*. New York: Vintage Books, 1956.

Thurman, Howard. *Jesus and the Disinherited*. Nashville, Tenn.: Abingdon Press, 1949.

Tillich, Paul. *The Protestant Era*. Chicago: University of Chicago Press, 1948.

Wilmore, Gayraud. *Black Religion and Black Radicalism*. New York: Doubleday, 1972.

Wilmore, Gayraud and James Cone. *Black Theology, A Documentary History, 1966–1979*. Maryknoll, N.Y.: Orbis Books, 1979.

Woodson, Carter G. *The History of the Negro Church*. 1921. Reprint. Washington, D.C.: Associated Publishers, 1945.

4

Folk Religion and Negro Congregations: The Fifth Religion

Joseph R. Washington, Jr.

In many places today, as in Montgomery in 1956, the reality of Negro folk religion can be seen in its uniqueness, supported in part by Negro Protestants and Negro Christians but in full by Negroes of the most diversified persuasions. The common suffering of segregation and discrimination is the crucible out of which the folk religion was created in the past; it creates the unity and power of Negroes in the present and in an effort to tap this resource Negro ministers have been particularly guilty of equating the folk religion with "the Negro church." The folk religion is not an institutional one. It is a spirit that binds Negroes in a way they are not bound to other Americans because of their different histories. Here and there this folk religion may be identifiable with a given congregation, yet wherever and whenever the suffering is acute it transcends all religious and socioeconomic barriers separating Negroes from Negroes. There are Negroes who are Protestants, there are Negroes who are Christians, there are Negroes in churches—but there is no Negro Protestantism, Negro Christianity, or Negro church. There are Negro religious institutions that developed out of the folk religion. And it is this historical folk religion that unites all Negroes in a brotherhood taking precedence over their individual patterns for the worship of God, or the lack thereof. The root of this folk religion is racial unity for freedom and equality. Every ecclesiastical expression of Negro congregations and institutions is but a variation or frustration of this theme.

It is unusual to think in terms of Negro folk religion, but it constitutes the fifth major religion functioning in the American culture. Generally acknowledged are Judaism, Protestantism, and Roman Catholicism.[1] The impact of these religions on the Negro has varied in quantity and quality. A religion less widely acknowledged, but nevertheless influential in American culture, is secularism. Secularism is rooted in humanitarianism, philosophical ideals, democracy, science, and human progress. Its impact upon the Negro, less widely heralded, has been impressive. In the sense that secularism is a religion, so also is the folk religion. The folk religion holds in common with secularism a non-ecclesiastical affirmation, but the singularity of the folk, or Black, religion is its heredity. As individuals, Negroes are adherents of the other dominant religions in this country. The majority are secularists; of those who have formal commitments the greater number are Protestants, usually in independent Baptist and Methodist communions —insitutionally and racially segregated from white congregations of the same name.

Black religion is unique to the Negro folk, born as it was of slavery, and it ties them each to the other in times of stress by a racial bond that cuts across all other variables. Given enough facts about his ecclesiastical affiliation and his status, we are often able to generalize accurately about the beliefs and attitudes of any particular non-Negro person with whom we are concerned. The fact that a Negro, however, is Protestant, Roman Catholic, or in rare instances Jewish, is of minor and less predictable value in determining his or her beliefs and attitudes.

Regardless of the congregational expression in which he may be involved side by side with his white neighbor, the Negro knows the dimension of separation from the white that leads him to seek fulfillment in fellowships primarily concerned with the folk religion: freedom and equality.

The white American prefers to repress, and the Negro American often does, the truth of a people involuntarily uprooted from their environment, herded together like animals and treated so on their way to an entirely different environment where the animal treatment was reinforced and its stigma perpetuated. This is the common history of the Negro from the early seventeenth century on. Once he landed on these shores he was quickly separated from his family and sold to the highest bidder. Thrown together with other slaves with whom he had in common only the bonds of slavery and race, he was forced to start a life without a history, a religion, or a family, and with a most precarious future. For the first two and a half centuries the majority of Negroes were denied freedom of body and for three and a half centuries they have all been denied freedom of choice (Negroes who have been able to advance on the basis of merit in one locale are still subject to being treated as undesirables when they move out of their restricted situation of privilege).

As a consequence, Negroes have chosen to make their way on pride of race as they strive to be respected on the basis of quality, since they are invariably viewed first as Black men rather than as men. This is especially true in congregational life.

Black religion began amidst polygamy in the cotton fields. It was an adaptation of the white master's religion. Slaves were not initially permitted to raise families of their own, nor to protect their women from the desires of the plantation owners and their associates. But they were permitted, from the earliest days, to work out their own peculiar religion. The slave songs which antedated the Negro family, and which the Negro used to articulate his overwhelming concern with freedom, were the key feature of this folk, or Black, religion. Deprived of the natural right of a family, exposed to moralities shorn of ethics through the religion the whites introduced into the lives of the slaves to ease the pain of a non-ethical system, Negroes fused race and the meaning they gave to slave songs into a religion which provided their sole sense of identity.

Born in slavery, weaned in segregation, and reared in discrimination, the religion of the Negro folk was chosen to bear roles of both protest and relief. Thus the uniqueness of Black religion is the racial bond that seeks to risk its life for the elusive but ultimate goal of freedom and equality by means of protest and action. It does so through the only avenues to which its members have always been permitted a measure of access: religious convocations in the fields or in houses of worship.

The genius of the Negro folk religion is not readily understandable apart from the awareness of the Black and white streams of which it is constituted. The white stream began with the missionaries who beat a path to the door of the Negro slave. Their main purpose was to extoll the virtues of the next world. From the earliest days the Negro was much more concerned with the freedom of this world than with the religion of the next. He listened attentively to the religious and moral teachings of the whites, but his mind was elsewhere. He was resourceful enough to perceive that the best way to freedom in this world was through the religion of the whites, sanctioned by his masters and overseers as a means of harnessing his energy for production.

The Black stream began under the camouflage of camp meetings during the day and singing at night, in which the religion of the whites and the concern of the slaves were blended to create the Negro spirituals, providing a cover for Negro preachers to lead insurrections and escapes. The fermentation of the folk religion began in the shadows of the plantation.

Inspired by the hope accompanying the end of slavery, the Negro created out of his Black religion a relief agency to aid the freedman centered in the congregation and the preacher. The hope of equal opportunity continued in the aftermath of Reconstruction, as well as the intention of the Negro that his religion of militancy and his minister serve him in the "advancement of the race."

This Black stream of the Negro folk religion was given leadership by the free Negro ministers of the North who had instituted Negro congregations independent of their white sponsors. This independent movement was a response to segregation in, and later exclusion from, white congregational communions, first in the North and then in the South. Frustrated by their inability to express in open ways the militant drive for freedom that in slavery was channeled through escapes to the North, the post-Civil War Negro folk put their trust in, and merged with, the independents, who like the folk, were instructed by whites, but unlike the folk, brought to this union the institutional procedures of whites. The independents intended and carried out no innovations in ecclesiology, doctrine, ritual, polity, or theology which distinguished them from white denominations; instead they assumed the names of white denominations, prefacing them with "African." Direction came from Negroes who had long yearned for freedom and equality; their folk religion supplied the independents with a needed, unique, inner dynamic. The union of the folk religion and independents created in the Negro congregation a center for the relief of the freedman. This was assumed to be a temporary need and the folk anticipated the day when the preacher and the fellowship would bring about freedom and equality.

But the hope for the minister and fellowship was not realized. Following Reconstruction the old practice of segregation was resumed with a vengeance in the South and discrimination continued in the North. These twin evils curbed the militancy of the folk religion. In that era of decline in the quest for freedom, the Negro minister remained the spokesman for the people with this difference—faced by insurmountable obstacles, he succumbed to the cajolery and bribery of the white power structure and became its foil. Instead of freedom, he preached moralities and emphasized rewards in the life beyond, in much the same manner as the white missionaries. The Negro minister increased his control and redirected the enthusiasm of the folk religion for the purpose of gaining personal power.

From this point on, the Black contribution lay dormant while the white contribution was active and dominant. The burning zeal for liberty and justice, the raison d'être of the folk religion, was dimmed in the darkness of the whole society's disarrangement. The dominant theme was stymied and could not be articulated in the society at large. Frustrated, the vitality of the repressed black religion was expressed through the hope of a world beyond —the only other outlet available to the Negro.

The disappointment with the Negro minister and the independent fellowships became apparent early in this century with the loss of widespread support of Negro congregations and the rise of organizations such as the National Association for the Advancement of Colored People and the National Urban League. These racial organizations, led by social workers, took over the leadership of the central concern of the Negro people and channeled their desires more satisfactorily in creative and positive achievements. Increasingly since the 1920s, the Negro minister has been an object of disgust. The deprecation of the Negro minister and his thwarting of Black religion reached its height during the Depression, as noted by St. Clair Drake and Horace R. Cayton in *Black Metropolis*:[2]

> You take some of these preachers, they're living like kings—got great big Packard automobiles and ten or twelve suits and a bunch of sisters putting food in their pantry. Do you call that religion? Naw! It ain't nothing but a bunch of damn monkey foolishness.
>
> Blood-suckers! they'll take the food out of your mouth and make you think they are doing you a favor.
>
> The preachers want to line their pockets with gold. They are supposed to be the leaders of the people, but they are fake leaders.
>
> Ministers are not as conscientious as they used to be. They are money-mad nowadays. All they want is the almighty dollar and that is all they talk about.
>
> I used to be active in the church; I thought we could work out our salvation that way. But I found out better. These Negro preachers are not bothered about the Race—about all they think of is themselves.

There were always a few ministers and congregations which continued to work along the lines expected of the folk religion:[3]

I am a member of the Solid Rock A.M.E. Church. Churches are a necessity, for I believe that it is through them that our people got the idea that we must co-operate with each other.

My whole family belongs to St. Simon's Baptist Church. I am of the opinion that the church fills a great need. It is hard to picture the amount of evil that would take hold of the world if the church were done away with. I also believe that many of our folks have learned from the church that big things can be accomplished only by the joining of forces of a large group of people.

It is precisely this function of religion, which Negroes everywhere have always adhered to, white Protestants do not understand, and Negro ministers forget, when they claim that Negro congregations are evidence of "the Negro church," instead of the affirmation of Black religion. They may have never realized or forgotten what the folk have always known, that the meeting house is the gathering point, where alone the brotherhood is free to be about its primary business: working together to pursue and achieve equal rights and opportunity for each and all.

Since the 1920s Black religion, the religion of the folk, has been dysfunctional. From this period on the once subordinate and latent stream of white Protestant evangelicalism has been dominant and manifest, relegating the uniqueness of Black religion to verbal expression from the pulpit in such a way that action was stifled. But all the while the folk religion has been seething. It came to a head with the nonviolent movement. Once again some of the Negro ministers resumed their expected roles as leaders of the race. With the protest movement Black religion has come full circle and its vitality has never been more pronounced. For historic reasons American Negro folk religion employs the meeting house to advance the race through brotherhood and to make its presence felt in politics, education, economics, and the fight for justice and equality. Black religion has never been primarily concerned with contributing to worship, liturgy, theology, or the ecumenical movement in Protestantism, nor has it assumed responsibility in the specific concerns of the Christian faith such as missionary work. Ecclesiastical expressions are rooted not in Black religion but in the white heritage.

The dysfunction of the folk religion was caused by its suppression within institutional and evangelical Negro religious organizations. Militancy was frustrated or considered repellent. On the strength of the repressed militant and folk religion, the independent movement among Negroes who adhered to white religion expanded into the major Negro institution. Today there are more than thirty Negro religious organizations, bearing names similar to the white institutions from which they are independent. But from the beginning the major ones were committed to double duty. To provide an outlet for equality in religious leadership and worship and to be the primary institution for the advancement of the Negro in the society, in the interim between freedom hoped for and freedom realized, was the raison d'être of the independent movement.

Unfortunately for several generations now Negro ministers and their organizations have misconstrued the historic intent of the folk religion. It is clear that Black religion has always been deeply committed to the central concern of Christianity, which was not learned from white Protestants—love-justice-equality. Instead of focusing on this concern and bringing it to fruition, Negro ministers have concentrated on the maintenance of independent organizations for the sake of independence. They have forgotten that Black religion is a tradition interested not in pseudo-Protestantism but in freedom with equality.

Surprisingly enough, while Negro religious institutions of the independent variety have been dysfunctional in the realm of the Black stream running through the folk religion, they have been equally dysfunctional in the realm of the white stream. Negroes have failed to make real contributions to Protestantism, the Christian faith, or the Christian church, or to suggest any ecclesiastical change in the white organizations after which they are modeled. The reason for this failure is not inherent inability; it is because of the fact that Negro institutions were not established to propound theology or liturgical matters. Negro independent religious life has been shaped within structures whose power is perverted, as clearly as Black religion perverted the historic Christian faith. Independent Negro congregations and institutions are ineffective among Negroes because they have failed in faithfulness to Black religion and to the communion they represent.

Of the independents, the Baptists are numerically in the majority and now boast of about 7,268,800 members—divided into two National Baptist Conventions (an indeterminate number exists in a third one organized in 1962). The African Methodist Episcopal Church lists 1,166,300 and the African Methodist Episcopal Zion Church 770,000. Each of these institutions grew out of conflicts within white bodies. They were the carriers of the Black religion with which they have infected latter-day independents, as well as dependent Negro congregations within white denominations. Congregations of Negroes in white Presbyterian, Episcopal, Lutheran, Roman Catholic, Methodist, and Baptist denominations have all been permeated with the dynamic of the Negro folk religion—most particularly in the sermons of the minister and the social fellowship. While these dependent institutions have been financially underwritten, to various degrees, in their educational and building programs by whites, the independents have been supported to a far less degree by the white communities. For instance, African Methodist Episcopalians claim they are a completely Negro organization with no white backing. Baptists in the South are sometimes aligned with, and more often supported by, the Southern Baptists (white), and Negro Baptists in the North are aided by the American Baptist Convention (white), but even among Baptists it is clear that congregations are largely independent.

Considering this independence, the dysfunction of Black religion is the more startling. A tremendous amount of energy is spent to keep these organizations alive for the sole purpose of providing a place of worship and fellowship for Negroes. Pride in the past history of these independent groups as militant communities aiding the advancement of the Negro is now only a ritual, recalled to support their continuation for religious exercises. The real purpose of Negro independents, promotion of freedom and equality, is no longer a primary concern. Indeed, in many ways, these independents have become separatists or reactionaries who dampen the contemporary drive for freedom, fearing it will disturb the institutional program. Against this lethargy the massive nonviolent protest movement has striven, and it has drawn into its ranks those Negroes who affirm Black religion and deplore the maintenance of institutionalism. Strange as it is, the protest movement represents the last "big push" for the justification of separate Negro religious organizations. Insofar as the movement is successful in pulling Negroes together, independents will have ammunition for the restoration of pride in racial institutions. It is accurate to state that racial pride and personal interests are now the distorted characteristics of independents and are the only reasons for which these organizations exist.

If we consider the role of the independents throughout the first half of this century, the dysfunction of the folk religion is a matter of record. The Negro's emotional involvement in Black religion has been manipulated by these organizations for their own benefit. In return they have provided an opportunity to worship, primarily through emotional release and fellowship.

But the vestiges of this once imaginative and unique Black religion are here and there identifiable. To see the present dysfunction of Black religion in proper perspective, it is helpful to recall this fact: it is as the Negro social organization for the advancement of the race—not the "Negro church"—that the folk intended the meeting house, although their belief in the divine sanction of their endeavors is obvious. In addition to their will to worship —though the majority of Negroes from the days of slavery have never been involved—there is good reason why Negroes have identified their destiny with the meeting house:

> The church was the first community or public organization that the Negro actually owned and completely controlled. And it is possibly true to this day that the Negro church is the most thoroughly owned and controlled public institution of the race. Nothing can compare with this ownership and control except ownership of the home and possibly control of the Negro lodge. It is to be doubted whether Negro control is as complete in any other area of Negro life, except these two, as it is in the church.[4]

By any theological standard "the church" is the people of God and cannot be "owned" as if it were a "community organization" unless it is intended to be the Negro's "community or public organization." In varying degrees, the meeting house is an honored symbol for some Negroes, an improvident one for others, and the source of imprecation for still others. However, the meeting house of the folk still enables one to see in isolated instances a once indispensable site for an experimental Black religion.

In spite of the failure of the folk religion, Negro congregations appear to flourish, a fact not explained by the white man's belief that the Negro is all emotionalism in religion. Given a Negro and a white person, or two congregations of the same socioeconomic background and cultural sensitivity, the emotional output in religion, as elsewhere, would not vary significantly. And while the degree of frenzy of religion varies in proportion to the class station of white and Negro Americans, the Negro may be slower but no less sure in abandoning this frenzy because he is impeded in his endeavor to participate fully in the culture. (The word "station" is deliberately used here to indicate the difficulty of using the term "status" when speaking of Negroes in America, because they have no status except as they make their own within Negro subcultures—and it is this imitation that reinforces the will to separate religious societies.) Moreover, the Negro is not inherently fixated upon the supernatural; there are, comparatively, at least as many Negroes as whites who do not feel this compunction. Whatever prosperity Negro congregations realize, in the near obliteration of Black religion, is due to the lack of choice and the curtailment of community diversions. Both the oldest and wealthiest organization in the Negro community, the religious fellowship has moved into this vacuum, offering a wide variety of activities which give a fundamental rhythm to existence. The obvious need filled by religious organizations is at once the glory and doom of the folk religion. Its glory lies in its proper function within the framework of the folk religion; its doom is in its being the consuming interest of the organization. These activities are stepped up in the large urban areas, whose milieu offers increasing competition to Negro congregations. In small towns, they meet less competition from the taverns, poolrooms, police stations, movies, clubs, and dance halls.[5] In rural areas the meeting house remains the dominant outlet for the excluded people.

Notes

1. See Gerhard Lenski, *The Religious Factor* (Garden City, N.Y.: Doubleday, 1961). Lenski does not include secularism as a religion, but emphasizes the importance of the other four.

2. St. Clair Drake and Horace R. Cayton, *Black Metropolis: A Study of Negro Life in a Northern City* (New York: Harcourt, Brace & World, 1945; Harper & Row, 1962).

3. Ibid., 422.

4. Benjamin E. Mays and Joseph W. Nicholson, *The Negro's Church* (New York: Institute of Social and Religious Research, 1933), p. 278.

5. Hylan Lewis, *Blackways of Kent* (Chapel Hill: University of North Carolina Press, 1955):64 ff.

The Religious Ethos of the Universal Negro Improvement Association

Randall K. Burkett

Several insightful Black intellectuals contemporaneous with Marcus Garvey have at least alluded to the religious motifs which were to be found in the program and propaganda of the Universal Negro Improvement Association. One of the first of these was Claude McKay, one-time correspondent for the *Negro World*, who wrote an article for the April 1922 issue of the radical magazine *Liberator* in which he suggested that the essence of the appeal of this new "Negro Moses" was Garvey's imitation of one Alexander Bedward, a West Indian cultic leader who flourished in Jamaica between 1891 and the early 1920s. The Bedwardites constituted "a religious sect . . . purely native in its emotional and external features," which was "the true religion of thousands of natives." McKay hypothesized that perhaps "the notorious career of Bedward, the prophet, worked unconsciously upon Marcus Garvey's mind and made him work out his plans along similar spectacular lines."[1]

McKay's readers, familiar with Bedward's career, were aware, of course, that he had recently been placed in a Jamaican mental institution. He was committed for having prophesied that as the Black incarnation of Jesus Christ, he would on a given day be whisked off to heaven in a white throne, returning after three days to wreak destruction upon the (white) non-elect.[2] Presumably McKay's implication was that the same fate might be appropriate for Garvey, or at least that Garvey, like Bedward, was best understood as an impostor and a fraud.[3]

A more suggestive, if still cursory, analysis of the religious aspects of the Garvey movement was made in a brief article by E. Franklin Frazier published in 1926. Writing in the *Nation*, Frazier called for a "closer examination of the ideals and symbols which Garvey always held up for his followers," and suggested that precisely this symbolism was the basis of Garvey's unique appeal. He pointed specifically to resonant religious themes such as the "redemption of Africa," which Frazier saw as formally analogous to the syndicalists' myth of the general strike. The "redemption of Africa" had become for the UNIA a central motivating mythos, an equivalent to the idea of paradise which had been lost, but which was "always almost at hand." Formative events of the Judeo-Christian tradition were likewise re-symbolized:

> Garvey, who was well acquainted with the tremendous influence of religion in the life of the Negro, proved himself matchless in assimilating his own program to the religious experience of the Negro. Christmas, with its association of the lowly birth of Jesus, became symbolic of the Negro's birth among the nations of the world. Easter became the symbol of the resurrection of an oppressed and crucified race.[4]

Such "naive symbolism," as Frazier termed it, ought not to blind one to the power the symbols possess in evincing commitment and devotion; nor need one conclude that Garvey was simply a "common swindler" capitalizing on the superstitions of a people for selfish gains, "when the evidence seems to place him among the so-called cranks who refuse to deal realistically with life."[5] Whether in spite of or because of his lack of realism, however, Garvey had achieved a dramatic goal: sustained grass roots support on a mass basis. As Frazier concluded, "He has the distinction of initiating the first real mass movement among American Negroes."[6]

It is not insignificant that, whereas the editors of the *Negro World* relegated to the back pages of their paper a brief reply to the "Bedwardism" charge leveled by McKay, they reprinted the full text of Frazier's article and reserved their own corrective assessment of certain aspects of his critique to a subsequent editorial column.[7] Evidently Frazier's intuition concerning the importance both of the movement itself and of the religious elements within it was in much closer agreement with the UNIA's self-understanding than was McKay's perspective.

Unfortunately no one developed the suggestions advanced by Frazier by way of a systematic investigation into the religious framework around which the UNIA was organized. Instead the typical application of the "religious" interpretation was made in a pejorative sense, the point being that Garvey's was but another in a long string of "escapist" or "utopian" cultic movements that have had the net effect in the Black community of siphoning off effective protest into an "otherworldly" and apolitical realm. James Weldon Johnson provided an example in his condescending description of the UNIA:

The movement became more than a movement, it became a religion, its members became zealots. Meetings at Liberty Hall were conducted with an elaborate liturgy. The moment for the entry of the "Provisional President" into the auditorium was solemn; a hushed and expectant silence on the throng, the African Legion and Black Cross nurses flanking the long aisle and coming to attention, the band and audience joining in the hymn: "God Save our President," and Garvey, surrounded by his guard of honour from the Legion, marching majestically through the double line and mounting the rostrum; it was impressive if for no other reason than the way in which it impressed the throng.[8]

While such men as McKay, Frazier, and Johnson were thus aware of the presence of religious motifs within the UNIA, they were mostly content to use this knowledge as a club with which to attack Garvey. One suspects that for all of these men religion was basically understood as synonymous with "escapism," or as compensation in another world for material rewards denied in the present world.[9] Simply to conclude that Garveyism was a religion was therefore to go a long way towards discrediting it or denying the need to take it seriously.[10] However, where religion is viewed more broadly as that universal phenomenon endemic to the human enterprise whereby one attempts to make sense of the world in face of the meaning-shattering events continually bombarding one, a more careful examination of these "religious elements" within the UNIA appears to be justified. The question then becomes whether these are isolated and/or extrinsic elements adopted only for their instrumental value or whether they have a larger significance. If the latter is the case, then it will become important to see how these elements are woven into a coherent view of the world.

This chapter provides a careful descriptive analysis of the religious ethos of the UNIA, examining the structure and format of its meetings, noting the vocabulary with which members addressed issues, clarifying the role of chaplains within the organization, and elucidating the religio-political symbols of nationhood by which its purposes were embodied. This discussion should therefore provide a foundation for the "closer examination of the ideals and symbols" of the UNIA called for by Frazier a half-century ago.

Typical UNIA Meetings

From the descriptive point of view alone, one can scarcely help being struck by the fact that meetings of the Universal Negro Improvement Association possessed many of the characteristics of a religious service. This was true of special rallies that were held in Madison Square Garden, of the regular Sunday evening meetings in Harlem's Liberty Hall, and of local division and chapter meetings that were held throughout the United States and the Caribbean. A typical example of the special rallies is one held in Madison Square Garden on March 16, 1924, on the occasion of the return to the United States of a delegation the UNIA had sent to Europe and Africa "to Negotiate for the Repatriation of Negroes to a Homeland of Their Own in Africa."[11] More than ten thousand persons attended the evening program.

The festivities opened with a colorful procession of officers of the association and a parade of units from the numerous auxiliary organizations of the UNIA including the Black Cross Nurses, the Royal Guards, the Royal Engineering Corps, the Royal Medical Corps, and the Universal African Legion. During the procession the officers sang "Shine on Eternal Light," one of the official opening hymns used by the association. It had been written by the bandmaster of the UNIA, Rabbi Arnold J. Ford. Next, the audience joined in singing the first, third and fourth stanzas of Reginald Heber's century-old missionary hymn "From Greenland's Icy Mountains," which was also used as an opening hymn. The chaplain-general offered a prayer and this was followed by an elaborate and carefully selected musical program. First the UNIA band played a march and the UNIA choir offered the "Gloria." There were three solos, followed by a quartet rendering of "Heaven," written by Black composer Harry T. Burleigh, and the musical presentation was capped by a stirring solo sung by Mme. Marie B. Houston. All of the numbers were explicitly religious in terms of theme and although this was perhaps a more elaborate musical program than usual, the UNIA meetings at both national and local levels invariably featured outstanding musical talent.[12]

Sir William Sherrill, the second assistant president-general, delivered the first speech of the evening, elucidating the purpose of the UNIA. Another musical interlude introduced the high point of the evening: Marcus Garvey's address, "The Negro and the Future." Garvey's speeches were always carefully timed to achieve the maximum impact and were delivered in a fiery and dramatic style that left no member of the audience unmoved. His talk was followed by a brief sermonette by Rev. Dr. William H. Moses, a New York City Baptist minister whose subject for the evening was the familiar biblical text, "Ethiopia Shall Soon Stretch Forth Her Hands Unto God." The speeches were followed by a presentation of delegates and announcements and the program was closed by the singing of the first verses of the African National Anthem and the Star Spangled Banner[13] and a benediction. The format of a religious service was followed even to the point of receiving an offering, the normal practice both at special rallies such as the one just described and at the regular Sunday evening meetings in the Harlem Liberty Hall.

While the massive rallies at Madison Square Garden were doubtless more elaborate in their planning and execution than the regular weekly programs at Liberty Hall, the spirit and tone of those weekly meetings were the same. A typical Sunday evening program is described in the following excerpt from a *Negro World* report:

> The meeting tonight opened with the customary religious service of congregational singing of anthem and prayer, followed by all repeating the Twenty-Third Psalm, after which the High Chancellor, the Rev. Dr. G. E. Stewart, the presiding officer, offered a special prayer for the safe return of the President-General. Then followed the musical program, the Liberty Choir and the Black Star Line Band performing their parts well. Mr. Samuels sang a baritone solo. Madame Fraser-Robinson was the soloist.[14]

The speakers for this particular evening included, in addition to Stewart, two other clergymen: William H. Ferris, a Harvard Divinity School alumnus and editor of the *Negro World*, and Frederick A. Toote, "Speaker in Convention" and one of the founders of the African Orthodox Church. Toote's speech was devoted almost wholly to the imminent return of Marcus Garvey, who was just concluding an extensive trip through the Caribbean on behalf of the UNIA. He closed with a "fervent appeal to all friends of the movement to help make the reception to be tendered to Mr. Garvey an unqualified success," and his appeal evidently did not go unanswered, as the paper reported, "This brought a voluntary response of nearly everyone present, who came forward and made a liberal contribution toward the expenses of the proposed welcome. Following this, the meeting closed, with everyone in a happy frame of mind, and elated over the glad tidings that had been heard."[15]

For a time Sunday morning programs were also held in the Harlem

Liberty Hall and these were evidently strictly worship services. On at least one occasion the morning worship service was reported in the Pittsburgh *Courier's* regular weekly section "Among the Churches," which published summaries of sermons delivered in Harlem's most prestigious churches. Reporting on the program "At Liberty Hall" for Sunday, May 23, 1924, the *Courier* noted that an "overflowing crowd" was in attendance at the eleven o'clock service. The Reverend G. Emonei Carter presided and Bishop George Alexander McGuire delivered the sermon based on a text from the book of Hebrews, chapter eleven.[16]

The meetings of local UNIA chapters and divisions across the country similarly reflected the tone of a religious service and followed a carefully ritualized pattern. The following item concerning the Los Angeles division, dated January 30, 1923, is typical of the reports appearing weekly in "The News and Views of UNIA Divisions" section of the *Negro World*:

> The Los Angeles Division, No. 156, met in their hall, 1824 Central Avenue, with the president, Mr. D. J. Henderson. The meeting opened by singing From Greenland['s] Icy Mountain[s], the motto being repeated by the chaplain. The front page of the *Negro World* was read by Mr. Henderson.
>
> Mr. J. J. Stafford, second vice-president was present as master of ceremonies. First on the program was a selection by the choir, next Rev. A. Brown, [on the] subject, "Love is the Greatest Thing." A paper [was read] by Mr. Hoxie stating what the editor of the "Los Angeles Times" (White) said: "That the great God who we serve is a Black Man," referring to the finding [recently of the] Egyptian King [Tut, who died], 3000 years ago. Mr. Hoxie said we, the Negroes that were brought to this country as slaves, never knew of anything, not until Marcus Garvey came. Go on, go on, Marcus Garvey, until victory shine upon the continent of Africa.[17]

Local UNIA meetings were normally held on Sunday evenings and some divisions held morning services as well. Almost always, when a division was first founded, meetings were held in the church of a friendly (or at least a neutral) minister in the community, though each local organization was strongly encouraged by national headquarters to build its own "Liberty Hall" as quickly as possible. Often, as in the case of the Los Angeles division, the prime mover on the UNIA's behalf was a prominent clergyman. In this instance it was the influential pastor of Tabernacle Baptist Church, the Reverend John Dawson Gordon, in whose church the Association held its meetings for over a year and a half.[18] Gordon soon became a national officer of the UNIA, and a large number of his congregation became active Garveyites.[19]

As was the case at the special rallies and in the Harlem Liberty Hall meetings, local UNIA meetings were characterized by hymn singing, prayers, and sermons by local clergymen. Special rituals were devised to give local groups a sense of identification with the national organization, such as public reading of the front page of the *Negro World*, which was always written by Marcus Garvey. A regular feature of the local meetings was the welcoming of new visitors and the introduction of prominent community leaders in the audience. The reports carried in the "News and Views" section of the *Negro World* invariably concluded with a listing of influential citizens who had attended the chapter or division meeting, and special prominence was given to testimonials of support from any clergymen present. In addition to these regular weekly features of local meetings, there were special ceremonies prescribed for unique events such as the "unveiling" of the charter of a new UNIA chapter or division, a practice not dissimilar from the dedication and consecration ceremonies found in many churches. Mortgage burning ceremonies were likewise held by local UNIA groups.

Vocabulary of the UNIA

There is another important sense in which the UNIA reflected a religious ethos, namely, in the language and the vocabulary on which the movement drew both to describe its own purposes and to evoke commitment and loyalty amongst its membership. Unquestionably the vocabulary of the UNIA was drawn from the religious realm, as can be attested by practically every issue of the *Negro World*.

Garvey himself provides a classic example in a speech he delivered in February 1921 at Liberty Hall. On that occasion he stated:

> I wish I could *convert* the world of Negroes overnight to the tremendous possibilities of the Universal Negro Improvement Association. It pains me every every moment of the day when I see Negroes losing the grasp they should have on their own. You of Liberty Hall I must ask you to *go out as missionaries* and *preach this doctrine* of the Universal Negro Improve-

ment Association. Let all the world know that *this is the hour*; this is the time *for our salvation*. Prayer alone will not save us; sentiment alone will not save us. We have to work and work and work *if we are to be saved* . . . the time is now to *preach the beatitude of bread and butter*. I have contributed my bit to *preaching this doctrine*.[20]

The "doctrine" of the UNIA to which Garvey continually referred, and which he here felicitously characterized as "the beatitude of bread and butter," was a combination of faith in oneself, in one's race, and in God. It included a political and an economic, as well as a specifically religious program, though all were expressed in religious terminology. The most widely touted element of Garvey's political program, for instance, was the "Back to Africa" demand, which was most frequently described in terms of the "Redemption of Africa." This theme has a venerable place in Black American history,[21] and Garvey was by no means using the idea in ignorance of its past history.

Garvey's speeches and editorials were sermonic in style, containing extensive use of biblical references and religious imagery. Every address was a call to commitment, determination, and sacrifice, with a not infrequent note of apocalypticism creeping in. Amy Jacques Garvey has recorded in her biography of her husband that as a boy, young Marcus learned his lessons in elocution by standing outside the opened windows of churches in Kingston —churches in which the most outstanding preachers of the day delivered their addresses.[22] Perhaps he learned more than lessons in rhetoric while listening at those open windows.

Another example of the tendency of Garveyites to express political programs in a religious vocabulary is found in this excerpt from a revivalist-style speech by the Reverend James W. H. Eason, who was the first chaplain-general of the UNIA, and later was named "Leader of American Negroes." Speaking on the topic, "The Significance of the Life Pledge," he remarked,

A life pledge makes a man out and out, a man all round, who stands four-square to every wind that blows. Play the man; the race demands it. Africa expects every man to do his duty. Liberia is calling to you for commercial development.

I want everyone in this building tonight to make a life pledge, come weal, come woe. I will count one in the uplift of my race; I will count one to glorify my God; I will count one to help put over the Liberian constructive loan. I will pledge my word, my money and my sacred honor to see to it that the Liberian constructive loan is a success, that the ideas of the provisional president may be advanced and spread abroad to the world.[23]

Such calls for "life pledges," Garvey's "vision of a redeemed Africa," and his hope to "convert the world of Negroes" did not go unheeded. Indeed numerous Garveyites have indicated that their decisions to join the UNIA were more than rhetorically analogous to a conversion experience. Some have provided descriptions of the process by which they were "grasped" and brought into the fold of Garvey's organization. One of these was William L. Sherrill, the son of a Methodist Episcopal minister in Hot Springs, Arkansas, who as early as 1922 accepted Garvey's call. Amy Jacques Garvey preserved the text of Sherrill's conversion experience as he recalled it many years after the event:

Here was I, a successful business man with a family, member of a church, a lodge, and fully insured to protect them. I did not have to join anything else. I subscribed to the anti-lynching campaign every time a Negro was lynched. I did not like to hear people talk about conditions of my people, as I had overcome many of them; let everybody else do likewise. I argued this way against the persuasion of friends.

One night on my way to a show, I saw a huge crowd outside a church. I went up and said, "What's going on in there?" A lady turned to me and said, "Man alive, don't you know that Marcus Garvey is in there talking? Yes, indeed, Garvey in person." "Shucks," I said, "I may as well see what he looks like." I could not get near the windows, so I had to get a ticket for standing room only. I squeezed in, until I could get a good look at him; then suddenly he turned in my direction, and in a voice like thunder from Heaven he said, "Men and women, what are you here for? To live unto yourself, until your body manures the earth, or to live God's Purpose to the fullest?" He continued to complete his thought in that compelling, yet pleading voice for nearly an hour. I stood there like one in a trance, every sentence ringing in my ears, and finding an echo in my heart. When I walked out of that church, I was a different man—I knew my sacred obligations to my Creator, and my responsibilities to my fellow men, and so help me! I am still on the Garvey train.[24]

It was not only the magnetism of Garvey's personality that was capable of eliciting such total commitment to the movement. Richard Hilton Tobitt, for instance, an African Methodist Episcopal clergyman in Bermuda, felt the call of the UNIA when reading the *Negro World*. As he observed in a biographical essay some years later,

> It was while giving a public lecture in St. Paul's A.M.E. Church, Hamilton City, Bermuda, on the subject, "Is Education Necessary to the Negro?" that a copy of "The Negro World" was placed in my hands for the first time. . . . Having carefully analyzed the program of the UNIA as set forth by its founder, Marcus Garvey, and believing in the integrity of the man and the righteousness of the course he espoused, I caught his vision and became a ready disciple of Garveyism, which I discovered was the "Master Key" . . . to the correct solution of the vexed race problem of the world and a sane and practical exposition of true religion. Without delay, I set to work to organize the Bermuda Division of the UNIA . . . and "left the court of Pharaoh, choosing rather to suffer affliction with my people than to dwell in the land of Goshen."[25]

Such conversions often came at a high price. Tobitt, for instance, in his reference to the "Court of Pharaoh" was no doubt alluding to his disbarment from the ministry of the A.M.E. Church in Bermuda as a consequence of having joined the UNIA. In addition, government funds for the school over which he presided were withdrawn, the governor of the island declaring that Tobitt had clearly demonstrated by his action that he was "no longer a fit person to be entrusted with the education of children."[26]

Religious vocabulary was consistently used by Garveyites in their Sunday evening speeches in Liberty Hall. A typical headline in the *Negro World* for February 26, 1921, quoted William Ferris, who "Says Gospel Message of UNIA Has Swept Over the World Like a Tidal Wave, Giving Hope and Inspiration to the Negro Everywhere."[27] One A. S. Gray spoke to an audience in Oakland, California, on the "Righteousness of the UNIA."[28] Marcus Garvey called upon his followers to "act as living missionaries to convince others,"[29] and on another occasion referred to the UNIA as "the great ark of safety."[30] Such language persisted in the pages of the *Negro World* to the paper's very last issue. In an editorial by Mme. M. L. T. De Mena, published in that issue on October 17, 1933, the paper's editor described "Garveyism as the guiding star of Ethiopia's restoration."

The Sacred few, the noble few, the gallant few, who . . . from a burning heart and languishing soul . . . felt the true zealousness and sublimity of race consciousness, the fundamentality of nationhood, the infancy of a great commonwealth, operated and governed by Negroes in yonder fragrant Africa's sunny fields; yea a modern heaven and refuge, a substantial environment, a solace wherein all Negro generations will be called blessed. This is our abiding faith, the eternal creed, the renovated religion, that now appeals and aches within the breast of our hundred million Negroes under the ethics of the Universal Negro Improvement Association.[31]

The *Negro World* itself was referred to as the "Testament of the UNIA" because, according to one official, it "has been the greatest missionary in building up divisions and making converts to the cause outside of New York City."[32] Indeed, one could go so far as to say that the *Negro World* began to take on the quality of a sacred text. As earlier noted, part of the ritual of each Sunday evening program in the local "Liberty Halls" outside of New York City consisted in reading aloud the lead editorial which comprised the entire front page of each issue of the paper. The public reading of this editorial gave Garvey regular access to all UNIA members and insured that all would receive inspiration and information directly from their leader.[33]

Chaplains in the UNIA

The religious ethos of UNIA meetings, which was set by the formal structure of the regular programs and by the language used by its officials, was further reinforced by the presence of chaplains at both local and national levels. Each chapter or division was required by the UNIA constitution to select a chaplain, whose duty it was to attend to the spiritual concerns of the members. All chaplains were under the direction of the chaplain-general, who was a member of the high executive council, the UNIA's ruling body.

By far the most able of the chaplains-general was West Indian-born George Alexander McGuire, who was elected to the post at the first annual International Convention of the Negro Peoples of the World in August 1920. Under his leadership the religio-political nationalism that was present in the UNIA from its earliest days was made ever more explicit and pervasive. One of his first deeds as chaplain-general, for instance, was to compile the *Universal*

Negro Ritual, published in 1921. The *Ritual* was modeled after the *Book of Common Prayer* on which McGuire was raised as a member of the Church of England and which he later used as a priest in the Protestant Episcopal Church.

All chaplains were obliged to follow and all members were encouraged to acquire and study the *Ritual*, which prescribed the standard order of service to be followed in UNIA meetings. The standard format, exemplified in the three services described earlier, opened with the hymn "From Greenland's Icy Mountains" and with one or more of the special prayers that McGuire compiled. These were to be followed by singing of either "O Africa Awaken" or "Shine on Eternal Light" (both hymns especially composed for the UNIA), prior to presentation of the featured events of the program. "These preliminaries," it was remarked on one occasion, "lend a religious air to the meeting, and the audience responds and participates with a fervor and zeal that is highly commendable."[34] The meeting closed with additional prayers and the African national anthem.[35] As will be detailed in a later chapter, in addition to standardizing the order by which meetings were to proceed, McGuire included in the *Ritual* a baptism and a burial service for UNIA members. On occasion, marriages also took place under Association auspices. Clearly, in McGuire's conception, the UNIA was an all-embracing institution ministering to the spiritual needs of its members from the cradle to the grave.

Under McGuire's leadership the role of the chaplains was broadened and clarified and efforts were made to upgrade the standards required of those who sought the post. At the time of his election as chaplain-general, McGuire was able to effectuate changes in the UNIA constitution in order to accomplish these goals. One such revision concerned Section 63 of the book of laws, which henceforth required that all chaplains of local divisions or chapters "must be ordained ministers or have their first license."[36] The implementation of this section presumed, of course, the membership of at least one ordained clergyman in every UNIA division in the country as well as the willingness of each division to grant a significant leadership role to that person. McGuire may have encountered some resistance to this rule, as is suggested by the following notice made in the "chaplain-general's Department" column in the *Negro World*:

The Chaplain-General hereby announces that in accordance with Section 63 that no Chaplains in the various Divisions will be recognized as qualified for such office unless they meet the requirements as laid down. Evidence must be sent to this office of the ordination of Chaplains to the ministry, or credentials of license as lay-readers or local preachers. *There can be no excuse for lack of qualification as His Grace the Chaplain-General is ready to issue a license to any layman who can pass a fair and reasonable examination in English and religious knowledge.*[37]

Opposition to the ordination requirement apparently persisted, and in the 1922 revision of the general laws the relevant section was made to read simply, "All Chaplains of the UNIA and ACL shall be intelligent persons versed in reading and interpretation of the Universal Ritual and the Scriptures."[38]

Another constitutional revision which McGuire discussed in the *Negro World*, and which required action by local UNIA chaplains, concerned the necessity of creating youth organizations in each UNIA division. The relevant section of the general laws required "That in every Division of the UNIA, a juvenile branch be formed *and only teachings of spiritual and racial uplift be taught.*"[39] The rules and regulations for juveniles, which were published as part of the *Constitution and Book of Laws*, indicate the type of training envisioned for children of UNIA members. A variety of classes were to be formed. The infant class included all children, ages one to seven, and they were to be taught the following: Bible class and prayer; doctrine of the UNIA and ACL; Facts about the Black Star Line Steamship Corporation, the Negro Factories Corporation, and history of Africa (in storybook fashion).[40]

Children aged seven to thirteen composed the number two class and they were divided by sex for their program. For the girls this included: how to make souvenirs with cloth, needle and thread for sale for juvenile department; Ritual of Universal Negro Improvement Association; write Negro stories, taught race pride and love; Taught Negro history and etiquette and be given disciplinary training by the legions.[41] Boys received the same training, except that they were to make souvenirs from wood rather than by needle and thread.

The cadets class consisted of youths aged thirteen to sixteen, who were required to study the *Ritual*, military training, flag signals, and Negro history. Books specifically recommended for study included J. A. Rogers's *From Superman to Man*; Sydney H. Olivier's *White Capital and Colored Labor*; Hubert H. Harrison's *When Africa Awakes*; and the book, *African Lure and Lyrics*. It was specified that the class was to be taught by a member of the Universal African Legions "who is acquainted with military tactics."[42]

Finally there was a preparatory nursing class under the direction of the Black Cross Nurses for girls aged fourteen to eighteen. Their responsibilities included: making uniforms for juveniles; Negro history; etiquette; talk on latest topics of the day; elementary principles of Economy; Negro Story Writing; Hygiene and Domestic Science.[43]

A lady vice-president was placed in charge as superintendent of the juvenile department and teachers were to be appointed by the division president. There is no indication as to how often classes were expected to meet, though it seems clear that the intent was to supplement rather than to replace the public education system. Coming out of the tradition of the Protestant Episcopal church, in which confirmation classes and catechetical training were long established, McGuire was aware of the importance of providing a mechanism whereby Negro youths could regularly and from an early age be taught the spiritual and racial values of the organization. In all cases it was the responsibility of the chaplains to provide religious training for juveniles. Not surprisingly, on completion of the *Universal Negro Ritual* McGuire turned to the task of devising a *Universal Negro Catechism* for use in the juvenile branches to assist in this task.

Finally, in one of his columns in the *Negro World* for the "Chaplain-General's Department," McGuire set forth the model of chaplaincy to which he hoped all would aspire, and listed the duties of the office as he perceived them. They were:

a. To conduct Divine Service according to the Universal Negro Ritual on Sunday mornings or afternoons where it is the desire of the members of the Division to have such Sunday service.

b. To conduct the Ritual as prescribed in the Ritual Book in connection with Mass Meetings or Members' Meetings.

c. To instruct the members of the Juvenile Branch in his Division in the knowledge supplied in the Universal Negro Catechism.

d. To see that every member of his Division purchase the Universal Negro Ritual and the Universal Negro Catechism.

e. To visit the sick and afflicted members of his Division and report to the proper officers any case needing charity.

f. To govern his own life and conversation in such manner as may prove him worthy to be a moral and spiritual guide to his fellow members.[44]

In brief, McGuire hoped that the chaplains would function as spiritual leaders to members, inculcators of racial and moral values for the young, counselors and comforters to the sick and needy, and models of the moral and righteous life for the entire community. Their presence in each local chapter or division was meant to insure that the religious ethos established as normative by the national organization would be carefully followed in every UNIA gathering across the country.

Garveyite Regalia and the Paraphernalia of Nationhood

We have thus far examined the rituals, both implicitly and explicitly religious, to be found in meetings of the UNIA; described the language, drawn primarily from the religious realm, by which its programs were presented; and observed the role of the "religious virtuosi" (to borrow a term from Max Weber) who were specially designated to inculcate the values and norms of the association. What remains to be noted, in this essentially descriptive discussion concerning the religious ethos of the Garvey movement, is the multitude of religio-political symbols of nationhood by which the UNIA fostered the idea of peoplehood and self-identity.

Nationhood was the perdurable motif around which much of the activity in the UNIA revolved. The constitution, first adopted in 1918 and amended in succeeding years, set forth the constituent elements of the nationhood motif in systematic fashion. The list of officers, for instance, included a president-general who was at the same time provisional president of Africa (the chief administrative position, which Garvey held himself). Assistant presidents-general also held the titles of "Titular Leader of American Negroes" or "Titular Leader of the West Indies, South and Central America." There were appointed ministers of African legions, of education, and of labor and industries, as well as ministers plenipotentiary, who were designated as ambassadors "to all regular governments" and to the League of Nations.[45] In addition to enumerating these titles of officials modeled after that of a national government, the constitution also authorized a variety of agencies to perform quasi-governmental tasks. These included a civil service, which gave regular exams and offered limited positions to be filled by UNIA members in good standing; a passports bureau, which issued passports to facilitate travel of members from one branch to another; and a bureau of justice, to insure the rights of Negroes wherever they might reside throughout the world. Even taxes were levied: in addition to the one dollar annual membership tax, there was a ten-cent per-month levy as a "death tax," in exchange for which members were to receive free burial by the association.[46]

Garvey took care to integrate religious imagery into his conceptualization of the "new nationality." The official motto of the UNIA was "One God! One Aim! One Destiny!" The motto was to be found emblazoned on the official banner, on UNIA stationery, and on the letterhead of the *Negro World*, and it was repeated at every meeting of the association. The notion of a unified religious faith for all Black persons implied by the words "One God" was a perennial topic for discussion at international conventions and was a theme to which Garvey frequently returned in his speeches. The official slogan, "Pro Deo, Pro Africa, Pro Justitia," was less widely used than the motto, although it also contained a God referent.

On the official letterhead of UNIA stationery was also printed the biblical injunction from Acts 18:26, "He created of one blood all nations of man to dwell upon the face of the earth." To be sure, Garveyites were unabashed in proclaiming the goals of their organization as being the uplift of one particular racial group, but this was always presented in the context of a demand for respect of the rights of all mankind and a commitment finally to the brotherhood of man and the fatherhood of God.

The most frequently cited biblical passage by far, and the one which most often served as a text for sermon topics in Liberty Halls around the country, was the one from Psalms 68:31, "Princes shall come forth from Egypt; Ethiopia shall soon stretch forth her hand to God." This biblical prophecy has been cited by Black churchmen in America at least since the eighteenth century, to specify God's special concern for men and women of African descent.[47] The concern for Africa that was so central to the UNIA, and the conviction that God was working in history through the instrumentality of the UNIA to create a nation, Africa, as a part of his larger purposes, rendered this verse from the Psalms uniquely appropriate to the Garvey movement. The meaning of the passage, as understood by Garveyites, was explicated in the *Universal Negro Catechism*:

Q. What prediction made in the 68th Psalm and the 31st verse is now being fulfilled?

A. "Princes shall come out of Egypt, Ethiopia shall soon stretch   -
forth her hands unto God."

Q. What does this verse prove?

A. That Negroes will set up their own government in Africa, with rulers of their own race.[48]

Here was biblical warrant and ultimate grounding for the association's political program, and irrefragable evidence that the UNIA's work was indeed of God.

The psalmist's prophecy concerning Ethiopia was also incorporated in the "Universal Ethiopian Anthem," another basic element in the UNIA's paraphernalia of nationhood. Written by Ben Burrell and UNIA choirmaster Arnold J. Ford, it again illustrates the mixture of religious and political elements that was so characteristic of Garveyite rituals and symbols. The text of the hymn, which was officially adopted as the anthem "of the Negro race," is as follows:

> Ethiopia, thou land of our fathers,
> Thou land where the gods loved to be,
> As storm cloud at night sudden gathers
> Our armies come rushing to thee.
> We must in the fight be victorious,
> When swords are thrust outward to glean;
> For us will the Vict'ry be glorious
> When led by the red, black and green

> Chorus

> Advance, advance to victory!
> Let Africa be free!
> Advance to meet the foe
> With the might
> Of the red, the black, and the green.

> Ethiopia, the tyrant's falling
> Who smote thee upon thy knees;
> And thy children are lustily calling
> From over the distant seas.
> Jehovah the Great One has heard us,
> Has noted our sighs and our tears,
> With His spirit of love He has stirred us

To be one through the coming years.

Chorus

O Jehovah, Thou God of the ages,
Grant unto our sons that lead
The wisdom Thou gav'st to Thy sages
When Israel was sore in need.
Thy voice thro' the dim past has spoken,
Ethiopia shall stretch forth her hand,
By Thee shall all fetters be broken
And Heav'n bless our dear Motherland.[49]

In sharp contrast to the much more familiar "Negro National Hymn," written by James Weldon Johnson some twenty years earlier. Ford's anthem was a call for military preparedness in anticipation of an inevitable conflagration which would be demanded before God's promise of freedom could be realized. Johnson's hymn, "Lift Every Voice and Sing," had breathed an air of determined hopefulness reflective of faith in the "harmonies of Liberty" that were working gradually but certainly toward a victory that was all but won. The God of whom Johnson had spoken was a benevolent if stern God, who has guided and is guiding the destiny of Black people to justice and to their promised land, to "the place for which our fathers sighed," which for Johnson was surely not Africa, but a just and truly democratic United States of America.[50] For Ford, however, Ethiopia was the object of the people's affection and it was the God of retribution, Jehovah, who would insure that just as he had long ago led his people, Israel, to freedom, so now would he work through the instrument of the Universal Negro Improvement Association to achieve the redemption of his people and of their homeland, Africa.

It should be evident from the foregoing that the religious ethos of the UNIA was pervasive, embracing nearly every facet of its organizational life. The religious elements we have described were not isolated or random occurrences, but are to be found everywhere one looks within the movement. And just as recent students of religion in America have insisted that the God-references, the ceremonial and the religious symbols of nationhood developed over the past two hundred years of this nation's existence cannot simply be dismissed as insignificant "ritualistic" expressions, but are "indicative of deep-seated values and commitments"[51] worthy of careful examination, so can it be argued that the rituals and symbols developed by the Universal Negro

Improvement Association are constitutive of a coherent way of viewing the world that deserves to be taken seriously.

Notes

1. Claude McKay, "Garvey as a Negro Moses," *Liberator* 5 (April 1922):8. In his autobiography, *A Long Way*, pp. 55, 67, 87, McKay reports it was on the urging of his good friend, Hubert H. Harrison, that he started sending articles to Garvey's paper from Europe. Harrison was at the time an active Garvey supporter and columnist/editor for the *Negro World*. (Hereafter Negro World is cited as *NW*.)

2. Bedward had specified December 31, 1920, as the date of his ascension. On Bedward, see Leonard E. Barrett, *The Rastafarians: A Study in Messianic Cultism in Jamaica* (Rio Piedras, Puerto Rico, 1968):55–57; Martha Warren Beckwith, "Some Religious Cults in Jamaica," *American Journal of Psychology* 34 (1923):32–45, especially pp. 40–45; and Roscoe M. Pierson, "Alexander Bedward and the Jamaica Native Baptist Free Church," in Randall K. Burkett and Richard Newman, eds., *Black Apostles: Afro-American Clergy Confront the Twentieth Century* (Boston, 1978).

3. McKay, "Garvey as a Negro Moses," p. 8. McKay does temper his judgment of Garvey by remarking on the UNIA leader's "energetic and quick-witted mind." As McKay goes on in the article to make clear, the real basis of his objection to Garvey was the latter's persistent anti-union and anti-socialist economic program.

4. E. Franklin Frazier, "Garvey: A Mass Leader," *Nation* 123 (August 18, 1926):148.

5. Ibid.

6. Ibid.

7. The *Negro World* reply to McKay is found in *NW*, June 3, 1922, p. 12. Frazier's article was reprinted in *NW*, August 21, 1926, p. 5, with an editorial reply in *NW*, August 28, 1926, p. 4.

8. James Weldon Johnson, *Black Manhattan* (New York, 1930),:255.

9. For a discussion of James W. Johnson's attitude towards religion generally, see the comments by Benjamin E. Mays in his book *The Negro's God as Reflected in His Literature* (New York, 1969):234–36. Frazier's negative assessment of the religion of the Negro, which he said has "cast a shadow over the entire intellectual life of Negroes and has been responsible for the so-called backwardness of American Negroes," was summarized in his influential essay *The Negro Church in America* (New York, 1963):86. Stanford M. Lyman, in his recent study *The Black American in Sociological Thought* (New York, 1972), places Frazier's critique of the Negro church in the context of his sociological framework developed out of the Chicago school of sociology under the tutelage of Robert E. Park. See especially his discussion in chap. 2, 55–67.

10. A similar association is made by August Meier in his *Negro Thought in America: 1880–1915* (Ann Arbor, 1966), where he concludes that "The escapist Utopian character of the Garvey movement as a response to economic deprivation is revealed in the fact that a large number of ex-Garveyites joined the Father Divine movement during the depression of the 1930's," 315 n. 39. Interpreters more sympathetic to Garvey have also been chary of calling attention to the religious elements for fear of lending credence to the earlier associated notion that Garveyism

was simply "an oversized sect or cult, an escapist pseudo-religion of which Garvey was God while many of his followers were only a cut above fools." Theodore G. Vincent, *Black Power and the Garvey Movement* (Berkeley: Ramparts Press, 1971), p. 1 is typical in this respect.

11. The text of the speech delivered by Marcus Garvey on this occasion is printed in *Philosophy and Opinions of Marcus Garvey* 2, ed. Amy Jacques Garvey (New York, 1969):118–123. A copy of the evening program guide is preserved in volume 32 of the "Alexander Gumby Collection on the American Negro," housed in the Department of Special Collections, Columbia University. *See also* the account in the *New York Times*, March 17, 1924, p. 2.

12. Amy Jacques Garvey, in her biographical study *Garvey and Garveyism* (London, 1970):47, observed concerning the place of music in the UNIA, "Our people love to sing; it is said they sang their way out of slavery, through their spirituals, which expressed their sorrow, and their firm belief that God was leading them, as He had led the children of Israel through the Wilderness, and Daniel out of the lion's den. So Garvey outlined a set of meaningful hymns, and [Ben] Burrell and [Arnold J.] Ford of the music department put them into proper verse and set them to music." Most of these hymns were published in Ford's *Universal Ethiopian Hymnal*.

13. Garvey always insisted that the UNIA was not a subversive organization intent on the overthrow of the United States government, and inclusion in the program of the Star Spangled Banner was meant to underscore this point.

14. *NW*, July 16, 1921, p. 1.

15. Ibid.

16. Pittsburgh *Courier*, May 31, 1924, p. 13.

17. *NW*, February 24, 1923, p. 7

18. Gayraud S. Wilmore's characterization of the Black Church as "the NAACP on its knees" might thus just as accurately be applied to the UNIA during the early 1920s. See his *Black Religion and Black Radicalism* (Garden City, 1972):197. The practice of allowing protest organizations to utilize facilities of Black churches as a forum for debate and a base of operations has a long history, extending from the anti-slavery period to the present day.

19. On occasion, when a minister was won over to the UNIA, his entire congregation would join the association. See for example the statement of R. H. Cosgrove of Natchez, Mississippi, who reported at an international convention of the UNIA that "he pastored a little church of about 500 members, and everyone was a member of the association, as he was of the opinion that if he was to be a spiritual leader he should also be able to lead them in their temporal affairs. He attended the convention to see things for himself so that he could take back to the people who trusted him a true report of the work of the movement." *NW*, August 18, 1924, p. 2.

20. *NW*, February 19, 1921, p. 4. Emphasis added.

21. *See* St. Clair Drake, *The Redemption of Africa and Black Religion* (Chicago, 1970).

22. Amy Jacques Garvey, *Garvey and Garveyism*, 5.

23. *NW*, November 6, 1920, p. 8. On Eason, see my *Black Redemption: Churchmen Speak for the Garvey Movement* (Philadelphia, 1978), chap. 3.

24. Amy Jacques Garvey, *Garvey and Garveyism*, 266. See also the biographical sketch of Sherrill in *NW*, September 15, 1923, p. 4 and George Alexander McGuire's remarks in introduc-

ing Sherrill at the fourth international convention, *NW*, September 2, 1922, p. 12.

25. *NW*, October 20, 1923, p. 10.

26. Reported by William F. Elkins in "Marcus Garvey, the *Negro World*, and the British West Indies: 1919–1920," *Science and Society* 36 (Spring 1972):71. All was not loss for Tobitt, however, for his conversion opened new horizons for the expression of his social and religious conscience. He was one of the signers of the famous "Declaration of Rights of the Negro Peoples of the World" in 1920, and was elected leader of the Eastern Province of the West Indies. He subsequently held numerous posts within the UNIA.

27. *NW*, February 26, 1921, p. 3.

28. *NW*, December 16, 1922, p. 8.

29. *NW*, February 26, 1921, p. 4.

30. *NW*, December 26, 1931, p. 1.

31. "Are We Discouraged?" *NW*, October 17, 1933, p. 4.

32. *NW*, April 2, 1921, p. 3. The speaker was George Alexander McGuire.

33. The point should not be pushed too far, however, so as to suggest that the *Negro World* literally replaced the Bible as the sacred text for UNIA members. An instructive comparison is available in the pattern followed in the Father Divine Peace Mission Movement, where, according to Arthur Huff Fauset, "The sacred text . . . is not the Bible, but the *New Day*, a weekly periodical issued by the organization. Followers invariably refer to this book [*sic*] rather than to the Bible when they wish to speak with authority." *Black Gods of the Metropolis* (Philadelphia, 1944):60. Divine, who gained prominence in Harlem in the years shortly after the decline of the Garvey movement, appears here to have radicalized an idea found in more moderate form in the UNIA. Similarly, Divine seems to have taken to an extreme other journalistic ideas originated by Garvey: whereas the *Negro World* published verbatim texts of many speeches delivered at Liberty Hall and most of the speeches delivered elsewhere by Garvey, the *New Day* published verbatim transcripts of practically every word uttered by Father Divine at his famous banquet meetings. And whereas the *Negro World* contained a regular Spanish column and (briefly) a French column, due to the circulation of the paper in Latin America and French-speaking Africa and the Caribbean, the *New Day* regularly carried translations of Divine's speeches in French, Spanish, German, and Russian. It is significant that when the *Negro World* at last folded on October 17, 1933, with publication of vol. 32, no. 11, its presses and remaining supplies were purchased by none other than Father Divine, who published as a predecessor to the *New Day* his *World (Peace) Echo*. At least the first fifteen issues continued to number their papers with a dual system: old series, vol. 32, no. 12 (following the *Negro World* numbering); new series, vol. 1, no. 1; etc. A careful study of the relationship between these two historically contiguous movements should be undertaken.

34. *NW*, June 5, 1920, p. 2.

35. The text of the anthem is printed below, p. 76.

36. *NW*, April 2, 1921, p. 7.

37. Ibid. Emphasis added.

38. *Constitution and Book of Laws Made for the Government of the Universal Negro Improvement Association, Inc., and African Communities League, Inc., of the World* (New York, July 1918; revised and amended, August 1922): General Laws, sec. 62, p. 57. Coincidentally or not,

McGuire by this time had been ousted from the UNIA.

39. *NW*, April 2, 1921, p. 7. Emphasis added. *See also* sec. 61 of the revised 1922 edition of the *Constitution and Book of Laws*, 57.

40. Ibid., 85.

41. Ibid.

42. Ibid., 86.

43. Ibid.

44. *NW* April 2, 1921, p. 7.

45. *Constitution and Book of Laws*, 56.

46. Vincent, *Black Power*, p. 167, lists these and other of the "trappings of nationhood" fostered by the UNIA.

47. Absalom Jones and Richard Allen, in their brief encomium to whites who were working to improve the condition of slaves in the United States, concluded with the words, "May he, who hath arisen to plead our cause, and engaged you as volunteers in the service, add to your numbers until the princes shall come forth from Egypt, and Ethiopia stretch out her hand unto God." *A Narrative of the Proceedings of the Black People, During the Late Awful Calamity in Philadelphia, in the Year, 1793*, in *Negro Protest Pamphlets*, ed. Dorothy Porter (New York, 1969), p. 23. This is the first written evidence I have been able to discover concerning the use of this passage by Black churchmen.

48. George Alexander McGuire, *Universal Negro Catechism* (Universal Negro Improvement Assn., 1921):11.

49. The text of the Anthem may be found in Garvey, *Philosophy and Opinions of Marcus Garvey* 2:140–41. The militancy evidenced by the anthem is typical both of the general mood of Harlem in the post-war period and also of the aggressiveness that especially in its earliest period was characteristic of Garveyite rhetoric. The circumstances of its writing are themselves indicative of the incidents which all too often were perpetrated on Black Americans and which they were increasingly unwilling to accept without resistance or retaliation. According to an article in the *Negro World*, the hymn was occasioned by the brutal slaying in 1919 of a young woman who had been working as a housemaid in New York City. The girl, aged 17, had been raped by the head of the household where she worked. When she reported to her mistress that she was pregnant as a result of the attack, the woman, a "Negro hater," became enraged and threw her out of the house. Soon thereafter, according to the article, "she was found dead, her body horribly mutilated." William A. Stephenson, "The Universal Ethiopian Anthem and How It Came to Be Written," *NW*, August 25, 1923, p. 2.

50. In his autobiography *Along This Way* (New York, 1961):154–56, Johnson described the circumstances of the song's composition, the score for which was composed by his brother J. Rosamond Johnson. The second stanza of "Lift Every Voice" seems to make clear that it is the new home in America which is the Negro's rightful heritage, as a result of his centuries of struggle here.

51. Bellah, "Civil Religion in America," *The Religious Situation*, ed. Donald R. Cutler (Boston: Beacon Press, 1968):333.

6

Black Spiritual Churches: Thaumaturgical Responses to Racism and Social Stratification

Hans A. Baer

The development of African American religion has not taken a simple, unilinear trajectory but has been expressed in a multiplicity of interrelated streams. This essay will focus on one of the most neglected of these streams, the one consisting of those groups that generally refer to themselves as "Spiritual churches." As Gayraud S. Wilmore observes, "The period between 1890 and the Second World War was one of the luxuriant growth and development for many forms of Black religion in the United States and Africa that challenged the bourgeois nature of the mainline denominations and the racist posture of the white churches."[1] The Black Spiritual movement was one of several sectarian developments that emerged during this period as a response to the shifting status of Blacks in American society.[2] In this essay I present a brief overview of the development, organization, and activities of Spiritual churches. This is followed by an analysis of the role of Spiritual churches in the Black community and the juxtaposition of protest and accommodation to the larger society.

Because all religious groups claim to deal with spiritual matters, the term "Spiritual" in referring to a specific category tends to be problematic. Just as members of other religious bodies call themselves Baptists, Methodists, Pentecostalists, Muslims, etc., members of certain religious groups among African Americans use the term "Spiritual" as a specific label of self-reference. Furthermore, they often include the term "Spiritual" in the title of their congregation (e.g., St. Dymphna Spiritual Kingdom of God) or association (e.g., Universal Ethiopian Church of Christ). In addition to their strong thaumaturgical orientation, another feature that distinquishes Spiritual sects from many other Black religious groups is their highly syncretistic nature. While there is a considerable degree of heterogenity within the Spiritual movement itself, even among congregations within the same association, essentially it blends elements from Spiritualism, Black Protestantism, Roman Catholicism, and Voo-doo or hoodoo. Specific associations or congregations add elements from New Thought, Islam, Judaism, Ethiopianism, and astrology to this basic ensemble.

The Development of the Spiritual Movement

The Spiritual movement, like other new sects that appeared among African Americans following the turn of the century, developed within the context of a changing political economy that forced increasing numbers of Blacks from the rural South to seek employment in urban areas. According to Oliver C. Cox, "on the whole, the 'push' of the Negro population from the rural South has been greater than the inducements or 'pull' of the cities."[3] Push factors in the South included the relative severity of labor exploitation, the boll weevil invasion that reached disastrous levels about 1910, soil erosion and depletion, the relocation of many agricultural endeavors in the West, and patterns of systematic intimidation.

Prior to World War I, the industrial North had relied primarily on Euro-pean immigrants for a cheap labor supply. World War I stimulated the econ-omy and increased the demand for labor, a demand in large part filled by the migration of southern Blacks. Although it fluctuated through succeeding decades, falling during the Depression and rising again during World War II, the migration pattern that started among Blacks in the 1910s continued well into the 1970s. While the North may have been presented by labor recruiters as the Promised Land, what most Blacks found in Detroit, Chicago, Gary, Pittsburgh, Newark, Harlem, and other cities was considerably less. In the rural South they had occupied the lowest rungs of a rigid caste-like system; in the industrial North—although theoretically possessing more legal rights —Blacks became a type of sub-proletariat, or underclass, manipulated by the capitalist class in dealing with the growing demands of white workers.

The process of urbanization that accompanies capitalist expansion has repeatedly been demonstrated to have unsettling effects on rural migrants, not only in industrial nations but also in the Third World today. Invariably rural migrants attempt to adjust to their new environment by creating a wide array of voluntary associations, including religious ones. Next to the family, the church had been the most important institution among Blacks of the rural South.[4] In addition to providing emotional release from the oppressive conditions of the caste system, the rural churches of the Baptists and Methodists served as social and recreational centers, maintaining strong ties with various benevolent, mutual aid, burial, and fraternal societies.

As Melvin D. Williams observes, "The migration to cities created a social crisis, for it separated masses of Blacks from their rural life style and destroyed the social organization which gave meaning to their segregated rural Southern society."[5] While many migrants apparently did find comfortable niches in the larger churches of the old-time denominations, others who had enjoyed leadership positions in the rural South found themselves relegated to the sidelines of the large urban congregations. In addition to seeming more bureaucratic, impersonal, formal, and sedate than their counterparts in the South, the mainstream congregations increasingly adapted themselves to the more secular concerns of a new Black middle class.[6] In the midst of the social crisis faced by the migrants from the rural South, Black religion became even more diversified than it had been before. According to Wilmore, "the Black community, by the end of the decade of the 1930s, was literally glutted with churches of every variety and description."[7] Although storefront versions of the large Baptist and even Methodist congregations were established, many Black migrants were attracted to the Holiness, Pentecostal, Spiritual, Judaic, Islamic, and other sects such as the Father Divine Peace Mission and the African Orthodox Church, which emerged in tremendous profusion in the industrial North, but also in many southern cities.

The origins of the Spiritual movement remain obscure. It appears to have emerged in various large cities of both the North and South—particularly Chicago, New Orleans, Detroit, Kansas City, and New York—during the first quarter of this century. The Spiritual movement cannot be viewed simply as a Black counterpart of white Spiritualism. While initially congregations affiliated with the movement referred to themselves as "Spiritualist," by the 1930s and 1940s most of them contracted this term to "Spiritual." As part of this process, Blacks adapted Spiritualism to their own experience. Consequently much of the social structure, beliefs, and ritual content of Spiritual churches closely resemble those of other religious groups in the Black community, particularly the Baptists and Pentecostalists. Furthermore Spiritual people in southern Louisiana, many of whom probably were reared as Catholics, added many elements from Catholicism and, at a somewhat more subtle level, hoodoo. Somehow Spiritual churches in other parts of the country incorporated these elements.

The first evidence of predominantly Black Spiritualist churches comes from Chicago—a city which remains the foremost center of the Spiritual movement. According to Allan H. Spear, several "Spiritualist" congregations were established in Chicago's Black community during the first decade of the twentieth century.[8] Mother Leafy Anderson, a Black Spiritualist who was destined to play an instrumental role in the development of the Spiritual religion in New Orleans, established the Eternal Life Christian Spiritualist Church in Chicago in 1913.[9] Some time prior to 1915, the Lake City Spiritualist Church in Cleveland, Ohio, began to attract poor Blacks, particularly recent southern migrants.[10] Regardless of whether or not Chicago is the birthplace of Black Spiritual churches as an institutional entity, New Orleans appears to have been of vital importance in determining their present content. Despite the strong opposition to American spiritualism in the South, it nevertheless spread to cities such as Memphis, Macon, Charleston and particularly New Orleans.[11] Perhaps in part because of its liberal stance on race, as well as its compatability with African religions, Spiritualism found an appeal among certain southern Blacks.

The institutionalization of Black Spiritualism as a church movement per se in New Orleans appears to have awaited the arrival of Mother Leafy Anderson from Chicago sometime between 1918 and 1921.[12] Mother Anderson established the Eternal Life Spiritualist Church in the Crescent City, and attracted not only Blacks but also some poor whites. She trained several women, who established congregations of their own, and eventually became the overseer of an association that included congregations in New Orleans, Chicago, Little Rock, Memphis, Pensacola, Biloxi, Houston, and some smaller cities.[13] Mother Anderson accepted elements from Catholicism and other Spiritual churches also accepted elements of Voodoo. While the number of Spiritual congregations in Chicago, Detroit, and possibly some other cities surpass the fifty or so reported in New Orleans, in a very real sense the crescent city continues to serve as the "soul" of the Spiritual movement.[14]

Like many other African-American sects, the Spiritual movement underwent a tremendous growth due to the Great Migration, particularly in northern cities but also in southern cities. In 1923 Father George W. Hurley, a self-proclaimed god like his contemporary, Father Divine, established the Universal Hagar's Spiritual Church in Detroit.[15] On September 22, 1925, in Kansas City, Missouri, Bishop William F. Taylor and Elder Leviticus L. Boswell established the Metropolitan Spiritual Church of Christ, which became the mother church of the largest of the Spiritual associations. St. Clair Drake and Horace R. Cayton note that the Spiritual movement flourished on the south side of Chicago between the world wars: "In 1928 there were seventeen Spiritualist storefronts in Bronzeville; by 1938 there were 51 Spiritualist churches, including one congregation of over 2,000 members. In 1928 one church in twenty was Spiritualist; in 1938, one in ten."[16]

Following the death of Bishop Taylor and a succession crisis resulting in a split in the Metropolitan organization, Rev. Clarence Cobbs, the pastor of the First Church of Deliverance in Chicago, emerged as the president of the principal faction, the Metropolitan Spiritual Churches of Christ, Inc. According to Drake and Cayton, although the First Church of Deliverance, "like other Spiritualist churches, is still considered lower-class by the 'dicties' it was rising in status during the late Thirties, and had begun to attract middle-class members."[17] The six-foot, slender Cobbs came to symbolize the gods of the Black metropolis with his dapper mannerisms and love of the "good life."

Since Cobbs's death in 1979 shortly following the fiftieth anniversary of his southside church, the number of congregations in the Metropolitan association decreased appreciably from a possible high of 125. Another succession crisis prompted many pastors to withdraw their congregations from the association and some pastors to establish their own associations. Dr. Logan Kearse, the founder of the Cornerstone Church of Christ in Baltimore (formerly a congregation affiliated with the National Baptist Convention, USA), became the international president of the Metropolitan Spiritual Churches of Christ. Given the tensions that exist between Dr. Kearse and various pastors in the Chicago area, church leaders proposed that the association's headquarters be moved to a more "neutral" site, namely, Indianapolis.

One of the most colorful Spiritual associations is the Mt. Zion Spiritual Temple, Inc., which was founded in 1943 by King Louis H. Narcisse, D.D. The international headquarters of the association is in Oakland, California, and the East Coast headquarters is the King Narcisse Michigan State Memorial Temple in Detroit. In addition to these two temples, Mt. Zion has seven other congregations, including a second temple in Detroit and temples in Sacramento, Richmond (California), Houston, Orlando, New York City, and Washington, D.C.

I met King Narcisse, a tall stately man who appeared to be in his sixties, in 1979. In keeping with his regal status, he wore a golden toga and cape with a white surplice, a white crown with glitter and tassel, eight rings on his fingers, and a ring in his left ear. King Narcisse arrived at the temple in a shiny black Cadillac limousine with his title and name inscribed upon the door. His two body guards rolled a white carpet down the center aisle of the temple to pave the way for King Narcisse's procession to his throne in the front of the sanctuary from where he conducted the second part of the service. For those occasions when he cannot be with his flock in Detroit, a large picture of "His Grace" faces the congregation, reminding its members of their spiritual leader. Ironically, in contrast to the massive sanctuary with its elaborate altar and chandeliers, the presence of some thirty individuals at the service suggested that the the kingdom of Louis H. Narcisse had seen better days.

Spiritual Churches as a Religious Movement

Like other movement organizations, the Spiritual movement manifests the principles of decentralization, segmentation, and reticulation.[18] The Spiritual movement has no central organization that defines dogma, ritual, and social structure. While many Spiritual congregations belong to a regional or national association, some choose to function independently from such formal ties. In many instances the formal leader of a Spiritual association exhibits a clear pattern of dominance over its local congregations, as was the case when Rev. Clarence Cobbs was president of the Metropolitan Spiritual Churches of Christ. Conversely the formal head of an association may be closer to a "first among equals" relationship with the various pastors of affiliated congregations, as is the case for the Great Universal Spiritual Unity Union, which has its headquarters in St. Louis. Despite the fact that I observed activities and interviewed individual members of two of this association's congregations in Nashville, I never heard any specific reference to its supreme bishop, either by name or title. I learned who the formal leader of the association was only by reading a copy of its manual. Associations charter churches and ordain ministers, elders and other religious functionaries.

Segmentation in a movement means that it is "composed of a great variety of localized groups or cells which are essentially independent, but which can combine to form larger configurations or divide to form smaller ones."[19] While associations sometimes try to impose certain rules, policies, and even dogmas upon their constituent congregations, for the most part they fail to exert effective control. Instead, like many other movements, the Spiritual movement exhibits an "ideology of personal access to power."[20]

Theoretically anyone who is touched by the Spirit can claim personal access to knowledge, truth, and authority. Although associations may attempt to place constraints on such claims by requiring individuals exhibiting a "gift" to undergo some process of legitimation, the latter may easily thwart such efforts, either by establishing their own congregations or associations or by realigning themselves with some other Spiritual group.

The final organizational principle of movements, reticulation, refers to the process in which the "cells, or nodes, are tied together, not through any central points, but rather through intersecting sets of personal relationships and other intergroup linkages."[21] Leaders of Spiritual churches are reticulated with leaders of other Spiritual congregations not only in their own association, but also in other associations. Such a linkage is illustrated by the friendship between Bishop F. Jones, the pastor of the Temple of Spiritual Truth in Nashville and Reverend Brown, the pastor of the United House of the Redeemer in Indianapolis. (The names of these pastors and their congregations have been changed for this article.) After the two pastors met Bishop Jones invited Reverend Brown to preach at a revival at the Temple of Spiritual Truth. Reverend Brown reciprocated some time later by inviting Bishop Jones and his congregation to visit the United House of the Redeemer. The exchange of visits between the two churches occurred despite their affiliations with different associations.

The Spiritual Congregation

Even more than their Sanctified (Holiness/Pentecostal) counterparts, Spiritual congregations tend to be housed in storefronts, apartments, house churches, and simple frame church structures. Spiritual churches are primarily located in large urban areas; some are found in small cities, but very few appear to be situated in rural areas. The Spiritual movement emerged and continues to function as an almost exclusively urban phenemenon. Although most Spiritual congregations are housed in modest quarters, some of them, particularly those that crosscut socioeconomic lines, are housed in impressive edifices that can accommodate several hundred people.

Social Composition of the Membership

Probably more so than even Sanctified churches, Spiritual churches have found their greatest appeal among lower- and working-class Blacks. Drake and Cayton found that members of Spiritual (as well as Sanctified) churches in Chicago's south side were "marked down 'low-status'."[22] Kaslow and Jacobs conducted a comparative survey of the social composition of two Spiritual congregations in New Orleans.[23] King David Universal Spiritual Church of Christ (pseudonym) is one of the older Spiritual congregations in the city. In contrast, Helping Hand Spiritual Church of Christ (pseudonym) was established around 1979. In keeping with the respective ages of these congregations, "At King David S.C., 51.5% of the members are over fifty years of age; at Helping Hand 50.0% of the members are in their twenties, and none is over fifty years old."[24] Sex ratios in the two congregations are almost identical. Of the sixteen adult "core and elite members" in Helping Hand, eleven (68.75 percent) are female and five (31.25 percent) are male.[25] All of the core and elite members in King David, except for a retired school teacher and an unemployed woman, hold or are retired from working-class occupations (e.g., printer, domestic, taxi driver, hospital attendant). Whereas most of the adult core and elite members of King David work or had worked in semi-skilled and unskilled occupations, all of their generally younger counterparts in Helping Hand, except for a law student, are employed in skilled working-class positions.

Although most Spiritual congregations are small and attract primarily working- and lower-class individuals, the larger congregations crosscut socio-economic lines. For example, St. Cecilia's Divine Healing Church No. 2 (pseudonym) in Nashville and the United House of the Redeemer in Indianapolis attract some lower middle class and even professional Blacks. Both congregations also count a few whites within their ranks.

Organization of the Local Spiritual Congregation

Although Spiritual churches draw their rituals and beliefs from a variety of religious traditions, the politico-religious organization of many Spiritual congregations strongly resembles that of many Black Protestant congregations. Church organizations and auxiliaries at the First Church of Deliverance in Chicago, which is probably the largest Spiritual congregation in the United

States, include the Trustee Board, the Lady Trustee Board, the Ministers Board, the Medium Board, the Acolytes, the Spiritual Union, the Sunday School Board, the Usher Board, the Senior Nurses Board, the Men's Group, the Women's Department, the Group Captains Club, the Christian Service Guild, the Community Enrichment center, the Rev. Mattie B. Thornton (Cobbs's assistant for many years) Memorial Group, the Luela Williams (Cobbs's mother) Memorial Group, the Rev. C. H. Cobbs Volunteer Group, and several choirs.[26] While most Spiritual congregations are considerably smaller than the First Church of Deliverance, they also exhibit an elaborate politico-religious structure. During the course of my fieldwork at the Temple of Spiritual Truth in Nashville between 1977 and 1979, offices included pastor, assistant pastor, elders, deacons, deaconesses, missionaries, ushers and junior ushers, nurses, choir members, secretary, and treasurer. Despite the fact that the Temple of Spiritual Truth is a small storefront congregation, both its pastor and assistant pastor carried the title of "Bishop." Some Spiritual sects grant more regal titles to their leaders. The Mt. Zion Spiritual Temple, Inc., includes within its ranks Reverend Princes, Reverend Princesses, Princes, Princesses, Reverend Ladies, Prophets, Reverend Mothers, Grand Duchesses, Ministers, and Junior Ministers.

Most Spiritual churches maintain the status or office of "medium," "spiritual advisor," "prophet," or "messenger." Mediums possess the gift of prophecy—that is, the ability to "read" people or tell them about their past, present, and future.[27] Pastors of Spiritual congregations are almost always mediums, but other prominent members may also be mediums. Some Spiritual groups, such as the Universal Hagar's Spiritual Church and Spiritual Israel Church and Its Army, have established auxiliaries for mediums. Mediums give "messages" in special religious services, referred to as "prophecy and healing," "bless," or "deliverance" services. They also give messages in private consultations, often to individuals who do not belong to a Spiritual church. For the most part mediums focus upon a wide variety of problems of living, ranging from finding a job or spouse to removing a spell or hex.

Religious Activities

Much of what transpires in Spiritual services closely resembles what occurs in many Holiness, Pentecostal, and the more exuberant Baptist churches. Conversely the syncretic nature of the Spiritual movement means that Spiritual services often include rituals from other religious traditions, particularly Spiritualism, Catholicism, and at a more subtle level, Voodoo.

Although some Spiritual people today recognize a historical connection between their religion and mainstream Spiritualism, there is a strong tendency among many of them to view the latter in a cautious, even disparaging manner. Many groups contracted the term "Spiritualist" to "Spiritual" during the 1930s and 1940s. The séance seems to have been an important ritual in many Spiritual groups, including the Metropolitan Spiritual Churches of Christ at one time, but it is only a minor aspect of the contemporary Spiritual movement.[28] Many Spiritual congregations, however, place a great deal of emphasis on a message session that is conducted as part of a religious service either on Sunday evenings or during the week. Like mainstream Spiritualism, the Black Spiritual movement places a great deal of emphasis on therapeutic activities.[29] Individual spiritual advising, counseling, and the healing of physical ailments are integral parts of both movements. Many Spiritual people believe in reincarnation. In marked contrast to Spiritual churches elsewhere, some Spiritual churches in New Orleans have statues of Black Hawk and conduct rituals of veneration and propitiation to this important Spiritualist guide.

It is difficult to determine whether Catholic elements in the Spiritual movement were derived directly from Roman Catholicism or indirectly from Voodoo. The sanctuaries of many Spiritual churches, particularly in southern Louisiana but also elsewhere, more closely resemble those of Catholic churches than of the Protestant groups to which African Americans traditionally have belonged. Spiritual churches make use of many Catholic articles, including crucifixes; statues of Jesus Christ, the Blessed Virgin, and the saints; incense burners; and holy pictures. Spiritual people often engage in routine Catholic rituals, such as making the sign of the cross, genuflecting while passing before the altar, and burning incense and candles. But for the most part such rituals are interspersed with activities more typical of Black Protestant services such as testifying, hymn-singing, shouting, and the long sermon. I have never seen or heard of anything resembling the Catholic mass occurring in a Spiritual congregation.

Both Voodoo and the Spiritual religion emphasize the acquisition of "mysteries" or "secrets." Bishop F. Jones of the Temple of Spiritual Truth stated that the Lord gives people "secrets" in order to help them overcome the adversities of life. Some Spiritual people use floor washes, perfume oils, special soaps, powders, roots, and herbs. Many Spiritual churches in New

Orleans during the 1940s bore the name of St. Expedite, a Voodoo saint who can be appealed to when certain endeavors must be done in a hurry.

The Role of Spiritual Churches in the
African American Community

In assessing the role of Spiritual churches, I consider briefly the parallels between them and other religious groups in the African-American community. Given their distinctive nature, however, I focus on their thaumaturgical approach to racism and social stratification in American society.

Like many other lower-class religious bodies, Spiritual churches are compensatory in that they substitute religious for social status. Although one may occupy a humble standing in the larger society, in a Spiritual church an individual may be recognized as a bishop, prophet, elder, deacon, missionary, or even as a royal personage. Drake and Cayton note that the ban on women pastors in Baptist churches "has increased the popularity of Pentecostal, Holiness, and Spiritualist churches where ambitious women may rise to the top."[30] Of the forty Spiritual churches that I have visited in various cities, eighteen had female pastors. Six of the eleven Spiritual churches in Nashville had female pastors during the period of my fieldwork there. Spiritual churches with their busy schedule of religious services, musical performances, suppers, and picnics also offer a strong sense of community for their adherents. Furthermore, Spiritual churches provide their members with a variety of opportunities such as testimony sessions and "shouting" to ventilate their anxieties and frustrations.

Despite the foregoing functional similarities between Spiritual churches and other religious groups in the Black community, particularly those of the Baptist, Methodist, and Sanctified varieties, the emphasis on the manipulation of one's present condition through the use of magico-religious practices distinquishes the former from the latter. The belief that events can be controlled through thaumaturgical practices is found in all walks of life, but especially among the poor who often find themselves in a powerless situation. The acquisition of the "good life" and a slice of the "American Dream" are central concerns of Spiritual people as they are for others of low socioeconomic status. The intended function of magical ritual is to put people in touch with supernatural power. As Robert Murphy asserts, magic usually promotes a sense of self-assurance and "produces the illusion that people are master of their fate, controller of their environment and not its pawn."[31] As has already been noted, the techniques with which Spiritual people attempt to manipulate their destiny include burning votive candles, praying before the image of a saint, the use of wide array of occult articles, and public or private divination by a medium. Spiritual churches occasionally also conduct special services, often referred to as "demonstrations." Bishop Stewart, the pastor of the now defunct St. Joseph's Spiritual Church in Nashville, was particularly well known for her annual "cabbage demonstrations." Three days after the cabbages were blessed, they were cooked and eaten during the course of the day. Each time an individual ate part of the cabbage, he or she asked for a blessing such as money, a new house, a new car, or success in love. Some Spiritual leaders have developed metaphysical systems. For example, the pastor of Unity Fellowship (pseudonym) in Nashville places great emphasis on the power of positive thinking and prescribes a number of rituals intended to raise the level of one's "consciousness."

Although the majority of Spiritual people are lower class, others—particularly some of those who belong to the larger congregations—appear to be relatively affluent working-class or middle-class individuals. The appeal of the Spiritual faith for the latter is not as apparent as for the former, but E. Franklin Frazier argues that members of the "new middle class" are often fascinated by "'spiritual' and 'psychic' phenomena."[32] The Spiritual religion with its positive-thinking philosophy may serve to validate the newly acquired status of some upwardly mobile Blacks. Such individuals are attracted to relatively large Spiritual congregations such as St. Cecilia's Divine Healing Church No. 2 and the United House of the Redeemer. The pastors of both congregations tend to promote affluent members to positions of leadership and present them as living proof of the efficacy of the Spiritual religion.

In part guided by Marx and Engels's recognition of the dual nature of religion, significant data in the literature on African American religion address the matter of whether it has been accommodative or emancipatory.[33] Unfortunately, statements as to whether Black religion tends to be an opiate or inspiration for militancy often overlooks its diversity. For example, one might expect a member of an Islamic sect to be more militant than a member of a Sanctified church. The thaumaturgical approach to problem-solving promoted in Spiritual churches tends to deny "political conflict by stressing the importance of the individual over society, the insignificance of social arrangement and plans, and the irrelevance of group conflict beside the paramount importance of the individual."[34] Furthermore, most Spiritual churches eschew social activism and often blame their members for their miseries. In this regard they function as hegemonic institutions which transmit the "cult of private life" championed by such agencies of socialization as the family, the schools, the media, advertisers, social workers, and psychotherapists, and deflects attention from the social structural roots of racism and poverty.[35]

Conversely, Spiritual churches occasionally exhibit overt elements of social protest, particularly in critical remarks made by Spiritual leaders on business practices, politics, and racism in the larger society. Social protest in Spiritual churches, however, usually assumes more subtle forms. In his discussion of the belief in Indian spirit guides among the Spiritual churches in New Orleans, Andrew J. Kaslow refers to their symbolic meaning: "Black Hawk is regarded as a warrior who can cause justice to be done, and his intercession is frequently sought in court cases, or in seeking the release of loved ones from prison. The role of the Indian as an opponent of white domination is an expression of protest against status inferiority in the larger society."[36] Another manifestation of protest occurs in the widespread belief among Spiritual people that heaven and hell exist in the here and now. Spiritual people often pride themselves that, unlike other religious individuals and groups, they do not subscribe to "pie-in-the-sky religion." While the thaumaturgical means used by members of Spiritual churches in attempting to attain heaven on earth contain a strong accommodative dimension, their refusal to wait for social rewards in some nebulous afterlife suggests some degree of rejection of existing social relations.

Furthermore, Spiritual people often reject the Protestant work ethic. This does not mean that they do not work hard; as is generally true of the poor, many of them do. Conversely, they have internalized mainstream notions of success and value the benefits of the good life and the status symbols of the American Dream. As Charles Valentine asserts, the values and aspirations of the poor may be very similar to those of middle-class people, but must be modified in practice because of the situational stresses that the former experience in everyday life.[37] Many Spiritual people have come to realize that hard work in itself does not guarantee upward social mobility or security in American society. Since many Blacks in America are denied access to strategies that may result in some modest degree of social mobility, many Spiritual people have come to reject mainstream platitudes about the Protestant work ethic that serve to legitimate patterns of class and racial stratification in American society. While they realize that financial prosperity rests upon somewhat capricious factors, Spiritual people are unclear on what these are. Consequently they tend to resort to thaumaturgical techniques in their attempts to cope with their lowly position in American society.

Conclusion

The assertion that 11 o'clock on Sunday morning is the most segregated hour in America is probably as valid today as it ever was. Bearing this observation in mind, much of the content of African American religion acts as a response to racism and social stratification in American society. Powerless groups have often turned to religion as a way of coping with social reality and in this regard African Americans are no different. In responding to the larger society, their religious response has not been uniform. While Black religion was characterized by a considerable diversity during the nineteenth century, a multiplicity of new sects, including some which vehemently rejected traditional Christianity, emerged among African Americans during the early decades of the present century. In large measure, these were in response to the displacement of many Blacks from the rural South and the stresses accompanying the processes of urbanization and industrialization that accompanied the rapid expansion of American capitalism.

The Spiritual movement described in this essay was one of a multiplicity of transformations of the rural Black church of the South. The religious sects that emerged in the African American community after the turn of the century provided a mechanism for preserving rural religious and social forms and values and served as a buffer against the anonymity of the city and the large mainstream congregations that tended to cater to the needs of the Black *petit bourgeoisie*. Like the rural Black churches, these sects often sublimated the frustrations of their adherents, created meaning out of meaninglessness, and self-respect out of the degradation of racial oppression, economic exploitation and marginality. All of these sects—Sanctified, storefront Baptist, Muslim, Judaic, and Spiritual—promised their followers some sort of salvation: otherworldly, temporal, or a combination of the two.

While Spiritual churches exhibit many of the same characteristics as other religious groups in the African American community, they are distinguished by their highly syncretistic content and their thaumaturgical approach to the structural situation faced by Blacks in the larger society. In their syncretism, Spiritual churches are the closest counterpart in this country to the African American religions in the Caribbean and South America. The Spiritual religion demonstrates the ability of Blacks to take components from diverse belief systems in order to create a new religion relevant to their needs.

Although Spiritual churches perform multifaceted roles for certain segments of the African American community, their greatest appeal lies in their emphasis on thaumaturgical techniques that promise spiritual power over their destiny. This emphasis attracts many Blacks who do not belong to specific Spiritual congregations. Many of them attend bless services and visit Spiritual prophets and advisors for private consultations. Spiritual churches attempt to provide immediate release from the stresses that the powerless, poor, and alienated Blacks feel as result of their structural position in a racist and class society.

African American religion has been characterized by a dual consciousness in that it has fostered both accommodation and protest. As Manning Marable so astutely observes, "the conservative tendencies within Black faith reach for a Spirit which liberates the soul, but not the body," whereas "the radical consciousness within Black faith was concerned with the immediate conditions of Black people."[38] The juxtaposition of protest and accommodation is present in all Black religious groups throughout the Americas. Certain messianic-nationalist sects have emphasized the first; Spiritual churches have given more attention to the second. Yet protest against the larger society has often been couched in Spiritual people's rejection of the myth that work in itself guarantees success and prosperity. Some Spiritual bodies, such as the Universal Hagar's Spiritual Church and Spiritual Israel Church and Its Army, have heightened their critique of American society by incorporating elements of messianic-nationalism to their generally thaumaturgical approach. For the most part, however, such groups, like their mainstream counterparts, have offered a limited critique of the American society by focusing primarily on its racist dimensions without recognizing how these are intricately connected to the political economy of capitalism.

Despite the persistence of the collective dimension of African American religion in the social activism of many Black mainstream congregations, the economic enterprises of various messianic-nationalist sects, and the Black Theology movement, the pattern of individuation so characteristic of religious life in the larger society has become part of the Black religious experience. A stress on individual rather than collective salvation is particularly pronounced among Spiritual churches and other thaumaturgical sects such as Reverend Ike's United Church and Science of Living Institute. The solutions that Spiritual churches provide for their members tend to be compensatory rather than corrective. Instead of encouraging Blacks to seek social change, the Spiritual movement strives to alleviate their alienation from society by promising financial success or the restoration of personal conflict in return for the enactment of certain magico-religious rituals. The problems that its adherents and clients experience in most cases will not be eradicated until there has been a drastic transformation in the political economy of American society.

Notes

1. See Gayraud S. Wilmore, *Black Religion and Black Radicalism: An Interpretation of the Religious History of Afro-American People* (Maryknoll, N.Y.: Orbis Books, 1983):152.

2. Between October 1977 and July 1979 while teaching at George Peabody College for Teachers, I conducted fieldwork among the eleven then-existing Spiritual churches in Nashville, Tennessee. While a post-doctoral fellow at Michigan State University during the 1979–1980 academic year, I conducted research on Spiritual churches in Detroit, Flint, and Saginaw. A teaching stint during the 1980–1981 academic year at St. John's University provided me with the opportunity to conduct research on four temples affiliated with the Universal Hagar's Spiritual Church in the New York-New Jersey megapolis. I have visited a total of forty Spiritual churches located in fifteen cities and ten states. For a more extensive overview of the Spiritual movement, see Hans A. Baer, *The Black Spiritual Movement: A Religious Response to Racism* (Knoxville: University of Tennessee Press, 1984). For an account of the temple affiliated with Spiritual Israel Church and Its Army, see Hans A. Baer, "Black Spiritual Israelites in a Small Southern City: Elements of Protest and Accommodation in Belief and Oratory," *Southern Quarterly* 23, no. 3, (Spring 1985).

3. See Oliver C. Cox, *Race Relations: Elements and Dynamics* (Detroit: Wayne State University Press, 1976):58.

4. See E. Franklin Frazier, *The Negro Family in the United States* (Chicago: University of Chicago Press, 1968).

5. See Melvin D. Williams, *Community in a Black Pentecostal Church* (Pittsburgh: University of Pittsburgh Press, 1974):9.

6. See E. Franklin Frazier, *The Negro Church in America* (New York: Schocken, 1974).

7. Wilmore, 222.

8. See Allan H. Spear, *Black Chicago: The Making of a Negro Ghetto, 1890–1920* (Chicago: University of Chicago Press):96.

9. See Andrew J. Kaslow, "Saints and Spirits: The Belief System of Afro-American Spiritual Churches in New Orleans" *Perspectives on Ethnicity in New Orleans* (New Orleans: Committee on Ethnicity):61.

10. See Kenneth L. Kusmer, *A Ghetto Takes Shape: Black Cleveland, 1870–1930* (Urbana: University of Illinois Press):96.

11. See Geoffrey K. Nelson, *Spiritualism and Society* (London: Routledge and Kegan Paul, 1969):16–17.

12. See Zora Hurston, "Hoodoo in America," *Journal of American Folklore* 44:319; Robert Tallant, *Voodoo in New Orleans* (New York: Collier, 1946):173; Andrew J. Kaslow, 61.

13. See Andrew J. Kaslow and Claude Jacobs, *Prophecy, Healing, and Power: The Afro-American Spiritual Churches of New Orleans* (A Cultural Resources Management Study for the Jean Lafitte National Historical Park and the National Park Service, Department of Anthropology and Geography, University of New Orleans):95.

14. Ibid., 20.

15. See Baer, *The Black Spiritual Movement*, 82–109.

16. See St. Clair Drake and Horace R. Cayton, *Black Metropolis* (New York: Harcourt, Brace, 1945):642.

17. Ibid., 645.

18. See Luther P. Gerlach and Virginia H. Hine, *People, Power, and Change: Movements of Social Transformation* (Indianapolis: Bobbs-Merrill, 1970).

19. Ibid., 41.

20. Ibid., 42–43.

21. Ibid., 55.

22. See Drake and Cayton, 670.

23. See Kaslow and Jacobs.

24. Ibid., 83.

25. Ibid., 80.

26. See *50th Anniversary, 1929–1979* (Chicago: First Church of Deliverance, 1979).

27. See Hans A. Baer, "Prophets and Advisors in Black Spiritual Churches," *Culture, Medicine, and Psychiatry* 5, no. 2 (June 1981).

28. See James Daniel Tyms, "A Study of Four Religious Cults Operating among the Negroes" (M.A. thesis, Howard University).

29. See Robert Gray Fishman, "Spiritualism in Western New York: A Study in Ritual Healing." *Medical Anthropology* 3, no. 1.; Baer, "Prophets and Advisors in Black Spiritual Churches."

30. See Drake and Cayton, 631–632.

31. See Robert F. Murphy, *An Overture to Social Anthropology* (Englewood Cliffs, N.J.: Prentice-Hall, 1979):170.

32. See Frazier, *The Negro Church in America*, 84–85.

33. See Gary T. Marx, "Religion: Opiate or Inspiration of Civil Rights Militancy among Negroes" in Marcel L. Goldschmid, ed., *Black Americans and White Racism* (New York: Holt, Rinehart, and Winston, 1970).

34. See John Wilson, *Religion in American Society: The Effective Presence* (Englewood Cliffs,

N.J.: Prentice-Hall, 1978):356.; Hart M. Nelsen and Anne Kusener Nelsen, *Black Church in the Sixties* (Lexington: University Press of Kentucky, 1975).

35. See H. C. Greisman and Sharon S. Mayers, "The Social Construction of Unreality: The Real American Dilemma," *Dialectical Anthropology*, 2, no. 1.

36. See Kaslow, "Saints and Spirits," 64.

37. See Charles A. Valentine, *Culture and Poverty: Critique and Counter-Proposals* (Chicago: University of Chicago Press, 1968).

38. See Manning Marable, *Blackwater: Historical Studies in Race, Class Consciousness and Revolution* (Dayton, Ohio: Black Praxis Press, 1981):203.

Part Two

Biblical Studies

The report of the American Association of Theological Schools Committee on the Black Religious Experience and Theological Education states that "Biblical study will continue to occupy a preeminent place in the Black curriculum."[1] This comes as no surprise in light of the importance of Scripture in the daily life of believers throughout the history of the African American Church. The Bible is a primary source for the words of the famed Negro spirituals. Hundreds of extant slave testimonies reveal a ubiquitous hunger to read the Bible. Many taught themselves to read and write by stealing away, at great risk, to pore over the pages of a well-worn Bible, pages in which they met a God of justice and compassion, learned about the heroes and heroines of Israel, and entered a sacred world they fused with the existential world of their bondage.

Yet, as Latta R. Thomas of Benedict College reminds us, today many African Americans raise serious questions about the Bible.[2] He notes a new wave of skepticism and even hostility toward a Bible that was deliberately distorted to make the slaves passive and dependent and was interpreted by white preachers as containing the divine revelation that dark-skinned descendents of Ham, second son of Noah, should be "hewers of wood and drawers of water."

Thomas, therefore, joins a chorus of African American biblical scholars when he writes that "Black people must find out for themselves, especially in these days, what the Bible is really about."[3] It is doubtful that popular television evangelists, or the mounting conservatism of American Protestantism, as evidenced in the Southern Baptist Convention, will help Black people make that discovery. For the past several years highly trained African American biblical interpreters have taken up the task of demonstrating that the Bible reveals a God who works in history for the liberation of the oppressed to free the world of all forms of injustice. Indeed one of the major concerns of these scholars is to show that far from ignoring the people of Africa, except to condemn them to perpetual servitude, the Bible has a place for Black people equal to that of the white race, despite strenuous efforts on the part of some American exegetes and commentators to prove the contrary.

We begin with an essay addressing this contemporary question about the place of Black people in the Bible. Chapter seven by Charles B. Copher was presented in the spring of 1987 by the author at the annual lecture series named in his honor at the Interdenominational Theological Center in Atlanta. Copher has justly earned the title of dean of African American biblical scholars. He was for many years a beloved teacher at I.T.C. and is now Emeritus Professor of the Old Testament. In this paper reprinted from the *Journal of the I.T.C.*, he undertakes to review three millennia of biblical interpretation related in various ways to African ethnicity.

For all that it has meant in the Black religious past, modern-day Bible students must understand that there is no simplistic convergence. Chapter eight examines the differences and similarities between the African American experience and the story of the Bible in the context of the Black freedom struggle. The author, Robert A. Bennett, is Professor of Old Testament at the Episcopal Theological School, Cambridge, Massachusetts. He has done intensive research in Egypt and the Sudan on the African presence in the ancient world.

How has the Bible been understood and interpreted in African American churches? In Chapter nine Vincent L. Wimbush, Assistant Professor of New Testament at the School of Theology at Claremont, California, recognizes the role of ethical and moral considerations in the way Blacks have interpreted Scripture and is critical of the failure of some to do the necessary historical and descriptive work with the text that makes contextualization —the discovery of the relevance of the text to a contemporary situation —possible. Wimbush warns that unless the Black Church is willing to talk with biblical scholars about a correct historical perspective, "no clear assessment can be made of any biblical ethical principle, nor any biblical 'world.'"

The issue of a Black hermeneutic and contextualization arises again in the final essay in this section. Indeed we will be meeting it throughout this book. Chapter ten is a previously unpublished essay by Cain H. Felder, who teaches New Testament at the Divinity School of Howard University in Washington, D.C., and is editor of the esteemed *Journal of Religious Thought*.

Felder begins by exploring the "experiential sympathy" Africans at home and in the diaspora have with the biblical witness, and the new skepticism he and others share about Eurocentric exegesis, hermeneutics and historiography. Calling for a radical revision of this scholarship, he goes on to discuss recontextualization as the necessary "process of rediscovering some essential features of the Black religious experience in Africa . . . and in so doing to enter a new dialogue of liberation and spirituality as found in the Bible."

It is significant to note that those who contributed to Part Two of this book belong to an intensive seminar of African American biblical scholars that has been held each summer since 1986 at the Ecumenical Institute in Collegeville, Minnesota, under a grant from the Eli Lilly Endowment for the purpose of advancing the work represented by these essays. Many will agree that the next step is an interdisciplinary approach that will bring persons from other fields into this promising effort to delineate an African American hermeneutic for Black Christians and the ecumenical community as a whole.

Notes

1. *Theological Education* 6, no. 3, supplement (Spring, 1970):44.

2. Latta R. Thomas, *Biblical Faith and the Black American* (Valley Forge, Penn.: Judson Press, 1976):11–12.

3. Ibid., 11.

7

Three Thousand Years of Biblical Interpretation
with Reference to Black Peoples

Charles B. Copher

Introduction

In the land of Palestine, known also from antiquity as the Holy Land, stand two mountains, which are not far apart and which face each other. In between lies a valley. One mountain, called Gerizim, was referred to by the ancient Hebrews as the "Mount of Blessing." The other, called Ebal, was referred to as the "Mount of Cursing." We may compare the Bible to the valley between the two mountains, and ask a question: To which of these mountains does the Bible—or rather, interpretations of the Bible,—belong? To the "Mount of Blessing" or to the "Mount of Cursing?"

Granted that the Bible, along with interpretations of it, have proved to be and continue to be sources of blessings to millions of people. It is also true that these have been and continue to be sources of some of the greatest curses humankind has known. Upon the basis of the Bible and interpretations of it Orthodox Jew has killed Orthodox Jew; Orthodox Jew has killed Christian Jew; Gentile has murdered Jew; Christian has murdered Christian. In no instance, however, have the Bible and interpretations of it led to such murder —physical, psychological, social, and spiritual—as in the case of Black peoples. As will be noted, such murder goes back to ancient times and is still being committed today.

This chapter has as its purpose to review the history of the Bible and its interpretation with reference to Black peoples, from the very beginnings of the Bible itself, as collections of literature at various times, to the Bible as it exists today primarily (in English translation), and as it is still interpreted today. Hence the title of the chapter: "Three Thousand Years of Biblical Interpretation with Reference to Black Peoples."

Foundational for a treatment of the subject is knowledge of the history of the Bible and its canonization: knowledge of the fact that, according to critical historical-literary study, what now constitutes the Bible came into existence in stages, across more than twelve hundred years; and that canonization consisted of a series of processes that occurred, say, roughly from 600 B.C. to A.D. 400. Following the collection of literature into what may be referred to as the sacred Scriptures at any given stage along the way came translation of the Hebrew Scriptures, first into Greek; next came the creation of Christian New Testament writings in Greek; followed by translation into Latin, English and other such languages as now exist.

Once there was a Bible, at whatever stage at a given time, interpretation began. Thus there appears in what is now the Bible *inner* or *intra* biblical interpretation.[1] This type of interpretation was succeeded by interpretation of the complete Bible, first of the Hebrew Scriptures, then of the Christian Scriptures consisting of the Hebrew Scriptures plus Christian writings regarded as Scripture.

Interpretation as a process, begun within the Bible itself, continues in all literature related to the Bible including translations of originals—as all translation is by its very nature also interpretation.

Bodies of extra-biblical literature, arranged in a more or less chronological order, include the following: the translation of the Hebrew Scriptures into Greek, the Septuagint (250–100 B.C.); the Apocrypha and Pseudepigrapha of the Old Testament (150 B.C.–A.D. 150); the Qumran Writings (150 B.C.–A.D. 150); the writings of Philo and Josephus (25 B.C.–A.D. 100); the New Testament books (A.D. 50–100); early rabbinical interpretations such as are found in the early Midrashim, Haggadah, and the Palestinian and Babylonian Talmuds, plus Targums (A.D. 200–600); New Testament Apocryphal and Pseudepigraphal writings, primarily of the second and third centuries A.D.; Targums, (A.D. 200 and later); Islamic Literature (A.D. 625 and later); Jewish and Christian interpretations of the Middle Ages (A.D. 600–1400); and for our purposes, primarily Christian interpretations of modern times, including interpretations by Black peoples (1400–present).

Discussion of so vast a body of literatures must of necessity be limited to a very broad outline at best. All an author can hope for is akin to that hope expressed by a Black biblical scholar of nearly a hundred years ago, Bishop Benjamin T. Tanner, in the dedication of his monograph, *The Color Of Solomon—What?*: "To the rising scholars of the colored race, the writer dedicates the monograph with the hope that the subject which it discusses, and others akin to it, will receive such treatment at their hands as will vindicate the colored races of the earth and save them from the delusion: 'The leading race in all history has been the white race.'"[2]

The Biblical Text and Intra-Biblical Interpretation

Before interpretation within the Bible with reference to Black peoples must come consideration of the presence of Black peoples, or of peoples whom the biblical writers regarded as Black, in the biblical text itself. Such a presence is determinable by the use of words or terms employed to designate Black when applied to peoples—in Hebrew, Greek, and Latin. Relevant words and terms are *Shahar* meaning black in Hebrew, and used twice denoting skin or complexion, apart from occurrences associated with color caused by disease; *Hum* of doubtful meaning in Hebrew, and limited to Genesis, chapter 30;[3] *Kedar* meaning black in Hebrew, and occurring some twelve times; *Cush* and related words such as *Cushite*, in Hebrew, which occurs some fifty times and bearing a color notion through most typical visual features; *Hoshek*, in Hebrew, which refers to darkness; *Ethiopia, melas, niger*, and related terms in Greek; and *Ethiopia* and *Niger* in Latin—all of which have to do with black color.

The Greek and Latin terms are used to translate the Hebrew word Cush and related terms in the Old Testament; the Latin term niger is used to translate the corresponding word in the New Testament. In treating the identification of Black peoples the use of words is limited to include primarily Cush and related terms in the Old Testament (disregarding Kedar, Ham, and even Phinehas, which for now over a hundred years has been stated to mean "the Negro"), and Ethiopia and Niger in the New Testament.

Of some fifty occurrences of the word Cush and related terms in the Old Testament, half refer to individual persons. In the main the references are factual statements. Of these the vast majority are judgments of God upon the Cushites (Ethiopians) similar to or identical with God's judgments upon other peoples, and without pejorative connotation based upon color. On this Black biblical scholars are in agreement. Thus in writing about the biblical text with reference to color, Robert A. Bennett states, "Blacks in the Bible are mentioned favorably and become a symbol of God's love for all people."[4] Similarly, the Reverend Jacob A. Dyer in his booklet, *The Ethiopian in the Bible*, writes:

I know of a certain author who has produced some excellent works. However, after reading a number of his books, I observed that his black and Jewish characters were never honorable Whatever part they played, there was something about them that one could not admire. If his books were historical, it could be contended that he had recorded the facts as he found them; but as a literary composer, the characters he produced simply reflect his own attitude towards certain groups. Neither in the Old Testament nor in the New does the literature which constitutes the Bible reflect any such attitude towards non-whites or persons of black or dark complexion.[5]

An exception to the opinions just stated may or may not appear in the Song of Sol. 1:5, with reference to the appearance of the maiden: whether she is black *and* beautiful, or black *but* beautiful. Again, despite the opinions, there are at least two instances of texts within the Old Testament that reveal themselves as being cases of intra-biblical interpretation. These are the explanatory glosses with reference to Ham's being the father of Canaan (Gen. 9:18, 22) and the explanatory comment at Num. 12:1 with regard to Moses's having married a Cushite wife.

If (as it appears now or will appear later), the word *Ham* did not mean *black* at the time the Noah story was written, and if the term *Hum* was not replaced by the term *Shahar*, which was used as a term of color during the exilic and post-exilic periods, as argued by Athalya Brenner in her book *Colour Terms in the Old Testament*, then Ham as the father of Canaan would mean nothing with regard to the color of the Canaanites.[6] This would come later, as will be seen, when we deal with interpretations of the rabbis, beginning in the second century A.D. where a different interpretation of the gloss "Ham the father of Canaan" is called for. And, to be sure, modern historical-literary scholars do have their interpretations, as did the scholars who preceded them, in deriving *ham* from *hamas* or a similar word and interpreting it to mean *black*.[7]

Two things may be said about the gloss at Num. 12:1. It appears out of context, and the problem appears to be related to Aaron's and Miriam's status as prophets over the status of Moses. Second, as has been observed by others, whatever the bone of contention among the siblings, God disapproved of the behavior of Aaron and Miriam and took sides with Moses.[8]

Interpretation in the Septuagint

From intra-biblical interpretation the next step is to interpretation of the Bible as it existed at the time of its first translation. The earliest translation of the original biblical text is that of the Septuagint, from Hebrew-Aramaic into Greek. As has been stated, every translation is an interpretation. It is necessary then to investigate how the translators dealt with the matter of black color. Two passages will suffice: Gen. 9:25, which has to do with the "curse of Canaan," and Song of Sol. 1:5, which has to do with the color of the maiden. With respect to the curse of Canaan it has often been observed that one manuscript of the Septuagint has "cursed be *Ham*." References to this one instance have been made by writers in modern times, some of whom argue that such a translation is proof that the original Hebrew text intended to place the curse on Ham rather than upon Canaan.[9] The latter assume, of course, that *Ham* in the original Hebrew meant *black*. What this one manuscript may show at best is a move in the so-called Intertestamental Period towards a curse-on-Ham position in some circles or by a translator or scribe, even though *ham* may not necessarily at the time refer to blackness.

The conjunction in Song of Sol. 1:5 may be translated as either *and* or *but*, in both Hebrew and Greek. Translated *and*, it is complimentary; translated *but*, it is pejorative. According to the intensive investigations of Frank M. Snowden, Jr., early commentators translated the conjunction *and*, as it appears in the Septuagint.[10]

Interpretation in the O.T. Apocrypha-Pseudepigrapha—and Qumran Writings

A study of the Old Testament Apocryphal and Pseudepigraphal writings, and those of Qumran, reveals an absence of interpretations of the biblical text with reference to Black peoples. All in all, there are thirteen references to Ethiopia or Ethiopians in the Apocrypha-Pseudepigrapha: six with reference to geographical locations; four with reference to historical events, without comment; two in the form of prophetic judgments; and one with reference to the Ethiopians as a stout-hearted people. Thus there is one complimentary passage, but it does not refer to a text in the Bible.

A prominent biblical scholar investigated these books with an apparent purpose of detecting any that might refer to Negroes, in particular. At first, he appears to have had a suspicion that one passage in Jubilees, called the "Little Genesis", might be relevant, but concluded that the passage in question, 10: 29–34, which reveals the story of Noah's curse of Canaan, does not connect the curse to the Negro race.[11] A question is inherent in his conclusion, however, for much depends upon the identity of Negroes in a given person's mind.

Upon the basis of a check of biblical references in the Qumran literature, using the list of Scriptural references compiled by Theodore H. Gaster, there are no interpretations of pertinent biblical texts referring to Black persons or peoples.[12]

Interpretation in Philo and Josephus

Once more, as in the instance of his study of the Old Testament Apocrypha and Pseudepigrapha, Jack P. Lewis asserts that neither Philo nor Josephus interprets the Old Testament passages under consideration here in a way derogatory of Black people.[13] Further, neither writer interprets "Ham" to mean *black*. For them the interpretation is "hot" or "heat." Philo's treatment of the Ham/Canaan story is allegorical.

In dealing with Ham's descendants Josephus singles out Cush in his *Antiquities Of The Jews* and writes: "time has not at all hurt the name of Cush; for the Ethiopians, over whom he reigned, are even at this day, both by themselves and by all men in Asia, called Cushites."[14]

In other parts of his *Antiquities*, a rewriting of the Old Testament history, Josephus recounts a story of Moses's marriage to an Ethiopian princess, an account that does not appear in the Bible, but will appear somewhat differently in later Jewish writings. Without interpretative comments he reproduces the account of the Cushite in 2Sam. 18, that of the Queen of Sheba whom he identifies as Queen of Egypt and Ethiopia, and those accounts of other Cushites—Zerah, Taharka, Ebed-Melech—all in a matter-of-fact manner, without interpretative comment.[15]

Anticipating the rabbinical interpretations of the Noah story that will later appear in Genesis Rabbah of the Midrashim, and in the Babylonian Talmud, shortly after the time of Josephus, it might be well to give another excerpt from Josephus, one dealing with Noah's curse: "but for Ham, he did not curse him, by reason of his nearness in blood, but cursed his posterity; and when the rest of them escaped that curse, God inflicted it on the children of Canaan."[16]

Interpretation in the New Testament

During the lifetime of Josephus the books that comprise the New Testament were being written. Of the twenty-seven books that constitute the canon, only one, the book of Acts, 8:26–39 and 13:1, contains references to Black peoples. Both passages are reports of matters of fact, without interpretative comment with respect to color.

Ancient Rabbinical Interpretation

Ancient rabbinical literature abounds with interpretations of the Old Testament both with respect to peoples who are considered Black in the Biblical text and those who are regarded as, or said to be Black by the rabbis. The interpretations that concern us appear in the collection of midrashim know as Midrash Rabbah-Genesis, dated variously A.D. 200–400, and the Babylonian Talmud, Tractate Sanhedrin, dated as early as A.D. 500, but as in the case of Midrash Rabbah-Genesis, containing material much older. Additionally there are Targums, dating from uncertain provenance but by some dated in final form from the fourth and fifth centuries A.D.[17]

Apart from the Targums, classical locations of interpretations with reference to Black persons and peoples are Midrash Rabbah-Genesis XXXVI: 7–8; Babylonian Talmud, Sanhedrin 108b; and Midrash Rabbah-Genesis XXII: 5–6. The first of these has a curse to fall on Ham, not directly but through Ham's fourth son, Canaan, who will be ugly and dark-skinned (the degree of color being dependent upon the translator of the original). The second asserts that Ham came forth from the Ark black, having been turned that color because, contrary to prohibitions, he, along with the dog and the raven, had copulated while aboard the Ark. The third locus deals not with a curse nor mark upon Cain but with his rejected sacrifice (Gen. 4:5).

As translated, Midrash Rabbah-Genesis reads in part: "R. Huna said in R. Joseph's name: (Noah declared), 'you have prevented me from begetting a fourth son, therefore I curse your fourth son.' R. Huna also said in R. Joseph's name: you have prevented me from doing something in the dark (cohabitation), therefore your seed will be ugly and dark-skinned." R. Hiyya said: "Ham and the dog copulated in the Ark, therefore Ham came forth black-skinned while the dog publicly exposes its copulation. . . ."[18]

It is to be noted that Robert Graves and Raphael Patai, in their book

Hebrew Myths: The Book of Genesis, relate the passage in Sanhedrin 108b to other sources such as Tanhuma Noah 13,15, and produce the following additional narrative: "Moreover, because you twisted your head around to see my nakedness, your grandchildren's hair shall be twisted into kinks, and their eyes red; again, because your lips jested at my misfortune, theirs shall swell; and because you neglected my nakedness, they shall go naked, and their male members shall be shamefully elongated. Men of this race are called Negroes."[19]

Midrash Rabbah-Genesis XXII: 6, translated, reads: "And Cain was very wroth [*wayyihar*] and his countenance fell: [His face] became like a fireband [with the editorial note, *Blackened*]."[20]

Upon these statements will hang later interpretations of the Bible with reference to Black persons and peoples among Jews, then Muslims, then Christians; and through them they will be spread around the world as a deadly poison. Thereafter all the children, not only of Canaan, but also of Ham, will be considered to be black: Cushites (Ethiopians), Mitzraimites (Egyptians), Phutities, and Canaanites.

Interpretation in New Testament Apocrypha and Pseudepigrapha

As in the case of the New Testament itself, there is no interpretation of biblical texts with reference to Black peoples in the New Testament Apocrypha and Pseudepigrapha.[21] However it is to be noted that some of these writings, dated as early as the second and third centuries A.D. by some authorities, do contain statements pejorative in nature with respect to Ethiopians. The books in question and relevant passages are: Acts of Peter, 305; Acts of Andrew, 400; and Acts of Thomas, 475, and 478.

Interpretation in Church Fathers

As Jack P. Lewis notes: "Though there are many parallels in the interpretation of the flood between the rabbis and the church fathers, it is in the spiritual interpretation that they went their separate ways."[22] However with Irenaeus (A.D. 185), we begin to see the influence of the Septuagint and of the rabbinical interpretation upon Gentile Christians wherein the curse of Canaan is transformed into a curse upon Ham, although with no reference to color as yet.[23] Origen, Jerome, Augustine, and others down to the seventh century interpret the Old Testament references to Black peoples frequently but in an allegorical and typological manner.[24] Although Ham is not yet black, Origen does associate Ethiopians with Ham.[25] And Jerome, who shows in his letters a dreadful aversion to black Ethiopians,[26] translates, for the first time according to Frank M. Snowden, Jr., the conjunction in Song of Sol. 1:5 as *but* rather than as *and*.[27]

Origen, it is said, set the pattern for patristic interpretation, so we cite some of his interpretations by way of example as they are treated by Snowden in his book *Blacks in Antiquity*. Snowden calls attention to the fact that early Christian writers, when commenting upon a given Scriptural passage involving Ethiopians, developed a type of exegesis which collated several familiar references to Ethiopians. And, with reference to Origen, he writes as follows: "Origen says that several passages suggest themselves to him as being in accordance with 'I am black and beautiful.' In this connection Origen first cites with brief comment and then presents a detailed exegesis of the following: (1) Moses' marriage to the Ethiopian woman; (2) the visit of the Queen of Sheba to Solomon; (3) 'Ethiopia shall stretch out her hand to God;' (4) 'from beyond the rivers of Ethiopia will I receive my dispersed ones; they shall being me sacrifice'; (5) the Ethiopian eunuch Abdimelech."[28]

Snowden then proceeds to give Origen's detailed allegorical exegesis of the passages. And, in describing part of the Song of Sol. 1:5, he notes that Origen makes, among others, the following points which appear in similar or modified form in commenting on the words of the bride to the young maidens of Jerusalem: (1) the bride who speaks represents the church gathered from among the Gentiles; (2) her body, black externally, lacks neither natural beauty nor that acquired by practice; (3) the daughters of an earthly Jerusalem, upon seeing the church of the Gentiles, despise her because she cannot boast the noble blood of Abraham, Isaac, and Jacob; (4) the bride's reply is that she is black and that though she cannot point to descent from illustrious men, she is nevertheless beautiful, for in her is the image of God and she has received her beauty from the word of God; (5) she is black by reason of her lowly origin but is beautiful through penitence and faith; (6) the daughters of Jerusalem in reproaching her because of her blackness should not forget what Mary (Miriam) suffered when she spoke against Moses because he had married a black Ethiopian woman.[29]

Against Origen and others, who followed an allegorical and typological method in treating the Black peoples in the Old Testament—members of the "Alexandrian School" of interpretation—stand the members of the "Antiochan

School" who employed a literal method of exegesis. It is interesting to view the manner in which a member of this school deals with the same passage, not only in order to see biblical interpretation, but also to see how some people in that period regarded the Egyptians with respect to color, just as St. Augustine refers to the Ethiopians as black in his commentary on the Psalms. For an example I take Theodore of Mopsuestia whom Robert M. Grant calls the greatest interpreter of the school of Antioch. Grant discusses Theodore's dealing with the Song of Solomon as follows: "Theodore's analysis of the Song of Songs is interesting. . . . Its historical occasion is the wedding of Solomon with the daughter of Pharaoh. At this point in his discussion a certain sense of decorum overcomes Theodore, and he insists that the wedding took place not for pleasure, but for the political stability of Israel. Moreover, since the princess *was black* and therefore not especially attractive to the court of Solomon, he built a palace for her and composed this song—so that she would not be irritated and so that enmity would not arise between him and Pharaoh."[30]

Interpretation in Targums

Martin McNamara in his book *Targum and Testament* takes note that Pseudo-Jonathan on Num. 12:1 explains that Moses was constrained against his will to marry the Ethiopian woman and that he later divorced her. Further McNamara observes that Targum Onkelos paraphrases "Cushite" as "beautiful" and that other texts of the Palestinian Targum retain the word "Cushite" but go on to explain at length that she was not a Cushite ethnically speaking, but merely *like* a Cushite in complexion![31] Henry S. Noerdlinger in his *Moses and Egypt* explains that the depiction of Moses's wife as white in the movie "Ten Commandments" was based upon rabbinic traditions, as reported in L. Ginzberg's *Legends Of The Jews* (VI: 90). According to the rabbinic tradition referred to, "Ethiopian," with reference to Moses's wife, means that she distinguished herself from others by her beauty and virtue, just as an Ethiopian distinguishes himself from others by his physical appearance.[32] In his book *Ethiopia and The Bible*, Edward Ullendorff makes reference to an ancient Gematria employed by the Targum which renders Cushite woman as beautiful woman and in so doing calls attention to Rashi.[33]

Interpretation in Muslim Writings

Although no curse of Ham or Canaan by which the one or the other was turned back appears in the Koran, Muslim interpreters borrowed heavily from the Jews and added some of their own. In this connection Bernard Lewis writes that a common explanation of the slave status of the Black man among Muslims is that the ancestor of the dark-skinned people was Ham the son of Noah who (according to Muslim legend) was damned black for his sin. The curse of blackness, and with it that of slavery, passed to all Black peoples who are his descendants.[34] In agreement with Lewis's observation on Ham's blackness among Muslims is the *Shorter Encyclopedia of Islam*, which alludes to Midrash Rabbah-Genesis.[35]

Jewish-Christian Interpretation During the Middle Ages

Jewish interpretation continued throughout the Middle Ages in the form of Midrashim, targumim, and commentaries, all dealing with a curse on a Black Ham or Canaan, with Black biblical characters, and with those made black by the earlier interpretations in Midrashim and Talmuds. By way of example, a Midrash on the Song of Solomon, dated by W. O. E. Oesterley and G. H. Box around A.D. 750, but containing very early material, interprets verse 1:5 allegorically thus: "I appear black in my deeds, but comely in those of my fathers. The congregation of Israel says, I appear black unto myself, but comely in the eyes of my Creator."[36]

Further, in the Midrashic collection known as *The Book of Yasher* one finds, as presented by the translator-editor, the following account of Moses' marriage to an Ethiopian princess—an account much like that given by Josephus: "So Moses took the city by his wisdom, and the children of Cush set him on the throne. . . . And they . . . gave him Queen Adonijah the Cushite . . . to wife. But Moses feared the Lord . . . and he went not in unto her. . . . For Moses remembered how Abraham had made Eliezer his servant swear, saying: 'Take not a wife of the daughters of Canaan, nor shalt thou make marriages with any of the children of Ham. . . .'"[37]

Saadya Gaon (892–942) translated the Hebrew Bible into Arabic, and in so doing made Noah's curse rest upon Ham rather than upon Canaan. This act added fuel to the fire that had been started with the same translation in the one manuscript of the Septuagint.[38]

Greatest of all the Medieval Jewish commentators was Rabbi Solomon ben Isaac of Troyes, better known as Rashi (1040–1105). In his treatment of Noah's curse he refers to the interpretation given in Midrash Rabbah-Genesis and other works prior to his time.

Hugo Fuchs notes that Rashi makes use of Targum Onkelos and of oral interpretations in his commentary on the Torah.[39] And with specific reference to Rashi's interpretation on Moses's Cushite wife, D. S. Margolioux, who calls Rashi's interpretation "frivolous," notes that it is as old as Targum Onkelos.[40]

Commenting on Rashi's influence upon the Christian world, Isadore Epstein writes, "Nicholas de Lyra (1265–1349), who is an important link between the Middle Ages and the Reformation, quotes Rashi constantly in his *Commentaries*, which, in turn, was one of the main sources used by Luther in his translation; and many of Rashi's interpretations entered into the King James version of the Bible."[41]

According to Louis Ginzberg, there is no evidence for the direct use of rabbinic literature by the Christian world before the twelfth century,[42] and this is the very time of Rashi.

At least by the twelfth century in Europe, Cain is depicted with Negroid features in art as well as in literature.[43] Such a depiction may well go back to as early as Beowulf who makes mention of Cain's monstrous descendants. Quite interestingly Cain's black color is attributed to more than the occasion of his sacrifice as in Genesis Rabbah. It comes to be attributed additionally to a curse because he murdered Abel and to the mark, or sign, that God placed upon him for his protection. Whatever the time and whatever the cause of Cain's being turned black, Cain as black became associated with Black peoples in the minds of Europeans as well as Jews and the association is in the minds of Europeans and their descendants worldwide today.

Despite the anti-Blackness among Jews and Gentile Europeans with which we have dealt, it must be recognized that for a time and in different parts of Europe the Ethiopian received favorable regard. The most that can be done in this chapter to support this view is to refer to the three-volume work by Jean Devisse and Michel Mollat, *The Image Of The Black In Western Art*, and Joseph R. Washington, Jr.'s, recent book, *Anti-Blackness In English Religion*.[44]

Toward the end of the Middle Ages, the anti-Black influence of Jewish interpretation on that of Gentile Christian Europeans may be noted in the writings of Sir John Mandeville who in 1336 refashioned the story of Ham.

Although he views Ham as the accursed one he regards him as the mightiest and richest of Noah's three sons.[45]

Interpretation in Modern Times

The fifteenth century, which saw the importation of West African Blacks into Europe in ever increasing numbers, marks the real beginning of the application of the Ham-Canaan-Cain accounts to Black peoples, as interpreted by the Jews. One of the first to make such application was Gomes Eannes Zurara, chronicler for Prince Henry the Navigator. Confusing Cain with Noah's cursed son, in his history on the discovery of Guinea, Zurara wrote, "You must note that these Blacks were Moors like the others, but were their slaves, in accordance with ancient custom, which I believe to have been because of the curse which, after the Deluge, Noah laid upon his son Cain [sic], cursing him in this way: that his race should be subject to all other races of the world."[46]

From this time forward, notes Ronald Sanders, in his book, *Lost Tribes And Promised Lands*, Noah's curse will serve as a standard excuse for Black slavery among Europeans as it had for Moslems.[47]

A view aberrant from those that held Blacks to be offspring of Ham-Canaan-Cain entered the picture with Paracelsus (1520), who expressed the opinion that Negroes and some others had a separate origin from those who had descended from Adam. This opinion would be adopted and elaborated upon by many who would come later.[48]

Returning to the curse of Ham/Canaan in the various and proliferating interpretations given to it, positive and negative, note may be taken of a sixteenth-century writer on the subject, George Best (1577). Relying upon Jewish interpretations well known by his time, and adding something new of his own, Best wrote concerning Ham and his descendants, "God would a sonne should be born whose name was *Chus*, who not onely it selfe, but all his posteritie after him should bee so blacke and loathsome, that it might remaine a spectacle of disobedience to all the worlde. And of this blacke and cursed *Cush* came all these blacke Moores, which are in Africa. . . . "[49]

Winthrop D. Jordan notes that Ham's curse became common in the seventeenth century as an explanation of the Negro's color rather than as a support for slavery.[50] And David Brion Davis observes a probable increasing tendency around 1676 for Americans to identify Negroes with the children of Ham.[51] This tendency, however, was contrary to the views of Sir Thomas

Browne (1605–1682) and many others who attributed the color to natural causes. Jordan regards Browne as the bridge between Medieval and modern times with respect to the Negro's color,[52] and from his time onward the matter will be discussed and debated until at last the Ham/Canaan curse, with or without the questionable *curse, mark*, or *sacrifice* of Cain, will be used to justify Black slavery, and still later, segregation.

While still in the seventeenth century, it must be noted that the aberrant view of Paracelsus in 1520 was developed further by Isaac de la Peyére. This author in 1655 wrote that the natives of Africa, Asia, and the New World were descendants from a Pre-Adamite race. According to him, it was from this race that Cain had chosen a wife, a view that will later be expanded upon until that wife comes to be designated a Negro woman.[53]

During the whole of the 1700s, as has been anticipated, debate continued about Ham and Canaan, as well as Cain. In the year 1700 Judge Samuel Sewall in his famous work *The Selling Of Joseph* argued against an opponent that the curse on Canaan had been fulfilled in the enslavement of the Gibeonites.[54] Nevertheless, according to David Brion Davis, by 1733 there was an increasing tendency to identify Negroes not only as children of Ham but also of Cain.[55]

Elihu Coleman (1699–1789) pointed out that Negroes could not be the posterity of Cain because all his descendants had perished in the flood, while still others of an opposite mind will develop views that will link Ham even with a daughter of Cain.[56] The wide currency of views with regard to Cain and blackness, again whether based upon his sacrifice, murder of Abel, or mark, may be observed as they existed at the end of the eighteenth century and the early years of the nineteenth in the writings of Phillis Wheatley and David Walker respectively. In her poem "On Being Brought From Africa To America" Wheatley writes:

'Twas mercy brought me from my
Pagan land,
Taught my benighted soul to under-
stand
That there's a God, that there's a
Savior too;
Once I redemption neither sought
nor knew.

Some view our sable race with
   scornful eye,
'Their color is a diabolic die.'
Remember, Christians, Negroes,
   black as Cain,
May be refined, and join th'
   angelic train.[57]

On the other hand, David Walker in his *Appeal* lambasts whites for calling Black people the seed of Cain, informing them that he has read his Bible too without finding such a reference there. Not finding it in his Bible, Walker turns the tables and accuses white people of being those who are Cain's seed.[58]

As has been anticipated, the nineteenth century saw continuing debates, especially about the Ham-Canaan curse, but with increasing fury as pro-slavery and anti-slavery writers contested with each other. In a general way we may here cite several of the numerous views and counter-views that were propounded:[59] (1) the old curse of Ham-Canaan doctrine with no reference to the achievements of Hamites as presented in Genesis, chapter 10; (2) a curse of Canaan view that held only Canaan was cursed and with attention paid to the sons of Ham as founders of ancient civilizations in Africa and Asia; (3) a new view that Ham had been *born black*, was later cursed outright, and that all his descendants partake of the curse; (4) a view that Cain, Ham, and Canaan were all tied together, making for a threefold curse on Black peoples; (5) a new view that there was, and is, no curse upon Ham and his descendants and that Canaan instead of having been Black was white; (6) a resurrected Pre-Adamite view that forged a link with a theory of polygenesis and removed the Negro from the Adamic-Noahite human family and declared him a beast; (7) a view that held Negroes to be descendants of Adam-Noah and accepted Genesis, chapter 10, as referring to Black folk and took note that Jesus was a colored man; (8) a multiple view that combined the whole or parts of several anti-Negro views; (9) a new and increasingly accepted view — a new Hamite doctrine, contributed to and accepted by the rising critical histor-ical-literary study of the Bible, that removed Blacks from the Bible altogether. According to this last view, Ham and all his descendants were white.[60]

All the afore-listed views, plus still others, continued on into the twenti-eth century with greater or lesser strength, varying according to different groups. And although the anti-Negro views might not have been as loudly voiced during the present century until 1954 and afterwards, they were hardly asleep. They were only dozing. The attention paid especially to the curse of Ham during the intervening years, even among mainline white denominations, was great, indeed.

As is quite well known, the Supreme Court decision of 1954, relative to separate and equal education, stabbed fully awake the anti-Negro Cain-Ham-Canaan views. On the other hand, it stirred into action advocates of the new Hamite doctrine. These, more or less sympathetic towards Blacks, did battle with protagonists for the old view.

Only in passing can we observe that after 1954 pro-segregationists revived every pro-slavery argument based upon Ham-Canaan-Cain in support of segregation. Such arguments continue today among some sects, some television ministries, and among such groups as the Ku Klux Klan.

On the other hand, some mainline white denominations have produced literature in refutation particularly of the Ham-Canaan doctrine. And several individual authors wrote similar books on the subject of segregation and the Bible. Such are the books *Segregation And The Bible* by Everett Tilson,[61] and *Segregation And Scripture* by J. Oliver Buswell III.[62] Both the denominational literature and the books were written from the position of the new Hamite doctrine which, as we have seen, does not view Blacks (Negroes) as having been among the peoples of the biblical world; and thus not subjects in the biblical accounts about Cain, Ham, Canaan, or any other biblical character.

To be noted also is the fact that in 1978 the Mormon Church admitted Blacks to the priesthood, apparently thus removing Negroes from a curse on Cain-Ham-Canaan?

In recent years a new and unique interpretation has been presented by a Canadian scholar, Arthur C. Custance. He regards the Genesis Table of Nations as historically trustworthy, and believes that Noah's three sons represent the three racial groups that make up the world's peoples. To the Shemites he assigns Hebrews, Arabs, Babylonians, Assyrians, etc.; to the Japhethites, those whom he calls Caucasoids; and to the Hamites he assigns the Mongoloid and Negroid peoples. He then suggests that the curse that was pronounced upon Canaan or upon Ham should be interpreted to mean a servant "par excellence," i.e., the servants would perform a great service to their brethren.[63]

Biblical Interpretation by Black Peoples

Up to this point reference has been made to only two Black popular interpreters. We turn now to view the subject as dealt with by Black peoples themselves. With respect to written documents one may go back to the year 1742 and the person of Jacob Elisa Capitein (1717–1742), then to Jupiter Hammond in 1760, and then continue in an unbroken line to the present.[64]

In his booklet, *The Redemption Of Africa and Black Religion*, St. Clair Drake paints a beautiful picture of early Black biblical interpretation by both literate and illiterate preachers, and by those whom he calls folk theologians. Ignoring Capitein, who aped the white pro-slavery advocates, Drake says that preachers and theologians were able to counterattack white anti-Black interpretation by invalidating Noah's curse. They insisted that the curse had been wiped out with the coming of Christ or by arguing that God is the father of all men and that all men are brothers. Further they were able to point to the Black peoples in the Bible (using the Genesis Table of Nations) and to individual Black characters in the Bible and glory in a great past history.[65]

True as Mr. Drake's picture may appear on the surface, it does not represent the painting in its entirety. The literature from 1742 to the present, as well as oral responses, reveals responses and interpretations relative to the curse of Ham-Canaan if not with respect to a curse upon Cain. These responses and interpretations range all the way from unquestioning acceptance, to ignorance about it, through uncertainty, to scornful rejection.

With such a general preliminary observation having been made, I shall deal first with Black reaction to, if not Black interpretation of, a curse upon Cain. Of Phillis Wheatley's acceptance of it and David Walker's rejection note already has been taken. Forty-five years after David Walker, in 1874, William Wells Brown wrote that Cain's curse relating to color was nothing more than speculation that falls to the ground when we trace back the genealogy of Noah, finding that he descended not from Cain but from Seth.[66] Nothing more appears about Cain in the writings of Black authors until the year 1883. In that year George Washington Williams published his *History Of The Negro Race from 1619 to 1880* in which he expresses the opinion that even among white people it had died out as an explanation of the Negro's color.[67] Indeed, it does appear to have died out among Black people in America even if it had not among whites. By 1883 the Mormons had crystallized the curse, or mark, upon Cain as referring to Black peoples as a doctrine. Later Black writers have referred to it only in passing.

Joel A. Rogers in his book, *Sex and Race*, published in 1944, reports, contrary to the view of the rabbis that Cain's face had turned black, that Black West Africans taught that Cain was originally black, but when he killed Abel and God shouted at him in the garden he turned white from fright.[68] Against this view, Marcus Garvey classified white people as descendants of Cain and Black people as the children of Abel.[69] James Baldwin, speaking for at least some Black people, states that just as we knew Blacks were in the eyes of white people cursed descendants of Ham, so *for us* white people were the descendants of Cain.[70] Olin P. Moyd makes reference to this report by Baldwin in his book, *Redemption in Black Theology*, published in 1979.[71] And between Baldwin and Moyd, George D. Kelsey, in dealing with the white racist views of the late Reverend Dr. G. G. Gillespie who had included the mark of Cain in comments about Negroes, made reference to it in 1965.[72] Finally Latta R. Thomas (1976) quotes David Walker's statement,[73] and Carl F. Ellis, Jr., refers to the mark of Cain as a myth.[74]

A discussion of Black interpretations of the Ham-Canaan curse might well continue with the observation that up to a generation ago Black writers boasted proudly of Negroes' being the children of Ham.[75] They either bypassed, hid, or ignored the curse and usually emphasized, as Drake points out, the glorious record of the children of Ham as set forth in the tenth chapter of Genesis. Additionally great emphasis was placed upon Psalm 68 with its assertion that Ethiopia would stretch forth her hands to God.[76] And Drake's observation has been applicable especially down to 1900.

In reviewing publications by Black writers from 1837 to 1902, one notes that, with few exceptions, every Black writer dealt with a glorious, ancient Black history, based upon the Bible which was viewed as factual. Thus so spoke and wrote the Reverend H. Easton in 1837; James W. C. Pennington in 1841; R. B. Lewis in 1844; Henry H. Garnett in 1848; Martin R. Delany in 1952; Alexander Crumwell in 1862; William Wells Brown in 1863; Edward W. Blyden in 1857 and 1871; William Wells Brown again in 1874; George Washington Williams in 1883; Edward A. Johnson in 1891; Rufus L. Perry in 1893; Benjamin T. Tanner in 1902; and J. J. Pipkin in 1902. All these were African Americans; all were traditionalists in their view of the Bible. Interestingly enough, the works of Perry and Tanner were written partly to refute the new Hamite doctrine that removed Blacks from the Bible.[77]

For some Africans who lived in the period just surveyed in America, interpretation of the old Hamite doctrine was not so healthfully handled. Claude Wauthier reports that as early as 1870, at the first Vatican Council, a group of missionary bishops produced a document asking the Pope to release the Negro race from the curse which, it seems, comes from Ham.[78]

Shortly after 1902 and continuing to the present, there are many Black writers of Black history based upon the Bible to be found. Most of these have been traditionalist and fundamentalist, unacquainted with or unaccepting of modern historical-literary biblical studies. On the other hand, an increasing number of Black biblical scholars who are trained in critical exegetical methods and who are interpreting the Bible from a Black perspective have arisen and are giving instructions to others on how to interpret the Bible through the use of critical methodologies. Among such scholars are Bishop Alfred G. Dunstan, Jr., the Reverend Jacob Dyer, Dr. Robert A. Bennett, and the Reverend Latta Thomas. This last author urges Blacks to hold on to the biblical faith despite such interpretations as those that insist upon a curse upon Ham.[79]

In Africa, the late Cheikh Anta Diop presented a non-traditional and critical treatment of the "Ham Legend" in his book *The African Origin Of Civilization: Myth or Reality*.[80] And E. Mveng of Cameroun treats what he calls the "Myth of Ham" in an article entitled "The Bible And Black Africa."[81]

Not to be excluded in an essay of this kind is an aberrant type of Black biblical interpretation that has existed for some two generations and is increasing among several groups. This type goes beyond Black identification of Black peoples with the biblical Hamites and claims that Black peoples are to be identified with the ancient Jews; or with the ancient Hebrews-Israelites, as different from Jews of modern times. For these the Old Testament especially is a collection of writings by and about Black peoples.[82]

Conclusion

Thus we come to the end of our general survey of three thousand years of biblical interpretation with reference to Black peoples. The survey has shown that the most probable original text of the Hebrew was free of pejorative statements about peoples regarded as Black by the original authors; and that, with one or two possible exceptions, the same holds true of inner-biblical interpretation. Further it has revealed that apart from extra-biblical interpretations by the ancient rabbis and others like them, whose interpretations appear in Midrashim, Talmuds, Haggadah, and targumim, there are no curses upon Cain, Ham, Canaan whereby they were cursed with blackness. Again, it has noted that early Gentile Christians failed to adopt the anti-Black interpretations of the Jews, while the Muslims did; and that later, Gentile Christians, particularly in Europe, adopted the interpretations and applied them to Black peoples whom they met in increasing numbers. And so it has continued unto this day. On the other hand, the survey has gone on to reveal that Black peoples, at times ambivalent, in the main have managed to invalidate the white interpretations of the old anti-Black Hamite doctrine; and at points have challenged the new Hamite view that removes Blacks from the Bible.

Two concluding observations may be attempted. Inasmuch as a curse of blackness whether upon Cain, or Ham, or Canaan does not appear in the biblical text, those who take the Bible, including the Old Testament, to be the Word of God, norm for faith and practice, would appear to be engaging in blasphemy when they substitute interpretations. Second, according to numerous Jewish scholars, many white Gentile Christians during modern times, and an increasing number of enlightened Black biblical scholars, the interpretations of the ancient Jewish rabbis are to be classified as legends and myths. Thus, legend and myth have been made to serve as actual historical fact to the damnation of Black peoples, except where Black peoples have believed and acted otherwise.

Notes

1. For a discussion of *inner* or *intra* biblical interpretation, consult James L. Kugel and Rowan A. Greer, *Early Biblical Interpretation* (Philadelphia: Westminster Press, 1986).

2. Benjamin Tucker Tanner, *The Color of Solomon—What?* (Philadelphia: African Methodist Episcopal Book Concern, 1895).

3. See Athalya Brenner, "Colour Terms In The Old Testament," in *Journal For The Study of The Old Testament*, supplement series, no. 21 (Sheffield, England: Department of Biblical Studies, University of Sheffield, 1982):57, 63, 95.

4. Robert Avon Bennett, *God's Work Of Liberation* (Wilton, Conn.: Morehouse Barlow Co., 1976):78f.

5. Jacob A. Dyer, *The Ethiopian in The Bible* (New York: Vantage Press, 1974):62.

6. Brenner, 57.

7. Ibid., 227. See also 58–64, nn. 19,20, 21, and 22.

8. For example, see Frank M. Snowden, Jr., *Blacks In Antiquity: Ethiopians In The Greco-*

Roman Experience (Cambridge: Harvard University Press, Belnap Press, 1970):202.

9. For example, Jack P. Lewis, *A Study Of The Interpretation Of Noah And The Flood In Jewish And Christian Literature* (Leiden: E. J. Brill, 1968):119; and Arthur C. Custance, *Noah's Three Sons* (Grand Rapids, Mich.: Zondervan Publishing House, 1975):25.

10. Snowden, 198.

11. Lewis, 31.

12. Theodore H. Gaster, *The Dead Sea Scriptures In English Translation* (Garden City, N.Y.: Doubleday Anchor Books, 1956):343ff.

13. Lewis, 73ff., 179.

14. Flavius Josephus "Antiquities of the Jews," vol. 6 chap. 2, trans. William Whiston in *The Works of Flavius Josephus* (Hartford, Conn.: S. S. Scranton, 1903):40.

15. Ibid., 225–308, passim.

16. Ibid., 41.

17. See Fred G. Bratton, *A History Of The Bible* (Boston: Beacon Press, 1959):236.

18. *Midrash Rabbah, Genesis*, eds. Rabbi Dr. H. Freedman and Maurice Simon, foreword by Rabbi Dr. Isidore Epstein (London: Soncino Press, 1939):chap. 36, 7–8, 293.

19. Robert Graves and Raphael Patai, *Hebrew Myths: The Book Of Genesis* (New York: Greenwich House, 1983):121. *Tanhuma Noah*, 13f. is also cited in C. G. Montefiore and H. Loewe, eds. and trans., *A Rabbinic Anthology* (London; Macmillan & Co., Ltd., 1938; Reprint. New York: Shocken Books, 1974):56.

20. *Midrash Rabbah, Genesis*, 184.

21. The source here used is Edgar Hennecke, comp., *New Testament Apocrypha*, ed. W. Schneemelcher, English trans. R. McL. Wilson, vol. 1, *Gospels and Related Writings*; vol. 2, *Writings Relating To The Apostles, Apocalypses And Related Subjects* (Philadelphia: Westminster Press, 1963, 1965).

22. Lewis, 156.

23. Ibid., 119.

24. See Lewis for *typological* interpretation and Snowden for *allegorical* interpretation.

25. Snowden, 202.

26. For Jerome's attitude, see Jean Devisse and Michel Mollat, *The Image of The Black In Western Art*, vol. 2, trans. William G. Ryan (New York: William Morrow, 1979):256, 299 n. 1.

27. Snowden, 198.

28. Ibid., 201.

29. Ibid., 199.

30. Robert M. Grant, *The Bible In The Church: A Short History of Interpretation* (New York: Macmillan, 1948):77f.

31. Martin McNamara, *Targum and Testament* (Grand Rapids, Mich.: William B. Eerdmans Publishing Co., 1972):72.

32. Henry S. Noerdlinger, *Moses and Egypt* (Los Angeles: University of Southern California Press, 1956):70.

33. Edward Ullendorff, *Ethiopia and The Bible* (London: published for the British Academy by Oxford University Press, 1968):8.

34. Bernard Lewis, *Race And Color In Islam* (New York: Harper & Row, Torchbooks, 1971):66f. The very same statement appears in Graham W. Irwin, *Africans Abroad* (New York: Columbia University Press, 1977), 128. Lewis depends heavily upon Gustave E. von Grunebaum, *Medieval Islam: A Study In Cultural Orientation* (Chicago: University of Chicago Press, 1946).

35. *Shorter Encyclopedia of Islam*, 1974 ed., s.v. "Nuh."

36. W. O. E. Oesterley and G. H. Box, *A Short Survey of The Literature of Rabbinical and Medieval Judaism* (New York: Macmillan, 1920; Reprint. New York: Burt Franklin, 1973):76.

37. Ben Zion Halper, ed. and trans., *Post-Biblical Hebrew Literature: An Anthology* (Philadelphia: the Jewish Publication Society of America, 1921):132ff.

38. For references to Ham as the accursed one in an Arabic Bible, see Adam Clarke, *The Holy Bible*, with a commentary and critical notes, vol. 1 (Nashville, Tenn.: Abingdon Press, n.d.):38; Josiah Priest, *Slavery As It Relates To The Negro, Or African Race* (Albany, N.Y.: C. van Benthuysen and Co., 1843; Reprint. Albany, N.Y.: Arno Press, 1977):77ff.; and Custance, 25.

39. *The Universal Jewish Encyclopedia*, 1954 ed., s.v. "Rashi," by Hugo Fuchs. H. Wheeler Robinson, ed., *The Bible In Its Ancient and English Versions* (Oxford: Oxford University Press, 1940; Reprint. Oxford: Clarendon Press, 1954):147 notes that Lyra made a literal translation of Rashi's commentary that preserved the rabbinical tradition of the Middle Ages into modern times.

40. *A Dictionary of The Bible*, 1911 ed., vol. 1, s.v. "Ethiopian Woman."

41. Isadore Epstein, *Judaism: A Historical Presentation* (Baltimore: Penguin Books, 1959):269.

42. Louis Ginzberg, *On Jewish Law and Lore* (Philadelphia: the Jewish Publication Society of America, 1955):67.

43. See Ruth Mellinkoff, *The Mark of Cain* (Los Angeles: University of California Press, 1981):76ff.

44. Joseph R. Washington, Jr., *Anti-Blackness In English Religion: 1500–1800* (New York: Edwin Mellen Press, 1984):n. 26.

45. Ibid, 42f.

46. Quoted in Ronald Sanders, *Lost Tribes and Promised Lands* (Boston: Little, Brown and Co., 1978):62.

47. Ibid., 63.

48. For aberrant views of Paracelsus and others, see Thomas F. Gossett, *Race: The History of An Idea In America* (Dallas, Tex.: Southern Methodist University Press, 1963; New York: Schocken Books, 1963):15.

49. Quoted in Washington, 114; Winthrop D. Jordan, *White Over Black: American Attitudes Toward The Negro, 1550–1812* (Chapel Hill, N.C.: University of North Carolina Press, 1968):41; Sanders, 224; and in other publications.

50. Jordan, 18.

51. David Brion Davis, *The Problem of Slavery In Western Culture* (Ithaca, N.Y.: Cornell University Press, 1966), 316f.

52. Jordan, 15ff.

53. Information concerning Peyére and his views is obtainable from encyclopedias and from popular writings such as those of Gossett, 15; Sabine Baring-Gould, *Legends of The Patriarchs and Prophets* (New York: Hurst & Co., n.d.):26 f.; Don Cameron Allen, *The Legend of Noah* (Urbana, Ill.: University of Illinois Press, 1963):86f.

54. See Davis, 316ff.; Louis Ruchames, ed., *Racial Thought In America*, vol. 1, *From The Puritans to Abraham Lincoln: A Documentary History* (Amherst, Mass.: University of Massachusetts Press, 1969; New York: Gossett and Dunlap, 1970):46ff.

55. Davis.

56. Ruchames, 89ff.

57. Quoted in Alan Lomax and Raoul Abdul, eds., *3000 Years Of Black Poetry* (New York: Dodd, Mead & Co., 1970):205.

58. David Walker, *Walker's Appeal In Four Articles* (1829); Reprint with a new preface by William Loren Katz. (New York: Arno Press and the *New York Times*, 1969):71ff.

59. T. Peterson, "The Myth of Ham Among White Antebellum Southerners," (Ph.D. diss., Stanford University, 1975):146, isolates four versions of the Ham myth among southern white Americans.

60. For a statement of this view, see William F. Albright, "The Old Testament World," in *The Interpreter's Bible*, George Arthur Buttrick, Commentary ed. (New York: Abingdon-Cokesbury Press, 1952), vol. 1, 233–277. See also Paul Heinisch, *History of The Old Testament*, trans. William G. Heidt (Collegeville, Minn.: the Order of St. Benedict, Inc., 1952):52.

61. Everett Tilson, *Segregation and The Bible* (New York: Abingdon Press, 1958).

62. J. Oliver Buswell, *Segregation and Scripture* (Grand Rapids, Mich.: William B. Eerdmans Publishing Co., 1964).

63. Custance, 120, 149.

64. Accounts of Capitein may be found in Henri Gregoire, *An Enquiry Concerning the Intellectual and Moral Faculties and Literature of Negroes*, trans. D. B. Warden (Brooklyn, N.Y.: Thomas Kirk, 1810; Reprint. College Park, Md.: McGrath Publishing Co., 1967):196–202; J. C. de Graft-Johnson, *African Glory* (New York: Walker & Co., 1954):158ff.; and Johannes Verkuyl, *Break Down The Walls*, ed. and trans. Lewis B. Smedes (Grand Rapids, Mich.: William B. Eerdmans Publishing Co., 1973):31f.

65. St. Clair Drake, *The Redemption of Africa and Black Redemption* (Chicago: Third World Press, 1970):48.

66. William Wells Brown, *The Rising Son* (Boston: A. G. Brown & Co., 1874; Reprint. New York: Negro Universities Press, 1970):46–47.

67. George Washington Williams, *History of The Negro Race In America From 1619 to 1880* (New York: G. P. Putnam's Sons, 1883; Reprint. New York: Arno Press and the *New York Times*, 1968):vol. 1, 19.

68. Joel A. Rogers, *Sex and Race*, 5th ed. (New York: Helga M. Rogers, 1944, 1972):vol. 3, 317.

69. Amy Jacques-Garvey, ed., *Philosophy and Opinions of Marcus Garvey*, with a new preface by William Loren Katz (New York: Arno Press and the *New York Times*, 1969):412.

70. James Baldwin, *The Fire Next Time* (New York: Dell Publishing Co., 1962):59.

71. Olin P. Moyd, *Redemption in Black Theology* (Valley Forge, Penn.: Judson Press, 1979):154ff.

72. George D. Kelsey, *Racism and The Christian Understanding of Man* (New York: Charles Scribner's Sons, 1965):26.

73. Latta R. Thomas, *Biblical Faith and the Black Man* (Valley Forge, Penn.: Judson Press, 1976):49.

74. Carl F. Ellis, *Beyond Liberation* (Downer's Grove, Ill.: Inter Varsity Press, 1983):41.

75. The number of Black writers who did so is legion.

76. See Drake; and Gayraud S. Wilmore, *Black Religion and Black Radicalism* (Garden City, N.Y.: Doubleday, 1972):166ff.

77. Speeches and books by the authors named are quite easily obtainable.

78. Claude Wanthier, *The Literature & Thought of Modern Africa*, trans. Shirley Kay (New York: Praeger Publishers, 1967):209.

79. The authors listed are as follows: Alfred G. Dunston, Jr., *The Black Man In The Old Testament And Its World* (Philadelphia: Dorrance & Co., 1974); Dyer; Robert A. Bennett, "Biblical Hermeneutics and The Black Preacher," *The Journal of The Interdenominational Theological Center*, 1 (Spring 1974):38–53; Thomas.

80. Cheikh Anta Diop, *The African Origin of Civilization: Myth or Reality?* ed. and trans. Mercer Cook (New York: Lawrence Hill & Co., 1974):245ff.

81. E. Mveng, "La Bible Et L'Afrique Noire" (Proceedings of The Jerusalem Congress On Black Africa And The Bible, April 14–30, 1972, eds. E. Mveng and R. J. Z. Werblowsky).

82. Among those that identify with the biblical Jews are Black Jewish groups such as Church of The Living God; Church of God and Saints of Christ; Commandment Keepers Congregation, alternately known as Royal Order of Ethiopian Jews; and the Black Christian Nationalist movement of the Reverend Albert B. Cleage, Jr. Identifying with the Hebrews-Israelites as distinct from Jews is the Original Hebrew Israelite Nation of Jerusalem. A rather voluminous body of literature concerning these groups now exists.

8

Black Experience and the Bible

Robert A. Bennett

Before examining the Black experience as religious experience, or discerning what is God's word for us in Black self-awareness, some note must be taken of the biblical themes of liberation and the creation of community. At the core of the biblical witness is the fact that disparate groups who were nobodies, existing on the fringes of ancient Near Eastern society and who were held in bondage, were liberated from their oppression and became somebodies in a newly formed community. That community, Israel, saw itself essentially as a "people" (Hebrew 'am; Greek laos) or religious congregation bound to its God. But it also recognized itself as a political expression of that unity in terms of a "nation" (Hebrew goy; Greek ethnos).[1] Central to the newly formed society was its covenantal relationship with the God Yahweh whom it believed was responsible for this change of events; this relationship was dependent more upon working out the divine intentions for the community than upon ritual worship of the deity. The Old Testament and the New testify to the conflicts as well as to the deepening awareness of what such a priority of responsibility meant. Christian and Jew have found it hard to define and express that community which God's interventions into human history would create, one where human relationships can serve as the paradigm for the God-to-man relationship.

The Bible, as revealed word, therefore, tries to communicate something about the purposeful ordering of society as a sign of God's intentions for his creation.[2] The literature of the old and new Israel is religious literature because it witnesses to God as the one not only creating but also maintaining and forcefully working out freedom for the oppressed in a community for the alien or alienated. Consequently the God-and-man relationship of peoplehood must be worked out in social and political institutions of nationhood. The quest for justice among men becomes the religious quest. Yet it is not only by the mighty acts of God himself, as at the exodus and conquest and in Jesus's life and resurrection, but also by human response to these divine motions that the model for society is forged. It is not simply divine fiat, but by conflict, struggle, and overt human choice that men are liberated and community is formed.[3] In all this the freedom sought and effected is both political and spiritual; the fellowship created is both social and religious.

I

The Black experience in America is not the Jewish-Christian experience in ancient Palestine. But as the tale of sorrows of a people awaiting deliverance, the Black narrative has a message consistent with the biblical witness though not to be found in that witness. It is a testimony of its own, distinct from Scripture even as it would proclaim its word to us in biblical images and in the categories of scriptural revelation. In this interplay of the new and old, of the familiar and the unique, the Black experience partakes of religious experience as it attempts to speak and thereby mediate to us something of God's intentions for us. Though not of canonical status, the story of the Black man in America is a self-validating account of faith that when heard and heeded, helps Black and white respond more creatively to the divine word for our present situation.

The hermeneutical task of proclaiming Scripture's meaning for today is based upon the prior descriptive task of determining what the biblical document said in its own day. This methodological sequence seems equally valid for getting at the message Blackness holds for contemporary America, namely, that the texts or documents of the Black experience be identified and allowed to speak for themselves within their given situation before dealing with their meaning for contemporary ears. Lest there be any caveat about treating this tradition of a people's faith as if it partook of divine revelation, it must be remembered that the book of Psalms became part of the divine word because it was such a fine mirror image of the revealed truth. Those hymns of faith were such a powerful response to the revealed truth that they became part of the witness itself. There is no need or intention to elevate these texts to a canonical status; they validate themselves because of the truth they reveal about men and about their faith in God. This literary tradition—oral and written—of prose, poetry, and song extends from the beginning of life on these shores into the present. Two articles by the historian Vincent Harding trace the continuity of fundamental belief through these texts: "The Gift of Blackness," *Katallagete* (Summer 1967), suggesting that the blues continue the affirmation begun in the spirituals; and "Reflections and Meditations on the Training of Religious Leaders for the New Black Generation," *Theological Education* 6 no. 3 (Spring 1970), calling on us to hear the words of the new poets as proclamation. Renewed interest in the slave narratives, the collection and study of sermons and orations, plus the reissuing of Black classics, to say nothing of the push for Black studies, all indicate the interest in gathering and hopefully finding the critical tools to let these texts speak for themselves.

The fixing of the tradition in which the Black experience has and is speaking today means more than collecting the literature and publishing anthologies. That tradition must also include the historical circumstances surrounding it and the theological interpretation which the community placed upon it. Consequently, there are disciplines such as Black history, Black theology, Black psychology, and Black politics, all contributing to making the past and present record of the Black experience intelligible and potent for its audience. Interest in Black history focuses on the *Sitz im Leben*, or social setting, of the Black experience, which though marked by oppression from without and powerlessness from within, is nevertheless a record of a people's trust in their destiny to be a community and to be free.[4] That account has a prehistory in the Black presence in the Bible itself and in the not-forgotten African past. There was a significant Black presence in the biblical history from Joseph's sojourn in Africa, to Solomon's transplanting an African court to rule his empire, to innumerable Jewish and Christian colonies in Africa.[5] There have always been ties between the Black American and the "old country."[6] Nevertheless even as we note these links with the past, the vital themes are those which focus on the present reality of the Black presence in white America, marked by that continuum of oppression between slavery and racism. The setting Black history helps reconstruct is one in which the word to be gotten across is freedom and community here and now.

An important historical as well as theological question is, "Why did the slave ancestors accept the religion of their oppressors?" Here too we must note what distinguishes the Black experience from the biblical record. Israel had been called out of bondage in order that she might become a people and nation, but the Black forefathers were brought into slavery to find the God of justice and freedom. A ready answer eludes us in this puzzle, though several suggestions have been put forward: (a) the slaves accepted the gospel as a means of survival—Gospel or the sword!—or of advancement in the repressive slave system; (b) our ancestors merely absorbed a veneer of Christianity, keeping much of their African heritage, as in the practice of voodoo; (c) many in fact did not accept the gospel. The last thesis supposes that it was house slaves who took on "massa's" religion with his hand-me-down clothes, but that more distantly removed field slaves did not. An extension of this hypothesis is that the secular songs and blues developed out of this supposed segment.

Professors Charles Long and Lawrence Jones assert that the "middle passage" and slavery did not destroy the African religious heritage but, being a highly developed and sophisticated awareness of creation as divinely ordered, it was able to survive in the similar expression of faith found in Christianity.[7] With his deep sense of God as creator, the slave heard in the Bible, particularly in the Old Testament, not a new word but ideas with which he was already more or less familiar. The new faith was not etched on a tabula rasa, nor was it merely seized upon as a means of survival. Though this old question is perhaps nearing solution with the study of African religious traditions and their relationship to the biblical word on God as Lord of creation, there is a contemporary taunt hurled at Black churchgoers that asks how they can accept the religion of the society which continues to oppress the Black man and insult his aspirations.

II

A new appreciation of the role of the Black Church within the Black experience may help in responding to the charge that the church as institution —white or Black—has hindered more than helped the liberation efforts of Black Americans. To begin with, it should be clear that the Black experience as religious experience is not synonymous with or at least not exhausted by the story of the Black Church. Nevertheless the history of this most vital institution is used here as a vehicle for bringing us up to date on the present situation of Black America. The story of the Black Church may be divided into three periods.[8] (a) The antebellum church sustained the community in its hope for freedom in the here and now as well as in the hereafter. The hymns that spoke of life "over Jordan" meant for their hearers the Ohio River or the Canadian border. It was no coincidence that the preachers who preached release were also the leaders of slave revolts and thus became restricted by their masters. (b) The Reconstruction church was an important political force and was the backbone of the community in establishing its necessary institutions. As W. E. B. DuBois noted, then and later the church was the only institution that white America let the Black man run for himself. (c) The modern church, which dates from the turn of the century, is presently entering a new phase beginning at mid-century with the Civil Rights movement. Up until these most recent decades, the church had to assume a compensatory role in the community as the government and society by "benign neglect" allowed the rise of violent intimidation, segregation, disenfranchisement, and the whole new oppression of the Black man. In this period of deep depression, the church became the one place of release from this assault and in this time of trauma it responded with a word of "peace." The contemporary church is learning that once again the vital message must be that of liberation and the building of community.

The most vital message in Scripture for liberation hope is that God acts in the course of human events to bring about his purposes for mankind. As Scripture would not separate what we now call sacred and secular, so the resurrection of Black history properly lets the Black experience speak its peace as *fana* which cannot be called profane. In its interpretation of events past and present this story of a people under oppression is redeemed from meaninglessness and infused with divine significance. The narrative of the sorrows and of the hopes of Black folk in America cannot be equated with the story of the people of God. Its potency lies elsewhere as a story of faithfulness to the message it received even in bondage, namely, that God's intentions were for men to be free, living in a just society. As much out of their African religious heritage as in the Gospel word, the slaves and their descendants learned something of God's intention, even when the color he gave became the occasion of oppression. Black awareness in Black history is a fundamental assent to God's justice within creation, but it is also an affirmation of God's lordship within history. In other words, this is no mere recounting or chronicling of events; it is a contemporary expression of salvation history.

This sacred-secular story helps us accept as valid the cries of Black revolution about America's consistent and deep-seated racist strain. It provides the perspective that grants liberation from oppression is indeed the right prescription in such a diagnosis. The American problem thus is seen not as the Black presence, but the white refusal to accept that presence, which is also a

refusal to deal with its responsibility for that presence. The resurrection of
Black history helps free Black minds of the lie that the problem is a pathology
of poverty and lawlessness stemming from cultural privation. If the latter
were true, then the social technicians of this society, such as Daniel Moynihan, might have something constructive to say about solving America's racial
crisis. But if oppressive policies of a racist society are the cause of the problem, then maybe Stokely Carmichael would be a better advisor on setting
right what is wrong. The right reading of events—events interpreted
—indicates that white racism and Black suppression are the problems to be
dealt with in this story of sorrows. Only then can the Black participation in
the American Dream be dealt with substantively.

III

The special significance of Black theology is that it is helping to form and
articulate the categories for our creative response in acknowledging God's
lordship in creation and in history. First of all, it is indebted to the witness of
faith already made within the Black experience. The church and community
that accepted its Blackness but rejected its enslavement has already confessed
to God's rule in the natural and social orders.

Although it is not in the compass of this study to deal with the emerging
discipline of Black psychology and making sense out of being Black and
proud in a racist society, two poems express the questioning and the acceptance of the creator's gift to us of Blackness. In the "Harlem Renaissance" of
the 1920s, the poet Countee Cullen in his collection *Color* lamented the cruel
irony of being Black in an oppressive white society:

> I doubt not God is good, well-meaning, kind. . . .
> Yet I do marvel at this curious thing:
> To make a poet black, and bid him sing!

There is now, however, a new sense of affirmation in the gospel music
that talks of respect and in the poems and political platforms that speak of
liberation. At the heart of them both is the acceptance of the gift of blackness,
with color now redeemed of racist perversions as a sign of God's love. A Black
G.I. dying in Vietnam movingly expressed this acceptance, placing it in the
context of his at-oneness with nature:

How sweet the darkness
   The darkness of my tomb
   How sweet the solitude
   No one to aim
   No one to squeeze the trigger
   No one to give pain
   To this
   Dead nigger.
Man, I'm back to earth
   They buried me down
   And I'm the same color
   A deep, dark brown. . . . [9]

Black Theology, therefore, carries on a traditional role of helping to shape and to articulate those expressions of faith that already exist, and in the Black experience, awareness is already an affirmation, a response in faith to God's providential hand in the natural order as well as in the course of human events.

Though not ignoring this theme of God's role as creator, Black theology has up to this date directed its attention toward the sociopolitical phenomenon of "Black Power," as indicated by the titles of two major efforts, James Cone's *Black Power and Black Theology* (Seabury Press, 1969) and Vincent Harding's "The Religion of Black Power," *The Religious Situation, 1968*, D. Cutler, ed. (Beacon Press, 1968). This enterprise and this emphasis is not new, however, since it represents the repetition of the liberation theme of the antebellum church and the upbuilding of community institutions as during the Reconstruction era. This theology would articulate the message of Black self-awareness, namely, that even in the midst of oppression, Black men will be free participants within white America. Despite the church's emphasis on withdrawal from the burdens and insults—but also the promises—of this life during the first half of the century, it was a Black Baptist preacher, Martin Luther King, Jr., who helped bring the Black community to its renewed thrust for emancipation. The life and witness of King and the new Black awareness indicate that the Black experience as religious experience reached a new stage. Black Theology, therefore, is not merely filling in the gaps left by the suspicious color-blindness of previous theologians; it more importantly is both helping to shape and to articulate the Black experience as a religious experience which has a divine message for contemporary America. The effort within Black Theology to formulate and to communicate what that word is, under the guidance of biblical revelation, is its hermeneutical task. The problem facing Black churchmembers, therefore, is how to express the cry coming out of Black America as an essentially Christian and redemptive word within an oppressive self-righteous society. The divine word spoken in the Black experience is one of hope and vindication within this life, but it is also one that judges America's racist society and religious establishment.

IV

Just before his death, Martin Luther King, Jr., began to deal with that most potent force within the Black community, Black self-awareness and Black Power. Vincent Harding's article, "The Religion of Black Power," deals sympathetically with Dr. King's cautious appraisal of this phenomenon. Harding himself raises several questions about the militants, particularly their call for "autonomous action" to secure Black liberation. He cites the dangers of taking on the mind-set of racist America, and the consequences for the Black psyche of attempting to ignore or make invisible the white man. Harding asks if the Black quest for guns, mass media, the atom bomb is not a suicidal attempt to fight on America's terms and to become like the enemy in his use of "conscienceless power."[10] And he bids us think how we shall break the psychological dependence upon whiteness so as not to impair the wholeness of our own human perception. It is at points such as these that the message coming out of the Black experience stands in real tension with the biblical witness. But first of all it must be recognized that the biblical tradition stands in tension with itself at many points, a palimpsest, or tradition made up of many traditions inscribed one upon another. Scholars speak of the prophetic tradition, the priestly tradition, the wisdom tradition, the gospel, and the early church traditions.[11] Each generation and school of faith responds to God's word in its own way while yet in the old or new covenantal relationship. God's power is expressed in the Old Testament as autonomous action, the might of armies, and of natural phenomena, while in the New Testament it is expressed in the weakness and surrender of Jesus. Israel appears earlier as a nation among the nations, but later as a subjugated people highly self-conscious of her identity over that of her neighbors.

Yet even as these nuances are recognized in Scripture, the Christian witness suggests God's definitive word as given in the life and mission of Jesus and the community he called into being. This being the case, where is Jesus in Black Power? While many would identify Jesus as the revolutionary who liberated the oppressed, he even more clearly is the one who questioned and attacked the socio-religious establishment of his day. And it was most clearly his demonstration of power in weakness which set all the more in contrast and in judgment the corrupt and calcified establishment he was attacking. So it is the New Testament witness which helps Vincent Harding ask his incisive question of militant Black Power—"Shall it seek the autonomous action of the Old Testament tradition or shall it follow that New Testament demonstration of power in weakness in a perhaps more powerful judgment of the conscienceless power of the American way?"

Jesus attacked the established norms of his society so that those oppressed by that society might be free. The Black self-awareness in this present situation seeks to free Black minds from white myths about Blackness.[12] A new form of liberation is taking place where a long nascent community is coming alive in this land, not waiting for its exile to end, longing to be a proud Black people. The biblical categories are reversed: men seek to establish community in bondage so they may become free; they reject the alien-exile theme of Israel and the pilgrims who looked for a new land to form their society. The Black experience has been one in which a community learned to sing the Lord's songs in a strange land and to pray for the peace of the land where they had been carried. While there is solidarity with Africa and it is seen as the Black *Kulturland*, the Black American does not see himself as an exiled alien, as did the Israelite in Psalm 137 who couldn't sing the Lord's song in a strange land. Indeed, despite the oppression he has been a patriot and, taking Jeremiah's advice, he has prayed for the peace of this land. This people does not conceive of itself as being in diaspora. There has been no successful Back to Africa movement nor anything equivalent to Zionism. The community has no illusions about itself; it is no chosen people; this is no promised land. Its "messiahs" have been few and transitory. It is convinced, however, by its experience on these shores, by its survival under the most oppressive of slave systems, that God does not intend that this people shall die. The Black experience is the realization of this as historical fact, and acknowledging God as Lord of creation, it has maintained its hope and communion with the world around it.

This essay has attempted to say that God's word in Scripture comes to us more clearly and forcefully when we understand it as expressing something

138 Robert A. Bennett

about the divine purpose for creation and human society not only in the period when it was given form in the witness of Israel, or in Jesus, or in the early church, but also in the forms of human witness today. The Black experience in America is such an expression of faith in God's involvement in life for freeing those who are not free and giving power to those who have none. The biblical story and the account of the Black man in America are not the same story. Nevertheless, the same hermeneutical process that confronts us with the message from Scripture also suggests those categories by which we can deal creatively with the word being spoken by the Black experience. It is assumed that God's final self-revelation given in Jesus Christ and under the old and new covenant has consequence for the whole course of human history, and that word and event continue as potent in conveying that revelation. As we deal with Blackness and Black history as potent word and event, we come to see Scripture as relevant not in the discovery of points of contact between the Bible and the Black experience, but as it leads us to discern and accept God as speaking to us in the givenness of our situation.

Notes

1. E. A. Speiser, "'People' and 'Nation' of Israel," *Journal of Biblical Literature* 79, no. 2 (June 1960):157–63; Cf. J. W. Flight, "Nationality," *Interpreter's Dictionary of the Bible*, G. A. Buttrick, ed. (New York: Abingdon Press, 1962) 512–15; E. J. Hamlin, "Nations," Ibid., 515–23; Leo Spitzer, "Ratio-Race," and "The Gentiles," *Essays in Historical Semantics* (New York: S. F. Vanni, 1948):147–69; 171–78; Eric Voegelin, "The Growth of the Race Idea," *The Review of Politics* 2, no. 3 (July 1940): 283–317.

2. G. Ernest Wright et al., *The Biblical Doctrine of Man in Society*, Ecumenical Biblical Studies No. 2 (London: SCM, 1954).

3. G. Ernest Wright, *The Old Testament Against Its Environment* Studies in Biblical Theology no. 2, (London: SCM, 1950); and *The Old Testament and Theology* (New York: Harper, 1969):chaps. 2–6.

4. Cf. Arna Bontemps, ed., *Great Slave Narratives*, with editor's essay, "The Slave Narrative: An American Genre," vii–xix (Boston: Beacon Press, 1969); Melvin Drimmer, ed., *Black History: A Reappraisal* (Garden City: Doubleday, 1968); Thomas Frazier, ed., *Afro-American History: Primary Sources* (New York: Harcourt, Brace, 1970); Dwight Hoover, ed., *Understanding Negro History* (Chicago: Quadrangle, 1968); William L. Katz, ed., *Negro Protest Pamphlets* (New York: Arno Press and the *New York Times*, 1969); August Meier and E. Rudwick eds., *The Making of Black America*, 2 vols. (New York: Atheneum, 1969).

5. Cf. A. Arkell, *A History of the Sudan from Earliest Times to 1821*, 2d ed. (London: London University Press, 1961); *Cambridge Ancient History*, rev. ed., vols. 1–2 (Cambridge: Cambridge University Press, 1963); R. Collins ed., *Problems in African History* (Englewood Cliffs, N.J.:

Prentice-Hall, 1968); A. Gardiner, *Egypt of the Pharaohs* (New York: Oxford University Press, 1968); F. M. Snowden, *Blacks in Antiquity: Ethiopians in the Greco-Roman Empire* (Cambridge: Harvard University Press, 1970); E. Ullendorf, *Ethiopia and the Bible*, Schweich Lecture (New York: Oxford University Press, 1968).

6. Cf. Alexander Crummell, *Africa and America: Addresses and Discourses* (1891); Reprint. (Miami: Mnemosyne, 1969); W. E. B. DuBois, *Black Folk, Then and Now* (New York: Henry Holt, 1939); Melville Herskovits, *The Myth of the Negro Past* (Boston: Beacon Press, 1958); St. Clair Drake, "Negro Americans and the African Interest," in *The American Negro Reference Book*, ed. J. P. Davis (Englewood Cliffs, N.J.: Prentice-Hall, 1966): 662–705; and "'Hide My Face?' On Pan-Africanism and Negritude," in *The Making of Black America*, vol. I, ed. A. Meier and E. Rudwick (New York: Atheneum, 1969):66–87; H. R. Lynch, "Pan-Negro Nationalism in the New World Before 1862," in *The Making of Black America*, vol. 1, 42–65.

7. Cf. *African Systems of Thought*, Third International African Seminar, Salisbury, Dec., 1960, (New York: Oxford University Press, 1965); Henri Frankfort, *Ancient Egyptian Religion* (New York: Harper, 1948); John S. Mbiti, *African Religions and Philosophy* (New York: Praeger, 1969); Geoffrey Parrinder, *Religion in Africa* (Baltimore: Penguin, 1969); Noel Q. King, *Religions of Africa* (New York: Harper, 1970).

8. Cf. E. Franklin Frazier, *The Negro Church in America* (New York: Schocken Books, 1963); Benjamin Mays and Joseph Nicholson, *The Negro's Church* (New York: Institute of Social and Religious Research, 1933); and Carter G. Woodson, *The History of the Negro Church*, 2d ed. (Washington, D.C.: Associated, 1921). Note also: W. E. B. DuBois, *The Souls of Black Folk* (1903; Reprint. New York: Fawcet Crest, 1961); James Cone, "Black Consciousness and the Black Church," *The Annals* 387 (January 1970), 49–55; R. T. Handy, "Negro Christianity and American Church Historiography," *Reinterpretation in American Church History*, ed. J. C. Brauer (Chicago: Chicago University Press, 1968); and Lawrence Jones, "Black Theology in the Ante-bellum South," (paper delivered at the N.C.B.C. Black Theology Consultation, Atlanta, April, 1970); Benjamin Mays, *The Negro's God* (1938; Reprint. New York: Atheneum, 1968).

9. Poem, 'Viet Nam," by Jack DiNola of Trenton, N.J., quoted by John Snow in lectures on "Preaching in an Apocalyptic Age," (Kellogg Lecture for 1970, Episcopal Theological School, Cambridge, Mass., February 1970).

10. Vincent Harding, "The Religion of Black Power," *The Religious Situation, 1968*, ed. D. Cutler (Boston: Beacon Press, 1968):3–38.

11. Cf. recent works emphasizing the importance of the history and variety of interpretation within the biblical material: Günther Bornkamm, *Jesus of Nazareth*, 3d ed. (New York: Harper, 1960); Ernst Käsemann, *Jesus Means Freedom* (Philadelphia: Fortress, 1969); Klaus Koch, *The Growth of Biblical Tradition* (New York: Scribners, 1969); Gerhard von Rad, *Old Testament Theology*, 2 vols. (New York: Harper, 1962, 1963).

12. *The Black Scholar* 1, no. 5 (March 1970) is devoted to the topic of Black psychology; *The Black Scholar* 1, no. 2 (December 1969) deals with Black politics.

9

Biblical Historical Study as Liberation: Toward an
Afro-Christian Hermeneutic

Vincent L. Wimbush

The Bible and the Theological Situation in
African American Christianity

In the sense that they have always sought to know and articulate "the biblical position" on all matters pertaining to existence, including liberation for their people, all African American leaders—predominantly, though not exclusively, Christian—have been biblical theologians.[1] But very few of these leaders have had as their major concern the *academic* study of the Bible apart from preparation for, and acceptance of, the presuppositions of confessional vocations. The paucity of African American biblical scholars only confirms the point.

Nevertheless, two clarifications are in order. First, although the academic study of the Bible is an ancient practice,[2] the historical-critical methods, now the common possession of "reputable" biblical scholars,[3] came to be applied to biblical texts on a wide scale in this country only in the late nineteenth and early twentieth centuries.[4] Obviously African Americans as a whole were otherwise disposed during this period, struggling for basic human rights. At any rate, they had very limited access to educational institutions in general, especially those institutions in which debates about methods were being waged.[5] Thus they were hardly in a position to engage the emergent critical methods. Second, and perhaps more importantly, African Americans had already begun in this period of the rise of the use of historical-critical methods to appropriate Christian symbols, concepts, and language in their own way. This appropriation made somewhat irrelevant for them the crisis that led to the adoption of the critical methods applied to the Bible in this country.

White-American Protestant, Catholic, and Jewish readings of the Bible were an admixture of doctrinalist, moralist, and pietist patterns of thought.

Among such groups, the Bible was seen either as a source for correct doctrine, a handbook for moral guidance and decision-making, or combinations of both.[6] Since the Bible had from the beginning of the European presence in America been given so central a role in American society, difficulties soon emerged from differences and conflicts in interpretations and translations, from perceived contradictions within accepted texts, and especially from attempts to square the literalist, mythopoeic reading of certain texts with a post-Enlightenment world.[7] Efforts to silence dissent were unsuccessful; there was a revolution in the making.

What was emerging was a change in the understanding of history itself, specifically, the manner in which educated men and women were beginning to understand the relationship between revelation and history.[8] This new understanding suggested a "transformation of human consciousness," which entailed holding the conviction that cultures (their ideals and institutions — including religious ideals and institutions) are the *products* of history and must be known and assessed *within* the realm of history or not at all. Such a conviction forced, especially in "high" Protestant circles, the acceptance of the historical-critical methods in the study of the Bible.[9]

By contrast, the African American appropriation of Christian symbols, concepts, and language developed along different lines. It did not fit neatly into either the doctrinalist, moralist, or pietist "reading" of the Bible. Such readings presuppose, perhaps even require, literate bourgeois classes.[10] Since most of the earliest African American Christians had been denied from the beginning of their experience in the Americas the opportunity to be fully human, including the opportunity to learn to read and write, the "letters" of the biblical texts were not crucial in their appropriation and redaction of Christian traditions. What became important was the *telling* and *retelling*, the hearing and rehearing of biblical stories — stories of perseverance, of strength in weakness and under oppressive burdens, of hope in hopeless situations. To these stories African Americans related. Identification with biblical heroes and heroines, with the "people of God," with the suffering, and ultimately with victorious Jesus constituted "faith." (Slave songs, Black preaching, and orations remain eloquent testimony to this assertion.)[11] The hearing and rehearing, the telling and retelling represented the beginning of development into "the Afro-Christian tradition."[12] This tradition was a blending of remnants of the (West) African "sacred cosmos," on the one hand,[13] and Euro-American Protestant evangelical Christianity on the other.[14] This Afro-Christianity was neither merely Protestant evangelical nor African; it was from the beginning a type of syncretism.

This syncretism was necessitated by the social existence (slavery) of Africans in the American context. The character of the syncretism which emerged was controlled by, and found coherence in, the African Americans' assessment of their social existence. Such assessment inspired the independent church movements,[15] and made African Americans conscious of the degree to which their situation belied "Christian teaching" about the kinship of humanity under God.

In a recent monograph Peter Paris argues that in order to justify their separate existence as racial entities, the Afro-Christian churches consistently embraced and highlighted the principle of the universal parenthood of God and kinship of humankind.[16] Two important examples are in order.[17] First, at the twentieth Quadrennial Session of the General Conference of the African Methodist Episcopal Church (held in Wilmington, North Carolina, in May 1896), the bishops made the saying of Bishop Daniel Payne—"God our Father; Christ our Redeemer; Man our Brother"—the official motto of the church. At the same time they stressed that the mission of the church universal should be consonant with that of the denomination: "This is the official motto of the A.M.E. Church, and her mission in the common-wealth of Christianity is to bring all denominations and races to acknowledge and practice the sentiments contained therein. When these sentiments are universal in theory and practice, then the mission of the distinctive colored organizations will cease."[18]

Dr. E. C. Morris, in his presidential address before the Forty-Second Annual Session of the National Baptist Convention in St. Louis, December 1922, made even more clear how Afro-Baptists understood and justified their separate existence and what was at stake: "We early imbibed the religion of the white man; we believed in it; we believe in it now . . . but if that religion does not mean what it says, if God did not make of one blood all nations of men to dwell on the face of the earth, and if we are not to be counted as a part of that generation, by those who handed the oracle down to us, the sooner we abandon them or it, the sooner we will find our place in a religious sect in the world. . . ."[19]

It is important to note that what these and countless other expressions reveal about Afro-Christian communities is that they understood and explained their existence not through exclusive theological propositions or

dogma, but chiefly on account of social—here including political and economic and educational—realities. Afro-Baptists and Methodists did not bolt
from their respective white ecclesiastical counterparts on account of differences in dogma; those who bolted did so on account of the racism of white
Christians.[20]

From the beginning of their separate existence, the Afro-Christian
churches defined their mission vis-à-vis African Americans in general as
survivalist in method and intention.[21] They existed to enable African Americans to survive with meaning the non-affirming, dehumanizing forces and
structures of American society. But these churches soon found themselves in a
theological dilemma that had the most serious consequences for their self-
understanding and ultimately for the quality of life for all African Americans.
Since the churches were founded in response to the social situation, they
assumed the appropriateness and innocence of adherence to the confessional
framework (creeds, liturgies, polities) of the white parent denominational
bodies. Afro-Baptists still adhered to Anabaptist and/or Calvinist statements
of faith; African Methodists continued to hold the line for Wesleyan doctrine
and piety, as well as episcopal polity. Both communities allowed the Euro-
American theological constructs and polities to stay in place while they
explained their existence on an altogether different basis.[22]

Thus a strange and frightening thing happened to African Americans on
their sojourn to independence, progress, and liberation—and obtains even
today. With more opportunities to become engaged in letters, as well as the
wherewithal to engage American society in general, the "letters" of the biblical texts came to assume more importance in shaping the religious life and
self-understandings of many Afro-Christians. This claim could easily be established by research beyond the scope of this article. Yet it might suffice here to
postulate that the basis of much of the internal criticism of independent
African American churches since their founding has been the perception of
such churches' weakness in "expounding the Word," or more generally, in
transmitting and inculcating "the great Christian tradition." That Joseph
Washington could in 1964 accuse African American churches of being no
more than mere social clubs or transmitters of primitive folk religious traditions, ignorant of historic Christian doctrines, is significant.[23] The virulent
cricitism of Washington aside, one suspects that he was and is no loner as far
as his critique of the African American churches is concerned.[24] Further
research will likely establish Washington's sentiments as those of a significant

number of African American Christians. The founding of independent African denominations and parishes, the Black control of Black colleges and seminaries notwithstanding, Afro-Christianity began—ironically, on the way towards "emancipation"—to concern itself with the creeds and doctrines of the white parent denominational bodies.

This "fall" away from experience-based religion was gradual at first. To some extent, book-dominated religion among African Americans has existed alongside culturalist Afro-Christianity since the founding of the independent churches. This coexistence continues to have important implications for African American religious self-understanding. What neither the intransigent South nor the hypocritical North could accomplish through legal strictures or customs, African Americans' uncritical embrace of confessional frameworks did accomplish.[25] That is, African Americans' embrace of the creeds, doctrines, and polities of the white parent denominational bodies has often frustrated collective and sustained efforts in African Americans' best interest.[26] Dogma, liturgy, and polity serve important social functions, including that of emphasizing solidarity and influencing personal and communal behavior.[27] No confessional framework should be embraced with innocence, that is, without an understanding of the social implications.

The foregoing discussion has pointed to an aspect of the challenge which contemporary Afro-Christian churches face with respect to the engagement of Christian traditions. Because of its importance in all interpretations of Christian existence, the Bible should be the focus of the challenge that Afro-Christian churches must begin to face in order to engage Christian traditions anew. Without an increased measure of *hermeneutical control* over the Bible, it will prove impossible for Afro-Christian churches to articulate self-understanding, maintain integrity as separate Christian communities, and determine their mission in the world.

Needed are both a defense from alien, imperialistic hermeneutical constructs (and with them symbols, concepts, rituals, social orientation) and the capacity to assume control over, to evaluate critically, and advance their own traditions. Basically *pre-critical* in their biblical hermeneutic, African American churches find themselves unable to fend off alien and competing claims from other traditions, especially those which court with the same doctrinal language and polity. They also find it most difficult to build on their own foundations, since self-criticism and constructive change are frustrated without critical facility in a post-critical age. Critical facility for the historical study of both the self, viz., the Afro-Christian tradition, and the Bible as the single most significant depository of Christian tradition, is required for self-defense and self-criticism, as well as the capacity for the construction of a more affirming, indigenous hermeneutic built on the tradition. Such an indigenous hermeneutic will emerge out of post-critical reading of biblical texts, which presupposes critical engagement. Let us now turn our attention to a possible way in which historical study of the Bible can facilitate a liberation-oriented Afro-Christian hermeneutic.

"From the Beginning It Was Not So": Historical Study of the Bible as Scripture

Perhaps as far back as the Enlightenment, but most certainly since the nineteenth century in the West,[28] the Bible has been understood and engaged as both Holy Scripture and as a classic. In some sense, it has been normative for the moral and ethical life, and it also has served as a literary document that has profoundly affected the imagination of western culture. That these two categories of understanding of the Bible have persisted for some time in the West is, perhaps, not debatable. What is debatable is the manner in which the two categories ought to interface.

In *The Uses of Scripture in Recent Theology*, David H. Kelsey assumes the two broad categories—text/scripture—of understanding of the Bible, and provides further differentiation:

> To exegete the texts simply as texts is to engage in one of at least two different kinds of historical inquiry. (i) One may study a biblical text taken as a historical source that itself has historical sources. "Exegesis" in this sense is part of the historian's craft wherein the history of the text is reconstructed or a part of ancient history is reconstructed using the text as a source of validating evidence. (ii) One may study a text simply as it stands. This enterprise differs from the first because its goal is different. The aim of the inquiry is not so much to discover the sources out of which the text came, but rather what interest shaped the work of the one who put it in its present state and how it would have been understood by its original audience in its original context.[29]

He continues with reference to the third type of engagement of the Bible—as (Christian) "scripture":

(iii) . . . Such an exegesis would result in judgements about it precisely as used in rulish and normative ways in the church's common life to help nurture and reform . . . self-identity. Taken that way, an exegetical judgement is part of the theological task. It is guided in important ways by theological judgements about the nature of the church's task and about just how scripture ought to be used in the church's common life. . . .[30]

Krister Stendahl, in his 1983 presidential address to the Society of Biblical Literature, has also assumed the same broad categories of understanding of the Bible in the West. But in a characteristically provocative manner, he goes beyond the positing of the categories to suggest what relationship ought to obtain between them.[31] He defines a classic as "any work that is considered worth attention beyond its time."[32] The Bible is a classic not merely as literature—this is too broad a category. The issue is what type of classic, even as one must ask how it functions as literature in western culture. Stendahl argues that the Bible is a classic above all as Holy Scripture. This entails recognition of the normative function of the Bible, in a way similar to the recognition of the function of the Koran and the Bhagavad Gita in other cultures. It is this recognition which distinguishes the Bible as a classic of Holy Scripture from other types of classics, such as the writings of Homer or those of Shakespeare in one cultural context; or the writings of James Baldwin, Countee Cullen, and Margaret Walker in another.

The Bible understood as a classic of Holy Scripture neither precludes the serious historical task about which Kelsey speaks, nor necessarily mandates the manner in which "normative" is to be understood. As for the former, Stendahl argues that descriptive, historical exegesis is all the more needed when the Bible is understood as a *classic* of Holy Scripture:

The more intensive the expectation of normative guidance and the more exacting the claims for the holiness of the Scriptures, the more obvious should be the need for full attention to what it meant in the time of its conception and what the intention of the authors might have been. But where the Bible is enjoyed in a far more relaxed mood as a classic, people do like to find its support or sanction for their thoughts and actions. The low intensity of the normativeness often makes such use of Scripture less careful.[33]

As for the latter—the question of the manner in which "normative" is to be understood when the Bible is understood as Holy Scripture—it is enough to say that it is not necessary to document either the historical diversity of understandings, or the contemporary diversity of understandings among religious groups.[34]

Stendahl and Kelsey among many others agree that acceptance of the Bible as Holy Scripture does not preclude critical engagement of it. Kelsey sees his three types of exegesis influencing one another and theological construction in different, often complementary, ways. As far as the relevance of historical exegesis is concerned, he concedes that a certain condition must be met, namely, a certain "construal," "a logically prior and imaginative decision" about how scripture should be used in any community before any biblical text is studied.[35] Stendahl goes beyond Kelsey insofar as he takes for granted a certain "construal" of biblical texts and argues that, as scripture, they be engaged critically, viz., as products of history. Both scholars hint that the descriptive task could well be applied to all "construals" to the good effect of tempering dogmatism and criticizing the status quo interpretation. This could be accomplished from a vantage point which historical study alone could provide, so that it can be said of non-affirming and prejudiced constructs, "from the beginning it was not so."[36]

It would be only reasonable not to be in general agreement with both Kelsey and Stendahl in the way in which they assess broad categories for understanding the Bible, as well as in the importance they attach to the historical, descriptive task for all categories of understanding of the Bible, including the Bible as scripture. Any discussion about the Bible and hermeneutics must either confront or assume the categories of understanding framed by Kelsey and Stendahl. But two caveats are in order. First, the descriptive task about which Kelsey and Stendahl speak should not be understood as objective or scientific inquiry, but as a genre of presentation. Such presentation is to be contrasted, not with the subjective, but with that presentation which seeks to prescribe vis-à-vis direct engagement of biblical texts. Historical exegesis might very well function as a resource for prescription at some level, and it always carried with it the baggage, or predisposition, of the historian. But it does not formally prescribe behavior on the basis of studying the texts. It seeks only to describe behavior, and the rationale behind it as such comes into focus in the texts. Second, historical exegesis must not be taken as a substitute for prescription, that is, as the final arbiter about how biblical texts should be employed as normative scripture. Historical inquiry must not lead to historicism. It is important what kind of historical inquiry is conducted.

Because the Bible has always been understood as scripture by African American Christians, and because they have been victimized by racist, imperialistic biblical hermeneutics, discussion about reading the Bible as scripture is most relevant for Afro-Christian churches.

The History of "World":
The Bible as Post-Ethical Disclosure

The Bible comes to us in literary categories—genres and forms—and through the editorial manipulation of materials in those categories (e.g., order, expansions, deletions, etc.) which betray the concerns and intentions of the writers. Since genres and formal elements are created and employed in particular *Sitze im Leben* (life settings), interpretation cannot ignore the diversity of situations to which, and out of which, biblical texts speak. Such regard should limit the range of application of any biblical text.

What soon becomes evident when biblical texts are respected for the diversity of types of materials in them, as well as the editorial manipulation on the part of the original writer and later editors, is that the function of the texts is not to convey timeless ethical and moral propositions, but to present a picture of individuals and communities struggling to discover what it means to strive—and very often to fail—to be human in the highest key. These struggles, these faith-journeys, get played out in, although sometimes superficially against, the social and physical worlds in which the individuals and communities live. Ethical and moral prescriptions are always localized and always serve only to help fill out the picture of the struggles inherent in the faith-journey, namely in the effort to understand and realize true existence.

It is inappropriate to engage biblical texts on the level of the rational ethical principle alone because biblical writers wrote only out of and for situations for which ethical principles are tied to shared self-understanding.[37] There are no autonomous moral or ethical principles apart from shared history and identity, or at least the effort to commend such. To the extent that there is movement, diversity, and conflict within biblical texts, such can be made evident through research into understandings of existence, not ethical or moral principles.

Moral and ethical principles loosened from their original contexts eventually become part of the history of ideas. Aside from the fact that there are more discontinuities than continuities in the history of ideas in biblical texts, little ground can be gained in the effort to discover the self-understandings of those trafficking in ideas through such inquiry. In a little-noticed article published in 1968 entitled " 'World' in Modern Theology and in New Testament Theology," James M. Robinson challenged the next generation of biblical scholars to forget efforts "to recover the lost threads of continuity in the history of ideas from author to author" and instead to trace the movement of "world" as it "comes into language." Robinson assumed the tracing of the movement of world to be a historical, descriptive work; one would be charting the "trajectory to which understandings of existence can be meaningfully and historically interpreted."[38]

"World" historically interpreted will allow a glimpse of how biblical communities understood themselves, what it meant to live in the social and physical world as a community of faith. Every world is relative—to some other world. Every world is partly a response to influences from the (social and physical) world. Every world is, thus, contextual and has a history.

The very movement of world in biblical texts dictates against any uncritical, dogmatic acceptance and aping of any world. No world should ever be simply recreated, since every world is the result of influences that bind it to specific historial contexts. A biblical world should and can only be either rejected outright or accepted as a *springboard* of sorts for the construction of another, more relevant, viz., indigenous world. Outright rejection should follow from recognition that a particular biblical world has either little affinity with, or positive support for, one's present situation in the world. African American Christians have historically rejected parts of the Pauline and deutero-Pauline letters because they have found the seeming indifference of the latter to the moral issue of slavery difficult to accept in their situation in the world. But it is important to emphasize that this rejection was *not* done on the basis of historical exegesis. So African Americans rejected the "Pauline" references to slavery, but tended to accept the ethos of Pauline Christianity. That this rejection/acceptance phenomenon could persist is due to the engagement of biblical texts on an exclusive ethical-principle level. So it was possible to misjudge the full meaning and import of this world by abstracting social and ethical teachings from theology. Without historical perspective, no clear assessment can be made of any biblical ethical principle, nor any biblical world. And no adequate self-defense—if needed—can be made against it.

The Liberating Hermeneutical Circle

Leaders of the Afro-Christian churches must be willing to talk with those biblical scholars who now finally see the methodological if, sadly, not also the moral and ethical imperative of raising questions about understandings of existence in biblical texts. Along with familiarity with the history of world as it comes into focus in biblical texts, what is needed is ability to assess the implications of efforts to build bridges between any particular biblical world and the present. Again, biblical worlds should never be recreated; a biblical world can be *translated* into a force appropriate for contemporary situations in the world. But such translations require a great deal of wisdom with respect to one's own physical and social world, as well as knowledge of what is contained in the Bible

Translation (i.e., hermeneutics in a post-critical age) would represent the unearthing of the relevant influences upon the responses to the social and physical world which betray "world." What in the physical and social world is rejected or accepted is illuminating of self-understanding. To the extent that reasons for (viz., intentions behind the rejection of, or accommodation to) the physical and social world are discernible, it is possible to understand and translate "world."

The "world" of much of Pauline Christianity of the first and second centuries—of the Pastoral letters, Polycarp, Luke, Clement of Rome, 1 and 2 Peter—was carved out of the physical and social world of urban Asia Minor, Greece, and Rome. The social orientation was characterized by a type of accommodation to that physical and social world—partly from an attempt to counter the anti-social attitudes and behavior (e.g., ascetic) of some Christians and other religious groups at the time and partly as an effort to commend the faith to the powerful and sophisticated in Greco-Roman culture.[39] Acceptance of this world of first and second century Christianity would require not so much an immediate application of its specific ethical and moral injunctions, as an understanding of, and resonance with, the intentions behind the response to the physical and social world. Recognition that the world of the first and second centuries, reflected in biblical accommodationist documents, was a more worldly world meant to counter less worldly attitudes and behavior will force respect for the history and contextualization, as well as for the applicability, of that "world." It should be applied only after it is understood as a worldly response over against specific types of challenges and problems.

But it would be the whole of the response in context, not particular injunctions, that would be appropriate for application in contemporary situations in the world. Thus it would be the resonance of, or need for, a more worldly model of spirituality which would commend the documents, not any particular injunction or proscription.

What biblical texts provide is not a smorgasbord of worlds from which only one is to be embraced. What they provide are pictures—incomplete though they might be—of the *movement* of worlds. It is the movement—the diversity, the conflict, the change—that is of greatest hermeneutical significance. It liberates from ethical principles not mandated by shared experiences. The very movement of worlds allows freedom to explore, to experiment with the testimonies of other communities of faith about what faith might mean in different situations in life. In every post-biblical generation, then, biblical texts might function as facilitations of discussion about appropriate understandings and models of existence in the world. The worlds of biblical texts cannot be ignored because they provide the historical tie that binds all post-biblical communities together. They provide the occasion for the process of questioning and discussion.

Biblical texts should serve Afro-Christian churches in their quest for the articulation of a clearer self-understanding based on their origins and social station. The texts should serve as prisms through which possibilities for world can be seen more clearly in the contemporary situation in the world. The process should, however, have no real beginning and no real end. The process should be radically, not viciously, *circular*. Communal engagements of the Bible should help sharpen and challenge self-understanding, but the Bible itself is not broached without the presuppositions of the tradition, i.e., the working, preliminary "construal" of biblical texts based on collective experience.[40] Minority religious communities especially need this circular method for self-defense and the exercise of the imagination in freedom. It allows such communities a vantage point from which they not only can say of alien, imperialistic readings of the Bible "from the beginning it was not so," but also to criticize themselves on the basis of their own history and present social situation.

Historical study of the sort outlined above is necessary not as an end in itself, but as an important step in the direction of construing the Bible as Scripture for the articulation of an affirming self-understanding and existence. Historical exegesis makes relevant and demystifies every "world"—both biblical and post-biblical—and makes room for minority constructs. Perhaps what liberation initially requires is exegetical room.

Notes

1. See Henry J. Young, *Major Black Religious Leaders: 1755–1940* (Nashville, Tenn.: Abingdon, 1977) and *Major Black Religious Leaders: Since 1940* (Nashville: Abingdon, 1979) for discussion of the thought of selected personalities on God and ethics, Black suffering and redemption, eschatology. More detailed research needs to be done in this area, especially as regards the role of the Bible in the thought of such leaders.

2. Origen, Dionysius of Alexandria in the third century, c.e. See E. Krentz, *The Historical-Critical Method* (Philadelphia: Fortress, 1975):6; W. G. Kuemmel, *The New Testament: The History of the Investigation of its Problems*, trans. S. M. Gilmour and H. C. Kee (New York: Abingdon, 1972):15ff.

3. See Joseph Cahill, *Mended Speech: The Crisis of Religious Studies and Theology.* (New York: Crossroad, 1982):39–43, 67, 72, 110, 140 for discussion of present state of Religious Studies, including biblical studies, in American higher education.

4. Grant Wacker, "The Demise of Biblical Civilization," in *The Bible in America: Essays in Cultural History*, ed. Nathan O. Hatch and Mark O. Noll (New York: Oxford University Press, 1982):121–38.

5. Krentz, 29ff.

6. Richard J. Mouw, "The Bible in Twentieth Century Protestantism: A Preliminary Taxonomy," in Hatch and Noll, 139–62, especially 142–57. Although Protestants primarily in view, the various "readings" isolated easily fit the Catholic and Jewish communities as well. Also see Gerald P. Fogarty, S.J., "The Quest for a Catholic Vernacular Bible in America," 163–80 in same volume.

7. Krentz, 33.

8. Ibid., 33ff.

9. Ibid., 22ff.

10. Max Weber, *Sociology of Religion*, trans. Ephraim Fischoff, 4th ed. (Boston: Beacon Press, 1963):66, 166ff. Weber argues that the religion of the urban, literate middle classes is characterized by a tendency to order and rationalize religious experience. Careful attention to the interpretation of religious documents is reflective of this type of religious self-understanding.

11. See Howard Thurman, *Deep River and the Negro Spiritual Speaks of Life and Death* (Richmond, Ind.: Friends Press, 1975); Benjamin E. Mays, *The Negro God* (New York: Atheneum, 1968); and James Cone, *The Spirituals and the Blues* (New York: Seabury Press, 1972), for classic discussions.

12. See Mechal Sobel, *Trabelin' On: The Slave Journey to an Afro-Baptist Faith* (Westport, Conn.: Greenwood Press, 1979):pt. 1, for development of this appellation and concept.

13. Ibid.; also, Albert J. Raboteau, *Slave Religion* (New York: Oxford University Press, 1978):3–92.

14. Gayraud S. Wilmore, *Black Religion and Black Radicalism* 2d ed. (Maryknoll, N.Y.: Orbis

Books, 1983):4–28.

15. Will B. Gravely, "The Rise of African Churches in America (1786–1822): Re-examining the Contexts," *The Journal of Religious Thought* 41, no. 1 (Spring-Summer 1984):58–73, especially 59–68.

16. Peter Paris, *The Social Teachings of the Black Churches* (Philadelphia: Fortress, 1985):10ff.

17. Paris focuses on National Baptists and the African Methodist Episcopal Church. Cf. xi.

18. Paris, 13.

19. Ibid., 51.

20. Gravely, 60ff.

21. Wilmore, 220–41.

22. Paris, 42–52.

23. See Joseph Washington, *Black Religion: The Negro and Christianity in the United States* (Boston: Beacon Press, 1964).

24. No more than Albert Cleage should be considered a loner in his critique of white Christianity and bold claims about the origins of Christianity.

25. Gravely, 68. Some criticism of and reshaping of inherited confessional frameworks is documented here, but not enough to affect the thrust of this writer's argument. Cf. also Gravely's summary statement on the matter, p. 69.

26. An example would be the difficulty Martin Luther King, Jr., encountered in getting the African American churches to lend consistent and sustained support to the civil rights activities of which he, a cleric himself, was principle spokesperson. See Aldon D. Morris, *The Origins of the Civil Rights Movement: Black Communities Organizing for Change* (New York: Free Press, 1984):11. Morris makes the point that despite the fact that the African American churches played a significant role in the civil rights struggles, they did so primarily through the charisma, authority, and freedom of individual clerics and some clerical associations. The national church bodies themselves never provided the type of official sponsorship so desperately needed for the struggle.

27. See Wayne Meeks, *The First Urban Christians: The Social World of the Apostle Paul* (New Haven: Yale University Press, 1983), for a good discussion on the social functions of rituals and certain beliefs among the Pauline Christians. The discussion draws on sociological and anthropological studies which make the conclusions relevant for contemporary Afro-Christianity.

28. Krentz, 16ff.

29. David H. Kelsey, *The Uses of Scripture in Recent Theology* (Philadelphia: Fortress, 1975):197–204; a very provocative book, but flawed on account of its complete lack of reference to the use of the Bible in the African American communities!

30. Ibid., 198.

31. Krister Stendahl, "The Bible as a Classic and the Bible as Holy Scripture," *Journal of Biblical Literature* 103, no. 1 (March 1984), 3–10.

32. Ibid., 5.

33. Ibid., 8.

34. See note 6.

35. Kelsey, 198–99.

36. Kelsey, 199; Stendahl, 9–10.

37. Allen Verhey, *The Great Reversal: Ethics and the New Testament* (Grand Rapids, Mich.: William B. Eerdmans Publishing Company, 1984):176–78.

38. J. McDowell Richards, ed., *In Soli Deo Gloria: Essays in Honor of William Childs Robinson.* (Richmond, 1968):88–110.

39. Dennis Ronald MacDonald, *The Legend and the Apostle: The Battle for Paul in Story and Canon* (Philadelphia: Westminster Press, 1983).

40. This proposal is for communal, not individualistic, biblical interpretation. The challenge is for African American biblical scholars, theologians, and church leaders to lead the way.

10

The Bible, Re-Contextualization and the Black Religious Experience

Cain H. Felder

When cast in its broadest application, "the Black religious experience" extends well beyond the parameters of the African American religious experience. The connotative sense of the Black religious experience is simply the religion of those persons whose parentage, self-understanding, and/or physical features fall within the Black (Negroid/Africoid) race. There is an astonishing diversity of religious beliefs and practices in the history of Black people around the globe. This religious experience includes the religions of ancient Africa (Cush, Punt, and to some extent, ancient Egypt). Black adaptations of Hebrew, Jewish, Christian and Islamic beliefs and rituals, not to mention Traditional African Religions and numerous derivatives (e.g., Candomble, Garifuna, Shango and Vodun) found in the Black diaspora. Despite this variety, the Black religious experience also has denotative coherence that distinguishes it from the religious experience of other racial groups. The Black religious experience typically considers the supernatural as a mere extension of the natural order.[1] It seeks harmony with (not dominance over) nature, reveres ancestors, rejoices in rhythm, and takes both spirituality and the afterlife seriously.[2] But, the impact of slavery, colonialism, and racism in the oppression of Black people gives further particularity to the Black religious experience as a designation for African Americans, especially those who represent the Black Church tradition in the United States of America.

As is well known, the Bible has come to occupy a central place in religions of the Black diaspora. Whether in slave religion or independent Black churches of the Americas and Caribbean, biblical stories, themes, personalities and images have inspired, captivated, given meaning, and served as a basis of hope for a liberated and thus enhanced material life. They have enriched the prospects for a glorious afterlife as well. Latta Thomas rightly observes that Blacks identified with daring heroes of the faith and perceived that the God who empowered those heroes would likewise empower them.[3] Thomas thinks principally of Black Christians, but his comments could apply to Black Hebrews, Jews, or even many Black Muslims who attach great significance to the Bible, particularly the revealed Law, Old Testament prophetic visions, communal solidarity motifs and biblical mandates for love, mercy, and justice. Even beyond the confines of African American religion, Black people are fundamentally people of "the Book." To affirm this centrality is not to suggest, however, that the Bible attains such stature as the result of efforts by Blacks to conduct systematic critical analysis of biblical texts. The fact is that in Africa and in the Black Western diaspora, the apparatus of the historical critical methods for biblical analysis and hermeneutics is still in a nascent stage.[4] Vincent Wimbush reminds us that for well over fifteen hundred years, the Bible was not so much analyzed critically, but confessed dogmatically through doctrinalist, moralist, and pietistic prisms and that the critical analysis of the Bible by trained exegetes is a phenomenon scarcely two centuries old.[5] He further indicates that the "high Protestant" adoption of critical analysis of the biblical text was a by-product of the new consciousness among the literate bourgeois classes of Europe and America that usually excluded Blacks:

> Since most of the earliest African American Christians had been denied, from the beginning of their experience in the Americas, the opportunity to be fully human, including the opportunity to learn to read and write, the "letters" of biblical texts, were not crucial in their appropriation and redaction of Christian traditions. What became important was the *telling* and *retelling*, the hearing and the re-hearing of biblical stories—stories of perseverance, of strength in weakness and under oppressive burdens, of hope in hopeless situations.[6]

The Black Church and others within Black religious traditions give allegiance to biblical faith and witness, primarily because their own experiences seem to be depicted in the Bible. Many of the biblical stories reflect the existential reality of the Black story for the last few centuries in an environment typically hostile to the interests of Blacks attaining their full sense of human potential. Blacks have become all too familiar with being oppressed by socioeconomic forces or political powers, foreign and domestic, arrayed against them. They have found in the Bible ancient symbols of their predicament, namely the saga of the Egyptian bondage, the devastation of Assyrian invasions, the exportation into Babylonian captivity and the bedevilment by principalities and powers of the present age. Blacks have consequently developed an experiential sympathy with much of the biblical witness to which they in turn give reverent attention as quite literally the revealed word of God.

Mindful of what *has been* the relationship between the Bible and the Black religious experience, we are at the juncture in history where new questions must be posed. We must ask what observations about this relationship have been made by other scholarly disciplines? What is emerging now from those other disciplines and how do conclusions from such research impinge on what *should* or *shall be* the relationship between the Bible and the Black religious experience? Hints at answers have appeared in the literature of Black intellectuals and scholars of religion especially since the turn of the present century. Many of these hints have gone unnoticed or have remained undeveloped, because neither Euro-American academics nor the mainstream publishing world found much that was either marketable within or acceptable to the dominant racial groups. The irony of this is clear. Too often the results of serious Black scholarship and research have only limited means of mass distribution; and the marks of oppression restrict a Black readership which is scarcely in a position to purchase, study, and otherwise benefit from that kind of research. Nevertheless Black scholars have offered hints for decades.

In 1900 Henry Sylvester Williams, a Trinidadian lawyer, organized the first Pan-African conference in London.[7] Later W. E. B. DuBois displayed relentless efforts on behalf of the Pan-African Congress.[8] Researchers have traced other developments in the Black nationalism of Marcus Garvey, the Rastafarian critique of the West, and a renewed focus upon the centrality of Africa in clarifying the foundations for African American cultural consciousness.[9] Then, too, there are the writings of William Leo Hansberry of Howard University, such as *The African Presence in Asia: Africans and Their History*; *Pillars in Ethiopian History* and his most recent *Africa and Africans as Seen by Classical Writers*; or Chancellor William's *The Destruction of Black Civilization*; George G. M. James's *Stolen Legacy*; and Cheikh Anta Diop's *The African Origin of Civilization*. Even the extensive, if controversial, research by Yosef

Ben-Jochannan, notably, *The Black Man's Religion*, belongs to this surprisingly large body of literature, albeit often suppressed and scorned by almost all of American higher education, that points to Africa again and again as the *crux interpretum* for the Black experience, and in many respects, the *home* of the Black religious experience.

Within the past few decades, Black theologians and Black scholars of religion appear to be turning revitalized attention to Africa. Professor Charles Long has repeatedly stressed the importance of aspects of African religions for a proper analysis and understanding of the Black religious experience.[10] Similarly Gayraud Wilmore, in his provocative volume *Black Religion and Black Radicalism*, speaks of "the creative residuum of African religions" as contributing "an essential ingredient of black Christianity prior to the Civil War."[11] I welcome Wilmore's call for more scholarly interest in "the church in ancient Ethiopia and Nubia."[12] James Cone (*For My People*) stresses the importance of the relationship between Africa and Black religion in the United States, finding himself regularly adopting the nomenclature of "African American churches" as a substitute expression for American Black churches.[13] Professor J. Deotis Roberts in *Black Theology Today* goes as far as calling for a new consciousness that would be informed by an African Black metaphysic.[14]

From all this, two things become clear. First, Black writers with increasing sharpness recognize the total inadequacy and racial tendentiousness of the West's intellectual tradition in its endeavors to provide allegedly universal conceptual and religious norms. In this respect, Cornel West's *Prophesy Deliverance* is an invaluable resource for tracing the implicit racist tendencies of the philosophical "giants" in Europe since the Enlightenment.[15] The implication is that, whatever one may wish to say about the Bible, there is a need for a disciplined skepticism regarding its Western appropriations. Second, many Black writers and scholars of religion, in turning their sights to Africa, are demonstrating that what Michel Foucault decries as an "insurrection of subjugated knowledges" may be applied to the quest for the Bible's future meaning in the Black religious experience.[16] Evidently that quest must be conducted in a new dialogue and solidarity with Africa and this of necessity means that Blacks must redouble their efforts in this "insurrection of subjugated knowledges."

At the heart of this instruction is an awareness of the centrality of Scripture in Black liberation. The future meaning of the Bible for this new scholarship requires first an international "African identity;" second, a new skepticism regarding prevailing Eurocentric exegesis, hermeneutics and historiography; and third, a renewed commitment to the New Testament vision of liberation as a self-perpetuating process. Each of these requirements involves a continuing self-critique and the establishment of a shared power for creating the beloved community not only among Blacks, but among all people.

The Dawn of the Black Religious Experience

Recent archaeological discoveries at Cemetery L in Qustal of Upper Egypt indicate that Nubian Pharaohs ruled six or seven generations before the First Egyptian Dynasty.[17] As Bruce Williams reports, this find revolutionizes our perceptions about ancient Egypt and its relation to other parts of Africa:

> The place is ancient Nubia at Qustul, where the investigation of archaeological materials recovered during the great 1960s rescue effort (an international team effort in 1962 to save the ancient remains threatened by the rising waters of the Aswan Dam) has recently unveiled a birth place of pharaonic civilization several generations before the first historic Egyptian dynasty. This finding is rendered all the more startling by the fact that advanced political organization was not believed to have come to Nubia, or anywhere south of Egypt for another 2,500 years.[18]

Heretofore, the dominant opinions of European scholars have been that the high culture of ancient Egypt derived from cultural sources outside of Africa and that such traces of Egyptian culture found elsewhere in Africa are of Egyptian origin. European and American scholars alike therefore have tended to prefer the Greek geographer Strabo (64 B.C.–A.D. 22), who believed that Egyptians settled ancient Ethiopia, rather than the opposite view taken by the Greek historian Herodotus (Cicero's "Father of History"). Herodotus's expeditions in Egypt are dated 460–455 B.C.[19]

Professor Robert Bennett calls this perspective, that the ancient Egyptians originate from peoples outside of Black Africa, "insidious racism." He attributes the classical formulation of the perspective to C. O. Seligman (*Races of Africa and Negro Africa*).[20] Bennett notes that other Western scholars like Merrick Posnansky have contested the Seligman thesis and have suggested that Nubia and Egypt influenced each other. We may go further and point out that as early as the late eighteenth century Count Constantin de Volney (1757–1820) insisted that "the ancient Egyptians were true Negroes of the same type as all native-born Africans."²¹ Despite Count de Volney and other dissenters, most Western Egyptologists have had great difficulty believing that ancient Egypt originated in Black Africa.

With the 1962 archaeological discoveries at Qustul, Upper Nubia, we now have strong evidence that ancient Egyptian civilization was prefigured and shaped by developments to the south in Nubia. This shed light on Isa. 11:11 where a threefold division of Egypt is evident even in exilic or post-exilic times: "In that day the Lord will extend his hand yet a second time to recover the remnant which is left of his people, from Assyria, from Egypt (Misraim = Lower Egypt), from Pathros (Upper Egypt), and from Ethiopia (Cush = Nubia), from Elam, from Shinar, from Hamath, and from the coastlands of the sea."²² While this attestation cannot be regarded as a scientific geographical fact, it does confirm other more ancient evidence that an integral relationship existed between Black Africa and ancient Egypt and that this was known well after the demise of the Pharaohs.

According to the historian, William Leo Hansberry, three ancient African territories constitute the geographical contexts for the emergence of Black religious experience. These are the land of Qevs (Kesh/Cush) or Ethiopia proper, the land of Punt or Greater Ethiopia, and Egypt.²³ Millennia before the earliest Hebrews or Christians, the Black religious experience flourished among the people of Cush and Punt. In fact, a fourth dynasty Egyptian text (2620–2480 B.C.) refers to Punt as "the end of the world," beyond it is "the land of the spirits."²⁴ Many Pharaohs treated Punt as a kind of holy land and also considered Punt to be the birthplace of the Egyptians as well as the original homeland of many Egyptian gods.²⁵ The recent discoveries at Cemetery L at the present day border of Egypt and the Sudan suggest that cultural and religious influence from Black Africa shaped the formative years of ancient Egyptian civilization. Thus it is likely that the extraordinary variety of local gods associated with independent tribal cults of Egypt more than 1,500 years before Akhenaton's monotheistic revolution (1375–1358 B.C.) have their antecedents in other parts of Africa.²⁶

Of course it is one thing to argue that *Black* Africa exerted cultural and religious influence upon ancient Egypt disproportionate to such possible influences from other parts of the world. It is an entirely different matter to argue that the ancient Egyptians were, for the most part, a *Black* people. Perhaps the best known African Egyptologist who argues extensively for the Negroid identity of the Egyptian Pharaohs is Cheikh Anta Diop who published his dissertation, completed at the University of Paris, on this subject. According to Diop, the Western world has falsified history with respect to the racial type of the ancient Egyptians. He argues that the West *invented* a hypothetical white Pharaonic race that imported Egyptian civilization from Asia.[27] In his view, Egyptian civilization originated in Africa and the indigenous Pharaohs of Egypt were Black Africans.[28] Diop draws upon archaeological, anthropological, linguistic, and other kinds of evidence to show parallels between the ancient Egyptians and Blacks from other parts of Africa. Particularly striking are the comparative photographic reliefs that indicate the similarities as evident between Pharaoh Ramses II and the physical features, together with the hairstyle, of a modern Watusi warrior.[29] If the resemblace is more than coincidence, it could mean that this Pharaoh, traditionally associated with Moses and the Exodus, was indeed a Black African.

But whether or not we conclude that the Pharaohs were Black, there is considerable information about the ancient Egyptian religious experience to connect it with the continent of Africa. Excellent examples are found in The Egyptian Book of the Dead, the Pyramid Texts, and the Coffin Texts.[30] These writings provide details about an elaborate henotheistic system of religious belief and practice. Clearly the ancient Egyptians believed in a Supreme Being, the Creator and *neter*; they also believed in the existence of other gods, including great cosmic powers and finite divine beings with supernatural powers.[31] The Egyptians had a sophisticated doctrine of salvation, concepts of the afterlife and a long-standing belief in the resurrection. The considerable impact which the Egyptian mystery system had upon shaping the mystery religions of the Greco-Roman world, though frequently minimized by Eurocentric scholars, is nevertheless very clear.[32] Doubtless the basis of the pharisaic notion of the resurrection derives from Egyptian teachings.

Blacks in the Judeo-Christian Tradition

Millennia prior to Jesus of Nazareth, there was sustained intermingling of Cushites and Egyptians. Indeed, as Professor Ephraim Isaac and I attempt to show, on linguistic, epigraphic and historical grounds in chapter three of my book *Troubling Biblical Waters*,[33] there was not just *one* land of Cush, but two; one south of Egypt and the other across the Red Sea, including the Arabian peninsula but extending toward the Mesopotamian (Tigris and Euphrates

Rivers) basin.[34] References to two different groups of Cushim may be in the table of nations in Gen. 10 and further mentioned from the eighth to the second centuries B.C. in writings from Homer to Strabo. Such material lends credence to Cheikh Anta Diop's observation that thousands of years ago Blacks were established in civilizations that spanned territories from the Nile to the Mesopotamian fertile crescent.[35]

Despite the reluctance of Euro-American or Ashkenazic Jewish scholars of the Bible to attribute much significance to explicit references or allusions to Blacks in the Old Testament, such mentions are instructive. There is an impressive array of Black people found in the Old Testament, beginning with those in Gen. 9 and 10, or 1 Chron. 1; Hagar's Egyptian origin in Gen. 16; the Cushite wife of Moses in Num. 12, Jer. 38–39, Isa. 37; perhaps even Zephaniah, the Son of Cushi (Zeph. 1:1; qv. 2:12; 3:10) and the Queen of Sheba (1 Kings 10; 1 Chron. 9)[36]; Aaron's grandson, regarded as ancestor of the Zadokite priesthood (Exod. 6:25, Num. 25:6, Ps. 106:30); one of the sons of Eli (1 Sam. 1:3; 2:34); and the Egyptian name Phienehas, literally meaning the Nubian.[37] Many of these passages attest to the greatness and power of Blacks in Africa and as participants within the salvation drama (*die Heilsgeschichte*) of ancient Israel. That modern Eurocentric scholars have so much difficulty acknowledging the existence of Black Jews in the biblical period before Jesus Christ has always struck me as truly incredible. The critical point, however, is not that Blacks are an integral part of the Old Testament witness, but that if one considers the Hebrew Exodus Story as in some sense a historical event, we have to reckon with the fact that these *liberated* Hebrews were themselves most probably a racially mixed stock of people, Afroasiatics. In our modern period such observations might seem startling to some, but this long-neglected aspect of the Old Testament is important in tracing the relevance of a new international African identity, even as such an identity is informed by the New Testament.

Let us now acknowledge some direct ways in which the New Testament mentions or otherwise highlights the Black religious experience. First, the New Testament presents us with two Black queens: "the Queen of the South" (*basilissa notou*) is mentioned in the Q source material of Matt. 12:42 and Luke 11:21; and the *Kandake*, Queen of Meroe, capital of Nubia or Northern Ethiopia in biblical times, receives notice in Acts 8:27. We should point out that the nomenclature "Queen of the South" is an early New Testament reference to the Queen of Sheba. In the New Testament she has become an eschatological figure who, in this saying of Jesus, will at the final judgment rise up and condemn the faithlessness of Israel. It is revealing that the New Testament merely called her "Queen of the South," omitting any reference to the land of Sheba, for the same omission is found in Josephus's extensive account about this person to whom he refers as "the Queen of Egypt and Ethiopia."[38] One also notes that both Origen and later Jerome considered this Queen to be a *Black* African.[39] Such testimonies lend credence to the view that the Queen of Sheba was a Cushite, a Black royal personage whom even Jesus could recast as an eschatological sign against those among his Jewish contemporaries whom He chastised as being "a faithless generation."

The second queen in the New Testament is also a Black Cushite, the Queen of Meroe. Luke refers to her as part of his narrative development in Acts 8 which depicts the gospel moving away from Jerusalem (cf. Acts 1:8), first to the Samaritan north (Acts 8:5–25) and then to the Ethiopian south (Acts 8:26–40). The pattern is an elaborated re-presentation of Luke 13:29 wherein Luke amends the Q saying about those who will come and sit at Abraham's table as found in Matthew 8:11–12 by adding "north and south." Luke is consciously more inclusive; he records, in a manner consistent with his intentional universalism, the expanding witness of the gospel as *definitely* including the south, i.e., Ethiopia and Egypt.[40] It may well be that the two queens of the New Testament are quiet reminders not only of the ancient glory of Africa, but also of the way in which ancient African rulers sought to affirm the wisdom of Solomon in order to become beneficiaries of the Holy Spirit. How appropriate it is to find the Ethiopian God-fearer in Acts 8:32–33 reading about the Suffering Servant of Isaiah 53:7–8 who "in his humiliation justice was denied him." His text in recent centuries has become *the story* of Black people in the West.

A few remarks about the conversion of the Ethiopian finance minister (Acts 8:26–40) are in order. Eurocentric New Testament scholars have been perplexed at times by this episode that may suggest the Hellenist mission was responsible for bringing Christianity to Ethiopia in the first century. The usual tendency on the part of such exegetes is to deny the historical reliability of this tradition in Acts, despite the fact that the same skepticism is not shown toward the conversion of Cornelius, the Italian, in Acts 10. Ernst Haenchen, however, struggles to be balanced by saying that Luke intentionally leaves the Ethiopian's status as Jew or Gentile God-fearer ambiguous; the Ethiopian is thus "a stepping stone between . . . the Samaritans and the Gentiles."[41]

Haenchen also suggests that the story of the Ethiopian eunuch is the Hellenistic parallel to the Hebrew Christian mission story of Cornelius's conversion by Peter—"its parallel and rival."[42] Martin Hengel is surprisingly more bold in asserting, without reservation, that the Ethiopian minister is a Gentile God-fearer who is not only converted, but becomes the bearer of the gospel to the extreme southern boundary of the known inhabited world, Ethiopia (that is, Africa in general as "Ethiopia" was then understood).[43]

Next we consider an aspect of the Matthean Infancy Narrative—the episode called "the flight into Egypt" (Matthew 2:13–22) in the midst of which is the often-quoted Old Testament passage of Hos. 11:1, "Out of Egypt, I have called my son." One could transpose the thought slightly but no less accurately and say, "Out of Africa, I have called my son." Unfortunately, such a change startles many Anglo-Saxons today, since the Eurocentric view creates a "Middle East", a non-Black Egypt, even a non-Black Ethiopia. In any case, more so in antiquity than even today, Egypt was intimately (culturally, linguistically, and racially) a part of Black Africa. When one thinks of the liberated Hebrew slaves as the corporate slave/son called out of bondage only to reimpose bondage on one another, we have a basis for contrasting that son with the New Testament Son also called out of Africa. For Matthew at least, it was a suffering servant king whose righteousness through commitment, struggle, and liberating activity made him also the Messiah, and by theological metaphor, *Black Messiah* and Son of God, as recently suggested respectively by James Cone and Allan Boesak.[44] Yet, not only does the Eurocentric domination of biblical interpretation tend to deny the African identity of the place *whence* the Son was called, but it also shows little understanding of what *kind* of new suffering "slave/servant" (*doulos*) was called, and on what basis he became King and liberator of the oppressed, and through them—of all humankind.

Contextualization and Re-Contextualization

The term "contextualization" would seem to describe precisely the biblical revolution that Professor Onwu of the University of Nigeria sets forth in his survey of biblical studies in part of Africa today. What he describes is in itself an example of the "insurrection of subjugated knowledges" that opens the way for Western-trained Africans, on the basis of insights from their traditional worldviews, to challenge the Eurocentric hegemony of modern biblical exegesis and interpretation. Unlike the apologetic rationalizations found in John Mbiti's effort to legitimate the African worldview, Onwu shows that Africans today are presupposing the legitimacy of the worldview of African Traditional Religions, but interrogating the Bible and its Western interpreters regarding the *latter's* legitimacy among Africans.[45] Whereas Mbiti wants to show the West the "weaknesses" of African Traditional Religions in relationship to Judaism and European Christianity, Onwu, Owolalu and Ikenga-Methu in Africa, and Wilmore, Roberts, Cone and other African American scholars in the United States desire to lay stress upon their strengths and draw implications therefrom.

I prefer to speak in terms of "re-contextualization." This term, rather than an uncritical return to African tribal religions, or romanticizing the African worldview, refers to a process of rediscovering some essential features of the Black religious experience in Africa, including, but not limited to African Traditional Religions, and in so doing to enter a new dialogue of liberation and spirituality as found in the Bible. It is this kind of process that will lend unity and new coherence to the future of the Black religious experience in direct relation to the Bible, particularly the New Testatment.

In two recent books, James H. Cone, *For My People: Black Theology and the Black Church*, and Robert McAfee Brown, *Unexpected News: Reading the Bible Through Third World Eyes*, remind us of Karl Barth's re-encounter with the biblical text years ago.[46] Barth spoke of "the strange new world within the Bible," and indeed there is always, for the privileged and powerful, a "strange" world in the Bible. However for many others the Bible, particularly the New Testament, depicts a world which in its radicalism is not strange at all. The process of "re-contextualization" helps us gain access to this brave new world. It is a world which, frankly, was rather favorably predisposed to Black people. As evidence consider only Acts 12:1, where Luke mentions among the prophets and teachers of Antioch Simeon, who was called *Niger* (i.e., "the Black man") in an apparent Latinism. It was a world that was indebted to the Egyptian doctrine of salvation, taking seriously the glorious afterlife (1 Cor. 15:12−58; Phil. 3:12−16).[47]

Implicit in the specter of the glorious afterlife in the New Testament is an invitation to a radical metaphysic that, on the one hand, Paul (Rom. 12:1−2) no less than Matthew (11:28−30) or James (1:26−27, 3:13−18) extends so that people of the faith might be *transformed, yoked together* and *unstained* by gross materialism and false wisdom that subjugates true knowledge. This radical metaphysic is really not an individualistic or interiorized spirituality only for "the other world"; it has first and foremost to do with the international collective solidarity of the *oikos tou theou* ("the household of God") and the *koinonia*—understanding within this world even as it anticipates the greater solidarity in the next world.[48] The glorious afterlife is integral to an apocalyptic metaphysical faith-stance; moreover, this faith-stance in the ancient New Testament brave new world is *always* directed to the other, especially the oppressed other, the brother or sister who is so determined on the basis of one's own faith and not necessarily merely by blood kinship (Matt. 12:50; Gal. 6:10; Phil. 2:5–9; James 2:14–17). In this first part of our concluding emphasis on "re-contextualization," I am suggesting that in the New Testament the afterlife/resurrection does not just point to an ethereal "new life" on the other side, it points also back to an empowered new life in *this world*, wherein one's own self-interest is defined in direct relation to the welfare of the socioeconomically *and* spiritually *oppressed* other (Phil. 2:3). In the Greek New Testament, the word "oppress" is rendered in terms of *thrauo*, i.e., "to pull down" as in Luke 4:18, which derives from the Septuagint (LXX) Isa. 58:6. As with another Greek word meaning "oppress"/press down" (i.e., *katadunasteuo*, for example, in James 2:6b) *thrauo* carries the sense of socioeconomic or political abuse. However, *katadunasteuo* in the New Testament had another usage as it also refers to "being overwhelmed" or "oppressed" by evil spirits/ forces (as in Acts 10:38). This New Testament intersection between the historical and supra-historical has affinity with an aspect of the ancient African worldview and evidently survives to some extent in African Traditional Religions. It runs contrary, however, to Western this-worldly exploitation and the ideologies of racism, capitalism, neo-colonialism and class stratification so often tacitly sanctioned by the institutional church. Clearly, there is a lesson *from* Africa here, but there is also a lesson *for* Africans who lack a metaphysic of international solidarity and often fail to acknowledge an appreciation of the scriptural mandate to place a priority on the welfare of the oppressed other in their midst.

The second part of our conclusion regarding re-contextualization centers on the way in which "the brave new world" of the New Testament demonstrates an interest in *solidarity* and *power* through the *oikoi tou theou*, building upon but going beyond the African concern for extended families. Consider, for example, Paul's collection for "the poor among the saints of Jerusalem" (2 Cor. 8, 9; Rom. 15:25–29; Gal. 2:19); in a word, Paul in this understanding gives concrete practical expression to the principle that "the strong" should help "the weak," not only in matters of faith but also in economic power (2 Cor. 8, 9; Rom. 14, 15). In 2 Cor. 8:14, Paul is quite explicit about the necessity of those households/communities with an abundance supplying the needs of those that face scarcity; he sees this explicity as a matter of fairness and "economic justice" (*isotes*).

The redistribution and sharing of economic power is implicit in the African traditional concern for the extended family. Conversely, in modern Western society, the focus is usually upon the nuclear family, irrespective of Bible or church teachings—Protestant, Orthodox or Roman Catholic. Again there are lessons *from* Africa, even as the new world of the New Testament goes beyond the African perspective. In addition there are lessons *for* Africa today where we are appalled by the Western individualism and materialism embraced by the African elite who hoard luxury goods and otherwise contribute to the disintegration of the extended family and the nation-states struggling to their feet from colonialism.

This leads to our third and final reflection upon re-contextualization in the New Testament. The aim again is to construct an agenda for the future of the Black religious experience. It is at this juncture that one can best speak about Jesus, the suffering slave king whose very *life* was the embodiment of *agape* and whose every *action* gave liberation its meaning and practical application. Although he foresaw the cross, he saw beyond it the resurrection that pointed to *new life*, first as it unfolded around him in his ministry and second as a continuous process of training for his disciples and followers who would be the future leadership for the church. Now, re-contextualization means self-perpetuating liberation and the perpetual self-critique of those who would lead in the process.

By contrast, there is the Egyptian Pharaoh of the Old Testament Exodus Saga; though probably black in skin color, he oppresses the racially mixed Hebrew children of God. In that context of oppression, the Hebrews of Egypt are indeed "the children of God." Yet, despite deliverance, a revealed law, Promised Land, nationhood, and periods of glorious prosperity, "the children of God" enslaved one another, forgot and neglected the substantive moral dictates of Law, experienced slavery again, were delivered, developed a Temple-fixation ("an edifice complex"), fenced in the compassion inherent in the Torah and separated themselves either in ascetic withdrawal (Qumran), militant nationalist death squads (Sicarrii, Zealots), or in the pietism of peaceful coexistence (post-A.D. 70 Rabbinic Judaism). Here we have one portrait of what can happen to the oppressed once they are liberated. Forgetting the substance of their actual roots, they become condemned to repeat socioeconomically and spiritually the horrors of their past. So today Israel has become for the Palestinians the New Pharaoh and paradoxically enough, we have come full circle. Surely in this, there are lessons *from* Africans and for Africans.

Lest I be accused of "anti-Jewishness" (an expression more accurate than "anti-Semitism," remembering that today the Palestinians are far more Semitic racially than the politically dominant Ashkenazic Jews of Israel), Christianity, in its Western captivity, also basks in a strong triumphalism which has little or no future in the world of the twenty-first century. The suffering slave-king and his liberating activity, as pictured in the New Testament, is substantially absent from contemporary Euro-American Christianity. Commercial American popular Christianity scarcely mentions, or otherwise identifies with, a liberating slave-messiah for the oppressed!

Re-contextualization, therefore, shapes an agenda of Black *agape* within the international African community as the vanguard of "the beloved Black community" thereby becoming a paradigm for the inclusion and participation of all humankind in the coming realm of God. However what seems to be crucial is that we envision liberation as a *continual process*, virtually a "permanent revolution," with a perpetual and insitutionalized self-critique built into its leadership style. It would appear that this is where "the victorious parties" of the triumphalistic church failed. When their version of Christianity became acceptable to the political establishment, even a status symbol, it lost its affinity with the *zeitgeist* of the early New Testament apocalyptic tradition. Consequently, that tradition did indeed become a "strange new world." Its radicality evaporated and the voice of the ideologically triumphant church became "a noisy gong and a clanging cymbal" (1 Cor. 13:1). Yet the Bible still seeks to infuse new meaning into a Black religious experience that refuses to be separated from its rich past. Our challenge today is to rediscover the ways in which the Scriptures impel us toward a new international identity, a re-conceptualization of the message of the Bible, and a Black *agape*—all of which represents the future brightness of the religious experience of African and African American people.

Notes

1. John S. Mbiti, *African Religions and Philosophies* (New York: Doubleday and Co., 1970):62–76; Gayraud S. Wilmore, *Black Religion and Black Radicalism* (Maryknoll, N.Y.: Orbis Books, 1983):15–19.

2. Mbiti, 135–42, 208–16, and 257–65; Aylward Shorter, *African Christian Spirituality*, U.S. edition (Maryknoll, N.Y.: Orbis Books, 1980):15–19.

3. Latta Thomas, *Biblical Faith and the Black American* (Valley Forge, Penn.: Judson Press, 1976):18.

4. See survey by N. Onwu, "The Current State of Biblical Studies in Africa" *The Journal of Religious Thought* 42, no. 2 (Fall-Winter 1984–85):35–46.

5. Vincent Wimbush, "Biblical-Historical Study a Liberation: Toward an Afro-Christian Hermeneutic," *The Journal of Religious Thought* 42, no. 2 (Fall-Winter 1984–85):10.

6. Ibid., 10–11.

7. W. E. B. Dubois, *The Seventh Son*, vol. 1, Julius Lester ed. (New York: Random House, 1971):78.

8. Ibid., 83.

9. See: Amy Jacques-Garvey, ed., *Philosophy and Opinions of Marcus Garvey*, 2 vols. (New York: Atheneum, 1969); and E. David Cronon, *Black Moses: The Story of Marcus Garvey* (Madison, Wisc.: The University of Wisconsin Press, 1969). Also Leonard Barrett, *The Rastafarians: Sounds of Cultural Dissonance* (Boston: Beacon Press, 1977).

10. Charles H. Long, "Perspectives of a Study of Afro-American Religion in the United States," *History of Religions* 2, no. 1 (August 1971):54–66 as cited by James H. Cone, *For My People* (Maryknoll, N.Y.: Orbis Books, 1984):p 26.

11. Wilmore, 26.

12. Ibid., 235.

13. James H. Cone, 83; cf. pp. 61–62, 72 and seriatim, chaps. 7 and 8.

14. J. Deotis Roberts, *Black Theology Today: Liberation and Contextualization* (New York and Toronto: Edwin Mellen Press, 1984):179–87.

15. Cornel West, *Prophesy Deliverance* (Philadelphia: Westminster Press, 1982):47–65.

16. Michel Foucault, *Power/Knowledge: Selected Interviews and other Writings*, ed. Colin Gordon (New York: Pantheon, 1980) cited by Lewis S. Mudge in *Theological Education* (Spring 1984):43–54.

17. Bruce Williams, "Lost Pharoahs of Nubia" in *Nile Valley Civilizations* (Proceedings of the Nile Valley Conference, Atlanta, Ga., Sept. 26–30, 1984) Ivan Van Sertima, ed. *Journal of African Civilizations*, Ltd. (1985, p. 35 [Reprinted from *Archeology Magazine*, 33, no. 5, 1980]).

18. Williams, 29, 31.

19. *Histoire universelle*, trans. Abbe Terrason (Paris, 1758), Bk. 3, p. 341 cited by Cheikh Anta Diop, *The African Origin of Civilization: Myth or Reality?* trans. Mercer Cook (New York and Westport: Lawrence Hill and Company 1974 [1955]):2, 278. Further on Herodotus and Strabo see: Brian M. Fagan, *Tomb Robbers, Tourists and Archeologists in Egypt* (New York: Charles

Scribner's Sons, 1975):14–31.

20. Robert A. Bennett, Jr. "Africa and the Biblical Period," *Harvard Theological Review* 64 (1971):483.

21. Diop, 27.

22. See R. A. Bennett, 489. On the dating of Isa. 11:11, see Otto Kaiser, *Isaiah 1–12F: A commentary*, 2nd ed. (Philadelphia: Westminster Press, 1983):264; Raymond E. Brow, Joseph A. Fitzmyer and Roland Murphy, eds., *The Jerome Biblical Commentary* (Englewood Cliffs, N.J.: Prentice-Hall, Inc., 1968):273; Matthew Black, ed., *Peake's Commentary on Bible* (London: Thomas Nelson and Sons Ltd., 1962):499.

23. William Leo Hansberry, *Africa and Africans as Seen by Classical Writers*, ed. Joseph E. Harris (Washington, D.C.: Howard University Press, 1977):9–13.

24. A conservative dating of the IV Dynasty is given by Sir Alan Gardiner, *Egypt of the Pharaohs* (New York: Oxford University Press, 1974 [1961]):434. Cf. Sergew Hable Sellassie, *Ancient and Medieval Ethiopian History to 1270* (Addis Ababa, Ethiopia, 1972):21.

25. Hansberry, 12.

26. On the variety of local deities in Egypt, see Gardiner, 214–16. For the significance of Akhenaton's revolution in relation to the Bible, see Donald B. Redford, "The Monotheism of the Heretic Pharaoh: Monotheism or Egyptian Anomaly?" *Biblical Archaeology Review* 13, no. 3 (May/June 1987):16–32.

27. Diop, 43.

28. Ibid., 78.

29. Ibid., 19.

30. E. A. Wallis Budge, *The Egyptian Book of the Dead* (New York: Dover Publications, 1967): *Osiris and the Egyptian Resurrection*, 2 vol. (1973).

31. Budge, lxxxii–lxxxiii.

32. See George G. M. James, *Stolen Legacy* (New York: Philosophical Library, 1954. Reprint. San Francisco: Julian Richardson Associates, 1976):21–24.

33. Cain H. Felder, *Troubling Biblical Waters: Race Class and Family* (Maryknoll, N.Y.: Orbis Books, 1988):chap. 2.

34. Ephraim Isaac and Cain H. Felder, "Reflections of the Origins of the Ethiopian Civilization," (prepared for the International Congress of Ethiopian Studies November, 1983, Addis Ababa, Ethiopia). See the extended discussion in chap. 2 as cited above.

35. Diop, 73.

36. See chap. 3 of my *Troubling Biblical Waters* (Maryknoll, N.Y.: Orbis Books, 1988). Also, my colleague, Dr. Gene Rice, Professor of Old Testament, has written on the subject: "The Curse That Never Was (Genesis 9:18–27)", *The Journal of Religious Thought* 29 (1972):5–27; "Two Black Contemporaries of Jeremiah," *The Journal of Religious Thought* 32 (1975):95–109; and "The African Roots of the Prophet Zephaniah," *The Journal of Religious Thought*, 36 (1979):21–31.

37. Rice, "The Curse", 19.

38. Flavius Josephus, *Complete Works* (Grand Rapids, Mich.: Kregel Publications 1960):180;

Antiquities, book 8, Chap. 6, 3, 5. Snowden, *Antiquity*, 334, states that Josephus was probably acquainted with some native Egyptian or Ethiopian rendition which connected the Queen of "The Arabian Kingdom" (*sic*) with Egypt and Ethiopia. More likely, however, is the observation that Josephus merely reflects contemporary Jewish exegesis of the Old Testament episode; see, Edward Ullendorf, *Ethiopia and the Bible* (London: Oxford University Press, 1968):135.

39. See Origen's commentaries in *Canticum Canticorum* 2, 367–70 and Jerome's "De Actibus Apostolorum 1" 630–707, cited in Snowden, *Antiquity*, 202–4.

40. The following observation is instructive: as a result of the expulsion of the 'Hellenist' from Jerusalem the gospel was passed on to Samaria and finally in the figure of the Ethiopian on his way home, reached out to 'the ends of the earth.' (Cf. Zeph. 3:10; Ps. 68:32; Luke 11:31). In ancient geography, Ethiopia was the extreme boundary of the inhabited world in the hot south: Martin Hengel, *Acts and the Ancient History of Earliest Christianity* (Philadelphia: Fortress Press, 1980):80.

41. Ernst Haenchen, *The Acts of the Apostles: A Commentary* (Oxford: Basil Blackwell, 1971):314.

42. Ibid., 315.

43. Hengel, *Acts*, 79–80; cf. 75. Yet, in another vein, notice the extreme hesitancy of Wolf Leslau (*Falasha Anthology: The Black Jews of Ethiopia* [New York: Schocken Books, 1951]:xliii) to admit the possibility of Black Jews in the biblical period.

44. See Cone's commentary on Albert Cleage's Black Messiah in *People*, 18–19 and further discussion of Jesus's Black identity, 65–67. Also, Allan Boesak, *Black and Reformed* (Maryknoll, N.Y.: Orbis Books, 1984):10–15.

45. Nlenanya Onwa, "The Current State of Biblical Studies in Africa," *The Journal of Religious Thought* 41, no. 2 (Fall-Winter, 1984–85). Further, Mbiti, *African Religions*, 36, 92, 128. Cf. Cone, *People*, 72–73, 227.

46. Cone, *People*, 41. Brown, *Unexpected News*, 12.

47. Not to mention the Passion Narratives of the Gospels, and the call to radical spirituality, even martyrdom, in the apocalyptic segments of the New Testament, not least Revelation.

48. Ernst Kasemann, *Perspectives on Paul* (Philadelphia: Fortress Press, 1971):q.v. "On Paul's Anthropology," 1–21. Also, J. Christiaan Beker, *Paul the Apostle: The Triumph of God* (Philadelphia: Fortress Press, 1980) and especially his *Paul's Apocalyptic Gospel: The Coming Triumph of God* (Philadelphia: Fortress Press, 1982).

Part Three

Theological and Ethical

Studies

No one knows precisely when the theological revolution called Black Theology broke out in the African American religious community. It did not come like a bolt of lightning, but like a gentle earthquake undulating across the theological landscape from 1958 to 1970, loosening subterranean connections between African American Christianity and the old evangelicalism. In the absence of a more exact dating most theologians and ethicists accept the publication of James H. Cone's first book, *Black Theology and Black Power* in 1969 as the beginning of one of the most innovative movements in the history of Christian thought in North America.[1]

Chapter eleven, by James H. Cone, begins with a quotation from African American Christian activists, working primarily in the northern cities during the civil rights period—the National Committee of Black Churchmen. This group issued the first statement on Black Theology from Atlanta on June 13, 1969.[2] Building on that definition Cone's essay reviews the history of the theme of liberation in African American religious thought, working backward from King to the earliest preacher-led slave revolts. By focusing on responses of others to challenges articulated in his early work, he indirectly presents here his own enormous contribution to contemporary Black Theology.

As the most prolific and celebrated writer in this field, Cone has produced eight books on Black liberation theology. Since 1969 he has taught at Union Theological Seminary in New York and is now the Charles A. Briggs Distinguished Professor of Systematic Theology. He is a founding member of the Society for the Study of Black Religion and the Ecumenical Association of Third World Theologians.

Perhaps Cone's most enduring contribution is the training of younger Black scholars who have taken doctoral degrees under him at Union. One of them, Jacquelyn Grant, author of chapter twelve, is Assistant Professor of Systematic Theology at the Interdenominational Theological Center in Atlanta and a leading exponent of Womanist Theology, the response of Black women theologians to Black Theology and the white Christian feminist movement.[3] This paper on Christology shows how Black women's "tridimensional reality" renovates traditional understanding of the person of Christ.

It is customary to regard theological eruptions in the Black community during the 1960s as an exclusively Protestant phenomenon. Chapter thirteen is a previously unpublished essay on the Black Roman Catholic contribution to Black Theology by M. Shawn Copeland, O.P. Copeland is an Adrian Dominican sister who formerly worked as staff for the Black Theology Project of "Theology in the Americas." She has published widely in Roman Catholic journals and presently teaches theology at Yale Divinity School.

With the exception of James H. Cone, among the several African American scholars who have published on Black Theology and its ethical implications, none has been more influential than J. Deotis Roberts, Sr., who has been a major figure in African American theological education for more than thirty years. Having been Distinguished Professor of Systematic Theology at Howard University Divinity School and president of the I.T.C. in Atlanta, Roberts now directs an independent foundation and is a member of the faculty of Eastern Baptist Theological Seminary in Philadelphia. His best known work is *Liberation and Reconciliation: A Black Theology* in which he presents a counterpoise to Cone's strong emphasis upon liberation as the central meaning of the gospel.[4]

As an experienced teacher with wide-ranging interests in African religions, the Black family, Eastern philosophy and Christian ethics, Roberts's contribution to Part Three is chapter fourteen, which roams over a broad expanse of African American intellectual history to posit the theory that the Black movement of the 1960s was based upon an ontological-existential decision to be Black and free, to take action in hope against deculturation and dehumanization.

It is not possible to include here a more representative sampling of the work African American theologians and ethicists are doing to free themselves from dependence upon Euro-American academic norms and methodologies; for example, studies in relation to Pan-Africanism, Faith and Order issues of the ecumenical movement, the social teachings of the Black churches, and the most recent work of the new African American women theologians are not included here. It is hoped, nevertheless, that these four essays from Protestant and Roman Catholic perspectives may suffice to suggest the creativity of African American religious thought during the past twenty years.[5]

Notes

1. James H. Cone, *Black Theology and Black Power* (New York: Seabury Press, 1969).

2. The full statement is in Gayraud S. Wilmore and James H. Cone, *Black Theology: A Documentary History, 1966–1979* (Maryknoll, N.Y.: Orbis Books, 1979).

3. See also, Katie G. Cannon, *Black Womanist Ethics* (Atlanta: Scholars Press, 1988).

4. J. Deotis Roberts, Sr., *Liberation and Reconciliation: A Black Theology* (Philadelphia: Westminster Press, 1971).

5. See James H. Evans, Jr., *Black Theology: A Critical Assessment and Annotated Bibliography* (New York: Greenwood Press, 1987).

11

Black Theology as Liberation Theology

James H. Cone

Black theology is a theology of liberation. It seeks to plumb the black condition in the light of God's revelation in Jesus Christ, so that the black community can see that the gospel is commensurate with the achievement of black humanity. Black theology is a theology of "blackness." It is the affirmation of black humanity that emancipates black people from white racism, thus providing authentic freedom for both white and black people. It affirms the humanity of white people in that it says no to the encroachment of white oppression. — National Committee of Black Churchmen, "Black Theology," June 13, 1969[1]

It is one thing to proclaim Black Theology and attack white churches as racist, but quite another to develop a systematic and comprehensive exposition of the Christian faith using the Black experience of struggle as the chief source. There were no Black systematic theologies that Black scholars could use as models. There were only a few Black theologians and scholars in ethics, biblical studies, religious education, and history. And most of them, like George Kelsey and Nathan Scott, Jr., were not interested in associating the Christian gospel with the Black experience. Their views were similar to those of their white teachers and colleagues who maintained that the *universal* character of the Christian faith precluded the very idea of a Black theology: it would reduce Christian theology to the *particularity* of one people.

In the absence of substantial theological texts on Black Theology and with most of the major established Black scholars remaining cool or openly rejecting such an idea, white Christians and almost all white theologians dismissed Black Theology as insubstantial. Because white theologians controlled the seminaries and university departments of religion, many Blacks had the impression that only Europeans and persons who think like them could define what theology is. In order to challenge the white monopoly on the definition of theology, many young Black scholars realized that they had to carry the fight to the seminaries where theology was being written.

Because the term "liberation" had already emerged as the chief symbol for expressing the meaning of Black freedom in politics and the churches, it was only natural that it would serve a similar function in Black Theology. In this chapter I shall examine the sources from which Black theologians and preachers derived the theme of liberation.

Black Power

Although I have discussed the impact of Black Power upon the creators of Black Theology, it may be useful to analyze the depth of their commitment to the civil rights movement and the events in it that produced such a radical change in their theological perspective.

Almost without exception (Albert Cleage being one), Black preachers and theologians had been thoroughly committed to Martin King's method of nonviolent resistance as the only way for Blacks to achieve justice in America and they were proud to go to jail with him. They were strong advocates of integration and firm believers in King's dream that the United States would soon truly become the "land of the free and the home of the brave." Like King, their hope was deeply rooted in the Declaration of Independence, the U.S. Constitution, and the Christian claim that all human beings are created to be free. They, like other Blacks, including SNCC radicals, believed that they were living in the age in which freedom would be actualized and that their children would inherit a society that would be defined by justice and equality, not by oppression and slavery.

The successful "stride toward freedom" by King and the Blacks of Montgomery in 1955–56 marked the beginning of their hopeful struggle, motivated by the 1954 U.S. Supreme Court decision on the unconstitutionality of segregated public schooling, reinforced by the sit-ins and freedom rides of the early 1960s. The high point of their hope came with the 1963 march on Washington and King's "I Have a Dream" speech. After that speech, they firmly believed that the arrival of justice in America, long-awaited by black Americans, would soon be realized.[2]

Unfortunately we did not listen to Malcolm X and his analysis of the depth of racism in American society. After the march on Washington came Selma (1965) and then Chicago (1966). When King made his move to Chicago (1966), the first major northern urban riot had already happened—in Watts (Los Angeles), August 1965. It occurred only two weeks after Lyndon Johnson's signing of the Voting Rights Act. The Watts riot and the other eruptions like it should have told Black preachers something about the inadequacy of their analysis—both in terms of the method of nonviolence and the goal of integration.

In contrast to the South, Blacks "up North" had always been able to vote and use public facilities; the riots were dramatic indications that they had nothing for which to vote and they could not afford to live outside the ghetto. The riots were shocking evidence that the oppression of Blacks was much more complex and deeply rooted than had been articulated by Martin King. Its elimination would take more than a moral appeal to ideas of freedom and equality in the American liberal tradition or the idea of love in the traditional white view of the Christian faith.

A much more radical analysis was needed if the depth of racism was to be understood, and a much more radical method of change was needed if it was to be eliminated. Although the 1965 Watts riot clearly pointed to the bankruptcy of the ideas of integration and nonviolence, Black preachers still did not read the message. They continued along the same path of trying to achieve the "beloved community" by turning the other cheek.

However when King took his nonviolent movement to Chicago and failed at almost every point, because he and Black preachers failed to analyze the complexity and depth of Northern racism, it began to dawn upon many radical Black preachers that King's approach had serious limitations. Malcolm X began to make sense to them. It was while King was struggling against Richard Daly's racist political machine that James Meredith was shot in Mississippi, "marching against fear." The shooting of Meredith once again reminded Black Americans of the deep roots of white racism. They had a long way to go before its elimination would be a fact.

In what became the last attempt to publicly display a symbol of unity in the Black freedom struggle, King (SCLC), Stokely Carmichael (SNCC), Floyd McKissick (CORE), Whitney Young (NUL), and Roy Wilkins (NAACP) convened in Memphis in order to continue Meredith's march.[3] By the summer of 1966, SNCC and CORE members had already decided, *before* their leaders' meeting with King, Young, and Wilkins in Memphis, that a *new* day had come in the civil rights movement. Sharp conflicts between the members of the SNCC and King's SCLC had already surfaced in Albany, Washington, Selma, and other cities in the South. Differences in goals, methods, and personalities had always threatened the unity of the civil rights movement. But it was not until the Meredith-Mississippi march that everything came out in the open for the world to see.

SNCC and CORE members insisted that no whites be allowed to participate in the march and they insisted they would make no pledge of nonviolence as a response to whites' violence. Young, Wilkins, and King were truly shocked into disbelief at such a suggestion. The manifesto that defined the march stated: "This march will be a massive public indictment and protest of the failure of American society, the government of the United States, and the State of Mississippi to 'fulfill these rights'" (referring to a slogan of the Johnson administration).[4] Criticism of the Johnson administration, insistence on the exclusion of whites, and refusal to promise adherence to nonviolence were clearly viewed by mainline civil rights advocates as outside the bounds of acceptable rhetoric and behavior.

Young and Wilkins were so disturbed that anyone would make such proposals that they left, saying that they would have no part in such a march. They withdrew NAACP and NUL endorsement of it. How were they going to continue to appeal to whites for support of NAACP and NUL goals if they participated in a march from which whites were excluded, nonviolence was rejected, and the president of the United States was severely criticized? But to Martin King's credit, he refused to leave. He debated with Carmichael and McKissick nearly all night trying to get them not to use the phrase "Black Power" and to allow whites to participate in the march under a pledge of nonviolence.

King succeeded in eliciting their commitment. The march began. But when the marchers reached Greenwood, Mississippi, the place where Carmichael had worked, he was arrested. Upon his release, Carmichael, who had been in many southern jails and the federal government had done nothing about it, mounted a platform and protested, "This is the twenty-seventh time I have been arrested—and I ain't going to jail no more!" He continued: "The only way we gonna stop them white men from whippin' us is to take over. We been saying 'freedom' for six years, and we ain't got nothin'. What we gonna start saying now is 'Black Power!'" At that moment, Willie Ricks, called "the preacher" because of his persuasive sermonic style, took over and brought the crowd to ecstasy, chanting "Black Power!" The crowd responded enthusiastically with the same phrase. Although King tried to stem the tide of the crowd's enthusiasm for "Black Power," he did not succeed and many of his own disciples followed Carmichael and Ricks. From that point on, "Black Power" replaced "freedom now," and "we shall overcome" was replaced by "we shall overrun" as slogans of young Black radicals.

The rise of Black Power created a radical change in the consciousness of many young radicals in the SNCC and their followers. Organized in the spring of 1960, they had adopted Martin King's nonviolent direct action as a strategy for social change, even though most did not accept it as an ideology. They had used King's method throughout the South—Mississippi, Georgia, Alabama, and Arkansas. By 1966, after attending many of their comrades' funerals, after being beaten and shot as the FBI took notes and did nothing, the complexity and depth of white racism became clearer to them. They wryly noted that northern Blacks burned the cities even though they had the "rights" that southern Blacks risked their lives to achieve.

The Black power cry was the response of young Blacks to white power that had camouflaged itself in the Christian garb of love. It was their way of saying to whites that they were "on to their tricks" and thus would no longer allow them to use Martin King's idea of Christian love to keep the Black revolution in check. They now sang:

> I love everybody,
> I love everybody,
> I love everybody in my heart,

but they quickly added:

> I just told a lie,
> I just told a lie,
> I just told a lie in my heart.[5]

Young Black preachers were placed in an existential dilemma. Their faith was closer to King's but their politics closer to Carmichael's. In an effort to resolve the conflict, they began to reflect on how the gospel can be reconciled with the Black Power politics of liberation, especially as articulated by young Black radicals who claimed that Blacks should take their freedom "by any means necessary." Although they respected King and admired his commitment to justice, they could no longer embrace nonviolence as an ideology, nor could they affirm integration as the goal of the Black freedom struggle. But inasmuch as King, along with white churches and theologians, had defined Christianity as being identical with love, and love as being identical with nonviolence and integration, how could they retain their Christian identity and also support the Black Power claim that Blacks should take their freedom "by any means necessary"? That was their theological dilemma. How could radical Black preachers retain their Christian identity and also be as committed, as Black Power advocates, to Black liberation, refusing to accept white brutality with a turned cheek?

Black Power advocates made no claim to an identity derived from Christianity. Most were secular university students or adherents of African religions and all tended to define Christianity as "the white man's religion." Black preachers, in their struggle to be Christian *and* support Black Power, had to develop a theology that was distinctly Black and also accountable to our faith. It was in this context that Albert Cleage wrote the *Black Messiah* and I wrote *Black Theology and Black Power*.[6] I wanted to show that Black Power and the gospel were identical and that both focused on the politics of liberation.

It was not easy to connect Black Power with the Christian gospel. The advocates of Black Power were not only un-Christian, they were hostile to Christianity, viewing it as a white religion. Furthermore, most Christians, Black and white, were hostile to Black Power, viewing it as the opposite of everything that their faith represented. When Black Power advocates emerged as leaders in the Black movement, they de-Christianized the Black struggle for justice by emphasizing Black separatism and self-defense. As long as Martin King was the acknowledged symbol and standard-bearer of the movement, it remained Christian, emphasizing love, integration, and nonviolence. But emergence of Malcolm's philosophy through Black Power meant the introduction of a radicalization that excluded Christianity.

Black Theology arose as an attempt to stem the tide of the irrelevance of Christianity by combining both Christianity and Blackness, Martin and Malcolm, Black Church and Black Power, even though neither side thought it was possible. The early interpreters of Black Theology were theologians "on the boundary" (to use Paul Tillich's self-evaluation) between integration and separation, nonviolence and self-defense, "love our white enemies and love our Black skins." They refused to sacrifice either emphasis; they insisted on the absolute necessity of both.

Black Church History

When Black preachers were confronted with the dilemma posed by Black Power, they began to search Black Church history for insights and models that would illustrate and support their claim that the gospel of Jesus is identical with Blacks' liberation from political bondage. Their search focused on their radical Black forebears, chiefly in the masculine line. To be sure, Black preachers sometimes mentioned Harriet Tubman and Sojourner Truth, but unfortunately Black women did not occupy a prominent place in their analysis.[7] Richard Allen, Daniel Payne, Andrew Bryan, George Leile, James Varick, and Christopher Rush emerged as significant advocates for an independent Black Church movement that began in the late eighteenth century.[8]

But these Black churchmen were not radical enough for the era of Black Power. It was Nat Turner, Gabriel Prosser, Denmark Vesey, Henry Highland Garnet, David Walker, Henry McNeil Turner, and others like them, who helped young Black radical preachers articulate a Black version of the gospel. It differed from an appeal to integration, love, and nonviolence and thus, to everyone's surprise, was quite similar to the message of Black Power in the 1960s.

Turner, Prosser, and Vesey were insurrectionists. They had organized slave revolts in 1800, 1822, and 1831, respectively, in the name of the gospel and Black freedom.[9] Garnet's "Address to the Slaves" in 1843 and David Walker's *Appeal* in 1829 sounded like Black Power music to our ears. They too had urged rebellion against the evils of slavery, comparing our condition in the United States with the Hebrew slaves' in ancient Egypt.[10] Henry M. Turner's claim that "God is a Negro" (1898) suggested a historical and theological depth to the claim that God is on the side of Blacks for freedom.[11]

Black theologians and preachers of the 1960s began to realize that they were not the first in the attempt to find theological meaning in Blackness and the gospel. Indeed, Blacks have a usable heritage, a revolutionary past, that can give direction in the search for the truth of the gospel in the struggle for Black freedom.

We also found out how little we knew about Black history, especially a Black history that correctly located the role of the Black Church. All we knew were a few denominational histories and as few names of nineteenth-century Black preachers. Our denominational histories could hardly stand the test of critical scholarship, for they were written from the perspective of a particular ecclesiastical history and for the purpose of glorifying its leaders. Some few other personages were hardly known beyond a few historical references: not enough to give us substantive guidance in the age of Black Power.

Unfortunately no serious research had been done on the history of the

Black Church since Carter G. Woodson's *The History of the Negro Church* (1921). E. Franklin Frazier's brief volume *The Negro Church in America* (1961) was helpful but was too much of a sociological reduction as defined by the University of Chicago school of sociology. "The Negro Church" (1903) by W. E. B. DuBois in his Atlanta University Publications was useful, but it was even older than Woodson's work. Benjamin E. Mays's *The Negro's God* (1938) and his volume with J. W. Nicholson on *The Negro's Church* (1933), though not as old as the works by DuBois or Woodson, did not adequately meet our historical needs. What we needed was a well-written, comprehensive, and scholarly history of the Black Church and religion that could meet the test of both critical historical scholarship and also be useful in our attempt to develop a Black Theology.

Gayraud Wilmore responded to that need by writing his *Black Religion and Black Radicalism* (1972). This text is one of the most important contributions emerging out of the Black Theology movement. A social ethicist by academic training and an ordained minister in the Presbyterian church, Wilmore has been the moving force behind the NCBC, serving as its historian and theologian. More than anyone else, he was deeply committed to uncovering our history, not just in the United States, but all the way back to our African past. He would not let young Black radicals remain content with sloganeering about Black Church heroes but pushed them to search for the religions of Africa before the whites came with their slave ships. He encouraged us to study African Traditional Religions, and he was one of the chief forces behind the NCBC creation of an African commission, which established dialogues with African church persons.

From the very beginning, Wilmore's concern was to create a Black Theology that was truly Black—that is, *African*—and not a white version of Western Christianity colored Black. He wanted the definition of Black Theology to be shaped by an African meaning of liberation and not simply by Western bourgeois ideas of freedom and equality or a Marxist idea of liberation. The key to Wilmore's new appreciation of the autonomy of the Black religious tradition—or at least one important and neglected stream of it— was W. E. B. DuBois's *The Souls of Black Folk* (1903). It was DuBois who pushed him toward Africa, and Wilmore then pushed us to read John Mbiti (*African Religions and Philosophy*;[12] *New Testament Eschatology in an African Background*),[13] Bolaji Idowu (*Olódùmarè: God in Yoruba Belief*;[14] *Towards an Indigenous Church*),[15] Harry Sawyerr (*Creative Evangelism*;[16] *God: An-*

cestor or Creator?),[17] and Kwesi Dickson and Paul Ellingworth (editors of *Biblical Revelation and African Beliefs*).[18]

Charles H. Long, then professor of the history of religions at the University of Chicago and later at the University of North Carolina at Chapel Hill, concurred with Wilmore as to the importance of the study of African religions.[19] Jerome Long, Charles's brother, also supported the same emphasis, as did my brother Cecil Cone in his *Identity Crisis in Black Theology*.[20] We had many spirited debates about the role of African religions in Black Theology, with some advocating it as a source equally important as Christianity in the definition of Black religion and others defending biblical Christianity as its primary source.

Two meanings of liberation emerged from our historical past. One emphasized socio-political freedom as derived from the biblical theme of the exodus and nineteenth-century Black freedom fighters. The other emphasized cultural liberation as derived from the black nationalism of H. M. Turner, Marcus Garvey, Malcolm X, and especially the religions of Africa. No one wanted to exclude either emphasis entirely, but there was much debate about which should be normative for the definition of Black Theology.[21]

Although we debated our differences about the precise meaning of liberation, we all agreed that it had to be defined by our Black past. There can be no creative theology without a tradition upon which to base it. We knew that if we were going to sustain our attempt to make a Black Theology of liberation, we had to find persons in our history who had laid the groundwork for us. Therefore the attempt to create a Black Theology of liberation meant searching for its meaning in our historical past.

The Bible

In addition to Black Power and Black Church history, many Black theologians and preachers turned directly to the Bible for the content of the meaning of liberation as a theological category. Realization of the usefulness of the Bible as a support for the liberation of the Black poor came partly from our study of Black Church history. Henry Garnet, David Walker, Nat Turner, Gabriel Prosser, Harriet Tubman, Sojourner Truth, and many other Black freedom fighters used the scriptures in support of their resistance to and rebellion against oppression and slavery. In addition there were the Black spirituals and their emphasis on freedom—both here and hereafter. Although the Black spirituals had been interpreted as being exclusively otherworldly and compensatory, our research into the testimonies of Black slave narratives and other Black sayings revealed that the theme of heaven in the spirituals and in Black religion generally contained double meanings.[22] "Steal away" referred not only to an eschatological realm, but it was also used by Harriet Tubman as a signal of freedom for slaves who intended to run away with her to the North, or to Canada.[23] According to Frederick Douglass, the song "O Canaan" referred not only to heaven but also to Canada and the North.[24] In these slave songs were found also unambiguous demands for freedom:

> O Freedom! O Freedom!
> O Freedom! I love thee,
> And before I'll be a slave
> I be buried in my grave
> And go home to my Lord and be free.

A similar emphasis is found in "Go Down, Moses." While many Black leaders from Harriet Tubman to Martin King have been identified with Moses, almost all Blacks in America—past and present—have identified Egypt with America, Pharaoh and the Egyptians with white slaveholders and subsequent racists, and Blacks with the Israelite slaves:

> Go down, Moses,
> Way down in Egyptland,
> Tell old Pharaoh
> To let my people go.
>
> When Israel was in Egyptland,
> Let my people go,
> Oppressed so hard they could not stand,
> Let my people go.
>
> Go down, Moses,
> Way down in Egyptland,
> Tell old Pharaoh,
> "Let my people go."
>
> "Thus saith the Lord," bold Moses said,
> "Let my people go;

If not I'll smite your first-born dead.
Let my people go."
Go down, Moses,
Way down in Egyptland,
Tell old Pharaoh,
"Let my people go!"

With the Old Testament sharply in view, the New Testament Jesus was defined as the liberator whose ministry was in solidarity with, and whose death was on behalf of, the poor. In our investigation of our own Black Church history, we were driven to Scripture itself so as to analyze its message in the light of our struggle for freedom.

Because white theologians and preachers denied any relationship between the Scriptures and our struggle for freedom, we bypassed the classic Western theological tradition and went directly to Scripture for its word regarding our Black struggle. Although whites looked down with a condescending intellectual arrogance at our attempt to uncover a liberation theme in the Scriptures, we were not discouraged. Intuitively we knew that we were right, and they were wrong. Furthermore some of us had been trained by them, with a few doctorates to our credit, and we did not internalize everything we were taught. Besides, some things we had been taught in the seminary had far more revolutionary potential than our white teachers had envisioned.

For example, almost every biblical and theological teacher I had encountered in graduate school, as well as most of the well-known biblical scholars I read, claimed that revelation was not an abstract propositional truth but rather a historical event, God's involvement in history. Many of us had read Ernest G. Wright's *Book of the Acts of God*, Oscar Cullmann's *Christ and Time*, Gerhard von Rad's *Theology of the Old Testament*, Bernard Anderson's *Understanding the Old Testament*, and many other neo-orthodox biblical scholars. We merely asked that if God is known by God's acts in history, what, then, is God doing in and through historical events? What is the meaning of salvation as an act of God? Basing ourselves on the exodus and the message of the prophets, we Black theologians agreed with our neo-orthodox teachers that God is known by God's acts in history and that these acts are identical with the liberation of the weak and the poor.

As long as we Blacks located the liberating acts of God for the poor in ancient Hebrew history, that was acceptable biblical exegesis from the view-point of white scholars. But when we tried to do systematic theology on the basis of our exegesis, applying God's liberating acts to our contemporary situation in the United States, focusing on the relations between Blacks and whites, white scholars vehemently rejected both the procedure and the message. They tried to get around our contemporary application of the biblical message by saying that there were other themes in the Bible besides liberation (which we never denied). Our concern was to locate the dominant theme in scripture and to ask what its message was for the Black struggle for freedom today.

We Black theologians contended that if God sided with the poor and the weak in biblical times, then why not today? If salvation is a historical event of rescue, a deliverance of slaves from Egypt, why not a Black Power event today and a deliverance of Blacks from white American racial oppression? When we pressed these questions on white theologians and preachers, they always turned to the white, meek, pale-faced, blue-eyed Jesus, as if we Blacks were expected to embrace him as our Savior. But we vehemently rejected that Jesus.

In place of the white Jesus, we insisted that "Jesus Christ is Black, baby!" That sent shock waves throughout the white seminary and church communities. Whites thought that Blacks had lost their religious sanity. It was one thing to identify liberation as the central message of the Bible, but something else to introduce color into Christology. They could even keep their composure as we discussed together whether the title "liberator" can be appropriately applied to Jesus or whether he was a revolutionary. But to color Jesus Black, that was going too far, and they could hardly sit still during the discussion. "That is racism in reverse!" they said, "and such a claim has no biblical warrant." But we did not listen to them. We merely searched the Scriptures with the resources we had, knowing that in time the truth of our claim would be demonstrated so clearly that even whites would have to take notice of it!

The vehement rejection of the Black Jesus by whites merely reinforced the determination of Black clergy radicals to develop a Christology that took seriously Jesus's Blackness—both literally and symbolically.[25] The literal significance of Jesus's Blackness meant that he *was not* white! He was a Palestinian Jew whose racial ancestry may have been partly African but definitely not European. Therefore white pictures of Jesus in Christian churches and homes are nothing but an ideological distortion of the biblical portrait. By making this point, Black clergy radicals wanted to show that the so-called scientific biblical exegesis of white scholars frequently was not scientific at all. For they have helped to maintain the white image of Jesus through their silence about his true color, thereby suggesting the European Jesus was the historical one.

The major importance of the claim that "Jesus is Black" rested on the symbolic meaning of that affirmation. We were strongly influenced by Bishop Henry M. Turner's claim that "God is a Negro" and Countee Cullen's poetic reflections on "The Black Christ" (1929), which Sterling Brown referred to as "a narrative poem about lynching."[26] The Blackness of Jesus had definite political implications that we derived from the New Testament witness. It was our way of saying that his cross and resurrection represented God's solidarity with the oppressed in their struggle for liberation. The oppressed do not have to accept their present misery as the final definition of their humanity. The good news is: God, the Holy One of Israel, has entered the human situation in Jesus and has transformed it through his cross and resurrection. The poor no longer have to remain in poverty. They are now free to fight for their freedom, because God is fighting with them. In the United States this claim meant that God was on the side of oppressed Blacks in their struggle for freedom and against whites who victimized them. For Black clergy radicals, the best way to describe that insight was to say that "Jesus is Black."

Of course, the Blackness of Jesus did not mean that he could not be described also as red, brown, yellow, or by some other characteristic that defined materially the condition of the poor in the United States and other parts of the globe. Black clergy radicals never denied the universal significance of Jesus's death and resurrection. We merely wanted to emphasize the theological significance of Jesus in the context of the Black liberation struggle in the United States. We wanted to expose the racism of white churches and also encourage Black churches to embrace the biblical Christ who looks much more like oppressed Blacks than white oppressors.

White theologians resented our refusal to listen to them, because they had taught us and they were the experts in the field. But I ask any fair observer, why should we listen to those who have done nothing to assist Blacks in their liberation struggle? White biblical scholars have not even bothered to train Blacks to acquire the skills that they regard as necessary for sound biblical exegesis. What right, then, do they have to say that our exegesis is unsound? We Blacks merely responded to white scholars by saying that the kingdom that Jesus embodied in his life, death, and resurrection was not promised to the learned but to the meek, the humble, and the poor. If white biblical exegetes think that the God of Jesus gave them a hermeneutical privilege in biblical interpretation, then they have not only misread Scripture but have substituted their scientific knowledge about the Bible for a genuine encounter with biblical faith.

Despite the prescientific approach by most Blacks to the Bible, we claimed that their focus on liberation was historically accurate and theologically sound.[27] A study of Black Church history, therefore, led us to a study of scripture, and once again the theme of liberation became the dominant emphasis.

European Political Theologies

In 1967 Jürgen Moltmann's *Theology of Hope*[28] was published in the United States. It emphasized the biblical theme of God's promise as embodied in the struggles of the poor for freedom. Later the works of Johannes B. Metz also stressed a similar eschatological theme.[29] The theology of hope with a political ingredient became a dominant theme in American theology, and many conferences were held in order to explore its implications. Moltmann and Metz lectured frequently in the United States.[30]

I remember well the excitement of reading Moltmann and Metz, one Protestant and the other Catholic. "Now," I said to myself, "my view of liberation in the Bible has some theological support from Germany—widely known as having the leading theological centers in the world. How will run-of-the-mill white North American theologians now be able to deny Black theologians' claims about the theme of liberation in the Bible?" The feeling that Moltmann's theology supported the liberation of the poor accounted for why he was quoted so liberally in my work; he provided "respectable" theological support for my claims regarding God's solidarity with the poor.[31]

Other Black theologians were also influenced by Moltmann and Metz. The title of the first book by Major J. Jones on Black Theology reflects this dependence—*Black Awareness: A Theology of Hope*.[32] The writings of J. Deotis Roberts refer frequently to Moltmann and Metz.[33] Black theologians quoted from European theologians because they had developed a theological language that appeared to support similar claims in Black Theology. White North American theologians could ignore our attempts to develop an argument for a Black Theology of liberation on the basis of our limited knowledge of scientific exegesis, but we knew that they would not (indeed, could not!) ignore major European theologians, for Europe is the continent of their origin and the place to which they and their students frequently return in order to deepen their theological knowledge. If a major European theologian said something, North Americans listened carefully, even if they strongly disagreed. As we Black theologians expected, white Americans did pay close attention to the European theology of hope (political theology).

But European theologians did not help us as much in developing a language for Black Theology as we had originally expected.[34] Indeed we Black theologians began to move away from the progressive theologies of Europe when we saw how easily they were adopted by white North Americans as a substitute for taking Black Theology seriously. How could white North American theologians devote so much attention to the hope thematized in European theology and completely ignore the hope emerging from the nearly three hundred and fifty years of Black struggle in North America?[35]

The songs of hope, the "Negro spirituals," seemed to be the logical place to turn for any North American theological reflection on hope. Why were they ignored by white North American theologians who claimed to be interested in applying the ideas of hope and promise to life in the United States? Their silence baffled me, because the spirituals played such a dominant role in the civil rights movement. Furthermore, many of these same theologians were present at the march on Washington and had marched with King in Selma, singing these songs as everyone else, because of the empowerment and the courage they bestowed upon the marchers. Why, then, did they ignore them when they sat down at their seminary or university desks to reflect on hope? Were white theologians too blinded by their own racism to hear the truth of the gospel that was erupting from the struggles of the Black poor?

It seemed that the silence of white theologians on Black Theology and religion was and is their way of saying that Blacks cannot think. But as Gustavo Gutiérrez has said, "Even the poor have the right to think. The right to think is the corollary of the human right to be, and to assert the right to think is only to assert the right to exist."[36] By ignoring our hopes and dreams in their theologies of hope, white progressive theologians were saying that Blacks cannot think, because they do not exist. That was why some of them could say, and still do, that there is no such thing as Black Theology.

The white theologians' claim that there is no such thing as Black Theology did not upset us; white acceptance was never our primary concern. Indeed, in one sense, I was pleased with their dismissal of Black Theology because it meant I was even more free to reread the Bible without having to answer the technical concerns of white theological academics. It also made me more determined to create a Black Theology of liberation that was not dependent upon my white theological mentors.

When whites asked me whether Black Theology was a "fad," I responded negatively, and with a theological confidence, and touch of arrogance that showed my disdain for anyone who asked such a question. I often said, "With over twenty million Blacks in the United States, most of whom are extremely poor, how can you be so insensitive as to ask whether reflection on their religious history is a passing fad?"

The Black theologians' move away from the political theologies of Europe was also motivated by our uneasiness over their tendency toward theological abstractions. Progressive theologians of Europe were not concrete; they did not name enemies.[37] It was the Latin American liberation theologians' critique of the progressive theologies of Europe that really demonstrated the Achilles' heel of European progressive theologies.

Gustavo Gutiérrez's distinction between the problem of the unbeliever as created by the European Enlightenment and the problem of the nonperson as created by European colonization and exploitation of the Third World clarified our unexpressed suspicion about the political theologies of Europe. "The poor," he writes, "are not, in the first instance, questioning the religious world or its philosophical presuppositions. They are calling into question first of all the economic, social, and political order that oppresses and marginalizes them."[38] And he also observes that "one of the best ways to refute a theology is to look at its practical consequences, not its intellectual arguments."[39] When we Blacks observed the practical consequences of European thought and its North American mirroring, it was quite clear that we could not base Black Theology upon a liberation derived from Europe.

We then decided to incorporate into Black Theology the challenge of Frantz Fanon, a West Indian deeply involved in the Algerian war for independence from France. Fanon helped us to realize that we must be suspicious of European intellectuals even when they use a language of liberation that appears to be supportive of the Third World. Not everything that is is what it appears to be. Underneath the European language of freedom and equality there is slavery and death. That was why Fanon said:

Come, then, comrades; it would be well to decide at once to change our ways. We must shake off the heavy darkness in which we were plunged, and leave it behind. The new day which is already at hand must find us firm, prudent and resolute. We must leave our dreams and abandon our old beliefs and friendships of the time before life began. Let us waste no time in sterile litanies and nauseating mimicry. Leave this Europe where they are never done talking of [humanity], yet murder [human beings] everywhere they find them, at the corner of their own streets, in all the corners of the globe. For centuries they have stifled almost the whole of humanity in the name of a so-called spiritual experience. Look at them swaying between atomic and spiritual disintegration.[40]

Fanon captured our imagination because his analysis rang true and he convinced us that Black thought could create no genuine future for its people by looking to Europe for support. Europeans created the problem that necessitated our need for liberation and it was naive of us to expect that our theological salvation could come from Europe: "That same Europe where they were never done talking of [humanity], and where they never stopped proclaiming that they were only anxious for the welfare of [humanity]: today we know with what sufferings humanity has paid for every one of their triumphs of the mind."[41]

Fanon's challenge involved more than turning away from Europe; it also involved a turning to the resources found in the victimized peoples of the world: "If we want humanity to advance a step further, if we want to bring it up to a different level than that which Europe has shown it, then we must invent and we must make discoveries. . . . For Europe, for ourselves, and for humanity, comrades, we must then turn over a new leaf, we must work out new concepts, and try to set afoot a new [humanity]."[42]

The application of Fanon's message to Black Theology affected our understanding of our theological task. We now realized it consisted in something more than simply ebonizing European concepts in theology. Gayraud Wilmore and Charles Long saw the necessity and complexity of this task much clearer than most of us. They took the lead in directing Black theologians to Africa first and then to Latin America and Asia.

Third World Theologies

When Black clergy radicals began to develop a Black Theology of liberation, they had no knowledge of a similar theological development going on in Africa, Asia, and Latin America. To be sure, like most civil rights activists, we had been influenced by the rise of the African movement toward independent nations during the 1950s and 1960s, and we had heard about a parallel movement in religion, creating a renewed interest in African Traditional Religions and indigenous churches. Missionary churches, implanted by European and white North American missionaries, were being critically evaluated through the newly created organization called the All Africa Conference of Churches (AACC). The AACC, founded in 1958, was similar to the NCBC in that it was ecumenical and it began to provide the context for the creation of an African theology that would question the Europeanization of the gospel.[43] But despite these creative political and theological irruptions in Africa, the early interpreters of Black Theology did not know much about them. Most of us had never been to Africa and had spent little time studying it.

Although Frantz Fanon's *The Wretched of the Earth* was the catalyst that drew our attention away from Europe, it was Gayraud Wilmore and Charles Long who accepted the radical implications of his challenge and pushed us toward Africa as the critical source for the development of a Black Theology based on Black religion. When we began to read African theologians, such as John Mbiti and Bolaji Idowu, their talk about "Africanization" and "indigenization" reinforced the importance of cultural liberation, which many North American Black nationalists had stressed.

Some of us, however, were greatly disturbed about the political conservatism of many African theologians. We knew that Fanon would not look favorably upon a cultural nationalism that did not radically transform economics and politics. But despite our reservations, we continued to listen carefully and viewed African theology as far more important to us than European political theology. When Black theologians of South Africa responded theologically to their situation of oppression by using the phrase "Black Theology," North American Black theologians became even more determined to learn from Africa in our efforts to develop a theology that was Black both politically and culturally.[44]

Many Black theologians were greatly surprised to discover that Latin American theologians were using the term "liberation" to define the heart of the gospel.[45] Almost none of us knew Spanish and thus were limited in our knowledge of Latin American theology. However, because American white religious radicals of a socialist bent (at least in language) adopted them, as liberal and neo-orthodox white theologians adopted the progressive theologies of Europe, we Blacks were very skeptical of this new liberation theology from Latin America.[46] Why were white religious radicals so interested in the poor in Latin America and so indifferent to the poor Black in North America? I was reminded of Sartre's comment: "The only way of helping the enslaved out there is to side with those who are here."

Furthermore, Latin American theologians' focus on classism and their silence on racism troubled many Black theologians. In Brazil alone, there are more than 40 million Blacks and in Latin America more than 70 million. Why, then, are there no Black or Amerindian theologians among them? I have written about the early encounters of Black and Latin American theologies elsewhere, and at another time I shall comment upon our mutual support, along with African and Asian theologies, in our efforts to create a common Third World theology.[47] My concern here is to emphasize that during the early development of Black Theology, we Blacks were much too suspicious to learn as much as we should have. An early incorporation of class analysis into Black Theology could have prevented some of its most obvious and excessive weaknesses, which I shall take up later.

Most of us did not know anything about Asian theology. Dialogue with Asian Christians is more recent, and it is quite promising.

Black clergy radicals began to develop a Black Theology of liberation springing from the particularity of our history, the urgency of our present struggles, and our creative hope for the future. Most of our ideas about liberation came from the depth of our political and spiritual struggle as we attempted to make sense out of Black existence in white America. Although Black preachers' formal theological knowledge may have been limited and most did not have the educational credentials that would have entitled them to teach in white universities and seminaries, yet they did have the prophetic vision that enabled them to discern the truth of the time. Black Theology, therefore, was created out of the sermonic imagination of Black preachers as they fought to establish the freedom for their people that white Americans had denied but that God had foretold and promised.

The Literature of Black Theology and Religion

Although Black clergy radicals were the chief initiators of the idea of a Black Theology, a small number of Black Theologians in seminaries, universities, and colleges were often present during their deliberations. Near the end of the 1960s, writings of Black professors began to be published.

The "dean" of Black scholarship in religion is without doubt C. Eric Lincoln, who was a professor of sociology and religion at Union Theological Seminary during the late 1960s and early 1970s and later took up a similar post at Duke University. He is the author of the classic study *The Black Muslims in America* (1961).[48] Additional texts include *My Face is Black* (1964),[49] *The Sounds of the Struggle* (1967),[50] *The Black Church since Frazier* (1974),[51] and (as editor) *The Black Experience in Religion* (1974).[52]

In addition to his many published books and articles on Black religion, no one has done more than Lincoln in encouraging Black scholars to write and to publish. His C. Eric Lincoln Series in Black Religion made it possible for Black scholars to publish their radical ideas.

Although Joseph Washington's *Black Religion* was strongly criticized by almost all Black scholars and preachers, the importance of the text should not be minimized. Its importance is not simply the negative function it served in motivating Black theologians to develop a Black Theology. It served a positive function that is not often emphasized. Washington's *Black Religion* was the first text to demonstrate the uniqueness of Black religion, separating it from Protestantism, Catholicism, Judaism, and secularism. This was a major scholarly achievement, and it should be recognized as such. Black scholars (Gayraud Wilmore, Cecil Cone, Henry Mitchell) used his arguments to demonstrate the uniqueness of Black religion even though they rejected his negative appraisal of it. Washington actually reconsidered his views in his next book, *The Politics of God* (1967).[53] His *Black and White Power Subreption* (1969)[54] was an important treatment of the theology of Black Power, and his *Black Sects and Cults* (1972)[55] represented a further investigation of the African roots of Black religion.

The first texts on Black Theology were my *Black Theology and Black Power* (1969) and *A Black Theology of Liberation* (1970). Both used liberation as the central theme of the gospel message and thus as the organizing principle for the systematic presentation of the Christian gospel from the standpoint of the

Black struggle for freedom. The next volume, with a similar purpose in mind, was *God of the Oppressed* (1975).

J. Deotis Roberts is an important scholar in Black Theology; he has published several texts and many articles on the theme, the most important being *Liberation and Reconciliation: A Black Theology* (1971) and *Black Political Theology* (1974). Roberts is best known for an emphasis on reconciliation along with liberation in contrast to what he regarded as my one-sided stress on the latter.

A similar treatment to Roberts's was Major Jones's *Black Awareness: A Theology of Hope* (1971) and his *Christian Ethics for Black Theology* (1974).[56] His ethics and theology are closer to those of Martin Luther King, Jr., with an emphasis on love and reconciliation in black-white relationships. Although I have been critical of both Roberts's and Jones's views in Black Theology —because of what I considered as overemphasis on white theological norms for Black Theology—they will always be regarded as among the major interpreters of Black Theology, bridging the gap between the Martin King era and the rise of Black Power in religion and in the churches.[57]

No one has provided a deeper challenge to Black Theology than has the philosophical critique of William Jones. His book, *Is God a White Racist?* (1973),[58] shook Black theologians out of their "liberation complacency" and forced them to deal with the problem of theodicy at a deeper level. If God is liberating the Black poor from oppression, as Black theologians say, where is the liberation event that can serve as evidence of that fact? The question has not been answered to anyone's satisfaction, and thus continues to serve as a check against the tendency of substituting liberation rhetoric for actual events of freedom.

Another text that sparked a great deal of discussion was that by Cecil W. Cone, *The Identity Crisis in Black Theology* (1975).[59] Along with Wilmore's *Black Religion and Black Radicalism* (1972) and important articles by Charles H. Long, Cecil Cone's book criticized Black liberation theologians for their emphasis on political liberation and also for their dependence on white theologians, thereby separating them from the religion of the "Almighty Sovereign God" of the Black people. He claimed that an authentic Black Theology must use Black religion as its chief source.

Although Wilmore agreed with Cecil Cone regarding Black religion as the chief source of Black Theology, he disagreed with him regarding *who* had the identity crisis. According to Wilmore, "the crisis is not in black theology but in the contemporary black church."[60] Wilmore's perspective on Black religion and theology is persuasively argued in his *Black Religion and Black Radicalism*.

Differing with Cecil Cone at a different point was Charles Long, who questioned whether a Black Theology of liberation is possible in any sense if one takes Black religion seriously. He claims that theology is a discipline of European conquerors and thus alien to the experience of Blacks who have been enslaved by them.[61]

I have already discussed the significant impact of Albert Cleage's *Black Messiah* (1968); his *Black Christian Nationalism* (1972)[62] is a practical analysis of his theological program. Other early interpreters of Black Theology and religion included Henry Mitchell (*Black Preaching* [1970][63] and *Black Belief* [1975]);[64] Lawrence Jones, who wrote important articles in history;[65] Preston Williams, Herbert Edwards, and Carlton Lee, who made contributions in social ethics;[66] Robert Bennett in Bible studies;[67] Bishop Joseph Johnson and Warner Traynham in theology.[68] Leonard Barrett's *Soul Force* (1974)[69] is an important study of Black religion in the United States, Africa, and the West Indies.

No list of literature in Black Theology and religion of the 1960s and early 1970s would be complete without mentioning the outstanding work of Vincent Harding. His essay "No Turning Back?" is required reading for anyone interested in a critical interpretation of the documents of the NCBC. His "Black Power and the American Christ" and "The Religion of Black Power" are important for an interpretation of the mood that gave birth to Black Power and the challenge it presented to a religion of love based on the typical American theological perspective.

Since the late 1960s and early 1970s many Black scholars have been writing in the area of Black Theology, dwelling on different aspects and variations on the theme of liberation. The Fund for Theological Education and the Society for the Study of Black Religion, both then under the direction of C. Shelby Rooks (later president of Chicago Theological Seminary), did much to support and to encourage young Black scholars.[70]

Although the number of Black theologians has increased since 1966, there are still significant problems to be addressed in relation to the strengths and weaknesses of Black Theology in terms of its origin and present state. And if we Black theologians are hesitant to critically evaluate our work, then we should ask: For whom do we do theology—for ourselves or the Black poor? If the latter, then we must critically evaluate our work in order to assess whether it is accomplishing what we claim.

Notes

1. G. S. Wilmore and J. H. Cone, *Black Theology: A Documentary History* (Maryknoll, N.Y.: Orbis Books, 1979):101.

2. Martin King's dream that the "beloved community" could be accomplished through nonviolent direct action was shared by most Black Americans, including younger members of the SNCC, even though many of the latter did not share its Christian orientation. It is necessary to know the depth of the commitment of young Blacks to the achievement of justice through nonviolence and their perceived betrayal by white liberals and the federal government if one is to understand why they turned to Black power. See especially Clayborne Carson, *In Struggle: SNCC and the Black Awakening of the 1960s* (Harvard University Press, 1981). Julius Lester's "The Angry Children of Malcolm X," in Meier, Rudwick, and Broderick, *Black Protest Thought* (New York: Bobbs-Merrill, 1971) is required reading. Vincent Harding's *The Other American Revolution* (Los Angeles: Center for Afro-American Studies, 1980) is also important. An excellent autobiographical account is that by James Forman, *The Making of Black Revolutionaries* (New York: Macmillan, 1972). See also the illuminating essay by Emily Stopher, "The Student Nonviolent Coordinating Committee: The Rise and Fall of a Redemptive Organization," *Journal of Black Studies* 8, no. 1, September 1977; and the important book by Howard Zinn, *SNCC: The New Abolitionists* (Boston: Beacon Press, 1964). Lerone Bennett, "The Rise of Black Power," *Ebony* (February 1969):36–42, is also useful. For an interpretation of the SNCC's move from Martin King's ideas to Black power, see Gene Roberts, "The Story of SNICK: From 'Freedom High' to Black Power," *New York Times Magazine*, September 25, 1966. An excellent interpretation of the need for Black power is Stokely Carmichael, "What We Want," *New York Review of Books*, Sept. 22, 1966.

3. For interpretations of the events surrounding the continuation of the Meredith march, see especially Harding, *The Other American Revolution*, chap. 28; Robert Brisbane, *Black Activism* (Valley Forge, Penn.: Judson, 1974), chap. 6; Harvard Sitkoff, *The Struggle for Black Equality* (New York: Hill and Wang, 1981), chap. 7; Paul Good, *The Trouble I've Seen* (Washington, D.C.: Howard University Press, 1975):247–72; Carson, *In Struggle*, chaps. 13 and 14.

4. Harding, *The Other American Revolution*, 186.

5. Ibid., 186–87.

6. Perhaps I should say a word about the differences between Albert Cleage and myself. There are many, but they all stem from one central difference: the theological value of skin color. I do not believe that God has created Blacks with more propensity toward the good than whites or any other people. All persons were created in the image of God and all have sinned against creation, claiming for ourselves more than we ought. Furthermore I do not share Cleage's historical judgment about the "Black Nation of Israel" or of the African origins of Jesus. Even if his interpretation was based on factual evidence, the theological conclusion must point to a God concerned about the salvation of all, including whites. Cleage's Black Christian National-

ism is such a reaction to white racism, as was Elijah Muhammad's Nation of Islam that influenced him, that he fails completely to recognize the oneness of all human beings. *What-ever else we may say about the methods that Martin Luther King, Jr., used in the civil rights movement, his "beloved community" is the goal of every genuine Christian, for without this element the gospel is no longer the gospel.* It is Cleage's inordinate focus on the particularity of Blackness that has led him to place the universalism of the gospel in jeopardy, turning it into an ideology. That is also why he rejects the letters of Paul and Jesus' resurrection as essential elements in his theological perspective. What Black Christian can take Cleage seriously when he appears to show no respect for genuine biblical Christianity?

Despite my differences with Cleage's theology, our similarities were and still are much more significant, the most important of which is the centrality of Blackness and its connection with liberation in the definition of the gospel for the Black community. This agreement between us made us allies in our common effort to make the Christian faith relevant to the Black struggle for freedom.

7. Sojourner Truth is best known for her speeches against slavery in the abolitionist movement, and Harriet Tubman has been called the "Moses" of her people because of her liberation of herself and more than three hundred other Blacks to freedom. See chapter 6 in this volume for an analysis of Sojourner Truth's involvement in the fight for women's rights. See also *Sojourner Truth: Narrative and Book of Life*, Ebony Classics (Chicago: Johnson, 1970); Jacqueline Bernard, *Journey Toward Freedom: The Story of Sojourner Truth* (New York: Dell, 1967); Hertha Pauli, *Her Name Was Sojourner Truth* (New York: Camelot/Avon, 1962). The best and most comprehensive treatment of Harriet Tubman's life is that by Earl Conrad, *Harriet Tubman* (New York: Paul E. Eriksson, 1969); see also Sarah Bradford, *Harriet Tubman: The Moses of Her People* (Secaucus, N.J.: Citadel, 1974, originally published in 1869).

8. Richard Allen was the founder and first bishop of the A.M.E. Church (1816). Daniel Alexander Payne was also a bishop and is best known for his emphasis on education and his initiative in purchasing and later serving as president of Wilberforce University, the oldest Black university in the United States. See his *Recollections of Seventy Years* (New York: Arno Press, 1969); *History of the African Methodist Episcopal Church* (New York: Arno Press, 1969). George Leile was a significant participant in organizing the First Baptist Church in Silver Bluff, South Carolina, in the 1770s, and Andrew Bryan of Savannah was also a significant Baptist of the late eighteenth century. See James M. Washington, "The Origins and Emergence of Black Baptist Separatism, 1863–1897" (Ph.D. dissertation, Yale University, 1979). James Varick and Christopher Rush were significant participants in the founding of the AMEZ Church (1821). See Carol George, *Segregated Sabbaths* (New York: Oxford University Press, 1973), and Bishop William J. Walls, *The African Methodist Episcopal Church: Reality of the Black Church* (Charlotte, N.C.: A.M.E. Zion Publishing House, 1974).

9. See Herbert Aptheker, *American Negro Slave Revolts* (New York: International Publishers, 1943); idem, *Nat Turner's Slave Rebellion*; Arna Bontemps, *Black Thunder: Gabriel's Revolt, Virginia 1800* (New York: Macmillan, 1936); John O. Killens, *The Trial Record of Denmark Vesey* (Boston: Beacon Press, 1970); Robert S. Starobin ed., *Denmark Vesey: The Slave Conspiracy of 1822* (Englewood Cliffs, N.J.: Prentice-Hall, 1970). Particularly significant for Black theologians was Vincent Harding's research, "Religion and Resistance among Antebellum Negroes, 1800–1860," in A. Meier and E. Rudwick eds., *The Making of Black America* 1:179–97; see also his more recent publication *There Is a River* (New York: Harcourt Brace Jovanovich, 1981). Gayraud Wilmore's "Three Generals in the Lord's Army," chapter 3 in his *Black Religion and*

Black Radicalism, captured the emphasis of our concern and research. Although we rejected Joseph Washington's claim that Black churches had no theology, we did agree with his emphasis (in *Black Religion*) that Black faith had identified the gospel with the struggle for freedom. His book was often quoted with approval on this point. He served as a corrective to the widely held contention that Black religion was primarily otherworldly and compensatory. This view is strongly emphasized by Benjamin Mays in *The Negro's God*.

10. Walker's "Appeal" and Garnet's "Address" had an enormous impact on the thinking of the early interpreters of Black Theology. They were quoted more often than any other leading figures of the nineteenth century.

11. The impact of the rise of Black consciousness made Henry M. Turner especially important for the young Black clergy. He was a bishop in the A.M.E. Church, and the only mainline Black churchman whose radicalism was competitive with that of Garnet and Walker. He was a major critic of Booker T. Washington and was even isolated in his own denomination.

12. New York, Praeger, 1969. This book had a profound impact on Black theologians, and Mbiti, despite his conservative Western approach to theology, emerged as the most quoted and influential of all African theologians. See his controversial essay "An African Views American Black Theology," *Worldview* (August 1974), reprinted in Wilmore and Cone, *Black Theology*, 477–82. See my response to Mbiti, "A Black American Perspective on the Future of African Theology," in *Black Theology*, 492–502, and that of Desmond M. Tutu, "Black Theology/African Theology—Soul Mates or Antagonists?" ibid., 483–91. Mbiti does not like the stress on race and color in North American Black Theology.

13. London: Oxford University Press, 1971.

14. London: Longman, 1962.

15. London: Oxford University Press, 1965.

16. London: Lutterworth, 1968. Harry Sawyerr, an older African theologian, has not been friendly to Black Theology either; like Mbiti, he does not like the emphasis on race and color. Sawyerr wrote one of the earliest essays on African theology: "What Is African Theology?" *African Theological Journal* (August 1971):7–24.

17. London: Longman, 1970.

18. London: Lutterworth, 1969. The collection of essays in this book was often referred to by young African American members of the clergy because of its influence in the development of an African theology.

19. Long was particularly influential as a teacher and lecturer on African religions in the Society for the Study of Black Religion. His most influential essay was "Perspectives for a Study of Afro-American Religion in the United States," *History of Religions* 2, no. 1 (August 1971):54–66. This essay and his active participation in the ssbr provided the most challenging critique of the dependence of Black Theology on Western theology. See also his "Myth, Culture, and History: An Inquiry into the Cultural History of West Africa" (Ph.D. thesis, University of Chicago, 1962), and "The West African High God: History and Religious Experience," *History of Religions* 3, no. 2 (Winter 1964).

20. Nashville, Tenn.: African Methodist Episcopal Church Press, 1975.

21. I have referred to this debate in several places. See especially my interpretation of the debate among Black theologians in Wilmore and Cone, *Black Theology*, 615–20. See also

Wilmore, *Black Religion*, chaps. 8 and 9.

22. Especially useful in this regard is Miles Mark Fisher, *Negro Slave Songs in the United States* (New York: Citadel, 1953), and John Lovell, Jr., "The Social Implications of the Negro Spiritual," *Journal of Negro Education* (October 1939), and his definitive study *Black Song: The Forge and the Flame* (New York: Macmillan, 1972). These works provided significant counterinterpretations of the typical view that the slave songs were exclusively otherworldly. The research of many Black historians also aided our this-worldly view of the spirituals and Black religion. See especially Vincent Harding's "Religion and Resistance" (note 9, above); "Beyond Chaos: Black History and the Search for the New Land," Black Paper no. 2 (August 1970, Institute of the Black World); and his "The Afro-American Past and the Afro-American Present," in Mitchell Goodman ed., *The Movement toward a New America* (New York: Knopf, 1970). No popular writer on the subject was more influential than the senior editor of *Ebony*, Lerone Bennett. See especially his *Before the Mayflower: A History of the Negro in America, 1619–1964* (Chicago: Johnson, 1966); and *Confrontation: Black and White* (Chicago: Johnson, 1965). The writings of W. E. B. DuBois are particularly useful, especially his classic *The Souls of Black Folk* (New York: Fawcett, 1961; originally published in 1903); see also his *The Gift of Black Folk* (New York: Washington Square, 1970; originally published in 1924). Another influential essay on the spirituals was that by Sterling Stuckey, "Through the Prism of Folklore: The Black Ethos in Slavery," in Jules Chametzky and Sidney Kaplan eds., *Black and White in American Culture* (University of Massachusetts Press, 1969). My *The Spirituals and the Blues* (New York: Seabury Press, 1972) was written in the light of this emphasis on *Black* rather than "Negro" history.

23. According to Richard Randall, "Once in America when we owned other men as chattels, Negro slaves chanted thinly-disguised songs of protest, set to the meter of spirituals—'Go Down Moses,' the fighting song of Harriet Tubman who came like Moses to redeem her black kinsmen from the 'Egypt-land of the South'; 'Steal Away,' which invariably meant a summons to sneak off to the woods for a slave meeting; and the militant 'Follow the Drinking Gourd,' which meant following the Great Dipper to the Ohio River and freedom" ("Fighting Songs of the Unemployed," *The Sunday Worker Progressive Weekly*, September 3, 1939, p. 2). Earl Conrad made a similar interpretation of the spirituals: "Song, or the spiritual, as a means of communication, was a definite part of each of Harriet's campaigns. The spiritual, with its hidden meaning, was employed usually when the situation was the most dangerous. The idea of song was, in itself, disarming; thus, when the Negro sang he pampered his master's understanding of him as a 'loyal, satisfied, slave.' With a melody on his lips to cloak words which held an important and immediate significance, it was possible to dupe the slaveholder" (*Harriet Tubman*, 76). Interpretations such as these gave us the perspective on the spirituals and Black religion we Black theologians needed to ground Black theology in the Bible and Black history. It is true that we were often not as careful in our interpretation as we perhaps should have been, but we achieved the *militant* reading of the Bible our times required and our own history suggested.

24. According to Douglass: "We were at times remarkably buoyant, sang hymns, and made joyous exclamations, almost as triumphant in their tone as if we had reached the land of freedom and safety. A keen observer might have detected in our repeated singing of 'O Canaan, sweet Canaan, I am bound for the land of Canaan,' something more than a hope of reaching heaven. We meant to reach the *North*, and the *North* was our Canaan" (*Life and Times of Frederick Douglass* [New York: Collier, 1962]:159; a reprint of the 1892 edition).

25. A fuller exposition of my views on the Black Christ is found in *God of the Oppressed* (chap. 6); *A Black Theology of Liberation* (chap. 6); and *Black Theology and Black Power* (chap. 2). For a description of the controversy and a variety of views on the subject during the 1960s, see Alex Poinsett, "The Quest for a Black Christ," *Ebony* (March 1969). Albert Cleage was the most controversial with his emphasis on the literal Blackness of Jesus as a historical fact. See also Gayraud Wilmore, "The Black Messiah: Revising the Color Symbolism in Western Christology," *Journal of the Interdenominational Theological Center* 2, no. 1 (Fall 1974):8–18; J. Deotis Roberts, *Liberation and Reconciliation: A Black Theology* (Philadelphia: Westminster Press, 1971); *The Black Messiah*, chap. 6; Vincent Harding, "Black Power and the American Christ," in Wilmore and Cone, *Black Theology: A Documentary History*, 35–42. For an exposition of the idea of a Black God, see chap. 4, "God in Black Theology," in my *A Black Theology of Liberation*. However, my *God of the Oppressed* is the most detailed explanation of my views.

26. See Sterling Brown, *Negro Poetry and Drama and the Negro in American Fiction* (1937; reprint, New York: Atheneum, 1969):71. For an interpretation of Cullen's poem, see also Jean Wagner, *Black Poets of the United States*, trans. K. Douglas (Urbana: University of Illinois Press, 1973):283–347.

27. It should be emphasized that the development of Christianity in both the New World and Africa among Blacks was inseparable from internal and external rejection of slavery. Black religions are unthinkable without this background since the sixteenth century. Hence whether the term "liberation" was used or not, Black Church history has been about liberation.

28. New York: Harper & Row.

29. See especially his *Theology of the World* (New York: Herder and Herder, 1969).

30. See the book that resulted from the Duke University consultation, "The Task of Theology Today," April 4–6, 1968, in which the major paper was given by Jürgen Moltmann: *The Future of Hope: Theology as Eschatology*, ed. Frederick Herzog (New York: Herder and Herder, 1970). Major responses to the Moltmann essay were by Harvey Cox, Frederick Herzog, Langdon Gilkey, John Macquarrie, and Van A. Harvey. Another conference was held in New York City, October 8–10, 1971, and a book was published with the title *Hope and the Future of Man*, ed. Ewert H. Cousins (Philadelphia: Fortress, 1972). Major speakers (whose essays were published) included Jürgen Moltmann, Wolfhart Pannenberg, Johannes B. Metz (all from Germany), John B. Cobb, Jr., Daniel Day Williams, Schubert M. Ogden, Carl E. Braaten, and Philip Hefner (all from the United States). More than a thousand persons turned out to hear the European theologians.

31. The influence of Moltmann's *Theology of Hope* and later his *Religion, Revolution, and the Future* (New York: Scribner's, 1969) was great. I read and then reread him: "The man who hopes will never be able to reconcile himself with the laws and constraints of this earth, neither with the inevitability of death nor with the evil that constantly bears further evil. The raising of Christ is not merely a consolation to him in a life that is full of distress and doomed to die, but it is also God's contraction of suffering and death, of humiliation and offense, and of the wickedness of evil. Hope finds in Christ not only a consolation *in* suffering, but also the protest of the divine promise *against* suffering. . . . Peace with God means conflict with the world. . . . If we had before our eyes only what we see, then we would cheerfully or reluctantly reconcile ourselves with things as they happen to be. That we do not reconcile ourselves, that there is no pleasant harmony between us and reality, is due to our unquenchable hope. This hope keeps man unreconciled, until the great day of the fulfillment of all the promises of

God. . . . This hope makes the Christian church a constant disturbance in human society" (*Theology of Hope*, 21–22). As I read this and so many other passages like it, I concluded that this is exactly what hope in the spirituals means.

32. Nashville, Tenn.: Abingdon, 1971. Note especially chap. 1, "Introduction: The Case for a Black Theology of Hope," and chap. 7, "The Implications of a Theology of Hope for the Black Community." In both chapters, Jones quotes liberally from Moltmann's writings.

33. See especially his "Black Consciousness in Theological Perspective," in J. Gardiner and J. D. Roberts eds., *Quest for a Black Theology* (Philadelphia: Pilgrim, 1971), especially pp. 79–81; see also Roberts's *Liberation and Reconciliation*, and his *A Black Political Theology* (Philadelphia: Westminster Press, 1974). The title of the last book reflects Roberts's interest in hope theology, which was also called political theology.

34. J. Deotis Roberts was one of the first to note the problem with hope theology. That was why he asked: "How hopeful is the theology of hope?" (see his "Black Consciousness in Theological Perspective," 79). In most cases Roberts did not see much hope for Blacks in hope theology: "Some who have been the most vocal advocates of a theology of revolution have not touched the racial crisis in the United States. I am highly suspicious when Paul Lehmann, who teaches on the fringe of the largest black ghetto in the world, can wax eloquent concerning revolutionary theology, which is his answer to the situation in Latin America. Surely a political theology to be meaningful must be applied to the local crisis situation. . . . Another American, Prof. Richard Shaull of Princeton Seminary, has spoken on 'Revolutionary Change in Theological Perspective,' but he has selected Latin America. A black theologian, aware of the suffering of his people . . . has the responsibility to speak *first* to the American situation" (ibid., 79–80).

35. It was revealing that no Black theologians were invited as major participants in the conferences on hope; the issue of racism and the Black struggle against it were almost completely ignored. Jürgen Moltmann raised this problem at the New York conference, "Hope and the Future of Man," in his response to papers by Carl Braaten, John Cobb, and Philip Hefner. He asked: "*Whose* future do we mean? . . . Whose hopes are we giving an account of? . . . A future which does not begin in the transformation of the present is for me no genuine future. A hope which is not the hope of the oppressed today is no hope for which I could give a theological account. . . . If the theologians and philosophers of the future do not plant their feet on the ground and turn to a theology of the cross and the dialectic of the negative, they will appear in a cloud of liberal optimism and appear a mockery of the present suffering. If we cannot justify the theme of this conference, "Hope and the Future of Man," before the present reality of the frustration and oppression of man, we are batting the breeze and talking merely for our own self-satisfaction" (Cousins, *Hope and the Future of Man*, 55, 59). Many American theologians were upset with Moltmann's response and some considered it inappropriate and in bad taste. But I was very pleased and thought his comments would help American theologians to recognize that one cannot speak of hope without grounding that speech in the struggles of Blacks for freedom. But American white theologians simply returned to theology as usual, even though they claimed to be *personally* concerned about justice. It was really strange to me, not to say disgusting, to listen to American white theologians speak of hope and ignore the hopes of the victims in their situation.

36. *The Power of the Poor in History* (Maryknoll, N.Y.: Orbis Books, 1983):101.

37. Roberts writes: "At the Duke conference on the theology of hope, I put the question to

Moltmann . . . as to the meaning of his theology for an oppressed people. His answer at that time was not very hopeful" ("Black Consciousness in Theological Perspective," 80). When Moltmann spoke at the hope conference in New York a few years later and in his later writings, as Roberts acknowledges, he was more explicit about the connections between his theology and the oppressed. But his concreteness and his naming the enemy still left something to be desired. José Míguez Bonino's critique of Moltmann caused a great stir, especially from Moltmann. See Míguez Bonino's *Doing Theology in a Revolutionary Situation* (Philadelphia: Fortress, 1975), chap. 7, especially pp. 144ff. See also Moltmann's response: "On Latin American Liberation Theology: An Open Letter to José Míguez Bonino," *Christianity and Crisis* 36, no. 5 (March 29, 1976):57–63. To Moltmann's credit, he also went to Latin America and encountered Latin American theologians on their own theological turf. One important meeting was held in Mexico (October 1977), which I also attended. The issue between Moltmann and the Latin Americans focused on the use of Marxism—i.e., social analysis and the naming of one's enemies. It was a spirited exchange but with each learning from the other. See an account of the conference in Jorge V. Pixley and Jean-Pierre Bastien eds., *Praxis cristiana y producción teológica* (Salamanca, Spain: Sígueme, 1979).

38. *Power of the Poor*, 191; see also his "Two Theological Perspectives: Liberation Theology and Progressive Theology," in *The Emergent Gospel*, S. Torres and V. Fabella eds. (Maryknoll, N.Y.: Orbis Books, 1978).

39. *Power of the Poor*, 196.

40. *The Wretched of the Earth* (New York: Grove, 1963), 252.

41. Ibid.

42. Ibid., 255.

43. Although the NCBC and the AACC were similar, they were also quite different. The AACC was made up of official representatives of churches. The membership base of the NCBC was individuals.

44. On black theology in South Africa, see Basil Moore ed., *Black Theology: A South African Voice* (London: Hurst, 1973); Allan A. Boesak, *Farewell to Innocence: A Socio-Ethical Study on Black Theology and Power* (Maryknoll, N.Y.: Orbis Books, 1977); and John W. de Gruchy, *The Church Struggle in South Africa* (Grand Rapids, Mich.: Eerdmans, 1979).

45. I have tried to demonstrate in this chapter that from its very origin Black theology was defined as liberation theology. We did not borrow the word "liberation" from Latin America. But because the problem of white racism has played the central role in creating the need for a distinctively Black theology, the word "Black" has been more visible in describing our theological enterprise than has the term "liberation." The focus on "Black" has provided many white North American and European interpreters with the option of identifying "liberation theology" as exclusively limited to Latin America, even though Blacks started using the word "liberation" in relation to theology about the same time as did Latin American theologians. The focus on liberation in terms of class in lieu of color gave white North American theologians yet another occasion for ignoring the problem of racism and what it means in the history of North America and Europe. As we Black theologians faced the problem of limiting our theological vision to issues of color, we felt that our perspective of the world, when seen in terms of the immediate, existential needs of Blacks, required that we focus on color as our central starting point in theology, even though we recognized the obvious shortcomings in

that initial point of departure.

46. For an introduction to the important theology of liberation movement in Latin America, see José Míguez Bonino, *Doing Theology in a Revolutionary Situation*. The classic and most important text on liberation theology in Latin America is still Gustavo Gutiérrez's *A Theology of Liberation*; see also his *The Power of the Poor in History*. For the best introduction to the variety of perspectives of the excellent theological work that is being done in Latin America, see Rosino Gibellini ed., *Frontiers of Theology in Latin America* (Maryknoll, N.Y.: Orbis Books, 1979).

47. The dialogue between Latin American and African American theologians began in Geneva at the WCC in 1973; see *Risk* 9, no. 2 (1973). For my report on the history of our dialogue with Latin American, Asian, and African theologies, and important essays on the themes, see Wilmore and Cone, *Black Theology*, p. 4, "Black Theology and Third World Theologies," 445–608; see also my "From Geneva to São Paulo: A Dialogue between Black Theology and Latin American Liberation Theology," in Sergio Torres and John Eagleson eds., *The Challenge of Basic Christian Communities* (Maryknoll, N.Y.: Orbis Books, 1981):265–81, and *My Soul Looks Back* (Nashville, Tenn.: Abingdon, 1982), chap. 4.

48. Boston: Beacon Press, 1973, rev. ed. (originally published in 1961).

49. Boston: Beacon Press.

50. New York: Morrow.

51. New York: Schocken Books.

52. New York: Doubleday.

53. Boston: Beacon Press.

54. Boston: Beacon Press.

55. New York: Doubleday.

56. Nashville, Tenn.: Abingdon.

57. See my *God of the Oppressed* and my "Interpretation of the Debate among Black Theologians," in Wilmore and Cone, *Black Theology*.

58. New York: Doubleday. See my response to Jones in *God of the Oppressed*, chap. 8, and "Interpretation of the Debate among Black Theologians."

59. See my response to Cecil Cone in "Interpretation of the Debate."

60. Wilmore and Cone, *Black Theology*, 255.

61. See especially his "Perspectives for a Study of Afro-American Religion in the U.S." and his "Structural Similarities and Dissimilarities in Black and African Theologies," *Journal of Religious Thought* 32 (Spring 1976). See my response in "Interpretation of the Debate."

62. New York: Morrow.

63. Philadelphia: Lippincott.

64. New York: Harper & Row.

65. See especially his "Black Churches in Historical Perspective," *Christianity and Crisis* (November 2 and 16, 1970):226–28; "They Sought a City: The Black Church and Churchmen in the Nineteenth Century," *Union Seminary Quarterly Review* 26, no. 3 (Spring 1971).

66. I have referred to several articles of Preston Williams in earlier chapters. His most influential

articles included "Black Church: Origin, History, Present Dilemmas"; "The Ethics of Black Power"; "The Ethical Aspects of the 'Black Church/Black Theology' Phenomenon"; "Shifting Racial Perspectives," *Harvard Divinity Bulletin* (Fall 1968):12–15; "Ethics and Ethos in the Black Experience," *Christianity and Crisis* (May 31, 1971); "Toward a Sociological Understanding of the Black Religious Community," *Soundings* (Fall 1971); "The Price of Social Justice," *Christian Century* (May 9, 1973). Herbert Edwards's most important and insightful essay was his "Racism and Christian Ethics in America," *Katallegete* (Winter 1971). See also his "The Third World and the Problem of God-Talk," *Harvard Theological Review* 64, no. 4 (1971). Carlton Lee played a major role in the origin of the NCBC. One of his most important essays was his "Religious Roots of the Negro Protest," in Arnold Rose ed., *Assuring Freedom to the Free* (Detroit: Wayne State University Press, 1964).

67. See his "Africa and the Biblical Period," *Harvard Theological Review* (Oct. 1971); "Biblical Theology and Black Theology," *Journal of the Interdenominational Theological Center* (Spring 1976).

68. Johnson's essay, "Jesus, the Liberator" was the most influential. See also his *The Soul of the Black Preacher* (1970) and his *Proclamation Theology* (Shreveport, La.: Fourth Episcopal District Press, 1977). Warner Traynham has also written an important text on Black Theology, *Christian Faith in Black and White: A Primer in Theology from the Black Perspective*. This text is valuable not only because of its interpretation of the meaning of Black Theology but also because of the important documents in the appendices on the early development of Black Theology.

69. New York: Doubleday.

70. His most important written contribution to Black Theology is "Toward the Promised Land," *The Black Church* 2, no. 1 (1972):1–48.

12

Womanist Theology: Black Women's Experience as a Source for Doing Theology, with Special Reference to Christology

Jacquelyn Grant

Introduction

This paper is an exploration into the experiences of Black women for the purpose of providing alternative sources for doing theology.

Black Theology and other Third World theologies of liberation have shown through their challenge of the methodologies of classical theologies that experience of the dominant culture has been the invisible crucible for theologizing. They have demonstrated that theology is not unrelated to socio-political realities of existence and that historically it has been used to maintain the social and political advantages of the status quo. The portrayal of the universal God was such that an affirmation of this God meant a simultaneous negation of all others' cultural perceptions of the divinity, as well as a nega-tion of those very cultures. Nowhere was this more clear than in the area of Christian foreign missions where conversion to Christianity implicitly meant deculturalization and acceptance of the western value system on the part of Asians, Africans, and Latin Americans. Upon conversion, one had to with-draw from indigenous ways of imaging the divine reality and embrace for-eign, western ways that often served to undergird oppressive religious, social and political structures.

This is true not only in the foreign missions field but also in the western world; it is reflected in the ways in which oppressors deal with oppressed people within their own territory. We see this with respect to Third World people in the first world context as well as with respect to women.

An illustration emerging out of Black Theology and feminist theology will make the point. Theologians in both these theological camps propose an alternative understanding, for example, of Christian love.

James Cone, in an early work, makes a distinction between a non-threatening love of many Christians and the radical love of Jesus which demands justice: "There is no place in Christian theology for sentimental love—love without risk or cost. Love demands all, the whole of one's being. Thus, for the black [person] to believe the Word of God about [God's] love revealed in Christ, he/she must be prepared to meet head-on the sentimental "Christian" love of whites, which would make him/her a nonperson."[1]

Cone insists that one cannot practice Christian love and at the same time practice racism. He argues:

> It seems that whites forget about the necessary interrelatedness of love, justice, and power when they encounter Black people. Love becomes emotional and sentimental. This sentimental, condescending love accounts for their desire to "help" by relieving the physical pains of the suffering blacks so they can satisfy their own religious piety and keep the poor powerless. But the new blacks, redeemed in Christ, must refuse their "help" and demand that blacks be confronted as persons. They must say to whites that authentic love is not "help," not giving Christmas baskets, but working for political, social, and economic justice, which always means a redistribution of power. It is a kind of power which enables the blacks to fight their own battles and thus keep their dignity. "Powerlessness breeds a race of beggars."[2]

Black people do not need a love which functions contrary to the establishment of Black personhood. This understanding of love was just recently affirmed by Black theologians (lay and clergy, professional and non-professional) in Southern Africa in their challenge to the church through "The Kairos Document." They cautioned, "we must also remember that the most loving thing we can do for both the oppressed and for our enemies who are oppressors is to eliminate the oppression, remove the tyrants from power and establish a just government for the common good of all the people."[3] Here, love is not defined in the interest of those who wish to maintain the present status quo. But it is defined from the point of view of those on the underside of history—the victims of the oppressors' power.

In a similar vein, feminists challenge traditional understandings of love. Valerie Saiving Goldstein expresses her suspicions of traditional theological works in the following way: "I am no longer certain as I once was that, when theologians speak of 'man,' they are using the word in its generic sense. It is, after all, a well-known fact that theology has been written almost exclusively by men. This alone should put us on guard, especially since contemporary theologians constantly remind us that one of man's strongest temptations is to identify his own limited perspective with universal truth."[4]

Lifting up the Christian notion of sin and love, Goldstein suggests that it would be equally unsatisfactory to impose universal understanding on those concepts. The identification of these notions with self-assertion and selflessness, respectively, functions differently in masculine experience and feminine experience. She explains further: "Contemporary theological doctrines of love have, I believe, been constructed primarily upon the basis of masculine experience and thus view the human condition from the male standpoint. Consequently, these doctrines do not provide an adequate interpretation of the situation of women—nor, for that matter, of men, especially in light of certain fundamental changes now taking place in our own society."[5]

Because of their feminine character, for women love takes the form of nurturing, supporting, and servicing their families. Consequently, if a woman believes "the theologians, she will try to strangle other impulses in herself. She will believe that, having chosen marriage and children and thus being face to face with the needs of her family for love, refreshment, and forgiveness, she has no right to ask anything for herself but must submit without qualification to the strictly feminine role."[6] For women too, the issue is one of personhood—are women to deny who they are in order to be saved?

Goldstein then argues that when experience in theology is scrutinized, we will discover that because it has been synonomous with masculine experience, it is inadequate to deal with the situation of women.

In other words, Black theologians and feminist theologians have argued that the universalism classical theologians attempt to uphold represents merely the particular experiences of the dominant culture. Blacks identify that experience as white experience; and women identify it as male experience. The question then is, if universalism is the criterion for valid theology, how is such a universalism achieved?

What I will be exploring here is how Black women's experiences can provide some insights into this question. In doing so, Black women not only join Blacks and feminists in their challenge of theology but they also provide an internal critique for Black men as well as for white women. In this chapter, I will focus primarily upon Black women's experience as related to the development of feminist theology. (In a rather limited way, I have addressed the issue of Black women's experiences and Black theology in an article entitled

"Black Theology and The Black Woman."[7] That subject certainly has not been exhausted, and shall be treated in more substantive ways in the future.)

But here I am interested in engaging feminist theology with reference to its constructive efficacy for Black women given the peculiarities of their experiences. The results will be the beginnings of a theology from a Black woman's perspective with special reference to Christology.

In order to create a common starting point, let's begin with a synopsis of the basic tenets of feminist theology. First, feminist theology seeks to develop a *wholistic theology*. Feminist theology rejects the traditional forms of oppressive and one-sided, male-dominated theologies which arise out of patriarchal religion(s).[8] Women have begun to see that their continuous oppression in the church and society has its basis in these patriarchal religions. Historically, the theologies of religions have emerged out of the experiences of men, making the theologies representative thereof. Because humanity comprises both men and women, feminist theologians seek to develop a more wholistic perspective in theology.

Second, in seeking to produce a wholistic perspective in theology, feminist theologians call for the *eradication of social/sexual dualisms* in human existence inherent in patriarchy. A patriarchy is characterized by male domination and female submission and subordination. In such a society, men are considered strong, intelligent, rational and aggressive; women are considered weak, irrational, and docile.

A third function of feminist theology is to *conceptualize new and positive images of women*. Throughout history, including the history of theology, women have been portrayed in negative ways. They have been sources of evil (snakes), authors of trickery (witches), and stimulants (therefore causes) for the sexual perversions of men (temptresses and prostitutes). These negative images must be changed to reflect reality.

Finally, feminist theology must *evaluate male articulated understandings of the Christian faith*. Doctrines developed in a system of patriarchy merely perpetuate patriarchal structures. As the patriarchal theological system is challenged, so are the doctrines, God, Jesus Christ, the fall, and the church.

Emerging Black Feminist Perspective

It has been argued by many Blacks that the women's liberation movement is a white middle-class movement. Therefore it is believed to be totally irrelevant to the situation of Black women since the majority of them are not middle-class.

Brenda Eichelberger gives several reasons for Black women's non-involvement in feminist causes. Among them are such things as class differences, the lack of Black women's knowledge about the real issues involved and the suspicion that the middle-class white women's movement is divisive to the Black community that claims prior allegiance.[9] In spite of these and other negative responses to the white women's liberation movement, there has been a growing feminist consciousness among many Black women and some Black men. This consciousness is coupled by the increased willingness of Black women to undertake an independent analysis of sexism, thereby creating an emerging Black perspective on feminism. Black feminism grows out of Black women's tridimensional reality of race/sex/class. It holds that full human liberation cannot be achieved simply by the elimination of any one form of oppression. Consequently, real liberation must be "broad in the concrete";[10] it must be based upon a multidimensional analysis.

Recent writings by secular Black feminists have challenged white feminist analysis and Black race analysis, particularly by introducing data from Black women's experience that has been historically ignored by white feminists and Black male liberationists.

In only a few of these articles do Black women employ only a gender analysis to treat Black women's reality. Whereas Ntozake Shange focuses chiefly upon sexism, Michelle Wallace, like Alice Walker, presumes that white racism has had an adverse effect upon the Black community in a way that confuses and reinforces the already existing sexism. Sharon Harley, Rosalyn Terborg-Penn, Paula Giddings, and Gloria Wade-Gayles all recognize the inclusiveness of the oppressive reality of Black women as they endure racism, sexism and economic oppression. Barbara Smith, Gloria Hull, Bell Hooks, and Angela Davis particularly explore the implications of this tridimensional oppression of Black women. In so doing, Black women have either articulated Black feminist perspectives or developed grounds for doing so.[11] These perspectives, however, have not led to the resolution of tensions between Black women and white women, and they even have brought to the forefront some tensions between Black women and Black men.

On the contrary, the possibly irreparable nature of these tensions is implied in Walker's suggestion that the experience of being a Black woman or a white woman is so different that another word is required to describe the liberative efforts of Black women. Her suggestion that the word "womanist" is more appropriate for Black women is derived from the sense of the word as it is used in Black communities:

Womanist, from womanish. (Opp. of "girlish," i.e., frivolous, irresponsible, not serious). A Black feminist or feminist of color. From the Black folk expression of mothers to female children, "You acting womanish," i.e., like a woman. Usually referring to outrageous, audacious, courageous or willful behavior. Wanting to know more and in greater depth than is considered "good" for one. Interest in grown-up doings. Acting grown up. Being grown up. Interchangeable with another black folk expression: "You trying to be grown." Responsible. In charge. Serious.[12]

Womanists were Sojourner Truth, Jarena Lee, Amanda Berry Smith, Ida B. Wells, Mary Church Terrell, Mary McCloud Bethune and countless others not remembered in any historical study. A womanist then is a strong Black woman who has sometimes been mislabeled as domineering castrating matriarch. A womanist is one who has developed survival strategies in spite of the oppression of her race and sex in order to save her family and her people. Walker's womanist notation suggests not "the feminist," but the active struggle of Black women that makes them who they are. For some Black women that may involve being feminine as traditionally defined, and for others it involves being masculine as stereotypically defined. In any case, womanist means being and acting out who you are and interpreting the reality for yourself. Black women speak out for themselves. As a Black feminist critic Barbara Christian explains, referring to Audre Lorde's poem about the deadly consequence of silence, Black women must speak up and answer in order to validate their own experience. This is important even if only to ourselves. It is to the womanist tradition that Black women must appeal for the doing of theology.

The Beginnings of a Womanist Theology with Special Reference to Christology

Womanist theology begins with the experiences of Black women as its point of departure. This experience includes not only Black women's activities in the larger society but also in the churches, and reveals that Black women have often rejected the oppressive structure in the church as well.

These experiences provide a context significant for doing theology. Those experiences had been and continue to be defined by racism, sexism and classism and therefore offer a unique opportunity and a new challenge for developing a relevant perspective in the theological enterprise. This perspective in theology which I am calling womanist theology draws upon the life and experiences of some Black women who have created meaningful interpretations of the Christian faith.

Black women must do theology out of their tridimensional experience of racism/sexism/classism. To ignore any aspect of this experience is to deny the holistic and integrated reality of Black womanhood. When Black women say that God is on the side of the oppressed, we mean that God is in solidarity with the struggles of those on the underside of humanity, those whose lives are bent and broken from the many levels of assault perpetrated against them.

In a chapter entitled "Black Women: Shaping Feminist Theory," Hooks elaborates on the interrelationship of the threefold oppressive reality of Black women and shows some of the weaknesses of white feminist theory. Challenging the racist and classist assumptions of white feminism, Hooks writes, "Racism abounds in the writings of white feminists, reinforcing white supremacy and negating the possibility that women will bond politically across ethnic and racial boundaries. Past feminist refusal to draw attention to and attack racial hierarchy suppressed the link between race and class. Yet class structure in American society has been shaped by the racial politics of white supremacy."[13] This means that Black women, because of oppression determined by race and their subjugation as women, make up a disproportionately high percentage of the poor and working classes. However the fact that Black women are a subjugated group even within the Black community and the white women's community does not mean that they are alone in their oppression within those communities. In the women's community poor white women are discriminated against, and in the Black community, poor Black men are marginalized. This suggests that classism, as well as racism and sexism, has a life of its own. Consequently, simply addressing racism and sexism is inadequate to bring about total liberation. Even though there are dimensions of class which are not directly related to race or sex, classism impacts Black women in a peculiar way which results in the fact that they are most often on the bottom of the social and economic ladder. For Black women doing theology, to ignore classism would mean that their theology is no different from any other bourgeois theology. It would be meaningless to the majority of Black women, who are themselves poor. This means that addressing only issues relevant to middle-class women or Blacks will simply not do. The daily struggles of poor Black women must serve as the gauge for the verification of the claims of womanist theology. Anna Julia Cooper makes a relevant point: "Women's wrongs are thus indissolubly linked with all unde-fended woes, and the acquirement of her 'rights' will mean the supremacy of triumph of all right over might, the supremacy of the moral forces of reason, and justice, and love in the government of the nations of earth."[14]

Black women's experience must be affirmed as the crucible for doing womanist theology. It is the context in which we must decide theological questions. More specifically, it is within the context of this experience that Black women read the Bible. A (brief) look at Black women's use of the Bible indicates how it is their experiences that determine relevant questions for them.

The Bible in the Womanist Tradition

Theological investigation into the experiences of Christian Black women reveals that Black women considered the Bible to be a major source of reli-gious validation in their lives. Though Black women's relationship with God preceded their introduction to the Bible, this Bible gave some content to their God-consciousness.[15] The source for Black women's understanding of God has been twofold: first, God's revelation directly to them, and second, God's revelation as witnessed in the Bible and as read and heard in the context of their experience. The understanding of God as creator, sustainer, comforter, and liberator took on life as they agonized over their pain and celebrated the hope that as God delivered the Israelites, they would be delivered as well. The God of the Old and New Testament became real in the consciousness of oppressed Black women. Of the use of the Bible, Fannie Barrier Williams quite aptly said, "Though the Bible was not an open book to the Negro before emancipation, thousands of the enslaved men and women of the negro race learned more than was taught to them. Thousands of them realized the deeper meanings, the sweeter consolations and the spiritual awakenings that are part of the religious experiences of all Christians."[16]

In other words, though Black people in general and Black women in particular were politically impotent and religiously controlled, they were able to appropriate certain themes of the Bible that spoke to their reality. For example, Jarena Lee, a nineteenth century Black woman preacher in the African Methodist Episcopal Church, constantly emphasized the theme "Life and Liberty" in her sermons which were always biblically based. This interplay of Scripture and experience was exercised even more expressly by many other Black women. An ex-slave woman revealed that when her experience negated certain oppressive interpretations of the Bible given by white preachers, she, through engaging the biblical message for herself, rejected them. Consequently she also dismissed white preachers who distorted the message in order to maintain slavery. Her grandson, Howard Thurman, speaks of her use of the Bible in this way:

> "During the days of slavery," she said, "the master's minister would occasionally hold services for the slaves. Always the white minister used as his text something from Paul. 'Slaves be obedient to them that are your masters . . . as unto Christ.' Then he would go on to show how, if we were good and happy slaves, God would bless us. I promised my Maker that if I ever learned to read and if freedom ever came, I would not read that part of the Bible."[17]

What we see here is perhaps more than a mere rejection of a white preacher's interpretation of the Bible: it is an exercise in internal critique of the Bible. The liberating message of the gospel is seen as over against the oppressive elements in the Bible.

The truth the Bible brought was undeniable, though perception of it was often distorted in order to support the monstrous system of oppression. Sarcastically responding to this tendency, Fannie Barrier Williams admonished, "do not open the Bible too wide." Williams, a non-theologically trained person, realized biblical interpretation had at its basis the prior agenda of white America. She therefore argued:

> Religion, like every other force in America, was first used as in instrument and servant of slavery. All attempts to Christianize the negro were limited by the important fact that he was property of valuable and peculiar sort, and that the property value must not be disturbed, even if his soul were lost. If Christianity could make the negro docile, domestic and less an independent and fighting savage, let it be preached to that extent and no further.[18]

Such false, pernicious, demoralizing gospel could only be preached if the Bible were not opened wide enough, lest one see the liberating message of Jesus as summarized in Luke 4:18. The Bible must be read and interpreted in the light of Black women's own oppression and God's revelation within that context. Womanist theology must, like Sojourner, "compare the teachings of the Bible with the witness" in them.[19]

To do womanist theology, then, we must read and hear the Bible and engage it within the context of our own experience. This is the only way that it can make sense to people who are oppressed. Black women of the past did not hesitate in doing this and we must do no less.

Jesus in the Womanist Tradition

Having opened the Bible wider than many white people, Black people in general and Black women in particular found a Jesus who they could claim and whose claim for them was one of affirmation of dignity and self-respect.

In the experience of Black people, Jesus was "all things."[20] Chief among these, however, was the belief in Jesus as the divine co-sufferer, who empowers them in situations of oppression. For Christian Black women in the past, Jesus was their central frame of reference. They identified with Jesus because they believed that Jesus identified with them. As Jesus was persecuted and made to suffer undeservedly, so were they. His suffering culminated in the crucifixion. Their crucifixion included rapes, and husbands being castrated (literally and metaphorically), babies being sold, and other cruel and often murderous treatments. But Jesus' suffering was not the suffering of a mere human, for Jesus was understood to be God incarnate. As Harold Carter observed of Black prayers in general, there was no difference made between the persons of the Trinity, Jesus, God the Father, or the Holy Spirit. All of these proper names for God were used interchangeably in prayer language. Thus Jesus was the one who speaks the world into creation. He was the power behind the church.[21] Black women's affirmation of Jesus as God meant that white people were not God. One old slave woman clearly demonstrates this as she prayed, "Dear Massa Jesus, we all uns beg Ooner [you] come make us a call dis yere day. We is nutting but poor Etiopian women and people ain't tink much 'bout we. We ain't trust any of dem great high people for come to we church, but do' you is de one great Massa, great too much dan Massa Linkum, you ain't shame to care for we African people."[22] Implicit in the description "nothing but poor Black women" and what follows is the awareness of the public devaluation of Black women. But in spite of that Jesus is presented as a confidant who could be trusted while white people could not be trusted. This woman affirmed the contribution of Abraham Lincoln to the emancipation of Blacks, but rejected Mr. Lincoln as her real or ultimate master. Quite a contrast to the master's (slave owner's) perception of his or herself.

This slave woman did not hesitate to identify her struggle and pain with those of Jesus. In fact, the common struggle made her know that Jesus would respond to her beck and call.

> Come to we, dear Massa Jesus. De sun, he hot too much, de road am dat long and boggy (sandy) and we ain't got no buggy for send and fetch Ooner. But Massa, you 'member how you walked dat hard walk up Calvary and ain't weary but tink about we all dat way. We know you ain't weary for to come to we. We pick out de torns, de prickles, de brier, de backsliding' and de quarrel and de sin out of you path so dey shan't hurt Ooner pierce feet no more.[23]

The reference to "no buggy" to send for Jesus, brings to mind the limited material possessions of pre- and post-Civil War Blacks. In her speech, "Ain't I a Woman," Sojourner Truth distinguished between white women's and Black women's experiences by emphasizing that Black women were not helped into carriages as were white women.[24] In the prayer, this woman speaks of that reality wherein most Blacks didn't even have carriages or buggys. For had she owned one, certainly she'd send it to fetch Jesus. Here we see the concern for the comfort of the suffering Jesus. Jesus suffers when we sin—when we backslide or when we quarrel. But still Jesus is identified with her plight. Note that Jesus went to the cross with this Black woman on his mind. He was thinking about her and all others like her. So totally dedicated to the poor, the weak, the downtrodden, the outcast that in this Black woman's faith, Jesus would never be too tired to come. As she is truly among the people at the bottom of humanity, she can make things comfortable for Jesus even though she may have nothing to give him—no water, no food—but she can give tears and love. She continues:

> Come to we, dear Massa Jesus. We all uns ain't got no good cool water for give you when you thirsty. You know, Massa, de drought so long, and the well so low, ain't nutting but mud to drink. But we gwine to take de

'munion cup and fill it wid de tear of repentance, and love clean out of we heart. Dat all we hab to gib you, good Massa.[25]

The material or physical deprivation experienced by this woman did not reduce her desire to give Jesus the best. Being a Black woman in the American society meant essentially being poor, with no buggy, and no good cool water. Life for Black women was indeed bad, hot and at best muddy. Note that there is no hint that their condition results from some divine intention. Whereas I am not prepared to say that this same woman or any others in that church the next day would have been engaged in political praxis by joining such movements as Nat Turner's rebellion or Denmark Vesey's revolt, it is clear that her perspective was such that the social, political, and economic orders were believed to be sinful and against the will of the real master, Jesus.

For Black women, the role of Jesus unraveled as they encountered him in their experience as one who empowers the weak. In this vein, Jesus was such a central part of Sojourner Truth's life that all of her sermons made him the starting point. When asked by a preacher if the source of her preaching was the Bible, she responded "No honey, can't preach from de Bible—can't read a letter."[26] Then she explained; "When I preaches, I has jest one text to preach from, an' I always preaches from this one. My text is, 'When I found Jesus!'"[27] In this sermon Sojourner Truth recounts the events and struggles of life from the time her parents were brought from Africa and sold "up an' down, an' hither an' yon . . ."[28] to the time that she met Jesus within the context of her struggles for dignity of Black people and women. Her encounter with Jesus brought such joy that she became overwhelmed with love and praise: "Praise, praise, praise to the Lord! An' I begun to feel such a love in my soul as I never felt before—love to all creatures. An' then, all of a sudden, it stopped, an' I said, Dar's de white folks that have abused you, an' beat you, and an' abused your people—think o' them! But then there came another rush of love through my soul, an' I cried out loud—"Lord, I can love even de white folks!"[29]

This love was not a sentimental, passive love. It was a tough, active love that empowered her to fight more fiercely for the freedom of her people. For the rest of her life she continued speaking at abolition and women's rights gatherings condemning the horrors of oppression.

The Womanist Traditions and Christological Reflections

More than anyone, Black theologians have captured the essence of the significance of Jesus in the lives of Black people, which to an extent includes Black women. They all hold that the Jesus of history is important for understanding who he was and his significance for us today. By and large they have affirmed that this Jesus is the Christ, that is, God incarnate. They have argued that in the light of our experience, Jesus meant freedom.[30] They have maintained that Jesus means freedom from the sociopsychological, psycho-cultural, economic, and political oppression of Black people. In other words, Jesus is a political messiah.[31] "To free [humans] from bondage was Jesus's own definition of his ministry."[32] This meant that as Jesus identified with the lowly of his day, he now identifies with the lowly of this day, who in the American context are Black people. The identification is so real that Jesus Christ in fact becomes Black. It is important to note that Jesus's Blackness is not a result of ideological distortion of a few Black thinkers, but a result of careful Christological investigation. Cone examines the sources of Christology and concludes that Jesus is Black because "Jesus was a Jew." He explains:

> It is on the basis of the soteriological meaning of the particularity of his Jewishness that theology must affirm the christological significance of Jesus' present blackness. He *is* black because he was a Jew. The affirmation of the Black Christ can be understood when the significance of his past Jewishness is related dialetically to the significance of his present blackness. On the other hand, the Jewishness of Jesus located him in the context of the Exodus, thereby connecting his appearance in Palestine with God's liberation of oppressed Israelites from Egypt. Unless Jesus were truly from Jewish ancestry, it would make little theological sense to say that he is the fulfillment of God's covenant with Israel. But on the other hand, the blackness of Jesus brings out the soteriological meaning of his Jewishness for our contemporary situation when Jesus' person is understood in the context of the cross and resurrection. Without negating the divine election of Israel, the Cross and resurrection are Yahweh's fulfillment of his original intention for Israel. . . .[33]

The condition of Black people today reflects the cross of Jesus. Yet the resurrection brings the hope that liberation from oppression is immanent. The resurrected Black Christ signifies this hope.

Cone further argues that this Christological title, "The Black Christ," is not validated by its universality, but in fact by its particularity. Its significance lies in whether or not the Christological title "points to God's universal will to liberate particular oppressed people from inhumanity."[34] These particular oppressed peoples to which Cone refers are characterized in Jesus's parable on the Last Judgment as "the least." "The least in America are literally and symbolically present in Black people."[35] This notion of "the least" is attractive because it descriptively locates the condition of Black women. "The least" are those people who have no water to give, but offer what they have, as the old slave woman cited above says in her prayer. Black women's experience in general is such a reality. Their tridimensional reality renders their particular situation a complex one. One could say that not only are they the oppressed of the oppressed, but their situation represents "the particular within the particular."

But is this just another situation that takes us deeper into the abyss of theological relativity? I would argue that it is not, because it is in the context of Black women's experience where the particular connects up with the universal. By this I mean that in each of the three dynamics of oppression, Black women share in the reality of a broader community. They share race suffering with Black men; with white women and other Third World women they are victims of sexism; and with poor Blacks and whites, and other Third World peoples, especially women, they are disproportionately poor. To speak of Black women's tridimensional reality, therefore, is not to speak of Black women exclusively, for there is an implied universality that connects them with others.

Likewise, with Jesus Christ, there was an implied universality which made him identify with others—the poor, the woman, the stranger. To affirm Jesus's solidarity with the "least of the people" is not an exercise in romanticized contentment with one's oppressed status in life. For as the resurrection signified that there is more to life than the cross of Jesus Christ, for Black women it signifies that their tridimensional oppressive existence is not the end, but it merely represents the context in which a particular people struggle to experience hope and liberation. Jesus Christ thus represents a threefold significance; first he identifies with the "little people," Black women, where they are; second, he affirms the basic humanity of these, "the least;" and third, he inspires active hope in the struggle for resurrected, liberated existence.

To locate the Christ in Black people is a radical and necessary step, but understanding of Black women's reality challenges us to go further. Christ among the least must also mean Christ in the community of Black women. William Eichelberger was able to recognize this as he further particularized the significance of the Blackness of Jesus by locating Christ in Black women's community. He was able to see Christ not only as Black male but also Black female.

> God, in revealing Himself and His attributes from time to time in His creaturely existence, has exercised His freedom to formalize His appearance in a variety of ways. . . . God revealed Himself at a point in the past as Jesus the Christ a Black male. My reasons for affirming the Blackness of Jesus of Nazareth are much different from that of the white apologist. . . . God wanted to identify with that segment of mankind which had suffered most, and is still suffering. . . . I am constrained to believe that God in our times has updated His form of revelation to western society. It is my feeling that God is now manifesting Himself, and has been for over 450 years, in the form of the Black American Woman as mother, as wife, as nourisher, sustainer and preserver of life, the Suffering Servant who is despised and rejected by men, a personality of sorrow who is acquainted with grief. The Black Woman has borne our griefs and carried our sorrows. She has been wounded because of American white society's transgressions and bruised by white iniquities. It appears that she may be the instrumentality through whom God will make us whole.[36]

Granted, Eichelberger's categories for God and woman are very traditional. Nevertheless the significance of his thought is that he is able to conceive of the divine reality as other than a Black male messianic figure.

Even though Black women have been able to transcend some of the oppressive tendencies of white male (and Black male) articulated theologies, careful study reveals that some traditional symbols are inadequate for us today. The Christ understood as the stranger, the outcast, the hungry, the weak, the poor, makes the traditional male Christ (Black and white) less significant. Even our sisters of the past had some suspicions about the effects of a male image of the divine, for they did challenge the oppressive use of it in the church's theology. In so doing they were able to move from a traditional oppressive Christology, with respect to women, to an egalitarian Christology. This kind of equalitarian Christology was operative in Jarena Lee's argument for the right of women to preach. She argued ". . . the Saviour died for the woman as well as for the man."[37] The Crucifixion was for universal salvation, not just for male salvation or, as we may extend the argument to include, not just for white salvation. Christ came and died, no less for the woman as for the man, no less for Blacks as for whites. For Lee, this was not an academic issue, but one with practical ramification: "If the man may preach, because the Savior died for him, why not the woman? Seeing he died for her also. Is he not a whole Saviour, instead of half one? as those who hold it wrong for a woman to preach, would seem to make it appear."[38] Lee correctly perceives that there is an ontological issue at stake. If Jesus Christ were a saviour of men then it is true the maleness of Christ would be paramount.[39] But if Christ is a Saviour of all, then it is the humanity—the wholeness—of Christ which is significant.

Sojourner was aware of the same tendency of some scholars and church leaders to link the maleness of Jesus and the sin of Eve with the status of women and she challenged this notion in her famed speech "Ain't I A Woman?"

Then that little man in black there, he says women can't have as much rights as men, 'cause Christ wasn't a woman! Where did your Christ come from? Where did your Christ come from? From God and a woman. Man had nothing to do with Him.

If the first woman God ever made was strong enough to turn the world upside down alone, these women together ought to be able to turn it back, and get it right side up again! And now they is asking to do it, the men better let them.[40]

I would argue, as suggested by both Lee and Sojourner, that the significance of Christ is not his maleness, but his humanity. The most significant events of Jesus Christ were the life and ministry, the crucifixion, and the resurrection. The significance of these events, in one sense, is that in them the absolute becomes concrete. God becomes concrete not only in the man Jesus, for he was crucified, but in the lives of those who will accept the challenge of the risen Saviour—the Christ. For Lee, this meant that women could preach; for Sojourner it meant that women could possibly save the world; for me, it means today this Christ, found in the experience of Black women, is a Black woman.

Conclusion

I have argued that Black women's tridimensional reality provides a fertile context for articulating a theological perspective wholistic in scope and liberating in nature. The theology is potentially wholistic because the experience out of which it emerges is totally interconnected with other experiences. It is potentially liberating because it rests not on one single issue that could be considered only a middle-class issue relevant to one group of people, but is multifaceted. Thus the possibility for wholistic theology is more likely. Feminist theology as presently developed is limited by virtue of the experience base for feminist theology. That is, when feminists say that experience is the crucible for doing (feminist) theology, they usually mean white women's experience. With few exceptions, feminist thinkers do their analysis primarily, and in some circles exclusively, based on the notion that because sexism is the longest and most universal form of oppression, it should claim priority.[41]

Black women by and large have not held this assumption. Many have claimed that because of the pervasiveness of racism and because of its defining character for Black life in general, racism is most important. Though Sojourner Truth never did develop a sophisticated social analysis she was aware of the fact that she (and her people) were poor because she was Black, and perhaps poorer because she was woman. I say "perhaps" simply because in the slave economy one could argue that there was relatively little distinction between the property status of slaves by virtue of gender; women were no less property than men. As property they were a part of the material distributed, rather than participants in the inequitable system of material distribution. Thus as indicated above in the Black woman's prayer, material possessions of Blacks were limited. In a sense one could say that by virtue of one's race, one was slave and by virtue of that status, one was poor.

Still as we see the issues today, class distinctions which have emerged even in the Black community, and sex differences, which have taken on new forms of institutionalization, must be addressed. For liberation to become a reality, race, sex and class must be deliberately confronted. Interconnected as they are, they all impinge greatly on the lives of Black women. Overwhelming as are these realities, Black women do not feel defeated. For Jarena Lee observed the hope of the struggle is based on the faith that Jesus died (and was raised) for the woman as well as the man. This realization gave inspiration for the struggle. Black women today inside and outside of the church still bring an optimistic spirit as reflected in the conclusion of Maya Angelou's poem, "And Still I Rise:"

> Out of the hut of history's shame
> I rise
> Up from a past that's rooted in pain
> I rise
> I'm a Black ocean, leaping and wide,
> Welling and swelling, I bear in the tide
> Leaving behind nights of terror and fear
> I rise
> Into a daybreak that's wondrously clear
> I rise
> Bringing the gifts that my ancestors gave
> I am the dream and the hope of the slave.
> I rise.
> I rise.
> I rise.[42]

Notes

1. James H. Cone, *Black Theology and Black Power* (New York: Seabury Press, 1969):53–54.

2. Ibid., 54–55.

3. The Kairos Theologians, *The Kairos Document: Challenge to the Church*, 2d ed. (Braarufontein, South Africa: Skotaville Publishers, 1985; Reprint. Grand Rapids, Mich.: Eerdmans Publishing Co., 1986): pp. 24–25.

4. Valerie Saiving Goldstein, "The Human Situation of a Feminine," *The Journal of Religion* 40 (April 1960):100.

5. Ibid.

6. Ibid.

7. Jacquelyn Grant, "Black Theology and The Black Woman" in *Black Theology: A Documentary History, 1966–1979*, eds. Gayraud S. Wilmore and James H. Cone (Maryknoll, N.Y.: Orbis Books, 1979):418–33.

8. See Sheila D. Collins, *A Different Heaven and Earth: A Feminist Perspective on Religion* (Valley Forge, Penn.: Judson Press, 1974); Mary Daley, *Beyond God the Father: Toward a Philosophy of Women's Liberation* (Boston: Beacon Press, 1973); Mary Daley, *The Church and the Second Sex: With a New Feminist Post Christian Introduction by the Author* (New York: Harper and Colophon, 1975).

9. Brenda Eichelberger, "Voice of Black Feminism," *Quest: A Feminist Quarterly* 3 (Spring 1977):16–23.

10. This phrase is used by Anna Julia Cooper, *A Voice From the South* (Xenia, Ohio: Aldine Publishing House, 1852; Reprint. Westport, Conn.: Negro Universities Press, 1969), cited by Bell Hooks, *Ain't I A Woman: Black Women and Feminism* (Boston: South End Press, 1981):193–94. I use it here to characterize Black women's experience. To be concerned about Black women's issues is to be *concrete*. Yet because of their interconnectedness with Black men (racism), white women (sexism) and the poor (classism), it is also to be, at the same time, concerned with broad issues.

11. See Ntozake Shange, *For Colored Girls Who Have Considered Suicide When the Rainbow is Enuf* (New York: Macmillan, 1975); Michelle Wallace, *Black Macho and the Myth of the Superwoman* (New York: Dial Press, 1978); Alice Walker, *The Color Purple* (New York: Harcourt, Brace, and Jovanovich, 1982); and *In Search of Our Mother's Garden* (Harcourt, Brace, and Jovanovich, 1983); Sharon Harley and Rosalyn Terborg-Penn eds., *Afro-American Women* (New York: Kennikat Press, 1978); Paula Giddings, *When and Where I Enter* (New York: William Morrow, 1984); Gloria Wade-Grayles, *No Crystal Stair: Visions of Race and Sex in Black Women's Fiction* (New York: Pilgrims Press, 1984); Bell Hooks, *Feminist Theory: From Margin to Center* (Boston: South End Press, 1984); Barbara Smith, Gloria Hull, and Patricia Scott, *All the Women are White, and All the Blacks are Men, But Some of Us are Brave* (New York: The Feminist Press, 1982); Angela Y. Davis, *Women, Race, and Class* (New York: Vintage Book, 1981).

12. Walker, xi.

13. Hooks, 3.

14. Cooper, 91

15. Cecil Wayne Cone, *Identity Crisis In Black Theology* (Nashville, Tenn.: African Methodist Episcopal Church Press, 1975): especially chap. 3.

16. Bert James Lowenberg and Ruth Bogin eds., *Black Women in Nineteenth-Century American Life: Their Words, Their Thoughts, Their Feelings* (University Park, Penn: Pennsylvania State University Press, 1976):267.

17. Howard Thurman, *Jesus and the Disinherited* (Nashville, Tenn.: Abingdon Press, 1949):30–31.

18. Lowenberg and Bogin, 265.

19. Olive Gilbert, *Sojourner Truth: Narrative and Book of Life*. (1850 and 1875; Reprint. Chicago: Johnson Publishing Co., 1970):83.

20. Harold A. Carter, *The Prayer Tradition of Black People* (Valley Forge, Penn.: Judson Press, 1976):50. Carter, in referring to traditional Black prayer in general, states that Jesus was revealed as one who "was all one needs!"

21. Ibid.

22. Ibid., p. 49.

23. Ibid.

24. Sojourner Truth, "Ain't I A Woman?" in *Feminism: The Essential Historical Writings* ed. Mariam Schneir (New York: Vintage Books, 1972).

25. Carter, 49.

26. Gilbert, 118.

27. Ibid., 119.

28. Ibid.

29. Ibid.

30. James Deotis Roberts, *A Black Political Theology* (Philadelphia: Westminster Press, 1974):138. See especially chap. 5. See also Noel Leo Erskine, *Decolonizing Theology: A Caribbean Perspective* (New York: Orbis Books, 1980):125.

31. Roberts, 133.

32. Albert Cleage, *The Black Messiah* (New York: Sheed and Ward, 1969):92.

33. James H. Cone, *God of the Oppressed* (New York: Seabury Press, 1975):134.

34. Ibid., 135.

35. Ibid., 136.

36. William Eichelberger, "Reflections on the Person and Personality of the Black Messiah," *The Black Church* 2, no. 1 (1972):54.

37. Jerena Lee, *The Life and Religious Experiences and Journal of Mrs. Jerena Lee: A Colored Lady Giving an Account of Her Call to Preach* (Philadelphia: n.p., 1836):15–16.

38. Ibid., 16.

39. There is no evidence to suggest that Black women debated the significance of the maleness of Jesus. The fact is that Jesus Christ was a real, crucial figure in their lives. However, recent feminist scholarship has been important in showing the relation between the maleness of Christ and the oppression of women.

40. Truth, 94.

41. This question is explored further in Jacquelyn Grant, "The Development and Limitation of Feminist Theology: Toward an engagement of black women's religious experience and white women's religious experience" (Ph.D. diss., Union Theological Seminary, New York, 1985).

42. Maya Angelou, *And Still I Rise* (New York: Random House, 1978):42.

13

African American Catholics and Black Theology: An Interpretation

M. Shawn Copeland, O.P.

This is a report on the pastoral and intellectual appropriation of Black theology among African American Catholics. First, it will look backward to that thirty-five year period between 1889 and 1924 that was the scene of two attempts by Catholics of African descent to enjoy the heritage of their faith; to win for themselves, their progeny, and their people, the attention, the respect, and the care of their church; and to help secure the rights of citizenship for their race. By the power and grace of the Holy Spirit, these men and women gave birth to an indigenous *African American Catholic church tradition of struggle for social justice*. The story of their dedication enriches the common memory of all African American Christians and provides the historical context for the current twenty-year-old movement of Black Catholics in the United States. Second, it will identify the chief catalysts that have promoted the resurgence of that tradition. Third, it will present some illustrations of African American Catholic pastoral and intellectual appropriation of the impulses and insights of Black Theology. For the sake of our movement, I will cite names, achievements, and events, but because of the limitations of space, the efforts of many valiant and worthy women and men must be omitted. Finally, I will offer some suggestions for the future of that movement and its talented, diverse, and complex company of women and men who are striving, in the words of Pope Paul VI, to enrich their church with their "precious and original contribution of 'Negritude' [Blackness] which she [the church] needs particularly in this historic hour."[1]

Contextualization

From 1889 until 1894 African American Catholic laity conducted an increasingly vigorous movement to importune their church to "take an active interest in what concerns, not only the spiritual but also the temporal welfare of all the people entrusted to your [its] care." The call for a meeting of "Colored Catholics . . . for the purpose of taking the status of the race in their relation to the church"[2] was the inspiration of Daniel Rudd, the publisher and editor of the *American Catholic Tribune*, the only national newspaper published by Catholics of African descent in the United States in the nineteenth century. On Tuesday, January 1, 1889, nearly one hundred Black delegates from thirteen states, the District of Columbia, and South America, along with invited and sympathetic members of the white clergy and the hierarchy, met in congress in Washington, D.C.

At the end of the nineteenth century, the general state of African American Catholics within their church mirrored their condition in the wider American society. Although unlike the Presbyterians, the Baptists, and the Methodists, the Catholic church did not split over the question of slavery, the church long had purchased the culture and custom of racism; and, but for rare exceptions, ignorance, benign neglect, and segregation obtained. Catholics numbered about two hundred thousand in an African American population of seven million. A survey taken by the first congress cited twenty churches most with its own primary school, sixty-five other schools providing instruction for approximately five thousand children, nine orphanages, approximately one hundred fifty sisters in the two religious congregations founded for and by women of color,[3] seven seminarians, and one priest, Augustus Tolton.[4]

Four congresses followed, convening in 1890, 1892, 1893, and 1894, each assembly of delegates growing in confidence and in militancy. Their concerns and discussions were political and economic, social and religious, national and international in scope: an end to all forms of civic, economic, and political discrimination at home; the abolition of slavery abroad; the Back to Africa movement; just and equal treatment in their church. From the first, delegates had been eager for some permanent scheme, and at the third congress they organized the St. Peter Claver Union. However, neither the Union nor the congress movement lasted. It is not precisely clear why, but there were increasing clashes and differences with the white hierarchy and clergy over the identity, the direction, the purposes, and the leadership of the congress movement and the Union. Still, if their concrete accomplishments were few, this courageous group "recorded for posterity the perduring hopes and aspirations of the people they represented and left an embarrassing reminder of a plea for simple justice that would not be heeded."[5]

A broad-based movement among African American Catholics did not surface again until the second decade of the twentieth century with the concern of Dr. Thomas Wyatt Turner to meet the social, personal, and religious needs of Black Catholic servicemen during the First World War. The Committee for the Advancement of Colored Catholics, formed for this end, led to the Federated Colored Catholics. Turner had sought an action-oriented group dedicated to ending discrimination against Blacks within American society and within the church. For nearly a decade he was assisted by the Rev. John LaFarge, S.J., and the Reverend William Markoe, S.J. But rather than turn the Federated Colored Catholics in a less activist and practical direction, Turner parted company with the two Jesuits.

Catalysts in the Resurgence of the African American Catholic Struggle for Social Justice

The resurgence of an African American Catholic church tradition of struggle for social justice was catalyzed by radical change: change in the social, political, economic condition of Blacks in the United States and change in the Roman Catholic Church itself. The civil rights movement challenged the dominant ethos and pattern of accommodation to segregation; the Second Vatican Council challenged the historic intellectual, theological, and cultural insularity of the Catholic church. Change in the social mood without change in the ecclesial mood might have forced Black Catholics in the United States to abandon their centuries-old religious tradition; change in the ecclesial mood without change in the social mood might have compelled them to barter their racial-cultural heritage for silver. There was a propitiousness to these times. This was God's time; this was *kairos*.

The civil rights movement gave the U.S. Catholic church a singular opportunity to witness concretely at home to the meaning of unity in the faith and diversity in race, culture, and ethnicity. The nonviolent determination of Blacks for just and equal regard under law challenged the conscience. Catholic lay men and lay women, sisters and priests, marched at Selma. True, the Catholic hierarchy had denounced the sin of racism; and some, though not all, Catholic bishops had begun either to integrate those parochial schools under their direct control or to condemn publicly the worst examples of discrimination. But, as a whole, as an institution, the Catholic church in the

United States made no significant contribution to the civil rights movement. Black Catholic scholar-priest Jerome LeDoux declared the failure of the church at this crucial moment as one of "the most shameful scandals of modern Christianity: the damning exposure of the Church as the tail-light in matters of justice where the civil courts did not hesitate to be a head-light."[6] And writing from Gethsemani, Trappist Thomas Merton uncovered the dominant Catholic attitude as a "fake Catholicism." It was, he wrote, a "parody of unity which is no unity at all but a onesided and arbitrary attempt to reduce others to a condition of identity with ourselves . . . one of the most disastrous of misconceptions."[7]

If the silence and indifference of their church wounded Black Catholics, the cry "Black Power" galvanized them. At least one Black priest, Lawrence Lucas, joined the predominantly Protestant National Committee of Black Churchmen. Around the country Black priests, Black sisters, and Black laity began informal, nourishing conversations and study-groups. They retrieved and consumed the work of Black cultural theorists, historians, and artists. All over the United States, Black Catholics stood up.[8]

Fourteen days after the death of Martin Luther King, Jr., a group of Black priests stunned the white Catholic hierarchy by publicly and collectively naming their church as "primarily a white racist institution."[9] Women were not among delegates to the congress in 1889 and Robert L. Ruffin of Boston lamented their absence in his address to that body. But a woman was present at the priests' deliberations—Sister Martin de Porres Grey (now Dr. Patricia Grey Tyree). The priests urged her to organize Black sisters and she did. In August 1968, following a national gathering of 155 women from seventy-nine different religious congregations, forty-five cities, the Caribbean, and Africa, the National Black Sisters' Conference (NBSC) was born pledging "to work unceasingly for the liberation of Black people."[10] The National Office for Black Catholics (NOBC) along with national assemblies of seminarians and laity soon followed.

But the contemporary movement among Black Catholics was not without dissension and conflict. Black Catholics were never in complete accord over the function and organizational structure of the NOBC. There were heated objections to its presumed role as an umbrella agency for the various national groups. The clergy, sisters, and brothers were well-schooled in ecclesiastical protocol; at times they used this to disadvantage the laity. The new emphasis on lay leadership was no less threatening to Black clerics and religious, than it was to their white colleagues. Long denied pastorates and other appropriate outlets for their talent, they were not always eager to share leadership with the laity. But still, always—then and now—our arguments focused on the best means to importune our church to address itself to racism, on the style and strategy of our self-determination, but never on the validity of these needs, on the legitimacy of our demands, or on their substance.

Pastoral and Intellectual Appropriation of Black Theolgy

The efforts at pastoral and intellectual appropriation of Black Theology by African American Catholics are, first of all, the products of the resurgence of an African American Catholic church tradition of struggle for justice in their church and in the wider society. Clearly the various projects and programs developed by African American Catholics derive inspiration from the pioneering theological and ministerial studies of Black Protestant theologians, church scholars, and pastors. But African American Catholic projects and programs also take impetus from the Black Power movement and Black cultural nationalism, from the Black separatism of the early Malcolm X and the Black Christian nationalism of Albert Cleage; from contact with the leaders and developments of post-Conciliar African Catholicism and the renewal of theology and pastoral ministry taking place in the universal church. On the other hand, two movements with deep Catholic roots, namely, the Theology In the Americas program (TIA)[11] and feminist theology, to date have exerted little influence on African American Catholic pastoral work and theological thinking as a whole.

The Black Catholic Clergy Caucus always has formed a visible and vigorous vanguard confronting ecclesiastical racism at every turn, collectively offering Black Catholics and our activities an offensive and defensive pastorate, and initiating communication with our counterparts in Africa. The increasing number and participation of Black bishops in the National Conference of Catholic Bishops keep the agenda of Black communicants before the wider American Catholic church. It is through the bishops' vigilance that the hierarchy issued the pastoral letter on racism, "Brothers and Sisters to Us."[12] But it was the establishment and staffing of the various national offices, especially those of the National Office for Black Catholics and the National Black Sisters' Conference, that put teeth and soul into the shaping of a distinctive African American Catholicism. These two organizations carved out space for the development of leadership, for study, for spiritual and psychological formation, for the creative intellectual and pastoral interpretation of the Black Catholic experience in the United States.

Pastoral Application of Black Theology

Liturgical Rites and Rituals. Catholics of African American descent will be forever indebted to the Reverend Clarence Joseph Rivers who singlehandedly revolutionized the hymnody, the ritual form, the symbols, the mood, and the atmosphere of their worship. Well before the Second Vatican Council, Father Rivers had begun to compose, perform, and lecture on Catholic church music in a Black cultural style. In his *American Mass Program, Mass Dedicated to the Brotherhood of Man*[13] and subsequent compositions and recordings, Rivers introduced the idiom of African American music into Catholic worship. In the late 1960s and early 1970s, in order to bring greater cultural coherence to the liturgy, he began to critically reexamine the relation of the various elements of the mass to the Black idiom. In his commitment to articulate an authentic African American Catholic liturgical aesthetic, Rivers challenged the diluted liturgical experimentation that attempted to pass for renewal in so many places in the wider U.S. Catholic church. To his achievements are joined the work of other Black Catholic composers including Rawn Harbour, Leon Roberts, Marjorie Gabriel-Burrow, Grayson Brown, Avon Gillespie, Eddie Bonnemere, and Ray East.

The earliest pastoral attempts of African American Catholics to incorporate the insights of Black Theology centered on the Sunday worship of the local parish. These individual and initially isolated efforts, usually by priests or sisters, to add Black cultural shadings to the Catholic liturgy distinguish a first phase of adaptation or acculturation. Under the directives of the Second Vatican Council, the process of acculturation opens the Roman liturgy to the inclusion, substitution, and symbolic representation of compatible elements from particular cultures.[14] Black Catholics dove into the treasure chest of African American sacred music lifting up the spirituals, plundering the Baptist hymnal, tracking down organists competent in the Black musical genre and idiom—often from the Baptist congregation across town! Ever so tentatively the laity began to sing these songs at the eucharistic liturgy, at prayer services, at Advent or Lenten devotions. The nationalist colors—red, black, and green—along with traditional African styles, patterns, and weaves were employed in the design of vestments, stoles, and altar linens used in the various ceremonies of the Roman rite. Crucifixes and statues of the mother of Jesus sculpted in African features, and Black cultural products began to appear on the walls and altars of Catholic parishes. Priests began to listen to and to appropriate the rhetorical style of their Black Protestant counterparts. It was not long before hand-clapping, call and response, the shout, the tambourine, and the drum sounded in the Catholic church. This phase of adaption or acculturation began a process of psychic healing as Cyprian Rowe observed:

> Catholics of African descent have suffered intensely from the sterility of liturgical rites, because they have somewhere in their bones a tradition of worship in which the sung and spoken word have been fused into cele-brations of joy. Afro-Americans are therefore among the first to realize that it is a certain cultural ignorance, and even cultural imperialism, that have resulted in their almost total exclusion from worship, except as spectators.[15]

During this period there were widespread attempts simply to make Black culture welcome in Catholic parishes and among Black Catholics; but some measure of evaluation was needed so that parishes did not become "inauthen-tically Catholic in their scope while becoming authentically Black."[16] Under the leadership of its executive director, Brother Joseph M. Davis, S.M., and his successor, Brother Cyprian Rowe, F.M.S., NOBC's Program for Culture and Worship furnished the means to evaluate and to share liturgical activities; hence leading to the phase of indigenization. Through conferences, work-shops, and the publications of monographs, the NOBC constructed a platform from which Black Catholic composers and liturgists could mold and direct an African American renewal of Catholic worship. The NOBC inaugurated an annual workshop, staffed by cultural specialists, dramatists, liturgists, musi-cians, gospel artists, and singers, to school liturgists, priests, musicians, choirs, and lectors in African American modes of worship. These workshops were attended by Black Catholic laity, sisters, brothers, and clergy, as well as white priests, brothers, and sisters who ministered in the Black community. Inten-sive sessions brought participants into contact with the slave moans and chants, the spirituals, traditional and contemporary gospel music, and free-dom songs. Finally, these workshops created a climate for mutual exchange and collaboration among Black composer and musicians, as well as a stimulus for their professional growth.

The recent appearance of *Lead Me, Guide Me: The African American Catholic Hymnal*[17] is a sign of some maturity in this long and ambiguous period of indigenization. Thoroughly Black and thoroughly Catholic, the hymnal preserves spirituals as well as Gregorian plain chant, Black arrangements of Dr. Watts-style hymns as well as Catholic standards, traditional as well as contemporary Gospel Songs, Freedom Songs as well as African American Catholic compositions. The hymnal also recognizes and affirms both the commonality and plurality of the Black Catholic experience since ". . . a Louisiana Black Catholic is not a West Baltimore Black Catholic; neither is a New York Haitian Catholic a Los Angeles Black Catholic or a Chicago Black Catholic."[18]

The eucharistic liturgy is at the heart and center of Catholic worship. Given the nature of the doctrinal position held by the Vatican on the ordination of women, there resides at the core of Catholic liturgical life a putative theological bias favoring men over women. In the Roman Catholic church, only celibate males may preside at the eucharistic ritual. Inevitably, this taints Roman Catholic liturgical life with a patina of clerical-centricism. Black feminist theologians of other Christian traditions will find this situation not so different from their own: for even if their churches are logo-centric, preaching is dominated by the male voice. In the effort to nourish its own membership at retreats and to foster the gifts of women like Sister Teresita Weind, S.N.D., and Beverly Stanton, the NBSC encouraged the design of non-eucharistic rituals in a Black cultural style. Litanies and chants, African customs and symbols, stylized gesture and dance interplayed to express purification and dedication, to celebrate points of passage or commitment, to mark repentance or resolve.

Spiritual Formation. Christianity is, above all, a way of life. Catholicism marks that way of life with features which differentiate its expression from those of other Christians. And Black Catholics—lay women and men, sisters, brothers, priests—were not long in identifying the need and ways to ebonize features of a Catholic Christian way of life.

A retreat, the setting aside of sustained and uninterrupted time for prayer, for meditation, for examination or refreshment or renovation of one's relationship with God, was an opportunity to transform a common Catholic practice in the light of Black Theology. The NBSC sponsored retreats for its own members, but it was not unusual for married or single women, brothers, and priests to join them. (And in the last few years, retreats either have preceded or followed annual joint conferences of the permanent deacons and their wives, sisters, brothers, seminarians, and priests.) Retreats included a variety of spritual disciplines—private and communal reflective reading and praying of the Scriptures, singing spirituals or other appropriate hymns, fasting, silence, quiet or guided meditation. Devotional conferences were the locus of nourishing formative reflection. From the perspective of Black Theology, these conferences examined such topics as prayer, spirituality, celibacy, suffering, loneliness, and the meaning of eucharist in the Black sociopolitical context. Often these conferences were prepared by non-ordained women and men who had formal training in Catholic theology or spirituality or who were well-read in Black Theology and in Catholic spirituality. These conferences attempted to work out new understandings of the Christian life by which Black Catholics could take their bearings.

In September 1969, Al McNeeley of Detroit's St. Bernard Parish, along with a team of lay leaders and priests, developed a pastoral training program to give Black men theological, spiritual, and personal formation and support to function in the Black community as lay or non-ordained ministers within their parishes. The program took Scriptural impetus from the work of deacons (Acts 6:1–7); it took pastoral theological motivation from the pressing socio-economic and cultural needs of the local Black community; and it took personal inspiration from the promotion and cultivation of Black self-concept and Black leadership. "Ministers of Service" fanned out into various city parishes, assessed needs, and generated innovative ways to meet them. They helped families cope with crises of all sorts, befriended Black youth, criticized crime and drugs, cheered bed-ridden and home-bound residents, comforted those confined to hospitals and nursing homes. They assisted at the eucharist, conducted Bible study classes, and prepared youth and adults for participation in the sacraments. These men carried the compassion, love, and mercy of God to people and places the institutional church neglected.

Education, Evangelization, and Catechesis. With the Gospel imperative, "Go into the whole world and proclaim the good news to all creation," all baptized Christians are summoned to the work of evangelization and catechesis. Evangelization and catechesis are concerned with "church-building," that is to say, with preaching the message of the good news of salvation in Jesus Christ, with building up that message in the lives of individuals, and with achieving a community of believers who support and challenge one another to live up to the Gospel. The commitment of contemporary African American

Catholics to evangelization and catechesis can be linked with that of the earliest Afro-American Catholic Congress. Proceedings of that first assembly record an eagerness "to cooperate with the clergy in the conversion and education of our race." Concerted measures to address the tasks of evangelization and catechesis from the starting point of Black Theology can be traced over the past fifteen years and take at least three forms: 1) education to African American and African American Catholic heritages, 2) the development of a theology of catechesis and of catechetical materials, and 3) the pastoral letter from the Black Catholic bishops on evangelization.[19]

I cannot recount here the dozens of educational task forces, ad-hoc committees, and study groups which made the contributions, achievements, and biographies of Catholics of African descent available to Black and white Catholics in parish, school, and diocesan settings. These women and men plowed and toiled alone, often with little encouragement or financial support. Their work was a labor of love, inspiring so many of us who now walk more proudly and less hesitantly in the field they cleared. An early educational effort to inform Black Catholics about their Catholic heritage was a monograph edited by Al McNeeley. *Afro-American and Catholic*[20] retrieved the African Catholic community of Christian antiquity—"Church Fathers" (Tertullian, Origen, Cyprian, and Augustine), popes (Victor, Melchiades, and Gelasius), saints, martyrs, and desert monks (Benedict the Black, Peter Claver, and Moses the Black). It retold the story of Black Catholic life in the United States and particularly in the archdiocese of Detroit. And while *Afro-American and Catholic* cannot be considered a critical scholarly history, it did what professional Catholic church historians and educators had not—made accessible to Black Catholics in the pew a record of their presence in their church. Such publications continue to make an important contribution to the work of professional historians. They preserve life stories, put face and flesh on events and trends vital to social history. But, more importantly, these works continue to fill gaps in the spiritual, psychic, and historical experience of Black Catholics.

Among the Black Catholic bishops who have spoken on catechesis and evangelization, the most notable is Bishop James Lyke,[21] while the most differentiated articulation of a Black Catholic theology of catechesis comes from the writings of Toinette Eugene.[22] Methodical mediation of just such a theology has been the work of Nathan Jones[23] and practical translation of that method for pedagogy has been assumed by Sister Eva Marie Loomis,

S.S.S.[24] Taken collectively and complementarily, these thinkers advance a type of catechesis that offers a liberating experience of religion, faith, and religious education—an education for the whole person, rooted in, attentive and faithful to the common and plural Black Catholic experience.

In his publications, lectures, and presentations, Nathan Jones is unparalleled in outlining the methodical programming of catechetical education. Tapping into African and African American folklore, music, poetry, aphorisms, history, theology, religious traditions, and Catholic doctrine, Jones has produced a program of catechesis corrective and remedial, faithful to both our heritages. The pedagogical translation of an African American Catholic catechetical program into learning aids and classroom tools for directors of religious education and catechists is Sister Loomis's contribution to this overall enterprise. Her ability to identify and to adapt resources, to demonstrate ways to employ Black cultural learning styles in a catechetical motif has been indispensable.

Through the IMANI Program, Loomis and her associate, Sister Addie Walker, S.S.N.D., have begun the collateral task of catechist formation —preparing catechists to work in the Black community. Loomis and Walker have shaped the IMANI curriculum under the influence of Black scholarship in psychology, sociology, culture, history, and theology as well as Catholic spirituality. Bishop Lyke's early ministry as a pastor was an important resource for his doctoral studies and consequent analysis and critique of the National Catholic Catechetical Directory. Lyke's contribution to the formation of catechists has been in underscoring the social context of catechesis. Catechists ought to be alert to the systemic injustice threaded through the Black community and eager to cooperate in practical schemes of social change. Indeed failure to do so, he insists, will "make a mockery of Christ and his transforming power." But the catechist is never a "social worker who is pious." The catechist teaches a new power and a new wisdom who is "Christ self-emptying and self-transcending, powerful with the power of God."

The most conspicuous example of the African American Catholic response to the challenge of evangelization is the pastoral letter by the Black Catholic bishops, "What We Have Seen and Heard." In this letter, the bishops have adopted a familiar and traditional format through which Catholic bishops convey their thinking on important matters to their communities. The letter integrates Black spiritual, cultural tradition and Catholic heritage to challenge decisively the pervasive notion that "Blackness" and "Catholicism" are inimical. Moreover, the letter is a sign of the "coming of age" of a people in their church: participation in apostolic succession, membership in the clergy and religious congregations of women and men, an increasing body of communicants, discernible models of Christian practice, programs and structures of institutionalization and maintenance, trained church scholars and theologians. The pastoral letter presupposes a maturing African American Catholicism by writing of evangelization as a challenge to Black Catholics to make a gift of their genius to the whole church.

There are countless other women and men who shoulder the theoretical, practical, administrative responsibilities of catechesis, and of evangelization, of spiritual formation, social ministry, teaching, and worship. But I cannot fail to mention African American Catholic cultural-spiritual griot, Sister Thea Bowman, F.S.P.A., whose preaching, lecturing, writing, and experimentation in ritual have gained international acclaim; or the Reverend Clarence Williams, who has pioneered the work of evangelization in television and video production; or the Reverend Boniface Harding and the Reverend Albert McKnight, who for more than twenty years have sought to realize the corporal and spiritual works of mercy among the poor, the hungry, the homeless, the neglected, the battered, the disenfranchised, the illiterate; or the members of the National Association of Black Catholic Administrators, the dozens of women and men all across the United States who are directors of diocesan offices, local secretariats, and programs designed for Black Catholics, who hold the key to the doors of the wider field of evangelization. Through all these as well as so many other women and men, through all these ways and in so many others, African American Catholics press forward the process of indigenization in every dimension of leadership, of collaboration, of liturgy, of education, of catechesis, and of service.

Theological Appropriation

The meeting of African American Catholic ministry and Black Theology has had fruitful results. Already, as I have indicated, this encounter has made distinctive and significant contributions to pastoral and social ministry by and among Black Catholics to the way liturgy is understood and celebrated by and among us, as well as to the wider renewal of liturgy and the liturgical arts in the Catholic church in the United States. In theology, however, the situation is quite different.

In his reflection on the relation of African American Catholics to Black Theology, James Cone has this to say: "Although black Catholics challenged the racist character of the Catholic Church in the U.S.A., they have not made a significant academic contribution in the field of black theology, and the reasons are at least partly obvious. The white power structure in the Catholic Church is so restrictive on what blacks can do or say that it is almost impossible to think creatively."[25] In the paragraph that follows, Cone notes that Black Catholics do not lack the "conflictive situation" that provokes new theological thought. But he bemoans the absence of "space" for the development of indigenous Black Catholic leadership so necessary for creating a theological perspective accountable to the Black struggle for freedom, rather than to oppressive white structures. Cone continues: "As a black Protestant who looks at the Catholic Church from the outside, the immensity of the task of trying to challenge the tradition of Catholic theology *and* also remain inside the church is so great that it overwhelms me."[26]

Insofar as theology has been a privileged meta-language to which African American Catholics only recently have had full access, Cone is correct. But his comments neither sufficiently appreciate the ways in which Black Catholic organizations have functioned over the past twenty years to provide occasions for leadership, followership, collaboration, and criticism; nor do they acknowledge the fidelity of Black Catholics to their own best interests. Moreover, we are *not* overwhelmed: this is precisely how we perceive our sacred task. His assessment also fails to situate Black Catholic thinkers within the larger international context of Catholic theologians, church scholars, and pastoral ministers who are women and men of color. Though perhaps this latter omission is also our own. Still: given the dearth of formal-academically trained African American Catholic theologians, our intellectual appropriation and particular contribution to the ongoing development of Black Theology await maturity. But some beginnings have been made.

In the fall of 1978, under the auspices of the National Black Catholic Clergy Caucus, the Reverend Thaddeus Posey, O.F.M., Cap., organized and chaired the first Black Catholic Theological Symposium. Coming only months after an attack on U.S. (Protestant) Black Theologians in the pages of *L'Osservatore Romano*,[27] the Vatican news organ, the four-day meeting was neither an exercise in apologetics, nor in posturing rhetoric. In his preface to the published proceedings, Posey placed the symposium in the context of basic theological praxis—faith seeking understanding. "Black Theology," he wrote, "is

. . . not only natural but a prerequisite to natural growth in Christ."[28] One of the more immediate outcomes of the symposium was the establishment of the Institute for Black Catholic Studies, a summer graduate program administered through Black Catholic Xavier University in New Orleans. Posey along with the Reverend Bede Abram, O.F.M. Conv., and the late Reverend Joseph E. Nearon, S.S.S., have guided this effort. The Institute is staffed by Black Catholic scholars and theologians, is open to all interested persons, and is another instance both of the theological creativity of Black Catholics and their commitment to controlling structures for Black intellectual development.

The papers from the Black Catholic theological symposium represent some good examples of pastoral and existential mediation of Black Theology in the ecclesial and socio-cultural contexts. Many of the participants are university and seminary teachers who lecture, research, and publish in their fields of theological specialization. Some have gained national and international attention. They form a cadre of scholars whom Cone admits "are determined to develop a black theology that is accountable to their experience in both the black and Catholic communities."

The work of thematizing a theology of African American Catholic spirituality has been carried on, in large measure, by Benedictine monk, scholar, and church historian Cyprian Davis. For nearly fifteen years he has presented monographs and lectures that retrieve, contextualize, and interpret both Black and Catholic models of sanctity and African American Catholic spiritual traditions of communal Bible study and prayer. By unsealing the neglected, antique and modern, history of Catholics of African descent and situating Black women and men within the stream of Catholic piety, Davis breaks open a tradition faithful to both Black religious experience and to multicultural Catholic spirituality. He suggests four characteristics of Black Catholic spirituality: it is contemplative, holistic, joyful, and communitarian. It is contemplative because the African American apprehension of religion mystically surrenders to the dark numinous power of God to hallow a home in the heart and soul, to infuse the whole person with awe at God's transcendent presence and with ecstatic joy at the intimacy of God's immanence. It is holistic because the African American personality is di-unital, and retains the capacity to manage ambiguity. This personality is gifted with a fundamental regard for person, for the human over products or things. Black spirituality is joyful resting in the power of God to protect, to defend, and to save; and this joy animates works of love and compassion, of reconciliation and peace.

Black spirituality is communal and expresses itself in social concern and social justice; and this communitarian dimension opens Black Christians to all, excludes none. Davis's work displays a harmony neither artificial nor forced. He is a careful, painstaking historian able to tell the African American Catholic story in a style that emboldens and edifies. Currently Father Davis is at work on an extended history of African American Catholics.[29]

A Black Catholic theology of catechesis is one of the projects which occupies the scholarship of Toinette Eugene. Taking as her point of departure the African American religious experience as well as Roman Catholic church tradition, she sets evangelization and religious education in the place where revelation begins for Black people—in our own specific culture and ethos. Eugene's overall project in this area has been to lay out moral, ethical, and religious directions for Black Catholic catechesis. Those directions advocate Black culture as the "framework for embracing and synthesizing Church and community," a Christian love engaged in "meaningful and gracefull praxis within the struggle for liberation," and a prophetic "self-sacrificial love and concern for others."[30] Eugene has done additional studies that focus the moral and ethical imperatives of Black Catholic catechesis on specific questions— family, sexuality, love, images and roles of women. Her participation on the committee of women advising the U.S. Catholic Bishops' Committee on their pastoral letter on the status of women, brings a nuanced and critical voice to predominantly white, middle-class, liberal feminist concerns.

Catholic theology as a whole still wants for dialogue with the social and human sciences. In exploring the psychosocial theme of Black self-concept, Black Catholic theologians contribute to furthering conversation with psychology. Dominican Sister Jamie Phelps has begun to delineate a prolegomenon to a fully differentiated theology of person that explicity adverts to and affirms Black self-concept.[31] Her doctoral studies were preceded by a graduate degree in psychiatric social work as well as extensive clinical experience; and her career has always included parish involvement. Hence, Phelps' writing and lecturing on Black self-concept are characterized by practical as well as theoretical relevance and a nuanced grasp of varieties of Black lived experience. Committed to interdisciplinary work, Sister Phelps has benefitted from the cultural studies of Cyprian Rowe and the psychiatric studies of Edwin Nichols. Recently she has begun to link work in psychosocial development with studies in ecclesiology in order to document and to interpret more comprehensively the concrete mystery of the diversity of the church.

Canadian Jesuit philosopher-theologian, Bernard Lonergan has influenced the theological work of the Reverend Edward K. Braxton and me. Both of us have devoted doctoral research to Lonergan's work—Braxton on its relation to symbol and myth, me on its relation to contemporary political and theological thought on the common good.[32] Both of us are critical interpreters of contemporary theological movements and draw freely on the heuristic categories that Lonergan's reformulation of method in theology affords.

Braxton has written several articles analyzing and commenting on Black (Protestant) theology, as well as a lucid, thoughtful interpretation of changes in the church initiated by the Second Vatican Council.[33] James Cone has praised the potential of Braxton's "theological imagination and discipline" to make a significant Catholic contribution to Black Theology. However, Cone suggests that classical and European theological motifs compete for Braxton's talent, evoking in him an "unresolved inner tension"[34] that prevents the flowering of his acumen. But, it is also possible that Edward Braxton is ensnared in that dilemma faced by all Black intellectuals seeking legitimation through an academy that is so inimical to their innermost concerns and so existentially and intellectually stultifying for them.

I served as Program Director for the first national consultation on Black Theology sponsored by the TIA Black Theology Project in 1977 and was Lonergan's teaching assistant during his final year at Boston College, where I have been associated with that university's group of Lonergan scholars. From the foundational categories of Lonergan's structure of the human good, I propose to rethink political theology in the American context with specific attention to issues of race, gender, and class.

Albert Raboteau's *Slave Religion*[35] is essential reading for an understanding of the Black religious experience. Here he made a study of the Herkovits-Frazier debate on the tenacity of African cultural elements in the life of the slaves. Raboteau argues a continuum of African influence, one of less degree in the United States than in Cuba, Haiti, and Brazil. And according to Raboteau, Catholicism accounts for this difference. In the Caribbean and Latin America, Catholicism offered points of contact with traditional African ritual and customs. In the United States, this was not the case as a de-ritualized Protestantism prevailed. Raboteau's historical interest in Black religion and Black religious experience complements the more specifically Catholic explorations of Cyprian Davis.

Archbishop Jean Jadot, the Apostolic Delegate of the Vatican to the United States, in an address to the Black Catholic Clergy Caucus, called for a corps of Black Catholic "scholars in theology, canon law and church history who can bring the reflection process of the black experience to the total affairs of the Church."[36] European educated Black Catholic scholars Diana L. Hayes and British-born Sheila Briggs promise to make significant contributions. But currently only a handful of African American Catholics are enrolled in graduate theological programs, with few obvious attempts on the part of American Catholic institutions of higher learning to recruit and challenge others to doctoral work. The need to cultivate and to support Black Catholic women and men in theological studies is even more compelling today than it was thirteen years ago.

Some Tentative Recommendations

Peter Sarpong, the Catholic archbishop of Accra, Ghana, has spoken on several occasions of the need to Africanize Christianity. Such a statement implies the need for a thorough-going re-formation: the refounding of the gospel in every age, in and by every culture. We, African American Catholics, have been doing just this: laying a new foundation—a new intellectual, moral, and religious basis for our reception and promulgation of the revelation of God in Jesus of Nazareth.

This is an ongoing task. I conclude with a few recommendations:

1. The newly created permanent Secretariat for Black Catholics will require the support of every one of this nation's 1.3 million Black Catholics. The Secretariat is a sign of the respect from the hierarchy for the potential of Black Catholics, and is a particular mark of respect for the Black Catholic bishops who played a major role in obtaining the office. No doubt Beverly Carroll, the Director of the Secretariat, will take up the national pastoral plan ratified at the 1987 National Black Catholic Congress. This plan deserves national, international, and ecumenical distribution, collaboration, and criticism.

2. Sexism still plagues the relations of Black Catholic women and men. In a certain sense, it cannot be (though it ought to be) otherwise: both the wider culture that adds its blows to our formation and the church we love are persistently patriarchal. Serious, informed, and frank dialogue is needed. New disciplines and asceticisms of love are required. Black men must choose

humility, repentance, self-sacrifice, firm purpose of amendment, and change. Black women must embrace anger, self-respect, courage, forgiveness, and change.

3. We must not be afraid of internal critique of our movement. Such critique is needed if we are to be faithful to our Black Catholic tradition and experience, if we are to honor our African American heritage, if our movement and our church are to be nourished and grow. At the same time, critique must be offered intelligently, rationally, responsibly, and lovingly: questioning, comparing, and understanding our experience; scrutinizing our analyses, planning, and judgments; critically reflecting on our evaluation and deliberation; and subordinating our decisions and action to the message and values of the gospel, to the common human good of the people of God.

Like their nineteenth-century ancestors, contemporary African American Catholics (1) have argued for inclusion and participation in the full life, maintenance, and direction of the Roman church in the United States; (2) have reiterated with righteous indignation their disappointment at the failure of the institutional church to live boldly its universal message; and (3) have demanded self-determination and self-definition in pastoral, educational, and theological affairs. In their Black consciousness, in their militant commitment to civil rights, and in their love of their church, these women and men are the "lineal descendants" of that earliest group of African American Catholics who spoke of their struggle as "an entering wedge in the breaking of the mighty wall of difficulties." When contemporary Black Catholics assert that they are "Black *and* Catholic," they stand (even when they do not know it) within a tradition of African American Catholic discourse of racial self-consciousness and self-identification. The participants in the congress movement spoke consistently of themselves and their co-religionists as "Colored Catholics" or "Afro-American Catholics." And when contemporary Black Catholics collaborate with other groups and organizations for the freedom, development, and welfare of the peoples of Africa and of African descent around the world, they carry on the work of those earliest African American Catholics who advocated the universal abolition of slavery. In these and countless other ways, contemporary African American Catholics uphold an indigenous church tradition of struggle for social justice that is one hundred years old.

Notes

1. Paul VI, "To the Heart of Africa," *The Teachings of Pope Paul VI–1969* (Vatican: Liberia Editrice Vaticana): 205; Reprint, *Catholic Mind* 67 (September 1969):62–65.

2. *Three Catholic Afro-American Congresses* (Cincinnati: The American Catholic Tribune, 1893; Reprint. New York: Arno Press, 1978):14, 13. See David Spalding, C.F.X., "The Negro Catholic Congresses, 1889–1894," *The Catholic Historical Review* 55 (October 1969):337–57, and Cyprian Davis, O.S.B., "Black Catholics in America: A Historical Note," *America* 142, no. 3 (May 1980):378–80.

3. The first pre-Emancipation attempt to found a religious congregation for Black women was in 1824 through the work of Father Charles Nerinck in Kentucky. But the insensitivity of clergy and diocesan officials forced the dismissal of the group. In 1829 the Oblate Sisters of Providence was founded in Baltimore; in 1842, the Holy Family Sisters was founded in New Orleans. There is also a third Black religious congregation, the Franciscan Handmaids of the Most Pure Heart of Mary, founded in 1917 to work in Harlem, New York. True to the meaning of Catholicity, i.e., universality, each of these congregations opened their ranks to white women who have joined them over the years.

4. Father Augustus Tolton is generally recognized as the first Black American Catholic priest, but there were three others: the Healy brothers—James Augustine, Sherwood, and Patrick. Sons of a slave woman and an Irish Catholic planter, they had been isolated by their father's money and social associations from the brunt of racism, but this left them with little explicit race identification and consciousness. By the time of the congress movement, Sherwood, a canon lawyer and theologian, was dead; James Augustine was the Ordinary Bishop of the diocese of Portland, Maine; and Patrick, a Jesuit, had served Georgetown University as vice president and president.

5. Spalding, 357.

6. Jerome LeDoux, "Christian Pastoral Theology Looks at Black Experience," in *Theology: A Portrait in Black* (hereafter *TAPB*), ed. Thaddeus J. Posey, O.F.M., Cap. (Pittsburgh: Capuchin Press, 1980):115.

7. Thomas Merton, *The Black Revolution* (The Southern Christian Leadership Conference in Atlanta 1963?).

8. For some personal accounts see Saundra Willingham, "Why I Quit the Convent," *Ebony* (December 1968):64–74; Lawrence Lucas, *Black Priest/White Church, Catholics and Racism* (New York: Random House, Inc., 1970); Sister Louis Marie Bryan, S.C., "History of the National Black Sisters' Conference," *Celibate Black Commitment: Report of the Third Annual National Black Sisters' Conference* (NBSC in Pittsburgh, 1971):3–9; Sister Mary Roger Thibodeaux, S.B.S., *A Black Nun Looks at Black Power* (New York: Sheed and Ward, 1972).

9. First printed in *Freeing the Spirit* 1, no. 3 (Summer 1972); Reprinted in Gayraud S. Wilmore and James H. Cone, ed., *Black Theology: A Documentary History, 1966–1979* (Maryknoll, N.Y.: Orbis Books, 1979), 322–34.

10. "The National Black Sisters' Conference Position Paper," *Black Survival: Past, Present, Future, A Report of the Second National Black Sisters' Conference* (NBSC in Pittsburgh, 1970):155.

11. The National Black Sisters' Conference was invited through me, its executive director, to

participate in the 1975 Detroit meeting of Theology in the Americas. I was unable to attend because of conference business and Sister Jamie Phelps, O.P., attended.

12. *Brothers and Sisters to Us* (Washington, D.C.: USCC, 1979).

13. World Library Publications, 1966. See also his *Soulfull Worship* (Washington, D.C.: NOBC, 1974), *Spirit in Worship* (Cincinnati, Ohio: Stimuli, Inc., 1978), "Thank God We Ain't What We Was: The State of Liturgy in the Black Catholic Community," *TAPB*:66–74, and "The Oral Tradition Versus the Ocular Western Tradition," in *This Far By Faith: American Black Worship and Its African Roots* (NOBC and the Liturgical Conference in Washington, D.C., 1977):38–49.

14. Vatican II, *Sacrosanctum Concilium*, Constitution on the Sacred Liturgy, 4 (December 1963): no. 14 and 37.

15. Cyprian Lamar Rowe, F.M.S., "The Case for a Distinctive Black Culture," *This Far By Faith* 27.

16. Rivers, "Thank God," 73.

17. *Lead Me, Guide Me: The African American Catholic Hymnal* (Chicago: G.I.A. Publications, Inc., 1987). The hymnal was authorized in 1983 by the National Black Catholic Clergy Caucus; its compilation and editing were coordinated by Bishop James Lyke, O.F.M.

18. J-Glenn Murray, S.J., "The Liturgy of the Roman Rite and African American Worship," *Lead Me, Guide Me* (n.p.).

19. "What We Have Seen and Heard": A Pastoral Letter on Evangelization from the Black Bishops of the United States (Cincinnati, Ohio: St. Anthony Messenger Press, 1984).

20. Al McNeeley, *Afro-American and Catholic* (Detroit: Institute for Continuing Education, 1975).

21. Bishop James P. Lyke, O.F.M., "The Catechist in the Black Community," *Origins* 13 (June 9, 1983):70 –73; see also his pastoral letter *So Stood Those Who Have Come Down Through the Ages: A Pastoral Reflection on the Family in the Black Community* (November 3, 1986).

22. See Toinette Eugene, "Training Religious Leaders for a New Black Generation," *Catechist* 6, no. 2 (October 1972):8–10; "Developing Catholic Belief: Catechesis as a Black Articulation of the Faith," *TAPB*: 140–60; "The Black Family That Is Church," in Sister Thea Bowman, F.S.P.A., ed., *Families Black and Catholic, Catholic and Black* (Washington, D.C.: USCC, 1985).

23. Nathan Jones, *Sharing the Old, Old Story: Educational Ministry in the Black Community* (Winona, Minn.: St. Mary's Press, 1982). See p. 286.

24. In addition to her post as NBSC catechetical coordinator, Sister Loomis is the executive director of BLOODTIES, a resource center for Christian education in the Black community.

25. Cone, *For My People* (Maryknoll, N.Y.: Orbis Books, 1984):50–51; see also his "A Theological Challenge to the American Catholic Church," in *Speaking the Truth: Ecumenism, Liberation, and Black Theology* (Grand Rapids, Mich.: William B. Eerdmans Publishing Company, 1986):50–60.

26. Ibid.

27. Father Bianbattista Mondin, *L'Osservatore Romano*, July 18, 1979.

28. Thaddeus J. Posey, O.F.M., Cap., "Preface," *TAPB*:3.

29. See Cyprian Davis, O.S.B., "The Christian Interpretation of the Black Experience,"

TAPB:91–102; also his "Black Spirituality," paper presented at the meeting of the National Black Catholic Congress, Washington, D.C., May 1987; "The Holy See and American Blacks in the Files of the Apostolic Delegation, 1904–1919," (Paper delivered at the American Catholic Historical Association, Washington, D.C., December 30, 1987).

30. Toinette Eugene, "Developing Black Catholic Belief," *TAPB*: 14; see also her "Moral Values and Black Womanists," *The Journal of Religious Thought* 44 (Winter-Spring 1988):23–34, and "While Love is Unfashionable: Ethical Implications of Black Spirituality and Sexuality," in *Women's Consciousness and Women's Conscience: A Reader in Feminist Ethics*, ed. Barbara Hikert-Andolsen, Christine Gudorf, and Mary D. Pellauer (San Francisco: Harper & Row, 1985):121–41.

31. Jamie Phelps, O.P., "Black Self-Concept," *TAPB*:52–65; "Doctrine: The Articulation of Soul," in *Tell It Like It Is: A Black Catholic Perspective on Christian Education* (Oakland, Calif: NBSC, 1983):108–23, "Women and Power in the Church: A Black Catholic Perspective," Proceedings *Catholic Theological Society of America* 37 (1982):119–23.

32. See Edward K. Braxton, "Images of Mystery: A Study of the Place of Myth and Symbol in the Theological Method of Bernard Lonergan" (Ph.D. diss. Catholic University of Louvain, 1975). My dissertation is still in progress and offers a more political interpretation of Lonergan's work. See my revision of *Prophesy Deliverance! An Afro-American Revolutionary Christianity* by Cornel West, *Cross Currents* 33 (Spring 1983):67–71, "Black Theology," in *The New Dictionary of Theology*, ed. Komonchak et al. (Wilmington, Del.: Michael Glazier, 1987):137–41; "The Interaction of Racism, Sexism, and Classism in Women's Exploitation," in *Concilium: Women, Work, and Poverty*, ed., Elisabeth Schussler-Fiorenza (Nijmegen, Edinburgh: Stichting Concilium and T. & T. Clark, 1987):19–27.

33. See his essay on Black Theology in *America* (March 29, 1980):274–77; "Reflections from a Theological Perspective," in *This Far By Faith*, 58–75; "Black Theology: Potentially Classic?" *Religious Studies Review* 4 (April 1978):85–90, "What Is 'Black Theology' Anyway?" *The Critic* (Winter 1977):64–70, and *The Wisdom Community* (New York: Paulist Press, 1980).

34. Cone, 52.

35. Albert Raboteau, *Slave Religion, The 'Invisible Institution' in the Antebellum South* (New York: Oxford University Press, 1978).

36. Jean Jadot, "An Address to the Black Catholic Clergy Caucus," *Catholic Mind* 74 (March 1976):8.

14

Religio-Ethical Reflections Upon the Experiential Components
of a Philosophy of Black Liberation

J. Deotis Roberts, Sr.

Blacks are reluctant philosophers. But the present essay is not an apology. It is rather an attempt to blaze a new trail. We believe that there is an implicit philosophy within the Black experience which needs analysis and interpretation.

Among highly advanced Asian people, the Japanese have been reluctant philosophers. Until they made contact with the West, their philosophy was limited for the most part to ethics and this was based upon Confucian principles imported from China through the Korean kingdoms.

Africans appear likewise to be reluctant philosophers in the formal sense. But recent writers on African religion and culture make a serious case for an implicit philosophy of the African experience.

Mbiti treats the concept of time as the central consideration for the African worldview. The African worldview is said to be anthropocentric. Everything is understood in terms of how man experiences events. Time consists of the past, the present and a short future. Whereas those of us in the West hold a three-dimensional view of time, Africans, according to Mbiti, have a two-dimensional understanding of time. All aspects of life, whether personal, social, economic, political, or religious must be comprehended in this context. The past is designated as "big time" while present and short future belong to "little time." Eventually the present and short future are absorbed by "big time." This means that Africans look to the past. This explains why so much is invested in the family system with its deep reverence for ancestors.

What happens when African culture meets Western civilization with its "belief in progress" based upon a profound belief in the future is that Africans want much of what this Western view yields in terms of material benefits, but they want these things *now*. Since African philosophy with its deep religious roots is essentially materialistic, the immediate expectation of earthly things is sought with religious zeal. So much for Mbiti in *African Religion and Philosophy*.

For a people transported to a new world in chains and shackled throughout their history in the new social environment in either physical or psychological bondage, *liberation* or *freedom* is the basis of reflection upon existence. I prefer liberation to freedom in this context because the word freedom has been so abused by the majority of oppressing groups in this society.

It is not easy to find "systems" of philosophy neatly packaged by Black scholars to indicate this constant concern of the Black man in the American environment. There are several reasons for this. The Black man has a different temperament from those rooted solely in the Euro-American milieu. He has what Carter G. Woodson describes as "an oriental mind." The Black man expresses himself in intuitive more than in rational or metaphysical terms. As a victim of oppression, he has not been afforded the luxury of reflecting upon reality in terms of pure thought. The Black man has had to deal with concrete life-and-death issues in view of confrontation or escape. Whatever reasons the Black man has as he reflects upon existence are practical rather than "pure" reasons. This explains why Black scholars are attached to existentialism. Novelists like Richard Wright and James Baldwin, no less than theologians like Nathan Scott and James Cone are fascinated by the philosophy of existence. Furthermore, the moral and social implications of philosophical reflection hold the field. Alain Locke, the Oxford- and Harvard-trained philosopher at Howard University, turned his attention to a philosophy of culture. His search for "The New Negro" led him to apply his expert knowledge of aesthetics to art and literary criticism with special reference to the race problem. One is likewise reminded of William Banner's concern for moral philosophy and E. Franklin Frazier's preoccupation with social philosophy. Whether the Black philosopher is conscious of his Blackness or not, his experience in this society inevitably leads him in the more pragmatic direction where he begins an interpretation of liberation from oppression. The very nature of the Black man's existence leads him to a philosophical search for meaning and a sociological analysis of majority-minority group relations.

An Existential Ontology

In my interpretation of the Black experience, I would like to combine the ontological and the existential. The very nature of the Black experience, as we have observed, requires a constant existential analysis of one's life. But this cannot be a mere navel-gazing activity. We must always deal with reality.

Existentialism is an introspective humanism or a theory of man which expresses the individual's intense awareness of his contingency and freedom. It implies self-examination and the search for meaning. It indicates freedom, dignity and responsibility in shaping one's destiny.

It is not difficult to understand why individuals belonging to a suffering race should be moved by an introspective philosophy. The question "why?" has been a part of Black reflection from the very beginning. The folktales of Black folks are motivated by this poignant question. A people who live in what Nathan Scott calls "an extreme situation" must seek to make sense out of it if life is to continue. Thus the existential posture is native to Black experience. White oppression and Black introspection are strange bedfellows, but they coexist in this society.

A people cannot live without hope based on purpose or meaning. Neither may they survive on rhetoric and myth. Blacks must find a philosophy of survival in their *lebens welt*—living world. I would prefer, at this stage at least, to be nonjudgmental regarding the "cleansing" value of violence or the search for "land," so characteristic of the language used by some Black spokesmen. It bears watching, however, that some white racists prefer the hot rhetoric of angry Black militants to the challenge presented by the Black caucus on Capitol Hill. White racists are content to let Blacks blow off steam if they are assured that they are able to offset such words or deeds by superior power. On the other hand, if they see a weakening of their control at the power base, they feel seriously threatened. A viable philosophy of the Black experience must demonstrate that its rhetoric is grounded in reality. It follows that a significant philosophy of the Black experience is ontological.

Ontology is derived from two Greek words "onta," the things which exist, and "logy" or "theory." Ontology is, therefore, a theory of being or reality. It is the branch of knowledge which investigates the nature, essential properties, and relations of being. Whereas existentialism is preoccupied with meaning, ontology is concerned about reality. Through their ability to survive under conditions which would have driven many whites to insanity or suicide, Blacks have indicated the ontological basis of their experience. In spite of everything, we have touched base with the realities of our existence. The "trickster" folk tales of Blacks is one example of how Black reflection has been based upon reality. The rabbit outsmarts the fox and symbolizes powerlessness overcoming power. This is a philosophy of survival under conditions which deny the humanity of Black life. The use of slave songs, both work songs and spirituals, understood by the oppressor to be comforting and escapist in other-worldliness, to convey a code message of escape to freedom north of slavery is an example of sound ontology. The Black man was "thinking" of an interpretation of his existence that would make it livable. But at the same time he was very much in touch with the realities of his existence. His outlook can be justly described as existential-ontological.

"Myth" from the Greek "mythos" explains some practice, belief, institution, or natural phenomenon. But "myth" may also refer to something that exists only in the imagination. Such myths, when held by individuals or groups, may be a powerful means for survival of the in-group. When held by an opposing group, myth may be used as a convenient means toward oppression—if the oppressed group believes what the oppressing group conveys through its myths. Myths abound in the black-white encounter in this society. Examples are the magnolia myth of the contented Negro held by whites and the Christlike myth held by Negroes concerning their saintliness vis-à-vis the brutal, corrupt white man. As these examples show, myth participates in the rational and the irrational, in reality and in the imaginary. But for a myth to have its impact, it only need be believed. And the believing of myth is based to a large degree upon the thinking, feeling, and words that send it forth.

In the black-white encounter, both races have used myth in a forceful way. Joseph Washington is correct in pointing to freedom as a constant concern of the Black man. I would agree upon the predominance of the "stride toward freedom" in the thought and life of the Black man. And yet Preston Williams has alluded to a necessary corrective to the absolutization of freedom as the Black man's only preoccupation. There have been times when mere survival has been his only objective. In this instance a myth like the Christlike myth is a means of self-respect, personal worth, and dignity. Myth may serve as a weapon against oppression as well as an instrument for liberation. Some scholars such as B. F. Skinner may be prepared to move "beyond freedom and dignity." Reality for the Black man has been a constant quest for freedom and dignity.

Rhetoric, like myth, has been a useful tool in the Black man's quest. Rhetoric is the art of expressive speech. It is a skillful, artistic, and eloquent use of language. An "oratory of the oppressed" or a "rhetoric of protest" has been forcefully used by the Black man to win his freedom and claim his manhood and his peoplehood in a society that treats him with a "benign neglect." A philosophy of language has developed to articulate the depths of the Black experience. One may correctly refer to this language as the "hermeneutics" of the oppressed in quest of liberation. One gets the feel of Black rhetoric as he or she reads the speeches of Frederick Douglass, as he ponders through DuBois's *The Soul of Black Folk*, as he reads Martin Luther King's *Letter from a Birmingham Jail* or listens to a recording of his "I Have a Dream." Listening to Benjamin Mays, Howard Thurman or Mordecai Johnson is the best way to capture the real power of the soul of the Black orator. This language is uniquely fashioned to convey the thirst for freedom and humanity that stirs in the depths of every Black person in his solitude as he seeks meaning in his life. The oratory of protest is existential-ontological. It lays bare the soul of the Black man—it is introspective. On the other hand, it is in touch with reality—it is related to the experience of oppression and the longing for liberation. The philosophy of the Black experience is subjective-objective. It expresses the "spiritual strivings" of the Black man as he carves out a philosophy of existence amidst the "extreme situation"—racism.

It is not surprising that DuBois became an ardent disciple of William James while studying at Harvard. It is characteristic of Blacks to find perception or intuition more appealing than rationalism. A Black man finds greater affinity with his own experience and needs in this type of reflection. Abstract metaphysics and arid rationalism have little appeal. Much of my personal search for a reasonable faith has led me through the history of philosophy as well as doctrine. Very early I found kindred souls like William James and Henri Bergson. I was impressed most, however, by Blaise Pascal's "reasons of the heart." Most recently Kierkegaard, Buber, Schleiermacher, and Macquarrie, in their several ways, have challenged me and aided me in my search.

While these august thinkers of the modern period have aided me, Black fathers of the church, like Origen and Augustine, have made through the years an indelible imprint upon my mind and spirit. It would be amiss to omit the riches which have flowed into my understanding of the human spirit and ultimate verities from Asian religions and philosophies. From the study of Zen, Sufism and other religions or movements within these great religions, I have gained a real appreciation for perceptive knowledge.

It has been, however, by moving from existentialism (both theistic and humanistic) into the depths of the souls of Black folks that I have discovered my true self. The philosophy of the Black experience is more like insight or intuition than abstract thought. It is closer to existentialism than rationalism —closer to "practical reason" than to "pure reason." When a Zen poet writes about a tree, he identifies with the life of the tree. He does not think of the tree as an object. The tree becomes a subject and in some mysterious way he absorbs the life of the tree into his own awareness of existence. In spite of the Black man's coexistence in a highly technocratic society, he has maintained much of this nature-mysticism native to both Asians and Africans.

It is clearly understandable why DuBois, Archibald Grimke and other Black Harvard men of their generation were lifted up by the transcendental-ism they breathed in the New England air. Howard Thurman to this day remains the Black poet, mystic, and philosopher of the Black experience. Trained as a theologian and serving as a minister, he is essentially a religious philosopher—and not a theologian. His *Search for a Common Ground* is a recent and mature statement of a philosophy of the Black experience that espouses the unity and reverence of all life. It is a philosophy of feeling. As one reads or listens to Thurman's message he is transported into the depths of reality—even unto the very bottom of his own soul.

Thurman is able to articulate a "soul" quality in the Black experience philosophically, which one "feels" as he communicates with the mass of Black folks. These mass Blacks share the same experience but are unable to express what they feel. The source of Thurman's philosophy is deeply rooted in the Black heritage. This is an African as well as an African American experience. One observes it in the slave narratives, in folktales, spirituals, blues, novels and poems. Under the genius of Howard Thurman one observes the Black experience taking shape not merely of perception, but reflection upon percep-tion. Thurman enables us to communicate what we have been feeling and to understand it. The philosophy of the Black experience is a type of knowledge. It is like *prajna* or non-knowing knowledge. That is to say, it is not rational knowledge, but insightful knowledge. It is knowing from the inside rather than from the outside. It is characteristic of Blacks that they have learned about life from living it. Knowledge of experience more than book knowl-edge has been the basis of the Black experience. And as we have observed, even the intellectual Black man eventually finds his greatest interest in philos-ophy at the point where thought touches life. We have had to learn about life by living rather than thinking about living. Thus our reflection is based upon the realities of our existence. It is ontological-existential reflection. Black thinking is always practical. Even mysticism, as in Thurman, becomes practical or ethical mysticism.

Meaning and Protest

All philosophies of Black experience must tackle the question of meaning. Not only the question: "Who am I?," but the question of purpose or teleology must be raised and dealt with. If the philosophy of the Black experience takes a religious turn, the problem of theodicy arises. The question: why there is so much unmerited suffering in a world in which the One said to be in charge is lovingly just?

All humans, from preliterate days, have been preoccupied with the whence and whither of existence. We understand that man as a self-conscious being is alone in his reflection upon where he came from and where he is going. He is likewise concerned about the purpose of his life between his coming into this existence and the going out of this existence. He is concerned about his origin and the beginnings of the universe in which he lives. He develops myths of creation and cosmologies to explain these concerns. But as the existentialists remind us, being-in-the-world is a being-toward-death. Hence man is concerned with the termination of his earthly sojourn. He even looks beyond physical death to immortality, personal or social, and in some instances both. Thus, like other humans, the Black man's search for meaning is three dimensional. He is concerned about where he came from, where he is going and the meaning of his existence here and now.

At various times, as an individual or as a race, one or the other of these concerns may have been in the ascendency. Even if all concerns have been in mind simultaneously, one teleological issue may have had the priority. There might be even an explanation for the present suffering in terms of what happened in the creation of man. For example, one Black folktale relates that when God created the world he dropped two bundles in the middle of the road. One bundle contained a pick and shovel and the other a pencil and paper. The Black man picked up the first and the white man the second. This explained to the slave *why* he was slave and *why* the white man was his master. Such simplistic answers will not stand up under critical examination, but it did provide the slave with an answer that made an otherwise unbearable existence livable.

Even belief in life after death is not merely "escapist" for the Black experience. For a people brought to the New World from a social environment with strong kinship ties, who had their family system destroyed, the belief that loved ones, torn from them by a cruel slave system of the auction block, would be united with them at another time and place gave meaning to their present existence. They brought with them the reverence for ancestors and the belief in a continuing bond between the living and the living dead. This was buttressed by their understanding of the Christian hope.

In the estimate of the people who enslaved them, their life was meaningless. They were a mere thing, property to be used. But deep within they knew that life was worthful. Death was not only relief from the "troubles of this world," it was the one thing that they could do out of a sense of freedom and therefore vindicate their humanity. They had no control over their life, but they did have control over their death, so far as their relation to the master was concerned. Whereas to the slave master their death was mere bookkeeping, to the Black slave "freedom to die" gave significance to his life.

Beyond this, the Black man was able to see death as an experience within life. This message is born in the spirituals. In a real sense the Black man's future broke into his present life and gave it significance. There is more to what appears to be a sheer other-worldliness than an escapism. The meaning derived from an abiding existence and continuing relationships with loved ones brought richness and hope into a given existence. How else may we explain the "gift of laughter" or even the survival of Black people under such intolerable conditions over such a long period of time?

Indeed, conditions still are unbearable for masses of Black people in this country. Whereas some very affluent, comfortable, intelligent Blacks "cop out" in sheer hopelessness through sex, drugs—even suicide, those who are rooted in the heritage we have just described are able not merely to survive, but to live meaningful and fulfilled lives. Recently a friend of mine, who is principal of a school in a southern state related some of his experiences during the first phase of desegregation. It was of interest to me that he observed white parents were the ones who encouraged him to hire more Black teachers. They had learned not only that they were well qualified, but also they observed that Black teachers had a "humaneness"—a dedication to their task, which made all the difference in the world. How may we explain this "humaneness?" How does a person victimized by the situation of racism, who has every human right to revenge and bitterness, find meaning in his life and express deep affection for the offspring of the oppressor? It is my belief that part of the answer stems from the kind of reflection we have just described. Things which whites have given Blacks as a noose have been reshaped in the understanding brought to oppression into a cornucopia of meaning and service.

Black philosophical reflection has not only been concerned about meaning; it has likewise been a philosophy of protest, a political philosophy. We have been determined to be free and thus our philosophical reflection has been uniquely a philosophy of freedom. Sometimes this reflection has moved to the point of defiance. Liberation has demanded the willingness to die. Revenge and revolt have been the content of this philosophy of freedom. The Black man has said to the white oppressor, "give me liberty or give me death." Too often the white man has obliged him with death. For example, lynching became a respectable sport for many God-loving, Bible-thumbing, patriotic Americans. Nat Turner's *Confessions* represent the philosophy of the violent Black "rebel." His philosophy of freedom reflects what Camus describes as "resistance, rebellion and death." Such a philosophy is not concerned about pragmatism. It is not preoccupied with winning. It affirms the dignity and freedom of the Black man even in death. Those who subscribe to this philosophy had rather die as free men than live as slaves. To be truthful, in their reflection, death was preferable to life, if life were to be the living death they endured. This philosophy still is alive among Blacks. Fanon's *Wretched of the Earth* and Camus' *Rebel* are sacred texts to these adherents. Nat Turner is a saint for those who hold this view.

This is a very natural philosophy for Blacks to hold, given a factual look at Black existence in the history of the United States. It is easy to understand and some cannot understand how Black men can hold any other view. To those who think thus, any alternative view is untenable on moral, practical, or any grounds whatsoever. Since my description of Black philosophical reflection is intended, at least, to be nonjudgmental we must let it be. It is worthwhile, however, to recall Aristotle's advice that courage is midway between cowardice and foolhardiness. Furthermore there are dead cowards as well as living ones. Goading a sadist cop into taking one's life, which he may be happy to do under the guise of heroism, may be, in some cases at least, the final "cop out." If one has something to live for, there is meaning in his death. If he does not have meaning in his life, his death may also be senseless. It is interesting that death, imprisonment and exile have taken so many Blacks who hold this view out of the Black revolution. But one may immediately recall that the fate of Nat Turner was likewise the fate of M. L. King, Jr., the apostle of the philosophy of nonviolence. Both became the victims of violence.

This leads us to consider the other manner in which Black men have expressed a philosophy of freedom. We have already alluded to the way folktales and spirituals were used by Black men to proclaim the determination to be free. Blacks, under oppression, used "veiled language" and double talk to speak of freedom. Folktales that whites considered humorous or charming, sermons that appeared to be otherworldly, and songs that spoke of heaven or heroes in the Bible were means of expressing the longing for earthly freedom —even escape to freedom.

There have been those like Frederick Douglass who beseeched Americans to be true to their promises to all citizens. Emancipation followed by Reconstruction led to great political thinking and activity with Black liberation in view. These hopes were aborted by the compromise between North and South in 1877 which exchanged economic gain for the Black man's freedom. Black thought turned from politics to economics. Booker T. Washington embodied the new vision. Freedom was to be won by self-help, thrift and skilled labor. The cordial acceptance of Washington's Atlanta Compromise in 1895 indicates that the group was prepared for his message—that many Blacks despaired of politics as an avenue to freedom and were now open to the alternative economic approach. The pot of gold at the end of the rainbow for which all Americans desire now haunted the dreams of the Black man. Economic security was his means to freedom.

DuBois represents a different departure for a philosophy of freedom. He espouses a cultural nationalism and would like to make room not only for the Black masses, the skilled laborer, but also the "talented tenth." This latter group would not be industrial workers and the like, but professional Blacks who would stand equal to all others in their chosen vocation. The diversity in the gifts of Black men would blend into the plurality of the total society. Knowledge and experience for the Black man would not be circumscribed by preconceived restrictions. He desired to see Blacks break through the ghettoization of Black experience and knowledge into the open field of opportunity available to all Americans. In his experience of "doubleness," as a Black man and as an American, he sought the true air of freedom. DuBois was said to mix mysticism with pragmatism and at times the mystic in him gained the upper hand.

While in Booker T. Washington we meet a faith in the Negro based upon an ideology of accommodation, in DuBois, we confront a cultural nationalism highly pan-African in flavor. He asserted that Blacks have a unique contribution to make to civilization; that they should support their own businesses; cooperate with each other and go to every length to organize our economic and social power.

A more cultural type of philosophy of freedom develops under Benjamin Brawley, Paul Roberson, Alain Locke, Kelly Miller, and James Weldon Johnson. Brawley spoke of the "peculiar genius" of the Black race and Locke the interpreter par excellence of the Harlem Black Renaissance of Arts and Letters speaks of "The New Negro." Johnson asks Blacks to cherish the faith that "that dark past has taught us" as he penned what has been called ever since the "Negroes' National Anthem."

Marcus Garvey arrived in New York from Jamaica in 1917 with a vision of Black Power as racial enterprise and solidarity. He taught self-help and self-reliance and gained popular support among Blacks. He moved the Black masses. Recalling the African heritage of ancient times, Garvey produced within Blacks a pride of race and provided them with hope. He expressed through his organizations, social, economic, and political, the longing of Blacks to be free. He asserted that the Black man wants to take his destiny into his own hands and will have the rights to which he is entitled. Garvey is important in his own right for his immediate influence (even if he appears defeated by white power), but also for his influence upon Black power at this time. Not an African American in the same sense as other leaders discussed, he nevertheless was in touch with the aspirations of the Black masses more than most other leaders of his day. His life and thought have come down to us through Elijah Muhammad, Malcolm X, Stokely Carmichael, and Albert Cleage. His "philosophy and opinions" are alive in the current Black liberation struggle.

The philosophy of the Black experience with its message of freedom is eclipsed by the Great Depression save for men like A. Philip Randolph, DuBois, and other kindred spirits who kept hope alive. Then the Supreme Court passed its landmark education decision in 1954. In that same decade M. L. King, Jr., assumed the mantle of the prophet of nonviolence. He developed a philosophy of freedom by combining the Gandhian principle of nonviolence with the Christian virtue of love. *Satyagraha*, "soul-force" and *agape*, self-giving, sacrificial love were welded together into a militant batter-

ing ram against the racist walls of American society. With the method of
Gandhi and the message of Jesus, as he put it, King sought the liberation of
his people. King's fame, influence, and fortune swept like a meteor across this
nation and throughout the world. The Nobel Peace Prize he won symbolized
the international esteem of this man who rose from the obscurity of a Baptist
pulpit in Alabama to a world leader in the field of human relations. No one
man in this century has been able to move "all sorts and conditions" of Blacks
as King did. He was equally at home among kings, queens, presidents, and
professors as among farmers, dishwashers, and janitors. He was at home in
the lecture halls of the great universities, but could talk to the share croppers
in the backwoods of Mississippi, and the gangs on the south side of Chicago,
in words and ideas they understood. For all his learning and popularity, he
maintained his common touch and his Baptist "hum."

He was influenced by the personalism of the Boston school, by Anders
Nygren, the Swedish theologian of the *Agape* motif school, by the Indian
philosophy of *ahimsa*, and many others including Reinhold Niebuhr, but his
focus was the Black experience of oppression and the longing of Blacks to be
free. King developed his own philosophy of liberation and applied it in the
racial struggle. He was existential and ontological in thought and practice.
He taught and practiced love but sought justice.

Like Roy Wilkins, Whitney Young, and others of his peers, he sought to
be "free and equal." His March on Washington highlighted by his "I Have a
Dream" speech was focused on integration as a workable policy in Black-
white relations. Under the pressure of Black militants, King became more
militant in a nonviolent sense. But his demonstrations in Selma, Memphis,
Chicago, and the Poor People's Campaign, all emphasized nonviolence and
integration. "Black and White together" in coalitions of power were to enter
the "kingdom of equality and justice." The philosophy of nonviolence
espoused by King moved SNCC, CORE, NAACP and his own SCLC. King was
the philosopher par excellence of the freedom rides, sit-ins, and all other "ins"
for Black liberation at the crest of his influence.

An unsung philosopher and theologian, King's thought as well as his life
now begs for careful appreciation and critical evaluation. But his very success
was his failure. He spoke in absolutist terms about moral ideals. Even his
program was based upon the pragmatic results of the application of these
ideals in what he called the stride toward freedom. What he was about in
Memphis, in Chicago and the Poor People's Campaign was to be the ultimate

vindication of his philosophy of nonviolence. He invested everything in the hope that nonviolence would win an immediate and sure victory for the Blacks and the poor. He had a lot of confidence in his ideology as well as the conscience of money-hungry, power-mad members of the economic and political establishment in this country. He was to this extent a dreamer and did not perceive what some of his ministerial colleagues of the National Committee of Black Churchmen rightly described as a situation in which "powerless conscience faces conscienceless power." This explains the immediate acclaim of Stokely Carmichael's cry for "Black Power," together with the decline of King's influence as he moved into the racial conflicts in the urban North—i.e., Watts and Chicago. A tragic realism had confronted the Black masses regarding the white power structure and their worsening conditions of oppression.

But as long as King lived, Black churchgoers, white liberals, and many others who had only a vested interest in the Black man's misery hoped that King would win out over the Black militants who were undermining his hold upon Black youth. Even middle-aged members of the Black middle class supported him, even if their own children were listening carefully to what Stokely was saying "loud and clear." Many "Anglo-Saxon Negroes," to use Nathan Hare's description, had just begun to breathe the air of freedom. They could care less about their Black brothers and sisters trapped in the "dark ghetto." King's death illustrated how much the high and mighty thought of his nonviolent integrationist approach to race relations, but it assured the triumph of "Black Power."

With King's death a hopelessness settled over the Black people of this country. Those who entrusted all to his dream now had no basis for hope. A people cannot live without hope. The fact that life had become meaningless as a result of King's untimely death may explain the sheer senseless character of the riots that erupted like brush fires across this land as slum after slum burst into flame. I was in Durham, North Carolina the night King was assassinated. While I was in the peaceful environment of Duke University, much of Durham was aflame. On the next night as I arrived in downtown Washington, much of the city was in flames and the rest a military camp. The "King was dead" as the song says, and much of his dream had also died.

It was perhaps fortunate that some had not staked everything on King's philosophy and program; and that a radically different philosophy of protest and liberation had its roots in the Black psyche. A different departure in race relations with its own philosophy and program swept across the country from a march in Mississippi where Stokely had shouted "Black Power." Immediately the philosophy of Black Power became an alternative to King's philosophy of nonviolence. It operated with different principles and by different methods. It made "separatism and violence" possible if not necessary. This turned some off, but for others it provided grounds for hope. As we move toward a conclusion, we shall discuss the positive aspects of a Black Power philosophy of the Black experience in the context of *survival* and *hope*.

Ideas have consequences as Marxism has taught us. Black Power is an ideology whose time has come. The only alternative to total despair for many Blacks is some assertion like "Black Power." All legal and moral efforts that could be expected of any humans, including those who accepted the myth of the Christlikeness of the Black person, had been employed to integrate this society. Within a decade Blacks had sued, prayed, marched, ridden, and sat for freedom. What they had discovered was that the majority group did not have the will to grant Black men and women their freedom. They were systematically rejected in all important ways. Even their appeals to the highest authority in the land were met by repression, indifference or "a benign neglect." Few choices were open. Even their sanity was being taxed and a way to psychological survival had to be found. Black Power inclusive of Black consciousness, Black pride and self-determination allowed Blacks to stir among the ashes of King's shattered dream and light the embers of hope. *A people cannot live without hope*.

When Yette reviewed his book, *The Choice*, at Howard University someone asked him if he saw any grounds for hope. His reply was that as a journalist, it was his task to report his findings and not to interpret his facts. But, he was informed, this is exactly what he had done. He asserted that Blacks were brought to this country and tolerated out of economic necessity. In this age of machines their labors are no longer needed and, therefore, they are expendable. Genocide is seen by Yette as a likely ultimate solution for the "Black problem." This is about where Yette leaves us. It is not surprising that his questioner was left without hope.

I find much of this pessimism among young Blacks, many of whom have had a rather comfortable life. This is the generation that cut teeth by the T.V. screen that revealed how cruelly sadistic the white man can be as a racist. Black heroes, like Dr. King, were beaten, chased by dogs, thrown into jail, and even killed as they sought justice and equality. This happened in the North as well as the South. What whites were willing to do to maintain a superiority position in this society was paraded before young Blacks' impressionable minds and sensitive spirits daily on national television.

The study of Black history has aggravated this awareness of the victimization of Blacks in this country. There is little comfort in assessing what whites have done to Blacks in the New World. The purpose of Black history is to provide what Vincent Harding calls "the new land"—a cultural home for a rootless people. Unfortunately what one comes out with is dependent upon the philosophy of the one who reads Black history and the purpose he has in mind. When one seizes upon the brutality of the white man vis-à-vis the Black man, it is almost natural to conceive of no relations between Blacks and whites which are not based upon the "revenge and revolt" answer to the racial struggle. One concludes that all whites are racists. Rap Brown is correct: "Violence is as American as cherry pie." The only question is whose violence and not violence vs. nonviolence. Put this way, Black power becomes a way of expressing a life-and-death struggle in which liberty or death is the Black man's portion. To accept these assertions absolutely is to be taken out of the revolution; for there are no grounds for hope. One who operates out of these suppositions accepts a self-fulfilling prophecy. What he does as he acts upon this philosophy may create the basis for his exile, imprisonment, or death. By such hopelessness one may be taken out of the struggle for Black liberation.

Whatever outlook one accepts in this society that has any promise of leading to Black liberation *must* allow for Black-white coexistence. Our destinies are bound together. Together we shall "nobly win or meanly lose" the struggle for Black liberation. What we need is an ideology that will strengthen Black power and humanize white power. It is not conceivable that wanton violence and irresponsible thought and action will accomplish either. We need an ideology and a course of action which reveal our strongest points and expose the white man's weakest points. It is not likely that confessing our love for him will accomplish this. Our propensity toward religion has already been exploited to our sorrow. Now, in this time of Black Power, we no longer have a sentimental understanding of love. There can be no love where there is no justice. These are the bases for all moralized relations between humans.

It is at this point that we need a philosophy of the future. A philosophy of hope has been developed in Germany by Ernst Bloch, a non-theist. Due to the Marxist-Christian dialogue, some major theologians have been captivated by the potential of a philosophy of hope for a theology of hope. Jürgen Moltmann of Tubingen has become known in this country, at least, as the theologian of hope par excellence. While he was at Duke Divinity School, a major theological conference was centered around his thought. Resulting from this confrontation with both a philosophy and theology of hope, there has developed in revolutionary thought a looking toward the future. Black and Third World theologians have been captivated by this "political theology" more than they have been by other recent philosophical or theological movements. Rubum Alves wrote his *A Theology of Human Hope* and Major Jones his *Black Awareness: A Black Theology of Hope* from this perspective. The "hope" motif has much to offer as we look at the Black experience.

Any use we make of the hope motif as a basis for a philosophy of the Black experience will need to be put in Black perspective. Here also a purely African understanding of time, if we take Mbiti seriously, will be equally problematic. Africans are said to pay attention to a long past and a short future. The concerns of Europeans and Latin Americans in applying a philosophy of hope to social and political problems are not our concerns. Our worldview is neither Anglo-Saxon nor African, it is both and more still. Our self-understanding is rooted in our experience as a people in this country. We have our own message of hope and any helpful explorations in this outlook must grow out of the Black experience. Our oppressed conditions have not provided grounds for hope and yet we have dared to hope and have passed it on to our children.

Whether the Black people's hope has been based upon myth or upon reality and what this trust in the future has done for them deserves careful consideration. There is evidence that much of the Black people's confidence has been misplaced. We have trusted undeserving whites, we have taken seriously the promises of Americans, and have too seldom trusted ourselves or our own race. But something has enabled Black people to make bricks out of straw—to bring the improbable within the range of possibility. I am sure religion has had something to do with this, but religion per se is a subject in its own right. I will turn, therefore, to what we have introduced as the ideology of Black Power and seek to indicate how this may yield for Blacks, out of their own experience, a philosophy of hope.

When I mention "Black Power" here, I do not have in mind a violent confrontation with white racists. I am aware that circumstances can push human beings to the breaking point where violence will result. Violence or counter-violence should not be programmed nor provided logical or ethical justification. Given sufficiently bad conditions of oppression, violence is inevitable. This is precisely why considerable attention should be directed toward the alleviation of oppression or talk of violence will be a self-fulfilling prophecy. Any consideration of the hope motif as a basis for a philosophy of the Black experience must include a "political dimension." By "political dimension" I refer to Black Power as a basis for massive social, economic and political changes, making life more human for Blacks. As long as life, for masses of Blacks, remains a living death, the grounds for hope are dim.

In a land of plenty, in the land of the free, the lot of the person in Black skin must no longer be crumbs from the rich man's table. Over against an escapist and sentimental religious hope based upon a crude Jesusology, Black Power juxtaposes a this-worldly, secular and tough-minded understanding of what can be done to humanize structures of power to enable Blacks to hope.

There is a question as to how Blacks are to relate to whites in a society where there must be coexistence and inexistence in the Black-white encounter, but the real issue remains *liberation from oppression*. Whether one espouses integration or separation, it is a fact that Blacks, *as a people*, long to be free. The one-by-one approach taken the Black middle class and the white liberal is outmoded. It is based upon the philosophy of whites over Blacks. It moves in one direction—toward the white mainstream as the promised land. It ignores the richness of the Black heritage and is based upon the assumption that Blacks will be decultrated from "Blackness" and acculturated into "whiteness" in order to be free and equal. Blacks must earn their right to be human according to the white agenda. White is beautiful and Black is ugly. This is symbolized by the lily-white beauty contests that represent the ultimate in female beauty. The fact that one Black girl is used as a token, since Blacks have their own contests, does not alter the situation since the judges are mostly white.

According to the ideology of Black Power, Black is beautiful in its own right. I can now look at my three daughters and appreciate their beauty. This is based upon a new awareness. We have transvaluated ourselves and have been led to a new self-understanding. This has brought a new meaning and purpose into our experience. We see our history, heritage, people, and ourselves as not needing to win their humanity by measuring up to white demands, but freedom is our birthright. We take seriously the ideologies of natural law and natural rights upon which the Constitution and Bill of Rights are based. *Equity*, based upon the belief that to be human is to have dignity, is the basis of Black Power. We believe this position to be based upon a theory of being as well as a theory of existence. It is rooted in reality and provides meaning for the Black experience. It is likewise the firm ground for hope and action.

This leads us to our conclusion. In this essay I have attempted to reflect creatively upon the existential-ontological aspects of the Black experience. I have described meaning and protest, survival and hope, in Black perspective. We have described Black reflection upon being and personal existence as a movement from oppression to liberation. Black philosophy is essentially a philosophy of liberation. These have been the first fruits of a religio-ethical examination of the experiential foundations of a philosophy of Black liberation.

References

DuBois, W. E. B., *The Souls of Black Folk* (New York: Fawcett World Library, 1968).

Fisher, M. M., *Negro Slave Songs* (New York: Russell & Russell, 1968).

Fullinwider, S. P. *The Mind and Mood of Black America* (Homewood, Ill.: The Dorsey Press 1968).

Goldston, R. C., *The Negro Revolution* (New York: Macmillan, 1968).

Jones, LeRoi, *Blues People* (New York: William Morrow, 1968).

Mbiti, J. S., *African Religions and Philosophies* (New York: Doubleday, 1970).

Thurman, Howard, *The Negro Spiritual Speaks of Life and Death* (New York: Harper, 1947).

Part Four

Historical Studies

No discipline of African American Religious Studies has received more attention and, perhaps, greater revision in recent years than history. This is partly because the Black Studies movement of the 1960s depended upon a radical renovation of African and African American history. We look back with amazement today on the white scholar who advised John W. Blassingame in 1963 that if he wanted a career as a professional historian he would have to discontinue his study of the Black past; or on the report of a graduate student at an Ivy League college in the 1950s who, upon announcing to his professor that he wanted to do a dissertation on "Negro Thought," received the bemused response: "Did they have any?"[1] But American theological education was even less prepared than secular graduate schools for serious work in historical studies of African American religion. As late as 1975 a leading white church historian remarked to the editor of this anthology, "It is doubtful that one can speak of Black Church history much before the Civil War."

This section begins with an essay by a philosopher-historian of Black culture who created *Kwanzaa* and is director of the Institute of Pan-African Studies in Los Angeles. He is Lecturer in Ethnic Studies at the University of California, Riverside. Maulana Karenga's analysis of African religions, and particularly the Egyptian legacy in chapter fifteen, is an example the best of the new scholarship that characterized the Black Studies movement and sent Black Christian historians back to the sources to correct deficiencies and distortions in church history.

The subsequent revival of African American church history in North American theological seminaries and universities is illustrated in chapter sixteen by Will B. Gravely, Associate Professor of Religious Studies at the University of Denver. Gravely unpacks the early history of African churches in the United States. He concludes that proscriptive practices by white Christians were the necessary causes of the separatist movements led by Richard Allen, Absolom Jones, and others. He also notes significant contributions to abolitionism by Black churches that, more often than not, were veritable antislavery societies—a fact previously ignored by most white church historians. "That fact," writes Gravely with piquant understatement, "makes for a crucial, qualitative distinction between Black and white Christian traditions in American history."

Chapter seventeen originally appeared in Manning Marable's *Blackwater: Historical Studies in Race, Class Consciousness and Revolution*. Marable, a political scientist in the Department of Black Studies at Ohio State University, writes with acute perception about the strengths and weaknesses of religion in American society.[2] In this extract he is unsparing in his criticism. He probes the meaning of the Black Church as the locus of a philosophy of life that decoded the slave master's world and transcended his oppression. Finally he reflects upon the relationship between post-King Black evangelicalism and Black Power to find that, in a time of increasing Black alienation from religion, this form of African American Christianity is an authentic praxis fusing social analysis and spirituality for political and social change. Here, therefore, is an example of interdisciplinary correlation between religious history and political science.

The last piece in Part Four was written by C. Eric Lincoln, author of the first essay in this book and considered by many to be the dean of African American Religious Studies. Trained as a sociologist of religion, Lincoln, as we have seen, is a skilled interpreter of African American history as the bedrock of theological education in North America. In chapter eighteen he revisits his earlier work on Black Muslims in the United States[3] with an update that contributes to our knowledge of permutations in a "new religion" responsive to the legitimating influences in middle class Black America.

The essays in this section demonstrate how much American church history, as a discipline of the theological curriculum, needs the cross-fertilization of the secular social sciences to provide an accurate picture of the past—a past now impossible to understand without a reordering of both familiar and unfamiliar data, new theoretical frameworks based on empirical studies, and new attention given to "the underside of history." It is now clear that what became of that ragtag, illiterate band of Blacks who dared to call themselves a church when most of them were still in chains is one of the most exciting and informative sagas of the Christian era.

Notes

1. John W. Blassingame, "Black Studies and the Role of the Historian," in *New Perspectives in Black Studies* ed, Blassingame (Urbana: University of Illinois Press, 1973):216–17.

2. For example, see his "The Black Faith of W. E. B. DuBois: Sociocultural and Political Dimensions of Black Religion," *Southern Quarterly,* 23, no. 3 (Spring 1985).

3. C. Eric Lincoln, *The Black Muslims in America,* revised ed. (1961. Reprinted. Boston: Beacon Press, 1973).

15

Black Religion

Maulana Karenga

Introduction

Religion has always been a vital part of Black life in both Africa and the United States. In Africa religion was so pervasive that distinctions between it and other areas of life were almost imperceptible. In the United States, the extent of Black religiousness is clear and has been well-documented. Although there are numerous definitions for religion, for the purpose of this chapter, religion can be defined as thought, belief, and practice concerned with the ultimate questions of life. Among such questions are those concerning human death, relevance, origin, destiny, suffering, obligations to other humans, and in most cases, to a Supreme or Ultimate Being. Within the context of the concern with the ultimate is also the clear division between the sacred, i.e., the set apart and exalted, and the profane, i.e., the common and non-exalted.[1]

The religion of Black people in the United States is predominantly Judeo-Christian, but Islam, both Black and orthodox, and African Traditional Religions are growing among African Americans. Given the fact that Black religion is so predominantly Judeo-Christian, the tendency is to see it as "white religion in Black face." However, as Lincoln and Wilmore contend, such an interpretation is grossly incorrect.[2] For regardless of what external details of white Christianity are similar to Black Christianity, the essence of Black Christianity is different. The essence of a people's religion is rooted in its own social and historical experiences and the truth and meaning it extracts from these translates into an authentic spiritual expression that speaks specifically to them. Thus Black religion represents in its essence not imitation but "the desire of Blacks to be self-conscious about the meaning of their Blackness and to search for spiritual fulfillment in terms of their understanding of themselves and their experience of history."[3]

African Models

General Themes

Black religion like Black people began in Africa so it is important to discuss its historical forms before turning to its current expressions. The study of African Traditional Religions is made difficult by Europeans' interpretations that exhibit a need to make Christianity seem superior and African religions primitive, and by African Christian interpretations that strive to make African religions more "normal" by making them look more Christian or Western.[4] To appreciate African religions one must admit similarities and differences without seeing the similarities as "less developed" and the differences as evidence of psychological or cultural defectiveness.

If African stories of creation and gods are myths, so are Christian, Jewish, and Islamic ones. Moreover, Jehovah, Yaweh, and Allah are no more arguable than Nkulunkulu, Oludumare, and Amma. And the *abosom* of the Ashanti and the *orisha* of the Yoruba are no less effective as divine intermediaries than Catholic saints like Jude and Christopher. All non-scientific approaches to the origin of the world and the forces operative in it are vulnerable to challenge. And the choice of one over the other is more a matter of tradition and preference than proof of any particular one's validity. Therefore my use of Western religious examples will not be to force comparisons or contrasts, but to demonstrate parallels where appropriate that would tend to lessen a student's tendency to reductively translate African religions in a mistaken assumption of superiority for his or her own.

Although African religions are complex and diverse, some general themes tend to appear in all of them. First, there is the belief in one Supreme God: Oludumare among the Yoruba, Nkulunkulu among the Zulu, and Amma among the Dogon. This god is the father in most societies, but also appears as the mother in matriarchical societies like the Ovambo in Namibia and the Nuba in Kenya. In Dogon religion Amma has both male and female characteristics, reflecting the Dogon concept of binary opposition as the motive force and structure of the universe.[5]

Second, in African Traditional Religion, God is both immanent and transcendent, near and far. In this framework Africans engage in daily interaction with divinities who are seen as God's intermediaries and assistants. These divinities are both similar to and different from Jesus, angels, and Catholic saints as intermediaries and assistants to the Supreme Being. It is this kind of deference and exchange with the divinities that made the less-critical assume Africans were polytheistic rather than monotheistic. However evidence clearly argues against this assumption.

Third, African religions stress ancestor veneration. The ancestors are venerated because of their contribution in life, as guardians of family traditions and ethics, and because they are viewed as "the best group of intermediaries between men and God."[6]

Fourth, African Traditional Religions stress the necessary balance between one's collective identity and responsibility as a member of society, and one's personal identity and responsibility. Like religion itself, a person is defined as an integral part of a definite community to which he or she belongs and in which he or she finds identity and relevance. Summing up this conception, John Mbiti states that "I am because we are, and since we are, therefore I am."[7] The Dinka have captured this stress on the moral ideal of harmonious integration of self with the community in their word *cieng* which means both *morality* and *living together*. In this conception, the highest moral ideal is to live in harmony, know oneself and one's duties through others and reach one's fullness in cooperation with and through support from one's significant others.[8]

Another key theme in African religions is the profound respect for nature. Because humans live in a religious universe, everything that is has religious relevance. The whole world as God's creation is alive with his/her symbols and gifts to humans, and bears witness to his/her power, beauty and beneficence. Thus there are sacred trees, rivers, mountains and animals (as in western religions). Nature is not only respected because of its association with God, but also because of its relevance to humankind. The stress, then, is to show it due respect, to live in harmony with it and the universe, and not abuse it.

Finally, the conception of death and immortality is an important theme in African religions. Death in African religions is seen in several ways. First, it is seen as another stage in human development. Humans are born, live, die, and become the ancestors. Death is thus not the end, but a beginning of another form of existence, i.e., as ancestor and spirit. Therefore it is seen as a disruption of life rather than an end to it. After a period of mourning, there is celebration for the human conquest of death. For after the funeral, the dead are "revived" in the spirit world, and as ancestors, are close and relevant. Second, death is seen as reflective of cosmic patterns, i.e., the rising and setting of the sun, and often graves are dug east and west to imitate this pattern. Third, death is seen as a transition of life to personal and collective immortality. Personally one lives after death through four media: (1) children; (2) other relatives; (3) rituals of remembrance; and (4) great works or significant deeds. The living remember and speak one's name and deeds and works speak of one's significance throughout time. Thus without relatives to keep one's memory or significant achievements and deeds alive, one is what Africans call utterly dead. Collective immortality is achieved through the life of one's people and through what one means to them. For as long as they live, the person lives and shares in their life and destiny.

The Dogon Model

One of the most complex and impressive African religious systems is that of the Dogon. The Dogon, who live in Mali, have astounded the world by their astronomical knowledge and impressed it with the logic and intricacy of their thought. So impressive is their knowledge, especially of the Sirius star system, that some Europeans have argued that the Dogon's knowledge was given to them by space beings or by mysterious Europeans. However, Europeans did not know themselves until the 1800s what the Dogon knew about the Sirius star system seven hundred years ago.[9]

The socio-religious thought of the Dogon evolves from an elaborate cosmogyny and an extremely complex cosmology.[10] It is these constructions around which the Dogon understand and organize their world and seek to carry out their social and spiritual tasks. For the sake of brevity and clarity, I have tried to cut down the story of creation to its most basic elements while at the same time trying to remain faithful to its logic and content:

In the beginning everything that would be already potentially was. The substance and structure of the universe was in Amma, the Supreme God, who was in the image of an egg and divided into four quarters containing the four basic elements of air, earth, fire and water, and the four cardinal directions —north, south, east and west. Amma was the egg of the universe, and the universe and Amma were one. As egg, Amma symbolized and was fertility and unlimited creative possibility. Through creative thought, Amma traced within himself the design and developmental course of the universe using 266 cosmic signs which contained the essence, structure and life principle of all things. Placing the four basic elements and sacred signs and seeds on a flat disk, Amma set the disk revolving between the two cosmic axes. But the spinning disk threw off the water drying up the seeds. The first creation was thus aborted and Amma began again, deciding that this time he would make humans the preservers of order and life in the world.

Placing a seed at the center of himself, the cosmic egg, he spoke seven creative words. From this the seed (matter) vibrated seven times unfolding along a spiral path, conserving itself on one hand and transforming itself on the other through alternations between opposites. The principal of twinness, or binary opposition, directed its movement and its form and established a pattern for the structure and functioning of the universe: up/down, man/woman, action/inaction, hot/cold, etc. From the infinitely small (seed, atom) the infinitely large (universe) evolved. The seed, vibrating seven times and turning in a spiral fashion, extended itself in seven directions in the womb of the world, prefiguring the shape of a human being, i.e., two directions for the head, two for the arms, two for the legs and one for the genital. Thus the world was created in the image of humans and would later be organized around them.

Transforming the egg into a double placenta, Amma placed two sets of twins, male and female in each, again underscoring the principle of opposites which informs the structure and functioning of the universe. In the twins, he placed the sacred signs, words, and seeds of creation. Before gestation was completed, however, one of the male twins, Yurugu (Ogo), feeling lonely and incomplete, burst through the womb to seize his female twin. Unable to acquire his twin, he rebelled against the established order of things. Imposing disorder on an orderly process, Yurugu descended into the void in an attempt to create a world himself. But his knowledge was incomplete and he could not speak the creative words. Then Amma, using the piece of placenta which Yurugu took as he broke from the celestial egg-womb, created the earth. This creation of earth restored the human shape of the world. The celestial egg became the head of man; the lower incomplete placenta now earth; forming an incomplete circle became the hips and legs; and the space and lines that divide and connect heaven and earth became the trunk and arms. Binary opposition is thus, again established in that heaven is the head (mind, spirit) and earth, the lower region of the body (the physical). Joined together they form the structure and essence of humans.

To restore order in the world, Amma scattered Yurugu's male twin, Nommo, or creative word, over the expanse of the universe. Also, he created four other Nommo spirits from Nommo and their offspring became the eight ancestors of the Dogon. Amma then sent Nommo and the eight ancestors down to earth, with all species of animals and plants, and all the elements of human culture thus, laying the basis for human development and a prosperous earth. Descending, Nommo shouted out the creative words, therefore transmitting the power of creative speech and thought to earth, making it available to humankind. Through this power, they would be able to push back the boundaries of ignorance and disorder and impose creative order on the world. To punish Yurugu for his disorder and revolt, Amma transformed him into a pale fox. Deprived of his female half, pale fox is an incomplete and lonely being wandering through the world in a vain quest for wholeness. But as he wanders, he leaves tracks through the mysteries of life, revealing the dangers humans must avoid. Finally, sending rain to Earth, Amma made the Earth flourish and humans began to cultivate the land and cover it with ever increasing numbers. Possessing creative intelligence through Nommo, humans walk the way of Yurugu as well, alternating between disorder and order, destruction and creation, rationality and irrationality, conformity and revolt.

There are several aspects of this cosmogonical construction which reveal the profundity of Dogon thought and its susceptibility to interesting and expansive interpretations. First, it stresses the binary oppositional character and functioning of the universe, i.e., creation/destruction, order/disorder, male/female, perfection/imperfection, self-conscious action/unconscious action, etc. This is essentially an African dialectic, posing opposites necessary to the explanation and functioning of the world. In fact each opposite explains and necessitates the other. Thus Yurugu rebels because he feels deprived of his female half, which he needs for his wholeness. He fails because he represents action without critical consciousness; and Nommo, who reflects the creative thought and action of Amma, succeeds in establishing order and promoting development. Second, the concept of God as the cosmic womb, already containing in the beginning everything that would come into being, reflects the scientific principle that matter was always here and only its forms changed and change.

Third, the concept of God as egg is a reflection of his fertility, productiveness and infinite creative possibilities. As infinite creative possibility in the universe and of the universe, God is infinite in a logical and meaningful way. Fourth, the Dogon pose God as making a mistake in the first creation and thereby maintain logical consistency even in discussing God. For God is both perfect and imperfect, male and female, thought and action and therefore reflects and reinforces the principle of binary opposition.

Also there is a clear contention that the world is not perfect either and is in the process of perpetual becoming. This process again is marked by binary opposition in structure and functioning and strives toward the creative and ongoing harmonizing of the two opposites. Especially profound and far-reaching is the concept that becoming of necessity requires rebellion or oppositional thought and action against the established order. Yurugu comes into being by breaking through the cosmic egg and thus sets up conditions for a new world. Breaking from Amma, God, he becomes truly man rather than a cosmic baby. In this action, he reminds one of the young adult leaving his or her parents' house in order to build a world for him or herself. In a word, independence and development requires a break from the established state of things. And even though Yurugu fails to make the world, he contributed to its origin and still leaves tracks through the mysteries of life humankind can read and from which they can learn vital lessons.

Finally, Dogon thought is clearly impressive in its stress on humans as the indispensable element in the world's becoming and functioning. As noted above, the universe was created in the image of the human personality; he/she is the world in microcosm, containing its basic elements, the four cardinal directions, and the sacred cosmic seeds, signs and words. Moreover Amma, God, could not make the world without humans, for not only did the world need man/woman to flourish, but so did God. For if God is idea and creative possibility, only man/woman can know and appreciate it. Only humans are capable of creative thought; trees will not pray or praise, and dogs do not discuss spiritual or social duties. But if God needs man/woman, the binary oppositional logic of Dogon thought requires that man/woman also needs God. For if idea and creative possibility (God) cannot exist without man/woman, man/woman cannot exist without idea and creative possibility (God).

The Egyptian Legacy

Egypt's contribution to Western religions and indeed to Western civilization in general is a well-argued and well-documented contention. In fact, given the deeply religious character of Egyptian society, all activities whether science, government, or art were informed and inspired by its religion. Within the context of continental African and African American intellectual history works by Cheikh Anta Diop, John Jackson, George G. James, Jacob Carruthers, and this author as well as others cogently and consistently represent this position.[11] Some European scholars such as James Breasted, E. Wallis Budge, Gerald Massey, Henri Frankfort, Flinders Petrie, and most recently Martin Bernal, have assumed a similar position in varying degrees. In fact it is Breasted, the U.S.' preeminent orientalist, who concedes as early as 1933 that "It is now quite evident that the ripe social and moral development of mankind in the Nile Valley, which is three thousand years older than that of the Hebrews, contributed essentially to the formation of the Hebrew literature which we call the Old Testament. Our moral heritage therefore derives from a wider *human* past enormously older than the Hebrews, and it has come to us rather *through* the Hebrews than *from* them."[12]

John Jackson cites several legacies of Egypt to Christianity. First, he argues that the concept of Virgin and Child in Christianity is clearly based on the Virgin Isis and Child Horus of Egypt. Jackson states that "Gods, heroes, born of virgins, were quite common in olden times and the sources of most, if not all of these divinities seem to have been Egypt." He then quotes Jocelyn Rhys's *Shaken Creeds*, which notes that "In the catacombs of Rome, black statues of this Egyptian divine Mother and Infant still survive from the early Christian worship of the Virgin and Child to which they were converted."[13]

Secondly, Jackson contends that Horus, the Egyptian Savior and light of the world, is the model for Jesus who has similar qualities. He points out that, as Charles Vail contends in his *The World's Saviors*, there were fifteen saviors of miraculous birth that precede Jesus including Krishna and Gautama (Buddha) of India, Tammuz of Babylonia, Zoroaster of Persia, Quetzalcoatl of Mexico, and Horus of Egypt. But of all the virgin-birth saviors, Horus appears to be the model for Jesus. In fact Jackson states that, on the inner walls of the Holy of Holies in the Temple of Luxor inscribed about two thousand years B.C.E., "the birth of Horus is depicted in four scenes which suggests how much Jesus' story is modelled after Horus."[14] These four scenes are: (1) the annunciation in which the god Thoth announces to the Virgin Isis she will bear a son; (2) the Immaculate Conception in which the god Kneph (the Holy Spirit) and the goddess Hathor mystically impregnate Isis by holding the ankh to her head and nostrils; (3) the birth of the son of God, Horus; and (4) the adoration with men and gods paying homage to the child, including three kings or magi who are giving him gifts.

Also Jackson notes how an ancient Egyptian passion play enacts the arrest, trial, death, burial, and resurrection of Osiris, often used interchangeably with Horus as savior, providing more evidence of Christianity's borrowing of models from Egypt. Finally, Jackson points out that even the celebration of Christmas on December 25 has its roots in Egypt. For "In Egypt, three thousand years ago, the birth day of the sun God (Ra) was celebrated on the 25th of December, since it was the first day to noticeably lengthen after December 21st (the day of the winter solstice)."[15]

No one to date has done as much work toward the rescue and reconstruction of the rich cultural legacy of ancient Egypt to the world as Cheikh Anta Diop. A truly Imhotepian man, he was a historian, linguist, anthropologist, and archeologist, and he used each of these fields to rescue and reconstruct this legacy and make it a vital part in the vindication, revitalization, and continued development of African culture. For him, as with those who build on his work, Egypt is Africa's paradigmatic classical culture in the same way Greece is Europe's. His *The African Origins of Civilization* (1974) and his last major work, *Civilisation ou Barbarie* (1981), were especially dedicated to establishing and explicating the richness, relevance, and African rootedness of this world historical legacy.

Diop argues cogently Egypt's contribution to science, math, philosophy, and religion, more precisely to the "revealed religions," i.e., Judaism, Christianity and Islam. For Diop Greek and Judeo-Christian thought borrows from and builds on an Egyption cosmogony expressed in the so-called Pyramid Texts, around 2600 B.C.E. "in an epoch in which the Greeks themselves did not exist and the notion of a Chinese or Hindu philosophy was nonsense."[16] From this cosmogony, Diop contends, one finds several key philosophical concepts informed Greek philosophy and Judeo-Christian thought: (1) a universe of uncreated eternal matter (Anaximander's and Hesiod's aperion); (2) archetypes of essences of all future things that would be called into existence (Plato's archetypical ideals); (3) the law of transformation and the principle of evolution through time expressed in the concept of Kheper (actualization of archetypes in Plato); (4) the emergence of Ra (God) (Plato's demiurge); (5) Ra's creation through the word, i.e., logos, in Greek and later Judaism, Christianity, and Islam.

Speaking of Christianity in particular, Diop states that the very term "Christ" "is not from an Indo-European root but comes from a pharaonic Egyptian expression, *kher sesheta*, 'one who is in charge of the mysteries' and which was applied to the divinities Osiris, Anubis, etc." He says "it was only applied to Jesus in the fourth century through religious . . . (diffusion)." Moreover, Diop points out that Osiris is the religious paradigm for the Redeemer "who three thousands years before Jesus, dies and rises from the dead to save humans." He is thus the "redeeming God of humanity: he rises in the sky on the right hand of his father, the Great God, Ra. He is the son of God." Also he notes that Egyptian religious philosophy provides a source of the concept of trinity: "the notion of trinity appears throughout Egyptian religious thought and is found in the many divine triads such as Osiris-Isis-Horus or Ra in the morning, at noon and in the evening," i.e., Kheper in the morning, Ra at noon, and Atum in the evening.

Finally, Diop posits that a ray of light the goddess Hathor receives from heaven that engenders the god Apis is clearly "a prefiguration of the immaculate conception of the Holy Virgin." He refers to J. Pirenne's *History of the Civilization of Ancient Egypt* for further explication. In one sense Diop's work is a scholarly and well-documented expansion of George James's work which was seminal in its conception and presentation at an early stage in the African project of rescuing and reconstructing the Egyptian legacy. James's work was essentially philosophical but Diop brought a multidimensional knowledge base as well as scientific field and lab work to prove his contentions and explicate the African/Egyptian legacy.

George James argues in his major work, *Stolen Legacy*, that it is out of Egyptian socio-religious philosophy that so-called Greek philosophy came. He contends at the outset that "The term Greek philosophy, to begin with is a misnomer," since it is essentially a derivative from the Egyptian socio-religious educational and philosophical system called "the Egyptian Mysteries System". Realizing the awesome burden of proof such a contention incurs, James develops historical, textual, and conceptual evidence to support it.[17]

In terms of historical evidence, James cites the following: first, the teaching of the Egyptian Mysteries System was the source of higher education in the ancient world, educating students from Europe, Asia, and other parts of Africa. Not only did the Greeks study in Egypt, but Jesus and Moses did also. As a result these students returned to their various countries to set up E.M.S. schools or variations of them. Second, Pythagoras, from whom all Greek philosophers borrowed, studied in Egypt as did Thales, Democritus, Plato, Diogenes, Timaeus and Herodotus, and all confirm this in their writings. Third, other Greek philosophers—Anaximander, Anximenes, Parmenides,

Zeno, and Melisus studied in Ionia in Asia Minor, a stronghold of E.M.S. schools. Fourth, immigration of Greeks to Egypt for education began as early as 525 B.C.E. after the Persian invasion of Egypt. Fifth, the conquest of Egypt by Alexander (332 B.C.E.) prepared the way for greater absorption of Egyptian knowledge from its schools and libraries. The schools of Aristotle moved from Athens to Egypt, converted the Egyptian Royal Library to a research center and university, and compiled a vast body of scientific and other knowledge from documents and oral instruction from Egyptian priests, calling it the history of Greek philosophy. Sixth, there is a historical and logical problem of establishing that Aristotle wrote four hundred to one thousand books and learned from Plato—who learned from Socrates—a math, science, politics, and economics Socrates did not know. Historical evidence says Alexander gave Aristotle money to buy books on science, but in order to obtain them they had to be in existence, and if they were in existence, he cannot be credited with having written them. In fact, he got them from the libraries of Egypt. Finally, the persecution of Greek philosophers for teaching *foreign* doctrines and the edicts of Roman emperors Theodius (fourth century) and Justinian (sixth century) that abolished E.M.S. in Greece as well as Egypt point strongly to the historical link between the two.

The textual and conceptual evidence shows also the historical link and borrowing. The Memphite Theology (c. 4,000 B.C.E.), with its three-part text on Gods of Chaos, Gods of Creation, and Primate of the Gods, contain within it concepts the Greeks appear to have borrowed: (1) the concept of summum bonum—highest good and discipline and cardinal virtues that make humans gods (Aristotle, Socrates, Plato); (2) the E.M.S. curriculum, i.e., the seven liberal arts, the sciences of the 42 books of Hermes, the sciences of the monument (architecture, masonry, etc.), the secret societies (numerical, geometric and religious symbolism), and the social order and its protection (social sciences); (3) proof of God used by Aristotle, i.e., purpose in the universe and God as the unmoved mover; (4) concept of the soul, immortality and salvation; (5) concept of the key elements—air, earth, fire, water; (6) the principle of opposites in the structure and functioning of the universe (dialectics); (7) the concept of creation as a product of Nous (mind, intelligence) and logos (creative utterance); (8) the concept of the atom as the basic building block of the universe (from the God, Atum, whose name and attributes are the same as those ascribed to the atom). "This is the legacy of the African continent to the nations of the world," James concludes. And since it is Egypt who "has laid the foundations of modern progress . . . she and her people deserve the honor and praise which for centuries have been falsely given to the Greeks."

J. A. Rogers credits Pharaoh Akhenaton (c. 1350 B.C.E.) with making significant contributions to world religious development. He states that 1,300 years before Jesus Akhenaton taught and lived "a gospel of perfect love, brotherhood and truth. Two thousand years before Muhammad, he taught the doctrine of One God." And "three thousand years before Darwin, he sensed the unity that runs through all living things." Breaking from the Egyptian stress on one God with many manifestations, Akhenaton stressed the worship of One God. Moreover, Akhenaton's God unlike that of Moses was not a jealous God, but a God of Perfect Love, a God compassionate even toward the chicken that "crieth in the egg shell." Others have suggested that his psalms were the model for David's, whose were written five hundred years later and Rogers points out the similarity. Rogers also notes that Akhenaton advanced the concept that "the Kingdom of God is within you" centuries before Jesus did.[18]

Finally, in the *Husia*, which is a collection of selected writings from the sacred texts of ancient Egypt, I present textual evidence of parallels and/or sources for many concepts in the Judeo-Christian tradition that emerge from Egypt.[19] In the Book of Knowing, the creation's several fundamental concepts appear. Here one finds the concept of logos, as Diop has observed, which in Medu Neter or the ancient Egyptian language would be Hu Sia, or authoritative utterance of exceptional insight. Ra (Ptah) conceives in his heart and mind and commands it to be. Thus "by means of the Word, all (things) are fashioned and created." One encounters the concept of free will and human equality also in Ra's statement of his four good deeds. Ra says, "I made every person like his or her fellow," and made wind, water, and religious consciousness, "so that the humble might benefit from it like the great." And he allowed free will in that he "did not command them to do evil." On the contrary, "it was their own hearts and minds which caused them to disobey that which I commanded."[20]

In the Book of Prayers and Sacred Praises, one finds psalms which predate and prefigure David's in conception and imagery, as Rogers noted. Ra is the good shepherd (more precisely good herdsman) who leads his flock to green pastures. He rescues the humble and the needy and hears and answers the prayers of the prisoner and the oppressed. He is the prime minister of the poor, judge that takes no bribes. "He makes the weak-armed into the strong-armed so that the multitudes flee from the feeble and one alone takes a thousand captive." Also noteworthy is Akhenaton's hymn to Aton, which Breasted and others have compared to Psalm 104.[21]

In the Book of Khun-Anup, one has the oldest text on social justice. The command is to "Speak justice and do justice. For justice is mighty. It is great; it endures. Its worth is real and it leads one to blessedness. Wrongdoing does not achieve its goal, but one who is just reaches dry land." Especially should this justice be directed toward the most vulnerable of society. For if there is no justice, the vulnerable cannot survive. Therefore, the righteous and just are commanded to be "the father of the orphan, the husband of the widow, a protective garment for the motherless," and to "come at the voice of the caller."

The Book of Declaration of Virtues reveals a similar stress on social justice and preference for the poor and vulnerable. One is instructed by example to give "bread to the hungry, water to the thirsty, clothes to the naked and a boat to cross over for those who have none." There is a call to "rescue the weak from the strong," honor one's mother and father, speak truth, do justice, support the aged, satisfy the needs of the have-nots so that one "may come before God blameless and without blemish."[22]

In the Books of Wise Instruction, one finds several seminal theological and ethical concepts as well as the source of direct Hebrew borrowing. The book of Ptah-hotep teaches the intrinsic worth and inevitable triumph of *Maat* (the way of truth, justice and righteousness), the central ethical and religious concept in Egyptian spirituality. "Maat is great, its value is lasting," he says. "Although wickedness may gain wealth, wrongdoing has never brought its ware safe to port. In the end it is Maat that endures. . . ." He also teaches due process, honor for father and mother, reciprocity, and the concept of the chosen of God based on righteousness, not race or ethnicity. Kheti teaches the *imago dei* along with the concept of human stewardship on earth saying: God "made the sky and earth for their sake. They are in his image and came from his body."[23]

From the Book of Amenomope (c. 1405–1370 B.C.E.) Solomon (c. 976–939 B.C.E.) borrows heavily for his Book of Proverbs. As Breasted has maintained, "All Old Testament scholars of any weight or standing now recognize the fact that . . . a whole section . . . of the Book of Proverbs is largely drawn verbatim from the Wisdom of Amenomope; that is the Hebrew version is practically a literal translation from the Egyptian."[24] In the following example he cites Amenomope first and then Solomon: (1) "Incline thine ears to hear my sayings (words). And apply thine heart to their comprehension." / "Incline thine ear and hear the words of the wise and apply thine heart to my knowledge"; (2) "(riches) have made themselves wings like geese and they have flown to heaven." / "riches certainly make themselves wings like an eagle that flies toward heaven"; (3) "Better is poverty in the hand of God than riches in the storehouse." / "Better is little with the fear of Yahweh, than great treasure. . . ." There are, of course, many more examples of this borrowing by the Hebrews as both Breasted and Griffith contend.[25] Griffith cites at least twenty other borrowings including the "planted by the rivers of water" analogy found in Ps. 1:3 and Jer. 17:18. He concludes that this borrowing was not abnormal for "when the Hebrews were becoming civilized under Solomon and his successors, they looked especially to Egypt and Babylonia for instruction in the arts of life."

In the Book of Neferti one finds the concept of the messianic king that precedes David of the Hebrews. The messianic righteous king is "One Ameni, the son of man, born of a woman of Nubia" who shall return *Maat* (righteousness and order) to its place and drive away *Isfet* (evil and chaos).

And finally, in the Books of Rising Like Ra, one finds the hall of judgment before the risen savior, resurrection, the immortality of the soul through righteousness, the celestial paradise of heaven, and a source or parallel of the Ten Commandments. In the Book of Coming Forth By Day, often called the Book of the Dead, one finds the forty-two declarations of innocence that clearly contain eight of the Ten Commandments; this was written thousands of years before Moses of the Hebrews lived. These were declarations of innocence one made to justify or vindicate oneself before God and thus indicate an ethical code key to eternal life through righteousness. These eight similar to the commandments are: (1) I have not blasphemed against God; (2) I have not told lies in the seat of truth; (3) I have not mistreated my family and associates; (4) I have not committed murder, ordered murder, or turned over anyone to a murderer; (5) I have not stolen; (6) I have not committed adultery; (7) I have not violated sacred times; and (8) I have not coveted other's property. The two missing from the declarations are the prohibition against graven images, which runs counter to African religious art and symbolism, and the prohibition against gods *before* God, which obviously was not a major issue for the Egyptians. Egyptians recognized one great God with many manifestations. The Book of Prayers and Sacred Praises says of Amen-Ra, "You are the only God and there is none like you," and other prayers speak of Ra in his many forms, i.e., Kheper, Atum, etc.

Thus in so many areas Egypt's legacy proves itself both profound and far-reaching. It is, therefore, racism that denies African contribution to the forward flow of human history, or teaches that Egypt was European or Asian rather than African in both color and culture. And it is the task of critical scholarship in Black Studies to correct this error and distortion so that truth can be served and Africa receive its due credit and place in human history.

The Christian Model

Reasons for Conversion

It is common knowledge that African Americans were converted to Christianity in slavery. But what is less known and less discussed are the reasons for the conversion both from the point of view of the slaveholders and the enslaved Africans. The slaveholders' reasons for Christianizing the enslaved Africans began with their perception of Christianity as a way to reinforce and maintain dominance.

In 1743 a white minister prepared a book of dialogue for slaveholders to teach enslaved Africans which stressed contentment and thanks for being enslaved and ended saying, "I can't help knowing my duty. I am to serve God in that state in which he has placed me. I am to do what my master orders me."[26] As the indoctrination progressed, then, slaveholders soon discovered that many of the most amenable and submissive enslaved Africans were those who were Christians.

And, the slaveholders were equally, and at times more so, interested in uprooting Africans from their own religious heritage, in order to deprive them of cultural distinction and motivation for revolt. As Frazier points out, "whites were always on guard against African religious practices which could provide an opportunity for slave revolts, and they outlawed such practices." Slaveholders also converted Africans because they and other whites believed it was their duty to bring light to "benighted and lost" heathens. It was, in a word, based on a culturally chauvinist assumption that their religion was the only real and correct one and that all others were pagan and an abomination to their intolerant and jealous God.

Although many Africans accepted Christianity, many others resisted it for a long time, maintaining their commitment to traditional African religion or Islam. Most of those who accepted Christianity transformed it in their own image and interests.[27] Given the importance of religion to Blacks and the reverence they had for their God, one must raise the question, what compelled them to exchange their God for that of the slaveholder? The first reason for African American conversion to Christianity was obviously the conquest and coercion by the slaveholder. Alex Haley's description of the brutally coerced transformation of Kunta Kinte into Christianized Toby in his popular family saga, *Roots*, is representative of the process.[28] As Frazier notes the slaveholder and the "missionaries recognized the difficulty of converting adult Africans and concentrated their efforts on children."[29]

Africans began to accept Christianity more as they gradually began to accept the slaveholders' religious and cultural contentions which posed Christianity and the Christian God more powerful. This gradual acceptance was encouraged by the fact of their enslavement, the religious doubt and self-doubt it raised, the gradual loss of historical memory, and the end of revivifying contacts from Africa through the end of the slave trade. Christianity came to be seen as a coping strategy on the social and psychological level. Socially, acceptance meant avoidance of humiliation, punishment, and beatings reserved for recalcitrant "heathens." Psychologically, it meant a transferred hope for deliverance, which the old religions seemed unable to fulfill.

Christianity and the religious meetings it allowed became, even under severe restriction, a means of establishing and maintaining a sense of community. This was a time for the enslaved Africans to meet, to reinforce bonds between them, discuss hopes, problems, and also, as in the Turner, Vesey, and Prosser revolts, a time to plan liberation strategies. Finally, after years of forced conversion and tentative and partial acceptance, Christianity became a heritage, and subsequent generations born in a Christian context simply accepted it. However it is important to stress that in spite of this conversion to Christianity, Africans did not accept it totally in its racist slavery-supporting form. In fact, "a distinctive African American form of Christianity —actually a new religion of an oppressed people—slowly took root in the Black community." This new "Black folk religion carried within its perspectives a definitive moral judgment against slavery and a clear legitimation of the slave's and later the freedman's struggle against the forces of injustice and inequality."[30]

The Historical Role of the Church

The role of the Black Church in African American life has been substantial and enduring since its inception.[31] Although Frazier divides the church into the "invisible church" in slavery and the institutional church that began with the founding of the African Methodist Episcopal Church in 1787 and the first African Baptist Church in 1788, for the purpose of this section and to stress historical continuity, the division will not be made. Although the Black Church has rightly been and continues to be accused of support for the established order at various times, it does have a history of social activism and social service of which it can be proud. And it is this history which will be stressed.[32]

The Black Church obviously began as a spiritual sanctuary and community against the violent and destructive character of the slave world. And even after slavery, it remained a wall of defense and comfort against racism and its accompanying attacks on Black dignity, relevance, and social worth. The Black Church served as an agency of social reorientation and reconstruction, providing reinforcement for the old values of marriage, family, morality, and spirituality in the face of the corrosive effects of slavery.

The church became a center for economic cooperation, by pooling resources to buy churches; building mutual aid societies that provided social services for free Blacks and purchased and helped resettle enslaved Africans; and by setting up businesses for economic development. The church engaged in both public and internal educational projects, setting up schools and training ministers and teachers, and raising funds to carry these projects. Finally, the Black Church, from its earliest days as an invisible spiritual community, supported social change and struggle, providing leaders and leadership at various points in the struggle for Black liberation and a truly higher level of human life.

The King Model

The death of Bishop Henry M. Turner left the Black community with "no clergyman of his stature who could, by temperament or ideology, assume the leadership role he played in a persistant but unsuccessful attempt to radicalize the Black church."[33] Turner had been an advocate of the social role and responsibility of the church and religion, had engaged in a merciless criticism of U.S. society, and advocated the Blackness of God, draft resistance, armed self-defense and emigrationism. Not until King did another Black Christian leader rise to his level of relevance and social effectiveness. "It was Martin Luther King," Lincoln observes, "who made the contemporary church aware of its power to effect change." He also revived its tradition of self-conscious social activism and thus broke it from the moderate accommodating tendency that was also a part of its history and that it had exhibited since the death of Turner.[34]

King developed a theory and practice which combined the best of Black religion with socially focused concepts borrowed from Ghandi, Thoreau, Hegel, Rauschenbush, Tillich, and others.[35] Within his sociopolitical philosophy, five key concepts stand at its core. First, King posed Blacks as a people whose suffering and social situation have prepared them for, and in fact give them, a divine historical mission of not only liberating themselves, but also of restructuring and spiritualizing the American society.

Second, King argued that Blacks had both the moral right and responsibility to disobey unjust laws in their resistance to social evil. This stress, as Walton notes,[36] combines David Thoreau's concept of "the rightfulness of civil disobedience;" Jesus's stress on humanity, forgiveness, and love; and Ghandi's stress on loving nonviolence as a method of social transformation. "Your highest loyalty is to God," King stated, "and not to the mores, or folkways, the state or the nation or any man-made institution." Thus when any of those "conflict with God's will, it is your Christian duty to oppose it."[37]

Closely related to the above concept is King's contention that it is immoral and cowardly to collaborate in one's own oppression. "To accept passively an unjust system is to cooperate with that system," he maintained. And in doing this, "the oppressed becomes as evil as the oppressor." What's more, such nonaction says "to the oppressor that his actions are morally right." He concludes acquiescence to oppression is not only morally wrong and corruptive, "it is (also) the way of a coward."[38]

Fourth, King posed the necessity of religion having a social as well as spiritual function. Having read Walter Rauschenbush's *Christianity and the Social Crisis*, he developed "a theological basis for the social concern" which he felt religion should have "as a result of his early experiences." Therefore he stressed that true religion was obligated to deal "with the whole man, not only his soul, but his body, not only his spiritual well-being but his social well-being."

A final core concept in King's sociopolitical philosophy was his contention that human nature is perfectable through struggle. He asserted that Hegel's "analysis of the dialectical process . . . helped me to see that growth comes through struggle." Central to this concept is the emphasis on "creative tension," nonviolence struggle which not only changes the oppressor, but also the oppressed in the process.

King's sociopolitical philosophy was important to Black religion and the civil rights movement in several ways. It gave religious sanction to social resistance—although of the nonviolent type—and thus spiritually inspired an oppressed people who would not have been moved as deeply by other doctrines in their quest for freedom. It made social passivity immoral, an act in contradiction with the will of God and His desire for truth, freedom, and justice in the world, and therefore reinforced the need to resist social evil. It placed on preachers a continuing responsibility and pressure to take an active stand in the movement and make religion more socially relevant. And finally, King's sociopolitical philosophy served as a transition in Black religion which encouraged self-criticism and pointed toward a Black Liberation Theology.

Black Liberation Theology

In July 1966 in the midst of the period of Black urban revolts, a group of Black clergy met in Harlem to develop a position on the struggle for Black Power in the United States. There they assumed a position which made a definitive contribution to the emergence of Black Liberation Theology. Breaking from King's negative position on Black Power as "nihilistic," they affirmed the right and need of Black Power, criticized the Black Church for too often steering "its members away from the reign of God in this world to a distorted and complacent view of the otherworldly conception of God's power" and committed themselves to "use more of the resources of our churches in working for human justice in places of social change and upheaval" where God is truly already at work. This statement and other highly significant Black Liberation Theology documents appear in Wilmore and Cone's excellent documentary history of Black Theology from 1966 to 1979.[39] Finally, the body of clergy who began in 1966 as the National Committee of Negro Churchmen changed their name to the National Committee of Black Churchmen and became the practical expression and representative of the new Black Liberation Theology.

Black Liberation Theology, however, did not come into being by itself. It evolved from several fundamental sources. First, it was developed in response to the dynamics of the decade of the 1960's with its stress on Blackness and social activism and struggle. The sixties demanded a redefinition of the world in Black images and interests and Black religion was no exception. Also, the sixties demanded active engagement in the Black struggle for liberation and a higher level of human life and challenged the church to participate or disband. Second, Black Liberation Theology was inspired by both emulation and criticism of King. King's stress on the social relevance and role of religion and on active engagement in the struggle against social evil were accepted and applied, but his stress on nonviolence was challenged or played down, his denunciation of Black Power rejected, and his emphasis on redemptive suffering translated as redemption through liberating struggle.

Third, Black Liberation Theology evolved from an ongoing internal criticism and push for a more relevant religion in light of the activist tradition of the Black Church as well as the temper of the times. This process was given support and intensified by the dynamics of the sixties and forced Black churchmen and women and theologians to redefine the meaning and role of God in history and his relationship to Black oppression and struggle for liberation. Fourth, Black Liberation Theology was shaped by the creative challenge posed by Malcolm X and the nation of Islam, especially Malcolm's uncompromising critique of society and integrationist approaches to Black history, religion, and struggle. Finally, Black Liberation Theology helped inspire and was in turn inspired by Third World theology. Especially key here is Latin American liberation theology represented by Gustavo Gutierrez and Sergio Torres who translate religion in the most socially relevant and demanding ways.[40]

One could argue there is a distinction between Black Theology and Black Liberation Theology, the former being all forms of Black systematic religious thought and the latter being one particular form of it. However this distinction will not be made; for the quest for a Black Theology is firmly and clearly rooted in the search for religious answers to the questions of Black Liberation. Many major writers have sought to pose and answer such questions.[41]

In addition to the above writers, two others stand out as definitive of the two trends in Black Liberation Theology, i.e., Black nationalist Christianity and Black Christian nationalism. These are James Cone and Albert Cleage, Jr.[42] Both Cone and Cleage were key to the development of Black Liberation Theology. Cone, a professor of systematic theology at Union Theological

Seminary, "more than anyone else . . . set the tone and described the context of Black Theology with the publication of his first book *Black Theology and Black Power* in 1969" and helped shape the movement as a practical project.[43] Cleage, the dean of Black Nationalist Christians and founder and head of the Shrine of the Black Madonna as early as 1963 "was also an active member of the NCBC almost from its inception and took part in the first theological discussions of the new movement of militant Black clergy in 1967."[44] Given their relevance to and work in this theoretical and practical thrust, their contentions can serve as a framework for discussion of Black Liberation Theology in general.

Establishing the bases for a Black Liberation Theology, Cone maintains that it must above all speak to the condition and struggle of Black people. "Black Theology has as its starting point the Black condition," he asserts. "It is a theology which *confronts* white society as racist Antichrist, communicating to the oppressor that nothing will be spared in the fight for freedom."[45]

Cleage argues that there is a dual aspect to the liberation struggle, an internal as well as external dimension. Given Blacks' history of oppression, they "have two beasts to fight: the beast within and the beast without." Externally their enemy is specifically whites, white Christians. For ". . . within the system in which we live, we are not only separate, we are in conflict. We seek our freedom in a power struggle against them and in the context of this struggle, they are the enemy." Internally, the struggle is against what white society has made them, i.e., individualistic, addicted to mysticism about God and using religion as psychic relief rather than inspiration to actively seek liberation.[46]

In sum then, Black Liberation Theology is centered around several core contentions that appear in varying and similar forms in most writings on it. Among these are: (1) the need for a God in Black people's own image and interest, i.e., Black and of and for the oppressed; (2) the imperative that religion must reflect the interests of Blacks and concretely and actively benefit them; (3) the contention that Blacks are a "chosen people" or "covenant community", i.e., have a special relationship with God; (4) the recognition of the Black Church's radical history and a call for its resuming this role in the liberation struggle of Black people; and (5) the indispensability of social struggle to liberate Blacks—socially and spiritually—and realize God's will to bring truth, freedom and justice to society and the world.

The Islamic Alternative

Islam is clearly the largest and most effective religious alternative to Christianity among Blacks. In fact, as Lincoln contends, "It has an evitable appeal to Blacks who have difficulty with American Christianity because of its racism, and with the Black Christian church because of its posture of accommodation."[47] Beginning in 1913 with Noble Drew Ali's establishment of the Moorish Science Temple and growing to its highest point in the early sixties in the context of the Nation of Islam, headed by the Honorable Elijah Muhammad, Islam has become a major religion among African Americans. It has served as a creative challenge to Black Christianity in its internal criticism and struggle to create a more socially relevant religion, as expressed in Black Liberation Theology.

The Moorish Science Temple

In 1913 Noble Drew Ali established the Moorish Science Temple in Newark, New Jersey, and began to teach a synthesized version of orthodox Islam, Garveyism, Christianity and various extractions from oriental philosophy.[48] From Newark Ali's teachings spread to the northern cities of Detroit, Harlem, Chicago, Pittsburgh, Philadelphia, and to various cities in the South, eventually embracing an estimated membership of twenty to thirty thousand.

The main contentions of Noble Drew Ali's religious nationalism were that the key to the salvation and liberation of African people in the United States lay in the discovery and acceptance of their national origin as Moors; that Islam was "the only instrument for (Black) unity and advancement"; whites were the opposite of and negative to Blacks and were soon to be destroyed; the need to obey the law and refrain from radicalism is necessary; and finally, the essentiality of love, harmony, and peace in the world and especially among Blacks.

As Essien-Udom maintained, Ali's basic contentions and principles laid a basis for the Nation of Islam that came into being after it.[49] His stress on name, land, and nationality, his division of the world into dark and white peoples, his political conservatism and his conception of divine retribution of Allah on whites all find subsequent expression in the ideology and practice of the Nation of Islam. However, although the Black Islamic tradition owes its origins to Noble Drew Ali, it realized its most definitive development and recognition under the Honorable Elijah Muhammad and the Nation of Islam.

The Nation of Islam

The Nation of Islam began in 1930 with the splitting into two factions of the Moorish Science Temple, one following a newcomer to Detroit, W. D. Fard, and the other faction remaining faithful to Ali. Those following Fard eventually deified him when he disappeared in 1933 and became the founding members of the Nation of Islam under the leadership of Messenger Elijah Muhammad.[50]

The first and most fundamental aspect of the socioreligious thought of Muhammad is the posing of Islam as the true religion of Black people and Christianity as the religion of their opposite and enemy, white people. Islam is a Black religion because it means submission to the will of Allah and Black people are submissive to God by nature. It is the "religion of freedom, justice and equality" and thus serves Black people's interests better than Christianity, which "is a white man's religion and . . . contains no salvation for the Black man."[51]

Another aspect of Muhammad's socioreligious philosophy is his contention that Allah (God) is in reality a Black man and the Black man is God. As Lincoln observed, "all Black men represent Allah or at least participate in Him for all Black men are divine." Muhammad argues that Black people are a chosen people who are "righteous by creation and by nature."

Reversing the religious and world order ideologically in a way no one else had done, Muhammad defined the white man as the devil. By this he meant two things: (1) that logically if God is Black, the devil of dialectical necessity must be white; and (2) that if the devil means the embodiment of evil, the historical record of the white man both exposes and confirms his true identity. Thus he states that the white man's claim to be God or his chosen is in fact a lie. It is this part of Muhammad's doctrine of deliverance, the God-devil thesis, which has proved the most controversial and at the same time and most effective organizing principle.[52]

Muhammad argued that separation on the social and political level from whites was a divine imperative. This, he argues, is necessary in order for Blacks to avoid the influence of white civilization which is "floating in corruption," to avoid the divine destruction Allah has for America, and to establish a nation in their own image and interests. Also Muhammad stressed the need for economic self-help and a racial solidarity. To accomplish this, Muhammad calls for "a united front of Black men of America" who will join hands in a program of economic, political, and spiritual upliftment of Black people. Lastly, Muhammad stressed the need for racial and Islamic solidarity throughout the world. He argued that all Third World people were original people and that they were destined to unite despite the evil influence of the West that divided them.

Malcolm X

Muhammad's message was raised and taught at a national and international level by the NOI's most eminent and competent spokesman, Malcolm X (Al Hajj Malik Shabazz). Malcolm not only translated Muhammad's message into its most trenchant and compelling form, but he also went beyond it to produce and articulate one of the most effective and cogent critiques of domination in U.S. history.[53] It is this severe incisiveness of his analysis, along with his bold stands and organizational ability, that make him the most definitive symbol of the Black liberation movement in the sixties.

Malcolm's critique of domination focused on the religious, racial and class restraints of Black and human freedom. He chastised white Christianity for its role in slavery, racism, and oppression and its hypocrisy in dividing the secular from the sacred. And he urged moral and spiritual regeneration in the color-blind religious community of Islam. He taught the social rootedness and responsibility of religion, its need to be an instrument and support of social change. His strategy for regeneration and liberation through struggle for the masses was to "wake them up, clean them up and then stand them up." He taught preference for the human interests of the masses against the narrow class interests of the middle class. For him, the masses were the core and conscience of the movement while the middle class was dedicated to integration, tokenism, compromise, and self-mutilation. Malcolm saw history as a field for both human and divine action and a need for African and other oppressed people to self-consciously struggle to regain their history and humanity and build a new world. He notes that the African American struggle as "part of a global rebellion of the oppressed against the oppressor, the exploited against the exploiter." And this was for him God's hand in history on the side of the righteous and truly human.

Schism, Transformation and Rebuilding

The Schism. In 1963 the NOI began to show signs of unravelling as evidenced by the underlying reasons for the suspension and eventual ouster/ resignation of Malcolm X from it. His ouster/resignation had a tremendous impact on the NOI and the Black Movement and indicated a series of problems that would eventually lead to factionalization and transformation of the NOI. Although the reason given by the NOI for Malcolm's suspension was his disobeying an order to not comment on the Kennedy assassination, the underlying political basis for it was the conflict between two major tendencies in the NOI. The radicals represented by Malcolm and the conservatives represented by the ruling stratum in charge of daily administration were both vying for, and dependent on, Muhammad's decisions and his support for victory in both the daily battles and the ultimate struggle itself. As I have argued in a paper on the conflict, four major factors appear to have shaped and fed the conflict.[54] First, the transformation of the NOI from a small marginal group to one with a multimillion dollar budget and huge bureaucracy changed both its political character and its conception of what was politically acceptable. The ruling stratum became increasingly conservative in its desire to protect its gains and Malcolm could not adjust to the new conservatism.

Second, then, the conflict was shaped by the ruling stratum's fierce opposition to Malcolm. Although they recognized his worth and significance to the NOI, they resented and opposed him because of (1) his moral posture against the corruptive materialism which permeated the ruling stratum; (2) his unwillingness to moderate his radicalism in the face of changed circumstances; and (3) the likelihood of his succeeding Muhammad and establishing a radical position.

Third, the conflict was shaped by the ruling stratum's ability to eventually alienate Muhammad and Malcolm in spite of their prior closeness. This was achieved essentially by their being in the pivotal position of daily administration and thus of briefing the Messenger every day and arguing Malcolm's refusal to moderate his disruptive radicalism and accept Muhammad's divine authority. Having been convinced of these charges, Muhammad suspended Malcolm at first and later denounced him. Malcolm in turn denounced the NOI and Muhammad and the ensuing conditions set the stage for his assassination.

Finally, evidence suggests that the FBI had a significant role in provoking and sustaining the leadership struggle within the NOI. As early as 1959 it had placed people in the leadership stratum. Cointelpro documents obtained through the Freedom of Information Act reveal the FBI's decision to divide the NOI and either transform it or destroy it.

Transformation. After Muhammad's death in 1975, the NOI underwent a drastic transformation and fragmentation involving severe criticism of Muhammad, rejection of early Muslim beliefs on whites, and the introduction of a strong Americanism and orthodox Islam.[55] This process had its roots in the unsolved political economic problems that shaped and fed the conflict between Malcolm and the ruling stratum. In other words, the nonengagement, isolation, and general conservatism Malcolm fought in the sixties expresses itself in similar forms in the seventies and today with the added dimensions of Americanism and orthodox Islam advocated by Muhammad's son Wallace. In addition, four other factors contributed to the transformation. A second factor was the ideology and structure of the Nation itself. The theocratic leadership structure based on divine wisdom and authority allowed for corrupt officials to act without check, denied mass participation in decision-making and debates, and prevented criticism necessary to check the transformation carried to its ultimate by Wallace and the ruling stratum. Also the ideological tendency toward nonengagement in social struggle, obeying laws, and the stress on material acquisition cultivated an appreciation for political conservatism and vulgar materialism of the ruling stratum.

A third contributing factor was the leadership style and problems of succession of Imam Wallace Muhammad who succeeded his father. Wallace's leadership style leaned toward decentralization and orthodox Islam even before his father's death. Once at the helm, he reshaped the Nation. Also his problems of succession were ones of establishing his authority, creating a new image of the NOI, and winning new converts and allies. So, he disavowed his father's divine authority and his God; disbanded the paramilitary arm, the Fruit of Islam; eliminated a possible challenge; and changed the military, or coercive, image of the NOI. He changed the doctrine of the NOI from religious Black nationalism to Americanism and orthodox Islam, winning new converts and allies who once opposed the race and earth-focused religious doctrine of his father. Finally, as argued above, there is evidence of the U.S. government's intervention and role in the process of transformation and fragmentation. From positions at the top it appears they not only provoked conflict and helped eliminate the radicals, but encouraged the transformation that insured an accommodationist religious structure.

The Rebuilding. Although Minister Louis Farrakhan, the national spokesman after Malcolm, had at first gone along with the transformation, he eventually objected. In 1978 he announced publicly that he could no longer accept the transformation of the Nation and its members in silence. He listed among other things the following, which he found intolerable: the ingratitude and disrespect for Messenger Muhammad which the transformed NOI was exhibiting; its open admission of whites; the deterioration of discipline and the emphasis on orthodox Islam as opposed to a people-specific Islam for Blacks that Muhammad had developed.[56]

To offset the disintegration he perceived in the NOI, which was then called the World Community of Al-Islam in the West, Farrakhan moved to rebuild the NOI in its original Black image. He formed discussion groups around the country, lectured, published, and republished the Messenger's works, reproduced tape recordings of the Messenger and himself, started a newspaper, *The Final Call,* and began to rebuild mosque structures and leadership cadres across the country. At the heart of his efforts to rebuild the NOI is the struggle to rescue and reconstruct the image of Messenger Muhammad. To accomplish this, Farrakhan argues the truth and currency of Muhammad's message, his moral and material achievement, and the praiseworthiness of his character as a leader. The success of Farrakhan in rebuilding the NOI will depend on several factors: (1) his own leadership capacity; (2) the extent of opposition from other Islamic groups claiming the Messenger's mantle; (3) his ability to relate positively and effectively to the larger Black community.

Notes

1. See John S. Mbiti, *African Religions and Philosophy* (New York: Anchor Books, 1970); C. E. Lincoln, *The Black Church Since Frazier* (New York: Schocken Books, 1974); Maulana Karenga, *Kawaida Theory: An Introductory Outline* (Inglewood, Calif.: Kawaida Publications, 1980); and Milton Yinger, *The Scientific Study of Religion* (New York: Macmillan, 1970).

2. Lincoln; and Gayraud Wilmore, *Black Religion and Black Radicalism* (Maryknoll, N.Y.: Orbis Books, 1983).

3. Lincoln, 3.

4. See E. E. Evans-Pritchard, *Theories of Primitive Religion* (London: Oxford University Press, 1965); E. Bolaji Idowu, *African Traditional Religion* (Maryknoll, N.Y.: Orbis Books, 1975); and Mbiti.

5. Benjamin C. Ray, *African Religions* (Englewood Cliffs, N.J.: Prentice-Hall, 1976).

6. Mbiti, 108.

7. Ibid., 141.

8. Francis Deng, *The Dinka and Their Songs* (Oxford: Clarendon Press, 1973).

9. For discussions of the remarkable sophistication of Dogon astronomy see Robert Temple, *The Sirius Mystery* (New York: St. Martin's Press, 1976); Carl Sagan, *Broca's Brain: Reflections on the Romance of Science* (New York: Random House, 1979); and Hunter Adams III, "African Observers of the Universe: The Sirius Question," *Journal of African Civilization* 1, no. 2 (Nov. 1–20).

10. Marcel Griaule, *Conversations with Ogoemmeli* (New York: Oxford University Press, 1978); and Griaule and Germain Dieterlen, "The Dogon," in *African Worlds* ed. Daryll Gord (London: Oxford University Press, 1955):83–110.

11. See Cheikh Anta Diop, *The African Origin of Civilization: Myth or Reality?* (Westport, Conn.: Lawrence Hill & Co., 1974) and *Civilisation ou Barbarie* (Paris: Presence Africaine, 1981); John Jackson, *Man, God and Civilization* (New Hyde Park, New York: University Books, 1972); George James, *Stolen Legacy* (San Francisco: Julian Richards Associates, 1976); Maula Karenga, *Selections from the Husia: Sacred Wisdom of Ancient Egypt* (Los Angeles: University of Sankore Press, 1984); Jacob H. Carruthers, *Essays in Ancient Egyptian Studies* (Los Angeles: University of Sankore Press, 1984); and Karenga and Carruthers, *Kemet and the African Worldview* (Los Angeles: University of Sankore Press, 1986).

12. James Breasted, *The Dawn of Conscience* (New York: Charles Scribner's Sons, 1933):xv.

13. Jackson, 123.

14. Ibid, 124.

15. Ibid, 134.

16. Diop, *Civilisation ou Barbarie*, 388.

17. James, 151.

18. See J. A. Rogers, *The World's Great Men of Color*, vol. 1 (New York: Macmillan, 1972): 57–66.

19. Karenga, *Selections from the Husia*.

20. Ibid., pp. 7–8.

21. See Breasted, 202 ff.

22. Karenga, *Selections from the Husia*, 91 ff.

23. Ibid., 52.

24. Breasted, 371 ff.

25. See F. L. Griffith, "The Teachings of Amenophis," *Journal of Egyptian Archaeology*, 12 (1926):191–231.

26. E. Franklin Frazier, *The Negro Church in America* (New York: Schocken Books, 1974):19.

27. John W. Blassingame, *The Slave Community* (New York: Oxford University Press, 1979); and Wilmore.

28. Alex Haley, *Roots* (New York: Dell Publishing Co., 1976).

29. Frazier, 15.

30. Wilmore, 36.

31. See the classic study of Carter G. Woodson, *The History of the Negro Church* (Washington, D.C.: Associated Publishers, 1945).

32. For supporting arguments in this respect see Joseph Washington, *Black Religion* (Boston: Beacon Press, 1964); C. Eric Lincoln; and Wilmore.

33. Wilmore.

34. Lincoln, 114.

35. See the works of Martin Luther King, Jr., *Stride Toward Freedom* (New York: Harper & Row, 1958); *Strength To Love* (New York: Harper & Row, 1973); *Why We Can't Wait* (New York: Harper & Row, 1964); and *Where Do We Go From Here: Chaos or Community?* (New York: Harper & Row, 1967).

36. Hanes Walton, Jr., *The Political Philosophy of Martin Luther King, Jr.* (Westport, Conn.: Greenwood Press, 1976):44.

37. King, *Strength To Love*, 128.

38. King, *Stride Toward Freedom*, 189.

39. Gayraud S. Wilmore and James H. Cone eds., *Black Theology: A Documentary History* (Maryknoll, N.Y.: Orbis Books, 1979).

40. See Gustavo Gutierrez, *A Theology of Liberation* (Maryknoll, N.Y.: Orbis Books, 1973); and Sergio Torres, *The Challenge of a Basic Christian Community* (Maryknoll, N.Y.: Orbis Books, 1981).

41. See, for example, Wilmore, *Black Religion*; Major Jones, *Black Awareness* (Nashville, Tenn.: Abingdon Press, 1971) and *Christian Ethics for Black Theology* (Nashville, Tenn.: Abingdon Press, 1974); William R. Jones, *Is God A White Racist?* (Garden City, N.Y.: Anchor Press, 1973); J. Deotis Roberts, *Liberation and Reconciliation* (Philadelphia: Westminster Press, 1971) and *A Black Political Theology* (Philadelphia: Westminster Press, 1974); Joseph Washington, *The Politics of God* (Boston: Beacon Press, 1967); and Joseph Johnson, *Proclamation Theology* (Shreveport, La.: Fourth District Press, C.M.E. Church, 1978).

42. See James H. Cone, *Black Theology and Black Power* (New York: Seabury Press, 1969), *A Black Theology of Liberation* (Philadelphia: Lippincott, 1970), *God of the Oppressed* (New York: Seabury Press, 1975); and Albert Cleage, Jr., *The Black Messiah* (New York: Sheed and Ward, 1968) and *Black Christian Nationalism* (New York: William Morrow, 1972).

43. Wilmore and Cone, 77.

44. Ibid., 67.

45. Cone, *Black Theology and Black Power*, 118.

46. Cleage, *The Black Messiah*, 55.

47. C. Eric Lincoln, *The Black Muslims in America* (Boston: Beacon Press, 1961).

48. Arna Bontemps and Jack Conroy, *They Seek a City* (Garden City, N.Y.: Doubleday, Doran and Co., 1945):175.

49. E. V. Essien-Udam, *Black Nationalism* (New York: Dell, 1964).

50. Lincoln, *The Black Muslims*, 181–82.

51. Elijah Muhammad, *The Fall of America* (Chicago: Muhammad's Temple of Islam, no. 2, 1965): 8.

52. Elijah Muhammad, *Message to the Black Man in America* (Chicago: Muhammad's Temple of Islam, no. 2, 1965): 134.

53. Malcolm X, *Malcolm Speaks* (New York: Merit Publishers, 1965); see also his *The Autobiography of Malcolm X* (New York: Grove Press, 1966).

54. Maulana Karenga, "Malcolm and the Messenger: From Psychological Assumptions of Political Analysis," *The Western Journal of Black Studies* (Winter 1982):5.

55. Wallace D. Muhammad, *As the Light Shineth From the East* (Chicago: Wallace D. Muhammad Publishing Co., 1980).

56. Luix Overbea, "Leader Quits Black Muslims," *Christian Science Monitor*, June 13, 1978.

16

The Rise of African Churches in America (1786–1822):

Re-examining the Contexts

Will B. Gravely

At the end of his anti-slavery pamphlet published in 1810, Daniel Coker, a Black Methodist preacher and schoolmaster in Baltimore, appended four significant lists. He named thirteen ordained Black clergy (including himself), another eleven licensed local preachers, and eight writers and orators whose public works had proven "their talents." His compilation of fifteen "African churches," representing four denominational polities and ten cities, is an early primary source of what has been called "the independent church movement" in Black American religion.[1] Despite the fact that he took pride in the enumeration of "African Methodists" at 31,884 in 1809, Coker downplayed denominational identifications.[2] At the time he wrote, all of the local Black churches were still linked to biracial denominational jurisdictions; however, Coker was emphasizing an African church movement spanning the Atlantic seaboard from Charleston, South Carolina, to Boston, Massachusetts.

Black churches and their ministers, for Coker, were a biblical embodiment of the cultural, and religious transformation of enslaved Africans into free African Americans. He indicated as much by framing the entire appendix of lists with biblical images drawn from 1 Pet. 2:9–10: "chosen generation," "royal priesthood," "holy nation," and "peculiar people." This passage gave Coker the symbolic references for "what God [was] doing for Ethiopia's sons in the United States of America." Indeed, another part of the biblical quotation—"which in time past were not a people, but are now the people of God"—testified to the emergence of an African American community in the new United States. Hence, Coker gave African American peoplehood biblical and theological sanction, calling attention to its institutional expression in the network of African churches and identifying the leaders of church and community.

The rise of the independent "African" churches has attracted the interest of several scholars with differing views. A classic debate concerning African survivals was first held by Melville Herskovits and E. Franklin Frazier. More recently their interpretive insights have been synthesized by Albert Raboteau.[3] But their concern is not the most fundamental historiographical issue in free Black church history. The terms of the debate have shifted from the degree of syncretism in Black Christianity to a consideration of *the causes* for racial separation in American religion, beginning in the late eighteenth century, continuing throughout the antebellum period (South as well as North), and culminating in the era of Reconstruction across the states of the old Confederacy.[4] It may well be, of course, that the assertion of Black religious independence, as an identifiable movement for more than a century, merely recasts the debate between Herskovits and Frazier, suggesting that Black religious sensibilities cannot be contained within biracial, Euro-American structures. This would keep alive the large question of how the peoples of European and African descent interacted in other ways besides their religious traditions. However, the linkage has not usually been made.

If the primary historiographical question regarding the rise of African churches is to search for *the causes* of racially based religious separatism, interpretive traditions have commonly emphasized one of two alternatives. The focus has either been on the story of white discrimination and the moral failure of American Christianity, or it has been a celebration of the origin of a Black culture with separate churches—an important feature of its infrastructure. Even though these two contexts are not mutually exclusive interpretive options, they have tended to function that way.[5]

One factor which is perennially relevant to a consideration of the origins of Black religious independence is white proscription, the conscious exclusion from positions of power of Black members in biracial congregations and denominations. This historiographical emphasis is based on the famous incident, traditionally dated as November 1787, when trustees from St. George's Methodist Episcopal Church in Philadelphia pulled several Black members and local preachers from their knees during prayer at a public service. Blamed for refusing to go to the seats set aside for their race in the gallery, they abruptly left the service. With Richard Allen and Absalom Jones as leaders, they embarked on a course that formed in 1794 the first two African congregations with their own buildings in the city.[6] Even though no contemporary account of the fracas at St. George's Church survives, it has been many times retold in Black religious and social history, serving by the 1960s as the historical impetus for kneel-ins during the civil rights movement's challenge to white churches.[7]

 Proscriptive practices by white Christians directed against Black members and auditors in local churches were potentially the motivation behind the separatist movement. Events less overt, but symbolically as powerful as the confrontation at St. George's Church, often provoked a schism. Incidents of white pastors refusing to take Black infants into their arms to christen them (Washington, D.C.), of Blacks having to wait until all whites were served the Lord's Supper before being admitted to the table (Ohio), of conflicts over access to burial grounds (Charleston, South Carolina) and of constraints on freedom of expression in worship (Cincinnati, Ohio) served to set off Black resistance.[8]

During the period from Richard Allen's first separate class meeting for Blacks in Philadelphia (1786) to the formation of the third Black Methodist denomination in 1822, examples abound which confirm a recalcitrant white opposition to equal privileges for Blacks in every denominational movement having a noticeable Black membership. Although Episcopalians were not far behind, Methodists were especially culpable. Their leading bishop, Francis Asbury, performed at least eight ordinations of Black local preachers to the office of deacon, but the Methodist Episcopal general conferences never officially recognized the anomalous rank, never accepted the deacons into annual conferences of the Methodist preachers, and never advanced the Black deacons (including Allen, who remained one for seventeen years) to eldership or full priesthood.[9] In 1822 the Mother Zion Congregation in New York eventually lost patience in its efforts to obtain full ordination for its pastors, who were local Black deacons, as Allen had been in Philadelphia. It had endured refusals from three white Methodist Episcopal bishops, the Protestant Episcopal bishop of New York, and two white Methodist annual conferences.[10] The Black Methodist movement for independence in Wilmington, Delaware, involved two secessions in eight years before denominational autonomy was secured by Peter Spencer and his followers. The issues involved arbitrary exercises of power against Blacks by the white elders and conflicts over seating and use of buildings.[11] The Episcopalians, on the other hand, did give full priestly orders to Absalom Jones in 1804, but refused St. Thomas African Congregation membership in its convention until 1862.[12] A similar exclusion (until 1853) hampered St. Philip's Church in New York, organized in 1809.[13]

Despite the contention of George Levesque that the origin of the first northern Black Baptist church did not lie in discriminatory treatment by whites, a contemporary source strongly suggests otherwise. Elias Smith, a white pastor in Woburn, wrote in 1804, "When Thomas Paul [the first pastor of the African Baptist church in the city] came to Boston the Dr. [Samuel Stillman, a Baptist minister] told him it was Boston, and they did not mix colours." Another white Baptist in Boston, Thomas Baldwin, concurred by saying, "There are some of my congregation who would leave the meeting if Paul should preach here."[14] Although the details are less clear, tensions between white and Black members of New York's Gold Street Church led to a Black exodus in 1808 to form the Abyssinian Baptist congregation.[15]

At many points in the evolution of Black religious independence, white control and Black assertion clashed. The struggle was a competition for power and a test of the viability of biracial religious community. Especially among Episcopalians and Methodists, less so with Baptists and Presbyterians, whites were unwilling to share authority with, and extend modes of participation to, Blacks. Many Black churchfolk, on the other hand, insisted that their religious freedom could not be compromised. The sacred power that they felt, shared, and mediated could not be contained or isolated from more mundane forms of power. They wanted to elect and be elected to church office, to ordain and be ordained, to discipline as well as be disciplined, to preach, exhort, pray, and administer sacraments—in sum, to have their gifts and graces acknowledged by the whole community. Where that acknowledgment was withheld, Blacks resisted and sought other alternatives. In their "Founders' Address" of 1820, three Zion Methodist preachers stated the dilemma. "So long as we remain in that situation [of being deprived of ordination]," they declared, "our Preachers would never be able to enjoy these privileges which the Discipline of the white Church holds out to all its Members that are called to preach, in consequence of the limited access our brethren had to those privileges, and particularly in consequence of the difference of color."[16]

A second historiographical tradition, less dramatic but no less significant, shifts the concern from Black reaction to white discrimination. This second interpretive context is seen as a natural part of an expanding Black community that had other racially separate institutions. Their origins must be explained in terms of the demography of Black communities, the effects of migration and economic change on their composition, the presence of intrareligious competition and social dissent from within. Preeminently, this interpretation posits the prior existence of Black communities within which separate churches were conceived and in which they would function.[17]

Black Philadelphia was also an example of this corollary interpretation of the emergence of the independent Black churches. Before the walkout at St. George's, Allen and Jones, with others, had formed the Free African Society as a benevolent voluntary association.[18] It both assumed and fostered a community consciousness among Black Philadelphians. Its religious dimension was so prominent that W. E. B. DuBois would later interpret it as an example of continuity with African communal life. When, after six years, it disbanded, the members catalyzed communal energies into new institutional directions by founding the St. Thomas African Episcopal and Bethel African Methodist Episcopal congregations.[19]

Outside Philadelphia, before there were independent African congregations, voluntary associations met some Black religious needs, besides those found in biracial churches. Early in 1776 Prince Hall, with fourteen other men, founded African Lodge No. 1 in Boston in connection with a British Army lodge. After the new organization got an official warrant in 1787, it regularly celebrated the Festival of St. John the Baptist on June 25, heard Hall and Chaplain John Marrant preach, and conducted masonic rites for public funerals of its members. In 1792 Hall's sermon recollected the time in Christian history when there was "an African church," referring to early church organizations in North Africa.[20] The hope of restoring an African Christian tradition permeated the petition signed by Hall and seventy-five other Blacks from Boston in 1787, asking the General Court for permission to emigrate. Their plan specified the formation of "a religious society, or a Christian church" in Africa, with "one or more blacks [to be] ordained as their pastors or bishops."[21]

Similar features marked the history of Newport's African Union Society, which, by 1783, began to hold religious services in members' homes. Constituted in 1780, and embracing women in the membership, it had by the end of the decade sponsored a unified scheme of emigration with comparable organizations in Boston, Providence, and Philadelphia. Appropriately the Society invited a common religious effort to seek God's guidance "by extraordinary fasting and prayer," naming on one occasion the first Tuesday in July 1789 for that purpose.[22]

The emigration schemes in Boston and Newport failed to develop beyond exploratory ventures, but the early benevolent societies had reached out to each other across several states, before the appearance of the first separate

Black congregation in the North in 1794, or the first independent Black denomination in 1813. By 1792, the Black masonic movement had new lodges in Philadelphia, Providence, and New Haven.[23] The Newport African Unionists in June 1793 sent a contribution to the African church building project in Philadelphia, which later became St. Thomas church.[24] Locally fraternal and benevolent associations had experimented with forms of religious life sponsored within their Black communities that were not yet fraught with denominational competition and schism. The next logical step, to organize a community or union church, never took hold at the time when a significant option to denominationalism could have been shaped. Implicit in Boston, Newport, and Philadelphia, the concept did not catch on, though it was resurrected in attenuated form nearly a generation later in Providence between 1819 and 1821, and in Newport in 1824.[25]

The Union Church, as a racially separate institution, embodied the elusive dream of Black communal unity. It expressed one form of religious freedom and demonstrated the persistent symbiosis between churches and other voluntary associations in Black life. Left behind by Black denominationalism, the local focus of the Union Church limited its contribution to the formation of independent churches, lacking what emerged in 1830 with the colored convention movement. The alternative, Black churches both within biracial and separate denominational structures, was a concession to the organizational religious patterns of the larger society.

At the same time, the formation of separate Black churches repeatedly made visible the Black community's maturation. They became the institutional core of free Black community life, serving as an educational venture, housing literary societies and libraries, and hosting schools and benevolent associations. Their buildings were the meeting houses of the black freedom —and often of the white abolitionist—movement. Mirroring the communities they served, the churches enabled Blacks to celebrate themselves as a collectivity, and they provided the protective space whereby each could contend with the other about common concerns. And always, the churches were houses of prayer, song, sermon, and sacrament in a distinctive African American medium.

Despite the fact of white discrimination, and beyond the reality of an evolving free Black culture, it is important also to remember that the founders of the African churches openly commended white sympathizers whose support they courted and received. Dr. Benjamin Rush drew up "sundry articles of faith and a plan of church government" in 1791 for a committee of "a dozen free Blacks" from the Free African Society. His Episcopal proposal was adopted three days later as another step toward the creation of St. Thomas church. Dr. Rush and other whites raised and contributed money from their community for the project, as Blacks were also doing.[26] In 1799, Richard Allen thanked Rush particularly for his assistance in building three African churches in the city.[27] When no one else would come to their aid, the Zion Methodists got their Black local deacons ordained by James Covel, Silvester Hutchinson, and William M. Stillwell, three supportive white elders, originally from the Methodist Episcopal organization but more recently founders of a new (Stillwellite) Methodist connection in New York.[28]

In the absence of Black preachers in the early years after their organization, the African and Abyssinian Baptist congregations depended on the supply of white preachers from the Philadelphia and New York associations.[29] White Presbyterians in the Evangelical Society of Philadelphia were primary sponsors of the African Presbyterian Church in that city, first as a mission in 1807 and then as a building with its congregation beginning in 1811.[30] Even after the formation of separate churches, especially for Baptists and Presbyterians, the new congregations held membership in biracial associations, presbyteries, and synods.

If the relationship of whites to the African church movement is more complex than first appears, the presence of Blacks in significant numbers in some aspects of biracial denominational structures before 1813 and after 1822 poses other interpretive problems. They may be seen within the contexts of three previous historiographical emphases during the period: the legal achievement and guarantee of religious freedom; the rise of denominationalism in the Second Great Awakening as part of an organizational revolution in American Protestantism; and the compromise within mainstream American religion before 1820 over slavery. A comprehension of how these factors interact with the rise of the African churches will help to explain how the patterns of racial organization set in the first generation still generally describe Black-white interaction in American Christianity.

The major motif, as seen in the influential career of Sidney Mead, is the celebration of the revolutionary development of religious freedom in the late eighteenth century. Curiously Mead never made any application of that achievement to the history of Black religion in America. That omission may have been because the first Black churches did not entirely correspond to his generalizations about religious freedom. "What individuals and groups do when given religious freedom depends upon what they are when such is offered," he wrote.[31] But for Blacks, religious freedom was neither offered nor given, but seized and implemented in the independent church movement.

The chronological correspondence between the legal securing of religious freedom and the idea, leading to the institutional embodiment of African churches, was not coincidental. The early Black churches met the legal requirements for incorporation of religious bodies, most of which were directed to the ownership and use of property. They passed articles of association, published their bylaws and constitutions, and amended their incorporation to further protect their own interests. They appealed unsuccessfully and successfully in court for their rights to religious independence. The legal structures within which they worked were newly enacted, so that they both tested and expanded the state's role in religious litigation. As they were solidifying new institutional channels for themselves, they were also contributing to a larger stream of religious freedom in the national polity.

Speaking before a jubilant audience in Baltimore on January 23, 1816, Daniel Coker claimed that the recent Supreme Court decision in Pennsylvania that freed Philadelphia's Bethel Church from Methodist Episcopal control vindicated religious liberty. "Contrary to the predictions of many," he declared, "we have found to our great consolation, that the wholesome and friendly laws of our happy country will give us protection in worshipping God according to the dictates of our conscience."[32] The court decision gave African Methodists, who later in the year would form the second Black denomination, "the opportunity . . . of being free," and that meant to Coker being able "to sit down under our own vine to worship and none shall make us afraid."[33]

If Blacks were employing the necessary legal tactics to defend and extend their own religious freedom, they were further involved in the organizational revolution of denominationalism, "new meaasures" revivalism, and other modes of church extension. In the post-Revolutionary War generation there was a fluidity in the process of forming denominations because of the new context of religious freedom. All of the denominational polities and structures within which African churches were formed were being shaped, revised, challenged, defended, and implemented. In the 1780s Episcopalians and Methodists were moving from a colonial to an American organization of church government. Presbyterians did not hold their first general assembly until 1789. Baptists were only regionally organized until 1813, when they established the first national network for the purpose of missionary cooperation called the Triennial Convention.[34]

Denominational formation, therefore, was coterminous with the first generation of the independent church movement. It was a complex process, fraught with conflict and debate. The Methodists, for example, endured between 1792 and 1822 three major secessions, *besides* the three African Methodist breaks, over questions like the powers of the episcopacy, the legislative function of the general conference, and the role of the laity and the preachers.[35] Those conflicts were occurring at the same time that African Methodists in Philadelphia, New York, and Wilmington were organizing at the local level and confronting white authorities about innovative ways to involve the growing Black constituency. Writing to inform the Philadelphia Conference of 1807 that they had legally adopted "The African Supplement" to their articles of association with the Methodist Episcopal Church, Richard Allen and the trustees of Bethel Church put the challenge bluntly. "Our only design," they claimed, "is to secure to ourselves our rights and privileges, to regulate our affairs, temporal and spiritual, the same as if we were white people."[36]

The rise of the African churches out of biracial connections cannot be isolated from such issues central to the internal life of Christian churches as access to ordination, representation in denominational governance, consultation about pastoral appointments and services, the ownership and use of property, and participation in congregational discipline. Those were the power factors being contended for generally in the shaping of the popular denominations, and Black members and preachers were in the middle of the conflict.

Black denominationalism became a reality in three African Methodist organizations between 1813 and 1822. In partial forms it expanded with the American Baptist Missionary Convention in 1840, the Congregational and Presbyterian evangelical associations and conventions of the 1840s and 1850s, and in regional Black Baptist associations and conventions in the Midwest, like the Western Colored Baptist Convention (1853ff.) and the Northwestern and Southern Baptist Convention (1864).[37] These Black church bodies usually maintained the government and doctrines of the denominations and local churches from which they separated. Because they had participated in the life of biracial congregations and denominations from the outset, Black Protestants who removed themselves from white supervision and connections were merely continuing their own experience. That experience was to affirm, audaciously to many whites, an elemental core within each denominational tradition, and behind that, within Christianity itself, which was not created or controlled by white Christians. That core was as accessible to Blacks as to whites, and it was thereby appropriated. In the process, black Methodists, Baptists, Episcopalians, Presbyterians, and later Congregationalists, were redefining, perhaps unwittingly, the nature of the American denominational families. Their very presence, within biracial connections or separately alongside whites, transformed the landscape of Christianity in the United States.

As the founders of the African church movement perpetuated their own experience in the organizational revolution of the Second Great Awakening, focused particularly on denominational formation, they also found themselves in competition with each other. Denominational differences in Black communities were assured from the time some members of Philadelphia's Free African Society became Episcopalian under Absalom Jones, and others became African Methodists under Richard Allen.

Some of the religious options resulted from the refusal of some Black Protestants to move into separate denominations. In 1796 a second Black Methodist congregation, Zoar, was established in Philadelphia as a mission in the northern part of the city. The congregation never desired the independence toward which the Bethel society worked. Hence, in 1816, it remained loyal to the Methodist Episcopal Church and did not join Allen's new denomination. Similarly, in Baltimore, where Daniel Coker led the secession of 1815, the two largest congregations with their own buildings, Sharp Street Church and Asbury African Church, continued within the Methodist Episcopal denomination and insisted on calling themselves, for another decade at least, "African Methodists." The separatists, who linked up with the Philadelphia independents, left behind all claims to church property.[38] In Wilmington, some Blacks in Ezion Church kept unaltered their denominational connection after Peter Spencer led thirty-nine of his followers into a new organization in 1813.[39]

Denominational differences were further extended, when Spencer, after attending the organizing convention for the Allenite denomination in Philadelphia in 1816, refused to merge the African Union congregations into the new movement. Likewise, in New York, the Zion Methodists, following an exploratory interview with Bishop Allen in 1820, refused to bring their organization under his authority.[40]

African Methodists were not alone in their competitive denominational styles, for schism and division marked the early histories of the African Baptists and Presbyterians. In 1816, the Philadelphia Association debated for three days the competing claims of two groups, each representing itself as the authentic African Baptist party. Turning aside a protest from the white First Baptist Church, the Association sided with the claimants who owned the meeting house and other properties.[41] First in 1824, with the creation of a Second African Presbyterian Church with Jeremiah Gloucester as pastor, and then two decades later with the founding of Central Church with Stephen Gloucester as pastor, Black Presbyterians in Philadelphia resolved problems in internal dissent by forming new congregations.[42]

There is a final context of white-Black interaction which affected the African church movement. Between 1785 and 1818, three of the Protestant denominations within which African churches were established backed away from explicit opposition to slavery, both in the larger social and political order and in the disciplinary norms for membership and ordination.[43] Without providing the primary documentation, Woodson rooted the birth of the African Baptist Church of Philadelphia in 1809 in the waning "anti-slavery ardor" of the First Baptist Church during pastorates of southern-born whites.[44] That factor may have weighed in the decisions of other Black secessionists during the period, though the evidence in the form of explicit justification is lacking. In other words, there is no document that defends Black separatism on grounds that the denomination's anti-slavery standards had been compromised. At the same time, the African Methodist Episcopal denomination did reassert the original, forthright condemnations of slavery, which the Methodist Episcopal Church had abandoned.[45]

It is likewise noteworthy, in the case of the Methodists, that all three African separations occurred *after* the failure of the general conferences between 1800 and 1808 to remove slaveholders from membership and from clerical orders. Indeed, the conferences of 1804 and 1808 printed expurgated copies of the church's discipline for the southern states without the legislation on slavery. Even Asbury, who had despised slavery from the first, gave in to pro-slavery pressures, conceding in his journal that it was more important to save the African's soul than to free his body.[46]

Those events were taking place during the same period when Richard Allen, Daniel Coker, and William Miller (with other Black Methodists in New York) were publicly condemning slavery. With Absalom Jones, Allen had published an appeal to slaveholders to set free their oppressed chattels in

1794. He echoed similar sentiments in an appendix to the Articles of Association of the Bethel Society in 1799.[47] In 1804 and 1805 he financed publication of two works by Thomas Branagan, a white anti-slavery author.[48] In 1810 Coker published in Baltimore his *Dialogue Between a Virginian and an African Minister*. On New Year's Day of that same year, one of the Zion Methodist ministers, Miller, was orator for Black New Yorkers to commemorate the second anniversary of the end of the foreign slave trade.[49]

These anti-slavery activities reinforce a reminder. Blacks, unlike other Americans, had to consider the issue of personal freedom as the first freedom. It was only after emancipation in the northern states, between 1777 and 1818, that the attention of free Blacks riveted on religious freedom, and their energies became directed to independent churches. Sometimes the separate churches became the routes to obtaining freedom for southern slave preachers. Henry Cunningham from Savannah, Georgia, served the African Baptist Church of Philadelphia from 1809 to 1811 in order to earn enough money to secure his freedom, to be ordained, and to return South. Josiah Bishop, an early pastor for the Abyssinian Church in New York, was formerly a slave in Virginia, who bought his own freedom and that of his family.[50] The first pastor of the African Presbyterian congregation in Philadelphia, John Gloucester, traveled widely to raise funds to purchase the liberty of the rest of his family. Worn out at age forty-six, he died in 1822, but not before inducing his three sons—Stephen, James, and Jeremiah—to follow in his footsteps as Black preachers.[51]

Always, the independent Black churches stood as institutional symbols of human liberation. They did not often get the headlines which marked white abolitionist activity, but within their communities they carried on a continual struggle to defend, protect, extend, and expand Black freedom.[52] Unlike white Christians of the period, Black churchfolk did not have a choice as to whether they would work for Black freedom, for their own liberty was inescapably bound up with the liberation of their people. That fact makes for a crucial, qualitative distinction between Black and white Christian traditions in American history. Efforts to ignore it negate the ethical ground for the study of Black and white interaction in American religion—a study which David Wills has appropriately requested.[53] Only when the fact is acknowledged can Sidney Ahlstrom's insight—that the Black religious experience is the paradigm for the reinterpretation of American church history—be appreciated. Such an agenda is clearly more than the simple matter of addition or inclusion, for the Black religious story has normative, fundamentally moral dimensions at its center.[54] To ignore it is to insure that we will never comprehend what Martin Delany, the inveterate Black nationalist, meant when he observed in 1849, "As among our people, generally, the Church is the Alpha and the Omega of all things."[55]

Notes

1. Carter G. Woodson, *History of the Negro Church* (Washington: The Associated Publishers, 1921): chap. 4; Daniel Coker, *A Dialogue Between a Virginian and an African Minister* (Baltimore: Benjamin Edes for Joseph James, 1810; Reprint. Dorothy Porter, ed., *Negro Protest Pamphlets*, New York: Arno Press, 1969).

2. Coker's figures correspond to the number of "colored" members in *Minutes of the Methodist Conferences, Annually Held in America: From 1773 to 1813, Inclusive* (New York: Daniel Hitt and Thomas Ware, 1813): 447–53 (for 1809).

3. Albert J. Raboteau, *Slave Religion: The "Invisible Institution" in the Antebellum South* (New York: Oxford University Press, 1978): 48–60, 86, 89.

4. See H. Shelton Smith, *In His Image, But . . . :Racism in Southern Religion, 1780–1910* (Durham, N.C., Duke University Press, 1972), chap. 5; Will B. Gravely, "The Social Political and Religious Significance of the Formation of the Colored Methodist Episcopal Church (1870)," *Methodist History* 18 (October 1979):3–25.

5. George A. Levesque's suggestive essay, "Inherent Reformers—Inherited Orthodoxy: Black Baptists in Boston, 1800–1873," *Journal of Negro History* 60 (October 1975):491–99, wrestles with both motivating factors.

6. See *The Life Experience and Gospel Labors of the Rt. Rev. Richard Allen* (1833; Reprint. New York: Abingdon Press, 1960); Sernett, *Black Religion and American Evangelism: White Protestants, Plantation Missions, and the Flowering of Negro Christianity, 1787–1865* (Metuchen, N.J.: Scarecrow Press, 1975):116ff., 218ff. Sernett revises the date for the confrontation to five or six years later.

7. *The Doctrines and Discipline of the African Methodist Episcopal Church* (Philadelphia: John H. Cunningham, 1817): 4. A dissident member, Jonathan Tudas, claimed that the event at St. George's never happened, forcing Allen to refute him in Trustees of Bethel and Wesley Churches, *The Sword of Truth* (Philadelphia: J. H. Cunningham, 1823):13. On the popularization of the event, besides denominational histories and publications, see Lerone Bennett, Jr., "Pioneers in Protest: Richard Allen," *Ebony* 19 (May 1964):142–52.

8. There were comparable conflicts over the segregated seating in Providence and Cleveland and of Black pewholders being harassed in Bridgewater and Stoughton Corner, Massachusetts. John H. Cromwell, "The First Negro Churches in the District of Columbia," *Journal of Negro History* 7 (1922): 65; B. W. Arnett, ed., *Proceedings of the Semi-Centenary Celebration of the African Methodist Church of Cincinnati, Held in Allen Temple, February 8–10, 1874* (Cincinnati, Ohio: H. Watkin, 1874):14, 16; Alan Peskin, ed., *North into Freedom: The Autobiography of John Malvin, Free Negro, 1795–1880* (Cleveland: Western Reserve University Press, 1966): 55–56;

Incidents in the Life of the Rev. J[eremiah] Asher (London: Charles Gilpin, 1850):44–48; William C. Nell, *The Colored Patriots of the American Revolution* (1855; Reprint. New York: Arno Press, 1969):33–34; *The "Negro Pew": Being an Inquiry Concerning the Propriety of Distinctions in the House of God, on Account of Color* (Boston: Isaac Knapp, 1837); Ulrich Bonnell Phillips, *American Negro Slavery* (1918; Reprint. Baton Rouge: Louisiana State University Press, 1966):420.

9. Reginald F. Hildebrand, "Methodist Episcopal Policy on the Ordination of Black Ministers, 1784–1864," *Methodist History* 20 (April 1982):125–27.

10. Christopher Rush, *A Short Account of the Rise and Progress of the African M. E. [Zion] Church in America* (New York: Christopher Rush et al., 1866):38–40, 42, 46, 61–67, 75, 77.

11. Lewis J. Baldwin, "'Invisible' Strands of African Methodism," (Ph.D. diss., Northwestern University, 1980); John D. C. Hanna ed., *The Centennial Services of the Asbury Methodist Episcopal Church, Wilmington, Delaware. October 13–20, 1889* (Wilmington: Delaware Printing Co., 1889):146; *The Discipline of the African Union Church of the United States of America and Elsewhere,* 3d ed. (Wilmington, Del.: Porter & Kukel, 1852):iii–v.

12. William Douglass, *Annals of the First African Episcopal Church, in the United States of America, Now Styled the African Episcopal Church of St. Thomas, Philadelphia* (Philadelphia: King & Baird, 1862):85–106, 140–71.

13. Leon Litwack treated the action of the New York diocese as setting the policy of excluding Black Episcopal congregations from convention membership; it had first been established in Pennsylvania. See *Leon Litwack North of Slavery: The Negro in the Free States 1790–1860* (Chicago: Phoenix Books, 1961):199–200; Rhoda Golden Freeman, "The Free Negro in New York City before the Civil War," (Ph.D. diss., Columbia University, 1966):352–53, 356–60.

14. Levesque, "Inherent Reformers," 498–99; Elias Smith, *Five Letters* (Boston, 1804):18, quoted in William G. McLoughlin, *New England Dissent 1630–1883: The Baptists and the Separation of Church and State* (Cambridge: Harvard University Press, 1971):765.

15. Mechal Sobel, *Trabelin' On: The Slave Journey of an Afro-Baptist Faith* (Westport: Greenwood Press, 1979):265–66; David Benedict, *General History of the Baptist Denomination in America, and Other Parts of the World* (Boston: Lincoln & Edwards, 1813): 542; *Minutes of the New York Baptist Association, Held in the City of New York, May 23 and 24* (1810) (n.p., n.d.):4–5.

16. From the first A.M.E. Zion Discipline, quoted in William J. Walls, *The African Methodist Episcopal Zion Church: Reality of the Black Church* (Charlotte, N.C.: A.M.E. Zion Publishing House, 1974):49.

17. See Theodore Hershberg, "Free Blacks in Antebellum Philadelphia," *Journal of Social History* 5 (1971–72):183–209; Ira Berlin, "The Structure of the Free Negro Caste in the Antebellum United States," *Journal of Social History* 9 (1975–76):297–318; and "Time Space, and the Evolution of Afro-American Society on British Mainland North America," *American Historical Review* 85 (February 1980):44–78; Emma Jones Lapsansky, "Since They Got Those Separate Churches: Afro-Americans and Racism in Jacksonian Philadelphia," *American Quarterly* 32 (Spring 1980):54–78.

18. Gayraud S. Wilmore, in his new edition of *Black Religion and Black Radicalism* (Maryknoll, N.Y.: Orbis Books, 1983):81, repeats the argument that Jones and Allen formed the Free African Society *after* the walkout at St. George's Church. David Wills has investigated the historiographical traditions about the incident, privately circulated as "A Note on the Origins of the A.M.E. Church" (May 1980, Amherst College).

19. Douglass, *Annals*, 10–11, 15–17, 46; DuBois, *The Philadelphia Negro: A Social History* (1889; Reprint. New York: Schocken Books, 1967):197.

20. For Hall's orations see Dorothy Porter ed., *Early Negro Writing 1760–1837* (Boston: Beacon Press, 1971):63–78, especially 68; see also John Marrant, *A Sermon Preached the 24th Day of June 1789. Being the Festival of St. John the Baptist* (Boston: The Bible Heart, n.d.).

21. Massachusetts State Archives, House Files 2358, quoted in Floyd John Miller, *The Search for a Black Nationality: Black Colonization and Emigration 1787–1863* (Urbana: University of Illinois Press, 1975):5.

22. Douglass, *Annals*, 25–29; Dorothy Sterling, ed., *Speak Out in Thunder Tones: Letters and Other Writings by Black Northerners, 1787–1865* (Garden City: Doubleday, n.d.):3–12; Miller, Search, 6–15.

23. Lorenzo J. Greene, "Prince Hall: Massachusetts Leader in Crisis," *Freedomways* 1 (Fall 1961):249; George W. Crawford, *Prince Hall and His Followers: Being a Monograph on the Legitimacy of Negro Masonry* (New York: The Crisis, 1915):49–50.

24. Manuscript records of the Free African Society of Newport, June 20, 1793, Newport Historical Society.

25. *Short History of the African Union Meeting and School-House, Erected in Providence (R.I.) in the Years of 1819, '20, '21: with Rules for Its Future Government* (Providence, R.I.: Brown & Danforth, 1821); Robert Glenn Sherer, "Negro Churches in Rhode Island before 1860," *Rhode Island History* 25 (January 1966):12–17.

26. David Freeman Hawke, *Benjamin Rush: Revolutionary Gadfly* (Indianapolis: Bobbs-Merrill, n.d.):336; L. H. Butterfield ed., *Letters of Benjamin Rush* (Princeton, N.J.: Princeton University Press, 1951): vol. 1, 602–3, 609–10, 716–17; vol. 2, 1071; George W. Corner, ed., *The Autobiography of Benjamin Rush* (Princeton, N.J.: Princeton University Press, 1948):202–3, 221; Douglass, *Annals*, 45–46.

27. *Articles of Association of the African Methodist Episcopal Church, of the City of Philadelphia, in the Commonwealth of Pennsylvania* (Philadelphia: John Ormrod, 1799; Reprint. Philadelphia: Historic Publications, n.d.):17–19.

28. Rush, *A Short Account*, 78.

29. *Minutes of the Philadelphia Baptist Association, 1810, 5; 1811, 6; Minutes of the New York Baptist Association, 1810–1822*, inclusive.

30. William T. Catto, *A Semi-Centenary Discourse, Delivered in the First African Presbyterian Church, Philadelphia on the Fourth Sabbath of May, 1857: With a History of the Church from Its First Organization* (Philadelphia: Joseph M. Wilson, 1857):19–27; Broadside, "To the Pious and Benevolent," Leon Gardiner Collection, and Minutes of the Evangelical Society, 1808–17, Pennsylvania Historical Society; Evangelical Society manuscripts, Presbyterian Historical Society.

31. Sidney E. Mead, *The Lively Experiment* (New York: Harper & Row, 1963):108.

32. *The Act of Incorporation, Causes and Motives of the African Episcopal Church of Philadelphia* (Whitehall, 1810); "The Articles of Association" of the African Union Church of Wilmington, 1813, Hall of Records, Dover, Delaware; *Articles of Association between the General Conference of the Methodist Episcopal Church, and the Trustees of the African Methodist Episcopal Church in the City of New York* (Brooklyn: Thomas Kirk, 1801); *Articles of Association* (Philadelphia): n.27.

33. Coker's sermon is apparently only available in an extract in Herbert Aptheker, ed., *A Documentary History of the Negro People of the United States* (1951; Reprint. New York: Citadel Press, 1969):67–69; and in summary form in Charles H. Wesley, *Richard Allen: Apostle of Freedom* (Washington: Associated Publishers, 1935); 141–42, 150.

34. Smith, *In His Image, But . . .* , 38, 58, 117.

35. The secessions were led by James O'Kelly, who founded the Christian Connection, William Hammet, who led a schism in Charleston, South Carolina, and William Stillwell of New York.

36. Elmer T. Clark et al., eds., *The Journal and Letters of Francis Asbury*, vol. 3 (New York: Abingdon Press, 1958):366–67.

37. *Minutes of the Organization of the Western Colored Baptist Convention. Held in the City of Alton, March 11, 12, and 13, 1853* (St. Louis: Charles & Hammond, 1853); *Minutes of the Northwestern and Southern Baptist Convention, Held in the Second Colored Baptist Church, St. Louis, Mo. June 16th, 17th, 18th, 19th, 20th, and 21st, 1865* (Chicago: H. A. Newcombe & Co., 1864 [sic]): *Reports of the American Baptist Missionary Convention, 1849, 1853–55, 1857–60.* Amos Gerry Beman Scrapbooks, Yale University, on Congregations and Presbyterian Conventions, 1844 (vol. 2, p. 57); 1859 (vol. 2, pp. 133, 136, 141); 1860 (vol. 2, pp. 103, 132). *Frederick Douglass' Paper* (Rochester), December 18, 1851.

38. James M. Wright, *The Free Negro in Maryland* (New York: Columbia University Press, 1921), 216; Baltimore City Station Class Records, Lovely Lane Museum, Baltimore; Glenn A. McAninch, "We'll Pray for You: Methodist Ethnocentrism in the Origins of the African Methodist Episcopal Church in Baltimore," (Master's thesis, University of North Carolina, Chapel Hill, 1973): 41, 50.

39. Hanna, ed., *The Centennial Services*, 160–61; "Articles of Association" of the African Union Church of Wilmington, 1813.

40. Daniel A. Payne, *History of the African Methodist Episcopal Church* (Nashville, Tenn.: Publishing House of the A.M.E. Sunday-School Union, 1891; New York: Arno Press, 1969): 13–14; Rush, *A Short Account*, 39–42, 57, 76.

41. *Minutes of the Philadelphia Baptist Association*, 1816, 4–6; William Keen, ed., *The Bi-Centennial Celebration of the Founding of the First Baptist Church of the City of Philadelphia 1898* (Philadelphia: American Baptist Publication Society, 1899): 86.

42. Catto, *A Semi-Centenary Discourse*, 78ff., 110.

43. Smith, *In His Image, But . . .* , chap. 1.

44. Woodson, *History of the Negro Church*, 74.

45. *The Doctrines and Discipline of the A.M.E. Church*, 1817, 190.

46. Will B. Gravely, "Early Methodism and Slavery: The Roots of a Tradition," *The Drew Gateway* 30 (Spring 1964):150–65; Smith, *In His Image, But . . .* , chap. 6. Copies of the expurgated edition of the Methodist Episcopal Disciplines are in the Rare Book Room of the Perkins Library, Duke University.

47. Jones and Allen, *A Narrative of the Proceedings of the Black People, During the Late Awful Calamity in Philadelphia in the Year 1793*, 19–21. Reprint, Porter, ed., *Negro Protest Pamphlets; Articles of Association* (Philadelphia):17–19.

48. James D. Essig, *The Bonds of Wickedness: American Evangelicals Against Slavery* (Philadelphia: Temple University Press, 1982):198–99.

49. Miller, *A Sermon on the Abolition of the Slave Trade, Delivered in the African Church, New York, on the First of January 1810* (New York: John C. Totten, 1810).

50. Sobel, *Trabelin' On*, 192, 324.

51. Catto, *A Semi-Centenary Discourse*, 35–41.

52. Carol V. R. George's study of Black preachers in the abolitionist movement carries this issue in new directions. See "Widening the Circle: The Black Church and the Abolitionist Crusade, 1830–1860," in Lewis Perry and Michael Fellman, eds., *Antislavery Reconsidered: New Perspectives on the Abolitionists* (Baton Rouge: Louisiana State University Press, n.d.):75–95.

53. For a recent essay which obscures this distinction see Winthrop Hudson, "The American Context as an Area for Research in Black Church Studies," *Church History* 52 (June 1983), 157–71. Cf. David Wills's perceptive assessment of the historiographical importance of Black religious history in its larger American context in his introduction to Wills and Richard Newman eds., *Black Apostles at Home and Abroad: Afro-Christians and the Christian Mission from the Revolution to Reconstruction* (Boston: G. K. Hall, 1982): xi–xxxiii.

54. Sidney Ahlstrom, *A Religious History of the American People* (New Haven: Yale University Press, 1972):12–13. The statement in his preface implies more than merely adding the Black religious story to the larger picture; but it has rarely been realized in the scholarship thus far. See Will B. Gravely review in *Journal of Religious Thought* 33 (Spring-Summer 1976):106–8.

55. *The North Star* (Rochester), February 16, 1849.

17

Religion and Black Protest Thought in African American History

Manning Marable

I

Black Christianity, as well as the totality of the Black religious experience within America, cannot be understood outside of the development of white racism and capitalist exploitation. America was largely created through oppression—the systematic genocide of native Americans, the use of indentured servitude, and most importantly the exploitation of a significant number of African people within the "peculiar institution" of slavery. The cultural or ideological vision of pioneer America was Christianity, a faith which stressed among other tenets the innate perfectability of man, compassion for the oppressed and fraternal love and acceptance of others. The tensions created by the ever-increasing contradiction between white spiritual rhetoric and white politics established the parameters for white consciousness and faith throughout our history. These spiritual contradictions were only resolved, in part, through the pursuit of Black Christianity.

Initially white Christians made sporadic attempts to act out the meaning of their faith. During the first major uprising of evangelical fervor, the Great Awakening of the 1740s, hundreds of colonial itinerants baptized men and women regardless of their color or culture. Gilbert Tennent, the Scotch-Irish Presbyterian evangelist, travelled to Charleston in April 1741, and spread "great consolation" throughout the city, "especially among the young people, children and Negroes."[1] Well into the nineteenth century many southern clergymen promoted religious instruction and conversion for Blacks. In 1819 the Board of Managers of the Charleston, South Carolina, Bible Society claimed that "upwards of one fourth of the communicants are slaves or free persons of color."[2] Savannah, Georgia, minister Charles C. Jones observed that his white colleagues made "it a part of their pastoral care to devote frequent and stated seasons for the religious instruction of catechumen from amongst the black population."[3]

Many white ministers "were motivated by a paternal concern for the black man's soul," wrote historian Ira Berlin, "a belief that religion would make it easier to control blacks, and a clear knowledge that their white parishioners had no desire to add to the already swollen Negro membership of their churches."[4] Still others, perhaps less mindful of the racial dilemma and the crucial political questions involved, simply evangelized among the Blacks as they had among the whites. The great majority of colonial white Americans cared little for the theological distinctions between the Baptists, Presbyterians, or Congregationalists, and "most of them knew not to which church they belonged." Ministers and townsmen, slave traders and prosperous bankers were committed mostly to the passion of religious conversion and to the witnessing of their faith, allowing their slaves to participate in the proceedings. Historian Perry Miller wrote on this early phenomenon of religious "enthusiasm":

> We miss entirely the dynamics of the great revivals of the early nineteenth century if we suppose them missions to the heathen: they got their demonic power because they were addressed to those already more or less within the churches . . . They were not so much aimed at subjugating a wilderness as at reinvigorating the force of what was already professed. The town atheist might come to scorn and remain to pray: the finely coiffed Episcopalian lady might end by jerking so violently that her hairpins fell out, and the revivalist would chronicle his victories. But the mass of those he preached to, whom he humbled and "converted," were those who offered no ideological opposition, who wanted the "wave of electricity" to flow through them.[5]

One minister noted in 1839 that "It may be well to state the religious mania is said to be the prevailing form of insanity in the United States."[6]

It was the enthusiasm or passion generated from the popular conversion of the masses that made this form of frontier Christianity peculiarly American. As early as 1746, the great New England minister Jonathan Edwards argued in *A Treatise Concerning Religious Affections* that "true religion, in great part, consists in holy affection." Any man who wished to be saved from eternal damnation had to embrace Christ's message within the "exercises" of the heart. Edwards did not reject completely the role of *nomos*, or law within the doctrines of faith, but he emphasized enthusiasm and an aggressive, personal relationship between men and their idea of the Lord. A Christian who "has doctrinal knowledge and speculation only, without affection, never is engaged in the business of religion," he insisted.[7] The passion of religious conversion continued to dominate the rational frame of the white American mind, determining the character of American popular philosophy, or common sense. As G. W. F. Hegel noted, "passion is so bound up with the person's will that it alone and entirely determines its direction and is inseparable from it. It is that which makes the person what he is. . . ."[8] White Americans during the nineteenth and twentieth centuries were "badly christened" insofar as they accepted and obeyed "the gospel only in a highly sublimated form—which leaves the reality unfree as it was before."[9] The passion of white Christianity transfers critical thought to an idealist or supernatural plane, removing individual Christians from making moral decisions within the secular world, allowing "the sadistic extermination of the weak" to continue. The purpose of white Christianity as a popular philosophy, therefore, is not to change the world, but to alter the prejudices and emotions of those who dwell within the world to tolerate their real conditions.

There were limits to white America's fraternal spirit and brotherly love, limitations imposed by the special relationship between whites and Blacks within the wilderness society. As early as the dawn of the eighteenth century, qualifications upon the gospel's applicability for Blacks were pronounced in Puritan New England. The Reverend Thomas Bacon informed Blacks that "they must obey their masters in all things, even when cruelly abused: 'your Masters and Mistresses,'" he explained glowingly, "'are God's Overseers.'"[10] The venerable biblical scholar Cotton Mather wrote in his volume, *The Negro Christianized*, "Indeed, their stupidity is a Discouragement. It may seem, unto as little purpose, to Teach as to wash an Aethiopian."[11] In the wake of the slave rebellions of Gabriel Prosser, Denmark Vesey and Nat Turner, whites became fully aware of the implicit dangers of their proselytizing efforts in the slave quarters, and radically reversed course. Almost to a man, white clergymen in the cotton South "swore allegiance to the racial status quo," and "they became more and more enamored with the 'positive good' defense of slavery." Episcopalians declared that their teachings had nothing that could "inflame the passions of the ignorant black class-leaders."[12] The white church universally regarded the Negro as a subhuman being. As southern theologian William Andrew Smith wrote on the eve of the Civil War, "the religious sentiment is strong in African(s)"; however, "they are religious beings in a low state of civilization."[13]

Christianity evolved as a philosophy of self-deception, a glorification of primitive humanism, egalitarian theory, and inhuman practice. White Christians could not turn their own principles of faith upon their slaves or themselves for serious examination, because they would be forced to denounce themselves as moral monsters. The culture of white racism transformed their faith into a bridge which nearly traversed the immense contradiction of the treatment of the Negro. White Christianity was limited to the realm of the pulpit and the pews; it would not nor could not take an aggressive stand on secular issues, such as human rights of Blacks, Indians or other ethnic minorities. In time passion replaced and eventually superimposed itself over the principles of the church. By the middle of the century, most white Americans no longer hated the Black man in a conventional sense; the white culture chose to love the state of passion hatred inspires. White racism became a faith in which millions subconsciously or willingly shared, because the orthodox religious institutions took no position in favor of Black humanity. The white church, in its writings, its pronouncements and practices, was relegated to an inferior role within the scope of interracial relations, as the passion of hatred consumed the white public conscience.[14] White Americans "developed a strong commitment to the Puritan work ethic—but only so far as their slaves were concerned," historian Eugene D. Genovese wrote. "Slaves ought to be steady, regular, continent, disciplined clock-punchers. God Himself required it."[15]

Slave masters constantly reinforced the conservatism of Christianity by encouraging slave preachers to emphasize the ideals of loyalty, obligation, and duty in their sermons. Some Black preachers, either out of fear or from indoctrination, acquiesced to their masters' demands. They reminded their Black brethren of the many "advantages they had in bondage, for when they were in their native country, they were destitute of the Bible, worshipping idols of sticks and stones, and barbarously murdering one another."[16] The master was actually envious of the slaves' peculiar status, Blacks were told, "because God's special blessing seemed to be over them as though they were a select people. . . ."[17] A slave's reward for working long hours in the field would not be found on earth, but in the glorious kingdom beyond death. Of course, white preachers who frequented Black religious meetings took a different view on racial restrictions that awaited the slaves in heaven. One white itinerant informed a group of Blacks that "If all you niggers be good servants and obey your master and mistress you will enter the kitchen of heaven, but never into heaven."[18]

Underlying the American conscience was the great love for the passion of hatred, the lust for degradation and the essential denial of humanity to another group of human beings. White Christianity not only tolerated this passion, but perpetuated it and gave it renewed vigor; the "aethiopian" could not be washed white in the eyes of the white God. Religious instruction could, of course, provide secondary benefits for perpetuating the racist social order, by reinforcing the will of the slave master over his unwilling Black flock. But the passion itself denied that the Negro was capable of full human feelings or emotions, the ability to achieve full spiritual consciousness. It is for this central reason that white Christianity failed to convert the masses of Black people in America.

Nineteenth century Black critics recognized the self-deceptive character of white Christianity, and the chasm between religious principles and racist practices of Christians. David Walker, a free man of color living in Massachusetts, expressed this sentiment best in his famous *Appeal* in 1829. White Christians possess "the firm conviction that Heaven has designed us and our children to be slaves and beasts of burden," Walker argued. "In fact," he declared,

. . . they were so happy to keep in ignorance and degradation, and to receive the homage and the labour of the slaves, they forget that God rules in the armies of heaven and among the inhabitants of the earth, having his ears continually open to the cries, tears and groans of his oppressed people: and being a just and holy Being will at one day appear fully in the behalf of the oppressed; for although the destruction of the oppressors God may not effect by the oppressed, yet the Lord our god will bring other destructions upon them. . . .[19]

The white vision of man's redemption through faith had developed a psycho-neurotic flaw, residing within America's repressed loathing of the Black presence and in its passion for hatred. "The whites have always been an unjust, jealous, unmerciful, avaricious and bloodthirsty set of beings, always seeking after power and authority," Walker noted. Turning to Blacks themselves, he asked his "brethren" whether "our Creator made us to be slaves" or whether "we (have) any other Master but Jesus Christ alone?" Like Nat Turner, Gullah

Jack and a host of other Black slave rebels, Walker denounced the master-slave relationship as being inconsistent with the principle that the Lord was the spiritual "master" of all men.[20]

By the middle of the nineteenth century, Black Christianity had broken with white religious institutions. Black house slaves quietly resisted attempts by their masters to attend the white family's church, and most field hands were less than enthusiastic when their owners built segregated chapels or "praise houses" on their plantations.[21] When forced to attend white Christian services, Blacks disrupted the placid sermons by gossiping in the back pews or by simply going to sleep. One Southern Baptist clergyman of the era admitted that when forced to attend white churches, "the usual African resort is a loud, comfortable snoring nap."[22] Without white supervision, Blacks constructed their own meaning of the Spirit—a Spirit rooted within the intellectual traditions and customs of Africa. Even into the twentieth century, Black folk religious rituals were a blend of Christian doctrines and "other beliefs and customs handed down by parents and grandparents," such as the belief in "haints" or spirits, the special significance of drums in worship and the espousal of charms and conjuring.[23] Reading between the lines, the slaves saw in the Old Testament an implicit indictment of the racist state and the caste system of segregation. "The condition of the Israelites was better under the Egyptians than ours is under the whites," David Walker asserted. "The Egyptians (did not) heap the insupportable insult upon the children of Israel, by telling them that they were not of the human family. Can whites deny the charge?"[24] The Spirit or "soul," as Blacks understood it, was a passionate affirmation of the human condition, a cry of defiance in the wilderness in favor of God's love and compassion, as opposed to the slaveholder's universal assertion of Black inferiority in the spiritual realm.

Through the rituals of the Black Church, the Spirit and aspects of its meaning are revived every Sunday morning across the country, translated to Black children and reinforced by the material realities of Black exploitation and racial oppression. The Spirit is emotion and energized thought; it is faith in the meaning of Christian love and an unyielding belief in man's ability to recreate himself and his history through an understanding of the gospel. Not unlike white Christianity, Black Christianity is fundamentally a passion, an expression of a deep psychological and physical need to believe in the tenets of a moral creed. But while white Christianity became a limited and often twisted vision of the human condition, Black faith provided the entire breadth of human hope and courage in the face of pain and suffering. The Spirit literally "moves" those who choose to believe toward their own consciousness rebuilding, becoming more humane beings. It denounces the sterile passion of white racism. It places Black people inside their own cultural traditions.

Yet the secular conservatism and acceptance of the status quo, found within white American Christianity, also found expression within Black faith. Throughout Black Christianity was a dual consciousness, one located within the quest for spirituality, and the other within the attempt to transfer morals to material reality. The Black conception of God is alternately and simultaneously a distant heavenly representation of an ultimate spiritual redemption and a creative symbol of emancipation in the present. The conservative side of Black faith conforms to traditional western philosophy by locating the concept of liberation with the *Geist*, or Spirit, rather than within the material world. Within Christianity, Marxist philosopher Herbert Marcuse observed, "true freedom is only in the idea. Liberation thus is a spiritual event."[25] Secular alienation continues to exist, the aim of complete human freedom is repressed and the logic of faith emphasizes "the need for doctrinal unity of the whole 'religious' mass, and struggles to prevent the superior intellectual elements (from) detaching themselves from inferior ones."[26] As in white Christianity, passion and emotionalism assume a central role in reinforcing the logic of conformity and the acceptance of secular alienation.

The setting for the passion, for the quest of the Spirit, becomes the Black Church. The rituals of faith, the hymns sung in unison by Black participants, are acts of self-affirmation and renewal. The spirituals reflect a personal and even intimate relationship between the slaves and their idea of God:

> In de mornin' when I rise,
>   Tell my Jesus huddy oh,
> I wash my hands in de mornin' glory,
>   Tell my Jesus Huddy oh.
> Gwine to argue wid de Father and chatter wid de son,
>   The last trumpet shall sound, I'll be there.
> Gwine talk 'bout de bright world dey des' come from.
>   The last trumpet shall sound, I'll be there.[27]

As Albert Camus observed in *The Myth of Sisyphus*, men "find freedom in giving themselves. By losing themselves in their God, by accepting his rules, they become secretly free." The spirituals speak to the need of freedom of the

Black slave community, its desire to lose itself within a Spirit which tran-
scends the day-to-day suffering of enslavement. Indeed one could say that the
Blacks *"feel* free with regard to themselves, and not so much free as liberated."[28]
The voices of Black faith granted Blacks a spiritual emancipation from their
oppression, which is still a primary element in the anatomy of contemporary
African American Christianity.

Black Christianity was formed within a period of fundamental crisis, a
factor which had and continues to have a deep impact upon its ritual forms
and its perspectives. Two different languages, the language of the southern
master versus the African-English *patois* of the slaves, merged and separated
from each other. Two distinct cultures and value systems in the slave quarters
and in the proverbial big house, clashed and often assimilated traits from each
other over time. On the larger national setting, the South's dependence upon
servile labor contradicted the remainder of the country's capitalist mode of
production, which inevitably promoted a cultural and political separation
between the regions. The numerous rumors of slave rebellions and actual
racial violence, the knowledge of abolitionist activism, the underground railroad and other slave escapes, and the near paranoia of the slaveholders contributed to a general feeling of crisis. As Regis Debray observed, "People who
live through a crisis situation, whether political, social, military or a combination of them all . . . find it at once intensely clear and intensely confused. It is
clear to everyone that something of vital importance is being determined,"
Debray wrote, "but no one can agree as to what the solution will be."[29] Black
faith expressed the idea that an end of the slavery system would mark the
beginning of a new Black history, but it was not clear what secular pedagogy
or distinct agenda was necessary. The climate of intense crisis reinforced the
conservative aspects of Black religion, encouraging Black Christians to sometimes react to political and social events rather than to initiate them; at the
same time, the radical impetus of Black religion provided Blacks with the
beginnings of a militant pedagogy.

The antebellum Black ministers were the living embodiments of the
Spirit. They "often commanded the respect of their masters as well as the
slaves, but no less often faced the whip or worse for their efforts," Genovese
writes. "The preachers walked a tightrope. As men of God who cared about
the spiritual life of the slaves, their unwillingness to separate theology from
sociopolitical questions did not arise from an indifference to theology but
from a holistic vision of life."[30] The preacher employed the Bible as his vehicle

for understanding the Spirit, and often drew practical lessons of brotherhood and love from the Old and New Testaments, which undermined the hegemonic influence of white racism. Despite repressive Southern laws which increasingly limited their mobility, Black men of faith made their voices heard in the fields, in the kitchens and in the slave quarters at night. "The preachers did not typically call for revolt and violence," Genovese noted, "for conditions overwhelmingly discouraged insurrectionary ideas among sober black men." But many could turn into revolutionaries if conditions changed.[31] W. E. B. DuBois wrote that "it is but human experience to find that the complete suppression of a race is impossible." The Black minister, inspired by the "mighty spirit" of his faith, fought against the omnipresence of "inner discouragement and (the) submission of others."[32]

It was through the means of his sermon that the minister united his congregation in the realization of the Black Spirit. The central focus of the sermon was not upon the individual minister or upon some obscure theological principle as in white Christian practice, but within the dynamic process of communion, over which the Black preacher presided. In the traditional West African religious ritual, the priest called forth a phrase or passage of special meaning, the congregation immediately responded, and was followed by a second statement by the priest. Similarly, the African American church incorporated the call-and-response into each sermon. The Black minister's primary responsibility was not to interpret the Spirit, but to conjure forth the passion, the explosive enthusiasm of realizing the Spirit within each member of the congregation. The dynamics of the religious service demanded that the preacher become a charismatic spokesman and representative of the living God, a role which few if any white preachers could begin to assume, and could scarcely comprehend. The oratorical style drew heavily from the African rhetoric and pattern of speech. "Every successful preacher knew the power of rhythmic progression of words and knew how, at first slowly and softly and then with deceptive quickness, to move his audience to a crescendo of frenzied response."[33] The Black preacher's sermons were never the same twice, nor could they be: like the beauty of improvisational jazz or the powerful melodies of the classic blues, the Black sermon was not an object, but an expression of Black faith. The sermon's words were not the art; rather, the intimate relationship which joined the congregation, its preacher and the call-and-response sermon to the Spirit in that given moment of history forms the dialectics of Black faith and was the art itself.

Christianity as an ideology is a uniquely tragic form of faith. For white Americans, their vision of faith provides an intellectual shield through which the oppressive essence of their economic and political systems are made virtually invisible. As Camus observed, "it is Christianity that began substituting the tragedy of the soul for contemplation of the world."[34] Black Christianity, on the other hand, accepts the meaning of Christian principles and simultaneously rejects the passion of racism which constitutes the state of existence within the secular world. The voices of Black faith point toward a higher vision for all humanity, but are limited by the overwhelming reality of oppression which Black Americans have endured for more than three hundred years. The conservative tendencies within Black faith reach for a Spirit that liberates the soul, but not the body.

On the other hand, the radical consciousness within Black faith was concerned with the immediate conditions of Black people. This other half of Black faith, which I shall refer to as "Blackwater," provides a spiritual equilibrium with its conservative counterpart. Blackwater is the consciousness of oppression, a cultural search for self-affirmation and authenticity.[35] Blackwater was the dialectical quest for the pedagogy of liberation, the realization that human beings have the capacity through struggle to remake their worldly conditions.[36] Like childbirth, Blackwater was a painful break from the consciousness of the master, in favor of creativity and collective emancipation. It was expressed implicitly in the songs of Black churches through such phrases as "Steal away to Jesus." Expressed by Jean Toomer in "Cotton Song," Blackwater becomes a poetic challenge to the patient Jehovah of the Old Testament:

> Come, brother, come. Let's lift it:
> Come now, hewit! roll away!
> Shackles fall upon the Judgement
> But lets not wait for it.
>
> God's body's got a soul,
> Bodies like to roll the soul,
> Can't blame God if we don't roll.
> Come, brother, roll, roll![37]

Blackwater was not a quest toward the Spirit, but a partial reaction to the otherworldliness of the Black ministry. If the rituals of the church conveyed a message of long tolerance of suffering and acceptance of secular oppression,

Blackwater was the impetus toward political activism and the use of religious rhetoric to promote the destruction of the white status quo. Within Blackwater were the beginnings of a more comprehensive Black worldview, or Black life philosophy, a method of understanding the world and in transcending oppression. Located within the message of Black religion but always going beyond the immediate questions posed within Black rituals and Christianity, this was "a view (which provided) the necessary impetus and methodology to take our liberation," wrote Jabari Mahiri. Yet Blackwater also "goes beyond this to specify the process for perfecting our social relationships and harmonizing our existence in nature."[38] Both Blackwater and the conservative aspects of Black faith were essential by-products of the ideological frame which constituted Black thought throughout slavery and beyond the plantation.

II

The parameters of faith among the oppressed are always established by the passion for violence by the oppressor. With the end of slavery came an end to the paternal forms of racism that servile labor promulgated. DuBois wrote in *Black Reconstruction* that "there had been contact between Negroes and white people in the old South; and in some cases beautiful friendship, and even warm love and affection. But this was spasmodic and exceptional," he observed, because of "the sense of inferiority on the part of the Negro, and the will to rule on the part of whites."[39] As the South began to progress economically with the introduction of heavy manufacturing in its major cities and with sharecropping in the countryside, the character of white racism grew more brutal and potentially violent.

Wilbur Cash captures the frightening "savage ideal" of white southerners in *The Mind of the South*. By the 1880s, "there appears a waxing inclination to abandon such relatively mild and decent ways" of murdering Black people such as lynching or shooting, Cash reported, "in favor of burning, often roasting over slow fires, after preliminary mutilations and tortures—a disposition to revel in the infliction of the most devilish and prolonged agonies." Despite almost three thousand hangings and public burnings in the South during the 1880s to 1920s, most whites could not be classified as murderers per se. Nevertheless the casual acceptance of these activities produced a culture in which white men "capitalized on every shadow of excuse to kick and cuff" the Negro; where the "nigger-killer" in town was considered by most decent citizens to be "a hell of a fellow." Simultaneously the white South experienced a sharp rise in evangelical religion. Southern faith retreated into "primitivism" and "hysteria" during and after World War I. Great camp meetings of white Baptists and Methodists featured "such practices as speaking in tongues," "holy rolling," "fits, jerks (and) barks." Cash suggests that the level of Christian culture declined into crass emotionalism as the age of industrialization and finance capitalism entered the region.[40] It did not escape the notice of Black Christians that many of the sanctified, barking, gospel-swearing white Christians were all too often found in lynch mobs and beneath the white uniforms of the Ku Klux Klan.

Entering into his personal covenant with God through passion, the white Christian is less concerned with the distinct articles of his official religion than with the emotional experience achieved through its rituals. It is relatively simple, for example, to believe devoutly that Jonah was actually swallowed by a whale, or that Jesus literally raised Lazarus from his tomb at Bethany, because religious belief is separated from scientific fact. Theological positions or the names of the apostles are less important than the total acceptance of faith within the confines of that religion. The normal Christian "does not remember the actual arguments and could not repeat them," Gramsci reflected. "The fact that he was once convinced, as if by a clap of thunder, is the permanent reason for the persistence of the conviction, even if he is no longer able to argue for it."[41] The Christian subconsciously evolves a religion which is inseparable from his irrational hatred for the Negro: his passion for hating complements and reinforces his passion for love. "The present attitude and action of the white world is not based solely upon rational, deliberate intent," DuBois notes in *Dusk of Dawn*. "It is a matter of conditioned reflexes; of long followed habits, customs and folkways; of subconscious trains of reasoning and unconscious nervous reflexes."[42]

Both the Catholic and Episcopal churches failed largely to abandon racism, either at the altar or through their secular policies. Before the emergence of Jim Crow legislation in the South, most Black Catholics were forced to attend white churches. Of course, church societies only admitted white members, and "the colored portion of the congregation was looked upon as intruders. . . ." By 1926 almost two-thirds of the 203,000 Black Catholics attended exclusively "colored churches." But even after segregation, white Catholics refused to treat Blacks humanely. When whites attended a Black Catholic church, they demanded that Blacks should not "(receive) Holy Communion with them," and ordered Blacks to sit "in a few rear pews" in their own church.[43] Similar practices occurred in the Episcopal church. DuBois addressed the problem in a letter to A. C. Tebeau in February 1940. The Episcopal church accepted slavery uncritically during the nineteenth century, and had offered southern Negro schools little financial assistance. "Considering the great wealth and prestige of the Episcopal Church," he suggested, "their work for Negro education has been pitifully small. My own grandfather was once a member of an Episcopal Church in New Haven, Connecticut but was asked with other colored people to withdraw."[44]

The northern states became the single hope for material improvement and personal dignity for Black people. The trickle of Black immigrants that arrived in New York's Sugar Hill or Chicago's south side grew into a great flood of humanity. "The North became the Promised Land, another Jordan," writes LeRoi Jones in *Blues People*, "not because of the tales of high-paying jobs for everyone but because the South would always remain in the minds of most Negroes, even without the fresh oppression of the post-bellum Jim Crow laws, the scene of the crime."[45] But the vision of final emancipation turned into another bitter illusion for Black people. The ghettoes were not a golden land of equal opportunity, but a place for permanent unemployment, juvenile prostitution, and petty crime. The riots and the civil rights marches provided only a few material advances for the bulk of Black working class people. Alienation and an acute sense of resignation, the nagging belief that nothing will ever change, destroys the ability of many Blacks to reassert their humanity or unique culture. "You can drink till screaming is not loud enough," Jones argues; "you can stand in doorways late nights and hit people in the head."[46] For many people, the Black Church became the way out, the forum in which each week's mountain of frustrations and tragedies are eliminated from one's consciousness, a holy place of peace in a world of utter madness and dark decay.

African Americans rejected the bogus beliefs of their former taskmasters. Within several years after the Civil War, thousands of Black congregations were established, and the older Negro churches in the North experienced a boom in membership. The African Methodist Episcopal church could claim only twenty thousand members in 1856, mostly in the mid-Atlantic states. Twenty years later, as ministers returned to their native land, the church claimed a national membership of two hundred thousand. The Colored Primitive Baptists in America seceded from a white parent organization in 1865.

The Colored Methodist Episcopal Church also separated from the white church and quickly initiated five conferences. Black members of the General Assembly of the Cumberland Presbyterian Church started their own separate organization in 1869.[47]

In both the northern ghettoes and in the South, the Black Church assumes a vital social and psychological role. Existing in an ever-changing and threatening environment, Black people call upon their church to provide them with a sense of belonging and self-worth. "For many black people, the church is the only institution they belong to which is decidedly and exclusively theirs," wrote Charles V. Hamilton. "The church service for many participants is one moment in their lives when they can be men, free, relaxed, themselves." The Spirit, having survived the rigors of slavery, assumes a new character in the urban, storefront setting or within the rural, backwoods church milieu. The preacher again reveals through call-and-response sermons the powerful message of transcendence and unyielding faith the gospel represents. For Black people to remove themselves consciously from their oppressed conditions, the Black minister must be as independent as possible from the contradictions inherent within the established social order. He must praise the word of the Lord, and not speak for the local political boss, the neighborhood loan shark, or for the power company. Blacks "must have complete confidence in the competence and integrity of the minister," Hamilton asserted.[48] The church becomes the foundation for independence, Black confidence and Black clarity at a time when few of these qualities are to be found among whites in their relations with the Black community.

The Black Church in the postbellum period attempted to seize permanent control over its own religious rituals and to redefine the relationship between the church and the culture of the Black community. It rejected the dominant white belief that slavery had been sanctioned by God and proclaimed that Christ's death and rebirth revealed a promise of spiritual liberation for the oppressed. The church naturally became the great repository for African American culture. The average Black congregation "is a singing church—a fact well documented by the legions who have risen to fame and fortune in the world of secular music, but who began their careers in the choirs of the local black churches," Hortense Spillers wrote in *The Black Scholar*. The transition from the pulpit to the local nightclub and back again says a lot about the secular significance of Black religious music and quite a bit more about the relationship between Black religious and secular institutions. "The difference between what happens when Mahalia Jackson sings and Aretha Franklin or Billie Holiday or Bessie Smith sings may be a matter of theme and setting but hardly a matter of essence."[49] The church assumed a defensive conservative role in the dialectically evolving culture of Blacks; by supporting "a distinct body of social art embodied in music, song, dance, folklore, poetry" and other areas, the church preserved the unique historical traditions of the Black community.[50]

However important its role within popular culture, the church also perpetuated its dual consciousness—the equilibrium that existed between spiritual conservatism and the radical consciousness of Blackwater. The contradictions within Black faith which create a paternal, benevolent but distant savior figure on one hand and, simultaneously, the images of an activist Lord and clergy on the other, were never resolved after emancipation. The traditional "down-home" church often "taught black people that they had been saved by a white Jesus because of the love of a white God," argues Cleage. The Jesus of the sharecropping and peonage society "could not come to grips with the black man's powerlessness."[51] Historically this was an inevitable by-product of the overwhelming exploitation and the dynamics of the Black population's introduction into America's political economy and caste system at its lowest levels. Africans who possessed a complex philosophical tradition were first introduced to Christ while they lay flat on the bottom of slave ships as they crossed the Atlantic. As Joseph A. Johnson, Jr., observed, "The blacks on the slave ship heard his name sung in hymns of praise while they died chained in stinky holes beneath the decks locked in terror and disease. When the black women were raped in the cabin by the white racists," he notes, "they must have noticed the Holy Bible on the shelves." The fact that Christ remained a relevant cultural figure to both the former masters and former slaves almost inevitably fostered an anti-Black bias within the American Christian church and profound Black ambivalence toward this racist image. "The white Christ of the white church establishment" became the "oppressor" and "enemy" of the Black man and woman.[52]

This dual search for the Spirit and for temporal civil and human rights continued to dominate the Black Church. Since the 1920s especially, there have been bold attempts by Black Christians to transcend the inherent conservative tendencies of their faith by emphasizing the activist, politically oriented consciousness of Blackwater. In the newly formed Black Harlem ghetto, Marcus Garvey conscientiously used religion "for furthering his program of race pride and self-reliance." Tony Martin, Garvey's biographer, noted that the Black nationalist leader "was attempting to recapture what he considered to be the progressive and revolutionary essence of the early Christian church. As far as he was concerned," Martin wrote, "Christ was the leader of a mass movement for the uplift of oppressed people, and so was he."[53] The civil rights movement, although explicitly integrationist in its cultural impetus, was also a secular movement which drew heavily from the expressions of Black rituals and Black faith. The movement was unique from other major political reform campaigns in American history because, as philosopher Hanna Arendt implied, it "did not simply carry on propaganda, but acted, and moreover, acted almost exclusively from moral incentives."[54]

In the seclusion of the Birmingham City Jail in 1963, Martin Luther King wrote boldly that "all segregation statutes are unjust because segregation distorts the soul and damages the personality." King's assertions that "a just law is a man-made code that squares with the moral law," and "an unjust law . . . is out of harmony" with God's law, provided a theoretical framework for thousands of committed Black men, women, and children to lie down in the streets in protest, to be arrested and physically beaten by white policemen.[55] Again, King-as-Black-minister is never overshadowed by King-as-political-activist, because the vision of his politics is drawn from his faith. Not unlike David Walker, both Garvey and King in different ways found ample room within Christianity to transform their followers into committed, moral advocates for social and cultural change.

Black ministers are now often among the first to deplore the conservative aspects of their faith and to articulate a pedagogy stressing human rights. William H. Bentley, president of the National Black Evangelical Association, admits that the Black Church has been unable "to speak meaningfully to the culture of the street people and others outside her communion" and has "failed to substantively identify with the poor."[56] Black religion is often viewed as the culprit, an agent of the oppressor, rather than a potentially liberating ideological force. The emphasis upon individual conversion within the rituals of the church as opposed to a collective attempt at spiritual awakening reinforced the tendency to splinter and alienate Black people from each other and from the demands of the political world. "Continued primarily by Christianity's western expression, black people in America, through the acceptance of a concept of God as an initiator and agent of change beyond the sheer force of our collective determination, have been rendered virtually incapable of effecting systematic change in our conditions," wrote Jabari Mahiri.[57] In its extreme form, conservative Black Christianity reinforces cultural dominance of the Negro elite over other segments of the oppressed Black community. Harold Cruse observed that in Harlem, "the ministers of churches advance" a reactionary "brand of community uplift (which) is best for soothing the tortured ghetto soul twixt Hell on earth and Heaven hereafter," without actually altering his real condition.[58]

The advent of Black Power as a political philosophy in the late 1960s did not shatter the hold of Black Christianity, but actually renewed its appeal for the majority of Black youth. Black ministers recognize correctly that "younger people will not be frightened into heaven out of fear of burning in hell. This group is not looking for saviors," Charles V. Hamilton observed, "but for solutions. They are not looking so much for princes of peace as they are for pioneers in protest."[59] The needs of the secular world reshaped the language of the pulpit, just as the peculiar demands of slavery directed the scope of Black antebellum religion. A host of young Black theologians, speaking to the Spirit of Black people, conclude that Black Power was a logical idealist expression of faith, the pedagogy of moral and secular liberation. James H. Cone asserted, "It would seem that Black Power and Christianity have this in common: the liberation of man! If the work of Christ is that of liberating men from alien loyalties, and if racism is . . . an alien faith, then there must be some correlation between Black Power and Christianity." At an existential level, Black Power is the assertion of the oppressed man and woman "to say no . . . to refuse to cooperate in their own dehumanization."[60] Black Power is an attempt by Black Christians to resolve the permanent contradiction between Black spiritual freedom by faith and Black secular oppression—an attempt which may succeed in the short run." "It is joyously difficult," historian Vincent Harding admits, "but part of the affirmation of Black Power is 'We are a spirtual people.'"[61]

The continuing presence of racial prejudice and class exploitation forces the new Black theologians to reject the "error of speaking of Christ without reference to black liberation." James Cone states that many of today's Black ministers believe "that the white Jesus has no place in the black community, and that it is our task to destroy him. We must replace him with the Black Messiah. . . ."[62] Several generations of Black ministers had forgotten "the radical and revolutionary nature of the Christian gospel," argued Calvin B. Marshall, a member of the Executive Committee of the National Committee of Black Churchmen. "They forgot that Jesus the Christ stood in opposition to the religious, political, and social status quo of his day because he found those positions to be oppressive and dehumanizing to his people." Christ becomes another Malcolm X, and the meaning of his death and rebirth now connotes the burden of suffering and a vital commitment to struggle. The rabbi of Nazareth becomes within contemporary radical Black religion the shining advocate of a ministry to the dispossessed and the poor. "Jesus comforted the mourner and offered hope to the humble," Cone wrote. "He had a message for the men and women who had been pushed to the limits of human existence and on these he pronounced his blessedness."[63]

Black Christianity now assumes the role of social praxis—the joining together of a theoretical framework for spiritual liberation with a secular impetus for radical political and social change. Blackwater has largely triumphed, for the time being, over the more conservative, accommodationist elements of Christianity. David Walker's fiery criticisms of white Christians have culminated in Cecil Cone's logical assertion "that black Christianity is the *only* Christianity that is Christian." Black people had become "open to the divine revelation in a way that people who can depend on the political order cannot." Although white Christians might protest that Cone's beliefs are simply a negation or a reaction to the racist excesses of the past, the idea that Black faith is by itself the real Christianity reinforces the Black Church's authenticity within the Black community in a time of increasing alienation from religion and fundamental social crisis. Blackwater's emphasis upon the existential capability of transcendence, the Black man and woman's historic ability to survive and to rise above oppression, places Black Christianity at the very center of Black life.

But Christianity as an ideology has assumed various roles throughout western history, both progressive and reactionary. As an idealist philosophy, it has comforted both slaves and their masters on all continents. It is possible that Black theology may provide Blacks with the intellectual and moral guideposts to transcend their oppressed conditions within the American state, to mount yet another organized challenge to racism and political corruption, such as the movement of the sixties attempted to become. Blackwater is the expression of that dialectical, cultural movement beyond the artificial idealist limitations of American Christian thought, toward a Black, collective consciousness of liberation. Yet nothing is permanent in history. One is reminded that the Baptists, perhaps the most conservative and potentially racist of all

American church groups, were viewed in sixteenth and seventeenth century England as the most radical, anti-establishment of all sects. The Catholic church's various holy representatives have blessed Italian bombs before they were dropped over defenseless Ethiopian villages during Mussolini's colonial war, and supported guerilla struggles to overthrow American-backed dictatorships in Central and South America. Black faith, similarly, has fostered both accommodation and protest, the nonviolence of a Martin Luther King as well as the fury of a Nat Turner and a Malcolm X. It seems inevitable, despite the vigorous secular orientation of Black Christianity today, that the current radical direction of Black faith may not be so predictably in harmony with the political goal of Black liberation than many now within the church suspect.

For all the aspirations and statements of Black Christians, the basic ideological dilemma which besets late capitalist society—in the West generally and in the United States specifically—is a crisis perpetuated by the bankruptcy of white consciousness and consciences. The passion for hatred and racism which is a by-product of the material inequities of the capitalist system preserve and promote the hegemony of white reality. White Christianity has failed and still fails to liberate the deluded conscience of white America; the principle victims of this failure have been African American people. White Christianity's God is still a white God. James Baldwin makes this clear in two works: "If the concept of God has any validity or any use," Baldwin argued in *The Fire Next Time*, "it can only be to make us larger, freer, and more loving. If God cannot do this, then it is time we get rid of Him." More pointedly in *Blues For Mister Charlie*, he wrote:

> that white man's God is *white*. It's that damn white God that's been lynching us and burning us and castrating us and raping our women and robbing us of everything that makes a man a man for all these hundreds of years. Now, why we sitting around here, in His house? If I could get my hands on Him, I'd pull Him out of heaven and drag Him through this town at the end of a rope.[64]

Notes

1. Edwin Scott Gaustad, *The Great Awakening in New England*, 2d ed. (Chicago, 1968), p. 35.
2. Milton C. Sernett, *Black Religion and American Evangelism* (Metuchen, N.J., 1975):37.

3. Ibid., 37.

4. Ira Berlin, *Slaves Without Masters* (New York, 1976):292–93.

5. Perry Miller, *The Life of the Mind of America* (New York, 1965):10–11.

6. Ibid., 15.

7. Gaustad, 97–98.

8. Georg Wilhelm Frederich Hegel, *Reason in History, A General Introduction to the Philosophy of History* (Indianapolis and New York, 1953):29.

9. Herbert Marcuse, *Eros and Civilization: A Philosophical Inquiry Into Freud*, 2d ed. (New York, 1962):64.

10. Winthrop D. Jordan, *The White Man's Burden* (New York, 1974):91.

11. Ibid., 89–90.

12. Sernett, 39.

13. Ibid., 61.

14. Perhaps the best philosophical explanation of the relationship between passion and racism is Jean-Paul Sartre's *Anti-Semite and Jew*, rev. ed. (New York, 1972). Sartre judges racism to be "something that enters the body from the mind. It is an involvement of the mind, but one so deep-seated and complete that it extends to the physiological realm, as happens in cases of hysteria." The major weaknesses of Sartre's logic stem from the lack of dialectical development and the ahistorical character of his concept of race throughout his writings.

15. Eugene D. Genovese, *Roll, Jordan, Roll: The World the Slaves Made* (New York, 1974):297.

16. Stanley Feldstein, *Once A Slave: The Slaves' View of Slavery* (New York, 1971):74.

17. Ibid., 74.

18. Ibid., 75.

19. "David Walker's Appeal," in Sterling Stuckey, *The Ideological Origins of Black Nationalism* (Boston, 1972):42–43.

20. Ibid., 55–56.

21. Genovese, 188–89.

22. Berlin, 293.

23. Georgia Writers' Project, *Drums and Shadows* (Garden City, N.Y., 1972):77–78, 85, 87, 88.

24. "David Walker's Appeal," 49.

25. Marcuse, 107.

26. Antonio Gramsci, *The Modern Prince* (New York, 1975):63.

27. J. B. T. Marsh, *The Story of the Jubilee Singers: With Their Songs* (Boston, 1880):132.

28. Albert Camus, *The Myth of Sisyphus* (New York, 1955):43.

29. Regis Debray, *Prison Writings* (New York, 1973):99.

30. Genovese, 256, 263.

31. Ibid., 259.

32. W. E. B. DuBois, *Black Reconstruction in America, 1860–1880* (New York, 1935):702.

33. Genovese, 266–67, 271.

34. Camus, 136.

35. Paulo Freire calls this consciousness of the oppressed "conscientizcao." See Paulo Freire, *Pedagogy of the Oppressed* (New York, 1970):20.

36. Ibid., 33.

37. Jean Toomer, *Cane* (New York, 1923):15.

38. Jabari Mahiri, "Beyond Black Religion: Complete Collective Consciousness," *Black Books Bulletin*, 4 (Spring 1976):43–44.

39. DuBois, 190.

40. Wilbur J. Cash, *The Mind of the South* (New York, 1941):125, 297.

41. Gramsci, *The Modern Prince*, 72.

42. W. E. B. DuBois, *Dusk of Dawn* (New York, 1940).

43. John T. Gillard, *The Catholic Church and the American Negro* (Baltimore, 1929):63, 68.

44. W. E. B. DuBois to A. C. Tebeau, February 20, 1940, in Herbert Aptheker, ed., *The Correspondence of W. E. B. DuBois, Volume 2* (1934–1944) (Amherst, 1976):212.

45. LeRoi Jones, *Blues People* (New York, 1963):95–96.

46. LeRoi Jones, *Home* (New York, 1966):95.

47. John Hope Franklin, *From Slavery to Freedom*, 3d ed. (New York, 1969):309.

48. Charles V. Hamilton, *The Black Preacher in America* (New York, 1972):21.

49. Hortense J. Spillers, "Martin Luther King and the Style of the Black Sermon," *The Black Scholar* 3 (September 1971):25–26.

50. Harold Cruse, *Rebellion or Revolution?* (New York, 1968):51.

51. Albert Cleage, *The Black Messiah* (New York, 1969):108–10.

52. Joseph A. Johnson, Jr., "Jesus, The Liberator," *The Soul of the Black Preacher* (Philadelphia, 1971):102–3.

53. Tony Martin, *Race First: The Ideological and Organizational Struggles of Marcus Garvey and the Universal Negro Improvement Association* (Westport, Conn., 1976):59, 68.

54. Hanna Arendt, *Crises of the Republic* (New York, 1972):203.

55. Martin Luther King, Jr., "Letter from Birmingham Jail," in *Why We Can't Wait* (New York, 1964):77–100.

56. William H. Bently, "Black Christian Nationalism in Evangelical Perspective," *Black Books Bulletin*, 4 (Spring 1976):26–31, 66.

57. Mahiri, 42–45.

58. Harold Cruse, *The Crisis of the Negro Intellectual* (New York, 1967):90.

59. Hamilton, 232.

60. James Cone, *Black Theology and Black Power* (New York, 1969):39–40.

61. Vincent Harding, "The Religion of Black Power," in Donald R. Cutler, ed., *The Religious Situation: 1968* (Boston, 1968):31.

62. James H. Cone, "Speaking the Truth," *Black Books Bulletin* 4 (Spring 1976):6–13, 62.

63. Ibid.

64. James Baldwin, *The Fire Next Time* (New York, 1963):119; James Baldwin, *Blues For Mister Charlie* (New York, 1964):15.

18

The Muslim Mission in the Context of American Social History

C. Eric Lincoln

The United States of America began as a Protestant Christian establishment and after two hundred years was still close enough to her religious origins for a prominent theologian to aver with confidence that "to be a Protestant, a Catholic or a Jew are today the alternative ways of being an American."[1] Among the vast array of challenging implications to be drawn from Professor Will Herberg's famous aphorism are the following: religion in the United States is so closely identified with cultural or civil values as to take on the character of nationalism; and being "American" presupposes the Judeo-Christian heritage or experience. There is an inescapable irony in both propositions. In the first place, to the uncritical observer the most prominent feature of contemporary American life is its secularism, not its piety. In the second place, the founding fathers went to extraordinary lengths to insure the religious neutrality of the emergent nation by constitutional fiat. There could be no religious establishment, and there could be no religious test or requirement for equality of participation in the full range of common values incident to American citizenship. Nor may the national legislature make any laws to the contrary.[2] Nevertheless a close examination of American secularism will reveal features that are startling in their religious tenor. The principal elements of this "new" religion are derived principally from the Judeo-Christian tradition and from the idealistic sentiments of what is commonly called "the American Dream." This is the religion I call "Americanity,"[3] and for all the prideful references to the separation of church and state in the United States, Americanity is the "established" faith, a fact of critical importance in understanding the implications of the Islamic presence in America.

However, despite a demonstrated sophistication in sociopolitical foresight, there is nothing to suggest that the founders of the United States of America had even a premonition of the eventual arrival of Islam upon these shores. While the first European settlers were themselves in search of religious freedom, their initial "errand into the wilderness" was to establish a Christian community—one which would become a beacon of perfection—a kind of religious demonstration project for all the world to see and emulate. But the "world" to which the notion of a "righteous empire"[4] was addressed was the turbulent, schismatic world of European Christianity. Islam, a "pagan" religion, was beyond consciousness and beyond contemplation. In the unfolding scenario of Western manifest destiny, the religions of the East, like the peoples of the East, belonged to an exotic history whose wheel had turned; in the peculiar balances of the historical order, the rise of the West meant the descent of the East. Eight hundred and eighty-eight years separate the Battle of Tours from the landing of the Mayflower at Plymouth Rock and in that interim of nearly a full millenium Islam had long been displaced in the critical concerns of those who found, in the New World beyond the Atlantic Ocean, a world from which to mold a more perfect image of the Old World. Although Islam had lingered on in the Spanish peninsula and was spread among the American Indians by Blacks serving in the Spanish expeditions in the Americas in the sixteenth century,[5] it has never been an aspect of the English experience and the American commonwealth was from the beginning a transplant of the Anglo-Saxon culture and expectations. That primary cultural impress has of course been modified by subsequent immigration and by the development of an indigenous experience. But it has not been supplanted. Anglo conformism remains the norm—indeed the sine qua non of American self-perception.

It is clear then that the religion of Islam is not in any substantial way a part of the critically valued American experience. It has no purchase in antecedent European-American traditions and it played no part in the critical development of the indigenous American culture. Exclusionist immigration policies were aimed at reserving the country for Caucasian people in general and people of western European descent in particular. In consequence, the development of the "Western Empire" proceeded in what must now be perceived as a deliberately created cultural vacuum, denying itself the wisdom and the culture of the East in the vain, short sighted pursuit of a chauvinistic racial chimera.

While American immigration policies excluded both Asians and Africans its commercial interests did not. Among the millions of Blacks who were made involuntary immigrants under the aegis of slavery, there were inevitably numbers of Muslims from the Islamic kingdoms of the West Coast of Africa.

How many thousands (or perhaps tens of thousands) we shall never know, for the slave masters had no interest in recording the cultural and spiritual achievements of their chattels. What is more, the slave trade required and maintained a determined myopia regarding the religious interests of its hapless human commodities: first to avoid the embarrassment of knowingly selling an occasional Black Christian, but more often in support of the fiction that the religious depravity of the Africans made them legitimate targets for spiritual rehabilitation through the dubious ministrations of chattel slavery. Under that convenient sanction even Africans recognizable as Muslims would fare no better than the rest, for Islam was considered the supreme cabal of infidels, when it was considered at all. In spite of all this, the evidence of a substantial Muslim presence among the American slave population is compelling, while in South America and the Caribbean that presence was common enough to be taken for granted and the cultural impress of Islam remains in high relief in those areas to this day.[6]

In sharp contrast to the prevailing practices of Roman Catholic Latin America, the Anglo-Saxon Protestant hegemony that defined the cultural and religious parameters of the slave-holding South considered it expedient to suppress all African religions of whatever kind. The fear of insurrection or revolt under cover of religion was deep and unremitting, and the common precaution was to disperse as widely as possible all those slaves known to have common tribal or language affiliations. This practice effectively precluded the cultic apparatus by which means religions survive and propagate themselves. In spite of such discouragements, accounts persist of Muslim slaves who committed the entire Qur'an to memory in an effort to keep the faith alive and to pass it on to others.[7] Inevitably, of course, such heroic efforts were unavailing, for the intransigence of the slave system, buttressed as it was by a formidable reticulation of customs and convention, could not and did not accommodate itself to the heroics of its victims. What the system did provide (after a hundred years of dereliction) was an alternative faith. As the generations succeeded each other, scarcely marked except by the momentary discontinuities of birth and death, Protestant Christianity eventually made its way into the vacuum left by the proscribed "native" religions of whatever sort of origin. It took the better part of a century—from 1619 to sometime after the Society for the Propagation of the Gospel received permission to proselytize the slaves in 1701.[8]

It was not a permission easily obtained. At stake in sharing a religion with the Blacks was the spectre of sharing a community with them. The implications for economic prerogative, social status, political power, and even the transcendent bliss of the heavenly rest were unknown and troublesome in their anticipation. But the benefits, it was argued, would be many—not the least of which would be more tractable, more reliable, more loving, and more dedicated servants.[9] Was it worth the risk? Opinion was divided, and the compromise was a severely edited version of the faith dominated by careful selections of Pauline doctrine, which offered divine approval of the lowly condition of the slave. From the beginning of the Black experience in American Christianity, Black Christians were separated by race and by destiny. The churches were segregated and remain so to this day. Sharing the faith has yet to accomplish the elementary principle of sharing the community. White churches and Black churches go their separate spiritual ways, while in the arena of social and political intercourse the mandates of the faith are still suspended in the interest of less respectable values.

Such is the backdrop against which Black Islam attempts resurgence. Why "Black" Islam? First, because it was the Black Muslims, that is the "Moors" among the Spanish conquistadores, who first introduced Islam to the New World.[10] Second, because in the English colonies the only Muslim presence was among the slaves imported from Black Africa. Third, while there had been small enclaves of orthodox Muslims in America for many decades, their presence had been characterized by clannishness and quietism, not by proselytism or public identity and involvement.

The orthodox Muslims were more a spasm than an outpost of Islam, inundated by the flood tide of militant Christianity, the spirit of the symbol of Western ascendancy. In consequence, these "white Muslims" maintained a low profile. Perhaps subconsciously they considered themselves the logical targets for a Christian jihad, unaware, or more likely unconvinced, of the protections afforded all religions by the Constitution of the United States. In any case they seemed content, or at least constrained, to keep Islam within the parameters of their ethnic associations. Certainly the white Muslims provided no more opportunity and even less incentive for Black participation in the religion of Islam than the counterpart white church provided for a meaningful Black involvement in Christianity. And while their respective statuses within the American social structure were hardly analogous, their responses to the Black presence were not at all dissimilar.

Fortunately the African has a genius for religion that cannot be expunged.

Blacks seldom wait to be won over by a religion. They take the initiative and whenever they adopt a faith they make it peculiarly their own. They had known Islam and Christianity in their homelands, a fact overlooked by their new masters. But in their new situation both were given new life and style; both became visible signs of a distinctive community.

The memory of Islam, however tenuous, was never completely lost to the slave experience. The major Black Christian denominations were formed long before the Civil War, and though routinely denigrated by the white church, were a recognized part of the Christian community. If they were considered exotic, it was because they were Black—not because they were alien—a problem Islam could not and did not escape.

There was no room and no occasion for a "new" religion in the post-Civil War United States. The Black Church, split between Methodist and Baptist denominations, offered the newly emancipated Blacks the chance for self-respect in the form of religious self-determination, that is, the opportunity to belong—to be a part of an independent Black organization. Drawn by so heady and so novel an opportunity, and pushed by the white churches in which they had previously held a debased and segregated membership, the new Black Americans surged out of the white church and became proud members of "their own" Black churches—the African Methodist Episcopal Church, the Colored Methodist Episcopal Church, the National Baptist Convention, Inc., and so on. Through all this, there was a memory of Islam, but its time was not yet. It was to be another half-century before that memory would find vocal and physical expression among the hapless Blacks struggling for a negotiable identity and searching for their cultural roots.

In 1913 a Black "prophet" from North Carolina established a "Moorish Science Temple" in Newark, New Jersey.[11] Timothy Drew was not an educated man, but he had somehow learned enough about Islam to consider it the key to what would fifty years later be called "Black liberation." Islam was the religion of the Moors, the Black conquerors from Africa who once ruled much of Europe. How could anyone with such a heritage suffer the debasement which was the common lot of Blacks in America? Drew had no training in the social sciences but he did have the perception to realize that there is a very definite relationship between what you are called and how you are perceived, and between how you are perceived and how you are treated. "It is in the name," he concluded; the Black man's problems began with accepting a pejorative nomenclature. Drew, who was born in 1866 and given the Christian name of Timothy, now proceeded to give himself a name indicative of his "Moorish" heritage—Noble Drew Ali. His followers were no longer to be known as "Negroes" or "Africans" but as "Moorish-Americans," thus preserving their newly won American citizenship, but making explicit their Islamic heritage. Each "Moor" was issued an appropriate name and an identity card making clear his religion and political status in a society where "Negroes," however pronounced their Christian pretensions, were not generally held in high esteem.

Drew Ali's movement spread to Pittsburgh, Detroit, Chicago, and a number of cities in the South. Although it made use of what was known of the more romantic paraphernalia of Islam, including the Holy Qur'an, the wearing of fezzes, Muslim names, and the repudiation of certain fundamental Christian beliefs, Noble Drew Ali's movement was essentially a mélange of Black nationalism and Christian revivalism with an awkward, confused admixture of the teachings of the Prophet Muhammad. It was not Islam, but it was significant recovery of the awareness of Islam.

After a violent eruption within the administration of his Moorish Science Movement, Drew Ali died of mysterious causes in 1929. Thereafter the movement languished, splintered, and was succeeded by a more vigorous, imaginative, and demanding version of Islam led by Elijah Muhammad.

Elijah Muhammad was born Elijah Poole in Sanderville, Georgia on October 7, 1897.[12] One of thirteen children born to an itinerant Baptist preacher, Poole was destined to become one of the most controversial leaders of his time. But controversy aside, in terms of the impress he made on the world he must be reckoned one of the most remarkable men of the twentieth century. Among his more commonly recognized achievements were his enormous contributions to the dignity and self-esteem of the Black undercaste in America. Beyond that and with perhaps infinitely more far-reaching implications, Elijah Muhammad must be credited with the serious reintroduction of Islam to the United States in modern times, giving it the peculiar mystique, the appeal, and the respect without which it could not have penetrated the American bastion of Judeo-Christian democracy. If now, as it appears, the religion of Islam has a solid foothold and an indeterminate future in North America, it is Elijah Muhammad and Elijah Muhammad alone to whom initial credit must be given. After more than a hundred years, "orthodox" Islam in America had not titillated the imagination of the masses, white or Black, and was scarcely known to exist before the "Black Muslims"—Elijah's

Nation of Islam—proclaimed Elijah's "Message to the Black Man" in the name of Allah.

Elijah learned what he knew of Islam from a shadowy, mysterious evangelist who went by a variety of aliases, but who was most popularly known as Wali Farrad, or Wallace Fard. Fard claimed to have come from the Holy City of Mecca on a mission of redemption and restoration of the Black undercaste. He taught that the Black African diaspora were all of Muslim heritage, "lost-found members of the tribe of Shabazz." The essence of his message was that Black debasement had occurred over the centuries because Blacks were separated from the knowledge of Allah and the knowledge of self. They were estranged from the one true God to whom they owed allegiance and ignorant of their own history and their previous high status in the hierarchy of human valuation. The problem was to restore to the lost-found Nation the truth, the only truth that could make them free. This was the formidable task bequeathed to Elijah Muhammad, when after three years of instruction, Fard ostensibly returned to Mecca after designating Elijah, "Messenger of Allah."

In his own words, Elijah set out to "cut the cloak to fit the cloth." The complexity of his task was beyond imagination, for as Messenger of Allah he had committed himself to nothing less than the restoration of the most despised and brutalized segment of American Christianity back to a level of dignity and self-appreciation from which informed choices about religion could be made. His methods were sometimes ad hoc, and usually controversial, but they were always addressed to the realities of the situation rather than to an abstract theory whose relevance to his peculiar task had nowhere been demonstrated. Against him was a formidable array of forces, not the least of which were three hundred fifty years of solid Christian tradition in an avowedly, consciously Christian society. His initial "parish" was the slums of the Black ghettos of the industrial cities, and his potential converts were the slum-created outcasts of a developing technocratic society. His "people" were those who were most battered by racism and stifled by convention, and whose experience of the white man's "invincibility" made the acceptance of Black inferiority seem as reasonable as it was pervasive. The Black intellectuals would scorn him, and the white-appointed Black leaders would denounce him; the Christian church would repudiate him. But Elijah Muhammad was a man for the times. He was as dedicated as he was fearless; he was as imaginative as he was charismatic. He persisted in challenging the formidable phalanx of forces confronting him, and ultimately he prevailed. In the midst of his harassment by federal agents, local police, and others determined to silence him, he declared with characteristic boldness, "I am not trembling. I am the man. I am the Messenger . . . I am guided by God. I am in communication with God. . . . If God is not with me . . . protecting me, how can I come and say things no other man has said?"[13]

Muhammad drew freely upon the Bible, upon religious and secular mythology, and upon his own unique pedagogical constructs fashioned from experience. He met his converts where they were, ministering as far as he could to a spectrum of needs that transcended the spiritual to find their cruelest expression in more immediate exigencies, psychological, economic, social, and political. His "book" was the Qur'an, but that was not the only book he found useful. His "law" was the law of Islam, but he created his own supplement to fit the limited understanding of his followers. His "God" was Allah, but how does one portray the reality of Allah to a people whose total experience is washed in the pus of racial oppression? He cut his cloak from the cloth available. Elijah Muhammad did not achieve orthodoxy for the Nation of Islam, but orthodoxy was not his goal. What he did achieve was a pronounced American awareness of Islam, its power and its potential. Because of him, there were temples or mosques in a hundred cities where no mosques had existed before. There was a visible religious presence in the form of a hundred thousand Black Muslims—conspicuous in their frequent rallies and turnouts, and in their little groceries and restaurants and bakeries and other small businesses. The clean-shaven young Muslims hawking their newspapers on the street, celebrating their ritual in the prisons, debating their beliefs in the media, gave to the religion of Islam a projection and a prominence undreamed of in North America. Suddenly the prison warden, and the social workers, and the people who depended on Black labor were saying that the Nation of Islam had done a better job of rehabilitating the Black déclassé than all of the official agencies addressed to that task. And there was a general, if grudging, awareness in the Black community that the Black Muslims had done more to exemplify Black pride and Black dignity, and to foster group unity among the Black masses than any of the more reputable, integration-oriented civil rights organizations.

By the close of Elijah's seigniory, the Nation of Islam was no longer exclusively a community of the poor, the fallen, and the déclassé. With Malcolm X as its chief public representative, the Nation of Islam had attracted a good number of college students and a showcase element of intellectuals and professionals, including doctors, college professors, and former Christian ministers. An increasing number of celebrities in the world of sports and entertainment, clearly influenced by the Nation, became Muslims. However most of them joined more "orthodox" branches of Islam to avoid the stigma of belonging to an exclusively Black communion. A notable exception was Cassius Clay, who, after becoming the world champion of heavyweight boxing, adopted the Islamic name of Muhammad Ali.

Under Elijah Muhammad, the Nation of Islam became the prevailing Islamic presence in America. It was not *orthodox Islam*, but it was by all reasonable judgments, *proto-Islam;* and therein lies a religious significance that may well change the course of history in the West.

After shaping and guiding the Nation of Islam for more than forty years, the Honorable Elijah Muhammad died on February 25, 1975. Shortly thereafter the mantle of leadership devolved on Wallace Deen Muhammad, Elijah's fifth son. It was a progression rather than a succession of leadership, for Wallace Muhammad was destined to walk in his own way rather than in the tracks of his father. While he himself had no illusion and no anxieties about orthodoxy, Elijah Muhammad had promised his people that the day would come when they would fully understand their religion and its book, the Holy Qur'an, and when they would be universally recognized as full members of the worldwide Muslim community. The choice of Wallace Deen, (later to be known as Warith Deen Muhammad), to head the Nation after Elijah's death seems intended to implement that promise.

Immediately following his election as chief minister of the Nation of Islam, Wallace began the decultification of the following he had inherited from Elijah. His procedures were bold and forthright, but they were fraught with dangers of many kinds. A distinctive feature of the cult phenomenon is that the allegiance of followers is largely a response to the personal charisma of the leader, and charisma does not lend itself to transfer or succession. This does not mean that a new leader may not have charisma of his own, but it does mean that Wallace did not necessarily inherit his father's ability to obtain obedience and respect. That is why the characteristic cult seldom survives the death of its founder. In the cult phenomenon, few "successors" are able to hold intact the disparate forces controlled by a charismatic founder. Wallace was no exception. The transfer of power was neither complete nor intact, and while the widely predicted catastrophic implosion did not occur, there was dissatisfaction, disillusionment, and an inevitable erosion of membership. An undetermined segment of the Nation either drifted free from involvement, or elected to follow the independent movement of Minister Louis Farrakhan, who remains the most prominent exponent of the original teachings of Elijah Muhammad. For the millions of Blacks whose lot has been measurably improved by almost three decades of America's "new" racial policies, the romance of Elijah Muhammad's Nation of Islam still represents challenge and identity; and above all, it is a visible expression of the rage and hostility that still pervades the Black undercaste. To them, it is quite clear that the denied and the disinherited are still Black, the deniers and the disinheritors are still white, and Armageddon[14] remains inevitable. They see no compelling reason now to doubt Elijah, or to reinterpret his teachings.

Wallace's task as chief imam is ultimately ordered by the magnitude of his own ambitions. Now that he is confirmed in his leadership role it is conceivable that he could, if he chose, fashion for himself a comfortable spiritual suzerainty that would demand little more of him than the normative political housekeeping needed to keep him in power. The models for such are many and familiar and whatever its directions, the Nation of Islam was a going institution when Wallace Muhammad took it over. However Wallace has made it clear that his first priority of office is to completely eradicate the Black nationalist image of the erstwhile Nation by a dramatic reconstruction of its social and political understanding. The sweeping changes implied in this effort alone are enough to give pause to someone less determined, but for Wallace social reconstruction is only an obvious and necessary prelude to a much larger and even more formidable task. His ultimate goal is, of course, complete orthodoxy for the cult Elijah fathered and made internationally famous as the Nation of Islam.

Wallace Deen Muhammad is a dreamer, but he is a dreamer-cum-realist, and gentle, sensitive, and self-effacing. History may yet prove him to be one of the most astute religious leaders of this age, regardless of communion. A lifelong student of Islam, fluent in Arabic, and well-conversant with the nuances of Qur'anic ideology and its institutionalized projections, Wallace is no less a keen and perceptive observer of the American scene. Therein lies his potential for achievement and service of Islam. If he can bring the erstwhile Nation of Islam into fully recognized communion with orthodox Islam, he will have accomplished more for the propagation of that faith than any mujjaddid in modern times. The implications of such a feat are enormous, for they transcend at the outset the mere matter of ready-made corps of new adherents, although a hundred thousand or so new additions to any religion is in itself a signal achievement. But beyond mere statistics, the presence of a prominently visible, orthodox Muslim community in the United States would have political, social, and economic implications, which might in time reverberate far beyond the realm of the spirit.

Ironically, perhaps the most imponderable obstacle between orthodoxy and the Nation of Islam is not the opposition of the purist keepers-of-the-gate inside Islam, but the far more elusive and impalpable body of tradition that defines Black religion in general. Black religion derives, in the first instance, from that aspect of the Black experience that made it difficult to resolve the apparent incongruities between Christianity and Black slavery. It was not only a repudiation of the concept that slavery was acceptable to God, but has always been a critical medium through which the Black community has institutionalized its efforts to effect Black liberation. Inevitably this has meant a certain estrangement of the Black Church from Christian "orthodoxy" as understood and practiced by the white church. Hence, the salient tradition of Black religion has always been the sufficiency of its own insight.

Since practically all members of the Nation of Islam trace their religious origins to the Black Christian church, there is little reason to believe that the notion of "orthodoxy" holds for them any values of overwhelming significance. Further, since Islam is no stranger to the enslavement of Blacks, even in contemporary times, many of those who came to the faith via the Nation of Islam may well view Islamic orthodoxy as the Islamic counterpart of white Christianity—a possibility probably not overlooked in the careful strategies of Elijah Muhammad. Since Blacks have had more than sufficient reasons to question "orthodox" interpretations of any faith in the long travail that is the Black experience, they have learned to rely on feeling—the direct experience of the divine—rather than on the official formulas and prescriptions of the experts. Indeed the traditional Black answer to questions of orthodoxy has always been:

> If we ain't got it right
> Ain't it a mighty wonder
> De Spirit's over there
> Instead of over yonder?
> If this ain't true religion
> How come I got the feelin'

My soul done caught on fire
And left this world a'reelin'?

Certainly there is impressive evidence that Wallace Deen Muhammad has given such probems the most painstaking scrutiny before determining his own strategy for making Islam, in a relatively short period of time, the major religion in America after Christianity.[15] The catalogue of changes Wallace has accomplished in only five years of leadership tenure is already long and detailed. There have been changes of doctrine, changes of structure and administration, changes of name, style, role, and office. There were changes of official attitude about race, political involvement, and military service. High-ranking members of the ruling hierarchy were demoted or reassigned; financing of the movement's superstructure was redesigned and a strict accounting system introduced. The Fruit of Islam was disbanded. Key elements underpinning Elijah Muhammad's mythological doctrines were either allegorized, reinterpreted, or quietly abandoned altogether, and the "blue-eyed arch-enemy," that is, the "white devils," were rehabilitated and welcomed into the movement as brothers. The American flag is now displayed in every Muslim school, and the Pledge of Allegiance is made before morning prayers are offered. Still, the chief imam confesses with the candor of new revelation:

The former leader, the Honorable Elijah Muhammad, taught something that was un-American and un-Islamic. Now that I am leading the Community, following the Sunni (the way) of Prophet Muhammad, I find it now more difficult because it seems that many Americans liked it better when we were isolated—separated from the American people. Many that I thought would congratulate me, have not.[16]

In opting for corporate legitimacy for his Nation rather than for the personal emoluments traditionally available to such offices as his, Wallace was never far from the risk of losing everything. That risk was defused to some degree by the nature of his investiture. Although his name was presented for consideration by the surviving members of Elijah Muhammad's family, his appointment to office as Chief Minister of the Nation of Islam was given unanimous ratification by twenty thousand members of the Muslim Nation already assembled in Chicago for the annual celebration of Savior's Day. Once he assumed office, the chief imam immediately moved to disassociate himself and his office from the commercial interests so long a feature of the Nation of

Islam. This strategy not only removed his office from the possibility of conflict of interest, but it freed the new leader for the implementation of the grand vision that he had held since the days he headed the temple in Philadelphia in the late 1950s.

The "Islamization" of the Nation of Islam reached deeper and deeper. Ministers of Islam became "imams"; temples of Islam became "mosques," and later "masjid." Black people, believers and nonbelievers alike, were redesignated "Bilalians" in remembrance of Bilal Iban Rabah, friend and confidant of the Prophet Muhammad. The fast of Ramadan, traditionally celebrated in December under Elijah Muhammad, was rescheduled to coincide with the lunar calendar used by other Muslims throughout the world; and the Nation's official newspaper, "Muhammad Speaks," was renamed "The Bilalian News." The roles of women were upgraded, military service was no longer forbidden, and believers were urged to take an active part in the civil process. Malcolm X was rehabilitated and the Harlem mosque was renamed in his honor. In October 1976, the Nation itself changed names, becoming thereafter The World Community of Al-Islam in the West (WCI). Four years later the name would change again to The American Muslim Mission, "which," the imam explained, "speaks more to our aspirations and thrust."[17] During the same period the imam changed his own name from Wallace to "Warith" Deen Muhammad. He explained that this change was necessary because the man for whom he was named, Wallace Fard, had invested the name Wallace "with symbolism and mysticism," and that it had "an un-Islamic meaning."[18]

Finally, Imam Warith Deen Muhammad[19] made it clear that while most of the Mission's commercial holdings had been sold or placed in the hands of individual businessmen, the interest in the provision of economic opportunities for all who needed them was undiminished. This interest was made tangible in a dramatic development, which also exemplified the movement's new understanding of its civil responsibilities and opportunities. In February of 1979 the World Community of Islam signed a $22 million contract with the U.S. Department of Defense; the Muslims are teamed with Allen A. Cheng and Associates, a Chinese-American entrepreneur, and doing business as the American Pouch Food Company in the manufacture of an updated version of the C rations previously used by the military. The marketing potential of the new industry is estimated at more than $60 million annually.[20]

Although the leadership of Warith Deen Muhammad has been aggressive and far-reaching, it has also been low-key. The Muslims are no longer "news" in the sense they were when Elijah Muhammad and Malcolm X were the regular sources of newspaper headlines or television commentaries. This may well be a blessing in disguise. The energy crisis and America's chief political crises are all centered in areas of the world where Islam holds sway, and a more pronounced visibility of the growing Muslim presence in America might well drench the efforts of Warith Muhammad in a backwash of anti-Islamic sentiment. No one is more aware of this possibility than is the imam himself, and while he has not retreated from the principles of his faith, he has been diligent in showing himself and his movement to consist of reliable and responsible Americans, open and receptive to dialogue and cooperation with all who are receptive to them. In a book called *As the Light Shineth From the East*,[21] the imam attempts to spell out his position on the more controversial issues that nag at his leadership philosophy, or which otherwise threaten the rapprochement he wants between the American Muslim Mission and the diverse publics it wants to impress. Where Elijah advocated a separate Black nation, for example, Imam Warith declares: "I am a patriot of . . . the true blood of the Constitution of the United States."[22] "Now we are balancing (Elijah Muhammad's teachings) so we can develop an awareness in the children (of Islam) that they are not only members of a race but they are citizens —members of a nation—we want to grow in the full dimension of our country."[23] "My greatest desire for our community AMM is to . . . one day hear that a Muslim, a real Muslim, a genuine Muslim from our Community has become governor, or senator, or head of some big American corporation."[24] The imam is a vocal supporter of the Equal Rights Amendment, and his work with prisoners and ex-convicts earned him an invitation to address the American Congress of Corrections composed of prison administrators from all across the United States and Mexico.

Obviously the old Nation of Islam has come a long way under Warith D. Muhammad, but exactly how far is a very critical question yet to be determined. It is probable that those reforms designed to bring the movement into closer alignment with today's version of the American Dream will eventually be accorded the recognition and applause the imam has thus far found elusive. (He has already been honored with the Walter Reuther Humanities Award and he shares the Four Freedoms Award with such laureates as Eleanor Roosevelt and John F. Kennedy.) Nevertheless, considering the increasing polarities between East and West, there is no guarantee that the same reforms will not militate against the prize the imam wants most—unqualified recognition for the American Muslim Mission (AMM) as a legitimate segment of world Islam.

The signals from the East appear to be encouraging. Warith Muhammad enjoyed cordial relations with former Egyptian president Anwar Sadat (as did Elijah Muhammad with Sadat's predecessor, General Nasser). A more weighty significance, however, may be suggested by the fact that Warith was the only American observer invited to the Tenth Annual Islamic Conference of Ministers of Foreign Affairs (which met in Fez, Morocco); or in Warith's new role as a conduit for Islam's varied missionary enterprises in America. In 1978 a number of the oil-rich Persian Gulf states, including Saudi Arabia, Abu Dhabi, and Qatar named the American imam "sole consultant and trustee" for the recommendation and distribution of funds to all Muslim organizations engaged in the propagation of the faith in the United States.[25] A mosque estimated at $14–16 million is on the drawing board for the south side of Chicago, to be financed by contributions from the international community of Islam. About two million dollars have already been donated by just two donors, with an additional quarter-million given to the imam by one of them to be used directly for his educational budget.[26] Such largess is not without its hazards. Some established Muslim groups in the United States are unhappy about the attention the American Muslim Mission has received since Warith Deen assumed leadership, and in their pique they are quick to dismiss him as a propagator of (Elijah Muhammad's) "lies," and "no Muslim." Also, the risk that the American Muslim Mission will be seen to be manipulated by international politics is inescapable. Certainly here is no lack of potential manipulators, as Imam Muhammad must readily admit; but the potential for manipulation is the critical test of both the man and the movement. If either should falter, Islam will be the loser in America once again.

Notes

1. See Will Herberg, *Protestant-Catholic-Jew* (New York: Doubleday, 1955):274.

2. See the *Constitution of the United States of America.*

3. C. Eric Lincoln, "Americanity, the Third Force in American Pluralism," *Religious Education* 70, no. 5 (1975):485.

4. Martin Marty, *Righteous Empire: The Protestant Experience in America* (New York: Dial Press, 1970).

5. For a discussion of Spanish (Roman Catholic) precautions against the threat of the spread

of Islam among the American Indians through Black proselytization and intermarriage with Blacks, see Clyde-Ahmad Winters, "Afro-American Muslims from Slavery to Freedom," *Islamic Studies* 17, no. 4 (1978):187–90.

6. Ibid., 190–205.

7. Such a man was Ayuba Suleiman Abrahima Diallo of Annapolis, Maryland. Diallo, also known as Job ben Solomon, eventually gained his freedom after 1731 through British interests impressed by his knowledge and his strict observance of the Qur'an. Winters, 191. Kunte Kinte, Muslim protagonist in Alex Haley's celebrated *Roots* (New York: Doubleday, 1978).

8. The Society for the Propagation of the Gospel in Foreign Parts was the missionary arm of the Church of England. Originally organized in the interest of converting the Indians, the society turned its attention to the Blacks after the Indians repeatedly rejected the "white man's religion."

9. Cf. Cotton Mather, *The Negro Christianized, An Essay to Excite and Assist the Good Work, The Institution of Negro Servants in Christianity* (Boston: B. Green, 1706). Mather catalogs a long list of benefits, including divine approval, to be gained by bringing the Black to Christ, while refuting the popular arguments for excluding them from Christendom.

10. Betty Patchin Green, "The Alcades of California," *Aramco World Magazine* (November-December 1976):26–29.

11. For an account of the Moorish-Science Movement, see the following: Arthm II Fausett, *Black Gods of the Metropolis*, (Philadelphia: University of Pennsylvania Press, 1944); Arna Bontemps and Jack Conroy, *They Seek a City*, (Garden City, N.Y.: Doubleday, Doran, 1945); see also C. Eric Lincoln, *The Black Muslims in America*, 1st ed. (Boston: Beacon Press, 1961):51–55.

12. See C. Eric Lincoln, *The Black Muslims in America*, 1973 rev. ed. (Boston: Beacon Press, 1973) for a definitive study of the development of the Nation of Islam under the leadership of Elijah Muhammad and of the impact of the movement on American racial and religious practices.

13. *Mr. Muhammad Speaks*, May 1960.

14. Elijah Muhammad taught that "the Armageddon," a final clash between the forces of good (i.e., Blacks) and the forces of evil (i.e., whites), must take place "in the wilderness of North America" before the Black nation could be fully restored. See Lincoln, *Black Muslims in America*.

15. Such a projection assumes that since Judaism has only about six million adherents in the United States, it could be numerically eclipsed by a crusading Islam in relatively short order.

16. For an interview with Dirk Sager, correspondent for Station ZDF, German television: "Communicating for Survival." World Community of Islam (WCI) news release, December 27, 1979.

17. WCI news release, April 30, 1980.

18. WCI news release, April 2, 1980.

19. His official title was changed later to Leader and President of the World Council of Islam in the West.

20. *The Bilalian News*, February 16, 1979.

21. Warith D. Muhammad, *As the Light Shineth From the East* (Chicago: WDM Publishing Co., 1980).

22. "Communicating for Survival," December 27, 1979.

23. Ibid., September 29, 1979.

24. From a personal interview with Warith Deen Muhammad, April 9, 1980.

25. "Communicating for Survival," "Imam Warith Deen Muhammad, a Biographical Sketch," n.d.

26. From a personal interview with Warith Deen Muhammad, April 9, 1980.

Part Five

Mission and Ministry

Studies

Many scholars in religion believe that the true test of seminary education is the graduate's ability to demonstrate the coherence between research and reflection and practical knowledge for effective and faithful action in the world. Indeed the concern for interdisciplinary scholarship for the Black Church is most applicable in mission and ministry studies, where seminarians are expected to integrate all the departments of learning, secular as well as religious, into the development of a new professional identity as a practitioner and strategist of a liberating mission. The primary task of the ordained minister in this view is not learning how to "tune" a sermon after the fashion of illiterate Black preachers of the antebellum period, or mastering all the stock phrases and gesticulations that stir emotions and make Black folk "get happy." It is rather to "equip the saints" for their own individual and corporate ministries (Eph. 4:11–12); to prove in one's own life and thought the mystery of God's liberating and redemptive message incarnated in the mundane affairs of the parish; helping the congregation to discover how preaching and prayer, music and worship, pastoral care and counseling, church administration and Christian education, are all informed by biblical and theological knowledge in dialogue with the human sciences and directed toward the fundamental transformation of persons and institutions of the society.

The essays in this final section are more or less informed by this perspective. The first, chapter nineteen, is by Henry H. Mitchell, who inaugurated Black Church Studies at Colgate Rochester Divinity School in 1969. He is founder of the Martin Luther King, Jr., Fellows, Inc.,[1] and Visiting Professor of Homiletics at both the School of Theology at Virginia Union University in Richmond and at the Interdenominational Theological Center in Atlanta. Mitchell is one of the few African American teachers of preaching who has sought to articulate a theory that combines the old-time Black tradition with contemporary elocution. In this essay he addresses himself to the theological assumptions of such preaching.

One conspicuous development in the African American Church today is the increasing presence of women in the pulpit.[2] In chapter twenty, Cheryl J. Sanders, Assistant Professor of Ethics at Howard University Divinity School, reports on her study of sermons by Black women and men and in the process presents her own theory of the art of preaching in the African American Church. Although this comparative study is based upon a small sample, it suggests some significant differences between women and men's preaching that have been suspected on the grounds of other data. In any case, Sanders finds that "God speaks with a feminine voice and with a masculine voice," a conclusion that should help disabuse the Black Church of its traditional sexism.

Without music the Black Church ceases to exist. In recent years scholars have attempted to understand more thoroughly the affinities between African and African American worship styles, particularly the role of group singing and dancing in both secular and sacred contexts. In chapter twenty-one, ethnomusicologist Melva W. Costen uses cross-cultural analysis to describe the differences and similarities in "singing praise to God" based upon her study of 419 African American congregations. Costen is Helmar Nielsen Professor of Worship and Music at the Interdenominational Theological Center. She is a frequent consultant on hymnody and liturgics for the Presbyterian Church, U.S.A.

Chapter twenty-two shifts the discussion to the critically important field of Christian Education with an essay by Sid Smith, manager of the Black Church Development Section of Special Ministries for the Southern Baptist Convention in Nashville. The mission of the church school can be properly pursued only where the congregation itself stresses education for all age groups and provides a total spiritual and institutional context for transformative ministries. Smith finds such an environment at the New Shiloh Baptist Church of Baltimore, under the pastoral leadership of Harold A. Carter, a King Fellow of Colgate Rochester whose doctoral dissertation, *The Prayer Tradition of Black People* (Judson Press, 1976), should be well known to all seminarians. Sid Smith describes the famous Saturday Church School at New Shiloh as a highly commendable alternative to the traditional model.

A neglected area of African American Religious Studies is the field of pastoral counseling. Although Black psychologists and psychiatrists have increased our knowledge of the impact of racism and oppression upon the mental health of the African American community, very few of their insights have passed into pastoral care and counseling instruction in the seminaries and Bible colleges. Chapter twenty-three, by Edward P. Wimberly, is an attempt to view the counseling task from the perspective of the African American Church and its milieu. The author emphasizes the importance of empathy, experience, expectation and respect in the emotionally charged atmosphere of the Black congregation caught in the web of oppression and struggle. Edward P. Wimberly has taught pastoral counseling at the I.T.C. and Oral Roberts University. He is now on the faculty at Garrett Evangelical Theological Seminary in Evanston, Illinois. His most recent book, *Liberation and Human Wholeness* (Cokesbury Press, 1986) is coauthored with his wife, Ann Wimberly.

The last essay in this book, chapter twenty-four, deals with the African American Church and social action, an aspect of mission and ministry considered indispensable by the late Dr. Martin Luther King, Jr., and taken for granted as "a pantomime of the gospel" throughout the history of the African American Church. The author, William A. Jones, pastor of Bethany Baptist Church in Brooklyn and another member of the King Fellows, Inc., has been president of the Progressive National Baptist Convention and a leader in social, economic, and political movements in New York. In the best tradition of the Black pastor-scholar, this extract from his book, *God in the Ghetto* (Progressive Baptist Publishing House, 1979) articulates the social analysis which informs the present generation of Black preachers whose congregations are at the forefront of social and political action ministries. Such analysis draws from many disciplines and is expressed in the preaching and teaching which inspire and motivate such congregations. In this essay Jones contends that struggle is second nature to the African American Church, a struggle that leads ultimately not only to liberation, but to reconciliation between the oppressed and oppressors.

Notes

1. The Martin Luther King, Jr., Fellows, Inc., was founded in 1970 among a group of "master pastors" and their mentors who were recruited for a special Doctor of Ministry program at Colgate Rochester Divinity School. Most of their dissertations deal with the correlation of "academic" and "practical" disciplines in mission and ministry and have been published by Judson or their own M. L. King, Jr., Press.

2. For a sample, see Ella P. Mitchell, ed., *Those Preaching Women: Sermons by Black Women Preachers* (Valley Forge, Penn.: Judson Press, 1985).

19

Toward a Theology of Black Preaching

Henry H. Mitchell

Black preaching is conditioned by the sociology, economics, government, culture—the total ethos—of the Black ghetto. It is also affected by (and producing and changing) both a Black *summa theologica* and, in particular, a theology about itself. Much of this body of thought is unconscious and unformulated, but the process of analysis and writing has begun. Professor James H. Cone's writings are especially good cases in point. It is necessary and appropriate here to consider the theology of Black preaching. This can only be a beginning, but it is very important to state this theological basis.

The Black sermon is produced in a process which has already been clearly established as deeply involving the congregation. Black folk-theology of the people has always gone a step further and assumed that there was a third personal presence in the process, even the Holy Spirit. Black congregations have literally claimed the promise that "where two or three are gathered together in my name, there am I in the midst of them" (Matt. 18:20).

However stated, it has clearly been assumed that the sermon came from God. It has seldom been stated in terms of God as preacher, but the implication that God has been speaking has always been clear. In an age of secularization and emphasis on human effort, this sounds out of step and behind the times. It is necessary, therefore, to develop a theology of preaching which properly takes into account this advance in the thinking of Christendom.

This requires a collateral assumption about preparation which would appear to some as not typically Black. Men must *prepare* to preach. Many Black preachers seriously hold that specific preparation is contrary to the concept that sermons come from God. But other Black preachers (certainly those who bother to get professional training) hold that God acts only after man has done all that he can do by way of preparation. The category "man," in this case, includes the congregation. In unwitting support of the concept of man's crucial participation, many of the preachers most committed to Black culture will say, when the sermon goes hard, "Somebody isn't praying!" Thus the often unconscious assumption of Black preaching is that man brings to God his very best and asks him to take both preacher and congregation and make between them a sermon experience in which his word and will are proclaimed, with *power*.

This is not to get the least bit technical about *how* one carries out his prior effort. Be it outline, verbatim notes or just concentrated thought, prayer, and study about the text, *there must be some serious effort to give God one's best in preparation*. To do less is like asking God to do one's homework, or to go to the store and buy a loaf of bread! It should be clear in *any* theology, Black or otherwise, that God will surely not do for man what man can do for himself. This is the point of secularization in recent thought and it must be faced. The fact that man has control now of many things for which he once had to ask in prayer must be seen to apply to every field. One of these is the field of preaching. What the unschooled and charismatic Black preacher once was literally given from on high has now to be sought in part in the modern preacher's library. *Then* may he ask of God the finishing touches. He who asks God to do the entire task hath not heard the command to subdue all things (Gen. 1:28), or to go wash in the pool of Siloam (John 9:7), or to pick up his own bed and walk (Mark 2:9 and 11). In all of these God does his part *after* man has done his.

The question immediately arises: What of the spontaneity so universally accepted as Black culture's greatest trait? The riff or improvisation on the melody, so characteristic of the Black jazz instrumentalist or vocalist, is Black spontaneity at its best. The same freedom applied to the melodic line in Black gospels or religious soul music is the very trademark of Black culture. One Black intellectual, who is a popular lecturer in colleges and universities, has so embraced the concept of Black spontaneity as to make each lecture an example of his own thing, created in dialogue with the class on the spot. Is not this collateral assumption about preparation the very antithesis of Black spontaneity?

The answer from this same model of music is most obvious. No jazzman elaborates on the theme until he has mastered the theme, the instrument and the diatonic scale. When he does his thing, creating and playing "from the bottom of his soul," he has already practiced the basics for hours. To be sure, he is creating, Black fashion, and he is in a dialogue with his audience, which is comparable to the Black preaching dialogue. But the least informed Black jazz buff can feel the difference if the artist has not done his homework. So it is with the Black preacher. His hearers want what God gives him on the spot. But they also prefer that he be properly prepared to receive God's gift, and that he should have gotten some of it in advance. God does not give by direct revelation or inspiration what man can procure of God's gifts by his own study.

These generalities about preparation require at least some more specific word with reference to the format in which one brings his man-made part of the sermon. The traditional phrasing of the issue is the old controversy between those who use a verbatim manuscript and those who use an outline, of whatever complexity or detail.

The first comment has to be that God can speak to a man at his desk as well as in his pulpit. Therefore, although the end product is a dialogue with the congregation, the beginning may well be in a dialogue between the preacher and his God. This can produce both manuscripts and outlines. The old-school idea that only man speaks on the prepared paper was usually a dodge to rationalize the unlearned preachers' nonconcern with books and writing. That the very Bible itself was *written* by men inspired did not seem to trouble the anti-book people. The argument against manuscripts as quenching the spirit is further riddled by the fact that in the Black pulpit there is never any such thing as a verbatim manuscript. One may read every word, but the interpretation will still be different each reading. A substantial aspect of meaning has to do with *how* it is read. This amounts to an impromptu reinterpretation each time a given manuscript is read, a creation which is still the product of the preacher, the congregation, and the Holy Spirit.

The prominent preachers whose tapes I studied used manuscripts very well. But virtually all of them engaged in interludes of completely spontaneous elaborations or illustrations. On the whole these were very plainly more effective than the passages that were read. In addition to the increased rapport with the congregation, born of the restoration of visual contact and the increased freedom and flow, there was the apparent influence of these passages as coming more from the preacher's "soul." Whether the Black manuscript preacher uses a variety of reading interpretations or lengthy, spontaneous interpolations (most use both), the fact is obvious that God uses the manuscript method in some Black preachers to his own glorification.

My own bias is a somewhat more purist approach to the spontaneity so clear in Black religious tradition. This suggests that these excellent manuscript preachers would have been still more effective if they had established their original "batting stance" in the outline tradition. (On the other hand, it's not a good idea to change the batting stance of a .350 hitter, either.) To return to the parallel of the improvisation on themes in jazz and gospel songs, the outline is comparable to the establishment of the theme. The outline helps the Black preacher to integrate the gift that God has already given in the moment of illumination in the study with what God gives directly and through the congregation when the preacher proclaims the gospel from the pulpit. In theory, at least, this outline approach seems best to provide the environment for an authentic worship-happening. In fact God gives happenings to his Black preachers in spite of their manuscripts, and no theological construction can honestly oppose what so authentically comes from God.

Or do the best of Black sermons actually come from God? Again the single statement begets reservation. A further collateral assumption is required. Even though the Creator does speak through the medium of the Black sermon, the process is, in fact, the product of a partnership. This partnership involves not only the preparation mentioned but the goals and the entire message and impact. Whether it be styled to save and sanctify, to help and lift needy mankind, to praise God, or to hasten the very reign and kingdom of God, this means that the process of creation of the sermon is not exclusively God's.

God, who does not need anything men do, has clearly left it up to men to accept the creative partnership. If one man or all men refuse, Black theology holds that the rocks will cry out the message (Luke 19:40). But this concept of inevitable proclamation has no application to a unilateral creation of a gospel happening in our time. Rather it is directed to the end of human humility.

The creative aspect of a partnership between God and the preacher is vitally important. The hermeneutic principle clearly demands that preaching be more than fiery repetition of ancient shibboleths. No golden age of preaching to which men can look back was known at its inception to be golden. It was too fresh and disturbing. It was recognized as golden more often only in retrospect. The Black hermeneutic, at its best, will also be very strange and new. Just as the jazz riff or the gospel song improvisation on the melody will be a brand-new creation of the moment, so must the Black sermon be fresh and immediately relevant. It is the joint enterprise of a Creator who declares, "Behold, I make all things new" (Rev. 21:5) and a Black preacher who makes himself the instrument of innovation.

Yet newness does not imply Black uncertainty. The modern, white, middle-class tendency to be tentative in the interest of intellectual honesty and integrity is a luxury ill-afforded in the religion of the Black ghetto. To be sure, there are intellectual areas where honesty demands this. The question is simply whether or not the church needs to be concerned with such. The Black worshipper is seeking the answers to visceral questions on which his very life depends. The solution of abstract problems can wait. His questions are more pragmatic and immediate. He will have to bet his life on a decision tomorrow. How shall he take his risks?

"If the trumpet give an uncertain sound" (1 Cor. 14:7–9), he will only be confused. It is to be assumed that the Black preacher has had to take the same risks. What decision did he make and on what grounds? If the grounds were adequate for so momentous a risk, they are adequate to be proclaimed with certainty and not cautiously offered alongside some casual ideas he wouldn't think of betting his life on.

There are, of course, limits to the trumpet figure. The Black preacher is not an army officer ordering men to their death. Rather he is a crucial witness declaring how men ought to *live*. If he has no certainty about where to attack the infringements on his personhood, how may his hearers begin to know? But the Black church (and it is not alone) craves and demands that the trumpet be informed and, after having done all to be informed, *certain*.

This should not be construed as meaning that open-ended questions have no place in the Black Church. It simply means that such cannot be the main vehicle of meaning of the pulpit message. It means that, when uncertain issues which are anxiety-producing must be plumbed, their onus should fall on, or should be addressed to, a congregation prepared to grapple with them.

Preaching or proclamation is the functional arm of dogmatic theology. "Dogmatic" is here used, in the best sense of the word, to mean the certain presentation of today's truth in its proper setting inside the historical message and meaning of Christianity. This is not to be construed in reference to the stereotyped, hysterical, pulpit-pounding opposition against science, reason, and modern thought in general. Of this Gerhard Ebeling says:

> Yet it fails to realize its true obligation of presenting this man [modern secular intellectual], whom it regards as the enemy whom it is incapable of loving, with the testimony which would bring him the gift of cer-

tainty. Church proclamation of this sort is *de facto* propaganda against the church. . . . What is really needed is that we should find a way of witnessing to the Christian faith which is so convincingly simple and radical as to overcome problems raised by the tension between the letter and the spirit, or at least to show that they are secondary problems.[1]

The Black hermeneutic, Black preaching at its best, has done this very thing time and again. Giving the primary emphasis to the immediate needs of men and putting the intellectual questions in their secondary place, the message for *now* has been proclaimed. An excellent illustration is found in the sermon done some years ago at Bishop College[2] by Dr. Sandy F. Ray of Brooklyn, New York:

> This spirit to move out into new areas grips a man here and there. Not all, but one once in a while. Remember that thrilling story of the disciples caught in the storm. It involved a man of whom I am extremely fond. Jesus appeared and saw them out in this boat, distressed. The waters were lashing, and it was terribly dark. And they wished they had waited on Him (because they had left Him behind). And someone raised the question "I wonder where He is; we should never have left Him!" "But He told us to go and He would be on later." "But now we are caught! We are caught in the grip of a storm and *we* can't manage this little boat."
>
> And Jesus came, and the lightning flashed and somebody saw Him, and when they saw Him, they screamed, "Ghost! It's a ghost! It means that we are going to be destroyed!" And then the lightning flashed again, and Simon Peter saw Him, and they all thought, "It's a ghost."
>
> But just in the height of the fear, Jesus said, "Stop being afraid . . . it is I." And this daring man, with reckless faith, said, "Lord, if it be Thou, suffer me to come to you walking on the water." He said, "Come on." So Simon started to leave the boat, and the other men laid a restraining hand on him and said, "Don't be stupid. . . . Be practical! . . . You've been about lakes all of your life. Haven't you had enough?" But he said, "*Jesus* told me to come." But he said, "Listen, we *all* love Him, and we all know He has great power, but that's *water*, Simon, and *no* man has ever walked on water!" But he said, "That's the *Lord*." He said, "I know it's the Lord, but be *practical*." But Simon said, "When the Lord calls, sometimes you lose the sense of what is practical, and right now my faith has

become reckless and daring, and I'm going." And the records said, "He walked on the water!"

Oh, I know, I know you're going to say, "But he sank." . . . But he walked! . . . He walked on the water! And when he started from the boat, the laws of nature said, "Here comes a man walking, Lord, on the water; and you know that this is against the laws of gravitation; what shall we do?" He said, "With faith like this, you might suspend the natural laws, because we have to meet a faith like this with an unusual suspension of the law. And if he has the faith to walk . . . let him *walk!*" And the records said, "He walked on the water." Oh, I know you said he sank. . . . But he walked! But you say he didn't make it. . . . But he walked! He walked long enough for it to go in his obituary that he walked on the water. But he was walking toward someone who could rescue him when he sank.

Let us make man . . . make him daring . . . make him venturesome . . . make him fearless . . . for he isn't completed yet and his task is not completed. There is lots yet to be done that calls for courage and strength and a daring and reckless faith. We won't all get it . . . but we can create a climate in which one man will walk on the water. We won't all try something great . . . but we can create a climate of faith in God that once in a while a prophet can grow up. Let us make man . . . he isn't finished yet. . . .

Thus did a Black preacher inspire a host of Black college students to attempt the theretofore impossible. Thus did he, in typical Black idiom, select his text for its message and not its scientific complexities. A *certain* sound was uttered about a certain issue, and the secondary matters were relegated to their rightful place.

This example also raises the issue of hope, so essential to the gospel as it must be preached to enslaved people. *All* men need both hope and certainty, but none so much as those who have so little other than hope. As the areas in which Black people can take up cudgels for themselves expand, their desperate need for hope may appear to diminish. But they will never be in the position to be numerically and physically in control, or even guaranteed justice, save by the hope that is in their faith. The most effective blows for freedom will still come from men who, like Martin Luther King, Jr., believe in so hopeful a concept as the "cosmic companionship" preached to foot-weary walkers in Montgomery.

This is an excellent example of Black preaching as help from God. It shares in the goals of God. The Presbyterian Shorter Catechism holds that the chief end of man is to glorify God and to enjoy him forever. Black preaching does not deny this. It simply holds that no sermon glorifies God which avoids his plan to uplift man. Far from a secular, humanistic requirement, this stems from the admonition that when men see and receive the help of the preacher they will in fact glorify God the Father which is in heaven (Matt. 5:16).

Black preaching of the Reconstruction Era could be considered a tremendous success when it simply enabled Blacks to survive massive brutality and injustice. The church-aided organization of Black insurance companies and other businesses was virtually a stroke of genius. E. Franklin Frazier's *The Negro Church in America* describes the church's role in this crucial, Black Power-type thrust. The Black pulpit simply cannot coast on this golden age of the Black pulpit. It must give Blacks the insights and inspiration to survive *today's* social jungle, while, at the same time, arming them with the insights and inspiration to liberate themselves and eliminate oppression.

For instance, the Black preacher must keep the vivid imagery of the eagle stirring her nest (Deut. 32:11), so loved in the Black Church. But, faced with the generation gap in the ghetto family, he must emphasize the awesome wisdom of the eagle, who knows when to insist that the eaglet fly on his own. He must also give a certain sound advice about emerging young adults, so that Black parents will not be threatened by the loss of the one being in regard to whom they have exercised any real power. Men will indeed glorify God in response, for parents will see their problems as they have never seen them in secular terms. Youth too will be grateful for having the rites of passage eased by seeing themselves in a new relation to the eagle's nest.

Alongside this very personal kind of preaching help, the Black preacher must also give the certain sound that helps by mobilizing the Black Church as the largest and most stable of all Black Power bases. In summoning the sisters to boycotts which they can make more effective than anyone else can, the clear implications of Esther must be heard. They are indeed in the kingdom for such a time as this. And if they are scorned or even roughed up, what is this alongside Esther who said, "If I perish, I perish" (Esther 4:14–16)?

Texts like these are familiar and pregnant with potential for both the help of the congregation right here and now and for the great joy that comes from the fresh expression and application of familiar Bible stories and their heroes. Emotional reinforcement is given to the point of application by means of the tremendous satisfaction and fulfillment that accompany the proclamation of the gospel in Black spiritual power.

The sermon which celebrates without giving help is an opiate. The sermon which tries to help without celebration is, at least in the Black Church, ineffective. The climax is a necessity. But this is not to canonize a cultural habit. Rather, it is to theologize concerning this aspect of Black preaching.

Highly liturgical churches refer to their priests as "celebrating" the mass. (The actual history of this term would be interesting indeed.) It is not necessary to legitimize joy and celebration in worship. The fruit of the spirit is joy (Gal. 5:22). The baby of Pentecostal joy must not be thrown out with the bath water of public glossolalia, or speaking in tongues. In modern times the joy of Black worship has been self-validating to all save the most closed-minded. The "trip" sought by the drug culture has been recognized by more than one hippie as akin to the joy of Black worship.

What is this mass expression theologically? To say that Black worship succeeds in developing joy is not to say that it is automatically right. Just as the joy of the *spiritus sanctus* (Holy Spirit) was confused with the joy of *spiritus frumenti* (alcohol) in the eyes of the unbelieving in Acts 2, so is it possible to confuse spirits in the church today.

At its best, however, Black worship must have joy in its highest and purest form. At his best, the Black preacher must be not only a teacher and mobilizer, a father figure and an enabler, but also a celebrant. He must have a little of the joy *himself*. It must be clear that he is filled by the same joy he declares to his congregation. If indeed the preacher has not tasted and seen that it is good, he has nothing, really, to say. The goodness of God must not be a distant theory; it must be a present fact, which to experience is to celebrate. The same can be said of the goodness of the life which God gives.

To sense the presence and total acceptance of God, especially when one lives in an unaccepting, hostile world, is to know joy unspeakable. If this is literally true, how may one hold his peace? Even if one has white-oriented cultural inhibitions, if he has an open mind, how can he fail to participate in the joy of his fellow celebrants, be they laity or clergy? In their pilgrimage through the torture chamber of three hundred and fifty years of oppression, this celebration of the goodness of God and his acceptance of man has been the strongest nourishment available to Black people. It has reinforced and celebrated identity scorned everywhere else. Indeed, the Black Church itself has been made to think of its emotional freedom as a sign of primitiveness. Witness the fact that Blacks sober up and get "dignified" in most churches when they have white company. Fortunately this kind of overt self-rejection has never prevailed sufficiently to destroy the catharsis and healing of the shouting, celebrating Black Church. If Blacks, who have had the best reasons for self-destruction, have traditionally left suicide to the white American, the Black preacher had better not stop celebrating now! And those who do not know how to celebrate had better learn the art. In Black worship celebration, selfhood is validated, identity is reinforced, and the courage-to-be is renewed in the accepting, healing, uplifting presence of God. Since little else in the world can accomplish this for Blacks, there seems to be a valid argument for holding on to so vital a tradition.

To assert so much about the Black preacher's role in a day of diminishing faith is to suggest a Black tradition about the call of the minister which is not shared in the standard white church. While they insist, in white middle-class religion, on the conversational tone in preaching, they also insist on the preacher blending into the background of congregational lay conversers. Black preachers know better. If Jeremiah (Jer. 1:5) could be called before birth, so can they. And if Jeremiah's call could sustain him through unbelievable trials and rebuffs, it can for Black preachers also. And it has. In a day when the Black preacher has to play many roles and be a multitude of things to *all* men, and especially to Black men, it would be easier to escape the call for a less taxing responsibility were it not for the "fire shut up in my bones" (Jer. 20:9). The priesthood of all believers is a fact, but the burden of the priesthood still falls heavily on the Black preacher. Today's educated young Blacks would probably avoid it in larger numbers were it not for the fact that "woe is unto me if I preach not the gospel!" (1 Cor. 9:16) is still a powerful stimulus in the Black tradition.

These, in brief, are some of the theological assumptions which underlie Black preaching. To engage in the business of Black preaching without such undergirding is either to be wanting in sincerity or to labor without support. In either case, it is to attempt the impossible, and fail. Black preachers cannot afford merely to *seem* Black. If they have not the Black theological frame of reference, then they ought to preach from the frame of reference which they do have.

Notes

1. Gerhard Ebeling, *Theology and Proclamation*, trans. R. Gregor Smith (Philadelphia: Fortress Press, 1966):19.

2. Dallas, Texas.

20

The Woman as Preacher

Cheryl J. Sanders

Introduction

When the Reverend Suzan Johnson was installed in 1984 as pastor of Mariners' Temple Baptist Church in New York, a "first" for Black women within the American Baptist Church, *USA Today* reported the event with the comment that "Johnson hopes to bring the 'feminine voice' of God to her parishioners."[1] That quote echoes the central concern of this chapter—do we hear the feminine voice of God when women preach? If so, how does the feminine voice of God differ from the masculine voice of God? In other words, what are the distinctive characteristics of the preaching of women as compared with the preaching of men?

I have sought to answer these questions by conducting a comparative analysis if women's and men's sermons taken from three sermon anthologies: *Black Preaching: Select Sermons in the Presbyterian Tradition*, edited by Robert T. Newbold, Jr.; *Outstanding Black Sermons* by J. Alfred Smith, Sr.; and *Those Preachin' Women*, by Ella Pearson Mitchell. My sample includes thirty-six sermons: eighteen by women and eighteen by men. I have used all fourteen women's sermons in Mitchell's collection, three from Newbold, and the one sermon by a woman judged to be outstanding by Smith. The eighteen men's sermons have been selected at random from Newbold and Smith. For ease of comparison, I have only studied sermons preached within the Black tradition. However, a broad variety of denominations is represented within the sample, including Baptists, Presbyterians, United Methodists, the African Methodist Episcopal Church, the United Church of Christ, and several independent groups. Most of these preachers are pastors, but the sample also includes lay preachers, professors, and those who are employed by agencies or denominational headquarters. Because written sermons only lend themselves to analysis in terms of content, no attempt will be made here to compare women's and men's preaching on the basis of style or delivery.

The purpose of this analysis is not to promote stereotypes or caricatures of women preachers. In a recent article entitled "Black Women Preachers: A Literary View," Betty Overton addresses the question of the distinctiveness of Black women preachers from the rather negative vantage point of Black literature:

> Are black women preachers any different from their male counterparts? Probably not. What one does garner from the few women ministers in black literature is a half view, a view characterized by an attitude that women do not belong in the pulpit and that they earn their suffering and problems by their daring to take on this role. For the most part they are not admirable characters but stereotypes of the worst that is in religious ministry.[2]

Although Overton's conclusion that in real life Black women preachers are probably not different from their male counterparts is a reasonable one, her statement reminds us that negative stereotypes from literature or other sources can produce a biased "half view" of women's preaching. Indeed actual sermons preached by Black women constitute the best resource for a realistic examination of the question of the uniqueness of the feminine in the tradition of preaching.

Analytical Procedure

I have analyzed and compared sermons preached by women and men in terms of five key categories: (1) sermon form, (2) biblical texts, (3) central themes, (4) the use of inclusive language with reference to God and persons, and (5) homiletical tasks. First, I identified each sermon with one of four basic sermon forms: expository, narrative, textual, or topical. Next, I categorized the principal biblical text chosen by the preacher by literary type and by Testament. In cases where multiple texts were cited, the one text that appeared to have the greatest relevance to the central concerns of the sermon was singled out for analysis. The literary types include narrative, prophecy, or poetry for Old Testament texts, and narrative, prophecy (i.e., apocalyptic), or epistle for New Testament texts. I also noted whether or not the text chosen deals specifically with women. As a third step, I examined the content of each sermon in an effort to discern its central theme, which was often, but not always, conveyed by the title of the sermon. The fourth category I took into consideration was whether the preacher used inclusive language or exclusively masculine terms when referring to God or to persons. The fifth and final step was to take account of the range of homiletical tasks the sermon was designed to perform, that is, to ask what the preacher was trying to accomplish in and by the sermon.

Sermon Form

The four basic sermon forms applied in this analysis are described and illustrated by James Earl Massey, who concludes that the most popular and traditional sermon form is the *topical*: "This design highlights the truth or importance of a topic or theme, letting the logical points or facets of that topic control the sequence of treatment and timing of the application. The topic can be chosen from any one of a number of sources, but it is usually backed or supported by a related scriptural text."[3]

Ranking second in "popularity" is the *textual* sermon form, in which the sermon is designed to follow the divisions or sequences of thought in the scriptural text. Third, the *expositional* sermon form addresses an extended passage of Scripture, centering attention upon some one emphasis in that passage, "purposefully treating a teaching, an insight, a promise, a hope, a warning, a character, an experience, a meaning, a prophecy, a virtue, a key word, and so on."[4] For the purposes of this study, the expositional form is distinguished from the textual form based upon the length of the scriptural text and the manner in which it is treated; a textual sermon focuses attention on the message contained within a short passage of Scripture, while the exposition takes a more extended passage and draws from it some particular aspect or application. A fourth sermon form is the *narrative*, which treats some biblical story with particular concern for atmosphere, character, plot, tone, and movement.[5] Both in content and in form, the narrative sermon is centered upon the telling of a story.

There appears not to be much difference between women and men in the selection of sermon form. In accord with Massey's description of the topical form as the most popular among preachers, the majority of sermons preached by both the women and men in the sample followed the topical form. In fact, the proportions were identical; 67 percent (about two-thirds) of the women's sermons and 67 percent of the men's sermons were topical sermons. Second in popularity among the women was the narrative form; 22 percent of the women's sermons were narrative sermons. The remaining 11 percent of the women's sermons were in the textual form, and none of the women preached expository sermons. On the other hand, the one-third of the men's sermons that were not topical in form were evenly distributed among the three other types—11 percent were narrative, 11 percent textual, and 11 percent expository.

Biblical Texts

The women and men in the sample appeared to be more alike than different in the selection of biblical texts for their sermons. Thirty-nine percent of the women preached from the Old Testament, and 61 percent from the New Testament, whereas 44 percent of the men preached from the Old Testament, and 56 percent from the New Testament. In terms of actual numbers, only one more of the women's sermons was preached from the New Testament than was preached from the New Testament by the men. There was more variation between women and men in terms of literary type. Forty-four percent of the women preached from narrative texts, in comparison with 61 percent of the men. The second most favored literary type among the women preachers was the epistle, and 33 percent of their sermon texts were taken from the epistles, primarily of Paul. By contrast, only 11 percent of the men took texts from the epistles. Seventeen percent of the women's sermons were preached from biblical prophecy, and an identical proportion of the men preached from prophetic texts. The Psalms and Proverbs were used as texts for only 5 percent of the women's sermons and 11 percent of the men's sermons, representing one and two sermons, respectively. Only two of the men's sermons (11 percent) and three of the women's sermons (5 percent) were based upon texts that made specific reference to women.

Sermon Themes

An effort was made to organize the central themes of these sermons into several general categories. Three themes were common to the preaching of both women and men: the church and its mission, Christian virtues, and racial identity. Twice as many men (six) as women (three) preached on the church and its mission, four of the women's sermons and three of the men's were preached on Christian virtues, and equal numbers of women and men (three each) chose racial identity as a central sermon theme. However no one theme was the dominant choice of women or men. The most popular theme, the church and its mission, was chosen by only 25 percent of all the preachers. The second most widely used theme, Christian virtues, was actually preached by 19 percent of the preachers. Only 17 percent of the women and men preached on the racial identity theme.

Three sermon themes peculiar to the women's preaching included survival, healing, and ministry. Two themes, preaching and the nature of God and/or Christ, were exclusively preached by men.

Inclusive Language for God and Persons

The fourth analytical category applied to the sermon sample was the use of inclusive language. As might be expected, the men were far more likely than the women to use words like *he*, *his*, and *father* with reference to God, and to speak of people in general as man or mankind in their sermons. In fact, the majority of the women and a minority of the men used inclusive language in both cases. Twice as many women as men referred to persons using inclusive terms; 89 percent of the women as compared with 44 percent of the men. With reference to God, 61 percent of the women consistently used other than masculine terms, in comparison with 39 percent of the men.

Homiletical Tasks

Homiletics is the art of preaching as a subject of theological study. Etymologically speaking, the term *homiletics* translates from the Greek as the "art of conversing" or "a conversation with the crowd."[6] Thus the expression "homiletical tasks," as used here, connotes the particular functions and objectives the preacher undertakes in the course of carrying on a conversation with the crowd. The homiletical tasks represent what the sermon has been designed to accomplish, which is perhaps the single most critical dimension of preaching.

I have identified seventeen homiletical tasks that the preachers in the sample have undertaken in their sermons. They are: (1) affirming; (2) celebrating; (3) criticizing the church; (4) criticizing the society; (5) exegeting Scripture; (6) exhorting; (7) interpreting Scripture; (8) inviting the hearers to Christian commitment; (9) observing a liturgical event; (10) proclaiming an eschatological vision; (11) quoting lyrics of hymns; (12) quoting lyrics of Negro spirituals; (13) quoting poetry or drama; (14) story-telling; (15) teaching; (16) testifying; (17) translating Scripture into the vernacular. It is possible that this list omits some homiletical tasks that would be germane to other types of sermons and preaching traditions. However, my intention has been to account for the specific homiletical tasks undertaken in the sermons selected for the present analysis. Each of the seventeen homiletical tasks will be defined and illustrated with examples taken from the eighteen women's sermons. I will use my discussion of these homiletical tasks as an opportunity to provide a sampling of the power and beauty and diversity of Black women's preaching.

Affirming. Affirming is the task of speaking in positive, encouraging terms to an individual or group, usually with reference to a declaration of belief or commitment in solidarity with others. This homiletical task can also be understood to mean affirmation of the promises of God as appropriated from Scripture and applied to personal experience. Here is an example found in "Beyond Ourselves," a sermon preached by Barbara Campbell to the members of Pioneer Church, a small, struggling congregation:

> I think Pioneer Church has a proving ground right here in this community. You have already made a good start in extending yourselves beyond the boundaries of your church. You are already in the field, helping those in your community to help themselves no matter what faith they may be.
>
> I say to you that progress is often slow and the race is not always won by the swift, but by the diligent. I marvel in your desire to minister to your community. I ask God to give you renewed vigor when you are tired, so that you will continue to go forward. I feel confident that you dedicated Christians will not let Pioneer Church die.[7]

Celebrating. Celebrating is the task of calling attention to the joy of worshiping and praising God. Mary Ann Bellinger incorporates celebration and praise into her sermon "Upright but *Not* Uptight," which deals with the healing of the woman who suffered from a spirit of infirmity:

> I entitled my sermon "Upright but *Not* Uptight," because all too often when we "get religion," we figure that no one else has it like we do. We become so goody-goody that we can't praise God. And if by chance we do praise God, we want to make sure the right people are there so they can see how holy we are!

Look at this woman once again. When Jesus called her, she went forward and received healing. When she was healed, she didn't hold onto her joy selfishly but immediately began to minister to those around her in the synagogue. Praise God! She sang! Praise God! She encouraged! What did you do when God did something in your life?[8]

Criticizing the Church. This is the task of pointing out the problems and shortcomings of a particular body of Christians, or of the church at large. Deborah McGill-Jackson offers such a critique in her sermon "To Set at Liberty," based upon Luke's account of how Jesus read and interpreted the prophecy of Isaiah in the synagogue at Nazareth: "We in the church cannot afford to reject the gospel that convicts us in our comfort. The church must loosen the shackles by which it is bound—the shackles of tradition, the irons of prejudice, the bars of isolation and suburban escapism—lest church people and their ecclesiastical palaces deteriorate in their own captivity, which is due to the sin of alienation."[9]

Criticizing the Society. This is the task of pointing out the problems and shortcomings of the society, and especially the unjust social structures and systems. In her sermon "Jesus Christ, the Same Yesterday, Today—Forever," Thelma Davidson Adair compares the problem of the oppression of women with the fight for civil rights and the abolition of slavery:

Many women of the Third World spend their lives in the fields, suffer malnutrition and cruel treatment, and have no access to education. The concerns of women in the United States and in the Third World are massively different, but the underlying thrust is the same. It is the quest for fulfillment, the recognition of personhood, and a consistent wish for self-development. . . .

Our church must constantly seek to support this thrust. The church must again, as it did during the fight for civil rights, actively seek the disorder, the drastic social change which some social scientists predict will come from restructuring our society. Some Americans feared the social chaos which they were certain would follow the disruption of a highly profitable societal and economic slave structure. But with Jesus as the stabilizer, the constant in the changing world, the institution of slavery was overthrown. Today we rejoice in that event. With regard to women's rights, not just in the Western world, but around the globe, we will rejoice to see women free at last.[10]

Exegeting Scripture. To exegete Scripture is to perform a critical analysis or examination of the text. Although exegesis normally connotes interpretation, in the present investigation interpretation is treated as a separate homiletical task in itself. Thus, for our purposes, the exegetical task is understood to be the analysis and examination of Scripture in an effort to present the text in its proper historical and literary context. Ellen Sandimanie offers a brief exegesis of 1 Cor. 4:2, the text of her sermon "On Being Faithful Stewards":

> Paul's letter to the church at Corinth was written for the purpose of correcting disorders that had arisen in the church and setting before the early Christians a standard of Christian conduct.
>
> The theme of this epistle is "Christian Conduct" in relation to the church, the home, and the world. . . .
>
> Paul had completed his formal warnings against the parties in the church at Corinth. Now he turns to the responsibilities of those who are to teach. They are servants of Christ, not subject to the whims of anyone.[11]

Exhorting. To exhort is to admonish the hearers to act or to exhibit some virtue. The task of exhorting differs from the task of affirming. Exhortation challenges while affirmation congratulates, and it carries an implicit critique that is absent from the affirming statement. Katie Cannon concludes her sermon "On Remembering Who We Are" by challenging the hearers to identify with the biblical character Hagar and to do what the sermon title suggests:

> If we know of a sister or a brother—wandering around lost unto herself or himself—who doesn't know which way to turn or where to go, who is bent on self-destruction and cut off from the joy of living because she or he has been cast out into the wilderness of life, then let us open ourselves to the Spirit of God so that we can help provide the spiritual water that that sister or brother needs to come back home. Let us open ourselves to the grace of God and share the many blessings that God has bestowed upon us. . . .
>
> In closing I challenge you to go forth remembering who you are. You are persons created in God's own image. You are sisters of Hagar. And, when in doubt, simply recall the word *WHO*—*W* for willingness, *H* for humility and *O* for openmindedness—and the God that

we serve, the true and living God, has promised to hear your prayers. Amen.[12]

Interpreting Scripture. To interpret Scripture is to expound the significance of a particular text with an emphasis upon application. Occasionally a preacher will interpret or apply Scripture without providing an exegetical basis for analyzing or understanding it. Marjorie Leeper Booker interprets and applies her text, Phil. 2:5–9, as "A Prescription For Humility," the title of her sermon:

> We have discussed the three ingredients that are required for true humility as set forth by Jesus Christ: the emptying of self, humility, and true obedience. Paul set forth these virtues, which Jesus had portrayed in his saving act. With this prescription one can acquire the mind of Christ.
>
> How will the mind of Christ benefit us? With the mind of Christ we will be able to live the life we talk about. We will be able to overcome the temptation to glorify and gratify ourselves. We will be able to hear the cries of the needy and the deprived and be sensitive to their needs. We will be able to deny ourselves and put the interest of others before our own. We will be able to pick up our crosses daily and follow Christ. We will be able to obey God and do God's will, saying, like Jesus, "Not my will but thine be done." With the mind of Christ, we will be able to rise up and speak out against injustice, wherever and whenever it may be found. With the mind of Christ we will be able to look at all God's children as sisters and brothers in Christ. We will be able to play together, grow together, live together, love together, and serve God together.[13]

Inviting Hearers to Christian Commitment. The invitation to Christian commitment is an appeal to the hearers to accept Jesus Christ as Savior and Lord. Typically it is presented at the conclusion of the sermon and designed to lead into an altar call. The task of invitation differs from exhortation in its sense of urgency; it is an exhortation to immediate response and action. Peggy Scott offers an invitation at the close of a sermon that is directed specifically to foster children and parents. This invitation calls the hearers to inner healing as a prerequisite to effective Christian commitment. Five steps to inner healing are outlined in her sermon, "God Has a Master Plan for Your Life":

> God has a master plan for our lives. If we, children or adults, are to become effective Christians, we must receive an inner healing for all our hurts, pains, resentments, feelings of rejection, and other negative emo-

tions. God wants to heal us; God cares about us. We can be healed today and begin to realize that God has a plan for us. But how can we be healed?

There are five steps in receiving inner healing. (1) *Believe and confess*— "If thou shalt confess with thy mouth the Lord Jesus, and shalt believe in thine heart that God has raised him from the dead, thou shalt be saved" (Romans 10:9). (2) *Acknowledge that you are a new creature*—"Therefore, if any man be in Christ, he is a new creature: old things are passed away; behold, all things are become new" (2 Corinthians 5:17). (3) *Acknowledge that your name is in heaven*—". . . but rather rejoice, because your names are written in heaven" (Luke 10:20). (4) *Acknowledge God as your true mother and father*—"When my father and mother forsake me, then the LORD will take me up (as his own)" (Psalm 27:10). (5) *Forgive*—". . . forgive, and ye shall be forgiven. . . . Love ye your enemies, and do good, and lend, hoping for nothing again; and your reward shall be great, and ye shall be the children of the Highest" (Luke 6:37, 35).

Accept your family's circumstances; do not let them interfere with your relationship to God and with your spiritual growth. It is not so much what has happened to you as how you react to what has happened that matters.

If your situation is too painful, too much of a burden, too heavy a load to carry, then ask for forgiveness, and yield to Jesus. Allow the love of Jesus and the indwelling of the Holy Spirit to heal you today. "King Jesus will roll all burdens away."[14]

Observing a Liturgical Event. This task involves citing the significance of a special liturgical event, such as the Lord's Supper or Pentecost Sunday. The sermon theme and texts are directly related to the occasion. Nan Brown's sermon, "The Mind of the Insecure," highlights the significance of Advent: "When Herod sent the wise men to Bethlehem to search diligently for the Christ child, he had no thought of worshiping him. Herod was intent on murdering him. I trust that in the Advent season we all remember whose birthday we are celebrating and give gifts to him who deserves them, worshipping him who gave us life."[15]

Proclaiming an Eschatological Vision. An eschatological vision is one that looks to the ultimate or last things. As a homiletical task, to proclaim an eschatological vision is to announce what the future holds in an ultimate sense, usually with reference to heaven or to some notion of the reign of God. The eschatological vision proclaimed by Effie Clark in her sermon, "How a People Make History," is a vision of Black nationalism. She quotes the militant imagery of Margaret Walker's poem, "For My People," to illustrate this vision: "Let a new earth rise. Let another world be born. Let a bloody peace be written in the sky. Let a second generation full of courage issue forth; let a people loving freedom come to growth. Let a beauty full of healing and a strength of final clenching be the pulsing in our spirits and our blood. Let the martial songs be written, let the dirges disappear. Let a race of men now rise and take control."[16]

Quoting Lyrics of Hymns. Preachers sometimes quote the lyrics of hymns in order to create a certain effect or to convey a particular mood in keeping with the sermon's message. Usually the hymn is familiar to the hearers, as is sometimes the hymn writer. These lyrics may function as authoritative sources or summaries of sermon content. Clara Mills-Morton quotes a hymn to dramatize an important point in her sermon "The Blessings and Burdens of the Divinely Chosen":

> The preacher preaches, and souls are saved. The teacher teaches, and learning and growth take place. The philanthropist gives resources, and vital improvements are made possible. The physician administers the proper care and treatment, and healing occurs. Yet they all realize that their resources are given by God and that the results are made possible because of the blessings of God. Beatrice Brown expressed this with tremendous clarity when she wrote, "Without God, I can do nothing; without God I would fail; without God my life would be rugged, like a ship without a sail."[17]

Quoting Lyrics of Negro Spirituals. The lyrics of the so-called "Negro spirituals" are sometimes quoted to illustrate and reinforce sermon themes. These songs serve as a repository of the sacred history and tradition of Christians who suffered as slaves in the United States. In a sermon entitled "Singing the Lord's Song," Yvonne Delk quotes spirituals to illustrate her central theme and text (Psalm 137) with reference to the Black experience of slavery and injustice:

> Black people know about singing God's song in a strange and foreign land because Black Americans' spirituality was born in the context of the

struggle for justice. We sang our songs on boats called *Jesus* that brought us to America. We sang our songs on auction blocks—"Over my head I hear music in the air; there must be a God somewhere." We sang our songs on plantations—"Walk together children, don't you get weary; there is a camp meeting in the promised land."[18]

Quoting Poetry or Drama. Some sermons make use of quotations from the works of great poets and playwrights that capture the essence of the thought being communicated. Carolyn Ann Knight begins her sermon "The Survival of the Unfit" by expounding upon a familiar quotation from the play *Hamlet* by William Shakespeare:

> "To be or not to be, that is the question." What was an existential question for Shakespeare's Hamlet as he stood at the crossroads of his life is, for us today, an ontological question as well. Hamlet's plight of survival is a universal one. In a society that is disgruntled by the contrary winds of desolation and degradation, in a world that is scorched by the burning suns of trials and pestilence, in a civilization that is bombarded by the falling rocks of mutilated humanity, we too must grapple with the question "to be or not to be." With each new day that dawns, we stand on the brink of nonexistence.[19]

Story-Telling. The story-telling task has rich biblical antecedents, most notably in the gospels where Jesus tells stories in the course of preaching and teaching. In many sermons, and especially in the sermons that follow the narrative form, stories from the Bible or from human experience are told to make the sermon's message "come alive." Laura Sinclair offers an exciting rendition of the familiar story of Ezekiel in the valley of dry bones in her sermon "Can Your Bones Live?":

> Ezekiel was in a valley that had nothing but dry bones all around. An arm here, a leg there, just dry bones everywhere. God looked at these bones and asked Ezekiel, "Can these bones live?" Now I'm sure that Ezekiel wanted to say no, for he knew how these bones became dry. He knew that their dryness was an indictment on Israel for specific sins that the nation had committed. These sins included cultic abuse, such as profaning of the sabbath, and ethical crimes, such as bloodshed, adultery, extortion, dishonor of parents, and the violation of the rights of orphans, widows, and sojourners. But Ezekiel also knew that the God he

served was merciful and compassionate and that anything was possible with God. So he said, "O Lord, thou knowest." And sure enough, the mercy and compassion of God came forth. God told Ezekiel to preach to the bones, to tell them to hear the word of the Lord, and he, God, would cause them to live.

Ezekiel was obedient to God, and he preached to the bones. He saw something happen that I am sure astounded him. Many times the Lord will give his servant a directive, and the servant will look at it and say, "I'll do it, but I know that it will only be an exercise because I know that nothing will happen."

Well, to Ezekiel's surprise, as he preached, he heard noise and saw the bones shaking; he saw them coming together. He saw toe bones connected to foot bones, foot bones connected to ankle bones, ankle bones connected to leg bones, leg bones connected to knee bones, knee bones connected to thigh bones, thigh bones connected to hip bones, hip bones connected to back bones, back bones connected to chest bones, chest bones connected to shoulder bones, shoulder bones connected to arm bones, arm bones connected to hand bones, back bones connected to neck bones, neck bones connected to head bones. All the bones were connected. He saw sinews come upon them, and he saw skin cover them. But they were not breathing; they still were not living.

I'm sure Ezekiel must have looked up to God in puzzlement. But God didn't keep him puzzled for long. God told Ezekiel to preach to the wind, and he did. Ezekiel told the four winds to breathe upon the bones so that they might live. And as he preached, the breath came into those dry bones that had come together and been covered with sinew, and men stood upon their feet as a great army.[20]

Teaching. As a homiletical task, to teach is to set forth a structured presentation of information within the sermon. Typically three points of information are offered, but the actual number of points is less important than the quantity and quality of content being conveyed. In her sermon "Our Spiritual Account," Margrie Lewter-Simmons presents her teaching on the subject of spiritual self-examination in four points, as summarized here:

(1) Let's look at some methods of bookkeeping that might help with the audit of our lives. Look over your records. Turn your pages in the ledger of life back to a year ago. Have you hurt anybody? . . .

(2) Still another category in good bookkeeping is found in Matthew 5, where Jesus speaks of a selected audit. Blessed are the meek. Have you been meek or have you been running off at the mouth, bragging and offending people? Blessed are the peacemakers. Did you keep the peace or disturb the peace? Blessed are you when you shall be "buked and scorned," reviled and persecuted, talked about and yet unwilling to fight back. These things happened for the Lord's sake. Blessed. Blessed—your books are in good shape.

(3) One other means of adjusting your spiritual account can be found in Paul's letter to the Galatians, chapter 5. There he talks about a special kind of bookkeeping he called the "fruit system." If you go through the books and see what has been produced, then you get your account settled and straight with a good running balance. . . .

(4) One final concept is your *balance*, the previous balance. Peter said that if you come to the end of the record year and you have less than the previous year, you're in big trouble. "But grow in grace and in the knowledge of our Lord and Saviour Jesus Christ" (2 Peter 3:18). So, however good your balance sheet looks, if you haven't grown in grace, if you haven't grown in the joy of the Spirit, if you haven't grown in your capacity to forgive, if your faith cannot be measured as being deeper and more abiding than before, then you're in serious trouble. You're in deficit.[21]

Testifying. The task of testifying offers a personal word of witness to the self-disclosure of God, usually with reference to conversion. Here testifying is distinguished from story-telling in that it is based strictly upon personal experience. Sharon Williams incorporates personal testimony into the dramatic climax of her sermon "Studying War Some More," which is based on Paul's description of the weapons of spiritual warfare in Eph. 6:

You see, Jesus puts out this fantastic helmet. It took him three whole days to make it up just for me. He began forging the metal one Friday in the scorching noonday sun. And he didn't finish it until Sunday morning in the cool darkness of a rich man's tomb. When the stone was rolled away, out came Jesus, carrying my helmet of salvation. . . .

And while Jesus was working on my helmet, he fashioned a sword, which he called the Holy Ghost. He didn't issue it with the helmet. That sword came special delivery to a crowded upper room some fifty days later. The sword came just as he had promised. I can't go to war without my sword.

And I can't go to war without the Word. I've got my Bible, and I've got my helmet. I've got some faith, and my new shoes feel good on my feet. My breastplate is strapped on and my loins are girded round about.
I'm waging war by forgiving all enemies.
I'm waging war by practicing gentleness.
I'm waging war by giving up jealousy and backbiting.
I'm waging war by walking in a meek and lowly way.
I'm waging war by telling the truth, even when I am threatened by violent liars.
I'm waging war by bringing peace.
I'm waging war by feeding the hungry.
I'm waging war by supplying the poor with what they need.
I'm waging war by healing the sick.
I'm waging war by having patience and reconciliation.
I'm waging war by having a contrite and broken spirit.
I'm waging war by a will surrendered to God.
I'm waging war.[22]

Beverly Shamana offers a more pensive testimony in her sermon, "Letting Go," as she reflects upon the disappointment of failing to receive what she felt God had promised:

Like many of you, I've gone through surgery. What an ordeal! Yet even after the bright prognosis and a clean bill of health, I felt a great sense of "But you promised": My body should have worked. My arm, my liver, my kidney, my uterus—it should have worked, according to the medical journals and books. And if not, why couldn't I go to a doctor and get it fixed? To remove it was so final. Now it will never work because it's gone. Anger. Guilt. Blame. Sadness. And finally, goodbye. What a long journey it was from a tight-fisted grudge match to an open hand! What an arduous journey it was from the former things to the new thing!

God indeed created something new. I've developed greater appreciation for these bones, this skin, this muscle, this chamber that I now have. I've found that I can even soar to new heights. For one thing, my body is lighter! I have surrendered the excess baggage of weight.[23]

Translating Scripture into the Vernacular. In general the term *vernacular* refers to the standard language of a particular locality. The task of translating Scripture into the vernacular means making use of idiom, jargon, and/or slang, to convey the meaning of biblical texts and ideas in terms that would be familiar to a particular audience. An example of this task is found in a sermon by Suzan Johnson entitled "God's Woman," based upon the story of Esther:

> Now, in our story the Persian king was looking for a new wife to replace Queen Vashti, whom he had cut loose because she refused to dance nude in front of him and his friends. So he sent a search team to look throughout all the land for a new queen. I imagine that as all the women gathered, the scene was something like the Miss America pageant that we see today—the most "beautiful" women on parade. And of all the women that the king saw, the one he chose as his new wife was Esther, this Jew who was living in Persia.[24]

Results. I have evaluated the entire sample of thirty-six sermons preached by women and men with regard to the seventeen homiletical tasks, although all the examples cited here were drawn from the women's sermons. The task analysis highlights some interesting distinctions between women's and men's preaching. The typical woman's sermon involved an average of seven homiletical tasks, listed here in order of frequency of occurrence: (1) interpreting Scripture, which was done in 100 percent of the women's sermons; (2) exhorting, 78 percent; (3) exegeting, 72 percent; (4) teaching, 67 percent; (5) affirming, 56 percent; (6) story-telling, 50 percent; and (7) testimony, 44 percent. The typical man's sermon encompassed an average of six homiletical tasks: (1) interpreting Scripture, 89 percent; (2) teaching, 78 percent; (3) criticizing the society, 61 percent; (4) exhorting, 56 percent; (5) affirming, 44 percent; and (6) exegeting, 39 percent. Judging by frequency of occurrence alone, it is clear that the single most important homiletical task in the preaching of both women and men is the interpretation of Scripture. Other tasks that are important to both groups, listed in descending order of frequency, include teaching, exhorting, exegeting, and affirming. Thus, based upon a comparison of women's and men's sermons in terms of those homiletical tasks deemed most important by both groups, we can conclude that, in general, women and men seek to accomplish the same things in their preaching.

However it would be appropriate at this juncture to ask whether these results signify even a slight distinctiveness in women's preaching. When the typical woman's sermon, comprising seven homiletical tasks, and the typical man's sermon, comprising six such tasks, are compared, several subtle distinctions emerge. First, the difference in the average number of tasks can be seen as an indication that the women sought to accomplish a greater variety of tasks than the men did in their preaching. Next, it appears that story-telling and testifying were generally more important to the women preachers than to the men, while criticizing the society seemed more important to the men than to the women. This is not to suggest that women's preaching is all story-telling and testimony while men's preaching is all social criticism. The point is that more men (61 percent) criticized the society than women (39 percent), and more women (50 percent) told stories as a key component of their sermons than men (33 percent). Testifying was the one homiletical task which showed the greatest discrepancy between men and women; only one man out of eighteen offered personal testimony in his sermon, yet eight out of eighteen women did so in theirs.

This last finding suggests that it might be useful to compare women's and men's preaching based upon those homiletical tasks that occurred with the least degree of frequency. There were four homiletical tasks that appeared less than 20 percent of the time in the women's sermons: only 11 percent of the women criticized the church, while 17 percent engaged in the tasks of celebrating, quoting poetry or drama, or observing a liturgical event. A somewhat different set of four homiletical tasks was of least importance in the men's sermons: only 5 percent of the men included testifying, inviting the hearers to Christian commitment, or observing a liturgical event in their preaching, and 11 percent gave attention to celebrating. Thus there seems to have been a consensus among both women and men preachers not to lend great importance either to celebration or to liturgical concerns. However it is interesting to note how the women and men differed with regard to the other least popular homiletical tasks: the women were reluctant to criticize the church and to quote poetry or drama, while the men shunned the tasks of testifying and inviting hearers to Christian commitment.

Final Conclusions

By way of summary, we have observed that women and men preach the same types of sermons, from the biblical texts, but differ slightly in their choices of themes and tasks, and differ greatly in their talk about God and persons in inclusive terms. Perhaps we can say that women and men preach the same Word but with distinctive *accents*—women tend to emphasize the personal and men the prophetic. If this assessment is accurate, it reflects that ubiquitous false dichotomy between the spiritual and the social that has plagued the Christian church for centuries. Yet, it may be that this small discrepancy between women's and men's preaching holds the key to a possible resolution of this dichotomy in our own age of rapid social and cultural change. Women's preaching calls for men to incorporate into their homiletical, theological, and christological themes such basic and practical issues as survival, healing, and the hardships of ministry. Women's use of inclusive language challenges men to demonstrate genuine appreciation of the presence and participation of women by adjusting their talk to address he and she, God the Father and God the Mother, instead of just talking to and about "man" all the time. Women's sermons can teach men to temper social criticism with compassion. At the same time, women can learn from men how to sharpen their own testimonies and calls for Christian commitment with the cutting edge of prophetic indignation.

What shall we say then? Does God indeed speak with a feminine voice? If so, how does the feminine voice of God differ from the masculine voice of God? My conclusion is that God speaks with a feminine voice and with a masculine voice. God speaks to women and to men in their particularity, and in their commonality as well. After all, preaching is the telling, interpretation, and application of God's story. It is more than proclamation alone—it is "a conversation with the crowd" that is consummated when that crowd hears and bears witness to that proclamation. And as long as that crowd includes both women and men, there will be a need for God's story to be proclaimed in ways that embrace the experience of both genders.

Some serious theological implications emerge from our comparative analysis of women's and men's preaching. In an article entitled "Preaching in the Black Tradition," the Reverend Leontine Kelly offers an insightful description of some key assumptions concerning the nature of God that are borne out by Black women's preaching:

The black woman preacher does battle sexism, but she draws upon the spiritual confidence traditional in her culture. She is theologically and experientially grounded in a God who is Creator and Sustainer of the universe, actively holding the "whole world in his/her hands." She draws her understanding of a father/mother God from the traditional expression of the spiritual of her people, "He's my father, he's my mother, my sister and my brother, he's everything to me."[25]

If we confess that God is creator and sustainer of the universe, and Father and Mother of us all, then we must also accept the masculine and feminine voices and the masculine and feminine vessels that God has ordained to equip the church to perform a truly inclusive and wholistic ministry in the world.

As I close, I am reminded of the Old Testament prophet Elijah, who, having run for his life from a woman named Jezebel, sought desperately to hear a Word from the Lord. And the Bible says: "behold, the Lord passed by, and a great and strong wind rent the mountains, and brake in pieces the rocks before the Lord; but the Lord was not in the wind: and after the wind an earthquake; but the Lord was not in the earthquake: And after the earthquake a fire; but the Lord was not in the fire: and after the fire a still small voice" (1 Kings 19:11–12). Sometimes the voice of God thunders, and at other times God whispers. If the Creator of the wind and the earthquake and the fire can choose to speak in a "still small voice," then that same God can surely give utterance in the voices of women as often as in the voices of men. For God calls daughters and God calls sons, some with the accent of testimony and others with the accent of critique, to be heralds of the same living Word of truth.

Notes

1. "Baptist Group Names Black Woman Pastor," *USA Today*, March 5, 1984, p. 2A.

2. Betty J. Overton, "Black Women Preachers: A Literary View," in *The Southern Quarterly* 23, no. 3 (Spring 1985):165.

3. James Earl Massey, *Designing the Sermon* (Nashville, Tenn.: Abingdon, 1980):21.

4. Ibid., 23.

5. Ibid., 35–37.

6. See definition of "homiletics" in *The American Heritage Dictionary* (New York: American Heritage Publishing Co., 1975).

7. Barbara Campbell, "Beyond Ourselves," in *Black Preaching*, ed. Robert T. Newbold, Jr. (Philadelphia: Geneva Press, 1977):51.

8. Mary Ann Bellinger, "Upright but *Not* Uptight," in *Those Preachin' Women*, ed. Ella Pearson Mitchell (Valley Forge, Penn.: Judson Press, 1985):75.

9. Deborah McGill-Jackson, "To Set at Liberty," in Mitchell, 39.

10. Thelma Davidson Adair, "Jesus Christ, the Same Yesterday, Today—Forever," in Newbold, 16–17.

11. Ellen Sandimanie, "On Being Faithful Stewards," in Newbold, 36.

12. Katie G. Cannon, "On Remembering Who We Are," in Mitchell, 50.

13. Marjorie Leeper Booker, "A Prescription for Humility," in Mitchell, 90–91.

14. Peggy R. Scott, "God Has a Master Plan for Your Life," in Mitchell, 110–11.

15. Nan M. Brown, "The Mind of the Insecure," in Mitchell, 66.

16. Effie M. Clark, "How a People Make History," in *Outstanding Black Sermons*, ed. J. Alfred Smith (Valley Forge, Penn.: Judson Press, 1976):31–32.

17. Clara Mills-Morton, "The Blessings and Burdens of the Divinely Chosen," in Mitchell, 97.

18. Yvonne V. Delk, "Singing the Lord's Song," in Mitchell, 58.

19. Carolyn Ann Knight, "The Survival of the Unfit," in Mitchell, 27–28.

20. Laura Sinclair, "Can Your Bones Live?" in Mitchell, 21–22.

21. Margrie Lewter-Simmons, "Our Spiritual Account," in Mitchell, 115–17.

22. Sharon E. Williams, "Studying War Some More," in Mitchell, 82–83.

23. Beverly J. Shamana, "Letting Go," in Mitchell, 105.

24. Suzan D. Johnson, "God's Woman," in Mitchell, 121.

25. Leontine T. C. Kelly, "Preaching in the Black Tradition," in *Women Ministers*, ed. Judith L. Weidman (San Francisco: Harper & Row, 1981):72.

21

Singing Praise to God in African American Worship Contexts

Melva W. Costen

Theologies of worship that shape the forms and styles of ritual action are determined to a large extent by the contexts in which the faith is experienced. Beliefs and practices are most often the result of existential conditions. This was obviously the case as a Christ-centered faith was experienced variously among Africans transplanted in American soil. New liturgical and musical forms emerged representing a variety of cultural and historical contexts.

Africans exposed to the word of God responded in ways shaped and fashioned by interpretations and symbols unique to Africa and subsequently to Afro-America. In keeping with their own African gifts for improvising and adapting to the experiences of life, Africans in America extracted the truth from Christian doctrine which was often distorted when presented by their oppressors. Armed with their African belief systems, thoroughly aware of an omnipotent, omniscient God, African Americans set about the awesome task of honing and shaping liturgical and musical styles commensurate with their abiding faith in God. As a result, a new religion and new form of Christian theology were born. The musical forms through which this faith was expressed also became a major source for the development of new liturgical styles.

Just as there was no single, unified African culture or one set of religious beliefs and rituals among all societal groups in Africa, there is no one clearly distinguishable set of beliefs and practices among Africans in America. On their own soil Africans created innumerable religious beliefs, customs, languages, and symbols which gave them unique and separate identities. In the United States today worship and musical forms among Blacks reflect variances according to geographic and cultural differences contingent upon the particular struggles and the extent of oppression experienced by segments of the Black population.

Amidst the diversity, however, there are commonalities which form the basis for an African American religious ethos out of which music continues to flow. Africans, too, share continent-wide traditional primal world views, cosmologies, ideals, symbols, and cultural expressions which provide a common bonding and identity. Recent research by African and African American scholars attests to the continuity and utilization of these and other elements of culture in an American environment. Equally significant is the awareness that "culture" itself is not a fixed condition. Culture is also a process which provides interaction and linkages between past and present. For this reason Africans and persons of African descent have responded creatively to the realities of life in whatever situation they find themselves. This creative gift prevented Africans from totally absorbing the religious beliefs and practices of the strange and alien people who took them away into slavery.

In all ages and conditions humans have expressed their spiritual aspirations and responded to the physical world about them through music. Nowhere is this more certain than in the songs of African American people. With the aid of music, Africans in America were lifted closer to God as they struggled to bear the conditions of a harsh slave existence. Singing, an artistic form inextricably interwoven into the fabric of all African cultures, provided a channel through which God could speak and believers could respond. For an African people, music is not merely a means of expressing feelings. It evokes the reciprocal activity of imagination and understanding of the soul. Since the soul is the center of God's human work, only the believer's love of God allows the soul to respond through and in music. Thus, as if in anticipation of W. E. B. DuBois's statement, "music is the soul of Black folks,"[1] the sound of music born of human breath bore witness to the presence and love of God in the being of Black folks from the beginning of time. Herein lies the foundation of the various forms of music which catalog the theologies of African Americans.

In traditional African cultures one is born, named, and initiated through music into various levels of existence—puberty, marriage, life, and death. Music is a vital part of domestic chores as well as religious and social events. It is considered functional as well as artistic. People of African heritage in America bear the cultural seeds of musicians, poets, and dancers that were planted and continue to grow out of an African American ethos.

The basic characteristics of African American musical expression, regardless of denominational orientation, are these: there is no clear line of demarcation between secular and sacred in language and performance; a strong sense of communal togetherness is evoked; existential situations provide the subject for the poetic language; and the common means of transmission are by way of the oral tradition. Traditional songs evolved as "folk music" transmitted by word-of-mouth and action and remain open to "re-creation" and "re-forming," according to the particular community involved. Music was and remains a participatory activity rather than an occasion for spectators. The songs emanating from the earliest poet-musicians were created and employed in "praise houses," in fields, and in other work arenas characterized by a strong sense of corporate identity and cooperation.

A theology of music for worship in Black religious traditions was formulated out of the context of God's revelation and providence as revealed in the history of an enslaved people. Such a theology takes fully into consideration the ways in the history of an enslaved people. Such a theology takes fully into consideration the ways in which God, incarnate in Jesus Christ, is understood in the light of survival strategies and efforts for freedom. A theological core is at the heart of the rich cultural heritage emanating from religious beliefs and practices in Africa. Embodied in this theology and music is also a record of human history and beliefs shaped by biblical understandings.

In addition to considering the reluctant and ambivalent attitudes of American slaveholders concerning the religious instruction of slaves, one must also be aware of the state of music among the transplanted Europeans. Church music during the seventeenth century consisted solely of the singing of metrical versions of the psalms. Only four or five tunes were in common use and these were handed down by oral tradition. Hymns other than paraphrases of psalms in such tunes as "Old Hundred," "York," and "Windsor" were not known until after 1740 when the hymns of the Wesleys and Isaac Watts were reprinted in this country.

Singing in the churches was considered "crude and barbarous." Alice Morse Earle described this singing among white Americans in these words: "Of all the dismal accomplishments of public worship in the early days of New England the music was the most hopelessly forlorn, not only from the confused versifications of the Psalms, . . . but from the mournful monotony of the few known tunes and the horrible manner in which these tunes were sung."[2]

The tunes were "miserably tortured and twisted and quavered in our churches," wrote Rev. Thomas Walter, and "left to the mercy of every unskilled throat to chop and alter, to twist and change, according to their infinitely diverse and less odd humours and fancies."[3] Congregational singing was conducted by "lining out" the tune by a precentor or a deacon. In New England African Americans were allowed special pews where they sat separate from whites. Along with other members of the congregation they waited for the precentor to line out the psalm and "set the tune." There is evidence that the singing of psalms was not confined to the church nor only for formal occasions. Wherever this form of singing occurred, the "crude effect" was still apparent. The desire for improvement was influenced by the 1698 publication of a new edition containing music. But attempts to improve musical performance were met with violent opposition, dividing congregations in extreme hostility against each other.

Out of these conditions and the urgent need for instruction in the basic rudiments of music emerged "singing schools" where singing was taught by "rule and art." Extant records indicate that slaves received regular instruction in singing schools operated by the Society for the Propagation of the Gospel in Foreign Parts (SPG) in Philadelphia as early as 1728, in Boston between 1758 and 1775, in New York from 1760 to 1775, and in other parts of the North.

Documents also attest to the activities of colonial clergymen among slaves, stating the number of African American adults taken into the church, the number of infants baptized, and the number given religious instruction, including the teaching of psalms and hymns. According to these accounts the slaves preferred the musical activities of the religious services above all else, particularly the psalms and hymns of Isaac Watts.[4] This was apparently true for some slaves in the North, since religious instruction for Blacks in the South never attained the level that it did in the North. At no time did this form of instruction reach a considerable proportion of the Black population. During the colonial period most Black Americans were rarely touched by missionary efforts. They lived in separate quarters away from whites, shaping original musical forms as they worked and worshiped. Blacks in the North participated minimally in the perpetuation of Euro-American forms. The "reformed" the tradition of the lined-singing of psalms and hymns, creating an art form which continues today, especially among Black Baptists in the South.

Two Distinct Contexts

African Americans who remained in denominations founded by Europeans and Euro-Americans are often considered propagators of white liturgical traditions.[5] Recent scholarly research among Blacks in white denominations affirms what have been identified as adapted forms of white liturgies. In most instances there were separate congregations where Blacks freely used music from Black oral traditions along with forms from the white "parent body." Contrary to the opinion of some historians who held the notion that Blacks were not attracted to the formality of Catholic, Anglican, Congregational, and Presbyterian styles of worship, there is evidence that Blacks found "ordered forms" also conducive to a satisfying worship experience. According to letters dated September 1745 and March 1751, "the singing of psalms produced a good effect; it engaged many of the Negroes to a closer application in learning to read," and "Blacks often meet in the evenings on a regular basis for instruction in the singing of the psalm tunes."[6] This could mean that music, even in the newly acquired psalm forms, contributed to a feeling of group solidarity. It would be highly unfair to assume that all Blacks preferred one form of musical style—that which allowed only emotional outlets reminiscent of the African heritage. Africans in contemporary theological and secular educational instructions show that their worship experiences are "at home," varied and often void of any physical display. This in no way denies the importance of feelings and emotions in worship. It is also true that many Africans do not consider the avoidance of overtly emotional displays as an intellectualization of ritual. It is clear, therefore, that Black Christians today need not apologize for their choice of denomination or forms of liturgy. Today, even among traditional Black churches, music and liturgical forms may range from "high church" with "smells and bells" to "spirit-filled free forms."

With the introduction of the organ in Black congregations, combined with a desire for music literacy, concerts of sacred music gained in popularity and frequency. While the repertories may have featured music by Europeans, these events became occasions for the introduction of music by Black composers and the development of Black artists. Standards of music were raised, not merely as means of displaying musical tastes comparable to that of whites, but as opportunities for the development of musical talent among Blacks. Music for worship, then, took on additional variety. The foundation was laid for the use of the organ and new Black forms of music in the twentieth century.

The African American Spiritual

The African American spirituals are the heart and soul of American music. The exact date of origin of this religious folk song form is not known. It is believed that originally these songs were indeed rooted in West African oral traditions. The traditional line of evolution in America extends from African chants, moans, field hollers, work songs, game songs, and jubilees to the use of the term "spirituals" as a unique religious form.

A contemporary rendering of spirituals can only superficially express the agony and ecstasy out of which such scriptural ideas and allusions were re-formulated. For the slave such poignant reflections could not be confined to a specific time or place, but were appropriated for any given moment in God's time. Many of the spirituals depict the worldview of those in bondage. When the possibility of adjusting to the inequities of oppression and the subsequent satisfaction of basic human needs were denied, the slave created a "new world" by attempting to transcend restrictions through the most creative means available. For many, such means were the creation of songs.

The spirituals record the history of a people who survived by internally and emotionally expanding their universe in poetry and song. The dominant "call and response" (antiphonal) structure of so many of the spirituals placed the slaves in continuous dialogue with God and the slave community. Through music the communality so prevalent in African societies was maintained and strengthened in the New World. The improvisations, characteristic of the African homeland, reinforced the person in the context of the community. An individual's new idea, whether musical or poetic, became the community's idea and continued in the reshaping process until frequently a new form was born. This creative process continues whenever spirituals are sung today. In this way spirituals are always in process of becoming. Each generation or new group of singers is free to add themes in the light of their existential situation.

Freedom to use the language and concepts of the Bible to retell their story was a birthright of African people in America. Many European scholars, reviewing this musical literature for consistency and coherence, are often confused by the coexistence of Old and New Testament characters and stories in the same song. What was often written off by early researchers as ignorance has now been affirmed as a creative use of imagery and symbolic language in order to communicate the "real good news" to a people who understood the gospel as a message of liberation.

Those in bondage receiving religious instruction were liberated by the power of God to sing of the hypocrisy of the slaveholder's preacher whose sermon exhorted "sinlessness" as a ticket to heaven. Thus the slave could sing, "Everybody talkin' 'bout heaven ain't going there. . . ." The singer continued the dual message: "I got shoes, you got shoes, All of God's children got shoes; when I get to heaven, gonna put on my shoes, gonna walk all over God's heaven! . . ."

While functioning as a means of communication, a documentation of theological concepts, and as a means of expressing yearning for a better life on earth, the spiritual is also evidence of "freedom in action."[7] The slave, oppressed by an unjust world, subjected to "man's inhumanity to man" was free to release some of this tension in song. The dual meaning also allowed the songs to remain open to be freely used.

The community could admonish Mary (Magdalene) not to weep and mourn "'cause Pharoah's army got drownded" and evidence prevails that God takes care of all situations in time. "Mary" could also have been a code name for those seeking freedom from bondage to meet Harriet Tubman, conductor for the "Underground Railroad," at the river, since the song continues with reference to a specific time: "One of these day's 'bout six o'clock, this old world's gonna reel and rock. . . ."

The singers did not allow chronology to hinder matters of the faith and hope since faith and hope were pertinent to contemporary existence. "There was an immediacy about their relationship to biblical persons which allowed intimacy in the midst of estrangement."[8] The community could ask "Were you there when they crucified my Lord?" affirming a close relationship with Jesus and answering affirmatively—"Yes," as they sang, "O, sometimes it causes me to tremble," recalling (anamnesis) the powerful death and resurrection event.

Jesus can be seen talking with Noah (in spite of the Old and New Testament cross references) just as easily as he is seen walking and talking with the slave. Rivers are frequently used to symbolize difficult obstacles on the earthly pilgrimage enroute to the Promised Land. The community understood eschatology in relation to existential events and could celebrate with Moses, Joshua, and the Hebrew children crossing through the waters. It surely must have been confusing to the "saved" soul at the water of Baptism when the oppressor reminded them that their Baptism did not set them free to be part of the covenant community.

No doubt the mixed metaphors, the frequent use of non-biblical materials, as well as the fact that slaves were creators of this body of musical literature, have hindered the inclusion of a wider variety of songs in denominational hymnals. This has not, however, prevented their inclusion in the liturgy of the Black folk in meaningful ways. Two denominational publications, *Songs of Zion*[9] and *Lift Every Voice: A Collection of Afro-American Spirituals and Other Songs*,[10] have further enhanced the use of this music in worship. Also in continual use are "anthemized" arrangements of spirituals perpetuated by choral departments in Black colleges and universities.

African American Gospel Music

An openness on the part of Black Americans to the "process of becoming" in the midst of continual oppression provides a climate for the evolution of the religious song form and style known as Black gospel. The texts are based on the Good News proclaimed in Jesus the Liberator, couched in a musical expression of twentieth century folk life. The major differences between Black gospel and spirituals are the identifiable composers of gospels and fewer references to Old Testament stories and characters. Equally important is the use of accompanying instruments to enhance the improvisation. The delivery is highly upbeat in tempo, with an important role for soloists.

Thomas A. Dorsey, a Black musician perhaps best known for his composition, "Precious Lord, Take My Hand," is acknowledged as the father of Black gospel music. He credits a personal experience with God and exposure to the music of Charles A. Tindley, a Black minister, as his source of inspiration. As a gifted blues pianist, Dorsey transported his highly developed improvisatory technique to the worship setting. From these beginnings, worshipers continue praising God with their total beings. The sounds, hardly distinguishable from jazz, ragtime, and blues, accompany vocal expressions about the goodness of God in Jesus Christ.

Gospel singing evokes a strong sense of communality as singers testify about personal experiences and God's saving grace and an urgency for the singer to "tell the story." This form and style transcend boundaries of age, as both young and old participate together in the presence of the Almighty.

When gospel music is new to a congregation that has long-established music practices in liturgy based on Western, or Euro-American forms, there can be some problems. This "free" form has to be introduced in a manner that encourages the development of an appreciation for the many ways of praising God through music. One cannot assume, therefore, that all African American congregations swing, sway, and understand Black gospel as the authentic musical form for worship. Nor can one expect that there will ever be a consensus as to its appropriateness in Black liturgy. Many congregations have experienced dissension among choir members over the addition of gospel choirs in an effort to balance the musical offerings. Requests for music workshops have increased as young pastors are faced with division within their congregations and as Black theologians highlight African American traditions with an emphasis upon ethnicity in worship expressions.[11]

The popularity of gospel music increased during the civil rights movement as poor and middle-class African Americans came together in the struggle. The earliest Black gospel period (traditional gospel) was confined basically to storefront churches in large cities. The emphasis in the late sixties on Black awareness resulted in new forms which were developed on college campuses and variously labeled "modern" and "contemporary" Black gospel. After exposure to this and other Black artistic forms, many young college graduates left churches where there was a paucity of what they called "authentic Black expression" in music and liturgy. Those who maintained membership encouraged contemporary and "rock" Gospel in worship. They have become the major exponents of the record industry which too often determines the choice of music used weekly for worship. Black Gospel remains a viable liturgical form, however, especially when it is used to glorify God in Jesus Christ, rather than merely as a performance to glorify the singer(s).

Soulful Singing

It is quite common to hear (and use) spirituals and hymns "gospelized" with upbeat rhythms and heavy instrumentation. Additionally many congregations enjoy a style of soulful singing in which hymns are altered by the congregation to "allow time for the working of the Holy Spirit." These styles vary according to the particular congregation and can best be understood in the communal context.

The history of the slow-sustained-soulful singing can be traced to the 1800s after the "Great Awakening." The songs of Watts had been successfully introduced to the colonies and captured the imagination of the Black folk because of the vitality and freshness of the words. The singing of psalms by the slaves was replaced by the singing of hymns of Isaac Watts. Black Baptists in particular recast the hymns in the manner similar to psalm singing where a leader "lined out" the words and the congregation "surged" in and sang the line in a tune which was twisted and turned almost beyond recognition. Meter signatures were completely ignored and rhythms were adjusted according to the movement of the spirit. This practice, know as "Dr. Watts" among Blacks, exists today, especially in the southeast, as an art form and a powerful religious expression. Such hymns may last for ten or fifteen minutes, as worshipers in an attitude of prayer invoke the presence of the Holy Spirit. The musical form is entirely free with the tunes shaped by local congregations and transmitted orally. An entire stanza may be hummed as individuals pour out their prayers in a language that only God can understand. Such musical moments are open to verbal and musical interpolations such as "yes, Lord," "thank you, Jesus," and "Hallelujah!" in keeping with the spirit of praise. The melody flows melismatically with underlying harmonies which progress in intervals of thirds, fourths, fifths, and sixths.

The Dr. Watts style is an example of hymns "brought from the floor" or "raised" by a leader who also signals the congregation to stand, indicating that the current stanza will be the concluding one. Hymnbooks are not needed for this style of singing since the precentor is free to determine each line of poetry and music.

Music in the Liturgy

A recent study of mine revealed diversity in worship and music styles among Black Presbyterians.[12] Prior to 1807 when the first Black congregation was established in Philadelphia, Black Presbyterians worshiped in segregated sections of white churches. As additional congregations developed, the style of singing and worship was patterned after that of the majority membership. The new congregational environment made it possible to recapture the covenant (familial) community so vital to an African people and worship began to have a power that was not experienced in reserved "balconies" of white Presbyterian churches.

Geographic location and exposure to the hard realities of American life determined the extent to which Black congregations maintained traditional

African forms and styles reflective of the community's response to injustices and oppression. Many rural churches reflect a unity with Black denominations in the area as well as a Presbyterian ethos. The traditions discussed above are evident in the rural South where I grew up as a fourth generation Black Presbyterian. The musical offerings within the Presbyterian order of service include hymns, psalmody, spirituals, and "soulful" expressions of praise. The use of gospel music was rare in the church, but the constant mobility among traditional Black (A.M.E., Baptist, and Pentecostal) churches provided exposure to and appreciation of the African American heritage.

A questionnaire distributed to 419 Black congregations in an effort to ascertain worship and music styles revealed changes in styles as a result of a new Black consciousness developed during the civil rights period. The stigma of "middle classness" attached to Black Presbyterians at worship is being erased as traditional Black forms are incorporated in the liturgy. *Songs of Zion* now supplements the *Presbyterian Hymnbook* and *Worshipbook*. The congregations assume their role as the true choir, singing music from the African American heritage along with Euro-American hymns and anthems. "Lift Ev'ry Voice and Sing," an anthem sacred to Black Americans, is as popular today as Handel's "Messiah." Andrea Crouch's "Bless the Lord, O My Soul," and Margaret Douroux's "Give Me a Clean Heart," supplement traditional psalmody. "Ride On, King Jesus" can be heard more frequently than on Palm Sunday; "They crucified my Lord, an' He never said a mumbalin' word" can be heard along with "There Is a Green Hill Far Away" on Good Friday, and "He Arose" precedes "Jesus Christ Is Risen Today" on Easter.

Today talented organists and hand bell choirs freely include music from the Black heritage and the growing body of literature by African and African American composers. Anthems by Black composers are included in the liturgy along with Black gospel arrangements. Skilled harpists, string players, and percussionists accompany congregations and choirs in expressions of praise in the liturgy. Oratorios and cantatas continue to be offerings of praise as congregations are introduced to such Black composers as Frederick Hall, J. Harold Brown, Lena McLin, and Clarence Rivers.

God is glorified through music in the Black Church in a variety of ways. The singing tradition inherited from Africa has taught us the importance of wholeness of mind, body, and spirit as a way of life under the guidance of the Holy Spirit. Therefore liturgy is truly the work of the people gathered and scattered.

The minister, as leader of worship, is encouraged to immerse herself or himself in a theology which lifts up Black liturgy as an authentic expression of the faith. Presbyterian students at the Interdenominational Theological Center are required to study worship and homiletics and are offered options in Advanced Worship and Liturgical Worship and Preaching, taught by qualified and experienced scholars. The ecumenical and international ambience of the I.T.C. campus provides further exposure to African and Black traditions. This setting in Atlanta is a reminder that much can be learned from exposure to and an appreciation of ethnic expressions in worship. Traditions that have emerged demonstrate God's mysterious intervention in the lives of people wherever they find themselves in the midst of crisis in their particular communities.

The African American community is traditionally a singing community. African Americans are a people of faith who sing jubilantly of God's loving presence in the midst of struggle. Like the early Christians, we gather in song to proclaim Christ's identification with us. Like our African forebears, we sing with our total beings in praise of the Almighty God by the power of the Holy Spirit.

Notes

1. W. E. Burghardt DuBois, *The Souls of Black Folk* (New York: Washington Square Press, 1970):206.

2. Alice Morse Earle, *The Sabbath in Puritan New England* (New York: Scribners, 1896).

3. William Arms Fisher, *Notes on Music in Old Boston* (New York: Oliver Ditson Company, 1918), quoted in Edward Bailey Birge, *History of Public School Music in the United States* (Washington, D.C.: Music Educators National Conference, 1966):5.

4. Eileen Southern, *The Music of Black Americans: A History*, 2nd ed. (New York: W. W. Norton, 1983):41–42.

5. See especially Wyatt Tee Walker, *Somebody's Calling My Name* (Valley Forge, Penn.: Judson Press, 1979).

6. Edgar Pennington, *Thomas Brays' Associates and Their Work Among the Negroes* (Worcester, Mass.: American Antiquarian Society, 1939):82, quoting S.P.G. series B, 13, no. 219 and S.P.G. series B, 19, no. 68.

7. This concept is developed further in an unpublished article by Melva Wilson Costen, "Thurman's Interpretation of Human Freedom as Reflected in Negro Spirituals," March 1982.

8. Christa K. Dixon, *Negro Spirituals* (Philadelphia: Fortress Press, 1976):2.

9. Songs of Zion (Nashville, Tenn.: Abingdon, 1981).

10. *Lift Every Voice and Sing: A Collection of Afro-American Spirituals and Other Songs* (New

York: The Church Hymnal Corporation, 1981).

11. Gayraud S. Wilmore, *Black and Presbyterian: The Heritage and Hope* (Philadelphia: Geneva Press, 1983).

12. Melva Wilson Costen, "Worship and Music Styles in Black United Presbyterian Congregations," (Study conducted at Johnson C. Smith Seminary at the Interdenominational Theological Center, Atlanta, Georgia, 1981).

22

The New Shiloh Saturday Church School

Sid Smith

First Encounter

The spire atop the mammoth Gothic sanctuary points majestically to the sky. The huge structure displays a subtle charm that invites passersby to channel their steps into the monument of intrigue which bears the name New Shiloh Baptist Church. The immaculate lawn conspires with the neat overall appearance to transmit body language that proclaims the message, "Here is a great church."

The physical plant at New Shiloh Baptist Church, Baltimore, Maryland, is impressive. It stands as a bridge between an exciting past and a brilliant future. Like an adolescent garment, it has outgrown its maximum effectiveness and anticipates its obsolescence for this congregation as plans have been drawn for an ultramodern new facility.

The sanctuary invites the worshiper into an inner sanctum of spirituality. The atmosphere of reverence reminds the visitor that he is in the presence of God. The multitude of colors, reflected in banners carrying messages about the Divine, emit the impression that this place is alive with the presence of the Lord. A creative mural depicting scenes from the historic Black experience surrounds the baptistry and testifies to the relevance of the gospel to the Black situation in America. This spacious sanctuary, with its historic cultural motif, reminds the congregation of the partnership between Christianity and social justice. It is a *kerygma* that preaches the good news that God is a liberator.

The immediate community of the church is typical of Baltimore's inner-city dwellings. Characterized by common walls, miniporches, and concrete yards, this redbrick neighborhood with narrow streets and scarce parking reflects the anonymity of urbanity which challenges so many churches. People can be seen sitting on their front steps watching life pass by. With houses sharing common walls, the neighborhood easily appears to be a collection of urban apartments insulated by the dynamics of crowded closeness. Yet despite this insulation and isolation in a sea of people separated by myriad lifeboat apartments, there seems to be a God-consciousness that permeates the atmosphere.

The general church community served by New Shiloh is not geographically definable but sociologically identifiable. The observer readily is impressed with the variety of persons in the membership of this church. The membership spans the various socioeconomic categories within the Black community. Although the intellectual elite are represented, one also feels that those with humble academic credentials feel comfortable. There is an atmosphere of warm acceptance that reaches out to newcomers. In fact, there appears to be a blend of committed theological scholarship and folksy, pragmatic need meeting in the mind-set of leadership at New Shiloh. An onlooker may easily be confronted with evidence that the people attracted to this church prefer qualitative pastoral leadership with a vision for ministering to the needs of the community. People from all social strata have this preference and they are found involved in the ministry of this church.

Church Roots

New Shiloh Baptist Church is a pioneer of creativity in religious education in the Black community. How did this church become a pacesetter whose model is emulated across the country? What is the story of its history? In his book *Determined: A Faith History of a People Determined to Live with Christ,* Dr. Harold A. Carter focuses attention on two relevant questions about the story of New Shiloh: "How could it be that this congregation, located in the heart of one of America's urban cities, Baltimore, Maryland, would survive, prosper, and continue to grow? How could it be that this congregation of 3,500 persons would band together as one and more forward from generation to generation as a church determined to live with Christ?"[1]

The New Shiloh story goes back to the beginning of the twentieth century, when there was a Black migration from the South to the urban North. Thousands of Blacks migrated to Baltimore in search of a better quality of life than offered by the system in the South.

These transplanted Southerners brought the religion of their culture with them. One of the practices endemic to the new migrants was the community prayer band. According to Carter, "Through prayer bands, Black people kept alive traditional folk songs, called on God without artificial restrictions, and quite often laid the foundation for churches to follow."[2] Perhaps inadvertently, the Black prayer band movement led to the expression of a distinct form of Black church planting.

New Shiloh Baptist Church was one of the churches that grew out of the prayer-band movement. In October 1902, Rev. Whit W. Allen organized and founded this church on a base that began with three persons in a prayer band. The first name selected was the Shiloh Free Baptist Church. In 1907 the name was changed to Shiloh Baptist Church, and in 1926 the word New was added to the name. During the ministry of "Dr. Allen," as he was affectionately known, the church experienced phenomenal growth, and its membership totaled some five thousand persons.

Allen served as pastor of this church for forty years and earned the designation of having been "loyal to the pew." His long, fruitful ministry endeared him to the hearts of his parishioners. He is remembered as "a powerful preacher," a firm believer in the absolute truth of the Bible, and a fatherly figure with a winsome personality with which people could identify. This charismatic leader led his church to win people to Christ with evangelistic zeal. He built a massive church with a broad appeal involved in ministering to the community. This deeply respected, loved, venerated, and emulated pulpiteer laid a strong foundation upon which the church would continue to build in the future.

On Palm Sunday, 1942, the Lord called Dr. Allen to his eternal reward. The mantle of leadership fell on Dr. J. Timothy Boddie, a pastor with theological training at Virginia Seminary and College, Lynchburg, Virginia. Dr. Boddie assumed the pastorate of New Shiloh in 1942. An assessment of the Boddie leadership has been stated thus: "This ministerial team was able to lead the church from a gathering of persons, loosely held together into a church of strong, biblical, purposeful discipleship where members began to understand and support some of the deeper demands of the faith."[3]

During the Boddie administration huge progress was made. Under the leadership of the pastor's wife, the talented Emory Boddie, missions emphases were given priority, and involvement of women in missions increased. A program of biblical stewardship was instituted which yielded systematically greater income for church programs. During this period the involvement of the church expanded into denominational and ecumenical circles. Dr. Boddie's twenty-one-year pastorate ended in 1963.

In 1964 New Shiloh called the twenty-eight-year-old Harold A. Carter to be pastor. The coming of the young pastor and his lovely wife, Weptanoma, brought a new sense of excitement to the church. The civil rights movement was at its zenith. Dr. Martin Luther King, Jr., was the unquestioned moral leader of the day in the estimation of the Black community. The church had been cast into a prophetic leadership role for the cause of Black liberation. Black churches had caught a vision of possibilities with young pastoral leadership. Harold Carter seemed to embody the best in the relevant Black pastoral tradition.

In Harold A. Carter, New Shiloh had called one of God's strong servants to be the spiritual leader. He had already graduated from Alabama State University and earned a divinity degree with honors from Crozer Theological Seminary. Yet his brilliant mind still sought more academic challenges. He had pastored the Court Street Baptist Church in Lynchburg, Virginia, one of America's oldest Black Baptist churches. He was an associate of Dr. Martin Luther King's and had been involved in "the movement." He was blessed with a talented wife whose gifts would enable her to have an impact in her own right. Blessed with a brilliant, analytical mind, Harold Carter would soon escalate the involvement of the congregation into new creative approaches to ministry, especially in the area of Sunday School.

New Shiloh Baptist Church has a rich history. Its roots go back to the turn of the century. It has experienced remarkable growth in members. It has been led by only three pastors in its eighty-three-year history. It has not been afraid of change. Perhaps a dominant view of the church may be seen through Carter's statement, "While the church has had its growing problems, it has always managed to maintain a great love for the proclaimed Word, a contagious sense of celebration, and a fierce love and loyalty to Jesus Christ."[4]

The Shepherd

Upon meeting pastor Harold A. Carter, one quickly becomes impressed with his spirituality. He seems to be a shepherd who walks close to the Lord. His conversation reveals the heart of a man deeply dedicated to God and committed to letting God do great things through his ministry at and beyond New Shiloh Baptist Church.

Carter was born in Selma, Alabama, and was reared the son of a minister. His proximity to a "man of the cloth" left him with the desire to strive for the best level of theological education. After graduating with honors from Cro-zer Theological Seminary in Chester, Pennsylvania, he pursued the rigorous task of taking two earned doctorates simultaneously. In May 1976, he had the distinction of earning the doctor of ministry degree from Colgate-Rochester Divinity School *and* the doctor of philosophy degree in theology magna cum laude from Saint Mary's Seminary.

Dr. Carter is in worldwide demand as a major speaker for evangelistic events. His preaching opportunities have taken him to some twenty-five different countries. Many places in Europe, Africa, the Philippines, Romania, and the Caribbean have been exposed to his messages. Major denominations in the United States such as Southern Baptists, American Baptists, Progressive Baptists, Methodists, and Assemblies of God use him frequently. He was one of the keynote speakers in 1981 at the American Festival of Evangelism in Kansas City, Missouri, at which fifteen thousand persons participated in an event to "call America to Christ."

Dr. Carter is a gifted pulpiteer. He is blessed with an appealing "preacher's voice" that allows its baritone message to be delivered with force. His voice has been described as sounding similar to that of the late Dr. Martin Luther King. This medium-sized prophet has been bequeathed a mighty voice that enables him to drill his point home convincingly. The content of his message is heavy but simple. "Carter seeks to grab the most unsophisticated minds in his congregation."[5] He says, "If I can reach the lowest common denominator, I believe I will have preached the authentic gospel. What's going through my mind is how do you make tangible the weighty truth of the Scripture so that the simplest minds can grasp it?"[6] To put it differently, he has the gift of discovering deep truths of God's Word and sharing the profound simply. Although he is unquestionably a gifted academician, his messages are not pedantic or stilted. He uses his brilliance to simplify the great mysteries of life.

As a preacher, Carter has managed to blend two powerful forces in the pulpit—intellectual ability and oratorical skill. Nobody will ever accuse him of being "an egghead," and nobody will say, "He can't preach." The evidence is too overwhelming in the other direction.

His pulpit skills have been widely recognized. Not only is he a word craftsman, but he has something to say forcefully. His messages have ministered to the thousands fed from their wisdom and spiritual power. His messages are interpretations of Scripture which bring hope to the individual with a heavy use of the anecdote wrapped in the sermonic style of the southern Black preacher. One of New Shiloh's members who has heard numerous sermons by Carter described the experience like this: "Creative counseling masses of people but also seemingly speaking with the thought of one person in mind. He preaches so as to bring the future hopes of a people into present reality. His knack of using ever-recurring anecdotes to drive home truths keeps his messages fresh and alive."[7]

Dr. Harold Carter not only is a giant in the pulpit, he is as able with the pen as he is with the Sword of the Spirit. Not only is he a great orator, he is also a great journalist. This prolific writer has authored several books including *The Prayer Tradition of Black People*, *Myths That Mire the Ministry*, *The Preaching of Jonah*, *Determined: A Faith History of a People Determined to Live with Christ*, and others in process. He has also contributed to numerous magazines and scholarly publications.

One cannot help but be impressed with the skills of the pastor in the area of teaching. The full weight of his theological training enriches the class taught by the pastor on Saturday mornings. Hundreds of adults flock to be fed by the shepherd each week in the Saturday church school class he teaches. Enthusiastic minds eagerly sit at the feet of this master teacher to soak up pearls of wisdom. One senses a reverence from the class for the great mind but humble spirit of the pastor. One senses that the audience does not hesitate to ask difficult questions because their teacher probably knows the answer. Sitting in Dr. Carter's class is like taking an expedition into the deep truths of God's Word. He brings out information rarely addressed in a class.

In summary, New Shiloh has been blessed by the continued tradition of being led by an outstanding pastor—in the person of Dr. Harold A. Carter. This scholar, educator, pulpiteer, and leader has a vision of where the Lord wants his church to go.

The Flock

New Shiloh Baptist Church is located in the heart of urban Baltimore. The congregation is composed of about 3,500 active members. It has a rich history and looks forward to a glorious future. Blessed with outstanding pastoral leadership, it is famous for its ongoing ministries of missions and evangelism. For more than a decade it has maintained multi-staffed ministries with a minister at large, minister of music, and minister of education. During the tenure of Dr. Carter more than forty persons have surrendered to the ministry. At least fifteen persons now serve as ministers who were ordained by New Shiloh under the Carter pastorate. With an annual budget of about $800,000, the church baptizes about 325 persons a year!

This church has a holistic approach to ministry, being concerned about the total person. It practices both fervent evangelism and aggressive social concern. Some of the ministries of the church include:

A *radio ministry* on at least three stations, including a broadcast in Haiti;

A *food co-op ministry* with deliveries every other week through the New Shiloh Food Co-op;

A *ministry of printed literature* including books by Pastor and Mrs. Carter;

A *scholarship assistance ministry* for high school graduates;

A *seminarian financial assistance ministry* for students pursuing theological training;

A *prison ministry* at penal institutions;

A *visitation ministry* at boys' homes;

A *financial-support ministry* for colleges, seminaries, and numerous social concerns;

A *Saturday church school ministry* which provides Bible, academic, worship, and spiritually artistic growth. This program has been a model for numerous churches across the nation.

Other traditional ministries are also carried on by the church.

The guiding principles of New Shiloh are reflected in a statement by the pastor which reveals the heartbeat of this great church:

New Shiloh therefore declares publicly to absolute belief in the Bible, God's Holy Word, the inherent sinfulness of all humanity, and the consequent necessity to preach the Gospel, calling men from a life of sin to fullness in the kingdom of God. New Shiloh believes in the Mystical Body of Christ, the fellowship of Saints, and the fact that born-again believers can live in peaceable love and holy fellowship. To this end, this church seeks to be a saving station, celebrating God and meeting human needs in the day and time God has called to serve. All officers and elected officials are called upon to publicly declare their faith and allegiance to Christ and His Word, year after year. This public service of reaffirmation and rededication is a source of renewed honesty and sincerity to the sacred cause of our Lord.[8]

The secret to the success of New Shiloh Baptist Church seems to be the powerful combination of a super pastor with a vision, a congregation with the commitment to follow God's leadership, and a determination to live for Christ on the part of both pastor and people.

The Alternative to Sunday School

One of the interesting programs at New Shiloh is the Saturday Church School. Whereas most churches have a *Sunday* School, New Shiloh has a *Saturday* church school! How did this alternative to Sunday School develop? Why did the church move Sunday School to Saturday?

The story goes back to 1972. That year the pastor became burdened about the existence of a mini Sunday school at New Shiloh. The church was most ineffective in reaching many of its members for Sunday School. Dr. Carter concluded, "But twelve years ago, as this urban congregation of three thousand members and fewer than 200 in Sunday School looked at its Christian education program, it had to admit that real attention needed to be given to this fundamental need."[9] In response to this conclusion, an exploratory committee was formed to develop specific recommendations for the improvement of the quality of the Sunday School.

The exploratory committee recommended that the church move its Sunday School program to Saturday beginning in October 1973. The overhaul of the religious education program at New Shiloh yielded other recommendations including:

(1) Become more Bible centered and supplement with reference books and Christian literature we would write ourselves.
(2) Discontinue Sunday School as an organized department and put all energies into Saturday church school development.
(3) Departmentalize the Saturday church school providing elective classes for academic enrichment, arts, and crafts.
(4) Go into the community and publicize widely making Saturday church school an outreach ministry.

(5) Follow the Christian year in worship emphasis, dramas, programs, and celebrations.

(6) Consciously seek to be evangelistic in Christian teachings and family-oriented toward building a new respect for parental authority, guidance, and the Christian pursuit of love.[10]

The church accepted these recommendations and moved to implement this mammoth challenge. The new Saturday church school idea was promoted and publicized through posters, radio announcements, word-of-mouth communication, and from the pulpit. On the first Saturday in October 1973, the Saturday church school became a reality at New Shiloh. Not only had a new concept in religious education been implemented, but some one thousand persons enrolled! With a change of meeting day and curriculum, the church school enrollment had increased 400 percent!

The implementation of the Saturday church school program had a tremendous impact on the congregation at New Shiloh. The huge success of this new approach brought several dividends to the church. The church was different in these ways:

First, an unexpected dividend was "a swelling tide of evangelism." The Saturday church school became a catalyst for soul-winning. The pastor reported, "Parents who sent their children to the Saturday school began coming to the church and were won to the cause of Christ."[11] After the Saturday church school started, baptisms at the church jumped from sixteen per month to an average of thirty-five per month.

A second benefit of the new arrangement was an increase in worship service attendance on Sunday. Greater involvement in Saturday church school generated more involvement in Sunday worship. New Shiloh had to add another Sunday worship service to accommodate the crowds stimulated by the Saturday experience.

A surprising phenomenon developed into a third dividend: professionals in the congregation, notably public school and college teachers, "rose to the challenge" and became willing to sacrifice for "the movement." Yet it was extremely difficult to enlist their participation in the local church, and especially in Sunday School. The Saturday church school created a challenge to academically trained minds to dedicate their talents to the Lord. These professionals enthusiastically became involved in the "renaissance of Christian education" at New Shiloh.

A fourth benefit to the church was an increase in fellowship between faculty and students. The sacrifices of Saturday for a weekly religious-education event have not proved to be a problem. Instead of shying away from attendance, teachers and pupils can often be found talking and fellowshipping after official adjournment. The traditional Sunday School schedule had not made this fellowshipping time practical.

A fifth point of impact was in the area of modifying the schedule. The Saturday church school schedule was set up as follows:

10:00 A.M. General worship

10:30 A.M. Bible study (all classes)

11:30 A.M. Second period classes
Bible
Recording/writing/arts crafts/typing/cooking/carpentry/computers/etc.

12:30 P.M. Assembly—A closing devotion from each class

1:00 P.M. Adjourn

During July, August, and part of September the schedule is reduced to two hours, from 10 A.M. to noon. The regular term runs from September through June. This combination provides opportunity for renewal, rest, and rejuvenation in preparation for an enthusiastic fall kickoff.

Dividend number six is the design and implementation of a nontraditional curriculum. Whereas traditional Sunday Schools usually restrict curricula to various Bible study emphases, New Shiloh has broadened class offerings. In the Saturday church school a participant can study courses ranging from Genesis to creative dance. Their curriculum focuses on training people to meet life's needs. It is practically oriented. It is more than an attempt to teach people the Word, it is an effort to supply the specifics of implementing the implications of the Word where people live.

A seventh characteristic reflected through the Saturday church school was a dramatic jump in enrollment and average attendance. Enrollment increased from below two hundred to about one thousand; average attendance ranged between four hundred to six hundred. One sure conclusion about the new approach is that it was effective in securing the involvement of many more people. The church creatively attempted to meet the needs of people, and the effort was met with a tremendous response.

The enrollment of adults was another surprising development as a result of the Saturday church school program. In most Sunday Schools in the Black community, the "children's syndrome" is operative. In this syndrome, adults are not expected to participate in Sunday School because "Sunday School is for children only." However, adult attendance jumped dramatically. On a typical Saturday, half the people present are adults involved in creative classes. For many adults the Saturday church school is the first formal learning experience within the context of care and concern.

Perhaps one of the most significant outgrowths of this creative approach was the ministry. Seventeen persons who came through New Shiloh's Saturday church school now pastor churches!

Once New Shiloh ventured into a creative alternative to its sparsely attended Sunday School program, exciting surprises were discovered. As a result of the Saturday church school, this servant church in the heart of Baltimore would never be the same.

A major distinction of New Shiloh's program is the creative curriculum. The church embraced the philosophy of expanding a traditional Sunday School curriculum. While their curriculum starts with basic Bible study, additional courses complement the biblical foundations. For example, courses are offered in recording, creative writing, arts, crafts, typing, cooking, carpentry, computer operation, and other areas. They have recovered the generalist curriculum emphases of the Black Sunday School movement of a century ago.

Several other ministries have grown out of the Saturday church school at New Shiloh. These spin-offs include:

(1) A tutorial program three days a week in which assistance is available in English, Latin, Spanish, French, math, reading, and typing;
(2) A "Youth Express" class in which current problems affecting teenagers are discussed from a Christian perspective;
(3) A class for the hearing impaired;
(4) The sponsoring of "festival days" by the church "where teachers set up booths, sometimes blocking off the street in front of the church for an old-time country fair usually built around a family theme;"[12]
(5) Marches involving two thousand people "celebrating family solidarity in Christ;"
(6) A weekly witnessing ministry in a home of delinquent boys.

What is the key to success for New Shiloh's Saturday church school? From the perspective of the church, three major factors may be mentioned.

The most evident dynamic that makes New Shiloh's Saturday church school successful is the leadership role of the pastor. The vision and charisma of Dr. Harold Carter permeate this ministry. Without his leadership and involvement, it probably would not thrive as it does. He says, "A further key is the total involvement of the pastor. I have taught a weekly Adult Bible class, sharing truths about various books of Scripture and concerns in Christian theology. This class of 100 has proved to be a nucleus of inner strength and power around which the rest of the program could build."[13] The New Shiloh testimony is that the most important ingredient in a church school program is the leadership of the pastor.

Another dynamic contribution to the success of the Saturday church school is an effective leadership-development program. Prior to serving as a teacher in the church school, prospective workers are required to complete a leadership development program. In the leadership-development program, future teachers are taught how to "be genuinely Christian, evangelical in their beliefs, and committed to the practice of soul-winning and serving others."[14] Furthermore, attendance at weekly teachers' meetings enables the faculty to discuss class-related problems, receive training in outreach, develop skills in retaining new members, and preview the upcoming lesson. Clearly a strength of the church school is trained leadership.

The opening worship service also provides a dynamic impact for the Saturday experience. Built with creativity in mind, the worship period involves guest choirs, musical groups, bands, and notable personalities. The worship period not only sets the mood for the educational experience but provides another opportunity for various components of the worship service to be exercised. The New Shiloh model assumes that proper learning occurs in the context of worship.

Would New Shiloh go back to the traditional Sunday School? The pastor responds with an emphatic "No! We have a catchall class for those who come to our church at 9:30 on Sunday morning, not knowing about our Saturday program. But our dedication is to the ongoing enrichment of the Saturday Church School." [15] This church has tried an alternative to Sunday School, and they like it.

An Analysis of Success

From the standpoint of Sunday School growth strategy, what appears to be the formula for effectiveness for this super church? What are some characteristics that make the Saturday church school effective at New Shiloh? The following seem to be components of New Shiloh's strategy:

1. *A pastor with the vision.*—The observer immediately becomes aware that the pastor of New Shiloh has a broad vision for reaching people through relevant religious education. An interview with Dr. Carter reveals a heartfelt burden for helping people achieve their potential. He sees the potential for people-building that rests in the resources of a congregation that dares to be relevant. He understands the opportunity for improving the quality of life for congregants who move beyond the usual worship experience to involvement in a first-rate training program. This shepherd has a grasp of the difference a church can make in the life of the community if it is willing to pay the price. This pastor knows: "Where there is no vision the people perish."[16]

2. *The personal involvement of the pastor.*—At New Shiloh the guiding force behind the Saturday church school is the pastor. He does not abdicate his leadership role. He leads; he does not point. He has credibility because he role models involvement; he avoids the subterfuge of token participation; he is physically present and significantly involved in the Saturday church school. This program is important to the life of the church because the pastor, the official legitimizer for the congregation, makes it his personal priority.

3. *A distinctive definition.*—The definition of the church school at New Shiloh is distinctive. It is not simply "the Bible-teaching arm of the church." It is broader. It involves the church preparing people for thorough ministry. Therefore, this church school program extends beyond the traditional definition. It does not simply help people understand the content of the Bible; it helps people prepare for life situations.

4. *A creative curriculum.*—The curriculum at New Shiloh's Saturday church school is creative. Geared to meet the needs of people, it dares to corral available resources to equip people for life. Practical courses such as carpentry, typing, and computer training entrance many people who would not likely be interested in the traditional Sunday school curriculum. The success of the creative approach to the Saturday church school at New Shiloh shows that people tend to respond when their needs are met.

5. *A preferred schedule.*—The scheduled time for the church school is apparently preferred by the New Shiloh congregation. The meeting time—Saturday mornings—is obviously better for this church. Perhaps some of the dynamics of the traditional meeting time for Sunday School worked against encouraging people to attend. Not only does the new schedule provide a different

meeting day, but it allows for more time spent in church school. Consequently, the participants can benefit from exposure to more training by virtue of spending more time in class per week. The response of the congregation indicates a preference for the new schedule.

6. *An emphasis on adults.* — Adults make up half of the average attendance at the church school at New Shiloh. The church has not written off the adults; it has challenged them. As a result, they are involved. At this congregation, church school is not for children only; it is for the family. It has discovered that if we reach the adults, the children will be brought also.

7. *A commitment to growth.* — This church was ready to make a definite commitment to grow through the church school. Growing out of a burden of the pastor to reach more people, the congregation embraced the concept that it needed to be willing to pay the price for growing. They realized that a fundamental component of growth strategy is making the commitment to grow. Commitment supplied the energy that propelled this new approach to church school.

8. *Proper worker enlistment and training.* — The selection and training of workers at New Shiloh's church school is a sacred task. Painstaking care is taken to enlist committed and dedicated teachers for the church school. In-depth qualitative training is provided. There is an atmosphere filled with the attitude that "we want to do our best." The weekly teachers' meeting provides opportunity for training to be effective.

9. *The provision of space and equipment.* — A major concern at New Shiloh is the provision of space and equipment. The church knows that space and equipment are major factors in the effective educational experience. Their new church building has a provision for even more educational space. This church understands the relationship between a maximum learning environment and the providing of adequate space and equipment.

10. *A Bible-centered evangelism.* — Although there are many courses in New Shiloh's creative curriculum, the basic foundation is built upon an appreciation for the word of the Lord. The Bible is the basic textbook in this church school. It is taught with a twofold emphasis: (1) winning people to Christ and (2) equipping them for service. Evangelism is the major thrust of this Bible-centered church school.

The above characteristics provide some insights into the success of the Saturday church school at New Shiloh Baptist Church. This creative alternative to the traditional Sunday School yielded with the combining of the classical Sunday School curriculum with a practical program of Christian social ministries. For this dually aligned Progressive Baptist and American Baptist church, an experiment with boldness and creativity paid off.

Notes

1. Harold A. Carter, *Determined: A Faith History of a People Determined to Live with Christ!* (Baltimore: Gateway Press, Inc., 1984):1.

2. Ibid., 3.

3. Ibid., 7.

4. Ibid., 9.

5. Ibid., 19.

6. Ibid.

7. Ibid.

8. Ibid., 101.

9. Ibid., 22.

10. Ibid., 23.

11. Quoted in *Leadership 100*, January-February 1983, 15.

12. Carter, 17.

13. Ibid.

14. Ibid.

15. Ibid.

16. Ibid.

23

Pastoral Counseling and the Black Perspective

Edward P. Wimberly

Introduction

The contents of this chapter are an attempt to lift up the unique aspect of pastoral care in the Black Church. The unique emphasis in Black pastoral care is a perspective which has been shaped by the existential, cultural, and historical conditions peculiar to Black people. This perspective reflects the cultural heritage of Black people, their history as a people in a land of injustice, racism, and segregation, and their struggle as a Christian people to make sense out of their existence in a hostile environment.

What, then, is this distinct emphasis that makes a Black perspective in pastoral care and counseling unique? This distinctive emphasis is the corporate nature of pastoral care and counseling in the Black Church. Of course there are white churches in Protestantism that have had a corporate emphasis in pastoral care and counseling, but the emphasis in white Protestantism has almost been exclusively individual, not corporate. It must also be added that many of the white Protestant seminaries are attempting now to bring the corporate emphasis into pastoral care, because the biblical emphasis is upon the corporate dimensions of human growth. It is also important to acknowledge that the history of American psychiatry shows a pendulum swing between the individual and corporate emphasis in the nineteenth century.[1] However the emphasis upon the individual and his self-sufficiency has been the dominant theme for most Americans including the psychological and religious communities. On the other hand, the corporate emphasis among Black Protestants has remained constant in their behavior, if not in attitude, due to the nature of Black society and its cultural heritage from Africa.

The purpose of this chapter is to analyze the corporate nature of pastoral care and counseling in Black Protestantism, which has its roots not only in

African soil and racial discrimination in this country, but also in the biblical conception of the nature of man and God's attempt to bring salvation to him. However there is no attempt in this chapter to give a systematic explanation of the biblical contribution to pastoral care and counseling in the Black Church. One goal is to establish the corporate function of pastoral care in the Black Church, and to discuss pastoral counseling in the light of the historical-social conditions of the Black Christian.

Corporateness

The nature of pastoral care and counseling in the Black Church is corporate for several reasons. We mean by the term "corporate" that the care of the individual is the function of the total community rather than the function of the pastor or any other specially designated person who possesses specialized skills. The two outstanding influences that have historically contributed to the corporate nature of pastoral care and counseling are segregation and unconscious African survivals.

Segregation, which is the direct result of a rational attempt to justify slavery upon the innate inferiority of Black people, excluded the Black person from participation in the total life of the community. It excluded him from the social life, the religious life, the economic life (except to the extent that he was allowed to be on the producing end of the economy rather than the consumer end), the educational life, and the political life. He was systematically excluded from normal access to participation in the community that would lead to the fulfillment of his potential as a total person. The consequence of all of this is the fact that many of the political social, educational, recreational, economic, and social needs of the Black person had to be fulfilled within the Black Church, his only institution. This was also true for the medical and mental health needs of the Black person. Often it was the Black Church that took care of the needs of the neglected sick and mentally ill. Because the hospitals and mental institutions were segregated, it was the Black Church that had to fulfill this function. These persons were cared for by a caring community because they could not be isolated from the community like the white sick and mentally ill. In fact it was through the efforts of the Black Church that the hospitals were established in the Black community.

Also segregation forced the Black community to see mental health as a problem related to their external condition. Beginning with slavery, the main concern of the Black Christian was his own freedom, but not only his own freedom, but the freedom of his friends and his people. Yes, for some freedom was in the world to come, but for others, freedom was something that would come sooner or later here on earth. The point is, much of their psychic energy went into thinking about freedom, freedom from injustice and slavery. As a result the Black person never saw mental illness or health as an individual matter, but he saw the context in which a person lived out his life.

The second influence that contributes to the corporate nature of the Black Church is the unconscious survivals of Africanisms. There are many African survivals which are present in the life of the Black community today. The writer relies heavily on the theory of the hereditary collective unconscious outlined by the eminent psychologist Carl Jung for his theoretical support for African survivals.[2] Melville Herskovits, a noted American anthropologist, has spent his career developing the theory of the survival of Africanisms while doing comparative field research.[3] The Africanisms for prime consideration in this chapter, then, are the African philosophical concept of unity with nature, and the ritualistic symbolic ceremonies that support the person in the crises of life.

The Africans believe that man exists in harmony with nature.[4] In this context man is not the manipulator nor controller of the forces of nature, but man is to cooperate with nature.[5] The result of this philosophy is that the African sees himself and his community as an integral part of nature and both have a mutual influence upon the other. Thus a person recognizes that his own identity is the result of the interaction with nature and his environment.

To the African not only is man's identity based upon the interaction with his physical environment, but it is also developed in relationship to the community. John Mbiti points out that a child must be born, named, initiated, married—which are all the function of the community—before he can be thought of as a complete person.[6]

The implication of the concept of unity with nature and with the community is obvious. The collective unconscious of Black people lends itself to the corporate concept of pastoral care and counseling. The corporate concept emerges from the background of the African emphasis upon unity with nature, forming the basis for an open systems approach to Black psychology. Black psychology sees man's identity developing in interaction with his environment, as opposed to a closed system equilibrium model, which forms the basis of some individualistic adjustment model of psychology.

Another important factor in African religion that is of interest is the corporate nature of the symbolic ritualistic ceremonies through which the African adjusted and coped with life crises in the past and survives in some of Africa today. Through the ritualistic ceremonies surrounding birth, child rearing, initiation at adolescence, harvesting time, and death, the African found himself in an ethos of ideological and emotional supports that helped him overcome the crises of life. The same kinds of support surrounding the life crises of Black people, which became part of the Black Church, are an inheritance from the collective unconscious reaching back to Africa. This support system is evidenced in the way the Black Church has been a real value in helping the Black person deal with the insanity of racism and injustice. Along with an ideological support system based upon the experience of Black people with God and Jesus Christ—a support system reflected in the Negro spiritual—the African past has helped the Black person and his community deal with the crises of life.

Pastoral Counseling and the Black Person

From the preceding section one would perhaps conclude that pastoral counseling, a specialized area of pastoral care focusing on the individual, is irrelevant to the work of the pastor in the Black Church. But it is conceivable that along with the corporate dimensions and methods of Black pastoral care, pastoral counseling can be used by the Black pastor. In fact, there is increasing evidence supporting the need for more training of Black pastors in the specialty of pastoral counseling to meet the needs of their parishioners.

One source of evidence concerning the aforementioned need of Black pastors to be tooled in counseling skills is a study done by Thomas Pugh and Emily Mudd. The study focuses upon the attitudes of Black women and men toward using community services.[7] One of the conclusions of the study is that many Black people turned to the family, kinfolk, and friends for help with their marriage problems, but most of the respondents felt this did not help them, and they said they would seek out professional help if it were available at a reasonable fee. One of the largest deterrents in seeking out professional help for the respondents was the cost factor, and perhaps a trained clergymen could help bring this needed service at low cost.

Another source of evidence was a study done on the Black middle class in Philadelphia.[8] The study reported the high degree of use by Black people of medical caretakers as opposed to nonmedical caretakers as well as a sophisticated knowledge of mental illness. Although the study reports the extensive use of medical personnel rather than nonmedical personnel, it does appear to me that a pastoral counselor with skills and reputation could utilize this mental health sophistication to great advantage.

However the evidence is not just limited to the Black middle class. Perhaps the most convincing evidence concerning the viability of pastoral counseling in the Black community comes from a study published in book form by Barbara Lerner called *Therapy in the Ghetto*. Her basic thesis is that individual psychotherapy, under appropriate conditions, is an effective method of helping not only the classical middle-class, highly verbal, intellectual client, but it also is a value to the so-called "non-classical untreatable" clients, such as the poor, the Black, and the severely emotionally disturbed. These "untreatables" were thought to be poor prognostic risks because of class distinctions. The treatables were the young and attractive who possessed a high degree of ego-strength, who were well-educated members of the upper class with the absence of deep characterological distortions and a willingness to communicate, and who had a value system congruent with the therapist. Lerner's whole study was to find out if psychotherapy—an attempt by one human being with specialized training to establish a genuinely meaningful, democratic and collaborative relationship with another person in order to put his special knowledge and skills at the second person's disposal for such use as he chooses to make of it—had any results with the so-called "non-treatables."[9]

The first conclusion of the study is that measurable results of the treatment of non-treatable clients, when compared to the same changes in the classical clients, have been achieved in less than thirty hours of treatment, or less than nine weeks.[10] It was found that ten to twenty-five sessions were the normal length for improvement to take place.[11] Not only had improvement been accomplished, but it was done in a short enough period of time to warrant the use of psychotherapy in the local church where the pastor has time only for short-term and crisis-intervention counseling.

The counselor variables were measured to ascertain what effect the counselor had upon the outcome of therapy. The four variables measured were counselor empathy, experience, expectation, and counselor's use of democratic values or respect. The conclusions were that all these variables were significant factors in the improvement of the clients.[12] However the empathy variable failed to show any results because of the inadequacy of the measurement instrument according to the author of the study.

It can be concluded from the study that the obstacles hindering the use of individual psychotherapy on the so-called "non-treatables" are neither unchangeable nor inherent in the client. A trained counselor, pastoral or otherwise, with empathy, respect, and the expectation that the client can grow as the result of his intervention, is a person who can help the so-called "untreatable" person.

Goals of Pastoral Counseling with Blacks

The pervasive influence of racism, segregation, and injustice upon the Black personality cannot be underestimated. These sinister forces have left their unmistakable imprint. The impact of these forces on the Black personality has been evidenced in the Black person's belief that he does not possess the power to effect change in his own life and in the lives of others—indeed, that he is powerless. In fact it is only the rare Black person who can escape this feeling of powerlessness. Thanks to the efforts of Dr. Martin Luther King and the civil rights movement as well as the Black Power movement that the Black person has begun to assess his real power. It is nonetheless clearly evident that the powerlessness the Black person feels as well as the current Black Power movement have significant implications for pastoral counseling with Blacks by the Black pastor.

The first implication is that pastoral counseling with Blacks must focus upon the liberation of the Black personality from any belief in his own powerlessness as a person to determine the direction of his own life according to his own internal frame of reference rather than helping the person adjust to an oppressive society.[13] The adjustment equilibrium model of dynamic psychology is an inadequate goal of pastoral counseling with Blacks, because it means adjusting to a society which must be changed to allow the Black personality to grow to fulfillment of its potential.

Second, the goal of pastoral counseling with Blacks must be action-oriented based upon an analysis of each individual's powerlessness. Often the goals of psychotherapy have been intrapsychic insight into the client's past, but there has been little emphasis upon the steps that a client could take to correct his own difficulties in the present. Pastoral counseling with Blacks cannot afford the luxury of inaction and backward looking by itself. It must focus not only upon the past, but also upon the present. Its focus must be upon the Black person's ability to act on his own behalf and in concert with others in order to change his own condition. It must help him to see that he is not totally powerless; there are some things that he can change. Consequently the goal of pastoral counseling with Blacks is action, insight, and growth, in the present rather than intrapsychic insight into the past.

Process and Pastoral Counseling with Blacks

As pointed out by Barbara Lerner in her study, there are certain core conditions that must be met for therapy to be effective. In reviewing these conditions, four elements will be considered. The first element is counselor empathy. A pastoral counselor, Black or white, must be able to enter into the experience of his client and be tuned in on the wavelength of the client. This has often proved difficult for white therapists.[14] Second, the counselor must have the expectation that the person can grow as the result of his intervention if therapy is to be successful. Certainly the counselor's expectation, whether positive or negative with regard to the client's ability to grow, will be communicated to the client through his attitude toward the client. This is particularly crucial if the counselor is white, because lack of expectation of growth toward the Black client is historically related to white racism.[15] Third, it is emphasized that the counselor must have respect for the client's potential to be a responsible person who makes responsible decisions. This means helping the client to be convinced himself of his own ability to make decisions based upon his own internal frame of reference. Finally, counselor experience and training are important in the outcome of therapy. All four of these core conditions must be present at the same time if therapy is going to be useful for Blacks.

It is the latter concept of experience that will occupy the remainder of this chapter. Beyond satisfying the core conditions of establishing a relationship based upon empathy, positive expectation, and respect, the counselor needs adequate experience in order to appropriately assess the problem of the client and to select the approach which will best help the client. For example, in the case of those clients who feel powerless, the pastoral counselor needs to be able to touch the motivational source of change that exists in the Black client's psyche; that is, Black rage. Black rage is the deep anger resultant from a realization that the control of one's life rests in the hands of others.[16] The counselor's experience with and his ability to reach this affect is crucial in helping the Black person move toward growth. But more than this, he has to move back and forth between the existential and behavioral modalities of therapy so that the client can not only experience his own anger, but also use this anger to do what he can to change the circumstances of his own existence. On the one hand, the existential approach to affect helps the client to experience himself as an angry person while at the same time helping him to discover his own internal meaning and value system. On the other hand, the behavioral approach will help him act upon his value system discovered through the expression and exploration of anger. To accomplish this, the counselor clearly needs training and experience.

This chapter is primarily addressed to the Black pastor. Through my contacts with whites it is clear to me that Black rage is the single factor with which many whites have a great deal of difficulty. This would be true for the white counselor also, especially, because the rage would be directed toward the white counselor. It would be hard not to take it personally. Thus dealing with Black rage may be an area that should be left to the Black counselor.

There are specific implications for the preparation of the Black pastoral counselor that deal with his own anger and value system. The Black pastoral counselor's ability to deal with the anger of the Black client depends upon the extent to which he has dealt with his own anger. If the pastoral counselor has not dealt with his own anger, chances are that he will not be able to facilitate the discovery and exploration of his client's anger. A Black pastoral counselor must necessarily be aware of his own rage toward white society, because, if he denies his own rage, he will not let it come up in the therapy with his client. Second, the Black pastoral counselor must have explored the implications of his own rage for his own meaning and value system and for his own behavior in the world. Finally, the Black pastoral counselor must feel sufficiently at home with his life-style based upon his own internal value system. When the Black pastoral counselor has achieved some degree of success in these personal areas, then he might be effective in helping the Black client or parishioner to move toward growth.

Conclusion

The purpose of this chapter has been to explore the corporate dimensions of pastoral care in the Black Church from a historical vantage point. Also there has been an attempt to explore the relevancy of pastoral counseling as an additional method of the Black pastor alongside the corporate methods of pastoral care. The conclusion is that pastoral counseling can be a viable method for the Black pastor's work with Black parishioners, especially when the core elements of empathy, experience, expectation, and respect are present and when the pastor has faced the implications of his own anger for his existence.

Notes

1. Ruth Caplan, *Psychiatry and the Community in the 19th Century* (New York: Basic Books, 1969).

2. Carl Jung, *Psychology of Religion* (New Haven: Yale University Press, 1938).

3. See Melville J. Herskovits, *The Myth of the Negro Past* (Gloucester, Mass.: Peter Smith, 1970).

4. John Mbiti, *African Religions and Philosophy* (Garden City, N.Y.: Doubleday, 1970):20.

5. Cedrick Clark, "Black Studies or the Study of Black People" in *Black Psychology*, ed. Reginald Jones (New York: Harper and Row, 1972):11.

6. Mbiti, 154.

7. Thomas J. Pugh and Emily Mudd, "Attitudes of Black Women and Men Toward Using Community Service," *Journal of Religion and Health* 10 (July 1971):256–77.

8. Stephen Ring, "Attitude Toward Mental Illness and Use of Caretakers in the Black Community," *American Journal of Orthopsychiatry* 40 (July 1970):711.

9. Barbara Lerner, *Therapy in the Ghetto* (Baltimore: Johns Hopkins University Press, 1972):10.

10. Ibid., 149.

11. Ibid.

12. Ibid., 144.

13. Edward J. Barns, "Counseling the Black student: The Need for a New View," in *Black Psychology*, ed. Reginald Jones (New York: Harper & Row, 1972):215.

14. William Banks, "The Black Client and the Helping Professionals," in *Black Psychology*, ed. Reginald Jones (New York: Harper & Row, 1972):205–12.

15. Kenneth Clark, *Prejudice and Your Child* (Boston: Beacon Press, 1967):85.

16. William Grier and Price Cobbs, *Black Rage* (New York: Basic Books, 1968):27.

24

Confronting the System

William A. Jones, Jr.

There are essentially three ways to look at the American system. One is through the lenses of telescopic idealism. This sometimes results in a view of American culture as the new Eldorado, and evokes intense feelings about the manifest destiny of America. It often leads to political messianism, as witnessed in the often-stated remarks about America's duty to "make the world safe for democracy." The rationale for American involvement in both the Korean War and the war in Vietnam was repeatedly expressed in these terms. America is continually lifted up by her political representatives as "the leader of the free world." Ironically the so-called free world is composed of that segment of the white world which exercises its power to dominate the rest of the world. Furthermore, the leaders of the nations which make up the "free world" have never agreed that America is indeed their leader. Charles V. Hamilton, Jr.'s book *The Nixon Theology* is a clear commentary on civil religion in America and its attending spirit of ethnocentrism. Commenting on former President Richard M. Nixon's reaction to the Apollo moonshot, Hamilton reports:

> In his euphoria following the splashdown, the President had said to a group of foreign students: "Any culture which can put a man on the moon is capable of fathering all nations of the earth in peace, justice and concord." In addition to the lapse of diplomacy involved in making such a chauvinistic statement in the presence of foreigners, Nixon's remark betrayed one of his most critical weaknesses. He seems so certain that the values of this country are universally binding that he could find even in the technological success of a moonshot the symbol of a transcendent mission.[1]

Telescopic idealism is at best replete with fantasy and mythomania. America is not the kingdom of God on earth.

Telescopic idealism is also reflected in the nation's posture of economic messianism. The inscription on the base of the Statue of Liberty is a clear example: "Keep, ancient land, your storied pomp!" cries she with silent lips. "Give me your tired, your poor, your huddled masses yearning to be free, the wretched refuse of your teeming shore, send them, the homeless, the tempest-tossed to me, I lift my lamp beside the golden door."

Messianic notions have resulted in the widespread attitude, even in pulpit and pew, that government policies and actions should not be subjected to sharp criticism and harsh judgment. The late Cardinal Spellman often declared: "My country, right or wrong." Others have repeatedly echoed his pronouncement in myriad ways. From a Christian perspective, an attitude of moral superiority over other nations vitiates any good that is done for the suffering peoples of the world.

A second way to view the nation is through the lenses of microscopic realism. This view can eventuate in a characterization of the nation as the seat of satanic power, hell on earth, and the perfect embodiment of the demonic. Those in this camp run the gamut from cynicism to nihilism.

The third approach is one of holding telescopic idealism and microscopic realism in a state of dialectical tension. This view recognizes and acknowledges the nation's virtues and its vices, its grandeur and its wretchedness. To do this is to be faithful to the prophetic function, to see the human order both as it should be and as it actually is. The prophet is one who has seen "the vision splendid," and then gauges and addresses the human order on the basis of that vision.

A close scrutiny of "The System" reveals that Americans are controlled and manipulated by a sinful minority that is neither young, colored, nor poor. They own the nation's wealth, rape the world's resources, make the political decisions, plan the nation's military ventures, hurt our humanity, and deface our divinity. Ferdinand Lundberg, in his exhaustive study titled *The Rich and the Super-Rich*, points out that the economic and political control of America is in the hands of a highly privileged few:

> 1.6 percent of the adult population own at least 32 percent of all assets, and nearly all the investment assets, and . . . 11 percent of households . . . own 56 percent of the assets and 60 percent of the net worth. It is even possible that 1/2 of 1 percent own more than one-third of all productive

assets as of 1965-67. It is evident that this leaves very little to be apportioned among 90 percent of the population.[2]

Lundberg further advises that "most of the productive activity of the United States is in the hands of a tiny number of very large corporations largely owned and completely dominated by a small coterie, almost a junta."[3] Their influence over the decision-making process of the government is tremendous. They are a tightly knit group of men who not only work together through interlocking corporate boards, but who also socialize together for purposes that are ultimately economic and political.

Not only are the big deals arranged in the comfortable privacy of the interlocking clubs . . . but . . . general policy governing the interlocking corporate world, as distinct from the specific policy of each company, is there determined. Even big tycoons must eat; and they eat together in their clubs. As it happens, during the meals, arrangements are made for organizing the world after their hearts' desires.[4]

The influence of big business in the political sphere is pointedly described by C. Wright Mills in his book *The Power Elite*. According to Mills, the military-industrial complex is controlled by "the inner core of the power elite."

Each member of the power elite need not be a man who personally decides every decision that is to be ascribed to the power elite. Each member, in the decisions he does make, takes the others seriously into account. They not only make decisions in the several major areas of war and peace; they are the men who, in decisions in which they take no direct part, are taken into decisive account by those who are directly in charge.[5]

Most Americans, prior to the Watergate era, sincerely believed that the nation's affairs were directed by men in government who were free from the pressures of powerful economic interests. Had they listened, they would have learned a serious lesson from Senator Russell Long's admission in a 1967 speech before the United States Senate. The Senator from Louisiana said:

Most campaign money comes from businessmen. Labor contributions have been greatly exaggerated. It would be my guess that about 95 percent of campaign funds at the congressional level are derived from businessmen. At least 80 percent of this comes from men who could sign a net worth statement exceeding a quarter of a million dollars. . . . Merely by assiduously tending to the problem of business interests located in one's own state, a legislator can generally assure himself of enough financial support to campaign effectively for reelection.[6]

The translation of economic power into political power is part and parcel of "the American way of life." By this process the interests of *the powerful few* are preserved and enhanced, while that which accrues to the well-being of *the powerless many* is almost accidental.

The actual (though unannounced) objective of the ruling triumvirate is to hold on to its power. Total control of the society is implicit in every decision and in every action. They control the systems of communication, define terms, put word labels on all forms of human behavior, and through skillful psychological manipulation, perpetuate and escalate already existing divisions and polarizations. By the use of linguistic devices, they cause certain words to generate terrible fears in most members of the larger society. For example, the words *liberal* and *radical* at one time were considered dirty words. For they applied, in the eyes of most Americans, to persons who were traitors to the best interests of the nation. In recent times, the words *militant* and *revolutionary* hold the preeminence as dirty words. They are distasteful for they are associated with the idea of the overthrowing of the existing governmental order.

To speak of revolution is to disturb domestic tranquility and threaten an already shaky sense of security. But there are some things, like them or not, that are part and parcel of the human pilgrimage. Revolution, in spite of its poignant, piercing character, falls into this category. It touches down not as some new bolt out of the blue. It is as ancient as man's initial estrangement, and stretches across the total mileage of man's marchings. Unlike *evolution*, which connotes gradual change, *revolution* is abrupt, and it involves the overthrowing of the established order rather than the development of its latent capacities for good.

About five centuries before Christ, Aristotle attempted in his *Politics* an explanation of the revolutionary posture in the human situation. "The universal and chief cause of this revolutionary feeling," according to Aristotle, is "the desire of equality, when men think that they are equal to others who have more than themselves."[7] The revolutionary spirit is rooted in the desire to be free, to experience and to enjoy equity, and it is grounded in certain ineluctable urgings of the human spirit. Men bound by oppressive brethren cry out, "I want to be free. Something deep, down within me—that mysterious something called 'the soul'—prods and pushes me, and demands of me that I break out of any unjust confinement to which sinful mortals subject me. Something good and God-like in me rebels and revolts against any and all forms of tyranny." Regardless of any derogatory interpretation given to the revolutionary spirit by the up-people, a genuine thrust toward personhood and/or peoplehood should be regarded as sacred. Victims of tyranny who refuse to acknowledge and actively work for the fulfillment of their God-intended destiny as real persons do violence to the sanctity of their own creation.

In the present world order, freedom is so rare and oppression so common that revolution is commonplace. Deep rumblings and uprooting social convulsions are the order of the day. From nearly every quarter there comes the word of uprisings against human powers that have become demonic. Youths are rebelling against military madness and morally bankrupt value systems. Blacks are revolting against the democratic myth and the plantation ethic. Almost everywhere, there is a rolling tide of resentment toward hindrances and obstacles to human existence. A generation, in some ways new and novel, has come into being. They often speak in rough and abrasive manner; their words are cutting and callous; the language is often crude and unpolished.

The fundamental issue, however, concerns the groanings beneath the linguistics. Are the groanings legitimate? That is the question, for the divine ear is ever alert to the cries of the afflicted. Those who groan, in this writer's view, are on the side of righteousness and make company with the eternal. In our world right and righteousness constitute a revolutionary posture. Wrong is so prominent and pervasive that it appears right to be wrong. Those who deem it their duty to challenge the emissaries of evil are relegated to the status of renegades, and the most bitter scorn is reserved for those who seek justice. The most vicious attacks are leveled at persons who strive to be actively Christian.

Against the backdrop of structured sin and institutionalized iniquity, righteousness is thus inherently revolutionary. If one is faithful to the gospel, one is revolutionary by definition. Arnold Schuchter states the case well:

For the revolutionary Christian, the message is that the future is his prime responsibility—to subject the earth and its institutions to human welfare, to build truly human communities of men as the physical and social context of that welfare, and to develop the potential of individuals within those communities to their fullest fruition. Obstacles that stand in the way of carrying out this responsibility are sins which should be removed. This is a vision of redress that has the kind of catalytic power requisite to revolutionary movements. It is a vision of the good society where the many will be favored over the few or the few will not be exploited or oppressed by the many.[8]

The things that belong to God are in such radical opposition to the human order as presently structured that God can be called without apology "God the Revolutionary."

The paramount question, historically and presently, centers on the methodology for dealing with the demonic. The writers of the Declaration of Independence recognized clearly the sanctity of revolution and declared forthrightly:

that whenever any Form of Government becomes destructive of these Ends, it is the Right of the People to alter or to abolish it, and to institute new Government, laying its Foundation on such Principles, and organizing its Powers in such Form, as to them shall seem most likely to effect their Safety and Happiness. . . . But when a long Train of Abuses and Usurpations, pursuing invariably the same Object, evinces a Design to reduce them under absolute Despotism, it is their Right, it is their Duty, to throw off such Government, and to provide new Guards for their future Security.[9]

But how does an afflicted minority exercise this right and this duty? Acceptance of its rightness does not necessarily prescribe the method. Morris describes the great need of revolution and the point at which most churchmen put on the brakes:

Nothing short of revolution will cauterize the stinking sores of the West. A fair slice of the Christian world is agreed about that—the Vatican, the World Council of Churches, bishops, theologians, and parish pump preachers. By revolution they mean many things, all important; drastic reform of the Church, more dynamic Christian witness, a new spirit in men's hearts—but they do not mean blood, bombs, and barricades.[10]

The question of method is basically the question of the moral status of violence versus nonviolence. Christians can be observed operating on both sides of the spectrum, with each side affirming its faithfulness to the gospel. Some embrace an ethic of violent revolution. Others preach a gospel of nonviolent revolution. The latter position is sometimes charged with being a middle-class phenomenon, embraced for security reasons by those who have something to lose. The foremost modern proponent of the nonviolent ethic was the late Martin Luther King, Jr., and yet it is difficult to place the label of absolute pacifism upon him. He said often that Hitler should have been fought because of the demonic nature of his deeds. And of course King did not refuse armed protection of himself by others. Emil Brunner's dictum is valid: "He who affirms the State, affirms violence."[11] This means, in a word, that those who refuse to take up arms may have to be defended by others who will.

In so-called Christian America, the national posture has been consistently contradictory in character. America has presented itself to the world as a peace-loving nation, but is simultaneously regarded by the outside world as a warmonger. The nation has never sought the nonviolent distinction in its foreign involvements, but has always urged nonviolence as the only proper course for aggrieved and afflicted citizens. A hybrid mentality exists, which perhaps explains the preponderance of hypocritical double-talk. Great concern has been voiced in recent years about an emerging ethic of violence in the land. Much of this talk is tied to the Black thrust for power. But to treat violence as a new thing is absurd, when just a scant trace of history reveals that violence is closely akin to Americanism. The roots of violence sink deeply in Western culture. America's beginning was on a bloody basis. The land was taken from the Indians by violence; independence was secured by violence; Blacks were enslaved by violence; and radical but necessary social change has often been prevented by violence. There is little wonder, then, that the victimized masses, here and elsewhere, have adopted as their motto: "By any means necessary!" Ted R. Gurr, co-author of the report of the National Commission on the Causes and Prevention of Violence, acknowledged the tendency of Americans to dismiss certain hard, historical realities: "Americans have always been given to a kind of historical amnesia that masks much of their turbulent past. Probably all nations share this tendency to sweeten memories of their past through collective repression, but Americans have probably magnified this process of selective recollection, owing to our historic vision of ourselves as a latter-day chosen people, a new Jerusalem."[12] Perhaps collective repression of facts pertaining to a violent past is to be expected from the heirs of those who engaged in collective oppression. But it does not spare the heirs the burden of dealing presently with the demands of the descendants of those who were oppressed and who consider themselves sorely oppressed.

How does one deal with the demonic? Methodologically speaking, to choose absolutely between violence and nonviolence is too simplistic. To embrace either ethic absolutely is to deny or to ignore the relativities of the life situation. Both violence and nonviolence are relative strategies in that both are morally ambiguous. The choice of either is necessitated by the absence of love, which is the only absolute ethic. The absence of love makes for the denial of justice, which insures the presence of injustice. José Bonino, president of Union Theological Seminary, Buenos Aires, sees the question of violence as "a subordinate and relative question." He explains:

> It is subordinate because it has to do with the "cost" of the desired change—the question of the legitimacy of revolution is not decided on the basis of the legitimacy of violence and vice versa. "Violence" is a cost that must be estimated and pondered in relation to a particular revolutionary situation. It is "relative" because in most revolutionary situations . . . violence is already a fact constitutive of the situations: injustice, slave labor, hunger, and exploitation are forms of violence which must be weighed against the cost of revolutionary violence.[13]

In other words, the methodology for dealing with injustice must be determined by the particular social situation and the degree of demonism therein.

In the course of history there have been instances where violence was redemptive. Prayer and fasting did little to stop Hitler and the Nazi juggernaut. Nonviolence has been, at least to date, the most rational and redemptive strategy for Blacks in racist America. But nonviolence appears utterly untenable as a means of dealing a deathblow to the apartheid of Southern Rhodesia and South Africa. The proper response to demonic power at the planetary level has to be determined situationally. The choice is not between purity and impurity; it is between differing degrees of sin. There is no social ethic that does not have to consider the sins of man and the relativities of human history, for every social policy is tainted by sin. Perfection is not possible within history.

There is another dimension to the debate over violence and nonviolence. Without the threat of violence (overt or covert, open or veiled), nonviolence is politically impotent. Martin Luther King, Jr., operated at one end of the continuum; Malcolm X and others operated at the opposite end. The almost total rejection of Malcolm facilitated a certain acceptance of King. The hallmark of nonviolence is its view of redemptive suffering, its activistic affliction endured in pursuit of truth and justice. This brand of behavior is noteworthy in its declaration that a profound relationship exists between the victim and the victimizer. Jacques Ellul argues,

> Only in the light of Jesus Christ's sacrifice of himself can man be compelled to live as man. In following the path appointed by Christ we show the other to himself. Camus understood this; he showed that there is a link between the victim and the executioner, showed how the victim can compel the executioner to become a man by recognizing his victim. Seeing the crucified Christ the Roman centurion said, "Certainly this man was innocent." Seeing Joan of Arc burned at the stake the English captain said, "We have burned a saint." At that moment they became men.[14]

Although a profound relationship does seem to exist between the victim and the victimizer, conversion from brute to man also seems to be the rare exception rather than the general rule. Most butchers remain butchers. Case studies in the Black-white experience, where butchers have been changed to brothers, have yet to be released. It must also be acknowledged that most victims of "The System" see the attainment of their freedom as primary and conversion of the victimizers as secondary or unimportant. Redemptive suffering is not the stated goal of the masses of men. It is the method of the saints who are as rare as righteousness itself. It is the conduct of those whose faith assures them that resurrection follows crucifixion, that funeral is followed by festival, and that Sunday will give answers to Friday's questions. In the final analysis, it is the posture of those who are willing to suffer for righteousness' sake, and who do so believing that they are workers together with God in his revolutionary, leveling process expressed to and through Isaiah: "Every valley shall be exalted, and every mountain and hill shall be made low: and the crooked shall be made straight, and the rough places plain: and the glory of the Lord shall be revealed, and all flesh shall see it together: for the mouth of the Lord hath spoken it."[15]

To recognize the inadequacies of nonviolence as a strategy does not necessarily lead to the unconditional advocacy of violence as the only strategy. The violent strategy is not a viable one for Blacks in America. The system may very well deserve a violent revolution, but there is a fundamental difference between militancy and insanity. Aggrieved and frustrated Blacks who urge the use of munitions in an armed assault on evil white structures do not understand the nature of the enemy. America is probably the most pathological killer in the history of the world and one does not go bear hunting with a switch. It would prove initially suicidal and ultimately genocidal. But over and above this, the inhumanity of whites is not worthy of imitation.

Within the ranks of ghetto dwellers, other voices can be heard. There are those who espouse an ethic of separatism or withdrawal from white society. The rhetoric runs all the way from the creation of a separate Black state within the continental limits of the United States to a modern exodus with an unspecified African destination. The separatist position is an understandable reaction to the failures of integration. Stokely Carmichael speaks for millions of Blacks when he declares:

> Integration . . . speaks to the problem of blackness in a despicable way. As a goal it has been based on complete acceptance of the fact that in order to have a decent house or education, blacks must move into a white neighborhood or send their children to a white school. This reinforces, among both black and white, the idea that "white" is automatically better and "black" is by definition inferior. This is a subterfuge for the maintenance of white supremacy.[16]

Integration is generally defined in terms of what is best for whites, which signals a fundamental absence of integrity. It is a one-way street, more monological than dialogical. It preserves paternalism, even within the churches. Integration is impossible in any cultural setting where racism is real to any degree. Separatism, too, is impossible, both ontologically and practically. An interim ethic of Black asceticism has already proven profitable. Blacks have withdrawn psychologically, spiritually, and even culturally, as witnessed by the widespread interest in Black history, Black art, Black music, Black religion, Afro hairstyles, and African dress. This has served to diminish significantly the Black identity crisis, and represents an eventful step in the movement from property to pride to power. Neither integration nor separatism is the goal of Blacks. The dominant desired goal is that of freedom and equity.

Existence without equity is the plight of Blacks throughout America. It is the major hurdle to be overcome. Passive submission to the status quo is the big barrier that stands in the way. A spirit of defeatism, born out of centuries of unfulfilled dreams, pervades the thinking of millions. The problem with this posture is its denial of the creative powers of the human spirit. It ascribes permanence to society's sinful structures and says that nothing can be done to reverse the downward spiral. Passive submission says "amen" to Samuel F. Yette's assessment: "Examination of the problem must begin with a single, overpowering socioeconomic condition in the society: black Americans are obsolete people."[17]

However if the majority of Blacks believed that they were in fact an obsolete people, hope would be on an unending holiday. The tremendous flux and ferment evident in the Black community are a sure indication that most Blacks have not surrendered to a spirit of hopelessness and helplessness. Many Blacks continue to "sing the Lord's song in a strange land." Whenever there exists within a people a residue of interest in and enthusiasm about the large possibilities of that people, their powerlessness is not absolute. The simple presence of twenty-five million persons of African descent after centuries of maltreatment, miseducation, and ghetto misery says clearly that Blacks have not thrown in the towel. The sheer size of the Black population undercuts and vitiates the charge of total powerlessness. There is sufficient power present to obviate the charge of obsolescence. The problem is essentially one of the nonutilization and misuse of power.

The point is that there is sufficient latent power in the Black community to provide fuel and fire for a strategy of creative coercion. Such a strategy entails, in simple terms, the proper use of existing power to coerce or force the oppressor into a just relationship with the captive community.

Nonviolent direct action as expressed in the campaigns headed by Martin Luther King, Jr., is a striking example of creative coercion. It resulted in the removal of the legal sanctions of segregation and gave Blacks throughout the South free access to the ballot. Beyond these, King's actions raised the vision of Blacks throughout the nation to the larger possibilities of creative coercion as a method for achieving economic justice. Creative coercion is a just means to a just end. It is a proven route to equity and power. Its spiritual basis is that of noncooperation with evil, an ethical stance deeply rooted in the Judeo-Christian tradition. Cooperation with evil is tantamount to an endorsement of evil.

The biblical narratives cite instance after instance where men were more concerned about the state of their souls than the well-being of their bodies. The Exodus is a shining illustration. During the Babylonian Captivity, Shadrach, Meshach, and Abednego, slaves of the empire, told Nebuchadnezzar: "O king . . . we will not serve thy gods, nor worship the golden image which thou hast set up."[18] They decided that it was better to burn than bow. In the midst of the same enslavement, the prophet Daniel refused to eat the king's meat.[19] Rather then betray their Lord, Peter and the other apostles told the Jewish council: "We ought to obey God rather than men."[20] Paul admonished the Christians in Thessalonica to "abstain from all appearance of evil."[21] Noncooperation with evil is fundamental to the liberation of any people. It is the launching pad for a program of creative coercion, for it affirms personhood and peoplehood. It admits to a dignity which is divinely derived, and it says that no man has the right to attempt its destruction.

Three components are absolutely essential to a meaningful program of creative coercion: (1) transformation of the Black leadership class; (2) collectivization of Black economic power; and (3) politicization of Black numerical strength. Let us look at each.

First, there is an urgent need for a transformation of the Black leadership class. Black leadership suffers from serious fragmentation. Division is deep not only between different professional groups but also within the various groups. Group interests and individual ambitions take precedence over the total well-being of Blacks in the nation. There is widespread difference of opinion about what the actual goals of Blacks should be, and about the strategies that should be implemented for the attainment of just goals.

Daniel Thompson, in his study titled *The Negro Leadership Class*, concluded that there are three types of Black leaders: "Uncle Tom," the "racial diplomat," and "the race man."[22]

"Uncle Tom," presently not as prominent as heretofore, existed on a large scale both prior to and during the era of the 1960s. He was the liaison person between powerful whites and powerless Blacks, and his primary allegiance was always to whites. The dispenser of limited favors to the Black community, he was expected to "bow and scrape" before whites to receive pitiable favors. Uncle Tom seemed satisfied with the system of segregation. Fortunately the mortality rate of Uncle Toms has been exceedingly high during the past decade.

The "racial diplomat" is the spiritual successor to Uncle Tom. Generally better educated and more sophisticated, he also serves a liaison function, but does not see himself in that role. He hugs the illusion that he is operating with whites on a peer basis for the good of his people. He is exhibit "A" in Black-white relations, a prominent personage at interracial affairs made up of people who have held back the tide of justice for the past fifty years. The racial diplomat can always be expected to mediate differences between the natives and the rulers, but always in a way that guarantees an outcome amenable to the rulers. In the ghetto, he is called an "oreo": Black externally but white internally. His social behavior says to ghetto dwellers that he prefers sipping cocktails with the oppressors to shaking hands with the oppressed.

The "race man" is the rare creature in the Black leadership class. Though not a racist, he is the embodiment of racial pride and has absolute distaste for the system. His primary devotion is to his brothers and sisters in tribulation. He begs no favors from the establishment, but demands justice for his people. While the up-people regard him as militant, revolutionary, and a trouble-maker, his own people see him as a spokesman for, and champion of, their cause. The task is one of increasing his tribe by sensitizing the "racial diplo-mat" to the reality, namely, that the ghetto is basically a cultural condition afflicting all Blacks in America, and even throughout the world. Only authen-tic "race men" can creatively confront a racist world.

Second, Black economic power must be collectivized. Many have con-cluded that the technological revolution has already rendered Blacks expend-able. The conclusion is utterly false. It is true that Blacks have limited produc-tion power; Blacks are mainly consumers and not producers. Though they are instruments of production, they are not producers in the sense of ownership of the means of production. However consumers are not a powerless group. In a capitalist system, consumption is ultimately more determinative than production. Production minus consumption equals economic chaos. Black consumption power in America is awesome, not simply because the collective annual earning power of Blacks is upwards of seventy billion dollars, but also because of the narrow profit margin at which many American businesses and industries operate. The great majority enjoy a profit figure of less than 10 percent. Most food companies realize less than 3 percent. Given the reality of narrow margins of profit, it is clearly understandable how the slogan "The customer is always right" has come into widespread usage.

What does this mean for Blacks who dwell at the base of the economic pyramid? It means that they represent the difference between profit and loss for many mass-consumption industries, and these constitute the very backbone and lifeblood of the nation's economy. In existential terms, Blacks can spell the difference between life and death for numerous industries and businesses. How can this reality be exploited for purposes that are morally just and equitable?

The ghetto has been previously described as an island of poverty in the midst of a sea of affluence. The ghetto is marked by economic starvation and stagnation. The outgo exceeds the income. Capital is the missing ingredient. The Japanese in California, when faced with the same problem following World War II, adopted a policy that stipulated that every dollar that entered their community had to pass through the hands of at least four Japanese before departing from their community. Such a strategy would certainly strengthen the economic life of the ghetto and is worthy of emulation.

Beyond this, if the larger business community returned to the Black community a share proportionate to what Blacks contribute in sales and profits, the status of Blacks would be appreciably enhanced. Such a "return" should include equitable employment at all levels; a proper percentage of bank deposits to Black banks; a just amount of the advertising budget to Black advertising companies and Black media concerns; an equitable expenditure of the insurance dollar to Black insurance companies and agencies; a proper use of Black service companies; and a just portion of the philanthropic dollar to Black causes. Although Black institutions in these categories do not now exist in sufficient strength to handle such a massive "return," white businesses, on the simple basis of the Black contribution, should be made to create and develop new Black business institutions.

The regularly recited response to this kind of request is that anything which smacks of a quota system or a percentage arrangement is patently undemocratic. The argument is absurd. The evils are too long-standing and too deeply entrenched for the gap to be bridged by any other means. Historically free enterprise has meant the freedom to deny fair employment, to ignore the pain of ghetto dwellers, and to exploit the ghetto's meager resources for the economic enhancement of whites. The system has been free to be undemocratic in its distribution of power. Powerful economic institutions cannot be expected to move volitionally toward equity. They must be creatively coerced.

The Reverend Richard Allen, founder of the African Methodist Episcopal Church, recognized the necessity of a program of creative coercion more than a century ago. Charles H. Wesley described it as follows:

> Richard Allen was active in the organization of a "Free Produce Society" of Philadelphia. The object of this organization was the purchase of produce grown by free labor only. Its members pledged themselves to make purchases only from merchants who refused to sell slave labor produce. This society grew out of an assembly of colored people at "Richard Allen's Church" on December 20, 1830. About five hundred persons assembled "to form an association to encourage the use of the productions of free laborers in preference to those of slaves."[23]

Allen's methodology was at once that of selective buying and creative coercion.

Two movements in this area have been attempted in recent years. The first was called Selective Patronage, a Philadelphia-based program spearheaded by Black clergymen to secure jobs for Blacks. The procedure was simple and direct. A minister's committee with an unnamed chairman would wait on the head of a major company and present specific job demands. If the company did not favorably respond within a specified time period, four hundred preachers would go to their pulpits and urge their congregants to cease patronizing the company in question. Selective Patronage resulted in many new jobs for Philadelphia Blacks and in the early 1960s gave birth to Opportunities Industrialization Centers (OIC), a national and international job-training and job-development program, headed by the Reverend Leon H. Sullivan. The selective patronage concept caught the eye of Martin Luther King's Southern Christian Leadership Conference, and a new program under SCLC auspices was born. Headed initially by the Reverend Jesse Jackson, it took the name Operation Breadbasket. The selective patronage concept was expanded beyond demands for jobs, to include banking, insurance, advertising, service contracts, and philanthropy. Chapters were established in ten major cities. Operating on the basic presupposition that "the earth is the Lord's, and the fulness thereof,"[24] the Breadbasket strategy is as follows:

1. *Investigation*—A target company is researched with respect to its total business posture, and then visited by a committee of clergymen. Data is requested of the president. The data includes items such as the latest report to the Economic Opportunity Commission, a complete breakdown of all jobs

according to race, and a listing of all concerns with which the company does business. If the company refuses to release the information, that is sufficient grounds for a withdrawal of patronage. If the information is given, the second step is taken.

2. *Education*—This is self-education. The chapter familiarizes its constituency with the facts and draws up a set of demands to be presented to the target company.

3. *Negotiation*—Demands are formally presented and a time period given for compliance. If good faith is evidenced within the designated time period, a covenant is agreed upon and signed by the principals, signaling a new relationship of respect and justice. If good faith is not demonstrated, the chapter moves to the fourth step.

4. *Demonstration*—While demonstration may include picketing and leafleting, it involves primarily the use of pulpits, public media, and word of mouth announcements to inform Blacks and other persons of goodwill that the target company has been declared off limits. As a rule, it is just a short while before the company feels the pinch and the loss of its "good" name, and thereupon agrees to the demands.

5. *Reconciliation*—The company and the community are reconciled. A covenant is signed, and Blacks are informed that it is now all right to patronize the company.

The Breadbasket strategy is a workable one. It is rational, responsible, and redemptive. However, there is one major drawback. Economic injustice is so widespread, and those equipped to carry on the struggle are so few in number, that it is difficult to implement the strategy on a wide scale. There have been instances where companies other than the one in immediate question invited Operation Breadbasket to look them over and set their house in order. It should be noted that Breadbasket does not concern itself with recruitment and training, which are viewed as company responsibilities. Operation Push, a split from Operation Breadbasket, employs a strategy identical to that of Breadbasket. Both stress the need for Blacks to support Black business wherever possible, and both have sponsored Black business expositions to raise the visibility level of Black businesses.

The Greater New York chapter of Operation Breadbasket ran up a string of successive victories over Taystee Bread, Wonder Bread, Drake's Bakeries, Mays Department Stores, Abraham & Straus, Martins Department Stores, Coca-Cola Bottling Company of New York, Canada Dry, Robert Hall, Sealtest

Foods, and Pepsi Cola Bottling Company. In most instances it was not necessary to call for a boycott. The mere threat of such an action caused company officials to accede to the demands.

The most formidable foe ever faced by the Greater New York chapter was the Great Atlantic and Pacific Tea Company, a company with sales in excess of 50 billion dollars per annum, and a net profit (after taxes) of less than 1 percent. After several unsuccessful attempts to meet with William Kane, president of A & P, the chapter's ministerial leaders decided on a course of direct action. Twenty-two clergymen gathered in Grand Central Station on the morning of January 27, 1971, and proceeded from there to the executive suite of A & P. A knock on the door resulted in its being opened, whereupon the preachers moved in and began an occupation of the offices, which lasted some thirty-six hours, culminating in arrests for criminal trespassing. The widespread publicity resulting from this action alerted the general public to the unjust dealings of A & P with the Black community. The company's products were declared off limits to Black appetites. Many whites joined in the struggle. Other mass arrests followed, including those of the Reverend Jesse Jackson and the Reverend Ralph Abernathy, president of Southern Christian Leadership Conference. As a result of such activities, a ground swell of support developed in the New York City area, extending even to Rochester, New York. Thirty-three major organizations gave the campaign unreserved endorsement. These included the United Farm Workers of America, the Congress of African Peoples, the National Council of Churches, the Catholic Senate of Manhattan, the Episcopal Diocese of Brooklyn and Long Island, the Catholic Senate of Brooklyn and Long Island, the Baptist Ministers Conference of New York and Vicinity, the Commission on Interfaith Activities of the Union of American Hebrew Congregations, the North Jersey Federation of Reformed Synagogues, the Harlem Ministers' Interfaith Association, the New York Inter-religious Clergy Coalition, the Brooklyn Catholic Inter-racial Council, the Long Island Council of Churches, the New Rochelle Council of Churches, the Council of Churches of the City of New York, the National Disciples of Christ, the Council of Black Elected Officials, the National Welfare Rights Organization, the Vulcan Society (Black firemen), the New York Urban League, Block Associations, and numerous other groups. Huntington Hartford, grandson of the founder and a major shareholder in A & P, gave his endorsement and called a press conference to publicly declare his support.

The impact was significant. A & P sales were dealt a severe blow. The value of company stock steadily fell. When the action began, A & P stock was selling at $34 per share. It has not risen above $8 in the past three years.

William Kane, the president who refused to meet with the ministers, and whose action brought about the boycott, was kicked upstairs to the position of chairman. This was either a case of elimination by elevation or a reward for recalcitrance. William Longacre was elected president and appeared more reasonable and seemed anxious to come to terms. Several meetings were held with him in a Manhattan hotel. It was obvious that he was not his own man; a ventriloquist was behind the scenes. He agreed to sign a covenant, but one drafted by the company with more shadow than substance, which was totally unacceptable.

The momentum generated by the mass arrests and the many endorsements picked up speed. Jackson and Abernathy scheduled press conferences and called for a national boycott. It appeared to the New York chapter that, for the first time in American history, Blacks were about to move collectively on a nationwide scale in the interest of economic justice. That hope was short-lived. Nothing was done at the national level to implement the announced action. Greater New York was the only area of regular activity. The chapter could have settled for a covenant that covered A & P operations in the New York area, but this was unacceptable since the originally stated goal was that of a national covenant covering all A & P operations and installations. It should be acknowledged that significant changes have taken place in A & P's behavior in the New York community. The percentage of Blacks has increased at all levels. Several Black companies have entered into a contractual relationship with the company. The boycott has not been lifted. Hence, many persons still refuse to patronize A & P. It should also be noted that for the first time in two years, the company realized a profit in the first quarter of 1974.

The lessons learned to date from the A & P encounter are crucial to the development of any program of economic justice. First, Blacks can effectively organize at the local level to challenge economic injustice. Second, the more obstinate the adversary, the greater the degree of public support. Third, it requires no more energy to fight a large company than it does to fight a smaller one. Fourth, it is not difficult, when the issues are clear and properly presented, to galvanize diverse religious and civic groups into an effective coalition.

Blacks in America have never moved in concert against any major business concern. Such an effort would serve well to inform and heighten the collective conscience of Blacks concerning their tremendous but latent consumption power. Economic equity spells power. Equity is owed to Blacks, but there is no disposition on the part of powerful economic pharaohs to grant it; it must be seized by means of creative coercion.

The third component in an effective program of creative coercion is that of the politicization of Black numerical strength. Ghetto dwellers have few representatives in government to plead their case. The gap between numerical strength and political power is greater than, though not as devastating as, the economic gap between Blacks and whites. At the national level, Blacks hold less than 4 percent of the congressional seats, and o percent of the senatorial seats. This is the picture at that level where primary decisions are made with respect to "Life, Liberty, and the Pursuit of Happiness."

The problem of low representation is due in major measure to the long period of disenfranchisement, brought to an end less than ten years ago with passage of the Voting Rights Bill of 1965. But in the North, where political action was an easier enterprise, Blacks demonstrated great apathy, mainly because of a basic distrust of the political system. Politics as a means of liberation is, at best, highly suspect in the eyes of the Blacks. It is a game of nonchoice, where no real differences can be detected in the two major parties. Furthermore, Blacks see little that politicians have done to ease their condition, not to mention the deliverance from that condition. It may be that Blacks who are politically disinterested, through some sixth sense, see politics as nonredemptive. If that is the case, they are correct, for "politics is means, not Messiah."[25] However, this does not negate the importance of the "means." Politics is not inherently uncaring. There are politicians who do not care. The surge for power on the part of Blacks has profound political implications for their general well-being. To dismiss or ignore this reality is to court cultural disaster. As evidenced by the election of Blacks in increasingly large numbers throughout the South, Black political leadership that is sensitive to human needs can and does make a difference. Through a process of critical examination and selection, Black communities the nation over can insure the production of a new breed of politicians, men and women who view themselves as protagonists for the poor, and interpret their mission as that of dealing with the greedy in order to heal the needy.

Important to the idea of a revolutionary confrontation with the system is the principle of coalition. Although Blacks are primarily concerned with the problems related to their ghetto existence, the reality of the class problem in America must be acknowledged. A commonality of affliction due to poverty affects many groups. Demonic structures are not only racist; they are also political and economic. If racism ceased to exist (and there is no indication that it will), the class problem would still persist. The economic well-being of the majority of Americans is very tenuous. Lundberg says at the outset of his book:

> Most Americans—citizens of the wealthiest, most powerful and most ideal-swathed country in the world—by a very wide margin own nothing more than their household goods, a few glittering gadgets such as automobiles and television sets (usually purchased on the installment plan, many at second hand) and the clothes on their backs. A horde if not a majority of Americans live in shacks, cabins, hovels, shanties, hand-me-down Victorian eyesores, rickety tenements and flaky apartment buildings.[26]

The vast majority of the nation's people live either in poverty or on the cutting edge of poverty. The average worker cannot afford an illness of a few months' duration. If such is the plight of the working class, how harrowing must be the lot of the unemployed. The September 1978 figures from the U.S. Department of Labor's Bureau of Labor Statistics reveal the following:

Unemployed Whites	16 and over	5.2%
Unemployed Blacks and others	16 and over	11.8%
Unemployed Males/White	20 and over	3.1%
Unemployed Males/Black	20 and over	7.1%
Unemployed Females/White	20 and over	5.7%
Unemployed Females/Black	20 and over	10.8%
Unemployed Teenagers/White	16 to 19	12.8%
Unemployed Teenagers/Black male	16 to 19	34.0%
Unemployed Teenagers/White female	16 to 19	15.9%
Unemployed Teenagers/Black female	16 to 19	39.7%

While the percentage of unemployed Blacks is twice the number of unemployed whites, the total number of unemployed whites exceeds the number of unemployed Blacks. Their common tribulation is in itself sufficient reason for forming an alliance for joint action. If the working class of people (Black and white) recognized their marginal existence at the mercy of the ruling class, they would unite to deal with their common enemy. They would also recognize their affinity with the unemployed and seek the formation of a coalition to work for an equitable distribution of the nation's wealth.

It is abundantly clear that Blacks are affected by the problem of color *and* class, while most whites are affected by the problem of class. Color is the chief obstacle to coalescence. The racist ethos has created for whites an illusory notion concerning their place under the sun. This is the primary problem standing in the way of coalition. So long-standing and widespread is the reality of racism that Blacks are naturally suspicious of attempts to form Black and white alliances. Well-meaning whites who truly desire justice for all will have to guard against all appearances of that brand of liberalism which is marked by a spirit of paternalism. Blacks would rather "hoe their own row" than relate to whites on anything less than a peer basis.

In this writer's view, the most logical arena for attempts at coalition is the religious community. The ecumenism demonstrated in the previously mentioned A & P confrontation is a strong indicator of the existing possibilities. In that situation, white churchmen entered the fray with a clear recognition and acceptance of the established Black leadership. Coalition can be effective, but only when respect is real and when the achievement of justice is recognized as the prelude to reconciliation. At any rate, the liberation of Blacks remains essentially a Black concern.

What instrumentality is available to Blacks for confronting the system and dealing with demonic structures? There is but one, that unique religio-social institution called the Black Church. In local terms, the church is a society of sinners hammering out its redemption under the auspices of grace. The church is social by definition. Why then is it necessary to speak of the Black Church as a religio-social institution? If Christianity is concerned about man in the totality of his relationships, why is such a characterization important? This tag of identification is used because of essential differences between the Black Church and the white church. Because of its origin, affliction, worship, witness, and mission, it has had to be more social than any other religious institution on American soil. A deep social consciousness was forced upon it by cultural conditions and circumstances.

Certain African antecedents made the process simpler and easier. Though apparently stripped of their African heritage, there remained in and with the slaves at least one ethical carry-over: the idea of the "together community." Basic to the African way of life is a view of society in terms of mutual obligation, as opposed to the western emphasis on individual rights. The statement "the wolf is in the pack and the pack is in the wolf" is applicable to the African situation. William Conton expresses well the African spirit:

> And then my father went on to remind me that I had started to climb a palm tree that was high and difficult to climb. That many were watching my progress, and much fruit awaited me on the successful conclusion of my climb. But then he went on to warn me that if I failed to reach the top, those both living and dead would curse me for having failed them. And if I reached the top simply to gorge myself with fruit, I would surely become sick and fall to the ground and die. But if I reached the top and returned to my people, to share with them the fruits of my labor, then all would honor and praise me and thank those who had brought me to life.[27]

No doctrine of rugged individualism has ever gotten off the ground in Africa. The sanctity of individual personality is inseparably tied to the sanctity of the group; and since all of life is fundamentally religious, religion is social and the social is religious.

These humans from Africa were brought to the New World with their souls (the essence of being) intact. Tribal units were broken up; families were disjointed; and persons from different tribes, speaking different languages, were thrown together to make easier the new socialization process. But with their souls intact, there remained an innate capacity for receiving the revelation of God in Jesus Christ. These motley groupings, strangers to one another, learned a new language, developed a new dialect, put it together in God's name, and became one of God's new creations: the Black Church. They were bound together by four distinctions: blood, Blackness, bondage, and the new birth. The Black Church was for the slaves, and to this day remains the American counterpart of the African extended family. It more closely resembles the Christian communities of the New Testament than any other church in the western world. *Koinonia* does not have to be designed and promoted. It derives quite naturally from the factors already cited. DuBois wrote eighty years ago:

> As a social group the Negro Church may be said to have antedated the Negro family on American soil; as such it has preserved, on the one hand, many functions of tribal organization, and on the other hand,

many of the family functions. Its tribal functions are shown in its religious activity, its social authority, and general guiding and coordinating work; its family functions are shown by the fact that the church is a center of social life and intercourse, acts as newspaper and intelligence bureau, is the center of amusements—indeed, is the world in which the Negro moves and acts. So far-reaching are these functions of the church that its organization is almost political.[28]

The development of a social gospel theology was not necessary for Blacks. James Cone's *Black Theology and Black Power* is mainly the restatement of positions that once flowered and almost died. It is a case of old wine having been put in new bottles. The religious and the social have been one for Blacks. Worship is a collective experience of the living Word. Singing is a union of body and soul in wondrous ecstasy. Preaching is antiphonal. One hour is not adequate for the public worship of God. When one experiences eternity, the clock has little significance. Persons touch each other before, during, and after the service proper. The African concept of community remains central. The emphasis is on "we" instead of "me." One's "me-ness" is authenticated only as it contributes to and participates in a glorious "we-ness" under God.

In the Lord's service, the kingdom comes on earth through a corporate, communal emphasis and experience. Karl Barth, in his *Church Dogmatics*, points out four levels of humanity on an ascending scale:

(1) "Eye to eye" relationship (seeing one another).
(2) Mutual speech and hearing (communicating: talking to and hearing one another).
(3) Mutual assistance (helping one another; sharing).
(4) All of the other three levels together with a spirit of joy (*koinonia* and *agape*).[29]

The Black Church is the most visible expression of this kind of humanity on the American scene.

The Black Church became the new Africa. It was "the extended family" restored, under the leadership of Jesus Christ, the great High Priest, and under the earthly direction of the Black preacher who was prophet, priest, and village chief. Conceived in the womb of social crises and born as a result of the disparity between Christian faith and social policy, it has been inseparably related from the beginning to the Black *sitz im Leben* (situation in life) to the sufferings and deprivations of an oppressed people. It has provided a sense of belonging and filled the need for approval. Since its inception it has been the largest and most significant of all racial enterprises. By and large, the social advances of the race have had their origins in the Black Church: the struggle for human rights, battles for economic equity, efforts for fair and decent housing, and warfare against the racist ethos.

The Black Church has been and still remains the connecting rod between Black history and Black hope. It is the only institution on the island that has historic continuity. It is the largest base of numerical strength. It is the one place where the vision of a nobler life is lifted up regularly. It views life as perennial struggle by people in pilgrimage. And because of its nondependence on the larger society, it is free to be prophetic. When compared with the white church in America, sharp differences are readily observable:

Black Church	White Church
church of the oppressed	church of the oppressors
theology of survival	theology of success
theology of immanence	theology of transcendence
prophetic	priestly
free pulpit	restricted pulpit
spontaneity in worship	rigidity in worship
social ferment	status quo oriented
activistic affliction	apathy
substance	shadow
heterogeneous	homogeneous

While the aforementioned differentiations do not apply absolutely to the Black Church and the white church, the preponderance of evidence weighs heavily in favor of such a typology. Racism has rendered the white church spiritually powerless. Many Black churches also have failed to exercise the prophetic function. Judgment is upon them for failure to act in terms of their freedom, a freedom that is inherently present in any community of believers that is not bound to the culture in which it finds itself. Black preachers, in particular, enjoy a status unlike that of all other clergymen. They are answerable, in the main, only to the God they serve. They need not ask permission to be prophetic. They and the churches they lead are the logical leaders in the encounter with systemic sin and entrenched evil.

The Black preacher, unfortunately, is often a hindrance to the advancement of the Black cause. Some are inactive in the struggle because of their failure to see the social implications of the gospel. They are unconscious allies of racistic religion. It is not uncommon to hear a Black clergyman say: "My task is to preach the gospel and win souls to Jesus Christ. Social betterment will come only through the salvation of men." Such a theological stance not only makes for ministerial apathy; it also can serve to render an entire congregation socially impotent.

To awaken many Black preachers to the prophetic task is an awesome but necessary responsibility. This difficulty was painfully dramatized at the beginning of the A & P struggle in New York City. While the Breadbasket clergymen were occupying the A & P executive offices, a Black ministerial conference was in session. It was decided that those attending the conference should be alerted and enlisted in the effort. The following letter was written:

My Brethren,

I'm sure you know by now that I along with 21 others of our ministerial brethren have occupied the Executive Offices of A & P at 420 Lexington Avenue since 9:30 A.M. yesterday. We are here in the interest of justice for our people. Since coming here to declare the truth and righteousness demanded of God, we have discovered that the A & P situation is worse than we had ever imagined. Nearly 500 people work here under the leadership of President William Kane. Only a handful are Black. Of 137 top executives working here, only *one* is Black. There are no Blacks at all in the Accounting Department. A & P operates out of a plantation ethic and has no intention of dealing justly with our people.

Brethren, we are here. We are tired and hungry, but absolutely determined. I appeal to you now for your active support. We need your presence here today. We cannot telephone out. A & P officials are attempting to keep the Press out. I pray that you will find it possible to leave the Conference around 2:30 or 3:00 and come here as a body in the name of Jesus Christ to press the just demands of our people who have been historically victimized by the economic evils of a wicked social system. You and I are comfortably situated. We are a privileged group. But for millions of our brothers and sisters, hunger pains dart through their bodies. We have to be here not for our sake, but for the future's sake. I am here because Jesus couldn't make it. If He were in town, I'm convinced that He would be here with us. I ask of you your prayers and your presence.

For the Brethren,
William A. Jones, Jr.

To the surprise of the Breadbasket clergymen and to the shame of the ministerial conference, only one preacher responded in a positive manner.

In order for the latent power of the Black Church to become manifest, it is essential that a wholistic understanding of the Christian gospel be at the top of the agenda for Black theological education. The Black preacher is easily the freest man in the American pulpit, but freedom devoid of understanding serves only to perpetuate Black powerlessness. By virtue of its calling, its strengths, its continuity, its freedom, and the power inherent in that freedom, the Black Church can readily become "reservation headquarters." The capability is present. Only the will "to be" is needed.

The collective power of members of individual congregations has been demonstrated over and over again. They have erected new edifices, established credit unions, built low-income housing, and served as rallying bases for movements in behalf of social justice. The great need is for the "people power" already evidenced at the congregational level to be extended to areas of community enterprise. Many local congregations are sufficiently strong to sponsor community-based institutions and enterprises that will lead to economic self-sufficiency within the ghetto. If and when the power of all Black churches is collectivized for a national thrust, the day of total liberation will be clearly in view.

Better than thirty years ago, Richard Wright wrote, "Our churches are where we dip our tired bodies in cool springs of hope, where we retain our wholeness and humanity, despite the blows of death from the Bosses."[30] The "blows of death" continue to come. The "bosses" of the system must be confronted with the demands of the Creator. The autocracy of pleasure must be replaced by the democratization of pleasure and pain.

If the struggle ends with the oppressor and the oppressed living in a climate of reconciliation, let God be praised. If not, let God still be praised. For he has placed himself on the side of the victimized masses; and, through their conquests in his name, the kingdom will come on earth as it is in heaven.

Notes

1. Charles P. Henderson, Jr., *The Nixon Theology* (New York: Harper & Row, 1972):38.

2. Ferdinand Lundberg, *The Rich and the Super-Rich* (New York: L. Stuart, 1968):13.

3. Ibid., 297.

4. Ibid., 358.

5. C. Wright Mills, *The Power Elite* (New York: Oxford University Press, 1956):290.

6. *Congressional Record*, April 4, 1967, p. S4582.

7. Aristotle, "Politics," *The Works of Aristotle*, vol. 11, *The Great Books of the Western World*, ed. Robert M. Hutchins (Chicago: Encyclopedia Britannica, 1952) 9:503.

8. Arnold Schuchter, *Reparations* (Philadelphia: Lippincott, 1970):69.

9. The Declaration of Independence.

10. Colin Morris, *Unyoung—Uncolored—Unpoor* (Nashville, Tenn.: Abingdon, 1969):82.

11. Emil Brunner, as quoted in Morris, 94.

12. Ted R. Gurr, as quoted in Schuchter, 32.

13. José M. Bonino, "Christians and the Political Revolution," *The Development Apocalypse*, ed. Stephen C. Rose (New York: World Council of Churches, 1967):108.

14. Jacques Ellul, *Violence* (New York: Seabury Press, 1969):167.

15. Isaiah 40:4–5.

16. Stokely Carmichael, "What We Want," the *Boston Sunday Herald*, October 2, 1966.

17. Samuel F. Yette, *The Choice: The Issue of Black Survival in America* (New York: Putnam, 1971):18.

18. Dan. 3:18.

19. Dan. 1:8.

20. Acts 5:29.

21. 1 Thess. 5:22.

22. Daniel Thompson, *Negro Leadership Class* (New York: Prentice, 1963):58–79.

23. Charles H. Wesley, *Richard Allen—Apostle of Freedom* (Washington, D.C.: Associated Publishers, 1969):239–40.

24. Ps. 24:1.

25. Will D. Campbell and James J. Holloway, *Up to Our Steeples in Politics* (New York: Paulist Press, 1970):71.

26. Lundberg, 1.

27. William F. Conton, *The African*, in the African Writers Series (London: Heinemann, 1960, 1964).

28. W. E. Burghardt DuBois, *The Philadelphia Negro* (New York: B. Blom, 1967):201.

29. Karl Barth, *Church Dogmatics* vol. 3, pt. 11 (Edinburgh: T. & T. Clark, 1936):250.

30. Richard Wright, *12 Million Black Voices* (New York: Arno Press, 1969).

Index

Abernathy, Ralph, 445, 446
Abolitionism, 229, 268, 306, 325, 378
Abosom, (Ashanti), 272
Abram, Bede, 241
Abyssinian Baptist Congregation, 304, 307
Accommodation, 96, 259
Adair, Thelma D., 378
Africa, 3, 5, 27, 102, 117, 131, 166, 271, 332, 396, 420–423; ancient, 155–161; Back to, 63, 75, 137; Black Catholics and, 231, 245; Egypt, 67, 75, 102, 155, 159–161, 164, 183, 186, 278–282, 341; Ethiopia, 6, 64, 75–77, 107, 109, 113, 122, 158–163, 301, 336; Ghana, 10, 244; history of, 267; Kenya, 272; Liberia, 67, 68; Melle (Mali), 10, 274; Nambia, 272; Nubia, 158–162, 284; Southern, 209, 436
African Americans, xxi, 1, 9, 27, 28, 46, 51, 69, 83, 95, 105, 107, 110, 112, 113, 120, 122
African American Catholics. *See* Black Roman Catholics
African American Christianity, 2, 140, 149, 268, 271
African American churches, viii–xxi, 25, 27, 32, 37, 102, 132, 156, 182–184, 268, 421, 427, 451
African American Church history, viii, 182–187, 190, 267, 302
African American culture, 59, 232–234, 238, 302, 306, 362
African American experience, 26, 38, 130–138, 156, 266, 350, 405; in Africa, 165, 168; philosophy of, 251, 253, 258; and religion, 1, 20, 96, 155, 157, 165, 167
African American religion, viii-xii, 2, 3, 47, 52, 55–59, 95, 267, 286; operational definition of, xxii n
African American religious studies, vii–xx passim, 22, 29, 35, 267, 268, 358
African American theologians. *See* Black theologians
African American theology. *See* Black theology
African American women, 210–213, 217, 219, 221, 235, 358
African culture, 249, 279, 302, 392, 421, 422
African diaspora, xii, 11, 137, 155, 156, 346. *See also* Black diaspora
African heritage, 396, 449
African Methodists, 56, 69, 142, 216, 287, 301, 308–311, 330, 344, 372, 402, 442
African Traditional Religion, ix, xv, 155, 165, 166, 184, 194, 249, 267, 271–273, 286, 392
Akhenaton, 160, 282, 283
Ali, Muhammad, 348
Ali, Noble Drew, 292, 344, 345
All Africa Conference of Churches, 194
Allen, Richard, 81, 183, 268, 302, 305, 307, 309–311, 442
American Academy of Religion, 2, 3
American Association of Theological Schools, 1, 101
American Baptists, 372, 409, 419
American Muslim Mission, 352, 353. *See also* Black Muslims
Amma (Dogon mythology), 274, 275
Ancestors, 10, 245, 273, 276, 403
Anderson, Mother Leafy, 85
Angelou, Maya, 225

Lanternari, Vittoria, 46
Latin America, 9, 192–194, 243, 264, 342
Ledoux, Jerome, 231
Lee, Carlton, 198
Lee, Jarena, 213, 216, 223
Lerner, Barbara, 424, 426
Levesque, George, 303
Levine, Lawrence, 40, 41
Lewis, Jack P., 112
Lewter-Simmons, Margrie, 384
Liberalism, 281, 432, 449
Liberation, vii, ix, 103, 133, 152, 159, 167, 178,
    183, 185, 187–197, 214, 220, 221–224, 250,
    253, 260, 265, 290, 294, 324, 331, 335, 336,
    350, 398, 408, 425, 447, 449
Liberty Hall, 62, 64, 80
Liele, George, 19
Lincoln, Abraham, 218
Lincoln, C. Eric, 3, 4, 34, 37, 42, 196, 268,
    271, 288, 292, 293
Linguistics, 433
Liturgy, 233, 239, 358, 376, 381, 388, 392–399,
    400–402
Living dead, 256
Local churches, 413, 424. *See also*
    Congregations
Locke, Alain, 250, 259
Lonergan, Bernard, 243
Long, Charles H., 2, 4, 132, 158, 185, 193, 194,
    197
Long, Jerome, 185
Loomis, Eva Marie, 237, 238
Love, 93, 181, 198, 208, 218, 219, 241, 263, 282,
    288, 292, 323, 328, 380, 436
Lucas, Lawrence, 231
Lundberg, Ferdinand, 430, 448
Lutherans, 11, 57
Lyke, James, 237
Lynching, 257, 328

McGill-Jackson, Deborah, 378
McGuire, George Alexander, 70, 81
McKissick, Floyd, 179
McKnight, Albert, 235
McNeeley, Al, 236, 237
Magi, 278
Malcolm X (Al Hajj Malik Shabazz), 178,

182, 232, 259, 290, 294, 295, 296, 335, 336,
    352, 437
Marable, Manning, xx, 96, 99, 268
March on Washington (1963), 178, 260
Marriage, 210, 287, 393, 423
Marshall, Calvin B., 334
Martin, Tony, 333
Marxism, 26, 184, 262, 263
Massey, James Earl, 374
Materialism, 167, 296
Mather, Cotton, 15, 320
Mays, Benjamin E., 184, 253
Mbiti, John, 165, 184, 249, 264, 273, 422
Meier, August, 78
Meredith, James, 179
Meroe, Queen of, 163
Merton, Thomas, 231
Messianism, 96, 137, 164, 220, 222, 429, 447
Methodism, 11, 18, 51, 57, 82–84, 92, 303,
    304, 308, 311, 344, 372, 409
Metropolitan Spiritual Churches of Christ,
    87
Metz, Johannes B., 190
Middle class, 93, 94, 268, 365, 370, 424
Migration, 85, 304, 406
Militancy, 55, 93
Mills, C. Wright, 431
Mills-Morton, Clara, 382
Ministers, 53, 54, 403, 446. *See also* Black
    clergy
Ministry, 223, 376, 411, 415
Mission and ministry studies, 357, 359, 375
Mitchell, Ella P., 372
Mitchell, Henry, 196, 198, 357
Moltmann, Jurgen, 38, 190, 263
Monotheism, 273
Montgomery, Ala., 50, 178
Moorish-Americans, 292, 344, 345
Moors, 117, 292
Morality, 273, 287, 320–324, 333
Mormons, 121
Morris, Elias C., 142
Moses, 110, 113–115, 161, 186, 282, 284
Moses, William H., 64
Moyd, Olin P., 122, 127
Moynihan, Daniel, 134
Mudd, Emily, 423

Permissions

Permission to reprint selections from the following sources is gratefully acknowledged (listed by chapter):

1   C. Eric Lincoln: From *Review and Expositor*, Summer 1973.

3   Charles H. Long: "Black Religious Scholarship: Reflection and Promise," October 1981; from Addresses at the Tenth Annual Meeting of the Society for the Study of Black Religion.

4   Joseph R. Washington, Jr.: From *Black Religion: The Negro and Christianity in the United States* (Boston: Beacon Press, 1964), pp. 30–42.

5   Randall K. Burkett: From *Garveyism as a Religious Movement: The Institutionalization of a Black Civil Religion* (Metuchen, N.J.: Scarecrow Press, 1978), pp. 15–44.

7   Charles B. Copher: From *Journal of the Interdenominational Theological Center*, Spring 1986, vol. 13, no. 2.

8   Robert A. Bennett: From *Theology Today*, January 1971.

9   Vincent L. Wimbush: From *Journal of Religious Thought*, Fall–Winter 1985–86, vol. 42, no. 2.

11 James H. Cone: From *For My People: Black Theology and the Black Church* (Maryknoll, N.Y.: Orbis Books, 1984).

12 Jacquelyn Grant: From *Journal of the Interdenominational Theological Center*, Spring 1986, vol. 13, no. 2.

14 J. Deotis Roberts, Sr.: From *Journal of the Interdenominational Theological Center*, Fall 1973, vol. 1, no. 1.

15 Maulana Karenga: From *Introduction to Black Studies* (Los Angeles: Kawaida Publications, 1982).

16 Will B. Gravely: From *Journal of Religious Thought*, Spring–Summer 1984, vol. 41, no. 1.

17 Manning Marable: From *Blackwater: Historical Studies in Race, Class Consciousness and Revolution* (Dayton: Black Praxis Press, 1981).

18 C. Eric Lincoln: From *The Muslim Community in North America*, edited by E. H. Waugh, B. Abu-Laban and R. Qureshi (Edmonton: University of Alberta Press, 1983). Reprinted with permission.

19 Henry H. Mitchell: From *Black Preaching* (Philadelphia: Lippincott, 1970).

20 Cheryl J. Sanders: From *Journal of Religious Thought*, Spring–Summer 1986, vol. 43, no. 1.

22 Sid Smith: From *10 Super Sunday Schools in the Black Community* by Sid Smith. Copyright 1986 Broadman Press. All rights reserved. Used by permission.

23 Edward P. Wimberly: From *Journal of the Interdenominational Theological Center*, Spring 1976, vol. 3, no. 2.

24 William A. Jones, Jr.: From *God in the Ghetto* (Elgin, Ill.: Progressive Baptist Publishing House, 1979).

About the Editor

Gayraud S. Wilmore is Professor of Church History and Afro-American Religious Studies at The Interdenominational Theological Center in Atlanta, Georgia. He has published numerous articles and books, including *Black Witness to the Apostolic Faith*, David Shannon, co-ed.; *Black and Presbyterian: The Heritage and the Hope*; and *Last Things First*. Professor Wilmore is the recipient of the Bruce Klunder Award of the Presbyterian Interracial Council (1969), the Award of the Interdenominational Ministerial Alliance of Harlem (1971), and various honorary degrees.

Library of Congress Cataloging-in-Publication Data
African American religious studies.
Includes bibliographies and index.
1. Afro-Americans—Religion.   I. Wilmore, Gayraud S.
BR563.N4A36   1989   277.3'008996073   88-33567
ISBN 0-8223-0904-1
ISBN 0-8223-0926-2 (pbk.)